Presidents, Vice Presidents, Congresses

President	Service	Vice President	Congress
1 George Washington	Apr. 30, 1789-Mar. 3, 1797	1 John Adams	1, 2, 3, 4
2 John Adams	Mar. 4, 1797-Mar. 3, 1801	2 Thomas Jefferson	5, 6
3 Thomas Jefferson	Mar. 4, 1801-Mar. 3, 1805	3 Aaron Burr	7, 8
Thomas Jefferson	Mar. 4, 1805-Mar. 3, 1809	4 George Clinton	9, 10
4 James Madison	Mar. 4, 1809-Mar. 3, 1813	George Clinton (1)	11, 12
James Madison	Mar. 4, 1813-Mar. 3, 1817	5 Elbridge Gerry (2)	13, 14
5 James Monroe	Mar. 4, 1817-Mar. 3, 1825	6 Daniel D. Tompkins	15, 16, 17, 18
6 John Quincy Adams	Mar. 4, 1825-Mar. 3, 1829	7 John C. Calhoun	19, 20
7 Andrew Jackson	Mar. 4, 1829-Mar. 3, 1833	John C. Calhoun (3)	21, 22
Andrew Jackson	Mar. 4, 1833-Mar. 3, 1837	8 Martin Van Buren	23, 24
8 Martin Van Buren	Mar. 4, 1837-Mar. 3, 1841	9 Richard M. Johnson	25, 26
9 William Henry Harrison (4)	Mar. 4, 1841-Apr. 4, 1841	10 John Tyler	27
10 John Tyler	Apr. 6, 1841-Mar. 3, 1845		27, 28
11 James K. Polk	Mar. 4, 1845-Mar. 3, 1849	11 George M. Dallas	29, 30
12 Zachary Taylor (4)	Mar. 5, 1849-July 9, 1850	12 Millard Fillmore	31
13 Millard Fillmore	July 10, 1850-Mar. 3, 1853		31, 32
14 Franklin Pierce	Mar. 4, 1853-Mar. 3, 1857	13 William R. King (5)	33, 34
15 James Buchanan	Mar. 4, 1857-Mar. 3, 1861	14 John C. Breckinridge	35, 36
16 Abraham Lincoln	Mar. 4, 1861-Mar. 3, 1865	15 Hannibal Hamlin	37, 38
Abraham Lincoln (4)	Mar. 4, 1865-Apr. 15, 1865	16 Andrew Johnson	39
17 Andrew Johnson	Apr. 15, 1865-Mar. 3, 1869		39, 40
18 Ulysses S. Grant	Mar. 4, 1869-Mar. 3, 1873	17 Schuyler Colfax	41, 42
Ulysses S. Grant	Mar. 4, 1873-Mar. 3, 1877	18 Henry Wilson (6)	43, 44
19 Rutherford B. Hayes	Mar. 4, 1877-Mar. 3, 1881	19 William A. Wheeler	45, 46
20 James A. Garfield (4)	Mar. 4, 1881-Sept. 19, 1881	20 Chester A. Arthur	47
21 Chester A. Arthur	Sept. 20, 1881-Mar. 3, 1885		47, 48
22 Grover Cleveland (7)	Mar. 4, 1885-Mar. 3, 1889	21 Thomas A. Hendricks (8)	49, 50
23 Benjamin Harrison	Mar. 4, 1889-Mar. 3, 1893	22 Levi P. Morton	51, 52
24 Grover Cleveland (7)	Mar. 4, 1893-Mar. 3, 1897	23 Adlai E. Stevenson	53, 54
25 William McKinley	Mar. 4, 1897-Mar. 3, 1901	24 Garret A. Hobart (9)	55, 56
William McKinley (4)	Mar. 4, 1901-Sept. 14, 1901	25 Theodore Roosevelt	57
26 Theodore Roosevelt	Sept. 14, 1901-Mar. 3, 1905		57, 58
Theodore Roosevelt	Mar. 4, 1905-Mar. 3, 1909	26 Charles W. Fairbanks	59, 60
27 William H. Taft	Mar. 4, 1909-Mar. 3, 1913	27 James S. Sherman (10)	61, 62
28 Woodrow Wilson	Mar. 4, 1913-Mar. 3, 1921	28 Thomas R. Marshall	63, 64, 65, 66
29 Warren G. Harding (4)	Mar. 4, 1921-Aug. 2, 1923	29 Calvin Coolidge	67
30 Calvin Coolidge	Aug. 3, 1923-Mar. 3, 1925		68
Calvin Coolidge	Mar. 4, 1925-Mar. 3, 1929	30 Charles G. Dawes	69, 70
31 Herbert C. Hoover	Mar. 4, 1929-Mar. 3, 1933	31 Charles Curtis	71, 72
32 Franklin D. Roosevelt (16)	Mar. 4, 1933-Jan. 20, 1941	32 John N. Garner	73, 74, 75, 76
Franklin D. Roosevelt	Jan. 20, 1941-Jan. 20, 1945	33 Henry A. Wallace	77, 78
Franklin D. Roosevelt (4)	Jan. 20, 1945-Apr. 12, 1945	34 Harry S. Truman	79
33 Harry S. Truman	Apr. 12, 1945-Jan. 20, 1949		79, 80
Harry S. Truman	Jan. 20, 1949-Jan. 20, 1953	35 Alben W. Barkley	81, 82
34 Dwight D. Eisenhower	Jan. 20, 1953-Jan. 20, 1961	36 Richard M. Nixon	83, 84, 85, 86
35 John F. Kennedy (4)	Jan. 20, 1961-Nov. 22, 1963	37 Lyndon B. Johnson	87, 88
36 Lyndon B. Johnson	Nov. 22, 1963-Jan. 20, 1965		
Lyndon B. Johnson	Jan. 20, 1965-Jan. 20, 1969	38 H	0
37 Richard M. Nixon	Jan. 20, 1969-Jan. 20, 1973	3	2, 93
Richard M. Nixon (12)	Jan. 20, 1973-Aug. 9, 1974	40	
38 Gerald R. Ford (14)	Aug. 9, 1974-Jan. 20, 1977	41	
39 Jimmy (James Earl) Carter	Jan. 20, 1977-Jan. 20, 1981	42	
40 Ronald W. Reagan	Jan. 20, 1981-	43	

(1) Died Apr. 20, 1812. (2) Died Nov. 23, 1814. (3) Resigned Dec. 28, 18[...] ...enator. (4) Died in office.
(5) Died Apr. 18, 1853. (6) Died Nov. 22, 1875. (7) Terms not consecutive. (8) Died Nov. 25, 1885. (9) Died Nov. 21, 1899.
(10) Died Oct. 30, 1912. (11) Resigned Oct. 10, 1973. (12) Resigned Aug. 9, 1974. (13) First non-elected vice president,
chosen under 25th Amendment procedure. (14) First non-elected president. (15) 2d non-elected vice president, sworn in
Dec. 19, 1974. (16) First president to be inaugurated under 20th Amendment, Jan. 20, 1937.

Alternate Edition
UNDERSTANDING AMERICAN GOVERNMENT

UNDERSTANDING

Alternate Edition
AMERICAN GOVERNMENT

ROBERT WEISSBERG
University of Illinois at Urbana-Champaign

HOLT, RINEHART AND WINSTON
New York Chicago San Francisco Dallas Montreal Toronto London Sydney

Senior Acquisitions Editor: Patrick V. Powers
Senior Development Editor: Rosalind Sackoff
Managing Editor: Jeanette Ninas Johnson
Senior Project Editor: Françoise D. Bartlett
Production Manager: Annette Mayeski
Text Designer: Betty Binns Graphics
Art Director: Robert Kopelman
Photo Research: Jo-Anne Naples

To my parents, Herbert and Frances

Library of Congress number: 81-997
ISBN 0-03-058038-2

© *1980 by Holt, Rinehart and Winston*
© *1981 CBS College Publishing*

Address correspondence to:
383 Madison Avenue, New York, N.Y. 10017

CBS COLLEGE PUBLISHING
Holt, Rinehart and Winston
The Dryden Press
Saunders College Publishing

(Continued on p. 754)

PURPOSE OF THIS BOOK

UNDERSTANDING AMERICAN GOVERNMENT is a comprehensive book designed for the introduction to American government course offered at most colleges and universities. Like many other books of this type, it covers in detail the standard features of U.S. politics – the Constitution, federalism, political parties, Congress, the courts, and all the other traditional "core" topics. In addition, several subjects usually given only scant attention in most texts – the biases of our electoral system and power in private organizations, to name but two – are given greater emphasis.

I believe, however, that *Understanding American Government* is not merely another traditional introductory text, albeit with some new subject matter. Underlying this book is a set of beliefs about how politics ought to be approached, as well as several techniques designed to help students grasp sometimes complex material. Four major beliefs or assumptions guided the writing of this book:

GUIDING ASSUMPTIONS

1. A major purpose of an American government text is to teach students how to *analyze* politics. This means showing students how to disentangle complex events and relate these events to their own values and preferences.

2. The best approach to the traditional subject matter of American politics is to focus on important debates and questions surrounding these topics. If students are to remember and integrate all of the factual detail of politics, such detail must be presented as part of an answer to an important question. Rather than assemble thirty pages of assorted information on the Constitution, it is much more productive to raise – and then answer – questions such as "Does the Constitution allow government by the people?" This approach not only helps students organize diverse facts, but even more important, shows them by example how a political analyst considers important questions rather than merely accumulates detail. Each chapter thus begins with a set of questions that helps organize and integrate the factual material of each chapter.

3. Most important political questions are not easily answered; and to present partial answers as unquestioned truth under the guise of helping students does not serve either the students or the truth. It is misleading, for example, to offer a single explanation of voting as *the* explanation

when experts disagree considerably on this subject. Provided all sides in a debate are described and illustrated, students are willing to accept conflict over what is true or false. Disagreements can *heighten* interest in politics while simultaneously helping students to develop their analytic skills. Throughout this book I have presented the various sides of key issues rather than give a false sense of certainty of knowledge.

4. One of the most effective methods of teaching politics is to illustrate abstract principles with actual political events and stories. Abstractions are necessary for intellectual structure, but such principles are much more likely to be remembered if they can be associated with memorable illustrations. *Understanding American Government* contains a large number of examples that are an integral part of an attempt to encourage analytical thinking. I further believe that numerous well-chosen stories will motivate students to read the chapters.

HELPING THE STUDENT

Together with these four overall perspectives, I have made use of several techniques to help students make more effective use of this book. All students need some assistance in a basic textbook even if the book is well written and about an interesting subject. Five features deserve particular mention:

1. "PREVIEWS" AND BRIEF CHAPTER SUMMARIES Each chapter (except the first) is organized around two to four broad questions. On a page preceding the chapter, these questions are stated and then briefly answered. This "Preview" provides students with a general overview of the chapter and gives them a sense of where they are headed and what is to be covered. A briefer version of the "Preview" is provided at the end of each chapter under the title "Major Questions Raised." This section too helps students to find and review material.

2. RUNNING GLOSSARY Technical and specialized terms appear in boldface type in the text. To insure that these terms are understood immediately, definitions are provided on the same page. The glossary terms are also set in boldface type in the index to facilitate an overall review of new terminology.

3. ANNOTATED "SUGGESTED READINGS" Following each chapter except the first is a list of books that may provide further information. Brief content summaries are given, and when necessary, an evaluation of the book's technical complexity, timeliness of material, and the special qualifications of its author.

4. "QUESTIONS FOR FURTHER DISCUSSION" Each chapter ends with three or four provocative questions that could be the basis of classroom discussions or written projects. These questions typically stress resolution of conflicting points of view, not the recalling of factual detail. On occasion they raise paradoxes that will encourage far-ranging analyses that go well beyond the traditional topics of American government.

5. HUMOR A special effort has been made in *Understanding American Government* to make the book interesting to students. A major part of this effort involves the use of humor. Humorous and outrageous events are a continuing part of American politics, and if they are relevant to the

analysis, they deserve mention. There is no conflict between learning from a book and enjoying the book.

FOR THE INSTRUCTOR

A SPECIAL NOTE TO THE INSTRUCTOR   Teaching the introductory American government course well is a formidable task. In terms of the scope of knowledge and the amount of administrative detail required, the course is far more demanding of an instructor than the most advanced graduate seminar. In writing this text I have tried to eliminate some of this time-consuming preparatory and administrative work. Of course, most introductory textbooks in political science routinely offer some aid, but this one differs in two key respects: (1) I have personally prepared all ancillary material, and (2) there is much more of this material than is usually the case. This assistance is provided in a test bank and separate instructor's manual.

The test bank consists of two parts. Over 1,500 multiple choice, true-false, sentence completion, and essay questions are provided. These questions all have descriptive titles that are listed in a table of contents. The test bank also discusses testing procedures. It includes tips on question construction, a formula for calculating how well items discriminate, guidelines for putting examinations together, and other useful information. The test bank not only provides test items but it also offers a concise introduction to testing and measurement as applied to political science.

Each chapter of the instructor's manual consists of four main elements. Given that many instructors have used several texts in recent years, I have provided a graphic display of the relationship between topics covered in this text and the location of similar topics in other leading texts. This should facilitate the transition between books. Each chapter also presents what I consider to be the major goals of the next chapter. This is a sort of "What I Tried To Do and Why" section. The core of each chapter in the instructor's manual is a suggested lecture topic that is compatible with the text chapter. This suggested lecture topic includes enough information so that it can be the basis of a classroom presentation without a great deal more material. Each chapter concludes with an annotated list of sources for additional lecture material. The instructor's manual also includes numerous government forms that illustrate the complex relationship between citizen and government. Many of these will be of interest to students.

Many people have contributed to this effort. As usual, the greatest thanks goes to Brian D. Silver, whose work is reflected in every paragraph of this book. Many people at Holt, Rinehart and Winston deserve a well-earned thanks. Rosalind Sackoff and Francoise Bartlett in particular deserve awards for their contributions. Jo-Anne Naples did a fine job of obtaining the many pictures and cartoons that add to the value of this book. Frank Graham played a major role in this project and deserves a great deal of credit, as does Robert Sandee, who was instrumental in making this a Holt book. Many of the fascinating stories of this book are the result of the work done by the extraordinary Stuart Pellish. All the effort, however, would have amounted to nothing without Judy Gallistel and Jean Baker, who transformed my longhand into error-free typescript.

Finally, there are the many reviewers of the manuscript. On countless occasions their comments were genuinely helpful and thought-provoking. For contributing their comments on a chapter-by-chapter basis I would like to thank Gottlieb Baer, American River College; Gregory Casey, University of Missouri-Columbia; Judith Gillespie, Indiana University; Roger Handberg, University of Central Florida; Patrick Kennedy, Seton Hall University; Oral E. Parks, East Carolina University; Randall Ripley, Ohio State University; and Martin Sutton, Bucks County Community College. I would also like to acknowledge the overall assessments provided by William Daniel, Humboldt State University; Peter DeGroot, City College of San Francisco; Jack Dennis, University of Wisconsin; James Fairbanks, University of Houston (Downtown Campus); John Gilbert, North Carolina State University; John Gillespie, Indiana University; Andrew Hacker, Queens College (C.U.N.Y..; Naphtaly Levy, Queensboro Community College; N.S. Levy, Los Angeles City College; Lawrence Longley, Lawrence University; Michael Maggiotto, University of Florida; Dale Ride, Santa Monica City College; Paul E. Scheele, State University of New York at Oneonta; Ronald Schmidt, California State University at Long Beach; Michele Shover, California State University at Chico; Al Stokes, Xavier University of Louisiana; Lonnie Turner, California State University at Northridge; Joseph Unekis, Kansas State University; Joel Verner, Illinois State University; William Weiss, West Valley College; Robert Whelan, Georgia Institute of Technology; Berry Woodson, Tarrant County Community College; and Samuel Yeager, Wichita State University. The number of inaccuracies and misinterpretations caught by these reviewers will remain a closely guarded secret.

The Alternate Edition reflects two substantial changes in the content of *Understanding American Government:* the addition of a chapter on state and local government and a chapter analyzing the 1980 election. As in the other chapters, the emphasis is on a few significant issues rather than encyclopedic coverage of any topic.

The basic structure and orientation of the book remain the same. In addition to the complete chapter on the 1980 election, a number of minor changes have been made throughout the text to reflect this national election.

I felt the changes that needed to be made were enough to call this an Alternate Edition. Not only has the text been changed, I have added chapters to the Instructor's Resource Kit. This also provided the opportunity to add about 1000 more test questions for the entire book.

Urbana-Champaign   —RW
January 1981

CONTENTS

PART TWO

CITIZENS AND POLITICS

PART THREE

INSTITUTIONS

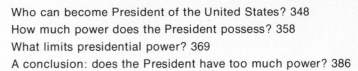

12 PRESIDENTS AND PRESIDENTIAL POWER 347

13 THE FEDERAL BUREAUCRACY 393

14 THE SUPREME COURT AND THE JUDICIAL SYSTEM 433

15 THE POLITICS OF CRIME AND JUSTICE 477

PART FOUR

POLICY

Alternate Edition
UNDERSTANDING AMERICAN GOVERNMENT

Part one

The basic framework

CHAPTER ONE

THE STUDY OF AMERICAN GOVERNMENT AND POLITICS

For most of you this is your second or even your third exposure to American government (or to the closely related subjects of American history and "civics"). You are probably wondering why—again—you have to read about the Constitutional Convention and memorize important political dates and events. Even if you have never had a course in American government, you may ask why you must learn how a bill becomes a law or what judicial review means. If these are your questions, they are reasonable ones.

Why study American government and politics—again?

The traditional answer to the question, "Why study American government?" has been a vague "It's good for you and the country." The underlying assumption is that to be knowledgeable about the political process makes one a better citizen, and the more informed citizens there are, the better off the country will be. Knowledge, according to this perspective, is defined largely in factual terms. One is an informed citizen, for example, if one knows the difference between the New Jersey and the Virginia plans proposed at the Constitutional Convention or can explain exactly how the Constitution can be amended. Just how having such factual knowledge makes one a better citizen is rarely spelled out. Perhaps for this reason many students in American government courses never quite see the use of acquiring vast quantities of detailed political information.

A DIFFERENT APPROACH TO THE STUDY OF AMERICAN GOVERNMENT AND POLITICS

This book takes a different approach. We reject the belief that the major purpose of civic education is to impart as much factual information as possible or to describe all major current events. Facts and current events are important, but more is required. We believe that politically well-educated citizens are persons who can intelligently relate their own political values to the issues and movements of the day. Our goal is to help citizens decide which policies to support or what actions to take. We emphasize the *analysis* of politics, not encyclopedic familiarity with details. It is one thing to know every law enacted in the last five years, but it is far more important (and more difficult) to be able to analyze the relevance of these laws to one's own values and activities.

We emphasize analyzing politics from one's own perspective for two reasons. First, in contemporary society virtually every aspect of our lives is affected by government actions. In the eighteenth century what government did probably made little difference to the average citizen. This is not so today. Where we live, what we eat, where we attend school – and what we are taught – the drugs we can take, and even our sexual behavior are all areas that to some degree come under government control. Even if one left civilization and moved to a remote mountain top, the air one breathed and the water one drank would be affected by the government's environmental policy. Contact with government is unavoidable.

Second, the American political system allows citizens the right to take part in the political process. This right may be exercised through such conventional means as voting or through unconventional channels such as civil disobedience, boycotts, or protest marches. The right to participate also means, of course, the right to abstain from political involvement. The consequence of having this right is that each citizen faces choices concerning whether to participate, how to participate, and for what purpose. These choices exist even for apathetic citizens – they have chosen not to participate.

Given the great impact of government policies and the extensive opportunities available to effect its policies, it should be obvious that a well-educated citizen must be a fairly sophisticated political analyst. Such would not be the case if government were limited to a few basic services, for example, building roads, or if citizens were excluded from the political process. In today's world educating citizens solely about the facts of American politics without teaching them how to interpret this information would be like teaching someone automobile mechanics to prepare them to drive the Los Angeles freeway system. Understanding the mechanics of the automobile is not the same thing as knowing how to navigate in 55-mile-per-hour bumper-to-bumper rush-hour traffic.

AN EXAMPLE OF POLITICAL ANALYSIS

To illustrate the distinction between merely accumulating factual material and knowing how to analyze this material, let us consider the following political issue: How much tuition should students pay at state-supported universities? The facts of this situation are fairly clear. First, the cost of educating students at state schools such as Los Angeles State or the University of Wisconsin is only partially covered by the tuition paid by students (tuition usually covers less than half the cost). Second, the difference between the cost of operating a college and the total amount collected as tuition is made up by the state from general tax revenue. Third, a college education is fast becoming a prerequisite to economic advancement. Because of the crucial role of education, some people argue that it ought to be provided free (or at very low cost) so that poor people can have the same opportunities as other citizens. Others disagree and claim that those who receive a college education ought to pay in full for this benefit.

On the basis of these facts, which position do you choose? Do you endorse lower tuition because you favor anything that is "free," and your savings could be applied to a new stereo set? Or do you support lower tuition because it would help poor people break out of their poverty through education? On the other hand, do you endorse setting tuition equal to the true cost of a college education on the grounds that state benefits ought not to be sold at huge discounts? A third alternative might be a system of variable tuition, with the poor paying less and the rich paying more.

Obviously, merely stating the facts of the issue does not automatically help you to take a stand. Indeed, not having any factual knowledge sometimes makes it easier to take a position on an issue. But if facts by themselves provide no clear solution, how do you decide what policy to endorse?

Deciding your political goals

The first step in analyzing the issue of college tuition is deciding what you want. This process is more complex than it appears. In this example there are several goals related to education that you might support. Among these are:

1. A society that provides everyone with an equal opportunity to obtain social and economic benefits. Equal opportunity, of course, may not result in everyone receiving the same benefits.
2. A society which insures that no individual receives any greater benefits than any other individual. All citizens receive the same benefits.
3. A society that allows those who have achieved positions of status and wealth to maintain their positions. There is neither equal opportunity nor equal benefits.

Suppose you come from a comfortable, middle-class family and you enjoy that life-style. You have no desire to compete with more people than necessary for life's economic rewards, and you certainly reject the idea of everyone getting the same benefits regardless of family background or occupation. You therefore conclude that the third goal—maintaining the social and economic position of people like yourself—is your objective.

Relating goals to specific policies

The next step is to relate this goal to the particular policy choices at hand. High tuition for the rich, no tuition for the poor is rejected as a direct potential threat to your values. High tuition for everyone would help keep many people out of college (and thus reduce the competition), but this policy means coming up with $6,000–$8,000 every year—hardly a proposal you could endorse with enthusiasm, even if you are reasonably well off. Equally important, it would probably be politically impossible to sell the idea of setting tuition at $6,000 a year at state colleges. The effect it would have of excluding the poor in favor of the rich is much too blatant.

What about zero tuition? But wouldn't such a policy help poor people to compete with you for good jobs? Yes, but *only* if they can get into college and graduate. The solution is becoming apparent: endorse the politically popular idea of "equal educational opportunity" and zero tuition, but also insist that traditional academic standards be maintained to insure the quality of public education. By traditional standards you mean such measures as high school class standing, scores on standardized tests, and extracurricular activities such as student council or debate club. You do not mean intangible things like commitment to helping one's ethnic or racial group advance or other nonacademic matters. Since these traditional academic characteristics are disproportionately found among middle-class students (like yourself), their impartial application will sharply reduce the entry of poorer people into college. Another plus is that because your tuition is covered by state tax revenue, you have the added pleasure of knowing that poor people help finance a system that disproportionately benefits middle-class citizens. You call your proposal free quality education and claim that it gives everyone an equal chance to pursue the American dream.

Assuming that you want to preserve the existing social arrangements that limit competition from persons economically less well off than you, your program of free quality education makes the most sense from your own perspective. There is nothing crass or inherently selfish about advocating this position. After all, you could have decided that equality of benefits was your goal, and this would have led you to advocate equal admissions of all groups to higher education, regardless of academic records, with large scholarships for poor students and high tuition for wealthy persons. The purpose of this exercise has been to show how an important political issue can be analyzed from the perspective of one's own values. Whether these values are socially desirable is, of course, an important but separate question.

Learning to analyze politics

It is hoped that this brief analysis of the politics of college tuition has demonstrated that going beyond the mere listing of facts can be a worthwhile endeavor. Unfortunately, there is no simple formula for analyzing complex political phenomena. Political education is not as simple as a consumer education program where you can be taught how to read labels carefully or to divide weight by price to get per unit prices. Ultimately, the ability to analyze politics comes from repeated exposure to such analysis and lots of practice.

Nevertheless, underlying the chapters that follow are four very general principles and perspectives guiding our analysis of American government and politics. These are not scientific mechanisms for unlocking the mysteries of politics. Rather, they provide a general perspective that can be applied to a very diverse set of subjects.

1. ALL POLITICAL ISSUES INVOLVE CONFLICT OVER WHO GETS WHAT

Political conflicts are not abstract discussions of good versus evil or of the ultimate meaning of life. Many political issues, for example, a woman's right to an abortion, have their roots in such philosophical differences; but politics is not a debate over philosophy. The fact that an issue is on the political agenda means that some values—for example, money, status, power—are at stake for certain groups or individuals. That politics involves conflicts among people over values may seem obvious, but this principle is frequently ignored when actual issues are being examined.

Determine who takes what side

The importance of this principle derives from the types of questions it leads us to ask. One such question is: Which people take what sides in the conflict? This is a simple but important question because, as in sports, the action is hard to follow unless you know who is on what side. Describing the participants can also be an important first step in understanding political outcomes. For example, the issue of political corruption is widely discussed, and virtually everyone is in favor of tougher anticorruption laws. Yet progress has been slow despite frequent scandals such as Watergate and bribery to secure foreign aid for Korea. Why is progress so slow? Part of the explanation may have to do with the fact that the chief beneficiaries of corruption are frequently responsible for writing the laws to change the situation. Moreover, those favoring weak anticorruption laws—for example, unscrupulous lobbyists—generally have a large stake in the final outcome, while opponents of corruption have much less at stake. In short, simply identifying *who* is involved and on what side in the conflict is an important first step in analyzing politics.

Examine what tactics are employed

Viewing politics as a conflict among interest groups over values also leads one to ask, What are the tactics in this conflict? What is being done by advocates of each policy to defeat their opponents? Frequently merely raising this question can make certain types of political actions more easily understood. What may appear to be inefficiency or lack of information can sometimes be merely a tactic in a political conflict. How might those in favor of lenient laws against corruption in government advance their cause when virtually everyone is against corruption? One possibility is to enact laws with high-sounding names (for example, "The Total End of Bribery Act of 1980") but allow so many well-hidden exceptions and ambiguities that their impact is nil. Another tactic is to conduct a lengthy investigation which delays all action and collects so much irrelevent information that the whole issue sinks under the weight of boredom and technical documents. Such actions are much easier to spot when you acknowledge that opponents and supporters of policies will advance their cause in *some* way. This advancement of objectives may be open and straightforward or highly deceptive. Recall that in the college tuition example your scheme to keep poor people out of college was called free quality education, a clever though perhaps misleading tactic.

Analyze the consequences of conflict

A third question that might be asked about a political conflict is, What are the likely consequences of victory of one side over the other? Here again, this may seem like an obvious question, though it is seldom fully explored. Again let us consider the case of tougher laws against corruption. What would be likely to happen if public officials had to live solely on their public salaries and could not accept bribes or "freebies" such as use of corporate jets or free theater tickets? One possible outcome of this reduction in income might be an influx of wealthy people into politics because they would not need cash contributions or fees from speaking engagements from banks, labor unions, or real estate developers. Another consequence might be a shift in power from interest groups that have supplied monetary rewards (for example, business groups) to those that could provide benefits that did not legally constitute corruption (for example, organizations that could supply thousands of volunteer campaign workers).

Asking about the consequences of different political outcomes is clearly a crucial step in viewing politics in terms of one's own goals. It is sometimes easy to get carried away with an idea or slogan without fully realizing its consequences. The slogan "Complete Honesty in Government" has enormous appeal, but its implementation may also involve an increase in government bureaucracy and extensive police surveillance of thousands of government employees and persons doing business with government. Pushed to the extreme it could also mean that public officials would have to adhere to a strict moral code well beyond the capacity of the average citizen. How many of us would want to be governed by such saints? On closer inspection, then, "Complete Honesty in Government" may not be as desirable as you first thought.

In sum, this book approaches politics as conflict over values such as money, power, status, and other things people are willing to fight over. In many respects politics can be viewed as a sports contest. The utility of this perspective is in the types of questions it leads us to ask. Given a political issue, a good place to begin our analysis is to ask questions such as who is on what side of the conflict, what tactics are being employed, and what are the consequences of one interest defeating the other.

2. POLITICAL CONFLICT IS GOVERNED BY RULES, AND NO RULE IS POLITICALLY NEUTRAL

Any description of American government and politics entails describing numerous political rules and their actual operations. Such rules include the procedures we follow in electing public officials, the requirements for amending the Constitution, the steps a case must follow to get to the Supreme Court, and the criteria by which members of Congress are assigned to committees. These examples only scratch the surface, and a complete description of them would fill hundreds of pages and read like a law book.

All rules have consequences

Learning many of these rules is inevitable in a course in American government. Our approach, however, will be to emphasize the political consequences of rules, not just their content. All rules favor some people at the expense of others. Rules such as the ones described above not only keep order but they also have a bearing on who wins and who loses. A political rule—even if enforced with complete impartiality—is biased.

Political conflicts are not limited to those who understand the issues. Here two children demonstrate over the construction of a nuclear power plant to be built at Seabrook, New Hampshire.

To appreciate this fact consider the requirement that we hold federal elections on the first Tuesday after the first Monday in November. At first glance this rule appears to be as neutral as, say, the rule requiring all motorists to keep to the right. Nevertheless, this date is advantageous to some people and disadvantageous to others. The holding of elections in November instead of, say, June increases the likelihood that bad weather will hold down voter turnout. A reduced turnout does not, however, affect all political interests equally. Candidates depending on the support of weakly motivated citizens—many of whom are poor or have little education—stand a greater chance of having supporters stay home than do candidates favored by highly motivated citizens. In addition, holding the election on Tuesday instead of, say, Sunday probably discourages turnout among those who cannot easily take off an hour from work to vote. Thus, a candidate appealing to factory workers will have a more difficult time getting his or her supporters to the polls than a candidate who appeals to businesspeople or professors. Overall, this seemingly innocuous regulation probably helps wealthier interests win elections.

To make this point even clearer, let us consider a rule whose impact is even less evident: limits on campaign spending. Several groups have recently pressed for state and national laws that would limit the amount of money that can be spent by candidates campaigning for office. Their basic argument is that by reducing the amount of money needed to campaign, candidates would have to seek less money, which in turn would reduce the influence of wealthy people in choosing our leaders. While this rule is designed to help the "average citizen" against "the rich," there are some less obvious consequences. For one thing, with less money to go around, incumbent officeholders increase their advantage, since they already have visibility, a paid staff, and many opportunities to provide benefits to voters (for example, jobs, community projects, introducing bills). Second, among challengers the reduction of money puts a premium on highly visible characteristics or celebrity status. If you are going to challenge an incumbent and you cannot spend much in getting yourself known, it helps enormously to be an ex-football star who had a movie career before becoming the first astronaut to land on Mars, or to have a name like George Washington. In other words, limiting campaign contributions can hinder voters from voting out present officeholders.

No rule is predetermined

In examining political rules it is important to realize that rarely is there only one way of doing something. In the United States the President is chosen by popular election (as filtered through the electoral college), but we could just as well have the Chief Executive elected by Congress or selected through a comprehensive examination. There is nothing predetermined about national popular elections for chief executives, and many democratic nations, for example, Great Britain, use a different procedure. When examining rules it is therefore perfectly appropriate to ask, Why do it this way? What are the alternatives? How do other nations handle this issue? In other words, rather than accept existing procedures as part of the background of politics, with people and issues in the foreground, we should treat procedures as part of the political process itself. Some of these rules may not be discussed, but they have a major impact on who wins and who loses.

A related, though rarely asked, question regarding any rule is, Why have it? Many features of American politics have become so deeply ingrained that we view them as akin to the eternal laws of physics. Take, for example, the widespread practice of requiring citizens to register before voting in elections. Most citizens took this procedure for granted for years, yet it was not always required in the United States, and other democracies have seen no need for it. In fact, this long-standing procedure has been successfully challenged in a few states, and abolishing registration prior to elections has not brought about any calamities. Similar questions can be raised regarding having a written (and difficult to change) Constitution, maintaining the civil service system, or even having two legislative houses instead of one.

Asking who benefits from a particular rule

It is also important to ask, Who really benefits from a rule? For example, who benefits from the requirement that voters must register to vote in September (or some other month) in order to vote in November? Obviously, this requirement may discourage citizens with little interest in the campaign—which is understandable, since the registration period is usually before the campaign is in full swing. Registration also allows local officials an opportunity to control who can vote in elections. In some instances this involves perfectly proper activity such as removing deceased voters from the electoral rolls. In other instances, however, this power can be employed to discourage certain citizens from participating. For many years the registration process was used to prevent southern blacks from voting. Typically, registration was possible only during a few hours a day and moved slowly, so blacks wishing to register had to expose publicly their intention to vote, thereby making harassment much easier. In short, having a registration requirement is a potential advantage to local officials who may wish to limit electoral participation.

3. POLITICS REQUIRES CITIZENS TO MAKE CHOICES BETWEEN CONFLICTING GOALS

We have argued that a key goal of political education is to help citizens relate their personal preferences to political action. There is more to political analysis, however, than figuring out what you want and how to get it. We all face the problem that many of the goals we advocate can conflict with each other if we push them to their limits. The situation is like the familiar conflict between having lots of money and enjoying one's leisure. Many people have discovered that in order to get things like expensive vacations, fancy automobiles, and the like, they have to work such long hours that they cannot use the things they worked for.

Deciding among competing values

We all face a trade-off in deciding what values are to be maximized. Take, for example, the issue of violent crime. Most Americans strongly oppose muggings, rapes, and armed robberies. Moreover, such crimes have increased substantially in recent years and have had a serious impact on social relationships in many urban areas. It is tempting to declare an all-out war on violent crime and at least to reduce it to levels found in other nations such as Japan or Great Britain. Advocates of an all-out war on crime sometimes fail to realize, however, that some of the necessary anticrime measures may be as objectionable as crime itself. Such a full-scale war might involve dawn-to-dusk curfews, the jailing without explanation of "suspicious characters," increased police surveillance (including reading of private mail and telephone wiretaps), and significantly larger expenditures to fight crime. Obviously, at some point the desire to reduce violent crime collides with one's desire for a reasonably free society. The point at which one says "too much war on crime, too little attention to personal freedom" will, of course, vary from individual to individual.

All public policies involve trade-offs of one kind or another. The most apparent conflicts involve questions of how money is to be spent. Despite our nation's enormous wealth, there is only so much money that can be raised through taxation without causing economic harm. Funding one desirable project may deprive a second and equally desirable project of needed funds. A dollar spent combating environmental pollution may be a dollar less for medical care for the disabled. Raising the second dollar by increasing taxes, and thus having both programs, would mean a dollar less than citizens could spend on food, housing, or their own medical care. Government borrowing of the dollar might increase inflation.

Allocating one's time and energy

Less obvious than the monetary trade-off are the trade-offs involving time and energy. There are just so many things public officials (and concerned citizens) can attend to in a year. It is probably impossible, for example, for a member of Congress to meet large numbers of constituents, be present for all legislative votes, develop innovative bills, and become an authority on several issues. Similarly, a President devoted to advancing world peace may leave himself open to the charge that he is giving too little attention to pressing domestic problems. Here again, every time we say something like "the government should do more in _____," we may be implicitly calling for government to do *less* in other areas.

In sum, politics involves conflict not only among competing interests but among an individual's own goals. When we are pursuing a goal we must also consider other goals that may have to be sacrificed or deferred. For this reason partial fulfillment of one goal may, under the circumstances, be good enough. For instance, although we might want perfectly clean air and water, we might accept some pollution as the necessary cost of having government devote other resources to different but equally desirable programs.

Political conflicts frequently occur over rights. Both pro- and anti-Equal Rights Amendment advocates have used many tactics to sway the public—including promoting their own definitions of "equal rights."

4. POLITICAL CONFLICT INVOLVES WORDS, AND MANY IMPORTANT WORDS MEAN DIFFERENT THINGS TO DIFFERENT PEOPLE

Perhaps in prehistoric times cave people resolved political disputes entirely by physical force. Physical force is still an important element in political conflict, but much of the contemporary battle is waged with words. To be a sophisticated analyst of politics requires that one pay attention to how words are used and what they really mean as opposed to the impressions they create.

Recall from our earlier discussion of college tuition that the phrase "free quality education" was employed to describe a situation in which (1) all citizens paid for tuition through their taxes, and (2) this state benefit was not enjoyed by everyone equally. Thus, "free" education was neither free nor was it equally enjoyed by all citizens. Political conflict abounds with appealing but somewhat misleading words or slogans like "free education." This situation in many ways resembles advertising in which a "free gift" is something you get *only* if you buy some merchandise and "large size" may be the smallest size you can get.

Unfortunately, there is no single list of words that are commonly employed to manipulate our thinking. A skillful manipulator sometimes uses innocuous, straightforward words to mislead. Nevertheless, for purposes of illustration we can identify some phrases that seem especially prone to creating false impressions. Consider, for example, the widely used word "reform." "Reform"—to make better by removing faults—is a highly regarded word in our political history. Not surprisingly, then, a wide range of new policies are labeled reforms, and the impression is thus given that these new policies are improvements and that anyone who opposes reform is against progress. Just how this new policy is an improvement is frequently left unclear. Nor do many people ask, "An improvement for whom?" On numerous occasions reform merely has meant changing the rules to shift power from one group to another without public policy becoming any more efficient or enlightened.

This use of "reform" was well illustrated in the debate over ward versus at-large elections that occurred in many American cities during the 1920s. The reformers proposed that members of city councils should be elected by all citizens (that is, at large). The nonreform position was that each city should be divided into separate districts or wards and that each ward would select one council member. Reformers argued that their at-large system would be better because each council member would represent all citizens instead of narrower district preferences. The major consequence of this "reform," however, was to change the social and economic composition of municipal leadership. Whereas the ward system usually encouraged election of a diverse ethnic and economic city council, the at-large system gave the advantage to middle-class, white business people who were known more generally in the community. Guess which type of individual favored the "reform" policy of at-large elections? Right.

A second word that can easily be employed to mislead is "democracy." Few words are as highly valued as "democracy," and few words have more definitions than "democracy." Because democracy involves so many complex and frequently ambiguous concepts—for example, competitive elections, freedom of speech, equality before the law—it is possible to label a great variety of goals as consistent with democracy. This strategy is helped by the fact that few citizens can precisely define "democracy." Proponents of greater government help to the poor may, for example, argue that such aid is essential if the United States is to be a true democracy. On the other hand, those opposed to such programs may claim that the high taxes and big government necessary to run the antipoverty program are a threat to democratic society. Each side employs "democracy" in support of its position, although democracy, as usually defined, may have nothing whatsoever to do with antipoverty programs. Their hope is that your general support for democracy will be extended to the particular policies being advocated.

Political analysis requires that we look beyond words and consider what is actually happening or is being proposed. Merely calling something an improvement does not make it an improvement. We must be especially careful when political conflicts involve such vague and high-sounding words as "reform," "democracy," "responsibility," "fair," and "efficient." Remember that when the five largest tobacco companies decided to launch a $5 million effort in 1978 to defeat an attempt in California to limit smoking in public buildings, they called their organization "Californians for Common Sense" and warned citizens against the unwarranted interference by "big government."

The purpose of our discussion is to help you to become a more sophisticated political analyst. Again, let us emphasize that these four perspectives are not a formula that will automatically reveal the true meaning of American politics. Political analysis is difficult, but one must begin by asking the right questions. Given a political event, one might proceed by asking:

Who is involved on what side of the issues?
What tactics are being employed?

What will happen if one side wins?
What are the rules governing the conflict?
Which side enjoys an advantage as a consequence of these rules?
What are the policy trade-offs involved in a set of issues?
How are words being used in this conflict?

These questions are only a few of many we might ask, but they are a good beginning.

The plan of this book

The chapters that follow describe important aspects of American government and politics. Each chapter is organized around a set of general questions presented at the beginning of the chapter. Some of these questions are fairly straightforward—for example, What is the federal bureaucracy? Other questions are far more difficult to answer—for example, Is the American system of criminal justice fair? In addition, each of these broad questions may raise several more specific questions. On many occasions we admit that answers to our questions may be informed guesses or subject to considerable controversy. In such instances we provide different viewpoints. Students seeking a single true answer to important political questions may thus occasionally find our presentation of differing answers somewhat frustrating. Nevertheless, we believe that such frustration is better than accepting an oversimplified and only partially correct answer as the complete truth.

The types of analytical questions we have raised in this chapter are found throughout the book. Obviously, for reasons of space we cannot consider every one in every chapter. They occur with sufficient regularity, however, to provide numerous illustrations of the utility of our approach. It is hoped that by the end of this course these questions will have become second nature to you. If so, they should be of considerable help to you in making intelligent political choices. This should be an improvement over once again memorizing the difference between the Virginia and New Jersey plans or how a bill becomes a law.

QUESTIONS FOR FURTHER DISCUSSION

1. In the last few years the National Taxpayers Union (NTU) has actively worked to have the states petition Congress to call a constitutional convention for the purposes of enacting a constitutional amendment that would prohibit deficit spending by the federal government. Under current rules the government can spend more than it receives in taxes (the estimated fiscal 1980 deficit is $29 billion). The NTU claims that a balanced budget would reduce everyone's taxes and slow inflation. In addition, limits on government spending would greatly constrain creating new programs because old programs are difficult to abolish. Given the fact that the major increases in government spending in recent years

has been in the area of social welfare, what kinds of people are likely to be attracted to an amendment requiring a balanced federal budget? What types of people are likely to support one of the opposing groups—Taxation with Representation—that favor reduced taxes by closing all loopholes in tax laws? If you were rich, which group would you support?

2. State election laws require that citizens vote where they legally reside. However, legal residence and where you actually live are not always identical. This is especially true for students—a student may live at his or her legal address only a few months a year compared to seven or eight months a year at his or her college address. Many local election officials have attempted to prevent students from voting in college town elections where students have a different legal home address. If you were given a choice on where to vote, would you and your fellow students be better off voting where your parents live or where you go to school? How would you respond to a city official who said that students should not be allowed to vote in college towns because, unlike other citizens of the town, they are not permanent residents?

3. Since the early 1970s several campaign reform laws have been passed designed to limit the role of special interests in campaigns. One common practice that has been attacked is allowing corporations to provide free use of company airplanes to candidates. Under present law, if Senator Foghorn wants to fly home from Washington on a corporate jet, the trip must be paid for in advance. In light of the burden placed on officeholders by this rule, which of the following government regulations also applies to the use of corporate airplanes (the correct answer is at the bottom of the page):
a. All paying passengers on airplanes owned by private companies must be provided hot meals if the flight lasts for one hour or more.
b. Public officials need not pay private companies for the use of their planes if the flight involves "official business."
c. The Federal Elections Commission, which enforces federal election law, has made the fine for nonpayment only $100.
d. The Federal Aviation Administration, an independent regulatory agency, forbids private companies to collect fares for use of their airplanes.

4. Political conflicts involve words, and a skilled competitor takes great care in selecting the right words. Consider the debate over whether areas such as federally owned land in Alaska should be "preserved as a national monument and wildlife refuge" or should be "opened to meet the pressing energy needs of the American people." Below are some of the expressions used by those who would prevent the Alaskan land from being used by oil and mining companies. If you were politicking on

[The correct answer to question 3 is d.]

behalf of the oil and mining interests, how would you counter these expressions:

a. The Alaskan wilderness belongs to the people of the United States; it is not something to be used for private economic gain.

b. Unless we preserve the scenic beauty of the arctic land, we will succeed in destroying one of the few remaining places untouched by civilization.

c. The federal government has a moral obligation to insure the survival of the sea lions, elk, reindeer, and other wildlife that would be destroyed by private exploitation.

PREVIEW

What are the origins of the American Constitution?

The Constitution is an attempt to resolve problems created by the Articles of Confederation. The government of the Articles did not rule the people directly and lacked the power to solve the financial and commercial problems of the day. Attempts to revise the Articles failed until delegates from eleven (later twelve) states assembled in Philadelphia in 1787. Originally charged with revising the Articles, the convention instead created a brand new government.

Much debate exists over whether this action was a conservative move designed to protect wealthy interests from attacks on property or a widely called-for remedy for serious political problems. Those who see the Constitution as an action of wealthy interests point to the backgrounds of those who drafted the Constitution, the procommercial interests of the Constitution, and the undemocratic nature of the ratification process. But Constitution Convention delegates supported the rights of the common people, and they were not a unified economic group; in addition, ratification was supported by many small farmers and tradesmen.

Does the Constitution allow government by the people?

The Constitution draws its authority from the people of the United States, who, according to the Preamble, created it. Yet, the Constitution does not easily allow for policy to be made by ordinary citizens. As the Constitution was originally designed, only the House of Representatives is directly elected by the people. In addition, several key features prevent a popular majority from acting quickly. Separation of powers and checks and balances impose barriers to the domination and control of government by one group. Gaining control of all three branches of government is difficult, and each branch can restrain the actions of the others. Federalism—the division of power between the national and state governments—also inhibits popular majorities from imposing their preferences. Finally, majorities are sometimes thwarted by constitutionally required "supermajorities" of two thirds or three quarters. If one trusts leaders not to abuse their power, these provisions are impediments to popular rule. However, if one places protection against tyranny ahead of popular rule, then these provisions are virtues, not defects.

Has the Constitution become politically outdated?

The changes that have occurred since 1789 raise important questions concerning the relevance of the Constitution. It can be argued that the present constitutional system is biased toward inaction, promotes unnecessary conflict among public officials, and gives minority interests disproportionate power. However, its defenders claim that the Constitution is flexible and adaptable because it gives leaders discretion through such provisions as "the necessary and proper" clause and the granting of "executive power" to the President. The Constitution is also a unifying symbol for all citizens. Perhaps the strongest defense of the Constitution is that it has allowed for the emergence of a strong, vigorous, nontyrannical government.

CHAPTER TWO

THE CONSTITUTION

The study of American government must begin with an examination of the basic rules regulating the political process. Ignoring these rules would be like trying to understand a baseball game without knowing that a batter is allowed three strikes or that each team is allowed three outs in an inning. Knowledge of such rules is a key step in making a wide variety of political behavior comprehensible and predictable. American politics is regulated by numerous rules, and new rules are constantly being created. Nevertheless, there is a core of rules of special significance, namely, the Constitution and the twenty-six constitutional amendments. Not only does the constitution define our basic political institutions—the presidency, Congress, the court system—but it also delineates key power relationships—for example, the limits of national power in state affairs. Moreover, the Constitution is more than just another set of regulations. It is the supreme law of our government, and if other laws conflict with it, as determined by the Supreme Court, these conflicting laws are declared invalid. In order to understand the significance and contemporary role of the Constitution, we shall seek answers to three important questions:

1. What are the origins of the American Constitution?
2. Does the Constitution promote government by the people?
3. Has the Constitution become politically outdated?

What are the origins of the American Constitution?

Continental Congress   Group of delegates from colonies that first met in 1774 to protest British rule. Eventually became first central government of the United States.
Articles of Confederation   Agreement creating a league of sovereign states ruled by a single-house legislature in which each state had one vote. Replaced by the Constitution in 1789.
Confederation Congress   The single-house legislature under the Articles of Confederation.

The Constitution defines the basic character of American government, but it did not come into existence until eleven years after America declared its independence from Great Britain. Between July 4, 1776, and May 28, 1787, when the drafting of the Constitution officially began, numerous events greatly affected the content of the document. The Constitution was not an expression of abstract political philosophy; it was an attempt to resolve several crucial problems that plagued American society following the Revolutionary War. To understand some of the important features of the Constitution, we need first to consider the failure of previous attempts to create a national political structure.

GOVERNMENT ORGANIZATION PRIOR TO THE CONSTITUTION

Though the Revolution was a conflict between the thirteen colonies and Great Britain, the colonies were not governed by a strong central political authority. The **Continental Congress,** which existed between 1774 and 1781, concerned itself with raising an army and conducting necessary diplomatic business. But since its orders were not binding on either state governments or citizens, it cannot be considered a true national government. The Continental Congress was more like a committee created to coordinate the actions of sovereign nations than a central government.

On March 1, 1781, the Continental Congress system of government was replaced by the **Articles of Confederation.** The central government created by the Articles of Confederation continued the tradition of the largely ineffectual Continental Congress. Under the Articles virtually all power was vested in a single legislative chamber, with no formal distinction between legislative and executive authority. Executive functions such as negotiating with foreign governments were performed by temporarily appointed committees or special officials. There was a provision for a national court, but its procedures were cumbersome and its jurisdiction was limited.

The central government under the Articles was subservient to the separate states. It did not directly govern the people of the United States; it could only request that state legislatures taken certain actions. In fact, delegates to the national Congress were selected and paid by the state legislatures—and each state had one vote. Some power to regulate international commerce was given the **Confederation Congress** (as the government under the Articles was called), but agreement with foreign governments could be (and was) overridden by individual states. The crucial area of interstate commerce was off-limits to central control. Attempts by the Congress to increase its powers were unlikely to succeed because major rule changes required approval by two thirds of all state delegations (and amendments to the Articles of Confederation required unanimous approval). The national government was especially weak in its power to raise money. Congress could not tax directly but had to make "requisitions" to state legislatures for funds. During its first two years the Confederation Congress requested $10 million and received $1.5 million from the states.

The central government created by the Articles of Confederation was virtually powerless to resolve the many problems that occurred in the post-Revolutionary period. Commercial competition among states frequently resulted in discriminatory taxation that undermined all commerce. The management of public finance was frequently chaotic or ineffectual. Payments on public debt were not regularly met, and some states resorted to printing more and more money to pay their bills. Inflation was rampant. What was most disturbing to established commercial interests was the growing strength of radical forces in several states.

THE REAL FIRST PRESIDENT OF THE UNITED STATES

The government under the Articles of Confederation has sunk into obscurity. Perhaps the greatest loser as a result of this neglect has been John Hanson. The Articles of Confederation came into existence on March 1, 1781, and John Hanson was subsequently elected President of the Congress of the Confederacy. This would make John Hanson—not George Washington—the nation's first President.

George Washington.

Hanson was active in colonial government and a leading advocate of resistance to British tyranny. In his native Maryland he helped raise troops, provided arms and ammunition, and otherwise advanced the cause of the American Revolution. After serving his year-term as President, he retired from public life.

John Hanson.

Peyton Randolph.

Hanson should not feel alone, however. An even more obscure first President of the United States is Peyton Randolph. Randolph was a prominent, highly respected Virginian who was appointed to that state's delegation to the Continental Congress. On September 5, 1774, he was elected the first President of the Continental Congress, but resigned seven weeks later to attend the Virginia state legislature. In 1775, he was again elected President of the Continental Congress, served for two weeks, and then resigned for health reasons.

Shays' Rebellion, which lasted from 1786 to 1787, pitted poor farmers against wealthier interests. This engraving depicts a brawl between a rebel and someone loyal to the Massachusetts government.

The most extreme manifestation of this radicalism was a rebellion of Massachusetts farmers, led by **Daniel Shays,** who sought relief from debt and foreclosures on mortgages. Shays' forces broke up court sessions involving debt cases and gained control of a number of towns. While Shays was ultimately defeated, other radical outbursts appeared imminent.

THE MOVEMENT TO REFORM THE ARTICLES OF CONFEDERATION

Though many people believed that the central government under the Articles of Confederation had to be strengthened, several proposals to accomplish this goal came to nothing. The first step in a change in governmental form and power began innocuously in 1785 when representatives from Maryland and Virginia met at George Washington's Mount Vernon home to discuss navigation problems on the Potomac River and Chesapeake Bay. This meeting resulted in agreements between the two states affecting currency, import duties, and commerce. (These agreements were technically illegal because they were not approved by the central government as required by the Articles of Confederation.) When the Virginia legislature subsequently ratified the agreements, it also pro-

Daniel Shays Leader of farmers' rebellion in western Massachusetts, 1786–1787 (Shays' Rebellion). Eventually it was put down, but the uprising scared established commercial interests.

posed a general meeting of all states in Annapolis, Maryland, to discuss their problems further. In September 1786, delegations from only five states actually showed up in Annapolis, but they issued a call for another meeting to resolve common problems to take place in Philadelphia in May 1787. The central government created by the Articles of Confederation first tried to ignore this call for a meeting but it ultimately approved the plan to modify the Articles. (Under the Articles the call for a meeting was illegal, but the issue was not forcefully raised.)

THE CONSTITUTIONAL CONVENTION OF 1787

The first session of the convention took place on May 28, 1787, and it quickly chose George Washington as its presiding officer. Seventy-four delegates to the meeting were selected by the states, but only fifty-five attended. Delegates from New Hampshire arrived two months after the convention began, and Rhode Island never participated. The delegates agreed that all deliberations were to be secret, and this secrecy was maintained for thirty years afterward. Compared to the general population, delegates were disproportionately well educated (half were college graduates) and came from higher-status professions such as law, medicine, and business. Many of the individuals closely associated with the Revolution, for example, Patrick Henry, Thomas Paine, Sam Adams, and John Hancock, were absent. In fact, of the fifty-six signers of the Declaration of Independence, only eight were present at Philadelphia.

The official purpose of the Philadelphia meeting was to revise the Articles of Confederation. Many advocates of a totally new form of government believed that state legislatures (which were dominated by small farmers and debtor interests) would never consent to a meeting designed to abolish the Articles of Confederation. Nevertheless, despite their formal responsibility to revise the Articles, the assembled delegates produced a completely new form of government. The weak single-house legislature was replaced by a two-house legislature that was explicitly given important power over taxation, currency, foreign trade, and interstate commerce. The executive was made less dependent on the legislature, and the newly created presidency was given several key independent powers such as the right to veto legislation and leadership of the armed forces. The Supreme Court was created, and the groundwork was laid for an extensive system of courts independent of state control. The Articles of Confederation had not been patched up; they had been abolished and replaced by what in its day was considered a strong central government.

RATIFYING THE NEW CONSTITUTION

The drafting of the Constitution did not automatically bring the new central government into existence. Considerable debate centered on the means by which the new government was to be implemented. Some people argued that the unanimous consent of all state legislatures was required (the required legal method under the still-existent Articles of

Confederation). This position was rejected as too demanding in light of Rhode Island's nonparticipation and the radical nature of several state legislatures. Eventually it was agreed that approval by specially selected conventions (not citizens acting directly) in nine of the thirteen states would bring the Constitution into force. Delaware was the first to give its approval in 1787, and by June 21, 1788, nine states had ratified the Constitution. Rhode Island was the last state to ratify (May 29, 1790). In

THE CONFLICT OVER PRINCIPLES OF REPRESENTATION

For many Americans the Constitution is viewed as the work of saints who labored to produce an almost perfect document embodying the highest virtues. While many delegates to the Philadelphia convention were knowledgeable and were motivated by a genuine concern for the public welfare, to view the convention as a gathering of altruistic men who were "above politics" would be a serious mistake. Most delegates were experienced in politics and understood the close connection between the rules of government and the benefits that could be realized from government. Like all good politicians, delegates frequently justified their own narrow goals in terms of lofty abstract principles. Moreover, the drafting was characterized by extensive bargaining, vote trading, manipulation, and threats to leave. The Constitution is a negotiated document, not a sacred stone tablet handed down like the Ten Commandments.

The bargaining aspect of the convention was especially pronounced in the conflict over representation. Who was to be represented and in what number in the new government were questions that evoked enormous conflict and animosity. Perhaps the most difficult question involving representation was the conflict over whether citizens or states were to be represented in the new government. This question almost destroyed the convention, and its solution has, justifiably, been called the "great compromise."

Under the Articles, states, not citizens, were represented in the single-house Congress. Although each state had between two and seven delegates, the delegates of each state voted as a unit; so Delaware, which had a small population, was equal to Massachusetts, which was much larger. This principle of one state, one vote had been under attack for years, and not surprisingly the issue surfaced again during the convention. The frontal attack on this system of representation was led by the Virginia delegation, which proposed a two-house legislature with representation in both chambers based on population. This plan, usually called the **Virginia Plan,** turned on an all-many states the conflict over the new Constitution was bitterly fought and the outcome close. Each side accused the other of bribery, trickery, and misrepresenting the facts. Nevertheless, on April 30, 1789, the first Congress convened, counted the ballots from the January presidential election, and declared George Washington President. The Confederation Congress disbanded and saved the United States the embarrassment of having two separate national governments.

New Jersey Plan The plan submitted by the New Jersey delegation to the Constitutional Convention. While strengthening the central government, this plan would have continued a one-house legislature in which each state had only one vote.

Connecticut Compromise A proposal by the Connecticut delegation that would have one house of the legislature based on population, while in the other house each state would be represented equally. Combined elements of both the West Virginia and New Jersey plans.

powerful lower house that would elect Senators who had previously been nominated by the state legislatures. The two houses would then elect an executive who would serve for seven years but would not be eligible for reelection. The executive, together with a council of national judges, could veto congressional and state legislation. Overall, it was a plan for a powerful national government representing citizens, not states.

Delegates from smaller states viewed the Virginia Plan as a serious threat to their interests. The Delaware delegation threatened to walk out when the plan was first introduced, and one delegate from that state called the plan a conspiracy of Virginia and Pennsylvania "in which they would have an enormous and monstrous influence." Several delegates from large states hinted that they might form a union without the smaller states. To counter the Virginia Plan the New Jersey delegation introduced its own plan. Like the Virginia Plan, it would greatly strengthen the national government, but it would continue the old confederation system of one state, one vote. For a while neither side seemed willing to budge, and delegates were subjected to many boring, repetitive speeches appealing to higher principles. Put to a vote, the **New Jersey Plan** lost, but the issue of representation remained unresolved.

Finally, after long arguments and numerous alternatives that failed, a compromise was reached. Sometimes called the **Connecticut Compromise,** after the delegation that proposed it, the proposal called for citizens to be the basis of representation in the House but for states to be equally represented in the Senate. Thus, both large and small states were given something in their battle over representation. What is important to realize is that our present House and Senate both resulted from lengthy and often bitter negotiations and compromises in which one or two votes were frequently decisive. This was a solution that was acceptable under those particular conditions; it was not a plan designed by experts to be the best possible system of government.

A more complete description of this debate is presented in Merrill Jensen, *The Making of the American Constitution* (New York: Van Nostrand Reinhold, 1964), Chaps. 7 and 8.

THE CONTROVERSY OVER WHICH INTERESTS CREATED THE NEW CONSTITUTION

These, then, are the key events surrounding the emergence of the Constitution. In terms of dates, personalities, and general conditions most historians agree on what happened. However, when it comes to evaluating the meaning of the change from the Articles to the Constitution, there is considerable disagreement among the experts. In particular, while most Americans revere the Constitution and those who created it, one point of view asserts that the whole process was an antidemocratic usurpation of power on the part of privileged interests. Those who hold this position argue that the Constitution was not a magnificently crafted, enduring solution to political chaos. Rather, certain well-off economic interests created the Constitution for selfish reasons and then imposed it on an unwilling population. Proponents of this view are usually associated with Charles Beard, who in 1913 published the widely acclaimed *An Economic Interpretation of the Constitution of the United States*.[1]

The evidence for the economic interpretation of the Constitution

1. *The business and professional interests of delegates to the Constitutional Convention.* In today's terms delegates represented the economic establishment. Small farmers and tradesmen were totally absent. The drafters of the Constitution were likely to gain financially from a strong central government that could protect their property from the more radical state legislatures. Moreover, most delegates owned public securities issued by the government, and these were practically worthless so long as the national and state governments were incapable of paying their debts. Clearly, most delegates stood to advance their own welfare by abolishing the ineffectual Articles of Confederation.

2. *The procommercial interest provisions of the Constitution.* The men of property who created the Constitution were not content merely to create a strong national government to counterbalance radical state legislatures. Provisions highly beneficial to their interests were directly incorporated into the Constitution. For example, Article VI, section 1 guaranteed that all public securities issued before adoption of the Constitution would be redeemed by the new government. This was a boon to speculators who had bought up these securities for a fraction of their face value. Several drafters of the Constitution also owned securities issued by the old government. Article I, section 10 prohibited states from making "any thing but gold and silver coins a tender in payment of debts" without the consent of Congress. A favorite tactic of debtors was to have states print so much money that their debts could be easily

---

[1] Charles A. Beard, *An Economic Interpretation of the Constitution of the United States* (New York: Macmillan, 1913). Additional support for the Beard interpretation is presented in Jackson T. Main, "Charles A. Beard and the Constitution: A Critical Review of Forrest McDonald's *We the People*," *William and Mary Quarterly*, January 1960, 17:86–102. It should be noted that when Beard published his analysis he admitted that many of his conclusions were tentative and required further research.

discharged. Section 10 of Article I also forbade states from impairing the obligations of contracts. That is, you and your fellow debtors could not have your debts (or any other contractual obligation) abolished by a state legislative act. In addition, the taxing powers of the national government could not be used to attack property interests directly. National taxes were to be apportioned on the basis of a state's population, not according to the wealth of people in that state. Rich and poor states of equal population were thus to be taxed equally. Concentrated wealth, at least until the advent of the federal income tax, was safe from attack by the national government.

3. *The undemocratic nature of the ratification of the Constitution.* The established economic interests won ratification of the Constitution despite widespread opposition from most ordinary citizens who realized the biased nature of the Constitution. This was accomplished by several methods. In some states poor citizens could not vote for electors to the ratification conventions because of restrictive property qualifications. In other states, for example, New Jersey, Georgia, and Connecticut, the ratification process moved so swiftly that the opposition had almost no time to organize. Holding the elections in late fall and winter made it difficult for rural residents, who were mostly opposed to ratification, to journey to the polls. Postmasters allegedly delayed or altered anti-Constitution material sent through the mails. In all, not more than a quarter or a fifth of all white males participated in the ratification process. Equally significant, the indirect system of ratification allowed antiratification majorities to be ignored. In New York, Massachusetts, and New Hampshire delegates violated voters' instructions and endorsed the Constitution. In South Carolina pro-Constitution forces never won a clear majority.

All in all, Beard and others have argued that the Constitution should be viewed as a victory of the wealthy over the vast majority of small farmers, tradesmen, and "common people." If the American Revolution was a rebellion on behalf of all citizens, the Constitutional Convention was a counterrevolution on behalf of economic privilege. Are these claims true? Is the Constitution a product of a conservative minority interested in selfish gain? Many historians have accepted this harsh verdict, but many others have vigorously challenged it. They have viewed this economic interpretation as either a misleading oversimplification or simply wrong.[2]

The evidence against an economic interpretation of the Constitution

Opponents of the Beard argument assert that a careful reading of the debates within the Constitutional Convention, which were recorded by

[2] The major attacks on the Beard position are Robert E. Brown, *Charles Beard and the Constitution* (Princeton, N.J.: Princeton University Press, 1956) and Forrest McDonald, *We the People: The Economic Origins of the Constitution* (Chicago: University of Chicago Press, 1958). Another informative book about this debate is Lee Benson, *Turner and Beard: American Historical Writings Reconsidered* (Glencoe, Ill.: Free Press, 1960).

Bill of Rights **Popular name for the first ten amendments to the Constitution. These amendments generally limit government actions against citizens.**

THE FIRST TEN CONSTITUTIONAL AMENDMENTS

When the Constitution went to the states for ratification delegates at state conventions raised numerous objections. In all, about 150 amendments to the Constitution were proposed in these conventions. Some called for greater constraints on Congress, for example, requiring a two-thirds vote to borrow money or to declare war, but the most popular dealt with guarantees of individual rights. The Constitution did, of course, contain many such guarantees, for example, the prohibition of bills of attainder, but the drafters of the Constitution emphasized the organization of power, not written guarantees, as the best protector of individual rights. This approach did not satisfy many of those concerned with individual rights.

The absence of such widely desired guarantees also gave new hope to opponents of the Constitution. In the summer of 1788, Patrick Henry, George Mason, and other opponents were proposing a second Constitutional Convention to remedy this situation. Of course, since such a convention would not be limited to individual rights, it could be used to rewrite the entire Constitution. Four states—New York, Virginia, North Carolina, and Rhode Island—agreed to call for a second convention, but support from the other nine states was not forthcoming

When the first Congress assembled in 1789, James Madison realized that the absence of guarantees of rights could be an effective rallying cry for those committed to undoing the Constitution through a second convention. In addition, many promises had been made regarding amendments in order to secure ratification. Drawing largely on the amendments suggested by the Virginia ratification convention, Madison proposed twelve amendments, which were then sent to the states after Senate and House approval. Only ten of them passed.

Only after many years did these first ten amendments become known as the **Bill of Rights.** Though these amendments have taken on a sacred quality, at the time of passage some people saw them as a very clever deception designed largely to stop a second Constitutional Convention. As Richard Henry Lee, an opponent of the Constitution put it, "How wonderfully scrupulous have they been in stating rights. The English language has been carefully culled to find words feeble in their nature or doubtful in their meaning."*

* Cited in Merrill Jensen, *The Making of the American Constitution* (New York: Van Nostrand Reinhold, 1964), pp. 149–50.

James Madison, shows that there was considerable concern for the interests of ordinary citizens. Numerous proposals were rejected on the grounds that ordinary citizens would not tolerate them. Moreover, several delegates expressed great confidence in the political good sense of urban workers. And while many delegates were primarily concerned with the protection of property, others were preoccupied with the protection of the rights of all citizens. James Madison, who probably had more of an impact on drafting the Constitution than any other delegate, clearly stated that if human rights and property rights were in conflict, human rights—such as the right to vote—had priority. Being wealthy does not automatically lead to the advocacy of schemes against those less well off.

Second, opponents of the economic interpretation point out that delegates to the Constitutional Convention were not a unified economic group. Delegates were not "*the* rich"; they were a diverse group, and their own economic interests were often in conflict. Southern slave-owning planters did not always agree with merchants from New England. Regional interests were sometimes more important than divisions between rich and poor. Moreover, many of these delegates supported policies that were against the narrow interests of the economic elite, for example, allowing states to issue paper money. A quarter of the delegates had participated in so-called radical state legislatures and had voted for prodebtor laws. Perhaps the most telling piece of information is the fact that several wealthy delegates—including the holder of the largest bloc of public securities—opposed ratification of the new Constitution.

Finally, it is asserted that the ratification process was not a conspiracy of the rich to defraud the poor. In most states the overwhelming majority of delegates to the ratification convention was small farmers, who supposedly opposed ratification, and not bankers or wealthy merchants. In Delaware, the first state to ratify, there was not a single manufacturer, banker, or security speculator at the convention. Nor was the vote very close in these ratifying conventions. Among the first nine in favor of ratification, the pro-Constitution forces received 66.75 percent of the total vote (only in New York and Massachusetts was the vote close). In short, the Constitution was not undemocratically imposed by the economic establishment on an unwilling citizenry.

Resolving conflicting interpretations

Which of these two positions is closer to the truth? Since both arguments rest on incomplete information and subjective interpretations, this conflict cannot be perfectly resolved. Nevertheless, despite many differences in interpretation, several facts are reasonably clear. First, the Constitution did not result from widespread, popular demands for a new form of government. Whether the advocates of a new form of government were exclusively the rich or a more diversified group does not change the fact that the demand was a minority demand. Second, the overall thrust of the new Constitution was to check the more radical, antirich policies of several state legislatures. Some historians interpret this as a conservative counterrevolution, but others see the same events as

Divine right   A theory used by some European kings between the fifteenth and eighteenth centuries asserting that their power came from God, and therefore they could not be overthrown by mere people. They ruled by divine right, not by citizen consent.

merely a reasonable corrective to a widely acknowledged problem. Finally, the proportion of citizens accepting the Constitution was minuscule. Women and blacks were automatically excluded from the ratification process, but even among those eligible to vote, most people chose to abstain. By today's standards a "mandate" by 2 or 3 percent of the population may seem meaningless. However, in the context of the late eighteenth century this might be considered a resounding endorsement.

Does the Constitution allow government by the people?

We have seen that the Constitution was not the result of widespread public desire, nor was it approved by the majority of citizens. We also know that most delegates to the Constitutional Convention greatly feared extensive participation in government by ordinary citizens. These historical facts, regardless of how they are interpreted, stand in sharp contrast to the popular current view of the Constitution as the basis for citizen control of government. Is it somehow possible that the Constitution promotes popular rule despite its origins? Or, on the other hand, are those who view the Constitution as providing rule by the people profoundly misinformed about the true nature of the Constitution? In order to understand this possible contradiction we must look at two aspects of the Constitution: its source of authority and the provisions that affect citizen control over government.

SOURCES OF GOVERNMENT AUTHORITY

All governments must somehow justify their rule. In the early seventeenth century King James I of England asserted that his power derived from God, so that he ruled by "**divine right.**" Ordinary citizens could not (supposedly) replace a monarch because they did not create the monarchy. Governments have also claimed that their authority rests on the innate superiority of leaders over subjects, for example, colonial regimes in Africa and Asia. Here too it would be wrong and contrary to "natural laws"—as defined by the rulers—for the ruled to overthrow the government.

Justifying government in America

The political philosophy that developed in America during the eighteenth century emphasized the people, not God or natural superiority, as the basis of government. The writings of the English philosopher John Locke were especially important in promoting the view that people create governments to serve their interests and that this authority can be withdrawn by the people. This view, which was the basis of the Declaration of Independence, was also accepted in the Constitutional Convention and was clearly expressed in the Preamble to the Constitution:

> We the People of the United States, in Order to Form a more perfect
> Union, insure domestic Tranquility, provide for the common de-

fence, promote the general welfare, and secure the Blessings of Liberty to ourselves and our Posterity, do ordain and establish this Constitution for the United States of America.

Basing the new government on the consent of the governed was more than just a gesture. A persistent theme throughout the constitutional debates was that no system of government would survive without popular support. After all, the delegates had seen the British colonial governments overthrown (as well as the unsuccessful Shays' Rebellion in Massachusetts) and thus knew that the divine right of kings was little protection against dissatisfied citizens. Many delegates also believed that the new government would be more effective if its authority came directly from the people. Recall that one of the weaknesses of the Articles of Confederation was that it drew its authority from the state legislatures, not the people themselves.

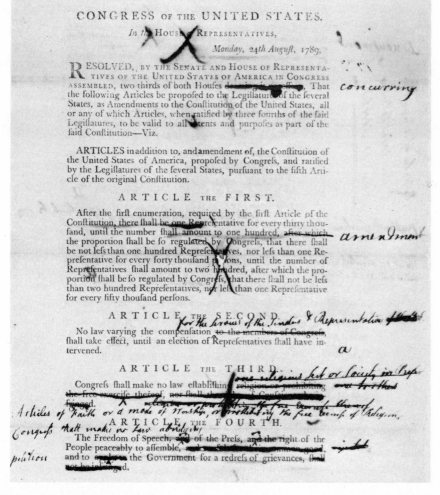

An early draft of the Bill of Rights. Note that the contemporary First Amendment (which protects free speech) was originally the Fourth Amendment. The original first two amendments were rejected and the Third and Fourth were combined.

BILL OF RIGHTS: U.S. VERSUS SOVIET

Like the U.S. Constitution, the constitution of the Union of Soviet Socialist Republics contains important provisions protecting individual rights. Here are some side-by-side comparisons of the U.S. Bill of Rights and the Soviet constitution.

U.S. Bill of Rights

I. Congress shall make no law respecting an establishment of religion, or prohibiting the free exercise thereof; or abridging the freedom of speech, or of the press, or of the right of the people peaceably to assemble, and to petition the Government for a redress of grievances.

Soviet Constitution (Adopted October 7, 1977)

Article 52—Citizens of the USSR are guaranteed freedom of conscience, that is, the right to profess or not to profess any religion and to conduct religious worship or atheistic propaganda.

Article 50—Citizens of the USSR are guaranteed freedom of speech, of the press, and of assembly, meetings, street processions and demonstrations.

Article 49—Every citizen of the USSR has the right to submit proposals to state bodies and public organizations for improving their activity, and to criticize shortcomings in their work.

II. A well regulated Militia, being necessary to the security of a free state, the right of the people to keep and bear arms, shall not be infringed.

III. No Soldier shall, in time of peace be quartered in any house, without the consent of the Owner, nor in time of war, but in a manner to be described by law.

Article 63—Military service in the ranks of the Armed Forces of the USSR is an honourable duty of Soviet citizens.

IV. The right of the people to be secure in their persons, houses, papers, and effects, against unreasonable searches and seizures, shall not be violated. . . .

Article 55 — Citizens of the USSR are guaranteed inviolability of the home. No one may, without lawful grounds, enter a home against the will of those residing in it.

Article 56 — The privacy of citizens, and their correspondence, telephone conversations, and telegraphic communications is protected by law.

V. No person shall be held to answer for a [serious] crime, unless on a presentation or indictment of a Grand Jury . . . . nor shall any person be subject for the same offense to be twice put in jeopardy of life or limb; nor shall be compelled in any criminal case to be a witness against himself, nor be deprived of life, liberty, or property without due process of law. . . .

Article 54 — Citizens of the USSR are guaranteed inviolability of the person. No one may be arrested except by a court decision or on the warrant of a procurator.

Article 160 — No one may be adjudged guilty of a crime and subjected to punishment as a criminal except by the sentence of a court and in conformity with the law.

VI. In all criminal prosecutions the accused shall enjoy the right to a speedy and public trial, by an impartial jury of the State . . . and to be informed of the nature and cause of the accusation; to be confronted with the witnesses against him . . . and to have the assistance of Counsel for his defense.

Article 156 — Justice is administered in the USSR on the principle of the equality of citizens before the law and the court.

Article 157 — Proceedings in all courts shall be open to the public. Hearings *in camera* are only allowed in cases provided by law, with the observance of all the rules of Judicial procedure.

Article 158 — A defendant in a criminal action is guaranteed the right to legal assistance.

(Continued on page 34)

VII. In suits at common law [greater than $20] the right to trial by jury shall be preserved, and no fact tried by a jury shall be otherwise reexamined in any Court of the United States, than according to the rules of the common law.

VIII. Excessive bail shall not be required, nor excessive fines imposed, nor cruel and unusual punishment be inflicted.

IX. The enumeration in the Constitution, of certain rights, shall not be construed to deny or disparage others retained by the people.

X. The powers not delegated to the United States by the Constitution, nor prohibited by it to the states, are reserved to the states, or the people.

Article 163—Economic disputes between enterprises, institutions, and organizations are settled by state arbitration bodies within the limits of their jurisdiction.

The people as the source of government versus the people as policy makers

Basing the authority of government on the people is *not*, however, the same thing as letting citizens decide government policies. The people were to be the *source* of political authority, but not the executors of policy. The power of citizens to influence the national government was to be greatly limited through a variety of constitutional mechanisms. Perhaps the most obvious limitation on popular influence concerned how public officials were selected. Only the House of Representatives was to be selected directly by citizens. Senators and the President were elected indirectly: state legislatures selected Senators and presidential electors (only by custom do citizens choose presidential electors). Justices of the Supreme Court were appointed and could be removed only for impropriety. Moreover, terms of office were staggered so that citizens could change only a portion of their leaders at any one election (no more than a third of the Senate could be changed at one time).

SEPARATION OF POWERS Besides frustrating citizen influence through the electoral process, the Constitution is designed to minimize the consequences should citizens gain control of one part of government. One way this is accomplished is through the **separation of powers** — the separation (but not complete independence) of legislative, executive, and judicial functions. If, for example, irate taxpayers revolted and gained control of the House, the impact would be muted by the fact that the House does not by itself usually possess sufficient power to create antitaxation policy. The House might pass antitax legislation, but the Senate might reject such legislation. House-Senate disagreements are even encouraged by the differences in what these legislatures represent: the House represents citizens while the Senate is intended to represent the states. Even if the two houses of Congress could agree, the legislature lacks control over the administration and the judicial interpretation of legislation. Similarly, a President opposed to Congress cannot impose his will on the other branch. If all powers were concentrated in one branch, controlling government would be much easier — a simple majority could make the laws, enforce them, and decide the resulting court cases.

CHECKS AND BALANCES A principle related to separation of powers is the doctrine of **checks** and **balances.** Whereas separation of powers divides governmental functions among different officials, checks and balances gives each official some power over the others. For example, Article II, section 2 gives the President the power to make treaties and to appoint ambassadors and Supreme Court Justices, but these appointments require Senate approval. Likewise, the President is commander-in-chief of the armed forces, but Congress is responsible for declaring war and authorizing the money to fight wars. The President is also given the power to **veto** legislation. A President who oversteps his powers or commits other crimes may be **impeached** (indicted) by the House and tried by the Senate. Checks and balances also apply to the courts. It is the President — with the consent of the Senate — who appoints all federal judges, while Congress creates new court systems and defines many areas of court jurisdiction. Here again the basic constitutional design allows some officials to resist or oversee the actions of other officials.

FEDERALISM A fourth feature of the Constitution that can thwart citizen control of the national government is **federalism.** Federalism means the division of power between the national and state governments. This principle is explicitly stated in the Tenth Amendment, which reads: "The powers not delegated to the United States by the Constitution, nor prohibited to it by the States, are reserved to the States respectively, or the people." This means that a national majority cannot demand action by the national government if that action falls in the domain of state power. If the American public demanded that Congress do something about the chaotic pattern of local traffic regulations, Congress could not act because this area is off-limits to national government; at best Congress might provide some economic incentives to change the laws, but it could

Separation of powers The principle by which power is dispersed among three branches of government, with each branch selected differently and having a different term of office.

Checks and balances The method of organizing government so that each component (the legislative, executive, and judicial) has some power over the actions of the other components. Also applies to relations between national and state governments.

Veto. Latin for "I forbid" The act of a President to prevent a bill passed by Congress from becoming a law. The President can be overridden by a two-thirds vote of each house.

Impeachment A formal process which states an accusation of a crime. Under the Constitution, the House of Representatives is responsible for bringing an impeachment.

Federalism The system of governing in which two or more levels of government rule the same people, with each level having some independence of policy.

FIGURE 2.1

FOUR DIFFERENT WAYS THE CONSTITUTION CAN BE AMENDED

	1.	2.	3.	4.
	2/3 2/3 2/3 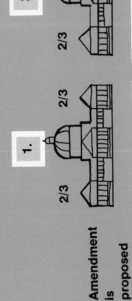	2/3 2/3 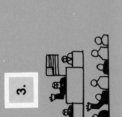		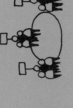
Amendment is proposed by	Two-thirds vote in both House and Senate	Two-thirds vote in both House and Senate	A national convention called for by Congress at the request of legislatures of two-thirds of states	A national convention called for by Congress at request of legislatures of two-thirds of states.
	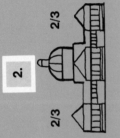	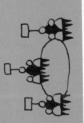		
Amendment must be ratified by	Legislatures of three-quarters of states (presently 38 states)	Specially convened conventions in three-quarters of the states.	Legislatures of three-quarters of states	Specially convened conventions in three quarters of states
When used	For all amendments except 21st (repeal of Prohibition)	For 21st Amendment	Never used	Never used

not legislate directly.[3] The practice of forbidding national action in certain areas is unknown in many other nations, for example, Great Britain, where all policies—even local traffic laws—can be made at the national level.

SUPERMAJORITIES   A fifth, and somewhat different, impediment to popular control of government is the frequent use by the Constitution of "**supermajorities.**" That is, to accomplish something one needs two thirds or three quarters of a vote, not a simple majority. Treaties with foreign governments, for example, must be approved by a two-thirds vote in the Senate. A simple House majority is needed for impeachment, but conviction by the Senate requires a two-thirds vote. The two-thirds requirement is also used for proposing constitutional amendments, while ratification of these proposals needs a three-quarters majority of either state legislatures or special state conventions (see Figure 2.1). The existence of such supermajority requirements frequently means that a minority of officials can effectively block highly popular proposals.

POLICIES OFF-LIMITS TO GOVERNMENT   Finally, the Constitution explicitly prohibits certain government actions, so that if people want the national government to pursue these policies, a constitutional amendment must be passed. For example, the passing of an **ex post facto** law (a law that makes a crime retroactive and has an adverse effect on the accused person) by Congress is forbidden (Article I, section 9). Nor can Congress permanently suspend the right to a **writ of habeas corpus** (a court order directing an official holding someone in custody to show cause for his or her detention to a court). The importance of such constitutional restrictions was made clear when the government's initial attempts at a national income tax were struck down as a violation of Article I, section 9, paragraph 4 that prohibited taxes or assessments on grounds other than state population. It required the Sixteenth Amendment to overcome this restriction.

THE CONSTITUTION AND CONTEMPORARY POLITICS

Clearly, then, the Constitution was designed to limit popular control over government despite the fact that it draws its political authority from the people. Two further questions arise concerning this situation: Have these original impediments to popular rule been significantly overcome? If not, can they somehow be justified?

The contemporary impact of the Constitution on popular rule

The original Constitution has been changed somewhat, but not drastically, to encourage greater citizen control of government. The most significant changes have occurred in the area of selecting public officials.

---

[3] Just how far the national government can go at the expense of state governments is a complex question that is analyzed in depth in Chapter 3. In contemporary politics Congress has considerable power if it chooses to act. This power is still not absolute, however, and for much of our history the Supreme Court did prevent the federal government from interfering with many state functions.

Supermajority   More than 50 percent plus one (which is called a simple majority). A super majority can be anything from 50 percent plus two to 100 percent.

Ex post facto law   A law that makes a crime retroactive and has an adverse effect on the accused person.

Writ of habeas corpus   A court order directing an official holding someone in custody to show cause for the person's detention to a court.

Presidential electors In presidential elections voters in each state technically choose slates of citizens called presidential electors, not one of the presidential candidates. The electors receiving the most votes then vote for the candidate they are pledged to support.
Poll tax A fee charged for voting. Commonly used to exclude poor people from voting.
Staggered elections The principle of not having all public officials elected on the same date or in the same year.

Since 1913, Senators have been directly elected (Seventeenth Amendment), and by custom **presidential electors** automatically follow voter majorities in their states (though exceptions can and do occur). Moreover, constitutional amendments have opened the political process to blacks (Fifteenth Amendment) and women (Nineteenth Amendment). The Twenty-fourth Amendment, passed in 1964, also forbids the use of a **poll tax** (a fee charged for voting) in federal elections.

Nevertheless, most of the constitutional features designed to limit popular control of policy remain intact. **Staggered federal elections** remain, thus always insulating part of the government from change, and judges and many other officials remain appointed, not elected. Separation of powers continues despite periodic pleas by members of Congress and the President for less bickering and more cooperation. Presidential complaints about "do-nothing" or "obstructionist" Congresses and congressional harping on presidential stubbornness have been regular features of twentieth-century politics. And both of these branches are frequently frustrated by judicial decisions. The principle of checks and balances is also very much alive. No President, regardless of his electoral success, has received total legislative cooperation on budgets, laws, and appointments. The 1973 impeachment proceedings against President Richard Nixon over Watergate underlined the contemporary relevance of this principle, but such dramatic events are only the tip of the iceberg of interbranch conflict.

The federalism principle preventing government action—even if desired by a national majority—remains relevant despite considerable blurring of purely national and state responsibilities. As we shall see in the next chapters, in such key policy areas as education, crime, and housing, state governments still dominate. A national majority might, for example, convince Congress and the President to legalize marijuana, but barring a constitutional amendment, each state could keep its own antimarijuana laws.

The supermajorities required by the Constitution remain very much in force. In the debate over whether President Nixon ought to be impeached a major consideration was the difficulty of getting two thirds of all Senators present to vote for conviction. The three-quarters rule for ratification of constitutional amendments has been a major impediment to the passage of the proposed Twenty-seventh, or Equal Rights Amendment (ERA). This amendment, which would forbid abridging rights on the basis of sex, was first proposed to the states by Congress in 1972. Between March 1972 and November 1978, thirty-five states ratified the amendment. Unfortunately for supporters of the ERA, however, this falls three states short of a three-quarters majority.

Finally, while the Constitution has displayed considerable adaptability to changing situations, as we shall see, it remains effective in keeping certain actions beyond the reach of today's citizens. What, for example, if there were a movement to elect former Secretary of State Henry Kissinger President? It would be forbidden by Article II, section 1, paragraph 5, which requires that the President be a native-born citizen (Kissinger's parents were German citizens). Abolishing the electoral college would also take a huge effort, merely because the procedure is spelled out in the Constitution. A similar difficulty would be encountered if we wanted to make Supreme Court Justices elected rather than appointed or to increase the terms of members of the House of Representatives from two to four years. All of these proposals have been widely considered and have much public support, but they have come to naught, in part because the constitutional obstacles to change are formidable.

Justifying constitutional restraints on majority rule

A second question regarding the Constitution's impediments to popular control of government concerns the desirability of these limitations. Since most of us highly value "government by the people," limitations on popular control might be viewed as obstacles to be removed. There is, however, another perspective that views these constitutional provisions

---

THE EQUAL RIGHTS AMENDMENT

Amending the Constitution can be a slow process. Frequently a proposed amendment languishes in Congress for years before it is sent to the states for ratification. The slowness of this process is illustrated by the history of the Equal Rights Amendment, which was officially proposed to the states by Congress on March 22, 1972, but has yet to be ratified.* To appreciate such delays, consider the following *New York Times* news item:

WASHINGTON, May 21 — The Senate Judiciary Committee approved a resolution today calling for a Constitutional amendment to guarantee equal rights to women.

The vote was 7 to 2. Before it can be put into effect it must be approved by a two-thirds vote of the House of Representatives and the Senate and ratified by thirty-six state Legislatures within seven years.

The amendment, an issue in Congress for years, would simply specify that the rights of a citizen shall not be abridged because of sex.

This story regarding the ERA appeared on May 22, 1951! Note from this report that even in 1951 the Equal Rights Amendment had been "an issue in Congress for years." In fact, it was first introduced in 1923.

* On average, once a constitutional amendment clears Congress, it takes one year and 136 days to be ratified by the states. The shortest ratification period was 100 days for the Twenty-sixth Amendment (the 18-year-old vote). The longest was three years and 240 days for the Twenty-second Amendment (limiting the President to two terms). The greatest source of delay, however, is securing ratification by both houses of Congress.

as necessary and desirable. This perspective, which underlies the Constitution, rests on the following beliefs:

1. The greatest of all political dangers is a tyrannical government. By "tyranny" is meant the arbitrary or unreasonable exercise of government power that results in the deprivation of some natural right such as the right to private property. Avoiding government tyranny is more important than any other political goal, including direct public control of leaders.

2. Unless somehow prevented, those in power will tyrannize those without power. Human beings are not angels, and thus nontyrannical government cannot depend on good instincts prevailing over bad instincts. Thus, the major problem faced in designing a government is avoiding this virtually inherent tendency toward tyranny.

3. The Constitution is designed to prevent tyranny in two general ways. First, since tyranny is likely to occur when one interest controls all political power, the system of separation of powers together with the various checks and balances and the need for supermajorities prevents tyranny within government. The desire for power on the part of one official checks the tyrannical tendencies of other officials. An ambitious, power-seeking President is held in line by the ambitions of members of Congress and judges. Tyranny is thwarted because no single interest can dominate government.

4. Second, the Constitution creates a large, diverse republic with a division of power between state and national governments. This diversity and dispersion of power will further prevent any single interest from achieving a dominating position. For example, a group of debtors intent on confiscating the property of the rich may have successes in some locations, but it is unlikely that they could ever capture complete political power in the United States. Because each interest can gain only a portion of power, it cannot tyrannize its opponents.

Evaluating the impact of the Constitution

It is clear that how one evaluates the limitations of the Constitution on citizen control of government depends on one's political priorities. If you believe that citizens will not tyrannize their fellow citizens, then such devices as checks and balances, separation of powers, federalism, and supermajorities are viewed negatively as impediments to citizen control of government. These features of the Constitution undermine democracy. On the other hand, if you are pessimistic about what individuals will do if given unrestrained political power, these same features are a necessary protection from a likely evil. Supporters of the second position do not oppose popular control of government; rather, accomplishing this goal is secondary to the goal of preserving our rights and liberties from a tyrannical government. Government by popular majorities is sacrificed in the name of protection from tyranny.

There are, then, several answers to our original question of whether the Constitution allows government by the people. Insofar as the government created by the Constitution draws its authority from the people, and insofar as most public officials are selected through elections, the answer is yes, the Constitution does provide for government by the people. On the other hand, many constitutional provisions are explicitly designed to thwart control of government by a majority of citizens. The Constitution does not automatically translate the preference of a popular majority into public policy. It does provide for popular influence, but it also contains many obstacles to popular control.

Has the Constitution become politically outdated?

The Constitution came into force on June 21, 1788. Two years later the first census reported a population of 3.93 million people living in 888,881 square miles. Much has changed since 1790. By 1977, the U.S. population had reached 216 million, the thirteen states had increased to fifty, and the United States had an area of 3.615 million square miles. More important, the world has become much more complex. Problems that are common today—nuclear weapons, disarmament, pollution, poverty, racial and sexual discrimination—were not major issues requiring government solutions 190 years ago. The transformation of society has understandably raised serious questions about the current political relevance of the Constitution. Some critics have even viewed the Constitution as an archaic force that is inherently undemocratic because nobody alive today ever explicitly agreed to it.

ARGUMENTS IN FAVOR OF CHANGING THE CONSTITUTION

Perhaps the most important argument in favor of a major change in the Constitution concerns whether the original design lends itself to solving contemporary problems. In 1788 the role of government was limited; it was concerned with securing peace, constructing roads and canals, and other housekeeping functions. Given this small role, the fear that government might acquire too much power was appropriate. Excessive power could result only in harm because the rightful duties of government, for example, issuing a uniform currency, did not require extensive power. Today, however, the fear that increased power will automatically lead to harm (or tyranny) may no longer be appropriate. In fact, the opposite may now be true—given the existence of pressing problems that *must* be solved, the *lack* of vast power could result in disaster. To constrain government, it is sometimes argued, is to make for ineffective government.

In addition, it is sometimes argued that the emphasis of the Constitution on conflict among public officials is more appropriate to a time when inaction was the normal government response to problems. In today's politics, the argument goes, the emphasis should be on cooperation among the branches of government, not conflict. Nobody really gains if the President has one plan to solve inflation, each branch of Congress has its own plan, and none can budge the others. Nor does it make any sense for Congress and the President to create and administer elaborate

"Necessary and proper clause" After giving Congress a long list of explicit powers, the Constitution states that Congress may also pass laws that are necessary to carry out these enumerated powers. Because the courts have broadly interpreted what is necessary, this clause has also been known as the "elastic clause."

programs under the ever-possible threat that their actions may be voided by the Supreme Court. Effective policy does not result from deadlocks and stand-offs.

Another contemporary criticism of the Constitution focuses on the power it gives minorities. A few individuals located in strategic positions can effectively block a clear majority. For example, fifty-one Senators representing only 18 percent of all Americans can block all legislation. Thirteen states can stop a constitutional amendment. Five Supreme Court Justices can insist that students be bused to achieve racial integration of public schools despite strong and extensive antibusing sentiment among citizens and other government officials. Such antimajority actions may have been acceptable in 1788, but some people claim that they cannot be defended in the twentieth century.

ARGUMENTS IN SUPPORT OF THE CONSTITUTION

The Constitution does, of course, have its supporters. Several arguments have been offered to defend the Constitution against the charge that it is outmoded. One important defense is that the Constitution does allow for flexibility and adaptation. Since its adoption, the Constitution has been amended twenty-six times, and these amendments have concerned such fundamental issues as abolishing slavery; providing blacks, women, and 18-year-old citizens the right to vote; and prohibiting congressional interference with free speech, freedom of the press, and freedom of religion. Nor has the Constitution prevented the national government from creating new organizations to meet new needs. The Constitution makes no mention of a Department of Commerce, a Federal Aviation Authority, a Federal Reserve Bank, or any other cabinet office or federal agency, yet all of these necessary organizations were created under constitutional authority. Important nongovernmental groups such as political parties and interest groups, which serve many political needs, have also developed apart from the Constitution. Thus, it cannot be claimed that the Constitution locks us into a late eighteenth-century style of government.

The Constitution provides flexibility

Flexibility is also provided by certain clauses in the Constitution itself. The delegates in Philadelphia realized that no document could ever anticipate in detail all future developments and emergencies, so discretion had to be granted to public officials. A well-known example of how such discretion is provided is Article I, section 8, clause 18, which gives Congress the power "To make all Laws which shall be necessary and proper for carrying into Execution the foregoing Powers, and all other Powers vested by this Constitution in the Government of the United States, or in any Department or Officer thereof." This provision, sometimes called the **necessary and proper clause** (or the elastic clause), follows a long section spelling out specific powers given to Congress and gives Congress the general authority to make whatever laws are necessary to implement these explicit powers.

This "necessary and proper" provision received its first, and most important, elaboration in the case of *McCulloch* v. *Maryland*, which came before the Supreme Court in 1819. The basic issue here was whether the national government could establish a bank to handle its finances despite no explicit constitutional authorization to create such a bank. Chief Justice John Marshall ruled that since the government was explicitly given the power to coin money, collect taxes, borrow money, and engage in other financial matters, the establishment of a bank is a legitimate, constitutional means to accomplish these ends. The "necessary and proper" clause is not a blank check. It allows great flexibility in executing specific grants of power. It does not permit the government to make any law on the grounds that it is "necessary."

Flexibility to meet changing circumstances is also provided by the constitutional responsibilities given the President. In particular, two key phrases in Article II have laid the groundwork for a wide variety of presidential actions not explicitly authorized in the Constitution. The first sentence of Article II states: "The executive power shall be vested in a President of the United States of America." This "**executive power**" has usually been broadly interpreted by all three branches of government. It has been the basis for presidential declarations of neutrality, removal of executive branch officials from office without congressional consent, the signing of executive agreements with foreign nations (which are legally equivalent to treaties), and various acts during emergency situations. None of these actions are explicitly mentioned in the Constitution, but each has been allowed as an exercise of "executive power."[4]

Executive power is not unlimited, however. In 1972, for example, the Supreme Court in *United States* v. *United States District Court, Eastern Michigan* ruled that the Nixon Administration had violated the Constitution in approving wiretaps to gather intelligence information on allegedly subversive domestic organizations. These surveillance actions were taken without a court order in the name of the President's inherent power to protect national security. Writing for the 8 to 0 majority, Justice Lewis F. Powell, Jr., wrote: "Unreviewed executive discretion may yield too readily to pressures to obtain incriminating evidence and overlook potential invasions of privacy and protected speech. . . . We cannot accept the government's argument that internal security matters are too subtle and complex for judicial evaluation."

A second important clause that allows considerable presidential flexibility is in Article II, section 3, which states "he shall take care that the laws be faithfully executed." Here again a certain amount of vagueness allows considerable discretion. The importance of this general grant of authority was illustrated several times in the conflict over the civil rights of southern blacks in the 1950s and 1960s. For example, when the governor of Arkansas refused to allow court-ordered integration of public high schools in Little Rock, President Dwight D. Eisenhower was able to order U.S. troops to Little Rock to prevent such interference. President John F. Kennedy took similar action to overcome southern defiance in 1962 and 1963. In all three cases it was up to the President to decide just how the

Executive power This concept has never been precisely defined, but it usually is interpreted to mean that the President can take whatever actions are necessary to preserve the public good.

[4] For an analysis of "executive power," see Edward S. Corwin, *The Constitution and What It Means Today*, revised by Harold W. Chase and Craig R. Ducat (Princeton, N.J.: Princeton University Press, 1973), pp. 111-13.

laws would be enforced. A variety of legal options were available, but the President's final decision depended on complex circumstances that could not have been anticipated by the drafters of the Constitution.

The value of the Constitution as a unifying symbol

The Constitution can also be defended on different grounds: it provides a valuable symbol that helps unite Americans of diverse political perspectives. It has been argued that all nations, if they are to remain united, must possess common, highly regarded symbols. For example, most Americans, whether Democrat or Republican, liberal or conservative, share positive feelings about the Declaration of Independence, the flag, the national anthem, the Battle of Bunker Hill, the Boston Tea Party, and perhaps most of all, the Constitution.[5] These objects and events evoke positive feelings even though many of us are only vaguely aware of what they are or what occurred. Politically, these symbols help to create a common national identity and thus moderate sharp disagreements.

The symbolic value of the Constitution can be seen when groups of citizens diametrically opposed on an issue each endorse the same Constitution. For example, many citizens opposed to the efforts of the national government to integrate public schools believe that their position is perfectly consistent with the Constitution. Black civil rights groups, who favor government-enforced integration, on the other hand, claim that all they want is *their* constitutional rights as they interpret them. Similar disagreements have occurred regarding the women's movement, with both sides pointing to the Constitution to support their positions. What is important here is that all sides share an admiration for the document that creates and defines our basic political structures. Conflict occurs over the meaning of phrases or the relative importance of provisions. The political system itself, embodied in the awe-inspiring, almost religiously worshipped Constitution, is not directly challenged. Without this document and the positive feelings that it generates, conflicts might be more acrimonious and even threaten the very system itself.

The argument that the Constitution has worked

A third broad defense of the Constitution is the most fundamental: it has worked. Especially compared to almost all other nations, government under the Constitution has worked exceptionally well. The major problem that the Constitution was designed to solve was the creation of a nontyrannical central government. Though there have been occasional acts of political repression—for example, the mass deportation of suspected radicals in the early 1920s—the United States has escaped the oppressive governments that have occasionally befallen Italy, Germany,

---

[5] The appeal of the Constitution to citizens is so great that in 1874 a composer named Greeler set the entire document, including the Preamble and the Bill of Rights, to music. The Constitution opened with the Preamble as a recitative for altos and basses and concluded with the amendments in the form of fugues. The whole musical drama took six hours and was frequently performed to widely enthusiastic audiences. This bit of history comes from David Wallechinsky and Irving Wallace, *The People's Almanac #2* (New York: Bantam Books, 1978), p. 1229.

Japan, and most countries in Africa, South America, and Asia. Of course, nobody would argue that only the Constitution prevented such tyranny, but it is likely that such mechanisms as separation of powers and checks and balances have played a significant role. In many ways the prosecution of President Nixon for abuses of power through constitutionally prescribed channels is persuasive evidence of the value of the Constitution in preventing tyranny.

It can also be argued that the effectiveness of the Constitution is demonstrated by the emergence of the United States as a world power. A major criticism of the Articles of Confederation was that it left the United States vulnerable to foreign domination. No unified commercial policies existed, and the central government lacked the resources to pursue American overseas interests vigorously. The government created by the Constitution clearly overcame these deficiencies. Moreover, in times of war and international crisis the government—despite separation of powers, checks and balances, and other impediments to action—has acted decisively. At least in foreign affairs a constitutionally limited government has not proved to be a weak, disorganized government. The American President, thanks to his position as commander-in-chief of the armed forces and his power in dealing with foreign governments, has been fully able to protect the United States in foreign affairs.

Finally, a good indicator of the soundness of the basic constitutional design is given by the subsequent modifications of this design through the amendment process. On the whole, while several amendments have had a profound impact on the rights of certain groups, the basic structure has been modified only slightly. For example, the Twelfth and Twentieth amendments settled some details concerning presidential elections and the taking of office, but they do not touch on the basic character of the presidency. The Fifteenth, Nineteenth, Twenty-third, Twenty-fourth, and Twenty-sixth amendments opened up the electoral process to blacks, women, residents of Washington, D.C., and 18-year-olds, and prohibited poll taxes, but left the electoral system untouched. The Seventeenth Amendment gave the people the right to elect Senators directly, but the Senate itself was left unchanged. Several policies, for example, federal income tax, the prohibition of liquor, and slavery, have been regulated through the amendment process, but these policies pertain to what the government can specifically do and do not affect the fundamental distribution of powers. If the basic design of separated powers, checks and balances, and so on, were defective, we would expect much greater changes. After all, if citizens could call a convention to overhaul the Articles of Confederation, they could do the same for the Constitution—and such a convention is explicitly provided for in Article V.

A conclusion: the Constitution

One of the most remarkable features of the Constitution is its appeal to so many people. Virtually every political group finds something of value in this document. Even citizens who could not recite a single constitutional provision if they had to probably believe that their freedom to do what they think is right is explicitly guaranteed in the Constitution. Citizens devoted to popular control of government have the Preamble (which proclaims the people as the ultimate source of power) plus the provisions for elections. Those fearful of popular influence are reassured by the provisions preventing a momentary majority from seizing control of government—for example, Supreme Court Justices are appointed for

AMENDMENTS THAT NEVER SURVIVED

The bias of the Constitution against fundamental political change becomes apparent when we examine attempts to make changes. Since the first ten amendments were ratified in 1791, only sixteen amendments have been adopted (and one of these—the Twenty-first—merely nullified the Eighteenth). Five more proposed amendments have received the necessary two-thirds vote in both houses, and four of the five have been ratified by a majority of the states, but not having reached the three-quarters requirement they have yet to become law. Two of these five were originally part of the first ten amendments. One dealt with the ratio between population and House seats and received only ten of the necessary eleven state votes. The other would have prohibited members of Congress from raising their salaries without an intervening election (it received only six votes). An 1810 proposal prohibiting citizens from accepting foreign titles or honors received eleven of the necessary fourteen votes. On the eve of the Civil War an amendment prohibiting future constitutional amendments from interfering with slavery was approved by Congress, but only three states ratified it. In the twentieth century two proposed amendments —one prohibiting child labor and one guaranteeing equal rights to women—have received clear majorities of support by the states, but thus far have failed to get three-quarters support. (This hurdle is sometimes compounded even further by supermajority requirements within the states.)*

Over the years several thousand attempts to change the Constitution have failed (as of the end of 1974, some 8,600 proposed amendments were introduced in Congress). One compilation of these failed efforts found, for example, that between 1889 and 1928, fifty-three amendments were proposed dealing with presidential elections. Despite several clear problems with the existing method—you can win, for example, with a minority of the popular vote—no change was made. Between 1790 and 1928, 210 amendments were introduced regarding

life. Advocates of freedom have the Bill of Rights and numerous other restrictions on government action—for example, prohibition of suspending the writ of *habeas corpus* except in emergencies. On the other hand, those who favor a strong, vigorous government are reassured by the vast powers given the President in military or crisis situations.

No doubt, this capacity to mean so many things to so many people helps explain the survival of the Constitution despite enormous political

the length of the President's term. One such proposal—the Twenty-second Amendment, which limits a President to two terms—finally made it in 1951. Before 1928, seventy amendments were proposed to give the President power to veto part of a bill (commonly called an item veto). None has yet succeeded. Between 1900 and 1928, there were thirty-nine proposals to limit the terms of federal judges, but these too failed.

Proposing constitutional amendments appears to be a popular, though virtually hopeless, legislative activity. Consider the work of the 84th Congress, which began in 1955. Within five legislative days of opening, fifty-nine proposals to amend the Constitution nineteen different ways had been submitted; the previous Congress made sixty-one proposals during its five opening days. Among the proposals in the 84th Congress were amendments to require a balanced federal budget, give states exclusive control over education, place a 25 percent limit on the income tax, limit Supreme Court Justices to twelve-year terms, make ex-Presidents "Senators-at-large," give states complete control over oil, limit government competition with private businesses, involve the House of Representatives in approving treaties with foreign governments, require all members of Congress to retire after twelve consecutive years of service, prohibit foreign aid except during wartime, abolish the electoral college, limit the President's treaty-making power, and give citizens over 18 the right to vote. Many of these proposals had extensive legislative support, but none made it except for the 18-year-old vote (the Twenty-sixth Amendment, ratified in 1971).

For an interesting description of failed amendments, see *Proposed Amendments to the Constitution,* prepared by M. A. Musmanno, 70th Congress, 2d sess. (Washington, D.C.: Government Printing Office, 1929).

* The fifth congressionally proposed, but not yet state-ratified amendment, calls for giving Washington, D.C. two Senators. However, since this proposed amendment has just recently gone to the states, it is too early to say what will happen to it.

changes in the last 190 years. Nevertheless, it would be a serious mistake to view the Constitution as a magic document that gives all interests an equal share of the benefits. As in contemporary supermarkets, we can all find something we like, but some tastes are better satisfied than others. No system of political rules is perfectly neutral, and the system of rules embodied in the Constitution is no exception.

Basically, when the provisions of the Constitution are considered as a group, it is clear that the system is biased toward the maintenance of the status quo. In this sense it is a conservative political force. Remember that for a bill to become law it must receive majorities in two legislative houses, and be signed by the President; and if the law is eventually involved in a court action, it must be favorably interpreted by the courts. Defeat at *any one* of these four steps usually means complete defeat. For a newly emergent political force to make a real impact it must exert electoral influence in numerous states and in several separate elections. Even if this new group did capture Congress and the presidency, it would still not possess a free hand to do whatever it pleased. The courts, supermajority requirements, and features of the checks and balance system would have to be overcome.

That the Constitution is a force inhibiting political change is clear. This conservative bias does not, however, automatically mean that advocates of certain issues are forever at a political disadvantage. Getting a new law adopted may be difficult under our constitutional system, but once your cause has become established, you are protected by the same inertia that was so difficult to overcome. You are now the beneficiary of the obstacles to change, even if your cause is considered liberal or even radical. The possibility that liberal causes will benefit from the status quo biases of the Constitution was well illustrated when many political conservatives brought to power in Richard Nixon's 1968 election were largely unsuccessul in dismantling the liberal policies established under the Presidents John F. Kennedy and Lyndon B. Johnson. President Nixon and his supporters might bemoan the liberal tendencies of the Supreme Court, but other than wait for new judicial appointments to occur, there was little they could do. Nor could Nixon order Congress to abolish all the established programs to help poor people without risking retribution on his other legislative goals (and several of Nixon's vetoes were overriden by Congress).

From a purely practical, self-interest perspective, a strong commitment to constitutional principles makes the most sense after you have won. With victory secure you can then talk about the dangers of impassioned popular majorities, the importance of checking the accumulation of political power, and the need for new proposals to pass through the traditional obstacle course of Congress, the presidency, and the courts. On the other hand, if your cause is on the outside looking in, these arguments have little appeal. Here you might want to emphasize such considerations as the need for quick action, the popularity of your cause, and the "obstructionist" tactics of those in power opposed to your position. Neither side is being deceptive; rather, the virtues of the Constitution can reasonably depend on whether your cause is helped or hurt.

Major questions raised

1. What are the origins of the American Constitution? The Constitution was created to remedy faults of the Articles of Confederation. It was not created or ratified by the overwhelming majority of citizens, and those who drafted it came from established economic groups. Disagreement occurs, however, over whether the Constitution was a conservative counterrevolution against the ordinary citizen.

2. Does the Constitution promote government by the people? The Constitution rests on citizen approval and provides for citizen influence in choosing leaders, but it is designed to thwart majority control of government policy. Provisions such as separation of powers, checks and balances, federalism, and supermajorities are intended to prevent tyranny, not facilitate responsive government.

3. Has the Constitution become politically outdated? Since the constitutional system is designed to prevent or to slow down government action, it could be argued that this system is obsolete in a world in which quick, decisive action is frequently necessary. However, defenders of the Constitution assert that the document has adapted to modern circumstances, and, perhaps most important, the system has worked for 190 years.

QUESTIONS FOR FURTHER DISCUSSION

1. Article V of the Constitution provides that "on the Application of the Legislatures of two-thirds of the several states Congress shall call a Convention for proposing amendments." Such a second constitutional convention has never been called, though there have been several near misses. In 1905, for example, two thirds of the states petitioned Congress for the direct election of Senators. Congress initiated the amendment itself rather than call a convention. In the 1960s a drive to call a convention to propose an amendment overturning the Supreme Court's decisions on the apportionment of state legislatures received widespread support, but came up one vote short. More recently, as of February 1979, twenty-six of the necessary thirty-four states have called for a convention to propose a constitutional amendment to prohibit deficit spending by the federal government. Once a convention is created, however, it can consider *any* topic, even rewrite the Constitution. Many leaders are nervous over this prospect. As Howard Jarvis, the organizer of California's Proposition 13, put it: "It would put the constitution back on the drawing board, where every radical crackpot or special-interest group would have the chance to write the supreme law of the land."[6]
If the Constitution represents the will of the people, what is wrong with letting the people, in a national convention, reexamine their basic law? Is the judgment of the men of Philadelphia 190 years ago so superior to current wisdom that we dare not tamper with the document except on a complex, lengthy item-by-item basis? Is such a constitutional convention a "crackpot" scheme?

[6] Quoted in "Balance-the-Budget Boom," *Newsweek*, February 12, 1979.

2. How would you answer someone who asserted that the system of government created by the Constitution is undemocratic because no living U.S. citizen ever gave it their consent? We have not chosen the Constitution; it has been imposed upon us by a small, unrepresentative, and long-dead minority. Right?

3. It is sometimes argued that one of the great virtues of the Constitution is that it is vague in key areas and thus can mean different things to different people. Key phrases such as "regulate commerce . . . among the several states" or "due process of law" are not spelled out and sizable gaps exist in such areas as presidential and judicial power. Given the need to interpret the Constitution in concrete situations (for example, in a criminal trial), to whose advantage is this vagueness and imprecision? Judges who must interpret the Constitution? Ambitious officials who can use vagueness to their own purposes? Should important sections that are vague be made much more specific to prevent them from being manipulated through devious interpretations? Of what use is a supreme law of the land that can be interpreted in many different ways?

BIBLIOGRAPHY

Beard, Charles A. *An Economic Interpretation of the Constitution of the United States.* New York: Macmillan, 1913.
    A path-breaking analysis of the philosophies and backgrounds of the men who drafted the Constitution. Presents considerable evidence to support—but does not conclusively prove—the contention that members of the economic elite, many of whom would benefit financially from ratification, were instrumental in creating the Constitution. Stops well short, however, of implying some diabolical conspiracy of the rich against the poor.

Brown, Robert E. *Charles Beard and the Constitution.* Princeton, N.J.: Princeton University Press, 1956.
    Brown provides an item-by-item refutation of the Beard interpretation of the origins of the Constitution. Much of the book focuses on the validity of detailed historical evidence used by Beard.

Earle, Edward Meade, ed. *The Federalist: A Commentary on the Constitution of the United States.* New York: Random House, n.d.
    Eighty-five essays by James Madison, Alexander Hamilton, and John Jay that defend the new Constitution as the best solution to the political problems of the day. While the essays were written largely to convince, they nevertheless provide a clear explanation and justification of the Constitution and its underlying philosophy. An important classic.

Farrand, Max, ed. *The Records of the Federal Convention of 1787*, rev. ed. New Haven, Conn.: Yale University Press, 1966.
    A running account of the Constitutional Convention as provided by the notes of James Madison. Invaluable for understanding the political nature of the Constitution. A detailed index allows one to find the debate on a particular question.

Fisher, Louis. *The Constitution Between Friends: Congress, the President, and the Law.* New York: St. Martins Press, 1978.
    An up-to-date treatment of the political impact of the Constitution. Considers the original meaning of the principles of separation of powers and checks and balances and then discusses the contemporary relevance of these principles. Excellent analysis of presidential power in terms of constitutional limits and grants of power.

Jensen, Merrill. *The Making of the American Constitution.* New York: Van Nostrand Reinhold, 1964.
> A brief but well-documented historical treatment of the origins of the Constitution. All the significant constitutional debates are clearly explained, frequently in the words of the participants. Contains copies of many important historical documents and a bibliographical essay.

Kenyon, Cecelia M, ed. *The Antifederalists.* Indianapolis: Bobbs-Merrill, 1966.
> A collection of essays written during the ratification period opposing the new Constitution. Many of these objections have proved groundless, but others are not easily dismissed. An interesting exercise is to compare the predictions made by opponents of the Constitution to what happened after ratification.

McDonald, Forrest. *We the People: The Economic Origins of the Constitution.* Chicago: University of Chicago Press, 1958.
> A detailed historical refutation of the Beard argument regarding the economic origins of the Constitution. Argues that delegates to the Constitutional Convention were a diverse group which represented most of the interests and areas of the nation. The Constitution was not a radical break with the past in order to protect threatened wealthy interests.

Peltason, Jack W. *Understanding the Constitution,* 7th ed. Hinsdale, Ill.: Dryden Press, 1976.
> After describing the background of the Constitution and giving an overview of its basic features, the author analyzes each section in detail (including recent court cases). An exceptionally useful book if you want to know what a specific portion of the Constitution has been interpreted to mean. Frequently updated.

Rossiter, Clinton. *1787: The Grand Convention.* New York: Macmillan, 1966.
> Rossiter is a superb writer and a leading authority on U.S. political history. He has written several books on early U.S. history, and this one provides a good feel for the people and debates of the convention. *Seedtime of the Republic* is another good Rossiter book on the beginnings of U.S. politics.

PREVIEW

What are the basic principles of American federalism?

Federalism exists when two or more levels of government rule the same people, with each level having at least one area in which it sets policy independently of the other. An important issue in U.S. federalism has been whether the national government or the states possess final authority. In *McCulloch* v. *Maryland* (1819) Chief Justice John Marshall ruled that on the basis of the supremacy clause and the necessary and proper clause of the Constitution, the national government was supreme in most areas. The doctrine of national supremacy has been challenged on numerous grounds, however. Current interpretations give supremacy to the government in Washington in almost all policy areas. A second important issue concerns the actual division of political responsibility between national and state levels. The Constitution provides some division of political labor, and custom has defined others. In areas such as regulating commerce authority is not clearly defined, and much depends on the outcome of political conflict.

How does contemporary federalism operate?

Over the years federalism has changed from a doctrine emphasizing the division of power between governments to a process by which the national government cooperates with states and cities to solve problems. Especially since the mid-1960s, federal aid to local governments, given through a variety of methods, has grown enormously. Categorical grants are provided for specific projects. Block grants are given for more general purposes and allow greater state or local discretion. A major issue in dispensing this aid is the degree of control the national government can, and should, exercise. In response to this conflict President Nixon instituted general revenue sharing, a program that gives the states large sums of money with no strings attached. State and local officials have also been involved in decisions that affect them. These questions entail far more than administrative details: they signify a redistribution of power and differences over policy.

Is federalism still politically relevant?

Federalism was originally justified as a means of preventing tyranny and as a price to be paid for a union of large and small states. If we accept the premise that it is a necessary protection against tyranny, then federalism is still relevant. In many policy areas states play an important role. It can also be argued that federalism is not a protection against tyranny. A debate in contemporary federalism concerns the administrative effectiveness of a federal system. Because of the federal system there is often confusion over applying the legal decisions of state courts, problems are caused by the existence of diverse state laws, and added layers of bureaucracy are a necessary part of the system. However, federalism can be defended on the grounds that diverse laws are necessary, Washington does not always know best, and state independence results in innovative policy.

CHAPTER THREE

FEDERALISM

When people think of *the* government, they often picture the national government in Washington, D.C. Though it may be our image of government, the President, Congress, and the Supreme Court do not constitute the only political authority of consequence in the United States. The national government may be the single most powerful government, but it does not monopolize political power. In addition to the fifty state governments, a 1972 survey reported a total of 78,218 other governments in the United States (with 66,000 having the power to tax property). The relationships among these governments, especially that between the national and state governments, are important and raise complex issues in American politics. The whole idea of a division of political authority between national and state governments—the principle of federalism described in Chapter Two—is an evolving rather than a fixed principle. Many important current controversies, for example, the efforts of the national government to impose racial integration on state and locally administered schools, are rooted in the issue of federalism. Our analysis of federalism will be in the light of three key questions concerning the division of power between the national and state governments.

1. What are the basic principles of American federalism?
2. How does contemporary federalism operate?
3. Is federalism still politically relevant?

FIGURE 3.1

DIFFERENCES BETWEEN UNITARY, CONFEDERATION, AND FEDERAL FORMS OF GOVERNMENT

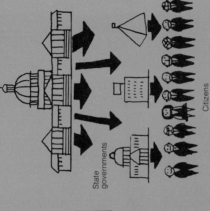

UNITARY GOVERNMENT

Central government

Regional or local administrative authorities

Citizens

Central government retains all political power. Regional and local officials have no independent power—they basically administer decisions of central government.

CONFEDERATION GOVERNMENT

Confederation government

Central government

Central government

Central government

Citizens

Two or more independent governments create new government to accomplish certain tasks. New government does not govern citizens directly. Confederation government can only request that central government take action.

FEDERAL GOVERNMENT

State governments

Citizens

Two or more governments share power and rule the same citizens. Each level of government maintains final authority over some policies.

What are the basic principles of American federalism?

Federalism can be defined fairly straightforwardly. A federal system exists when (1) two or more levels of government rule the same people, and (2) each level of government has at least one area in which it sets policy independently of the other.[1] The United States is a federal system because the national and state governments both have direct authority over citizens, and both governments enjoy autonomy in certain policy areas. A federal system is usually contrasted with a **unitary government** and with a confederation (see Figure 3.1). In a unitary government all political power ultimately resides in a central government. Some powers may be delegated to regional or local officials, but these can be modified or withdrawn at the discretion of the central government. Great Britain, France, and Italy are unitary governments. A **confederation** is a government created by other governments but it has no direct authority over citizens and remains subservient to the governments that created it. The United Nations is a confederation because UN officials cannot rule citizens of member states; they can only request the cooperation of national leaders. The government created by the Articles of Confederation was a confederation because the Confederation Congress was ultimately subservient to the authority of the member states and could not govern citizens directly.

While defining federalism may be simple, applying the principle is complex. In a unitary system questions involving who has what powers and who makes the final decision are easily answered: the central government decides everything, though for convenience it may delegate some power to local units. The principle of federalism, however, says nothing about how specific powers are to be divided or how conflicts between two levels of government are to be resolved. Federalism merely means some (unspecified) division of political labor. The precise way power is divided and the rules for deciding conflict are not inherent in the meaning of federalism. Let us consider two key aspects of the federalist principle in American politics: Which level of government—the national or the state—retains *ultimate* political power? How is political responsibility divided between the national and state governments?

THE QUESTION OF ULTIMATE POLITICAL POWER

When the Constitution was drafted the idea that two sovereign governments would rule the same people was frequently greeted with skepticism. The principles of unitary and confederation governments were theoretically and historically clear. Many people, however, doubted whether two governments could be coequal in terms of sovereignty. As a practical compromise necessary to enlist state cooperation in ratifying

Federalism A system of government in which two or more levels of government rule the same people, with each level having at least one area in which it sets policy independently of the others.

Unitary government A form of government in which all power ultimately resides in the central government, though for convenience some tasks may be delegated to local or regional officials.

Confederation A government created by other governments which has no direct authority over citizens and which remains subservient to the governments that created it.

---

[1] Adapted from William H. Riker, *Federalism: Origin, Operation, Significance* (Boston: Little, Brown, 1964), p. 11.

Supremacy clause Article VI, section 2 of the Constitution, which states that the Constitution and the laws made under it are the supreme laws of the United States.

"Necessary and proper clause" After giving Congress a long list of explicit powers, the Constitution states that Congress may also pass laws that are necessary to carry out these enumerated powers. Because the courts have broadly interpreted what is necessary, this clause has also been known as the "elastic clause."

the new Constitution, federalism—with its promise of sovereignty to both levels of government—was an attractive plan. Yet, 190 years after ratification the possible internal contradiction of the federalism principle is still with us: if both levels have sovereignty, who has the ultimate power in a conflict?

Early attempts to resolve the ultimate-power question

The question of who has ultimate power has been answered in many different ways over the years. In fact, the answer we generally accept today has not always been the most popular one. One important answer was given by Chief Justice John Marshall in the landmark case of *McCulloch* v. *Maryland* (1819). This case involved an action of the national government—establishing a bank—that was being hindered by a Maryland state tax. Marshall saw the issue of a state tax on a national government activity as basically a conflict between national and state power.

The Chief Justice ruled that the national government did not have to pay Maryland's tax because doing so would open the door to state domination of national government: a state that objected to a national program could, theoretically, tax the program out of existence. Marshall's decision in McCulloch came down strongly on the side of national government supremacy when the national government was acting within its constitutional authority. This decision rested on two important provisions of the Constitution. The first is Article VI, section 2, usually called the **supremacy clause,** which says:

> This Constitution, and the Laws of the United States which shall be made in Pursuance thereof; and all Treaties made, or which shall be made, under the Authority of the United States, shall be the supreme Law of the Land.

This provision means that if the laws of the national government made in accordance with the Constitution conflict with state legislation, national law prevails. But the power to establish a national bank is not explicitly granted to the national government by the Constitution. Can national law be supreme even if it does not rest on power explicitly mentioned in the Constitution? As we saw in Chapter Two, the power to create a bank is implicit in the constitutional grant of powers to the national government. It is implicit, according to Marshall, through the **necessary and proper clause** (Article I, section 8, paragraph 18) because creating a bank may be necessary for collecting tax money and paying debts (both of which are explicit powers). Marshall's position—sometimes called the national supremacy position—essentially means that the authority of the national government is final when the latter acts in accordance with explicitly *or* implicitly constitutionally granted power. Given the wide meaning of the "necessary and proper" clause, this position gives the national government considerable final authority.

It is possible, however, to take an entirely different approach to the question of which level of government retains ultimate power. One might focus on the nature of the original agreement between the states and the national government. It could be argued that since the states created the national government for particular purposes, for example, to regulate commerce, the states are not bound by actions of the national government if those actions go beyond the original purposes of the unifying agreement. The Constitution, like a contract, specifies obligations; it can enforce only obligations that are spelled out.

This type of reasoning has appeared many times in conflicts between the national and state governments. It first appeared when the national government passed the unpopular Alien and Sedition Laws in 1798 which made it a crime to criticize the government or its officials. These laws outraged many citizens. The Kentucky legislature went so far as to pass a resolution (drafted by Thomas Jefferson) declaring that national laws not specifically authorized by the Constitution have no force and that each state retains the right to judge for itself the laws that are unauthorized and what should be done about them. James Madison— who helped draft the Constitution—concurred with this judgment in a similar resolution passed by the Virginia legislature. He argued that a state could block the enforcement of unauthorized laws by "**interposing**" itself between its citizens and the national government.[2]

In 1832, the issue of ultimate power surfaced again when South Carolina declared federal tariff acts null and void and refused to allow federal agents to collect tariffs in the state. President Andrew Jackson responded to these **nullifications** of national law by sending gunboats into Charleston harbor to collect the tariff. Eventually the issue was resolved by a compromise on tariff rates.

The strongest claims for state power were made in the context of the debate over slavery. Southern spokesmen such as John C. Calhoun and Jefferson Davis argued that in the case of repressive action by the national government, the states could reassume even powers explicitly given the national government by the Constitution. Secession from the Union was permissible, it was argued, because the states had not surrendered their sovereignty for eternity. The Civil War settled the issue of whether a state, like a sovereign nation, could withdraw from the original compact. Some of the doctrines supporting the position that states can nullify national law reappeared in the 1950s when southern states resisted court decisions banning school segregation. Again, this extreme version of state sovereignty came to naught.

Dual federalism as an answer to the ultimate-power question

In the late nineteenth century a different perspective developed regarding the comparative power of the national and state governments. This perspective—usually called **dual federalism**—was highly influential until the late 1930s. Based largely on the Tenth Amendment, which says that powers not given the national government are reserved for the states or the people, the dual-federalism principle asserted that states and the na-

Interposing Application of the doctrine which states that a state can place itself between its citizens and the national government to prevent the enforcement of an illegal or unconstitutional national law.
Nullification The doctrine holding that states can declare national laws and orders null and void.
Dual federalism The doctrine holding that the states and the national government are co-equal in sovereignty. Maintains that, unless power is clearly given the national government by the Constitution, the states retain final authority.

---

[2] These laws were probably unconstitutional, but despite their enforcement and the fact that several people were jailed, they were never reviewed by the Supreme Court. When Jefferson was elected President in 1800 the issue was settled through nonenforcement.

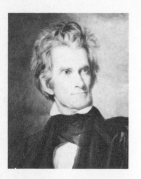

Portrait of John C. Calhoun (1782–1850). Calhoun was a leading politician and political thinker who provided much of the intellectual support for the rights of states to secede from the Union.

tional government are coequal in sovereignty. Whereas the nullification arguments of the first half of the nineteenth century rested on an interpretation of the purpose of the Union, the principle of dual federalism stressed that for the national government to be preeminent, the power must be explicitly granted by the Constitution. The link between the "necessary and proper" and supremacy clauses formulated in the McCulloch decision by Chief Justice Marshall was greatly weakened. On numerous occasions the Supreme Court, using this principle, ruled that national regulation of economic activities within states was a violation of state sovereignty. The most famous of these cases was *Hammer* v. *Dagenhart* (1918) in which the Supreme Court decided that a national law restricting the interstate shipment of goods produced by child labor went beyond the power expressly granted the national government by the Constitution.

The decline of the dual-federalism approach

This notion of two autonomous levels of government, each with its own wide political autonomy, came under increasing attack in the 1930s. Today duel federalism is almost entirely rejected, and most judges and legislators have returned to the interpretation first offered by Marshall in *McCulloch* v. *Maryland.* The national government is supreme whether its power is precisely enumerated, for example, the power to coin money, or is implied, for example, the power to create a national bank. Laws made under both types of power prevail if they conflict with state laws. Moreover, the Tenth Amendment – contrary to claims of dual federalism – does *not* say that powers not expressly given the national government belong exclusively to the states. Rather, the contemporary interpretation of the Tenth Amendment is that the states retain the ultimate power only where *no* power – explicit or implicit – is given the national government. For example, because the Constitution makes no mention of the social security program, this does not mean that the states reserve ultimate power in this area (this program may be justified in terms of implicit power).

Does all of this suggest that the federal system has really become a unitary system in all but name? Are state officials little more than agents of the Washington government? That is not quite the case. As we shall now see, the powers of the national government still do not cover everything, and in many issues the states still have a major voice.

HOW IS POLITICAL RESPONSIBILITY DIVIDED BETWEEN THE NATIONAL AND STATE GOVERNMENTS?

Our previous discussion concerned who possesses the final power in the American federal system. We saw that, according to current thinking, when the national government acts on the basis of its explicit or implicit constitutional powers, it has final say. Yet this doctrine does not automatically mean that the national government can dictate to the states on any and all issues. The "necessary and proper" clause may grant broad power, but it does not extend to everything. Even today, when the national supremacy position is widely accepted, there remains a division between the national and state levels which prevents officials in Washington from behaving as though ours was a unitary government.

Constitutional divisions of state-national power

To understand the division of political responsibility between the national government and the states we must begin by considering how the Constitution attempts to decide this issue. Experts have usually viewed the Constitution as dividing authority three ways: (1) policy domains that belong exclusively to the national government; (2) those that belong entirely to the states; and (3) those in which both governments exercise authority (commonly called **concurrent powers**). Moreover, the Constitution also speaks in terms of positive and negative power in each of these domains. Combining this positive and negative distinction with the national only, state only, and concurrent division of responsibility provides a sixfold categorization of national and state power. This sixfold classification is complex, and the courts have frequently interpreted it several different ways. These divisions are as follows:

1. *Exclusive (positive) national powers.* These include such matters as coining money, declaring war, making treaties with foreign nations, admitting new states to the Union, establishing rules for citizenship, regulating commerce among the states, establishing post offices, and creating new national courts. Some of these powers, for example, establishing post offices, are concretely spelled out in the Constitution. Others, for example, the power to negotiate with foreign nations, are considered inherent national powers because only the national government can represent the United States in such negotiations.

2. *Exclusive (positive) state powers.* The Constitution does not specify these areas. Rather, implicitly and through the Tenth Amendment it grants the states exclusive power when the central government is not delegated power. Traditionally, exclusive state powers have included powers to regulate such areas as the maintenance of internal order, public health and morals and laws governing contracts and property, fire and police protection, local elections, marriage and divorce, the content of education, and the licensing of professions.

3. *Concurrent (positive) power.* The Constitution grants the national government powers in such areas as imposing taxes, creating courts, chartering banks, and building roads, but the states may also engage in such activities. Of course, as we have seen, if governments conflict over concurrent powers, the supremacy clause allows the national government to override state activity.

4. *Powers denied only to the national government.* Article I, section 9 of the Constitution contains a lengthy list of things the national government cannot do. For example, it cannot tax exports, pass **ex post facto** laws or **bills of attainder**, grant titles of nobility, and so on. The first eight amendments also place limitations on the national government: it cannot, for example, abridge freedom of speech.

5. *Powers denied only to the state governments.* Article I, section 10 in particular lists activities the states, but not the national gov-

Concurrent powers Where both the national and state governments can legislate in the same policy areas, they have concurrent powers. Where conflicts occur, national policy prevails.
Ex post facto A law that makes a crime retroactive and has an adverse effect on the accused person.
Bill of attainder A law that declares a particular individual to be guilty of a crime and punishes him or her without a trial.

ernment, are forbidden to engage in. No state can coin money, pass laws impairing the obligation of contracts, or enter into an agreement with other states without the consent of Congress.

6. *Powers denied to both state and national governments.* Article I, section 10 also repeats some of the prohibitions stated in Article I, section 10 that applied to the national government. Thus, no government—state or national—can grant titles of nobility and pass *ex post facto* laws or bills of attainder.

This sixfold constitutional division of authority in principle appears to settle many of the questions concerning which level of government has primary responsibility for what policies. In practice, however, this division is far more complex. What may appear to be an exclusive national power might be interpreted by some people to be a concurrent power. In addition, the "necessary and proper" clause could conceivably be extended to dominate virtually every activity implicitly reserved to the states. The sixfold division of authority, then, is only the starting point for resolving many issues of federalism. To appreciate this complexity let us consider, as an example, the power to regulate commerce.

Regulating commerce as an example of the fluid nature of federalism

Article I, section 8, paragraph 3 of the Constitution gives the national government the power "to regulate Commerce with foreign nations, and among the several States, and with the Indian Tribes." At first glance this grant of power may seem straightforward, but it has been the subject of great controversy, and each time interpretations of it changed, so has the nature of American federalism. The first and third domain— foreign commerce and commerce with Indians—has generally been interpreted as an exclusive (positive) national power (category 1 above). It is "Commerce among the several states" that has been interpreted by different people in different ways.

To begin with, what is meant by "commerce?" If you are the proprietor of Goldberg's Pizzeria, are you engaging in commerce? Does it make

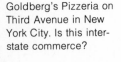

Goldberg's Pizzeria on Third Avenue in New York City. Is this interstate commerce?

a difference constitutionally whether you not only manufacture but also deliver pizza? Might it also make a difference whether your pizzas are delivered in more than one state? Suppose someone buys a pizza and carries it across state lines (but you yourself do not ship across state lines)? Moreover, what does "regulation" imply? Would a national law setting the diameter of small, medium, and extra large pizzas be consistent with the constitutional power to regulate commerce? What about a regulation stating that you cannot discriminate among customers in your business? Obviously, if the commerce clause allowed the national government to specify every detail of your pizza business, the nature of federalism would be quite different from what would be the case if the national government could affect only the most limited aspects of your business.

Sherman Anti-Trust Act   A law passed in 1890 that forbade contracts, combinations, or conspiracies to restrain trade or commerce.

The first of many answers to these key questions was given in the landmark case of *Gibbons* v. *Ogden* (1824). The case came about when New York State granted Robert Fulton and Robert R. Livingston a monopoly to navigate the waters of New York. They, in turn, granted Ogden a license to operate in New York waters. Meanwhile, Gibbons had been granted a license by the national government to operate steamboats between New York and New Jersey. Ogden—who had authority from New York—brought suit to stop Gibbons, who had been licensed by the national government. When the case reached the Supreme Court, Chief Justice Marshall had to decide how the commerce clause would apply to this conflict. First, Marshall interpreted "commerce" broadly—to mean all commercial transactions. Second, Marshall asserted that commerce "among the states" may involve transactions wholly within the bounds of a state. At this point it appears that Marshall's view was that Congress can regulate just about anything by virtue of the commerce clause. Marshall drew back from this conclusion, however, and observed that such regulation would be "inconvenient" and "unnecessary"—but not unconstitutional.

Marshall never mentioned, or drew a sharp line between, *inter*state commerce and *intra*state commerce, but the ultimate impact of *Gibbons* v. *Ogden* was to exclude almost all intervention by the national government in commerce that takes place wholly within a state. The commerce clause was for many years the "interstate commerce clause." Especially in the late 1800s, "interstate commerce" was construed very narrowly. When the national government under the **Sherman Anti-Trust Act** sought to break up one company's monopoly of the sugar industry, its actions were overruled by the courts on the grounds that sugar *manufacturing* was not part of interstate commerce. Only the *transportation* of sugar was interstate commerce; therefore as long as shipping sugar was not monopolized, the national government could not touch the manufacturing monopoly (*United States* v. *E. C. Knight Co.* [1895]).

Current interpretation of the commerce clause allows national regulation of almost every aspect of commerce (broadly defined), even when commerce occurs solely within a single state. This change in interpretation has its roots in a changed definition of "interstate commerce." The broadening of the commerce power first occurred in the early twentieth century when the Supreme Court acknowledged that when intrastate and interstate are inseparable commercial transactions, the entire process becomes part of *inter*state commerce. For example, if you buy cattle in Chicago that have been shipped from Texas (and the processed meat may continue on to all fifty states), your purchase is part of *inter*state commerce even though it takes place completely in Chicago. Moreover, even if the cattle were raised in Illinois and are to be eaten in Illinois, the transaction can be regulated by the national government if these intrastate transactions will have a substantial effect on interstate commerce.

In the late 1930s and early 1940s, a series of Supreme Court decisions greatly reduced the constraints on the use of the commerce power by the national government. In the key case of *National Labor Relations Board* v. *James & Laughlin Corp.* (1937), the court ruled that the national government can regulate labor practices within manufacturing plants because labor conditions in manufacturing clearly affect the nation's commerce. In *United States* v. *Darby Lumber Co.* (1941) the court ruled that it was legal for Congress to prevent all goods produced in violation of nationally set wage laws from being shipped in interstate commerce. This reversal of the *Hammer* v. *Dagenhart* doctrine in effect gave the national government the power to regulate employment in virtually all industries in the United States, even in small, largely local businesses. Other key court decisions during this period also allowed the national government extensive power in the regulation of agricultural products, hydroelectric power, and the insurance industry (though in practice insurance is still largely a state matter). Perhaps the most extensive use of the commerce power has been in the area of civil rights. On the basis of the commerce clause Congress banned racial discrimination in hotels, inns, restaurants, theaters, and employment. In 1963, employers were forbidden to pay men higher wages than women for the same work, and this law too was based on the commerce clause. In 1968, the commerce clause was again relied upon to prohibit discrimination based on race, color, religion, or national origins in the sale or rental of housing.

This evolution of the meaning of the commerce clause tells us something very important about the federalism principle: the division of political labor between the national government and the states is neither sharply defined on all matters nor forever fixed. On some issues, for example, prohibition of the coining of money by states, there is a clear division of labor, but on crucial questions such as regulating commerce no such clarity exists. Federalism is thus what political leaders, especially Supreme Court Justices, say it is.

Even the most explicit constitutional language regulating national and state powers can be transformed by the political process. For example, the First Amendment says that Congress shall make no law abridging the freedom of speech. It would seem that this wording still leaves the states free to abridge speech (this is an example of category 4 of our sixfold classification of constitutional grants of authority described earlier). In 1925, however, the Supreme Court ruled that states too are forbidden to abridge free speech (thus putting the regulation of

FEDERALISM AND CONFLICTS BETWEEN THE STATES

A continual problem of American federalism is disputes between the states. Since 1789 more than 120 disputes have wound up in the courts, and in at least four there was a show of armed force. Many of these cases have involved water rights. Several court cases have involved Arizona, California, and Colorado and the question of what state has what claim on the water from the Colorado River. Many cases have also involved the pollution of sewage from one state of the water of another state. Despite the supposedly fixed nature of state boundaries, conflicts over the exact locations of state lines continue to occur (in 1970, Arkansas and Tennessee had such a dispute).

Acting under its constitutional grant of original jurisdiction, the Supreme Court deals directly with such cases. The Constitution or other national laws are frequently of little help in resolving questions of water rights, the movement of pollution, and border disputes. The response of the courts to this problem of federalism has been to rely on certain principles of international law (modified when necessary) plus its own precedents.

The continuing difficulty associated with resolving conflicts between states is illustrated by the lengthy battle between Iowa and Kansas over birds and flowers. In 1970, the Iowa legislature proposed a bill to declare the sunflower—the state flower of Kansas—a "noxious weed." Kansas struck back by trying to declare the goldfinch—the state bird of Iowa—a public nuisance. In 1977, the Iowa legislature again proposed legislation to make the sunflower a noxious weed. Kansas is still mulling over its response.

speech into category 6—powers or policy domains denied both levels of government).

We can return now to the general question posed at the beginning of our analysis: What are the basic principles of American federalism? These principles may be summarized as follows:

1. The American political system is a federal one because there are two levels of government, each with its primary areas of responsibility, and citizens are governed by both levels.
2. Where the Constitution, explicitly or implicitly (through the "necessary and proper" clause), grants the national government authority, the authority of the latter is supreme if there are conflicts with state laws.

Cooperative federalism The general name given to contemporary federalism, since it emphasizes cooperation among the national, state, and local governments to solve common problems.

3. The central government cannot, however, act as a unitary government. The Constitution makes certain actions off limits, for example, the passing of *ex post facto* laws, and states are granted both concurrent and (implied) exclusive powers.[3]
4. This division of political labor is far from fixed, however. In 1800, an attempt by the national government to decide wages and working conditions in local businesses would have been considered a violation of federalism. Today such national power is widely viewed as consistent with the principles of federalism.

How does contemporary federalism operate?

Until fairly recently the history of federalism has been characterized by state-national conflicts. As we have seen, the issue of who possesses ultimate political authority surfaced on several occasions. During the nineteenth and the first half of the twentieth centuries the Supreme Court continually had to act as umpire on economic issues as a consequence of divergent interpretations of the commerce clause. Such conflict was, in part, intended by the very design of the Constitution. Recall that federalism was considered an important safeguard against one interest completely dominating the political process.

CHANGES IN THE MEANING OF FEDERALISM

In the mid-twentieth century the basic practice of federalism has been greatly altered. As social and economic problems have multiplied and as we have come to expect government actions in these problem areas, federalism marked by conflicts has given way to what sometimes is called **cooperative federalism.** In the nineteenth century federalism meant the division of political authority between the national and state governments. Today federalism has come to mean the process by which governments at all levels—including city, county, and special district governments, such as sewage treatment districts—interact in order to solve common problems. Divisions of sovereignty between the national and state governments remain, of course, but the precise legal definition of this division has become far less important than the question of how national and state officials can best cooperate.

Reasons for the change in federalism

This change has occurred for several reasons. Problems that were once purely local in nature now may involve several states or even the nation

---

[3] It is sometimes asserted that the states maintain their sovereignty in name only. This is not true. In the 1976 case of *National League of Cities* v. *Usery*, the Supreme Court held that Congress lacked the power to set national minimum wage and overtime standards for state and local employees. The majority opinion stated, "We have repeatedly recognized that there are attitudes of sovereignty attaching to every state government which may not be impaired by Congress."

as a whole. When travel was a largely local affair, it was reasonable to give the states or towns the main responsibility for building and coordinating a transportation system. Today, of course, roads, harbors, railroad terminals, and airports do not exist largely to serve local or state needs. The cost of providing many government services has also outgrown state fiscal capacities. Education, in particular, has become a very expensive government-provided service. Likewise, cleaning up lakes and rivers, a national goal, is frequently beyond the financial capacity of the states with the severest pollution. Finally, thanks largely to the personal income tax levied by the national government, Washington now possesses the financial resources to help states and cities.

Grants-in-aid program A program involving transfers of funds, land, or other resources from national to state or local authorities.

The emergence of the grants-in-aid program

In this transformation of federalism into a cooperative venture between state and national officials, the most prominent feature has been the national **grants-in-aid program.** Giving aid to the states is not an entirely new idea. In 1785, four years before the Constitution was ratified, the Confederation Congress provided money for schools in the Northwest Territory (today the upper Midwest). The Morrill Act of 1862 authorized national government money and land for public colleges. Several pioneering nationally funded programs in the areas of vocational education, road construction, treatment of venereal disease, and infant and maternity care were established in the World War I era. In the late 1930s, there was another spurt in grants-in-aid programs, but the real explosion in this type of federalism did not occur until the mid-1960s. In 1965, for example, the national government gave state and local governments $10.9 billion for programs in agriculture, transportation, education, and public welfare (to name but a few areas of assistance). By fiscal 1977, this figure had risen to $70.4 billion.[4]

Grants-in-aid from the national government to state and local governments cover almost every activity imaginable. In the mid-1970s, state and local officials could attempt to get financial assistance through almost 600 national grants-in-aid programs.[5] In many policy areas there exists a wide variety of nationally financed programs. For example, a state public official interested in nationally supported jobs and vocational training had fifty different grants-in-aid programs to select from in 1969. There were also thirty-five programs in housing and twenty-eight in the field of recreation. National grants-in-aid have been especially prominent in programs designed to alleviate poverty and hardship. A large proportion of community and state efforts in urban renewal, low-rent housing, aid for educationally deprived children, community action programs, vocational training, mental health facilities, assistance for poor families, health care for the aged, and the prevention of juvenile delinquency has been supported by funds from Washington. Substantial national assistance has also been given in the fight against pollution: na-

[4] *Statistical Abstract of the United States, 1978*, p. 284.
[5] Parris N. Glendening and Mavis Mann Reeves, *Pragmatic Federalism: An Intergovernmental View of American Government* (Pacific Palisades, Calif.: Palisades, 1977), p. 265.

A large-scale housing project with financing provided by the U.S. Department of Housing and Urban Development in cooperation with New York City.

Flat grant A grant for a certain amount of money given without regard to need, population, or other characteristics of the agency receiving the money.

tional aid has been instrumental in the building of solid-waste treatment facilities, air pollution controls, local sewers, and water-purification facilities. Perhaps the most visible results of these programs have been the systems of major highways that surround our large cities. In 1978, one out of every four state and local dollars spent came through various national grants-in-aid.[6]

Administering the grants-in-aid program

These grants-in-aid are given out according to several, frequently very complex, criteria. The simplest kind of grant is the **flat grant** that is allocated to states or localities on an equal basis. Certain programs for vocational education fall into this category and are distributed without regard to financial need or state/local contribution to the program. Most national grants-in-aid, however, are dispensed according to a wide variety of formulas that usually take into account local resources, the willingness of local authorities to make a financial commitment, the number of people affected by the program, and the total cost of the project.[7] Since rarely is there any self-evident formula for deciding who is to get how much from a new national grant program, many states and large cities organize extensive lobbying efforts to obtain the formula that is most beneficial to their interests. For example, President Nixon's 1974 mass transit plan would have allocated funds solely on a population basis. Congress came up with a plan that was based on population plus number of passengers carried and miles traveled. To New York City the difference between these two formulas was $80 million, and the New York City congressional delegation strenuously lobbied on behalf of the more complex formula.

[6] For a comprehensive description of this flow of aid from Washington to states and cities, see Deil S. Wright, *Understanding Intergovernmental Relations* (North Scituate, Mass.: Duxbury Press, 1978), especially Chap. 6.

[7] A good description of the different types of grants is found in Daniel J. Elazar, *American Federalism: A View from the States*, 2d. ed. (New York: Crowell, 1972), Chap. 3.

One of the most important consequences of the grants-in-aid program is to blur the neat hierarchial relationship among the national, state, and local governments.[8] Nineteenth-century conflict over federalism involved only two types of political authority—national and state. Local governments did not count politically because they were legally completely dependent on the states and could do only what was permitted by the states. It was inconceivable for local authorities to deal directly with Congress or for national bureaucracies to bypass the states in working with local government officials. Present-day federalism has changed much of this.

First, the grants-in-aid program has allowed municipalities to exercise some financial independence from state control. If Chicago cannot get state aid for a new subway system, it may go to Washington for the money. The present system of grants has also created a large array of new semipublic and public governmental organizations that do not fit into the traditional national-state-local pattern. For example, as a result of grants-in-aid to rural agricultural areas, there now exist over 3,000 soil conservation districts, many of which operate as independent political authorities.[9] Grants designed to combat poverty created innumerable semiautonomous community action organizations which followed national, rather than local, policy guidelines. In many instances cities and states formed new government authorities in order to comply with grant requirements—several communities might, for instance, create a sewer district to get antipollution funds. Both the increase in financial independence and the multiplicity of different political authorities have replaced the simple national-state relationship with one of much greater complexity (and confusion).

Controlling grants-in-aid money

The proliferation of programs, special government districts, and billions of dollars of expenditures have raised a dilemma regarding control over this enormous enterprise. On the other hand, since the purpose of these grants is to help, not subvert, subnational governments, it may be argued that it would be inappropriate to use grants to force national policy on unwilling states and cities. Grants are not intended to transform a federal system into a unitary one. On the other hand, it could be argued that because the national government is paying the bills, it has a right to insure that money given for remedial instruction for disadvantaged students, for example, is not used to build tennis courts for teachers. Balancing the need for some local autonomy with the need for some degree

[8] Morton Grodzins, a long-time observer of federalism, has proposed that our system be viewed not as a neat three-layer national-state-local cake but more as a marble cake. That is, on some functions (for example, urban renewal) there is one mixture of government involvement, while in another policy area (for example, education) there is an entirely different government combination. Frequently, as in a marble cake, it is difficult to tell where one layer ends and another begins. Morton Grodzins, "Centralization and Decentralization in the American Federal System," in Robert A. Goldwin, ed., *A Nation of States* (Chicago: Rand McNally, 1963), pp. 1–23.

[9] Glendening and Reeves, p. 263.

UNCLE SAM MAKES AN OFFER WINTER PARK CANNOT REFUSE

One of the consequences of the grants-in-aid program is that states and cities sometimes have to work hard to come up with "problems" so they can get their piece of the grant action. This is not always simple, as the following story illustrates.

TOWN GETS MILLIONS IN FEDERAL WINDFALL

(AP)

WINTER PARK, Fla. — Still puzzled over what to do with a $2.65-million federal windfall, officials of this small but fashionable central Florida town are trying to come up with 20 projects so the money won't be withdrawn.

A municipality with a population of slightly more than 20,000 adjacent to Orlando, Winter Park received word a couple of weeks ago that the money was in a grant that had been allocated by the Economic Development Administration.

Winter Park will not get the $2.65 million — or other amount — until the EDA approves the allocation.

"Nobody's got anything yet," EDA spokesman Bernie Jenkins said in Washington. He said the amount of a grant is determined by a formula based on unemployment statistics.

Winter Park had requested $883,500 for a new library. City commissioners, who were shocked to learn that federal officials wanted them to have three times that much, were given until July 13 to come up with a list of projects or lose the funds.

The $2.65-million allocation is more than half the size of the city's fiscal 1978 budget of $4.98 million.

Several officials said the money will lead to waste and profiteering, and one commissioner suggested only half seriously Tuesday that the city refuse it as a matter of patriotism.

But commissioners decided to declare a "state of emergency" to circumvent public hearings so they can get bid requests on 20 projects by the July 13 deadline.

"Maybe we ought to pioneer this thing of turning the money down," Commissioner Harold H. Roberts said at a meeting called to discuss the possible projects. But later, Roberts said he was just "being philosophical."

Among the 20 projects the commission is considering are the library, construction of a second floor to the police station, a parking lot for the fire department, tennis courts, a bike path, a $400,000 grandstand at the city's baseball field, $200,000 worth of repairs to the sewage treatment plant and paving and draining several streets and intersections.

The *Champaign-Urbana News Gazette*, July 10, 1977, p. 10.

of national control has been a continuing problem in contemporary federalism.

CATEGORICAL GRANTS   One solution is the so-called **categorical grant.** Here a state or local government is given money for a specific project, say a highway between two cities, with the precise details spelled out; if the state or city wants the money, it must follow rules made in Washington. The project will also be monitored by the national government, and deviations from the original agreement can result in a withdrawal of funds. The power to cut off funds has been employed on numerous occasions. For example, when several southern communities in the 1960s refused to implement racial integration in nationally funded facilities—schools—Washington withdrew its assistance. In fact, the Civil Rights Act of 1964 makes it illegal to provide national money for segregated activities or facilities. This approach can perhaps be described as national control through financial bribery.

STATE AND LOCAL INVOLVEMENT   A second, and different, approach to balancing national and subnational interests is to involve political leaders at the state and local levels in the administration of grant programs. This method has had a particular appeal to governors and mayors who felt threatened when Washington created new programs over which they had no control in their jurisdictions. Leaders like Mayor Richard Daley, the powerful boss of Chicago from 1958 to 1976, were not pleased when they found themselves the targets of attempts by nationally funded antipoverty groups to oust them. In response to such feelings of being left out, the Intergovernmental Cooperation Act of 1968 was passed requiring that state legislatures or the governors be informed of all national government grants in their states if they want this information. More recently, legislation has been passed that allows governors to veto antipoverty program grants to their states. This veto power, which has been used, exists in addition to the traditional state power over municipalities that could be used to prevent nationally funded projects. Officials in Washington might also consult with organizations of state and local officials such as the Council of State Governments, the National Governors Conference, or the National Association of County Officials. Such veto power or consultation is, however, a far cry from joint decision making.

"NEW FEDERALISM"   A third and more comprehensive solution to the problem of central government control versus state and local autonomy is the "**new federalism**" proposed by President Nixon in September 1969. The key feature of new federalism is the transfer of considerable decision making from Washington to state capitols and city halls. The national government continues to be the great financial benefactor, but state and local officials are no longer told precisely what they must do and how, who must be hired, and so forth. It was no accident that this new federalism was first proposed at the National Governors Conference, a group that has traditionally opposed interference by Washington in state affairs.

This "responsible decentralization" (as President Nixon called his program) involves several important changes in intergovernmental rela-

Categorical grant Funds given for a specific project to be done according to explicit rules determined by the agency providing the funds.
New federalism A program created by President Richard Nixon that emphasizes granting state and local authorities much greater power in deciding how money collected by the national government will be spent in their areas. Also called responsible decentralization.

Block grants Money given by the national government to state agencies for general purposes instead of on a project–by–project basis.

General revenue sharing The transfer of national-government-collected money to the states with few or no stipulations as to how the money is to be used.

tions. First, the categorical grant (money for a specific project to be performed according to strict guidelines) is replaced by **block grants.** Block grants have two important features: (1) they are given to states, as opposed to municipal, private, or special district authorities, and (2) they are given for general purposes rather than for specific projects. Whereas a categorical grant might give $1 million to a community action program to fund a neighborhood summer sports program for potential juvenile delinquents, under a block grant system the State Department of Corrections might get $50 million to help combat juvenile delinquency statewide.

A second feature of the new federalism is a greater emphasis on cash payments directly to individuals, thereby lessening the need for intervening agencies at different levels of government. In the past Washington might have provided housing for the poor by establishing independent housing authorities that would, in cooperation with state and local officials, build and manage subsidized public housing. The new federalism solution is to distribute the housing subsidy directly to people, letting them choose their own housing (this principle of direct payment underlies the social security program).

An important feature of the new federalism, however, is **general revenue sharing,** which became law in 1972. Under this program funds from the national government are distributed directly to the states on the basis of population and taxes collected by the states themselves. In turn, two thirds of these funds are distributed to government units like cities and counties within the states, although special purpose units like air pollution control districts and sewage districts are excluded. Though various bookkeeping requirements exist, states and localities generally can spend these revenue-sharing funds as they choose. In fiscal 1977, some $6.8 billion in general revenue-sharing funds was distributed and used for a wide variety of purposes, including reducing local taxes.[10]

Though President Nixon's new federalism has received wide publicity, it has not completely transformed national, state, and local relationships. The national government has not abandoned the system of categorical grants and replaced them with block grants and revenue sharing. Even in the mid-1970s, several years after the emergence of the new federalism, the categorical grant overwhelmingly remains the most common form of national government financial assistance. On several occasions President Nixon attempted to reduce the number of categorical grants and replace them with block grants or revenue sharing, but he met stiff congressional opposition. Moreover, the $6.8 billion given back to the states remains a small part of the total national aid given to states and localities (9.6 percent in fiscal 1977).

CONTINUING CONFLICTS IN CONTEMPORARY FEDERALISM

It should be clear that although federalism in the 1970s is a far cry from federalism in the 1870s, it remains a subject filled with complexities and unresolved questions. Instead of controversies over whether Congress

[10] *Statistical Abstract of the United States, 1978,* p. 284.

can pass laws regulating manufacturing, the debate is now likely to be over whether Congress can tell the states just how to construct roads that are to be built with national government funding. As before, however, these issues of federalism are more than just technical or legal questions. Behind each issue in the contemporary administration of federalism are conflicting interests, and solutions will favor one interest at the expense of the other. Rarely, if ever, are problems purely technical or constitutional.

Consider, for example, the new federalism program offered by President Nixon. Its defenders argue that giving greater policy discretion to state and local authorities will improve government performance by (1) eliminating paperwork and bureaucracy and (2) giving authority to leaders closer to the situation, who are thus more knowledgeable. What defenders neglect to mention is that "responsible decentralization" would involve a shift of power from Congress – which in recent years has been controlled by Democrats – to state capitals where Republicans are more likely to have political control. Thus, instead of money going to causes and groups favored by Democrats, more money would find its way into Republican-approved projects.

As many groups have discovered, *who* administers a program can be a major factor in who benefits from the program. For many years civil rights groups, groups representing senior citizens, and other organizations with an economically disadvantaged following have viewed national officials as their allies. In contrast, they have perceived state and local officials as more concerned with holding down taxes and catering to more established economic interests. To a certain extent the general revenue-sharing program has confirmed the fears of those economically less well off. The rise of revenue sharing has been accompanied by a decline in categorical grants-in-aid for education, public health services, drug-control programs, and summer youth programs. Equally important, states and cities have not used revenue-sharing funds to provide a higher level of services to needy citizens. These newly available funds, which probably would have been used for social services if spent by Washington, were typically spent on existing services, such as police and fire protection, so as to maintain or reduce state and local tax rates.[11]

In sum, regarding the broad question of how does contemporary federalism operate, the system can best be described as a complex flow of financial assistance from Washington to states, cities, and other governmental units. The prominent questions concerning American federalism are no longer who has ultimate sovereignty or what is the precise division of political labor. Rather, the debate now revolves around how these extensive transfers of funds should be administered. Several mechanisms exist, but many problems are unavoidable in such a vast enterprise. What is important to remember is that each solution helps some interests more than others.

---

[11] An excellent review of the issues in the debate over revenue sharing is presented in Michael D. Reagan, "Revenue Sharing: The Pro and Con Arguments," *Annals of the American Academy of Political and Social Sciences*, Vol. 419 (May 1975), pp. 21–35.

Creative federalism The federalism program of President Lyndon Johnson, which emphasized new ways of solving state and local problems with national government help.

PRESIDENT CARTER'S APPROACH TO FEDERALISM

As Washington has become more involved in state and local affairs, the management of contemporary federalism has become a prominent public issue. Not surprisingly, each new President has felt a need to offer his own program to cope with the complexities of federalism. Moreover, each of these solutions has been given a name. For example, President Lyndon Johnson offered the nation **"creative federalism,"** which emphasized new ways of involving the national government in previously state and local problems. Money was even given to private companies like Litton Industries to accomplish tasks once performed by state governments. Under Presidents Richard Nixon and Gerald Ford we had "new federalism," which stressed fewer restrictions on nationally supplied money. The key programs of new federalism were block grants and general revenue sharing.

President Jimmy Carter's approach to contemporary federalism has been to emphasize direct cooperation of public officials at all levels of government in both the formation and administration of policy. Several concrete steps have thus far been taken to accomplish this goal. Under Executive Order 11297 the President has created a group of officials drawn from cabinet-level departments charged with ex-

Is federalism still politically relevant?

The original justification of a federal system of government rested on two arguments. First, since tyranny results from the concentration of all political power in one person or institution, a division of authority between state and national governments (as well as separation of powers and checks and balances within government) would help prevent tyranny. Second, a federal form of government was a practical necessity if the thirteen original states were to ratify the Constitution. The division of powers was one of the prices to be paid for creating a central government. The first justification is merely an assumption—concentrated power automatically brings tyranny—while the second justification is a purely practical consideration, relevant only in 1789.

It can be argued that since the government in Washington now faces problems undreamed of in 1789, the whole idea of federalism must be critically reexamined. In seeking the contemporary relevance of federalism one must be concerned with two district issues. The first has to do with the original justification that federalism is a necessary protection

amining policies relating to urban and regional problems. This group, in turn, has created several task forces to study specific problems. A second step is to include advisers with state and local experience on the staff of Jack H. Watson, the President's assistant for intergovernmental relations. Watson is a highly regarded aide, and thus people concerned with national-state relations have a key White House contact. Third, through Watson Carter had undertaken a thorough review of the ten regional councils (these councils are supposed to coordinate national programs). Finally, the President himself has warmly received numerous state and local officials in the White House and reassured them of his commitment to involve them in policy making.

Clearly, both President Nixon's new federalism and President Carter's shared-responsibility federalism are designed to make government more effective, but they differ in their view of national control. Nixon's plan allows state and local officials considerable discretion in spending Washington's money (they do not even have to spend it). Carter's program, however, while encouraging consultation with state and local officials, keeps the final say in Washington. Whereas President Johnson's "creative federalism" sought to accomplish national goals by putting specific requirements in grants-in-aid, and Nixon stressed freedom from Washington's interference, President Carter hopes that extensive consultation will produce effective policy.

against tyrannical government. This involves the questions of whether or not modern federalism remains a defense against the complete concentration of power as well as whether tyranny does occur if all power is concentrated in one person or institution. The second issue concerns whether a division of sovereignty between national and state governments is a workable, effective way of running a government today. Here the focus is on the administrative costs and benefits of federalism. Let us begin our analysis by considering the original claim that federalism is necessary for political freedom.

FEDERALISM AND POLITICAL FREEDOM

The original justification for federalism was that a division of political labor between the national and state governments, by preventing the concentration of all political power in a few hands, would prevent tyranny. This argument still has its defenders, especially among conservatives. Moreover, almost all of those who accept this argument also believe that the government in Washington has exceeded its constitutional role and that we are thus living under a system in which the national government is unchecked by state authority. Hence, even the proprietor of the local pizzeria finds himself being told by the national government whom he must serve, the minimum wages he must pay his employees, and how he can advertise his products, as well as having to comply with a bewildering number of tax and antipollution laws. If he should complain to state or local officials about all of these regulations, he is likely to be told "go fight the government in Washington." To some people this power constitutes tyranny.

Contemporary state government power as a check on national government tyranny

For the moment let us accept the premise that federalism is a necessary protection against tyranny. The question we now face is, Has this protection been so seriously breached that the United States is on the verge of tyranny? Several facts run contrary to the claim that federalism as a barrier to national authority is completely dead. First, the bulk of the grants-in-aid system is essentially voluntary. Washington may attach stipulations to its money, but states or communities are not legally required to apply for these grants. Indeed, officials have sometimes refused to seek funds from Washington because they have objected to the attached strings. Recently, for example, the upper house in Wyoming voted to end the 55 mile per hour speed limit in that state even though this would mean a loss of some $40 million in highway money from Washington. Moreover, states and localities in need of money but wanting to avoid national rules can still raise the money themselves by increasing taxes.

Second, the Supreme Court in the last forty years may have given the national government vastly expanded powers, but states still maintain control over key policy areas. In such important areas as marriage and divorce laws, crime control, the control of firearms, the licensing of professions, the regulation of liquor, the financing of education, the regulation of utilities, and traffic laws the states still exercise the predominant power. States still possess considerable power over many policy areas that affect personal freedom. If you feel oppressed by the laws of one state regarding liquor, narcotics, and driving, you can always move to a state with different laws.

Third, the tendency begun in the 1930s of the national government expanding into state and local policy domains is not an irreversible process that will ultimately end in all subnational governments being absorbed by Washington. While the states must depend on the national government for things like national defense and negotiating with foreign leaders, the same dependence does not exist for building highways or providing police and other essential services. If the national government *did* become oppressive, citizens *could* remedy the problem. Indeed, several prominent political leaders have strongly opposed increasing the size of the Washington government. (Remember that it was President Nixon who initiated the general revenue-sharing program that allows states much more discretion in spending.) The next twenty years may see a flow of influence back to the states.

Challenging the assumption that strong state governments check national government oppression

Finally, the assumption that federalism is a necessary protection against tyranny is open to question. The voluntary nature of national aid, the existence of state power over important bodies, and the reversibility of growing centralized power were interpreted as evidence that federalism is still a viable protection against an oppressive government. It can be argued, however, that federalism and political freedom are *not* necessarily connected. That is, one can have a unitary government but yet not have an oppressive government.

Support for this contention can be found in the existence of numerous nonoppressive unitary governments. Many European democracies, for example, Great Britain and France, are not federal systems; others, like West Germany and Switzerland, are federal and nontyrannical. Moreover, powerful dictatorships in federal systems *have* occurred, as in Brazil. Additional proof regarding the federalism-protects-freedom argument emerges when we look at how this contention has been used in the United States. The most recent defenders of this argument have been white southerners who saw the civil rights activity on the part of the national government as tyranny from Washington. In other words, Washington's ruling that blacks be treated as equals in education, housing, and employment was labeled tyrannical. Also recall that may persons who favor turning more decisions over to state governments are Republicans, who have had greater electoral success at the state level.[12]

RESISTING THE LURE OF WASHINGTON MONEY

The voluntary nature of the grants-in-aid program was recently illustrated when the city of Coeur d'Alene, Idaho, returned $12,800 to the U.S. Economic Development Administration. The money was intended for a new roof, storm windows, and additional insulation for the city firehouse. Was this refusal an act of defiance against national encroachment in local independence? Not quite. It seems that the check arrived with a 400-page instructional book on the use of the money. An accompanying note stated that more instructions were on the way. When the city manager calculated that it would cost more than $12,800 to follow Washington's instructions, Coeur d'Alene asserted its independence.

The *Chicago Sun-Times*, May 6, 1978.

---

[12] Further analysis of the supposed relationship between federalism and freedom is presented in Riker, pp. 139–145.

"Full faith and credit" clause
Article IV, section 1 of the Constitution, which stipulates that
a civil court decision made by
one state court must be accepted as valid by all other
state courts.

In short, if we accept the argument made in 1789 that tyranny results when all power is concentrated in a single person or institution, then the United States remains nontyrannical. However, it can also be argued that the existence of federalism proves nothing about the existence of tyranny. The federal system could well be abolished, and citizens would suffer no loss of freedom. If federalism is to be justified, it must be justified on grounds other than its contribution to political freedom. It is to this justification that we now turn.

FEDERALISM AND ADMINISTRATIVE EFFICIENCY

Federalism was originally defended when both the number of governing bodies was small and the scope of any one of these bodies was comparatively narrow. Today, in addition to fifty states and some 78,000 other governing units, the scope of government action has expanded enormously. Needless to say, whenever several political bodies rule the same citizens, each having some independence from the other, a degree of confusion and inefficiency is bound to prevail. Such confusions and inefficiencies have taken a variety of forms.

Problems resulting from differing state court decisions

One source of problems related to federalism concerns how states treat the legal actions of other states. Article IV, section 1 of the Constitution requires that "Full Faith and Credit shall be given in each state to the public Acts, Records, and judicial Proceedings of every other State." This means that states are obligated to respect the civil (but not criminal) court decisions of all other states. A California court decision in a civil suit will be recognized as valid in all other states, but a California law making certain acts a violation of California criminal law does not automatically apply to the same behavior in other states. (But if you violate California criminal law and flee to another state, the Constitution [Article IV, section 2] requires that you be returned to California by the authorities of the state to which you fled even if your actions are not a crime in that state.)

In practice the **"full faith and credit" clause** has not eliminated the inevitable legal confusion that occurs when you have fifty states, each with its own distinct set of laws. The classic illustration of confusion in this area occurred over divorce laws. Until 1906, if a husband and wife lived in separate states and one got a divorce (even if the other party was not involved in the legal action), the divorce was valid in every state. In *Haddock* v. *Haddock* (1906), however, the Supreme Court ruled that each state could decide for itself whether to honor the divorce actions of another state. In this particular case when both husband and wife were in New York State they were considered married; when both were in Connecticut they were divorced; when he was in Connecticut and she in New York, he was legally single while she was legally married. Not until 1942 did the court rule that states must respect each other's divorce decisions. Even today lingering, unresolved issues exist regarding whether divorce settlements reached in one state are binding on ex-spouses residing in a different state. For example, if a husband leaves his wife in New York and gets a divorce under California law, does the California property settlement law apply to the ex-wife, who never set foot in California?

Problems caused by different laws and administrative regulations

Besides creating uncertainty over the nation-wide enforceability of state civil court decisions, state sovereignty creates confusion regarding what is or is not a crime. Despite efforts to create national unformity in criminal law, substantial variations still exist. Take, for example, the bewildering array of state and city laws regarding marijuana. A citizen of Maine is subject to a maximum fine of $200 if he or she is caught with any quantity of marijuana (the offense is comparable to a traffic violation). In Nevada, however, possession can result in a six-year jail term and a $2,000 fine. In Arizona possession of marijuana can bring a ten-year prison term and a $50,000 fine (the most one can get for possession in Wyoming is six months in jail and/or a $1,000 fine).

Such legal variations also hinder effective enforcement of state and local laws. For example, many cities and states have strict gun control laws. Because citizens living in strict gun control areas can drive to less strict areas, fill their cars with guns, and return home, however, strict gun control laws have been seriously undermined. Variations in liquor laws can also cause law-enforcement problems. When the author of this book attended high school in New Jersey (where the legal drinking age was 21), it was common for students to drive to New York State, which had an 18-year-old drinking age, for Friday and Saturday night parties. The drunken exodus back to New Jersey when the New York bars closed resulted in numerous deaths.

Differences in state regulations have also been blamed for exacerbating social and economic problems. For example, in the 1950s and 1960s, many poor southerners migrated to wealthier northern states in part because of higher welfare and unemployment benefits (some southern states even encouraged this migration). Efforts by northern states to require lengthy residency requirements before being eligible for public aid were struck down by the Supreme Court as a violation of the constitutionally protected right to interstate travel. Simultaneously, wage and labor policies in southern states caused numerous northern industries to abandon their northern facilities. The net result of both trends was a financial drain on cities like New York, Newark, and Philadelphia. No doubt uniform welfare and labor policies across all states would have prevented many of our present-day urban problems by removing the incentive for migration.

Federalism as a source of needless bureaucracy

Finally, it can be argued that maintaining the federalism system increases the amount of needless bureaucracy, delay, and administrative confusion. The involvement of state agencies, which have their own political perspectives, in national programs frequently results in unnecessary competition for control over programs, conflicts over administrative

FEDERALISM AND MARIJUANA

Perhaps the classic illustration of the consequences of having states regulate most criminal offenses is the vast disparity in rules regulating marijuana. Differences occur in virtually every aspect of the law: the distinction between small and large quantities, whether a sale is involved, the range of penalties, and differences between first and second offences (to mention only a few of the complexities). Similar variations exist for laws regulating other drugs, as well. Purely for purposes of educational illustration, here are some of the state laws as of May 1979.

State	Amount	Possession	Sale
Alabama	any amount	0–1 yr. and $1,000	2–15 yrs. and $25,000
Alaska	any amount in private for personal use	$0–$100 fine	0–25 yrs. and $20,000
Arizona	any amount	0–10 yrs. and $50,000	5 yrs.–life and $50.000
Arkansas	any amount	0–1 yr. and $250	3–10 yrs. and $15,000
California	up to 1 oz.	$0–$100 fine	2, 3, or 4 yrs.
Colorado	up to 1 oz.	$0–$100 fine	3–14 yrs. and $10,000
Connecticut	up to 4 ozs.	0–1 yr. and $1,000	0–7 yrs. and $1,000
Delaware	any amount	0–2 yrs. and $500	0–10 yrs. and $1,000–$10,000
District of Columbia	any amount	0–1 yr. and $100–$1,000	0–1 yr. and $100–$1,000
Florida	up to 5 gms.	0–1 yr. and $1,000	0–5 yrs. and $5,000
Georgia	up to 1 oz.	0–1 yr. and $1,000	1–10 yrs.
Hawaii	up to 1 oz.	0–30 days and $500	0–1 yr. and $1,000
Idaho	up to 3 ozs.	0–1 yr. and $1,000	0–5 yrs. and $15,000
Illinois	up to 2.5 gms.	0–30 days and $500	0–6 mos. and $500
Indiana	up to 30 gms.	0–1 yr. and $5,000	0–1 yr. and $5,000
Iowa	any amount	0–6 mos. and $1,000	5 yrs. mandatory and $1,000
Kansas	any amount	0–1 yr. and $2,500	0–10 yrs. and $5,000
Kentucky	any amount	0–90 days and $250	0–1 yr. and $500
Louisiana	any amount	0–6 mos. and $500	0–10 yrs. and $15,000

procedures, and inaction due to a lack of communication.[13] In some cases this filtering of nationally created programs results in redirections (or misdirection) of goals. For example, because of the need to secure the cooperation of innumerable state and local officials, national antipoverty programs in the 1960s did not always reach the individuals most in need of assistance. This implementation of national programs is further undermined by considerable variation across states in their rules and administrative capacities. For example, some national programs require that projects like hospitals be licensed by state authorities, but a state may not have an appropriate licensing agency.

[13] The problems of state-national program coordination are further described in Richard H. Leach, *American Federalism* (New York: Norton, 1970), Chap. 7.

State	Amount	Possession	Sale
Maine	any amount	$0–$200 fine	0–1 yr. and $500
Maryland	any amount	0–1 yr. and $1,000	0–5 yrs. and $15,000
Massachusetts	any amount	0–6 mos. and $500	0–2 yrs. and $5,000
Michigan	any amount	0–1 yr. and $1,000	0–4 yrs. and $2,000
Minnesota	up to 1.5 ozs.	$0–$100 fine	0–5 yrs. and $15,000
Mississippi	up to 1 oz.	$100–$250 fine	0–20 yrs. and $30,000
Missouri	up to 35 gms.	0–1 yr. and $1,000	5 yrs.–life
Montana	up to 60 gms.	0–1 yr. and $1,000	1 yr.–life
Nebraska	up to 1 oz.	$0–$100 fine	0–5 yrs. and $2,000
Nevada	any amount	1–6 yrs. and $2,000	1–20 yrs. and $5,000
New Hampshire	up to 1 lb.	0–1 yr. and $1,000	0–15 yrs. and $2,000
New Jersey	up to 25 gms.	0–6 mos. and $500	0–5 yrs. and $15,000
New Mexico	up to 1 oz.	0–15 days and $50–$100	1–5 yrs. and $5,000
New York	up to 25 gms.	$0–$100 fine	0–1 yr. and $1,000
North Carolina	up to 1 oz.	$0–$100 fine	0–5 yrs. and $5,000
North Dakota	any amount	0–1 yr. and $1,000	0–10 yrs. and $10,000
Ohio	up to 100 gms.	$0–$100 fine	6 mos.–5 yrs. and $2,500
Oklahoma	any amount	0–1 yr.	2–10 yrs. and $5,000
Oregon	up to 1 oz.	$0–$100 fine	0–10 yrs. and $2,500
Pennsylvania	up to 30 gms.	0–30 days and $500	0–5 yrs. and $15,000
Rhode Island	any amount	0–1 yr. and $500	0–30 yrs. and $50,000
South Carolina	up to 1 oz.	0–3 mos. and $100	0–5 yrs. and $5,000
South Dakota	up to 1 oz.	0–30 days and $100	0–1 yr. and $1,000
Tennessee	up to .5 oz.	0–1 yr. and $1,000	0–1 yr. and $1,000
Texas	up to 2 ozs.	0–6 mos. and $1,000	2–10 yrs. and $5,000
Utah	any amount	0–6 mos. and $299	0–5 yrs. and $5,000
Vermont	any amount	0–6 mos. and $500	0–5 yrs. and $10,000
Virginia	up to .5 oz.	0–30 days and $500	0–1 yr. and $1,000
Washington	up to 40 gms.	0–90 days and $250	0–5 yrs. and $10,000
West Virginia	any amount	90 days–6 mos. and $1,000	1–5 yrs. and $15,000
Wisconsin	any amount	0–30 days and $500	0–5 yrs. and $15,000
Wyoming	any amount	0–6 mos. and $1,000	0–10 yrs. and $10,000
FEDERAL LAW	any amount	0–1 yr. and $5,000	0–5 yrs. and $15,000

This chart contains the penalties for first offense possession and sale of marijuana.
The 11 states which have decriminalized possession are indicated as follows: Alaska.

Many states have increased penalties for subsequent offenses. A number of states also have separate penalties for offenses not included in this summary chart, including possession with intent to distribute and cultivation of marijuana.
Source: The Marijuana Laws published by The Center for the Study of Non-Medical Drug Use, Washington, D.C.: May 1979.

Defending the federal system of government

Can the federal system of government be defended against the charge that it promotes administrative inefficiency? Basically, three arguments can be used to defend the present system. First, the innumerable variations in state policies are required to fit the enormous diversity of the American people. Why should citizens of South Dakota and California have the same laws? It might be that divorce laws, liquor laws, and traffic rules that work well in South Dakota would be a disaster in California. A certain degree of inconsistency is the price we pay for the right of citizens to choose rules that best fit state and not national needs. Federalism is necessary in a diverse society.

Second, there is no logical reason to believe that the centralization of policy making in Washington would necessarily result in better, less expensive policies. State independence is a problem only if one is convinced that the national government is always in the right. Take the efforts of the national government to help cities clean up their water. Between 1972 and 1978 the national government spent $9.4 billion in grants-in-aid to help clean up sewage. At Washington's insistence some of this money has been used to construct complex "advanced water treatment" plants (AWT), which so far have cost $2.2 billion in federal funds and over $700 million in state and local money. The problems are that the AWT plants do not always work, and they cost a great deal to maintain. One Maine community found that its AWT plant cost $125,000, not the expected $28,000, a year to operate; so it is selling off the AWT and going back to its old system.[14] Such experiences with "made-in-Washington" policy are not isolated exceptions. Many a nationally conceived and funded program has had a fate similar to the advanced—but frequently nonoperating—sewage treatment facility.[15]

Third, the ability of the states to act independently has occasionally allowed them to develop new and successful policies, which were then adopted nation-wide. States are thus "laboratories of experimentation" where innovations are initially tested. Important national policies such as unemployment compensation, civil sevice, conservation laws, the income tax, regulatory commissions, and regulation of labor-management problems were first implemented at the state level. When the national interstate highway system was in its early stages officials in Washington drew on the experiences of New York and Pennsylvania. More recently policies such as no-fault automobile insurance, decriminalization of marijuana, no-fault divorce laws, liberalized abortion, and allowing professions to advertise have been tested in a few states before being adopted more widely. Such innovations would undoubtedly be more difficult if all important decisions were made in Washington.

In answer to the question of whether federalism is still politically relevant, what can we now say? Our answer is a clear "yes" if by "relevant" we mean that federalism still exists. As we have seen, despite a considerable transformation of the operation of federalism in recent years, the United States is far from a unitary government. Federalism remains important in understanding American politics. But if by "relevant" we mean necessary, then the relevance of federalism is less clear. Certainly the original argument that federalism is essential if political freedom is to be enjoyed is most likely false. Regarding the usefulness of federalism in administering public policy, here the evidence is mixed. Federalism undoubtedly adds numeorus complexities to American politics, but it is difficult to say which complexities are worth it. For example, are varia-

14 James S. Byrne, "Thanks a Lot, Uncle Sam," *Forbes*, October 30, 1978.

15 A virtual catalog of national government ineptitude is provided in Terry Sanford, *Storm Over the States* (New York: McGraw-Hill, 1967), Chap. 9. Part of this problem is that one part of the national government may not know what another part is doing. In one famous case, while one agency was planning a housing project in a city a second agency was planning a major highway for the same land.

**BUT JUST WAIT
UNTIL YOU SEE
THE COMFORT
STATION THAT
GOES WITH THE
RECREATIONAL
CENTER**

One consequence of the large grants-in-aid program is a blizzard of paperwork and the need to satisfy numerous layers of bureaucracy. A city wanting assistance to build a recreational facility might have to make separate requests to get money for the land, build a swimming pool, plant trees, operate a senior citizen's center, and purchase sports equipment. Sometimes funds for an identical project can come from different agencies depending on the size of the city.

One of the frustrating features of the grant system is that requisitions must pass through several different hands before they are approved. A small town might apply for money for a new jail, but several state and national officials could change the request as it moves (slowly) toward final approval. Naturally, with so many people involved, a breakdown in communication between the original need and the actual grant can readily occur. The following story about a proposed recreational facility illustrates this problem:

Stages of a Grant-in-Aid Project as It Advances through the Approval Process

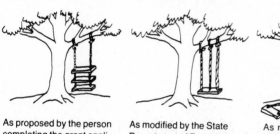

As proposed by the person completing the grant application

As modified by the State Department of Recreation

As modified by the Department of Health and Human Services, Washington, D.C.

As finally approved in Washington

Actual construction of project

What town originally wanted

tions in marijuana penalties good because they allow citizens a choice in the laws they live under, or is this variation bad because it confuses interstate marijuana smokers? What might be an innovative state policy to one observer may be a dangerous manifestation of local insanity to another. What we can say for sure, however, is that since abolishing federalism would require rewriting the Constitution, and rewriting the Constitution would require overwhelming state approval, federalism is likely to exist well into the future.

A conclusion: the politics of federalism

American federalism has undergone enormous changes. It has been transformed from a doctrine emphasizing conflict and sharp divisions of political authority into a system of intergovernmental cooperation to accomplish a wide variety of social and economic goals. Those who drafted the Constitution would probably not recognize contemporary national-state relationships as being consistent with their idea of federalism.

This change in American federalism is, however, more than just a change in governmental procedure. The present system of multibillion dollar grants-in-aid programs, national guidelines, and other features of this "new federalism" is not just the old system supplied with more money to do more things. Contemporary federalism has resulted in major shifts in political influence. Weak groups have gained new strength, and many traditionally powerful interests are now frustrated.

Under the old system of federalism a powerful group in one state could not necessarily affect policies in other states. A reform group might secure antipollution legislation in New York, but this success would have no bearing on policy in New Jersey. Appeals to Washington would be pointless because the national government takes little action with respect to pollution and many other areas. Similarly, railroad interests might dominate one state, but even the domination of several states did not equal domination of national policy. For better or worse, old-style federalism limited the national impact of strong state and local interests.

Today, however, a few citizens who may not constitute a majority in any state or city can influence national policy. For example, suppose that you and your friends oppose putting billboards alongside highways. In the past when highway construction was handled by hundreds of semi-autonomous governments your goal would be pretty hopeless. Thanks to contemporary federalism, however, you may accomplish your goals if you can convince a comparatively small number of national officials that all grants-in-aid for highway construction should contain a provision prohibiting billboards within 100 feet of a nationally funded highway. Hence, if a state wants funds from Washington, it must comply with national billboard placement requirements. You also now have the benefit of having your policy enforced by the powerful national government.

Not every interest has suddenly found its influence multiplied a thousandfold because it can now act through one central government rather than fifty separate governments. Many groups that were especially strong in a few states have lost influence to groups more adept at influencing Congress or Washington-based bureaucracies. Consider how present-day federalism has affected blacks in the South. Until the early 1960s, southern blacks were virtually at the mercy of unsympathetic state officials. The Supreme Court could order schools and other facilities to integrate, but resistance was difficult to overcome. The national grants-in-aid program, however, provided a powerful weapon for civil rights groups. These groups received a warmer reception in Washington than in, say, Jackson, Mississippi, and they were successful in incorporating antidiscrimination provisions in national grants-in-aid. Thus, if Georgia state hospitals practiced discrimination and wished to receive financial aid from Washington, discrimination had to stop. In short, civil rights groups with their congressional and bureaucratic allies now had the advantage over once-powerful state officials.

The lesson we draw from this shift in power is clear: federalism is not a fixed, well-defined legalistic principle beyond the conflict of who gets what in politics. Federalism can mean many things, and each of these different meanings benefits some people at the expense of others.

Major questions raised

1. What are the basic principles of American federalism? The American system is based on a division of power between the national and state levels. If the national government operates on the basis of either its explicit or implicit constitutional power, it overrides state action. The line between national and state power is frequently unclear, however, and has changed over time.

2. How does contemporary federalism operate? Present-day federalism emphasizes intergovernmental cooperation instead of conflict and sharply drawn lines of authority. The national government plays a major role in state and local affairs through its extensive financial contribution. It is also a system of many conflicts and unresolved issues (for example, how much control should Washington exercise?).

3. Is federalism still politically relevant? Despite much centralization of power in the national government, important elements of traditional federalism survive. However, it is open to debate whether federalism can be justified as preserving political freedom or providing an effective means to administer public policy.

QUESTIONS FOR FURTHER DISCUSSION

1. The principle of federalism is sorely tested when a strong local interest collides with a national policy. If you were a judge how would you resolve the following conflict between the Federal Aviation Administration (FAA) in Washington and the San Diego, California, airport authority? Here are the facts:

a. When the Airline Deregulation Act was passed in 1978, three airlines (TWA, Braniff, and North Central) took steps to begin service to San Diego.

b. The San Diego airport instituted a one-year moratorium on new airlines using the airport to stop the three airlines from coming to San Diego.

c. The San Diego airport currently violates California and national standards on acceptable noise levels. Additional airline service would add even more noise.

d. The state of California requires an environmental impact study to be done before airport traffic can be increased. This takes time.

e. The airport is presently being sued by local home owners on the grounds that existing noise levels unlawfully deprive them of their property rights.

Should national law, which allows all airlines to fly to San Diego, be enforced even if the result is more illegal noise, violation of California's environmental protection laws, and more lawsuits from San Diego home owners? What would be a fair decision?

2. Imagine you are working for greater financial aid for college students. What level of government should administer the program? The local government, because local officials are better able to make adjustments for the unique situations faced by each student? The state government, because higher-education finances are a traditional domain of state government, and state officials thus have the necessary experience? The government in Washington, because it has the resources, and a nationally oriented policy would promote equal opportunity for all citizens regardless of residence? Would you have all three levels of government share in the dispensing of scholarship funds? Could students on scholarship simply be given monthly checks with no stipulations on how the money is to be used?

3. A frequent criticism of the present grants-in-aid system is that it is an elaborate and costly means to give money back to the people. First, the money is extracted through heavy taxation and then much of it is shipped back to states and cities via grants and revenue sharing. In the interim money is spent on administration, and Washington is given the opportunity to tell people how to run their lives. What would be wrong with simply reducing the taxes paid to Washington as a form of "instant" revenue sharing?

BIBLIOGRAPHY

Elazar, Daniel J. *American Federalism: A View From the States*, 2d. ed. New York: Crowell, 1972.

   A widely read and broad treatment of American federalism. Elazar explores both the political nature of contemporary federalism (for example, how grants are administered) and the cultural basis of the American system. Here he distinguishes among the different political cultures of the United States and their consequences. Contains a bibliography (which includes government reports).

Glendening, Parris N., and Mavis Mann Reeves. *Pragmatic Federalism: An Intergovernmental View of American Government.* Pacific Palisades, Calif.: Palisades Publishers, 1977.

   A fact-filled analysis of relations among governments. Examines the roles of elected leaders, the courts, parties, and interest groups in the operation of federalism.

Goldwin, Robert A., ed. *A Nation of States: Essays on the American Federal System.* Chicago: Rand McNally, 1963.
Contains seven diverse essays on federalism. These include essays for and against a stronger national government, historical analyses of the Constitution's treatment of federalism, and a description of how contemporary federalism works.

Leach, Richard H. *American Federalism.* New York: Norton, 1970.
A comprehensive examination of many aspects of federalism. Describes the various theories of federalism from colonial times to the present, the power of the national government, problems associated with metropolitan areas, how federalism is administered, and financial aspects of federalism. Education policy is considered in depth as a case study of how federalism functions.

Macmahon, Arthur W. *Administering Federalism in a Democracy.* New York: Oxford University Press, 1972.
Macmahon is a well-regarded expert on federalism. This analysis focuses on legal and administrative issues in present-day federalism (for example, the growth of interstate and regional compacts). Considerable attention is given to financial aspects of federalism and coordination of national, state, and local policies.

Nathan, Richard P., Allen D. Manvel, and Susannah E. Collins. *Monitoring Revenue Sharing.* Washington, D.C.: The Brookings Institution, 1975.
A thorough, scholarly investigation of how revenue sharing worked in sixty-five diverse governmental units. Tries to assess who benefits and loses through the revenue-sharing program. An appendix provides a good historical description of the program and a wealth of data on how revenue-sharing money was spent.

Reagan, Michael D. *The New Federalism.* New York: Oxford University Press, 1972.
The clearest and best-written book on contemporary federalism. Provides an excellent review of the consequences of present state-national relations with attention to both legal changes and financial necessity. Good discussion of grants-in-aid and the politics of revenue sharing. Factual but not technical.

Riker, William H. *Federalism: Origin, Operation, Significance.* Boston: Little, Brown, 1964.
Riker is especially good at describing how non-U.S. federal systems operate (for example, Pakistan, Nigeria, and Switzerland). Chapter 6 examines the pros and cons of keeping the federal system from a practical and theoretical perspective. Contains a comprehensive bibliography of studies of non-U.S. federal systems.

Sanford, Terry. *Storm Over the States.* New York: McGraw-Hill, 1967.
Sanford was governor of North Carolina from 1961 to 1965 and writes from firsthand experience in state-national relationships. Though the author is sympathetic to the state perspective, he presents a balanced picture of state capabilities and examines where the national government can be of assistance. Provides numerous illustrations of how policies at all levels of government have succeeded or failed. Sanford concludes by suggesting several changes in the present system of state-national relations.

Wright, Deil S. *Understanding Intergovernmental Relations.* North Scituate, Mass.: Duxbury Press, 1978.
A detailed, well-documented analysis of how governments at all levels interact with each other. Good coverage of intergovernmental financial relationships, the roles played by different officials, and the impact of recent changes in federalism. An appendix contains texts of important laws and documents, and there is a glossary of terms commonly used in intergovernmental dealings.

Part two

Citizens and politics

PREVIEW

What is public opinion?

Public opinion is the position taken by a large number of people on a politically relevant issue. To analyze public opinion we must be able to measure it. The most common measure of public opinion is a public opinion poll. All polls use samples of people selected from a larger population.

Are opinion polls accurate? Polls differ in their accuracy, but all of them contain some distortion. Citizens may give inaccurate answers, the poll may be poorly designed, and the results may be improperly interpreted.

Do political leaders follow public opinion?

A prior question is: Should leaders follow public opinion? We could argue that heeding public opinion is a requirement of democratic government. On the other hand, it could be argued that leaders should advance people's interests instead of their opinions, and that their interests are not necessarily the same thing as the preferences they express, so that leaders should be free to interpret public opinion. Moreover, this argument would continue, public opinion is frequently too vague to guide leaders, and ordinary citizens lack the knowledge to formulate effective policies (but we could also argue that many people are informed on many issues).

Do leaders act in accord with public opinion? On broad issues, such as whether our economic system will be maintained, the answer is yes. However, on many specific issues there are discrepancies between what government officials do and public opinion. Why do leaders often ignore public opinion? Among the more important reasons are that not all opinions are equally relevant politically, leaders view public opinion messages skeptically, messages conveyed by polls are not politically feasible, and leaders are unaware of public opinion.

Is the U.S. public basically liberal or conservative?

If we pose this question in terms of how people perceive themselves, the vast majority of citizens would characterize themselves as middle-of-the-road rather than as liberal or conservative. Yet one could say that these terms have no concrete meaning to most people, and therefore such a question has to be answered on an issue-by-issue basis. Using this approach, we find that each issue has its own distribution on a liberal-conservative scale. On the question of legalization of marijuana, for example, most people take the conservative position (harsher penalties for use of the drug, not legalization). On women's rights, most citizens take the liberal stance. Moreover, people with liberal leanings on one issue do not always take the same position on other issues. Most citizens are inconsistent in their political thinking.

CHAPTER FOUR

PUBLIC OPINION

Like atmospheric pressure, public opinion seems to be a powerful but not easily observable force. Many things in U.S. politics are said to be caused by "public opinion," yet there is no general agreement on what public opinion is. Nor can we always agree on how public opinion works. Why do some unpopular laws survive while others are abandoned because of public opinion? How can leaders pledge themselves to serve the people and then make decisions opposed by the vast majority of citizens? Public opinion in U.S. politics is far more complex and subtle than the results of any opinion poll suggest. This chapter explores three crucial aspects of public opinion:

1. What is public opinion?
2. Do political leaders follow public opinion?
3. Is the U.S. public basically liberal or conservative?

What is public opinion?

Our use of the term **"public opinion"** implies several distinct characteristics. First, public opinion concerns issues that are *political* in nature. If the American public prefers vanilla to chocolate ice cream, we would not call this preference part of public opinion. A desire for less spending by the national government, however, concerns a political matter and is

Public opinion A preference concerning a political issue on the public agenda.

thus part of public opinion. Of course, an issue that was clearly nonpolitical at one time can also become political with changing circumstances. For example, the question of big cars versus small cars was once strictly a matter of personal opinion. However, because of the energy shortage, the gas consumption of automobiles is now affected by government regulations, and the question "Should we allow gas guzzlers?" is now also a public issue.

A second characteristic of public opinion is that it involves a *preference* for a policy. If you think that the government should invest more money in solar energy research, you have a preference for a particular policy. However, if you feel that most public officials are incompetents, you are not calling for any particular government action. Feelings such as these are usually called beliefs, and while they may be relevant to politics, they are usually distinguished from political opinions. Your preference for more government research in solar energy, for example, may be based on the belief that we shall soon run out of oil and coal.

Finally, the preference must involve some policy of general public concern. You may want government to build you a new house, but since this issue is of no concern to anyone else, it is not part of public opinion. This criterion stresses the *public* nature of public opinion. Issues can come and go as part of public opinion. In the 1950s, for instance, the question of whether the government should build an extensive network of bomb shelters was a major public issue. Today this question is no longer an item on the public agenda. In sum, when we say "public opinion" we mean a preference on a politically related policy of concern to a large number of citizens.

MEASURING PUBLIC OPINION

"Public opinion" is different from related phenomena such as beliefs and private opinion. By itself, however, it is of little help in telling us what politically relevant issues are of concern to people and how people differ on these issues. To analyze public opinion we must be able to measure it accurately. Otherwise anyone could claim that the public wants a particular policy, and we could not prove him or her right or wrong. How, then, do we determine public opinion?

Over the years public opinion has been measured in several different ways. Historians, for example, have relied on the written record to determine the opinions of our ancestors. By using newspaper stories, personal letters, novels, and documents, scholars have tried to piece together what people thought during a particular period. By this method it is possible to get some idea of the political issues and conflicts of ancient Athens or Rome. Unfortunately, the written record, though frequently the only evidence available, rarely presents a good overall picture of public sentiment. Until fairly recently illiteracy was widespread, so the written record expressed the concerns of only a small number of citizens. And even then, items such as newspaper editorials or personal letters may not have reflected the views of all persons who could write.

A second popular method used to ascertain public opinion has been to travel and talk with ordinary people. This approach is especially popular

Two leading pollsters, George Gallup (left) and Louis Harris. Gallup started in journalism and identifies with the Republican Party. Harris became prominent by doing campaign work and considers himself a Democrat.

with certain contemporary journalists who crisscross the country chatting with homemakers, students, workers, businesspersons, taxi drivers, and just about everyone else to get a feel for the "national mood." Author Studs Terkel and Charles Kuralt of CBS-TV are two leading practitioners of this technique. Here again, however, we face the problem of overall accuracy. Even the most industrious correspondent lacks the time to interview a wide cross section of the public. Moreover, these interviews can fill thousands of pages or miles of tape, and selecting "typical" passages can be a real problem. Despite its personal touch, determining public opinion by traveling and talking to ordinary citizens is of limited use.

OPINION POLLS

A third method of determining public opinion has a greater potential for accuracy. This is the opinion poll made famous by George Gallup, Elmo Roper, and Louis Harris. Today hundreds of organizations run opinion polls, and the results are widely reported and sometimes given great significance by political leaders. Though numerous variations exist, all opinion surveys follow four basic procedures.

Formulate questions
Questions may range from extremely specific ones requiring a simple yes or no response to such open-ended ones as "What should we do about the energy problem?" Careful researchers will test questions several times to eliminate unclear terms or misleading implications.

Draw a sample
Pollsters have discovered that it is unnecessary to ask everyone's opinion to get an accurate reading of overall opinion. A random **sample** of 1,500 people can give a good picture of how the entire population would answer a question. Though using a sample instead of asking everyone will produce some errors, the amount of error can be estimated, and the financial savings are enormous.

Ask questions
Organizations like Gallup or Roper usually ask questions in face-to-face interviews. Other popular ways of asking questions are by telephone interviews and mailed questionnaires. Face-to-face interviews are usually preferred but are expensive and time consuming.

Sample In public opinion polling, a sample is a selection of a small number of people from a larger group. In a random sample every person has an equal chance of being included in the smaller group, or "sample."

91

Tabulate the results

Hundreds of separate responses must be condensed, or the results would be bewildering. When questions are of the yes-no variety, the process is straightforward. However, when responses are more elaborate, judgments must be made concerning how to present the information. These judgments can involve decisions about including "don't know" responses in the tallies or combining similar answers.

PROBLEMS WITH OPINION POLLS

There is no one right way to conduct an opinion poll, and the quality of opinion surveys can differ significantly. The result is that it is usually difficult to evaluate the truthfulness of poll results; in addition, the practice of omitting technical details from the published reports further compounds the problem. Here we touch on the most basic issue in polling: Do opinion polls present a truthful picture of public sentiment? Do polls significantly distort and mislead? The answer is that to a greater or lesser extent *all* polls contain a certain amount of distortion. Distortion derives from three main sources: (1) people give inaccurate answers; (2) polls may be poorly designed; and (3) results may be interpreted inaccurately by the polling organization or the press.

DISAGREEMENT OVER THE MEANING OF "BLACK POWER"

Public opinion polls can be especially misleading when questions use terms that are unclear. For example, two people can answer yes to a question on racial integration but actually differ with one another if they disagree on the meaning of "racial integration." The variety of meanings given to controversial expressions is well documented in a study by Aberbach and Walker of how people defined "Black Power," a concept widely used in the 1960s.

Among Detroit whites in 1967, many (39 percent) interpreted "Black Power" to mean blacks dominating whites. Some typical definitions were:

Nasty word! That the blacks won't be satisfied until they get complete control of our country by force if necessary.

The colored are going to take over and be our leaders and we're to be their servants. Yes, that's exactly what it means.

On the other hand, about 22 percent of the black sample said the term was meaningless. Some responses were:

Inaccurate answers

One reason for errors in measuring public opinion is that people lie. Especially on controversial issues such as sexual likes and dislikes, questions involving racial prejudices, and unpopular political opinions, lying is probably fairly common.

Why do people lie? In some instances they are ashamed to give their true feelings. After all, even if you did favor discrimination against blacks, would you admit it to a stranger? How many students would admit that they favor cheating? A related reason for lying is that people do not know how the information they provide is going to be used. What would you do if someone asked you: "I'm from the Opinion Research Corporation, and I would like to know whether you favor communism?" People can have good reasons for giving false answers when questioned about such sensitive areas as their incomes, personal lives, or political activities because the information could be used against them.[1]

[1] People may also purposely give false information to avoid a sales pitch. In recent years, because of the great publicity given to public opinion polls, many salespeople have found it convenient to pose as public opinion pollsters to gain access to potential customers. During political campaigns propaganda pitches are sometimes hidden behind phony opinion surveys. Someone calling you to ask, "Do you know the name of the nineteenth President of the United States?" could be someone who wants to sell you an encyclopedia rather than a Gallup pollster.

It means nothing! A word coined by some nut. There is only one power and that is God.

It doesn't mean nothing. Biggest joke in the 20th century.

However, among Detroit blacks the most common interpretation (42 percent of all definitions) stressed themes of black unity and getting their fair share of political benefits. "Black Power" to these people meant:

Negroes getting the same opportunities as whites when qualified.

Give us an equal chance.

People getting together to accomplish things for the group.

It means being true to yourself and recognize yourself as a black American who can accomplish good things in life.

Obviously, because of differing interpretations of "Black Power," a poll question such as "Do you favor Black Power?" would produce meaningless results.

Joel D. Aberbach and Jack L. Walker, "The Meaning of Black Power: A Comparison of White and Black Interpretations of a Political Slogan," *American Political Science Review*, 64 (1970), pp. 367–388.

Providing false information to an interviewer is not always intentional. People sometimes misunderstand questions and therefore answer inaccurately. This point is illustrated by a survey conducted during World War II that asked whether the government should control wartime profits. Some citizens said no, but further investigation showed that these people thought the question referred to *religious prophets*, not *business profits*.[2] Studies of public thinking have shown that people frequently differ in how they interpret complex terms like "right to work law" or "socialized medicine." Hence, people may give misleading answers in opinion polls because they do not understand the questions.

Poorly designed polls

Measuring public opinion, like measuring temperature or wind velocity, requires an accurate instrument. One common source of distortion is poorly constructed questions. For example, a question like "Do you think the government should help poor people and promote greater economic equality?" really contains two separate questions. A person can favor government help for the poor and *not* favor greater equality, so one cannot be sure what an answer to this question really means. Another common type of misleading question is the one that uses "loaded" terms to steer answers in a certain direction. Compare the following questions on the same subject: "Do you think that suspected offenders deserve all the legal rights they are entitled to?" and "Does our legal system now overprotect criminals at the expense of innocent victims?" Obviously, both questions use certain words (for example, "suspected offenders" and "criminals") to manipulate responses.[3]

A second way an opinion poll can distort public opinion concerns the impact of the person asking questions. Without the proper training an interviewer can unintentionally push respondents toward some answers and away from others. A smile when the answer is "correct," a change in

[2] Cited in Lindey Rogers, *The Pollsters* (New York: Knopf, 1947), p. 110. Another illustration of such confusion turned up in an early Gallup poll asking about ownership of stock. Many people in the Southwest answered that they owned stock, but they had livestock in mind. The word "stock" was eventually changed to "securities or stock listed on any stock exchange." Cited in Charles W. Roll, Jr., and Albert H. Cantril, *Polls: Their Use and Misuse in Politics* (New York: Basic Books, 1972), p. 106.

[3] The use of poorly drafted questions can be intentional. The person paying for the poll may want questions that bias the results. In his study of pollsters Michael Wheeler suggests that even the President may occasionally want poll questions that produce misleading results. Wheeler relates the story of Louis Harris' 1971 White House-sponsored poll of national opinion. Just before the final questionnaire was to be printed, Harris received the following questions from the White House: (1) "Too many people are constantly trying to run this country down; instead, they should be positive and build up the country" (agree or disagree); (2) "The government should get rid of its give-away programs and reduce taxes" (agree or disagree). Some people close to the situation believed that President Nixon himself wrote these questions to elicit greater public support for his Administration. See Michael Wheeler, *Lies, Damn Lies, and Statistics* (New York: Liveright, 1976), pp. 7–8.

WHO ASKS THE QUESTION CAN AFFECT THE ANSWER

The impact of an interviewer on the answers people give to poll questions is exemplified by studies done in Detroit in 1968 and 1971. What happens when a black rather than a white interviews another black on matters involving racial feeling? Does the race of the interviewer make a difference in the answers people give? On sensitive matters of race, the answer seems to be yes, as the following results indicate.

Opinion	Interviewed by white	Interviewed by black
Among blacks (1968)		
Most whites can be trusted.	35% said yes	7% said yes
Detroit riots were step forward for Negro cause.	30% said yes	54% said yes
Should there be Negro principals in schools with mostly Negro students?	26% said yes	42% said yes
Among whites (1971)		
Not mind if relative married a Negro.	26% said yes	72% said yes
Negro and white students should go to same school.	56% said yes	91% said yes
Would *not* be disturbed if Negro of same social class moved into neighborhood.	69% said yes	100% said yes

Not every race-related question was affected by the race of the interviewer. In general, however, the more sensitive and controversial the issue, the greater the likelihood of an impact.

From Howard Schuman and Jean M. Converse, "The Effects of Black and White Interviews on Black Responses in 1968," *Public Opinion Quarterly*, 35 (1971), pp. 44–68; and Shirley Hattchett and Howard Schuman, "White Respondents and Race of Interviewer Effects," *Public Opinion Quarterly*, 39 (1975), pp. 523–528.

an interviewer's tone of voice, a look of boredom, all can have such an effect. Even an interviewer's style of dress, length of hair, or other personal characteristics can affect how questions are answered. The best polling organizations spend weeks training their interviewers to avoid these problems, but such training is not universal.

In 1948, the *Chicago Daily Tribune,* encouraged by misleading public opinion polls, declared Thomas E. Dewey the victor over Harry S. Truman. The polls had erred by not properly taking into account people's intention to vote.

Finally, even if well-constructed questions are asked by well-trained interviewers, the poll can still yield misleading results if the sample is poorly designed. Recall that all surveys use samples rather than poll everyone. A good sample is an accurate cross section of the group whose opinions one wants to measure. Most political polls use samples designed to represent national opinions, but unfortunately, many samples are not accurate cross sections. In some instances hard-to-find people, for example, isolated rural people, are simply omitted. In other instances interviewers shy away from "unpleasant" types, for example, poor inner-city residents, and concentrate instead on "safer" middle-class people in suburban shopping centers. Many opinion polls underrepresent the opinions of racial and ethnic minority groups, poor rural residents, and persons in the armed services and in institutions.

Inaccurate interpretation of results

Asking 1,500 people fifty questions produces an enormous amount of material. If these data are to be comprehensible they must be boiled down. Here again, public sentiment can be distorted. Some errors in interpretation stem from the alternative answers from which one must choose to answer a poll question. To save time and money, many surveys give two to four alternative answers for each question. Thus, for the question "What should the United States do about the energy problem?" the choices might be: "raise gasoline prices," "stress conservation," or "develop nuclear power." In responding it is obviously much easier to analyze three alternatives than dozens of possible answers.

The problem is that the choices given may not reflect the respondent's position. Suppose that on the energy question 75 percent of people polled favor the answer "find more oil," an answer not included with the question. Some people will answer the question by saying they don't know which answer is best, while others may choose the alternative that appears closest to their first choice. In this case the person who formulated the predetermined answers seriously misjudged public opinion *before* asking the question. In many instances such erroneous prior interpretations lead to distorted overall results.

One way to avoid the problem of preconceived interpretations is to offer respondents many different possible answers. Here the odds of excluding a person's real preferences are much lower. Nevertheless, while this approach can provide a more accurate portrait of public thinking, the result of having numerous choices can be confusion. Take, for example, the information on public attitudes toward U.S. Vietnam policy depicted in Table 4.1. Respondents are given *seven* possible responses — enough to reflect most opinions. What, then, does this poll prove? Since no single position receives majority support, one could argue that the public has no clear preference on Vietnam. On the other hand, like many professional pollsters, we could combine similar answers to provide a sharper picture. Table 4.1A shows that by combining categories 1, 2, and 3, 45 percent favor some degree of U.S. withdrawal from Vietnam. Table 4.1A also shows that by combining categories 5, 6, and 7, 30 percent favor some kind of increased military action, and 25 percent (category 4) favor the in-between position. Unfortunately, still no majority position has emerged. Fear not, however, for a majority position *can* be created by moving the middle position around. Table 4.1B "proves" that:

1. A majority rejects more military intervention (categories 1–4 equal 70 percent).
2. A majority rejects military withdrawal (categories 4–7 equal 55 percent).
3. A majority endorses a moderate position (categories 3–5 equal 51 percent).

In other words, by manipulating the results we can show that the public endorses any one of three contradictory positions on U.S. involvement in Vietnam.

TABLE 4.1

PUBLIC PREFERENCES ON VIETNAM POLICY, 1972

	Immediate and complete withdrawal			In-between		Greatly increase military effort	
Categories	1	2	3	4	5	6	7
Percent	21	10	14	25	12	6	12
Table 4.1A (combining three extreme answers)		45		25		30	
Table 4.1B (combining the middle response with the extremes)		70		51		55	

Source: Center for Political Studies, University of Michigan, Ann Arbor.

In depicting all of the problems of obtaining a true measure of public opinion our goal is not to discredit opinion polls. No doubt some surveys purposely mislead or engage in outright fraud, but most of the polls that ordinary citizens see (for example, Gallup results in newspapers) are honest efforts to project accurate information. But even the best efforts are likely to contain distortions. No poll can completely eliminate the distortions created by lying respondents, misleading questions, or inadvertent errors of interpretation. Moreover, the problems we have described are only a small sample of the kinds of difficulties associated with opinion surveys. In short, the opinion poll is probably the best way of determining what the public thinks, but it still presents only a reasonable approximation.

Do political leaders follow public opinion?

Before we consider whether public opinion actually affects the decisions of government officials we must explore a prior question: *Should* leaders follow public opinion? Might it be reasonable for leaders to ignore public sentiment on many issues?

EXTENT TO WHICH LEADERS SHOULD FOLLOW PUBLIC OPINION

One argument in favor of leaders obeying the majority is that such a response is fundamental to democratic government. After all, the argument goes, this is what "rule by the people" is all about. We certainly could not call a government democratic if it repeatedly violated majority preferences. Moroever, why have elections and free speech if the sentiments expressed through these channels count for nothing? Hence, it is sometimes argued that democratic government means government by public opinion.

Despite the appeal of this line of thinking, there are people, even supporters of democratic government, who would greatly limit the influence of public opinion. They claim that leaders should follow the *interests* of the majority and that these are not necessarily synonymous with the preferences people express in public opinion polls. To illustrate the difference between a person's *interest* and a *preference*, consider how most people would answer a question on the tax rate. If asked "Do you want higher or lower taxes?" most people would probably say lower taxes. Should the government then lower taxes? Some leaders might say no because lower taxes would increase inflation, and this would be against the *interests* of the majority.

People who do not want government officials to follow public opinion slavishly frequently argue that even democratic leaders must always *interpret* public opinion. Without such interpretation there would be no need for leaders—government would consist of clerks who would mechanically follow the results of opinion surveys. Because public opinion is subject to interpretation by political leaders, there will always be a gap between what the public wants and what the public gets. For example, a leader might interpret public desire to eliminate pollution to mean "eliminate as much pollution as possible without causing economic disruption." This reasonable interpretation could, of course, mean that there is a disparity between opinion poll results and government action on pollution.

Problems leaders face in interpreting public opinion

Moreover, public opinion may be of little value to leaders because of its vagueness. Opinion polls focus on general preferences, but leaders must make specific decisions. For example, during the period of U.S. involvement in Vietnam, the public was frequently asked to choose between such general alternatives as "increase military effort" and "eventually withdraw." Though each citizen may have had a specific desire, the final survey result was of little help to a decision maker faced with detailed choices. If a majority of the public said "increase military effort," how were legislators to know by *how much* this effort should be increased? Should the President send over another 10,000 troops? 100,000 troops? use nuclear weapons?

Asking more specific questions on polls does not solve the problem. Many people simply lack opinions on policy matters, so that giving them more concrete choices would probably be met with blank stares. Even if they did have opinions, there are so many possibilities for disagreement on details that a consensus would probably be impossible. Suppose this question were asked: "What exactly should the President do to reduce unemployment? Be as concrete as possible." This type of question would yield so many different answers that it would be very unlikely that even a third of the respondents would agree on a particular course of action. How then could the President be held responsible for following what the majority wants?

The capacity of citizens to give informed opinions

Of all the arguments against government by public opinion, perhaps the strongest is that the average citizen is too politically ignorant to offer wise judgments. In a nutshell, it is argued that while citizens may offer their opinions, they frequently don't know what they are talking about. To follow such uninformed opinion is to court political disaster and to act irresponsibly.

Advocates of this position can offer considerable evidence to support their case. One study done in 1956, for example, found that on several important foreign and domestic issues only between one half and two thirds of the public held an opinion on these issues *and* knew what the government was doing in these areas. Another study, conducted in 1968, reported that most citizens were relatively ill informed about how much money the federal government spends on national defense, social welfare, and foreign aid.[4] Nevertheless, many of these ill-informed people would probably willingly offer their opinions on what the government should do in these areas. Would any sensible leader follow the polls when he or she suspected that a large proportion of the responses was based on ignorance? Would *you* follow the opinion of someone who knew very little about your situation?

Of course, defenders of government by public opinion oppose the position that the public cannot offer informed opinions. They claim that while citizens may be ignorant on some questions, they are knowledgeable in other areas. Particularly on concrete, close-to-home issues, such as those having to do with tax rates or racial integration of neighborhoods, people are sufficiently knowledgeable to provide valid opinions. These opinions *are* politically relevant, it is claimed. Even more important, however, is the contention that even if people are ignorant on details, their opinions on issues are still worth following. For example, a poll result that shows people are opposed to gasoline rationing is a genuine message to political leaders even if most citizens know nothing of the complex economics of supply and demand. After all, one does not have to go to cooking school to give a worthwhile evaluation of a meal.

In sum, whether leaders *should* follow public opinion is difficult to answer. Advocates of government by public opinion claim that in a democracy the people must play a role in shaping policy and that citizens are capable of offering opinions that are worth following. Opponents of this view say that the public interest, and not mere opinion, should be followed. They place little value on the results of opinion surveys because they see them as imprecise, frequently contradictory, and commonly based on ignorance. We shall have more to say about this perplexing issue in our concluding section.

[4] These and other findings concerning public knowledge of government policy are presented in Robert Weissberg, *Public Opinion and Popular Government* (Englewood Cliffs, N.J.: Prentice-Hall, 1976), pp. 32–43.

TRAVELS WITH FARLEY

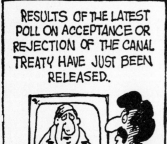

4-3

"I'LL FOLLOW PUBLIC OPINION IF YOU LET ME MEASURE IT"

If leaders were legally required to follow public opinion, a real danger would be a sudden increase in manipulated poll results. Measuring public opinion involves so many decisions that unscrupulous persons could rig survey outcomes without people even realizing it. Most pollsters would not knowingly engage in such deception, but some might. In their study of opinion pollsters, Charles W. Roll, Jr., and Albert H. Cantril relate the following stories of "poll results for hire":

In a Senate primary contest, two polling firms were bidding for a client's business. When a decision became imminent in favor of one firm, the head of the other firm took the client aside to offer a service no one else could offer. He would provide two surveys: one for use with the press for publicity and fund-raising purposes and one to report on how things really stood in the state.

In one of the larger Eastern states, a poll taker amassed poll findings and manipulated them to exaggerate the unpopularity of an incumbent governor. He then threatened the release of these findings to the press unless a poll was commissioned through his organization. In another state, this same poll taker did, indeed, release the alleged unfavorable findings when the client switched from his firm to another firm.

In 1970, the *New York Daily News'* Straw Poll showed incumbent Charles Goodell running a poor third in the Senate race. According to a public statement by an aide to the former senator, shortly after the Straw Poll was published, the senator's staff was contacted by a polling firm asking if there would be any interest in purchasing a poll which would show Goodell ahead.

Cited in Charles W. Roll, Jr., and Albert H. Cantril, *Polls: Their Use and Misuse in Politics* (New York: Basic Books, 1972), pp. 12–13.

PUBLIC OPINION AND PUBLIC POLICY

Are the actions taken by legislators, executives, judges, and administrators consistent with public opinion? Because government makes thousands of important decisions each year, the answer to our question must be yes and no. In some cases leaders do follow public opinion, and in other instances their decisions are contrary to the preferences of most citizens. The main question, therefore, is *what* decisions are consistent with public opinion? What policies run contrary to public opinion?

Policy and opinion agreement on broad issues

We find the greatest agreement between public opinion and government policy in overall political goals—those that both citizens and leaders take for granted. National defense is such an issue. While many political leaders as well as private citizens may disagree on the specifics, for example, exactly how much money to spend, it is fair to say that most people favor maintaining U.S. military strength. Similarly, leaders and citizens agree that our present form of democratic government—with a President, a two-house national legislature, and a Supreme Court—should be preserved. Another area of agreement concerns the role of government in society. Here again, differences on specifics occur, but the consensus is that government possesses major responsibilities for promoting the general welfare.

Citizens' and leaders' preferences are also in accord on several general economic questions. The most obvious is a shared commitment to economic prosperity and growth, though disagreements exist concerning the means of implementing these goals. A second point of agreement involves the maintenance of our system of free enterprise. In the United States, unlike in many other countries, the government does not own the banks, utilities, transportation and communications systems, and large industries. A leader committed to such socialistic policies would have a very short career. At the same time, however, most government officials as well as most citizens believe that some degree of government economic control needs to be exercised in these areas. Neither citizens nor leaders want a system in which economic interests are completely free to do whatever they wish.

Policy and opinion agreement on specific issues

Thus, on many broad political and economic questions government policy is in accord with public opinion. Though we rarely think about these issues, they are important politically. In fact, in many developing nations these kinds of questions are still openly debated, with disagreements leading to violence or even revolution.

Leaving these settled issues aside, however, what about more specific policy questions? Do leaders follow public opinion on the types of issues debated in legislatures or discussed in the mass media? The answer is that on a few specific issues leaders do follow public sentiment, but on most others there is little or no agreement. For example, one study examined eleven major issues that were on the political agenda for several years.[5] On only one question—whether the United Nations should admit the People's Republic of China—was there clear agreement between what the public wanted and government policy. On a second issue—U.S. involvement in Vietnam—the evidence was extremely complex, but public opinion and government action usually went hand in hand. On the other nine issues, however, there were numerous contradictions between opinion and policy.

[5] Weissberg, Chaps. 6 and 7.

One good illustration of the contradiction that exists between popular desires and government policy concerns government assistance for medical expenses. Between the mid-1930s and the early 1960s clear majorities of the public wanted such assistance, yet government action was virtually nil. Only during the sixties and seventies, when the government enacted the Medicare program and made major expenditures on medical research, did opinion and policy begin to show agreement. Overall, for a period of roughly forty years, citizens and leaders were in agreement about a quarter of the time.

Even sharper opinion-policy disagreements arise when we consider the issue of allowing prayers in public schools. In 1962 and 1963, the Supreme Court ruled that religious observances in public schools were unconstitutional. Numerous subsequent lower-court decisions have reaffirmed this ruling. Nevertheless, between 1962 and 1975, seven opinion polls indicated that the public overwhelmingly wants prayers to be said in public schools. Various legislators have introduced proposals to amend the Constitution so as to permit school prayers, but thus far no concrete change has been enacted.

Another clear-cut issue on which public opinion and government policy disagree is gun control. Numerous surveys taken between 1959 and 1974 showed overwhelming public support for a law requiring a police permit to buy a gun. Despite such sentiment, however, leaders have not taken decisive action on gun registration. At both the national and state levels, attempts to regulate the sales of handguns have met stiff opposition. Clearly, the preference of a national majority is not being implemented.

In general, such evidence indicates that as we move away from broad issues like preserving the existing system of government and into specific policy areas, the greater the likelihood that public opinion and government action will diverge. While few leaders would propose broad policies inconsistent with public opinion, these same leaders might ignore the results of opinion polls when considering more specific programs. For example, a President who, like every other citizen, supports the general principles of economic growth and prosperity may nevertheless call for such unpopular economic policies as higher taxes or wage controls. In short, the extent to which leaders follow public opinion depends on the level of generality at which we are talking. On broad issues leaders almost always *do* follow public opinion. However, on more specific day-to-day questions we find numerous discrepancies between public opinion and leadership behavior.

WHEN LEADERS IGNORE PUBLIC OPINION POLL

Why would an elected official faced with clear public support for such measures as tougher gun control or allowing prayers in public schools choose to ignore these demands? Doesn't such behavior risk electoral punishment? Further analysis of this question shows that there are good

GARBAGEMEN
USE POLLS TO
STAMP OUT
SMUT

A public opinion poll is not limited merely to measuring public opinion. Some politicians have found polls to be useful means of creating and manipulating public opinion. A few years ago Mayor Ralph J. Perk of Cleveland used the opinion survey technique to generate support for his antipornography crusade. Perk wanted to know how the people of Cleveland felt about pornography. Rather than hire a pollster to administer a thousand or so interviews, however, the mayor used city garbagemen to distribute questionnaires to 200,000 homes. In the questionnaire's cover letter the mayor stated: "I am shocked by the shameful, pornographic materials which are invading our city and our neighborhoods. . . ." Only 13,000 of the 200,000 questionnaires were returned, and Perk claimed that 80 percent supported his antipornographic position. It also just so happens that Perk was up for reelection the following November (he lost).

Reported in *Playboy*, November 1977, p. 70.

explanations for leaders ignoring opinion poll results. Let us briefly consider four reasons why a leader might act contrary to majority opinion.

Not all opinions are equally relevant politically

Suppose that a public opinion poll in a congressional district showed that 65 percent of the people favored a particular bill. Would it be wise to follow the majority? Not necessarily. It is possible that among those voting for the member of Congress (or those likely to vote for him or her the next time), a *minority* favors this bill. Support for the bill might therefore alienate the very people who put the representative in office. More generally, a public official's career may depend on keeping certain people satisfied, and these certain people may not be among the majority in an opinion poll. This situation has been well illustrated over the years by the special attention given to black citizens by Democratic Presidents. Because black voters played such a crucial role in the victories of Presidents Kennedy, Johnson, and Carter, these leaders sometimes ignored overall public opinion in order to satisfy the preferences of the black voters.

A related argument concerns the differences in the *intensities* of opinion. What should leaders do if the 65 percent who favor a bill are only mildly in favor of it while the minority opposes the bill very strongly? Can you equate a weak and an intense opinion? Because those holding intense opinions are more likely to act on the basis of their opinions, an intense minority will sometimes outweigh a weak majority in a leader's thinking. Perhaps the classic instance of this occurs with citizens opposing handgun registration. Though a small minority, these people are so committed to their cause that numerous members of Congress, fearful of their actions, strenuously avoid offending them. Such representatives commonly reason that voting for something favored by an apathetic majority has few benefits, while opposing an intense minority can incur great costs.

Messages conveyed by opinion polls are viewed skeptically

We have already seen that when the public speaks it does not always make precise, informed, and useful suggestions. Leaders are aware of the problems associated with conducting accurate polls and are thus reasonably cautious in following the results. A frequent claim leaders make about poll results is that citizens would offer different opinions if they were fully aware of the situation. Perhaps for this reason many leaders, if confronted with a poll result contrary to their own position, will not alter their position but rather insist that the public needs to be educated. In many cases, especially on complicated issues, unwillingness to follow poll results because of citizen misinformation is probably well justified.

An interesting example of this process is illustrated by President Carter's stand on the Panama Canal treaty. During much of 1977, President Carter staunchly defended a new treaty with Panama. From the beginning public opinion was very much opposed to Carter's position that turning the canal over to the Panamanians was the best policy. Why didn't the President follow public sentiment? On several occasions he stated that he would *not* follow the majority because it did not understand the treaty. If the public were "educated," according to President Carter, it would favor the treaty. In effect, the President was saying, "I will follow informed opinion, and informed opinion will support me." He was right. In October 1977, a Gallup poll showed that uninformed citizens opposed President Carter's position by a 2 to 1 margin. However, among those acquainted with key details of the treaty, 51 percent favored the treaty and 46 percent opposed it.[6]

We must also realize that leaders have many other indicators of public opinion besides the opinion poll. Public opinion can also be gauged by reading newspapers, talking to ordinary citizens, reading the mail, observing events, and contacting friends. Because some of these techniques are more trusted than national opinion polls, leaders may place greater reliance on them. If the messages conveyed by these sources differ from those derived from national opinion polls, it may appear that a leader is violating public opinion. Actually, the leader may be heeding a different version of public opinion and *is* following public sentiment *as he or she perceives it.* In fact, it is even possible for two people relying on

[6] Cited in the *Champaign-Urbana News-Gazette,* October 23, 1977, p. 6A.

national survey results to disagree, and yet both can claim to be following public opinion since national surveys occasionally differ on what the majority favors.

Messages conveyed by polls are not politically feasible

All political leaders—from a small-town official to the President of the United States—operate under constraints. U.S. politicians are not dictators. Action is limited by legal constraints, the power of other officeholders, budgetary limitations, and numerous other factors. Citizens answering poll questions, however, do not operate under such limitations. Hence, it is not unusual to find a majority of citizens demanding policies that are difficult—if not impossible—to enact.

Consider the issue of prayers in public schools discussed earlier. In view of court decisions stating that school religious observances are unconstitutional, the only way leaders could satisfy public demands for school prayers would be to enact a constitutional amendment. In fact, hundreds of congressional bills and resolutions have been offered to allow prayers in public schools, but to change the Constitution to permit school religious observances would be complex and time consuming.

A related problem is when polls provide contradictory messages to political leaders. This problem is particularly relevant when people demand that government spend less money while simultaneously providing more services. Polls conducted in the mid-1970s, for example, found clear majorities favoring cuts in federal spending, a smaller federal government providing fewer services, and less power for the national government. At the same time, however, overwhelming majorities favored a national health insurance program, increased aid to large cities, more aid to education, greater government effort to provide jobs for everyone, and more government aid for blacks. In the abstract most citizens want less government spending.[7] But when it comes to solving specific problems, most people call for solutions that require more spending and greater government power. What are leaders to do? It would be nice if the government could do more for less money, but this solution seems highly unlikely.

Leaders are unaware of public opinion

Every year tens of thousands of polls are conducted on a variety of issues. Yet despite all these efforts, on many contemporary issues surveys of public thinking do not exist. There are just too many issues, and polls are just too expensive for public opinion to be measured on every question. This is especially true of the detailed, specific issues, which are precisely the ones on which leaders must make decisions. On many topics leaders must therefore function with only a rough knowledge of public sentiment, and misjudgments can easily occur.

This lack of knowledge about public opinion becomes even more severe at the state and local levels. Results from national studies of

[7] Data are presented in Everett Carll Ladd, "What the Voters Really Want," *Fortune*, December 18, 1978, p. 44.

public opinion cannot be generalized for separate states and localities. That 75 percent of a national sample favors a particular policy does *not* mean that 75 percent of the citizens of each state favors that policy. Consequently, for all elected officials except the President, a national poll says little about how an official's own constituents feel on an issue. State or local surveys would be required to answer these questions, but such surveys are rarely available on more than a few issues. Members of Congress, governors, and mayors must therefore make educated guesses about public opinion instead of using poll results.

In general, the cost of informing each public official about how citizens feel on every issue would be staggering. We would probably need a government-administered survey organization to ask tens of thousands of questions. Leaders might therefore have a better knowledge of public feeling, but given the problems associated with following public opinion described earlier, all this new information might not make much political difference. Officials would probably continue to rely heavily on their own judgment. After all, our present form of government does not allow us to force a leader to follow majority opinion on a particular political controversy.

Is the U.S. public basically liberal or conservative?

Since the development of public opinion polls, much has been written about the content of the U.S. public opinion. The most common question in these discussions has been: Are U.S. residents basically liberal or conservative in their political opinions? This is an important but very complex question. The answer we get depends on how we define "liberal" and "conservative," the issues we ask people about, and when the research is conducted. Naturally, because of the many different approaches to this question, analysts offer many different answers to it.

ASKING PEOPLE WHETHER THEY ARE LIBERAL OR CONSERVATIVE

One way to answer the question is very simple — ask people whether they consider themselves to be liberal or conservative. Figure 4.1 presents the results of such a question asked in 1972, 1974, and 1976. The results show two things: (1) most people (about 75 percent) can apply "liberal" or "conservative" to their political positions, and (2) most people place themselves near the "middle-of-the-road" position. Though year-to-year variations occur, the middle position is always the most popular. Measured this way, then, we can say that most people are moderates, not extremists, on the liberal-conservative scale.

Does the information in Figure 4.1 provide a conclusive answer to our question? Some analysts would say no. In particular, they would claim that many people who use terms like "liberal" or "conservative" have little understanding of what these labels mean. That is, many citizens do not know that liberalism means support for greater government effort

FIGURE 4.1

**POSITIONS OF
AMERICANS ON LIBERAL-
CONSERVATIVE SCALES,
1972, 1974, 1976.**

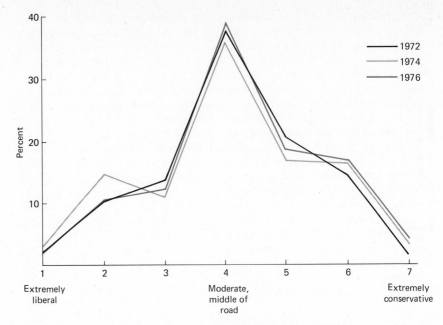

Source: Center for Political Studies, University of Michigan, Ann Arbor.

to solve social and economic problems, while conservatism means support for limited government and an emphasis on private enterprise to solve problems.[8] Hence, when people label themselves liberal or conservative, this says little about the actual policies they favor.

Do ordinary citizens understand this key difference when they use the terms "liberal" or "conservative"? On the basis of several studies, the answer seems to be no.[9] For example, a 1970 Gallup poll asked people, "What is the first thing that comes to your mind when you think of some-

[8] This definition of liberalism and conservatism is the most common one, and it stresses the role of government in economic matters. For example, someone favoring more government financial assistance to poor people is a liberal. However, on noneconomic issues this more-government versus less-government distinction becomes less clear. On the abortion controversy, for instance, the liberal position is usually associated with no government intervention while conservatives endorse government regulation. Many conservatives are also in favor of a strong government when it comes to supporting the military and the police. Liberalism-conservatism is also sometimes defined in terms of attitude toward change—liberals favor change, conservatives oppose change. Here too there are many exceptions. Overall, however, most experts would agree that liberalism means favoring government intervention while conservatism emphasizes private enterprise.

[9] See, for example, Philip E. Converse, "The Nature of Belief Systems in Mass Publics," in David E. Apter, ed. *Ideology and Discontent* (New York: Free Press, 1964), pp. 219–227.

FIGURE 4.2

PUBLIC OPINION ON GOVERNMENT-GUARANTEED EMPLOYMENT, BUSING TO INTEGRATE SCHOOLS, LEGALIZATION OF MARIJUANA, AND WOMEN'S RIGHTS, 1976.

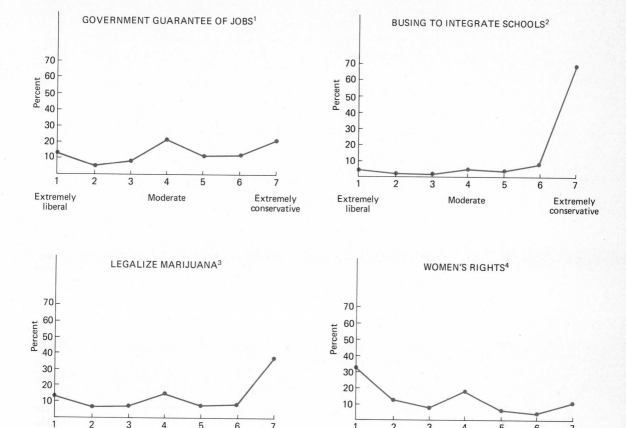

[1] The extremely liberal alternative was: *The government in Washington should see that everyone gets a job and a good standard of living.*
The extremely conservative alternative was: *The government should let each person get ahead on his or her own.*

[2] The extremely liberal alternative was: *Children should be bused out of their own neighborhoods to achieve racial integration.*
The extremely conservative observation was: *Keep children in neighborhood schools.*

[3] The extremely liberal alternative was: *Marijuana should be made legal.*
The extremely conservative alternative was: *Set penalties higher than they are now.*

[4] The extremely liberal alternative was: *Women and men should have equal roles in running business, industry, and government.*
The extremely conservative alternative was: *Women's place is in the home.*

Source: Center for Political Studies, University of Michigan, Ann Arbor.

109

one who is a liberal (conservative)?" Many responses were vague and had little to do with government action. Common answers were "open-minded, fair," "gives things away, spends too freely" or "cautious." About a third of the respondents could offer no definition of the terms. Such answers suggest that we must be cautious in interpreting what people mean when they describe themselves as liberal or conservative.[10]

LIBERALISM VERSUS CONSERVATISM ON SPECIFIC ISSUES

Whether the public is liberal or conservative can, however, be approached from yet another perspective. Specifically, we can examine public opinion on a variety of separate issues to see whether most citizens prefer the liberal or conservative alternative on each question. Thus, we might ask whether they are liberal or conservative on pollution policy rather than whether they are liberal or conservative in general. Then, by looking at the results of several questions, we can reach an overall conclusion.

To examine the degree to which the public is liberal or conservative on specific issues, let us consider poll results on four policies: (1) the government's role in guaranteeing employment; (2) the use of busing to integrate schools; (3) the legalization of marijuana; and (4) women's rights. Although we choose these particular questions to illustrate our argument, it seems likely that four different questions would yield roughly comparable results.

Figure 4.2 shows public preferences on these four issues in 1976. It is obvious that each issue has its own liberal-conservative pattern. For example, most citizens placed themselves on the liberal end of the scale when asked about women's rights. On the legalization of marijuana and busing to achieve racial integration of schools, however, a clear majority took a conservative position. Regarding government guarantees of jobs, there is no clear-cut conservative or liberal majority, though the conservative position was somewhat more popular.

Consistency on specific issues

It is also true that a person holding the liberal position on one issue may hold the middle-of-the-road or conservative position on others. That is, a person may favor equal rights for women (a liberal position) yet also oppose the legalization of marijuana (a conservative position). In fact, on these four issues only about 21 percent of the respondents gave consistent liberal, moderate, or conservative answers across all issues (and almost all of the consistency—19.8 percent—was a consistent conservative response). In short, on some issues most people take the conservative stance; on others, a majority may endorse the liberal alternative; and few citizens consistently take the liberal or conservative side on several different issues.

---

[10] *Gallup Poll: Public Opinion 1935–1971*, vol. III (New York: Random House, 1971), pp. 244–245.

To return to our original question of whether citizens are liberal or conservative, the answer is—it depends. If we simply ask people to describe themselves as liberal or conservative, we find that most consider themselves moderate or middle-of-the-road. If we claim that liberal or conservative labels mean little to most people, and examine opinions on an issue-by-issue basis instead, no simple pattern emerges. Depending on the issue, people tend to be liberal, conservative, or middle-of-the-road. A person's political preferences are complex, and to say that a liberal on one issue will be a liberal on all other issues is a mistake. The problem is even further complicated because many people who use terms like "liberal" or "conservative" disagree on what they mean.

A conclusion: public opinion

In recent years there has been much talk about making government more responsive to citizens. More than one candidate for office has run on a platform of "giving the government back to the people" or "making the people's voice heard in Washington." Government by public opinion may be an attractive idea, but do we *really* want it? On deeper analysis many people would probably reject such a system.

First, to have government act solely on the opinion of the majority, as expressed in an opinion poll, would require drastic constitutional changes. Recall from Chapter Two that many key features of the Constitution (for example, checks and balances) are designed to *prevent* majorities from deciding policy. Why have a Supreme Court if major policy decisions are decided by asking citizens? Clearly, government by public opinion would mean a radically different institution of government, not a mere adaptation of the existing system. Ironically, many people who want government by public opinion also want to keep the present constitutional system, which thwarts government by public opinion.

Second, many citizens are ambivalent about leaders slavishly following public opinion. Along with our veneration of public opinion we also admire leaders who make "tough" decisions that run contrary to popular sentiment. A President who conducted a poll before each action and then always took the majority position would probably not earn the respect of many voters. This ambivalence on the part of the public was well illustrated in answers to a 1960 poll conducted in Detroit. People were asked if a President should commit U.S. troops overseas *even if a majority of the public opposed such action*. Three quarters of the public approved of the President's defying public opinion.[11]

Finally, though the public may be venerated as an enlightened source of great wisdom, there is no guarantee that government by public

[11] Roberta S. Siegel, "Image of the American Presidency: Part II of an Exploration into Popular Vision of Presidential Power," *Midwest Journal of Political Science*, 10 (1966), pp. 123–137.

opinion would be an enlightened government. Policies chosen by 100 million citizens can be just as oppressive as policies enacted by a few irresponsible officials hidden in a massive Washington bureaucracy. Indeed, over the years numerous polls have indicated the willingness of a majority of the public to infringe upon the rights of unpopular political and religious groups.[12] If political freedom were solely decided by asking every citizen what he or she thought, the United States might well have less freedom than in a system in which leaders can ignore public opinion.

Who would gain by having government run in accordance with public opinion? Such a change would bring enormous power to those (nonelected) individuals who control the mass media. Top TV and newspaper executives would become the new political elite by virtue of their direct access to the public. Clever advertising and public relations people who can package and market new public policies would also gain in political power. The professional politician who currently survives by his or her ability to provide benefits to comparatively small groups of citizens would probably be the loser in government by public opinion. In short, advocating following the opinion of citizens on issues makes the most sense only if one has access to a means of shaping public opinion.

Major questions raised

1. What is public opinion? Public opinion is a widely shared preference on a politically relevant policy. A key problem is how to measure public opinion accurately. The public opinion poll is the best, and most common, approach, but even the best polls contain distortions because people may lie in responding, polls may be poorly designed, and the results may be misinterpreted.

2. Do political leaders follow public opinion? An important prior question is: Should leaders follow public opinion? It can be argued, for example, that leaders should follow the interests of citizens, not their opinions, and that public opinion is a poor guide to policy making. Regarding whether leaders do follow opinion, in general, the broader the issue, the greater the likelihood of leader-public opinion agreement. There are many good reasons, however, why leaders often violate the preferences of a national majority.

3. Is the U.S. public basically liberal or conservative? If we ask citizens to classify themselves as "liberal" or "conservative," we find that most say "middle-of-the-road." However, if we approach this question on an issue-by-issue basis, the answer varies depending on the particular question examined. Moreover, many citizens who are liberal on one issue are conservative on others.

[12] For a general review of such polls, see Hazel Erskine, "The Polls: Freedom of Speech," *Public Opinion Quarterly*, 34 (1970), pp. 483–496.

QUESTIONS FOR FURTHER DISCUSSION

1. A 1978 Gallup poll reported that 57 percent of the people interviewed supported a constitutional amendment that would allow citizens to put an issue to a national vote. Under this plan, if 3 percent of all voters in the previous election signed a petition, the issue would be up for a vote (on the basis of the 1976 presidential election, you would need approximately 2.5 million signatures). In fact, this proposal is presently before both houses of Congress for official consideration (it is called the Voter Initiative Amendment). Do you think the results of such a national vote should be binding on leaders or merely advisory? Should *any* proposal be allowed? Even one that was based on faulty knowledge (for example, Congress should repeal the law of gravity so Americans can save more energy)? What should be the necessary majority for such a vote? A majority of all those who bothered to vote, or a majority of all citizens over 18?

2. Conducting a well-run poll is very expensive. Many of the commonly read contemporary polls (for example, the Gallup poll) are basically commercial, profit-oriented enterprises. On occasions the need to stay financially solvent means cutting corners—substituting telephone interviews for face-to-face interviews, say. It has been suggested that only the national government has the resources to conduct numerous high-quality polls. But it can also be argued that there is an inherent conflict of interest if the government conducts the poll and then follows the poll results. Under such conditions political leaders might be tempted to manipulate the polls to further their own goals. Is there a solution to this problem? Should the government establish an autonomous agency whose job would be to conduct opinion polls? Or could we depend on several of the polling organizations established at universities?

3. One of the major issues in evaluating public opinion is deciding whether the opinions of some people ought to count more than the opinions of others. Suppose you do a national survey on whether children should be bused in order to achieve racial integration in public schools. Do you count all opinions equally, or do you give extra weight to the opinions of parents whose children will be bused? What about the opinions of the children? Is the opinion of a 7-year-old relevant, since he or she will bear much of the burden of the policy? Do you ignore the opinions of people who have no direct stake in the issue (for example, people with no children)? Should the opinions of those with strong feelings be given more weight than those who are almost indifferent?

4. *Mind-Boggler Special:* If a majority of the public said in a survey that the President should *not* follow public opinion, and the President claimed that he was *not* following public opinion, wouldn't such action constitute following public opinion (which, of course, the public opposed!)? *Caution:* repeated pondering of this problem can be dangerous to your mental health.

BIBLIOGRAPHY

Bogart, Leo. *Silent Politics: Polls and the Awareness of Public Opinion.* New York: Wiley, 1972.
  A nontechnical analysis of the uses and misuses of public opinion research written by a distinguished pollster. Contains many illustrations of how polls are interpreted by political leaders.

Cohen, C. Bernard. *The Public's Impact on Foreign Policy.* Boston: Little, Brown, 1973.
> Examines how officials in the State Department perceive and use public opinion. The first chapter is an excellent review of some of the problems in relating public opinion to government policy.

Converse, Jean, and Howard Schuman, *Conversations at Random: Survey Research as Interviewers See It.* New York: Wiley, 1974.
> Provides a behind-the-scene view of how opinion surveys are actually conducted. Especially useful for describing the interactions between the interviewer and the respondent.

Erikson, Robert S., and Norman R. Luttbeg. *American Public Opinion: Its Origins, Content, and Impact.* New York: Wiley, 1973.
> A comprehensive review of recent public opinion research. Contains several chapters that deal with the possible impact of public opinion on leaders through the electoral process.

Gallup, George. *The Sophisticated Poll Watcher's Guide.* Princeton, N.J.: Princeton University Press, 1972.
> Expert advice from an expert poll watcher on how to interpret poll results. Considers such problems as the accuracy of samples, government regulation of polls, and the use of polls in forecasting elections.

Harris, Louis, *The Anguish of Change.* New York: Norton, 1973.
> A wide-ranging analysis of American politics from 1960 to 1973 drawing upon several hundred public opinion polls. Covers such topics as Vietnam, women's rights, organized labor, the opinions of young people, and race-related attitudes.

Hennessy, Bernard C. *Public Opinion,* 3d ed. North Scituate, Mass.: Duxbury Press, 1975.
> The most comprehensive text on public opinion—everything you want to know from numerous definitions of public opinion to the relationship between democracy and public opinion to the many technical steps in survey construction and analysis.

Lehnen Robert G. *American Institutions, Political Opinion and Public Policy.* Hinsdale, Ill.: Dryden Press, 1976.
> A wide-ranging analysis of public opinion on numerous topics. Contains extensive information on citizen attitudes toward political institutions such as Congress.

Mueller, John C. *War, Presidents and Public Opinion.* New York: Wiley, 1973.
> An exhaustive analysis of public opinion on the Korean and Vietnam wars plus presidential popularity. The analysis can get complex, but different arguments are clearly stated and well documented.

Roll, Charles W., Jr., and Albert H. Cantril. *Polls: Their Use and Misuse in Politics.* New York: Basic Books, 1972.
> A readable and nontechnical introduction to opinion poll interpretation. Contains numerous examples of proper and improper use of opinion polls.

Weissberg, Robert. *Public Opinion and Popular Government.* Englewood Cliffs, N.J.: Prentice-Hall, 1976.
> Emphasizes the relationship between public opinion and government actions. Examines this relationship on such issues as income tax, school desegregation, and U.S. involvement in Vietnam. Also considers some of the different ways opinion can affect public policy.

Wheeler, Michael. *Lies, Damn Lies, and Statistics.* New York: Liveright, 1976.
> A nontechnical and critical analysis of the polling industry. The book describes several instances in which opinion polls were manipulated for political purposes. Contains a brief, but excellent, section on how to read opinion poll results.

Collections of poll results can be found in several places. *Public Opinion Quarterly* is a professionally oriented journal that usually has a section devoted to polls on one general subject (for example, presidential power). These articles are particularly good for polls conducted years ago and polls that have not been widely distributed. *Public Opinion,* published by the American Enterprise Institute, contains nontechnical articles on contemporary political issues plus a section ("Opinion Roundup") that reviews poll results on several issues. Results from Gallup polls are published in monthly reports (the technical name of the Gallup organization is the American Institute of Public Opinion, and these reports are usually listed under this title in libraries).

PREVIEW

What is political participation?

Political participation means taking part in political activity. Defining "political activity" is difficult. A behavior defined as "political" in one nation may be characterized as a criminal act or a psychological disorder in another. The Americans who threw tea into Boston Harbor considered themselves to be political activists. The British, however, viewed them as common criminals. Such differences in how behavior is characterized are important politically. Most Americans view political participation in terms of nondisruptive, conventional activities.

How much political participation exists?

Beyond voting, few citizens are active in electoral politics. Nor do very many of them participate in violent, unconventional behavior such as rioting. However, even a small percentage of the population can have a major impact. Activists are disproportionately drawn from the wealthy and the college educated and are most likely to be white males.

What are the benefits and costs of political participation?

Some of the important reasons people become involved politically are personal benefits (for example, a job), psychological needs, and the desire to implement a policy. Among the major reasons for apathy are legal restrictions, the absence of political competition, the disruptive effects of activism on one's personal life, the psychological disturbances caused by political conflict, and the absence of necessary skills. However, even if you wanted to participate, it might be rational to be apathetic. Such might be the case if you could benefit from other people's participation, if your own participation would harm your cause, or if nonpolitical options were a better means of reaching your goals.

Does political participation make any difference?

Just because you took part in politics and your cause won does not automatically prove that your participation made the difference. Evidence showing the impact of political activity comes from two sources: studies of how leaders view public opinion and a look at the changes in the quality of city services blacks in Tuskegee, Alabama, began to enjoy once their political clout was strong enough to capture positions on municipal councils. In general, political activism depends on such factors as the nature of one's goals, the strength of the opposition, and the costs of not satisfying one's demands.

CHAPTER FIVE

CITIZEN PARTICIPATION

It is fair to say that most people view political activity the same way they view regular physical exercise, good eating habits, and yearly health checkups—they heartily endorse such a regimen in the abstract, but they probably do not incorporate these practices into their own lives. From early childhood we are barraged with messages telling us that we should be active in politics, that it is shameful to shirk our civic responsibilities, and that democracy depends on political involvement. Most of us accept these propositions or at least feel guilty when prominent leaders (and scholars) chide us for our "dangerous" apathy. The fact is, however, that many of the traditional arguments about the nature and value of political participation are questionable. This chapter examines some of the key issues that lie behind the common, but frequently unthinking, exhortations to be active in politics. We shall concern ourselves not only with what occurs in contemporary politics but with why some things do not happen. Our analysis seeks to answer four general questions:

1. What is political participation?
2. How much political activity exists?
3. What are the benefits and costs of political participation?
4. Does political participation make any difference?

Political participation Taking part in political activity.

What is political participation?

Defining **political participation** may seem like an easy task. One might say: political participation means taking part in political activity. This simple definition is fine, but it obscures an important fact; namely, in some political systems certain politically relevant activities may be labeled political participation that in other systems may be classified as nonpolitical, criminal, or even mentally disturbed behavior. How "political activity" is viewed in a society is *itself* an important political fact. A dictator, with the dictator's perennial worry that people are plotting against him or her, might deal with political opponents by defining their activities as not involving politics at all but as evidence of criminal intentions or mental disturbances. This technique of manipulating the meaning of "political activity" may not appear applicable in the United States, but there is more of such definition manipulation in our society than is obvious.

THE IMPORTANCE OF HOW POLITICAL PARTICIPATION IS DEFINED

To understand the importance of how participation is defined, let us take a familiar example – high school "politics." During the author's high school days, we had a so-called student government that was formally elected but whose most important power seemed to be holding an annual meeting. Of course, there was an elected city government with real power over teachers and administrators, but we students had nothing to do with that. In fact, students had no real way of participating in such important matters as teacher selection, choice of curriculum content, and formulation of school rules. Legally, students were shut out of power.

Did this mean that students had no voice in school decisions? No. Some important types of political participation did occur, but they were not labeled participation. Usually such activities were called delinquent or disruptive behavior. For example, some students reacted to poor teachers by systematically boycotting their classes, being insubordinate, and otherwise promoting an occasional early retirement or transfer to a different school system. In effect, behavior was calculated to change school power relationships, but these actions were not officially recognized as political. Had we instead organized a march or circulated a petition to accomplish the same ends, our activities would have been described as political actions. (It is interesting to speculate which strategy is more effective in getting rid of a poor teacher – organizing a rally protesting him or her or driving the person crazy in class.)

The classification of political behavior as nonpolitical "disruption" is not limited to high school disputes. During the 1960s many cities experienced severe racial disturbances in which stores were looted, buildings burned, and bystanders killed. Was this a large-scale outbreak of *criminal* behavior, as some people believed, or was it a *political* insurrection directed against an oppressive political system? Both views have a certain amount of credibility.

How should we view violent terrorism directed against innocent people? There has in recent years been a dramatic world-wide increase in terrorist activity, which has taken such forms as the random killing of policemen and the bombing of public places. Are these the actions of deranged people, or are these terrorists no different politically from those brave patriots who, disguised as Indians, dumped British tea into Boston Harbor? Especially in nations with a revolutionary tradition, many a dangerous lunatic—if the cause is successful—becomes transformed into a hero of political history.

A fair question to ask is: Does it really make any difference whether we call a particular behavior political participation or, say, lunatic behavior? It probably makes some difference. To the extent that word usage affects how we relate to things, the use of negative-sounding words to describe activities helps keep those activities in low esteem. Whereas a radical might describe a protest demonstration as a "popular and spontaneous uprising," a conservative might call it "a bunch of dirty hippies running wild." If the latter description becomes popular, the activities are reduced to comparatively minor social problems calling for mundane solutions, such as greater police protection or soap and water. One of the major problems faced by new and different groups—whether radical or conservative—is to convince people that their actions *are* indeed political actions and not some kind of pathological behavior. In the Soviet Union one of the most effective means of combating political dissent is to call the dissenters insane and lock them away in asylums.

Boycott Exerting pressure by refusing to buy products manufactured, distributed, or sold by a company or individual. Usually effected by a group of citizens.

COMMON NOTIONS OF POLITICAL PARTICIPATION

Consider what most of us think of as political participation—activities like voting, running for office, organizing a petition drive, donating money, or making speeches on behalf of a cause. Perhaps the most disruptive acts one usually thinks of are holding a protest march, instigating a legal suit, or organizing a **boycott.** It is significant that few people readily come up with devious or disruptive actions when they think about political activity. This is not to claim that these ordinary citizens might never engage in such activity; rather, socially acceptable political actions in the United States are usually narrowed down to a few nondisruptive activities.[1]

[1] One recent illustration of devious political participation occurred near Minot, North Dakota, where the federal government wants to construct a dam that would flood some 30,000 acres of farmland. About half of this land belongs to some fifty farmers who don't want to sell it to the government. To prevent a government takeover, each farmer has taken an acre of his or her land, divided it into 4,840 separate parcels (each about a square yard), and offered the parcels for sale at $20 each. By mid-1978, about 1,000 of these square-yard parcels had been sold. The purpose of this action is to create a paper-work nightmare for the government, which now must negotiate with each of the 1,000 landowners. It remains to be seen whether the plan will work. See "A Dam Nuisance," *Time,* August 14, 1978.

Let us return to our initial question: What constitutes political participation? Political participation means taking part in some political activity. The real issue, obviously, is what is a political activity? Rather than argue over this philosophical question, however, it is far more interesting to ask *how a society defines some acts as political and some as nonpolitical*. We must keep in mind that nothing tells us for sure what is or is not "political" action: in the United States, those who speak out against their leaders are frequently called unhappy Republicans; in the Soviet Union they may be classified as insane and be put under psychiatric care.

How much political participation exists?

Are the people of the United States very active in politics or are they apathetic bumps on a log? Obviously, any assessment depends on what one means by "activist." Does one include violent, illegal tactics or only nondisruptive, legal behavior? These are important and knotty questions on which little agreement exists. It is clear, however, that most citizens do *not* play an active role in ordinary *electoral* politics. Table 5.1 presents some data on involvement of citizens in various activities between 1952 and 1976. It should be noted that these are unverified reports of participation, and given social norms supporting activism, these reports are probably exaggerated.

The data in the table certainly dispel any illusions of a nation of political activists. Moreover, despite some recent talk about the "new politics" and greater citizen involvement, no sudden and dramatic upsurge in participation has occurred since the early fifties. What about less-conven-

TABLE 5.1
POLITICAL ACTIVITY OF U.S. CITIZENS, 1952–1976

Activities	1952	1956	1960	1964	1968	1972	1976
Belonging to a political club or organization	2%	3%	3%	4%	4%	3%	*
Contributing financially to parties or candidates	4	10	12	11	8	10	16%
Attending political meetings, rallies, or dinners	7	10	8	9	9	9	6
Working for party or candidate	3	3	6	5	6	5	4
Wearing campaign button or displaying bumper sticker	*	16	21	16	15	14	8
Trying to change vote of another person	27	28	33	31	33	32	37

*Data not collected.
Source: Center for Political Studies, University of Michigan, Ann Arbor.

A. *Urban Riots.* In 1967, several cities experienced severe racial rioting in which buildings were burned and many people were killed. While it is impossible to say precisely how many people were involved in rioting, careful analysis suggests the following figures:

TABLE 5.2

UNCONVENTIONAL POLITICAL PARTICIPATION

City	Number of black rioters	Percent of area residents between 10 and 59 years of age who rioted
Detroit	16,900	11%
Newark	6,900	15
Cincinnati	1,800	4
Grand Rapids (Mich.)	900	16
New Haven (Conn.)	1,800	35
Dayton (Ohio)	800	26

Source: Robert Fogelson and Robert Hill, "Who Riots?: A Study of Participation in the 1967 Riots," in *Supplemental Studies for the National Advisory Commission on Civil Disorders* (Washington, D.C.: Government Printing Office, 1968), pp. 230–231.

B. *Anti-Vietnam War Protests.* During the 1960s, in response to growing U.S. involvement in Vietnam, many people participated in peace marches, demonstrations, teach-ins, and other collective activity intended to influence government policy.

PARTICIPATION IN MAJOR DEMONSTRATIONS

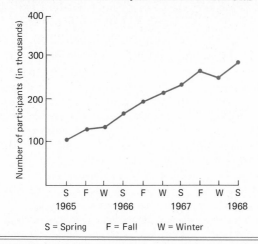

S = Spring   F = Fall   W = Winter

Source: Jerome H. Skolnick, *The Politics of Protest.* A Staff Report to the National Commission on the Causes and Prevention of Violence (Washington, D.C.: Government Printing Office, 1969), p. 24.

tional action such as taking part in urban riots, refusing to pay taxes, or engaging in violent protest? How much of this type of activity occurs? As Table 5.2 notes, such unconventional behavior received extensive media coverage, but it hardly represented a mass uprising. Even the urban riots of the 1960s, which were sometimes viewed as extensive, typically attracted only a small portion of people living in the immediate areas.[2]

Although the numbers given in Tables 5.1 and 5.2 are not large, one should not forget that even a very small portion of the population can represent in absolute terms a very large number of people. On August 23, 1963, 250,000 citizens gathered in Washington, D.C., for a civil rights demonstration which had a dramatic impact, despite the fact that only a very small percentage—0.22 percent of persons over 18—of the population was represented. Many a "popular" and "massive" revolution involved less than 1 percent of the population!

What about participation in local, close-to-home activities? After all, we expect greater activity on matters that directly affect our lives. Evidence from a 1967 nation-wide survey indicates that even on this level participation is limited. For example, only 20 percent of persons interviewed said that they had *ever* contacted a local official about a community problem, only 14 percent had *ever* formed a locally oriented organization, and only 30 percent had worked with others to solve a community problem.[3] Although these low percentages nevertheless indicate involvement by tens of millions of citizens, the fact remains that most people are not very active.

CHARACTERISTICS OF POLITICAL ACTIVISTS

What kinds of people are overrepresented in the activist group? In the eighteenth century, when the idea of ordinary citizen participation in government was first seriously considered, it was assumed that the more numerous downtrodden would take advantage of participation in order to obtain gains from the rich. In U.S. politics, however, the opposite has occurred: *those with social and economic advantages have been the most active participants.* On almost every indicator of "normal" political activity (for example, voting, writing letters) whites are more active than blacks, the rich are more active than the poor, and men are more active than women (other characteristics are examined in Table 5.3). The old aristocratic fear that the "lower orders" would swamp their "betters" through extensive participation has not come true. We will examine why this is so when we discuss the causes of political apathy.

[2] The relative lack of violence in U.S. politics becomes more evident if we compare our political violence with political violence in Italy. In 1977, Italian police reported that there were 2,128 acts of political violence ranging from arson to stabbings and shootings that resulted in thirty-one people being killed. During the same year there were also more than 2,000 political bombings. If the United States had this rate of political violence, we would experience about 16,000 such incidents a year! These data are reported in "The Lawless Society," *Newsweek*, March 27, 1978. The United States has also been spared other kinds of violence. For example, recently 4,000 residents of a Mexican town, enraged by the police shooting of a worker, seized the town's mayor and forced him to write his resignation. Then they made him eat twelve pounds of bananas. Reported in the *National Review*, June 9, 1978.

[3] Sidney Verba and Norman H. Nie, *Participation in America* (New York: Harper & Row, 1972), p. 21.

More active	Less active	
Whites	Blacks	
Men	Women	
Jews	Catholics, followed by Protestants	
Middle-aged people	Young and old people	
Nonsoutherners	Southerners	
Rich people	Poor people	
College educated	Grade-school educated	

No clear relationship exists between city size and participation, although the most rural people are the least active.

TABLE 5.3

POLITICAL PARTICIPATION VERSUS NONPARTICIPATION IN THE UNITED STATES[a]

[a] For a more complete analysis of differences in rates of political participation, see L. Milbrath and M. L. Goel, *Political Participation,* 2d ed. (Chicago: Rand McNally, 1977).

What are the benefits and costs of political participation?

Given that political participation takes time and effort, a fair question to ask is why some people do get involved. As in all human behavior, the motivation for action is complex and rarely determined by any single factor. There are, however, at least three general reasons why citizens become involved in politics.

FACTORS ENCOURAGING PARTICIPATION

Personal benefits

Many activists will admit that there are concrete and personal benefits to be gained by participation. It has been noted, for example, that novice lawyers occasionally engage in politics because such participation is a good way to meet people and thus build up a legal practice (in most states advertising by lawyers is very limited). Similarly, political activity in some places is a good way of obtaining a job or getting favored treatment from the government. Social benefits also flow from participation. Campaigns can offer excellent opportunities for meeting members of the opposite sex or improving one's social life. No doubt many activists stay in politics because of the enduring relationships that are part of their work or because of the economic incentives.

Psychological needs

Politics, especially for those who enter it on a full-time basis, provides ample opportunities to satisfy psychological needs for power, deference, and attention. Not surprisingly, psychological studies of leaders show that powerful political offices often attract aspirants with high achieve-

LONG-FORGOTTEN UNCONVEN-TIONAL PARTICI-PATION

Most analyses of U.S. political participation emphasize conventional, routine
activity. No doubt this constitutes the
bulk of citizen involvement, but it should
not be allowed to obscure a long and
varied tradition of occasionally violent,
unconventional, and sometimes eccentric
behavior in U.S. history. Unconventional
participation has taken a variety of forms.

Armed insurrections

In 1794, farmers in western Pennsylvania, upset over taxes on whiskey, organized what has been called the Whiskey Rebellion and
burned down the offices of tax collectors. This insurrection was put
down by military force. The early part of the nineteenth century also
witnessed several large-scale slave revolts. For example, a slave
named Denmark Vesey organized a revolt of 9,000 South Carolina
slaves before the plot was discovered. In 1842, after failing through
"normal" channels to remove restrictions on the right to vote,
Thomas W. Dorr and his followers proclaimed a new "People's Constitution" for Rhode Island. Elections were held, and Dorr's armed
supporters attempted to seize the state arsenal before being defeated. In 1917, the so-called green corn rebellion occurred in Oklahoma. There, 450 poor farmers, dissatisfied with government policy,
planned a long march to Washington to seize power (they hoped to
survive on green corn and barbecued steer). Detachments of farmers
were assigned to blow up bridges and pipelines. After two days of
rebellion they were defeated. During the 1960s and 1970s, in the
wake of racial turmoil and the movement protesting U.S. involvement
in Vietnam, several secret, terrorist-type organizations such as the
SDS, the **Weathermen,** the **Symbionese Liberation Army,** and elements of the Black Panther party engaged in militaristic, violent activities designed to overthrow the existing system.

Utopian rejections of existing politics

Many political radicals have sought to create totally new societies
rather than attempt to work within existing institutions. This strategy
was particularly popular in the first half of the nineteenth century.
For example, in the 1820s, Fanny Wright built the **utopian** community
of New Harmony in Nashoba, Tennessee, dedicated to freeing slaves,
promoting free love and abortion, and advocating a society of complete equality. Equally ahead of his time was John Noyes, who in
1834 in Putney, Vermont, organized the Oneida Perfectionists. The
Perfectionists followed primitive communistic principles of common
ownership of all property and enjoyed considerable success in farming and manufacturing. Their communistic philosophy also extended
to sexual relationships, so that every man was the husband of every
woman and every woman the wife of every man. Experiments such as
these numbered in the hundreds before the Civil War. Only one such

effort—the Mormon Church—had lasting success. This utopian spirit experienced a slight revival in the late 1960s with the commune movement. Such rejection of the "outside" world is clearly political, although violent conflict with society may be minimal.

A print published in 1774 shows how colonists dissatisfied with British regulations take matters into their own hands. The tax collector has been tarred and feathered, and a more extreme solution is presented by the "Liberty Tree." Such activities are usually discouraged today.

Extremist political sects

The United States possesses a long history of cases in which a few citizens with highly unconventional political views have formed societies that engaged in bizarre behavior. One early such organization was the Anti-Masons, who labored against the "evil" influences of the pope, Catholics, Jews, atheists, Jesuits, the French Revolution, Irish immigrants, and, of course, the Masons. For much of the first half of the twentieth century the Ku Klux Klan played a major role in the political and economic repression of southern blacks. In the 1960s and 1970s, the American Nazi Party engaged in numerous well-publicized political acts. Among other things, they picketed the White House with signs that said "Save Ike from the Kikes," dressed in monkey outfits in counterdemonstrations against blacks, and proclaimed Adolf Hitler the savior of the white race. Their policies called for genocide of Jews and the forced migrations of blacks back to Africa. Equally extreme is the Minutemen organization, which believes that the only way to prevent the United States from becoming Communist is to arm citizens heavily and train them in techniques of guerrilla warfare. Minutemen in various states have conducted field exercises with mortars, bazookas, and millions of rounds of ammunition. Membership in the Nazi Party and the Minutemen is probably less than a few thousand and is not a serious threat to existing politics. Yet these small numbers should not obscure the fact that such groups are numerous and have had a long (and sometimes vocal) existence in U.S. politics.

Temperance movement The general name for several groups advocating policies ranging from reduced consumption of alcoholic beverages to laws prohibiting the sale or manufacture of liquor, beer, or wine.

Women's suffrage Suffrage is the right to vote; the women's suffrage movement was the movement to give women the same voting rights as men.

ment needs and strong desires for power.[4] Even brief exposure to the power and deference associated with politics can frequently ignite an addictive need for more and more power and deference. Many people have claimed to be going into politics temporarily and reluctantly, but some find themselves enjoying the power and then try to make a lifetime of it. Many forms of unconventional politics, such as student demonstrations, draw people with distinct psychological needs.[5] It is not that politics draws abnormal types; rather, politics provides a good outlet for certain types of ambitions and needs.

Policy objectives

One of the most common explanations for participation offered by activists themselves is that they are working toward a policy goal. The political landscape has always been heavily populated by such policy-oriented people. Among some major recent issues that have stimulated heightened participation are the civil rights movement, environmental concerns, tax protests, and the women's movement. The mobilization of citizens over "big issues" is not, of course, a new phenomenon. There have been many "big issues" in U.S. history that have generated massive involvement. The abolition of slavery, the **temperance movement, women's suffrage,** the war in Vietnam, and trade unionism all motivated many citizens to play a more active political role than they usually did.

Most politically active citizens are active for more than one reason. For example, a person strongly committed to women's rights may remain politically apathetic for years until becoming socially involved with activists, whereupon the social relationship leads to active participation. Once involved, people may sustain the activity if it satisfies certain psychological needs, such as a need to belong. In short, it is important to understand that political involvement is not caused by a single factor; many, many factors encourage participation, and these vary from person to person.

FACTORS INHIBITING PARTICIPATION

If there are so many reasons for people becoming active in politics, why do most people remain apathetic? The answer is simple: despite all the things that encourage citizen involvement, there are probably even *more* forces in our society that inhibit participation. A complete list of factors discouraging participation would be long, but among the more prominent are the following.

Legal restrictions

Although *in principle* universal suffrage exists in the United States, *in practice* voting (and certain other activities) is legally restricted in a va-

[4] For one study of how political activity meets certain important psychological needs, see Rufus Browning and Herbert Jacob, "Power Motivation and Political Personality," *Public Opinion Quarterly*, 28 (1964), pp. 75–60.

[5] Several studies of student radicals in the 1960s suggest that activists differed from nonactivists in many psychological characteristics. These studies are summarized in Seymour Martin Lipset, *Rebellion in the University* (Boston: Little, Brown, 1971), pp. 102–113.

riety of ways. For example, preelection registration requirements reduce voter turnout; certain state and local residency rules discriminate against mobile people; and in most states convicted felons are barred from voting.[6] The Supreme Court has struck down the most obvious requirements restricting participation, such as property requirements and the payment of a tax to vote (the "poll tax"), but even the remaining minimal requirements can discourage weakly motivated citizens.[7]

Absence of political competition

Many U.S. elections are not competitive, and thus the motivation to participate is small. Even a presidential election that is closely contested nationally may not be very competitive on a state-by-state basis (where the electoral college actually decides the race). As a consequence, many citizens may see no value in working in even the most exciting electoral event. After all, if you are a Democratically oriented voter in an area completely dominated by Republicans, not much incentive exists to be active (unless you enjoy hopeless causes). In some political systems the electoral rewards received are proportional to the votes received, but in the United States the winner gets everything, so if you know you are going to lose, there is nothing concrete to be gained by participating. Moreover, in many elections the differences between candidates are so small that the outcome makes little difference—so again, why get involved?

[6] For a detailed analysis of how requiring registration can depress citizen participation, see Stanley Kelley, Jr., Richard E. Ayers, and William G. Bowen, "Registration and Voting: Putting First Things First," *American Political Science Review*, 61 (1967), pp. 359–379.

[7] Restrictions on political participation are further described in Burt Neuborne and Arthur Eisenberg, *The Rights of Candidates and Voters* (New York: Avon Books, 1976), especially Chaps. 2–3. The Voting Rights Act of 1970 limits the registration period to thirty days prior to a presidential election. On several occasions the Supreme Court has ruled on the time between registration and voting. It has rejected a year or three months as too long but accepted fifty days as reasonable (the court case was *Burns* v. *Fortson*, 1973).

To protest laws requiring separate eating facilities for blacks and whites, in the early 1960s blacks would sometimes request service at lunch counters. Occasionally angry whites would pour ketchup on them or otherwise attack the protesters. This incident took place at a Woolworth store in Little Rock, Arkansas, in 1962.

Disruptions of one's private life or job

As one moves away from simple political acts such as voting or putting a bumper sticker on one's car, political activity can be highly disruptive of family or employment relationships. There are only so many hours in a week, and for most people – even for citizens deeply concerned with political issues – eating, sleeping, earning a living, taking care of children, and other essential activities all come before politics. A frequent complaint among highly active citizens is that their political life almost destroys their outside social relationships.

The economic costs of participation are probably most severe for working-class citizens, who typically holds jobs with inflexible schedules and who lose pay if they miss work. It is not surprising, then, that political activists come disproportionately from groups whose occupations allow them flexible time with no severe economic costs – lawyers, middle-class homemakers, professors, and businesspersons. In addition, support for controversial candidates or issues – for example, the legalization of marijuana – can result in economic and social harassment.[8]

Psychological threat

Politics typically involves conflict, animosities, agonizing decisions, and the ever-present possibility of defeat. While some people thrive on conflict and uncertainty, most of us try to avoid them. If one wants to minimize disappointments and frustrations, one should stay out of politics and instead concentrate on such activities as stamp collecting or bird watching. Election outcomes will not disappoint us if we avoid politics completely. This is similar to our experience with our favorite sports teams: when the team is regularly winning, our interest is keen, but when things start going badly, many of us avoid the anguish by becoming less involved.

Skill requirements

It has frequently been noted that politics resembles a game, and so, as in any other game, certain skills are essential. Of course, which skills are politically useful depends on the particular situation. In some corrupt cities during the nineteenth century, physical strength was sometimes needed to get out the vote; in contemporary politics, being an effective public speaker is probably more relevant. Whatever the necessary skills, some people have more of them than others. Especially in modern campaigns requiring high levels of organization and handling of the news media, middle-class, well-educated people are at a distinct advantage. It

---

[8] The fear of economic or physical retribution was particularly important in explaining low political participation among blacks in the South (and even in some nonsouthern areas). For many years prior to the 1960s, southern blacks seeking to participate in politics frequently ran a real risk of losing their jobs or being beaten up. The role of fear in black apathy is discussed further in Lester M. Salamon and Stephen Van Evera, "Fear, Apathy, and Discrimination: A Test of Three Explanations of Political Participation," *American Political Science Review*, 67 (1973), pp. 1288–1306. For an analysis of purely personal reasons for apathy, see Morris Rosenberg, "Some Determinants of Political Apathy," *Public Opinion Quarterly*, 18 (1954–1955), pp. 349–366.

is probably true that many people have tried their hands at political participation (for example, organizing a demonstration), but gave up when they realized that they had little ability for such activities.

BEING APATHETIC CAN BE RATIONAL

Thus far we have considered factors that prevent a would-be activist from getting involved. It was assumed that the citizen *wanted* to participate, but for one reason or another was unable to become involved. But are there circumstances when, even if one *could* freely participate, it would make good sense *not* to get involved? Put another way, *can apathy be rational?* The answer is definitely yes. Specifically, there are three situations when staying out of politics would be a reasonable course.

First, apathy may be reasonable if other citizens are already actively pursuing a policy you desire and their success will benefit you regardless of your participation. Imagine that you live in a college dormitory that serves very poor food and that several residents want to stage protests to get better meals. Will you join? One can argue that since *everybody* — not just the activists — will benefit from improved food if the protests are successful, it would make good sense to let someone else do the hard work. The same situation holds in politics more generally. Policies such as civil rights or sexual equality apply to all people in a class, not just to those who actually worked toward obtaining those rights. Hence, if other people are already working for one's cause, one can get the benefits without any of the costs.[9] Of course, if everyone adopts this strategy, no one gets anything.

Second, one's active involvement may only make matters worse, so one might actually benefit more by being apathetic. This situation sometimes occurs when unpopular groups debate whether to work openly for a political cause. Imagine what might happen if heroin addicts organized a political-action group to campaign openly for a Senator. Such "support" might be a political kiss of death, with the end result that the cause of narcotics reform would be harmed far more than helped. A situation like this existed during the 1940s and 1950s in the South with respect to black voters. Several prominent southern politicians such as Senators John Sparkman of Alabama and William Fulbright of Arkansas had a more liberal attitude toward blacks than many other southern politicians. Blacks, however, were circumspect in their open support for these leaders lest the Senators be labeled candidates too favorable toward blacks, a characterization leading to sure defeat. In short, then, one does not get involved if one believes that such involvement may do more political harm than good.

A third rational reason for staying out of politics is if one can accomplish one's purpose more effectively by nonpolitical means. Suppose that you are the victim of job discrimination. What options are available to

---

[9] The problem of receiving benefits from the actions of others while remaining apathetic is examined in Mancur Olson, Jr., *The Logic of Collective Action* (New York: Schocken Books, 1968), especially Chap. 1.

you? Of course, you can use politics through voting, contributing money to your candidate, or organizing protests. You can also solve your problem by going into business for yourself or becoming a criminal. Depending on your skills and opportunities, any one of the above may be a better alternative than entering politics. That politics is only one of many ways to solve social or economic problems becomes clear if we examine how different ethnic groups have sought to overcome obstacles. Some, like the Irish, and more recently the blacks, have stressed advancement through political means; others, such as the Jews, the Chinese, and the Italians, have placed comparatively greater emphasis on private mechanisms such as family businesses or charitable organizations.

Does participation make any difference?

In the United States citizens are traditionally urged to become politically involved. If we don't like the way things are, we have all been told, get involved and change them! Underlying this advice is the belief that political participation makes a difference. That is, one is more likely to succeed in politics by being active rather than apathetic. Is this true? Unfortunately, despite all the research on citizen political activity, there is no precise, definitive answer. Nevertheless, there is some evidence that while participation does not automatically lead to political success, it frequently helps. People sometimes get what they want without lifting a finger, and others fight long and hard only to lose; but in general, participation probably increases the chances of winning.

Demonstrating that citizen activity makes a difference is difficult. Just because citizens were active and the government did what they wanted does *not* mean that the activity caused the result. After all, just because the sun rises after a rooster crows does not prove that the rooster caused the sunrise. Let us consider, however, two aspects of U.S. politics that lend support to the contention that participation helps. The first concerns the importance of participation in determining how leaders perceive public desires. The second examines the impact of black participation in southern politics.

PARTICIPATION AND THE SHAPING OF LEADERS' PERCEPTIONS

Every political leader—from the President to small-town officials—is concerned about what people think. Of course, many officials have no desire to follow public opinion precisely, but even so, staying in office requires being in touch with the voters. Public officials employ numerous methods to determine public thinking. They conduct opinion polls, read their mail, read newspapers, talk to people who visit them, and so forth. Do leaders get an accurate picture of people's thinking by using these techniques? If the citizens who actively communicate their opinions were a cross section of the U.S. public, such channels of communication would probably produce a fairly accurate picture. It turns out, however, that participants do not necessarily hold the same opinions as nonparticipants. Officials frequently get a biased picture of public feeling when they read their mail or listen to political activists.

The unrepresentative nature of activists' opinions is illustrated by a 1967 study of public opinion of U.S. involvement in Vietnam.[10] Recall that in the late 1960s many political leaders—including Presidents Lyndon Johnson and Richard Nixon—asserted that most citizens supported U.S. intervention policies. This was true because those favoring U.S. involvement in Vietnam outnumbered opponents by about a 2 to 1 margin. However, among activists these proportions were different. Among those who were actively doing something about the Vietnam issue—trying to change the opinion of others or writing to newspapers or their congressional representatives—support for intervention was even stronger. Hence, had officials heeded the messages coming in from these people, they probably would have exaggerated the strength of the pro-Vietnam intervention position.[11]

In general, given our knowledge of who participates the most in politics, it is fair to say that the messages conveyed by activists are usually biased in a conservative direction.[12] Poor people participate less than rich people, and thus the liberal opinions of poorer people on economic issues are underrepresented. Blacks participate less than whites, so when an official listens to what participants say, the message does not accurately reflect overall public opinion. It seems more than likely that many of the discrepancies between public opinion and government policy described in Chapter Four are a result of the nontypical opinions conveyed by active citizens.

PARTICIPATION AND THE WINNING OF CIVIC BENEFITS: BLACKS IN TUSKEGEE, ALABAMA

There are many reasons for taking part in politics, but perhaps one of the most basic is to obtain the benefits that governments dispense. Among these benefits are adequate police and fire protection, education, paved streets, sewers, garbage collection, and many other public services that one gets from tax money. These services are usually provided by local governments, and until recent times, municipalities in much of the South rarely gave blacks their proportional share. Black sections of communities frequently were denied such basics as sidewalks, nearby fire protection, or public transportation. Thus, in the 1960s when blacks

[10] Sidney Verba and Richard A. Brody, "Participation, Policy Preferences, and the War in Vietnam," *Public Opinion Quarterly*, 34 (1970), pp. 325–332.

[11] This pattern was not, however, found among those who had taken part in demonstrations. Here, prowithdrawal sympathy dominated. In short, if a leader looked to some types of activists, for example, letter writers, he or she would get an impression biased in the prointervention direction. On the other hand, by following just demonstrations, the bias would be in the opposite direction.

[12] Other studies examining the unrepresentative opinions of political activists are Philip E. Converse, Aage R. Clausen, and Warren E. Miller, "Electoral Myth and Reality: The 1964 Elections," *American Political Science Review*, 59 (1965), pp. 321–336; and Verba and Nie, Chaps. 15–20.

became more active politically, the improvement of such city services was a major goal.

The Tuskegee experience

The use of political activity to achieve concrete goals is exemplified in the town of Tuskegee, Alabama. Tuskegee is a heavily black city, and prior to the late 1950s, blacks were largely kept from voting through intimidation or the poll tax requirement. Despite these and several other obstacles, however, by 1962 blacks had succeeded in becoming a majority of the registered voters. In 1964, this voting strength, plus the efforts of the federal government, allowed Tuskegee blacks, for the first time, to capture positions on the city council, the county board of revenue, and the board of education, as well as to be elected to the positions of tax collector and sheriff. What were the concrete payoffs resulting from this participation?

According to William R. Keech, who studied the consequences of this "takeover," the results were substantial. For example, blacks received better treatment in court, many "Negro streets" were paved, city-supplied garbage removal was equalized, recreational facilities were desegregated, blacks were hired in nonmenial public positions, and the police force recruited blacks.[13] Judged against the pace of most social change, what happened in Tuskegee can be considered almost a revolution.

The Tuskegee experience does not, however, show that increased participation by a previously excluded group is an automatic and instant cure for whatever political problem exists. This new-found power reduced the most blatant inequalities but barely touched basic social and economic differences between blacks and whites. Paved streets are important, but they do not have the same significance as economic or social equality. Moreover, the experience of Tuskegee has *not* been repeated in every southern town. Especially where blacks remained a minority, increasing the black share of the votes—say from 5 percent to 25 percent—had little tangible benefit. In general, then, the Tuskegee experience illustrates what *might* result from greater participation; it does not prove that participation always works as intended.[14]

THE USE OF PARTICIPATION: SOME GENERAL CONSIDERATIONS

Thus far we have considered specific instances in which political involvement made a difference. Are there, however, some general guide-

---

[13] William R. Keech, *The Impact of Negro Voting: The Role of the Vote in the Quest for Equality* (Chicago: Rand McNally, 1968), pp. 47–51.

[14] A good illustration of how political participation can have unintended consequences occurred in municipal responses to the black urban disturbances of the 1960s. Many blacks hoped that these riots would result in greater expenditures on schools, public housing, and other welfare benefits. However, according to an analysis of city expenditures made by Susan Welch, the major impact of the riots was to increase the amount of money spent on police protection, not on benefits for black people. See Susan Welch, "The Impact of Urban Riots on Urban Expenditures," *American Journal of Political Science*, 19 (1975), pp. 741–760.

Marching to Washington to present one's grievances to government has now become common. A crowd of 1,800 Native Americans gathered on July 15, 1978 to protest legislation that threatened their way of life.

lines that suggest *when* such involvement will make a difference? Given the nature and organization of U.S. politics, three general factors may affect one's chances of winning.

The nature of one's political goal

As a rule, participation directed toward accomplishing a broad, abstract goal has less chance of paying off than that aimed at a more concrete and immediate objective. For example, organizing a movement to bring about world brotherhood and equality has less chance of succeeding than trying to have a stop light installed at a dangerous intersection. It is also true that owing to the decentralized nature of U.S. politics and its multiple points of access, it is much easier to *prevent* things from occurring than to convince government to act. Action requires the cooperation of many people; inaction can be brought about by a few people doing nothing.

The strength of the opposition

As in sports, the outcome in politics depends on the strength of the opposition. The first question one asks is: Is there any organized opposition? In some situations, for example, passing a legislative resolution in favor of ideals such as freedom or progress, virtually no opposition exists. Most of the time, however, there is opposition. Where one's opponents are well entrenched and deeply committed, political participation will accomplish little unless enormous efforts are made. This argument may appear self-evident, but would-be activists sometimes fail to assess their opponents when they first get involved. The history of U.S. politics is filled with (now forgotten) failures in citizen involvement. As a rule of thumb, success is *less* likely when one's participation is directed at some goal which will directly reduce the economic or social position of others. In short, if one wants to be successful, find causes that other people are indifferent about or in which your potential opponents are weak.

The costs of nonsatisfaction

A basic question all political leaders ask when confronted with citizens demanding something is: What happens if they are ignored? It is obvious

133

that different people vary in their political and/or economic importance, and this factor too can greatly affect the success of participation. Consider political protests made by truck drivers versus those made by college professors. Professors may have all the advantages of education and prestige, but nobody suffers from lack of food or other necessities if they do not show up for work. This is not so with truckers, and thus it is not surprising that when truckers staged protests in 1979 over sudden increases in fuel costs, they received prompt attention. A similar crucial position is sometimes occupied by groups of voters where elections are close and a small shift separates victory from defeat. The government has also found that members of certain occupations, for example, doctors, are more powerful politically than their numbers warrant, because their cooperation is essential to government programs involving health care, such as Medicare.

A conclusion: political participation

This chapter began by observing that citizens are constantly being encouraged to be more active politically. We also noted that few people think much about admonitions to "get involved." What has our analysis told us about the benefits of getting more and more people involved? Let us first consider the case *against* citizen participation.

THE CASE AGAINST GREATER PARTICIPATION

As we saw, many of the reasons for apathy are concrete and personal. Hence, many people may have to be forced *against their will* to become involved. One can well imagine a situation in which reluctant participants view their activity as similar to their regular visit to the dentist. Certainly the right to be apathetic is as important as the right to participate.

Increased participation may result in no perceptible impact on government policy despite a lot more commotion. One's effort to get a bill passed may bring into existence other organized groups who oppose the bill, and the net result may be a standoff. It is conceivable that one could be *worse* off because of participation, especially if a much stronger opposition is awakened.

Increased participation may result in political chaos and inefficiency; therefore, in the long run everyone stands to lose. This is especially likely if citizens resort to extralegal or violent means of participation. Imagine what life would be like if every time the government considered an issue large numbers of people became politically involved. Leaders would spend most of their time dealing with people trying to influence them (and these would run into the tens of thousands).

THE CASE FOR GREATER PARTICIPATION

On the other hand, there are several arguments in favor of increased political participation. Perhaps the most obvious is that involvement will reduce inequities in the way political benefits are distributed. We have seen that participants are presently drawn disproportionately from the better-off social groups, and this bias probably explains why many (but not all) policies favor the middle class over the lower class. If the less well educated, the poor, blacks, and other less active groups were more involved, they too might get their fair share.

A second argument is that political participation is more democratic than nonparticipation. Many people believe that apathy is a serious defect in a democratic society. Would greater participation increase the amount of democracy in the United States? Unless one holds the simplistic notion that democracy equals participation, the answer is no. Most conceptions of democracy entail far more than the *amount* of citizen political involvement. Democracy also involves the types of participation, for example, voting versus bomb throwing, as well as the legal rights enjoyed by citizens, for example, freedom of speech; hence, simply having more political participation does not necessarily make for more democracy.

The third and final argument in favor of greater participation is a devious one. Specifically, as long as most citizens are actively engaged in conventional, "safe" forms of participation (such as writing letters to their representatives in Congress) they are less likely to gravitate toward unconventional, politically dangerous participation (for example, assassinating government leaders). This contention is similar to the justification for organized athletic programs for children—it is better to have them engaged in organized activity, because if they are left idle they will get into mischief. Voting, campaigning, and organizing neighborhood groups are the safe activities—terrorism, insurrection, and civil disobedience could occur if citizens were not otherwise engaged. We shall have more to say about this argument in the next chapter.

One last question worth raising is: Should I personally support more extensive political participation in the United States? It is probably fair to say that most readers of this book have more to *lose* than gain if more people become politically involved. On the whole, most readers of this book *are* members of those groups, for example, the middle class, that *have* benefited from existing arrangements. It is not that we readers have won every battle; rather, if the poor were suddenly vigorously competing on an equal footing, many of us would stand to lose such benefits as subsidized higher education and valuable income tax deductions. Hence, perhaps our position should be: everyone should take part in politics unless such participation is harmful to our own political interest.

Major questions raised

1. What is political participation? At a minimum it means taking part in politics, but there is no single universally accepted definition of "political activity." Political activism varies from nation to nation, and it is important to ask how a particular political system defines some acts as political and others as criminal or psychological disturbances. Most citizens view participation in terms of "safe" activities such as voting, talking politics, or writing letters.

2. How much political participation exists? Whether measured conventionally or unconventionally, not much participation exists in terms of the percentage of citizens who are active. However, several million citizens do regularly engage in a variety of actions. Generally, those who are already better off in society are the most active.

3. What are the benefits and costs of political participation? People are both active and apathetic for a variety of personal and political reasons. Some of these reasons, for example, legal barriers, are easily changed. Others, such as fear of conflict or family obligations, are much more deeply imbedded.

4. Does political participation make much difference? Sometimes. Overall, it seems that one has more to gain than lose by getting involved, and dramatic instances of getting goodies by participating do occur. There is, however, no one-to-one relationship between political participation and political success.

QUESTIONS FOR FURTHER DISCUSSION

1. Nonconventional forms of political participation can sometimes be more effective than voting, writing letters, or signing petitions. For example, black civil rights groups once used a "run-out-of-gas-and-tie-up-rush-hour-traffic" tactic as a way of bringing attention to their cause. More recently, angry farmers turned several of their animals loose near the Capitol in Washington. Should school children, along with learning about voting and petitioning, also be taught about such disruptive tactics? After all, wouldn't you be training future citizens in truly effective participation? On the other hand, would you instruct young children *never* to engage in violent, disruptive political action?

2. Many Communist nations make it a crime to fail to vote or attend a political meeting. It has also been argued that democracies should also provide concrete incentives to increase political participation (for example, allowing a tax deduction for voting). Does the government have an obligation to encourage political participation in the same way it has an obligation to encourage traffic safety or public health measures? Or is apathy as basic a right as the right to participate?

3. What types of people should be legally forbidden to participate in the American political process? Mentally unbalanced citizens? People who owe their loyalty to foreign governments? Those committed to violent actions? If some people are to be excluded, who should decide the criteria for exclusion? Could we trust incumbent officials not to prohibit their enemies from taking part in politics?

4. Citizens are frequently exhorted to write their representatives in Congress, yet rarely do more than a few hundred citizens make their opinions known on an issue. What would happen if most citizens regularly wrote their representatives on most issues? Each week a member of Congress might receive 250,000 or so letters on an issue. Would this increased participation make for greater democracy? What would be some of the benefits and costs of such increased citizen involvement? If you were the representative, how would you handle 250,000 letters a week?

BIBLIOGRAPHY

Alinsky, Saul D. *Rules for Radicals: A Pragmatic Primer for Realistic Radicals.* New York: Vintage Books, 1972.
> A classic analysis of how to use participation to accomplish social and economic change. Filled with numerous fascinating examples.

Almond, Gabriel, and Sidney Verba. *The Civic Culture.* Princeton, N.J.: Princeton University Press, 1963.
> An extensive analysis of the roots of democracy in five nations—the United States, Great Britain, West Germany, Italy, and Mexico. Based on surveys conducted in 1959, this book presents extensive information on many different forms of political activity, including participation in school decisions.

Bollens, John C., and Dale Rogers Marshall. *A Guide to Participation: Field Work, Role Playing Cases and Other Forms.* Englewood Cliffs, N.J.: Prentice-Hall, 1973.
> A specific guide intended to help students become involved in government decision making. Especially relevant for those interested in local government and community problems.

Cobb, Roger W., and Charles D. Elder. *Participation in American Politics: The Dynamics of Agenda Building.* Boston: Allyn and Bacon, 1972.
> Addresses the question of why particular issues are on the public agenda while others are excluded. Presents some case studies, but it is largely theoretical in its orientation.

Davies, James Chowning. *When Men Revolt and Why: A Reader in Political Violence and Revolution.* New York: Free Press, 1971.
> A wide-ranging collection of articles dealing with explanations of political violence. Articles range from writings of Aristotle to Karl Marx to modern psychological theories of aggressive behavior.

Lens, Sidney. *Radicalism in America,* new updated edition. New York: Crowell, 1966.
> A thorough, but highly readable, historical treatment of radical political movements from the Colonial period to the black power and student revolutions of the late 1960s. The book also has a good bibliography and many pages of excellent photographs.

Matthews, Donald R., and James W. Prothro. *Negroes and the New Southern Politics.* New York: Harcourt, Brace and World, 1966.
> The definitive study of political participation among southern blacks in the early 1960s. Especially relevant for describing the impact of local attitudes and institutions on levels of black political activity.

Milbrath, L. W., and M. L. Goel. *Political Participation: How and Why Do People Get Involved in Politics,* 2d ed. Chicago: Rand McNally, 1977.
> After a discussion on conceptualizing political participation, several chapters review the major conclusions of other studies in political participation. The emphasis is on explaining why people participate in politics.

Verba, Sidney, and Norman H. Nie. *Participation in America: Political Democracy and Social Equality.* New York: Harper & Row, 1972.
> Based on a 1967 survey of citizens and community leaders, this is an exhaustive (and frequently technical) treatment of participation. Most of the book concerns the variety of political activity in the United States and what types of people participate. The last few chapters examine the impact of citizen involvement on the extent to which citizens and community leaders agree on the priority of issues.

PREVIEW

Why have elections?

Though they are popular in the United States, elections are not the only method of choosing leaders. They can, however, be defended on the grounds that (1) elections allow citizens to replace objectionable leaders; (2) they legitimize the transfer of political power; (3) they help channel disruptive behavior into safer participation; and (4) they enhance feelings of political solidarity. The electoral system has persisted in the United States because most citizens are deeply attached to it.

Elections have been challenged on the grounds that (1) they provide only the illusion—not the substance—of citizen political power, and (2) they discourage highly qualified individuals from seeking public office. Both arguments contain some truth. However, these defects may not be inherent in elections, and if citizens wanted changes, they could bring them about. Overall, elections help maintain the existing system of government.

What are the alternatives to elections?

There are several methods other than the electoral system for selecting leaders: (1) a government could be by a hereditary aristocracy; (2) leaders could be chosen on the basis of their performance on examinations; and (3) they could be appointed, as Supreme Court judges and some other officials are now. States vary in which offices are elective, which are appointive, and which are filled on the basis of examinations.

How are U.S. elections organized?

By organization of elections we refer to such things as the timing of elections, who votes for what offices, and the procedures for counting votes. These decisions can have a major impact on election outcomes. For example, in our system elections are staggered—that is, not all public officials are up for election in the same year. Thus, it can take years to replace present leaders. U.S. elections are also determined by the calendar, so we must wait until the fixed election date to vote on issues and candidates. A third rule is that representation is on the basis of geography. Because geographically defined districts are often made up of very diverse groups of people, representatives may find it difficult to discern their constituents' opinions. Our election system also operates on the winner-take-all principle, which allows victories by candidates with less than 50 percent of the vote. Finally, the electoral college also makes for inequities in the value of votes.

Whether our electoral system is acceptable or defective depends on what one believes it is supposed to accomplish. It is designed to allow citizens to choose leaders while preventing a tyrannical government, not to translate accurately citizen votes into government policy.

CHAPTER SIX

THE ELECTORAL SYSTEM

n the United States, elections are perhaps the most dramatic form of political activity. Regardless of how they feel about politics, few people can escape the commotion surrounding an election. Moreover, we in the United States seem to like the idea of holding elections. In 1978, for instance, we elected 35 U.S. Senators, 435 U.S. Representatives, 36 governors, 6,113 state legislators, and innumerable local officials, judges, superintendents of education, and dog catchers. Quite understandably, most of the attention given the electoral process is focused on the behavior of candidates, campaign issues, and explanations of victory or defeat. This is the perspective of the mass media, and it appeals to people who view politics as they do sporting events. There are, however, many important questions about the very nature of elections that are ignored during the heat of battle: Why are some officials elected while others are appointed? How should elections be conducted? How should votes be added up? These crucial questions are far more important politically than merely asking who won the election. In this chapter we shall consider three fundamental aspects of elections:

1. Why have elections?
2. What are the alternatives to elections?
3. How are U.S. elections organized?

Legitimizing Making in accordance with accepted rules, principles, or standards. A child born to an unmarried women is illegitimate.
Anarchy A condition of society without government or law.

Why have elections?

Elections may be as American as apple pie and motherhood, but as everyone knows, there *are* alternatives to apple pie and motherhood. Merely because we make extensive use of elections does not mean that they need no justification. If it seems unnecessary to justify having elections, remember that historically elections have been a rarely used method of choosing leaders. We may annually hold thousands of elections, but throughout history elections have been uncommon. Even one of our Founding Fathers—Alexander Hamilton—seriously doubted the value of elections. When the Constitution was drafted it was widely believed that the electoral system would not produce the best leaders and that unscrupulous politicians would use elections to manipulate citizens. Even today there are probably some people who view the electoral process as a farce. It is fair to ask, then, why have elections?

TO REPLACE UNPOPULAR LEADERS

Perhaps the most important benefit of elections is that they provide an opportunity to replace objectionable leaders. Thanks to regular elections we do not have to be stuck forever with a corrupt, incompetent official. This does not mean that elections insure the selection of good leaders. After all, voters may replace a corrupt incompetent with an unscrupulous psychopath. Moreover, more than once voters have returned to office people convicted of crimes, leaders guilty of sexual misconduct, and even public officials who have served time in jail (voters have also elected dead people). The opportunity to throw officials out of office may seem obvious, but this self-evident characteristic should not detract from its political significance. Just think of what might have happened had the colonists had the opportunity to vote King George III out of office.

TO LEGITIMIZE TRANSFER OF POWER

A second advantage of elections is that they are an efficient means of **legitimizing** (making acceptable) the transfer of political power. When one political leader replaces another as the result of an election outcome, virtually all citizens—even supporters of the ousted leader—accept the change. To most of us, accustomed to the process of new leaders replacing old ones without much fuss, this legitimizing benefit may not seem like much. Yet if one looks at history or at many contemporary third world nations, the value of having regular elections becomes clearer. In countries without an established electoral tradition, new leaders have had to continue fighting their opponents, citizens have not accepted the laws proclaimed by new officials, and general **anarchy** has prevailed. All governments must have some means to insure the smooth transfer of political power—even a dictatorship when the dictator dies—and of all the mechanisms that have been devised to deal with this problem, holding elections is perhaps the most efficient.

TO CHANNEL DISRUPTIVE BEHAVIOR INTO "SAFE" PARTICIPATION

A third important benefit of elections is that they channel political dissatisfaction into politically "safe" and routine behaviors. Given that election campaigns frequently appear tumultuous, this claim may initially appear false. Yet consider what might happen if we did *not* have regular, routinized election opportunities open to practically all groups. Suppose that the only way you could capture political power was to be of royal blood or to pass a difficult **civil service** exam. What could you do if you were extremely dissatisfied with a government policy? In circumstances in which citizens do not possess a routine and quick access to political influence, they must improvise outside of existing channels. Typically, such behavior ranges from petty violations of the law to organized terrorism.

On the other hand, because it is easy to "vote the rascals out," organize election campaigns for sympathetic candidates, or even run for office oneself, politically disruptive hostility is channeled into safe, "in-the-system" activities. Recall our analogy in Chapter Five about organized, as opposed to improvised, participation. By providing a routine, Little League-type of recreation, adults direct children away from unsupervised, potentially dangerous play into exhausting but safe participation. Elections serve a similar function.

To see the effect of the easy availability of elections, consider what occurred to two of the most potentially disruptive movements in recent years: the struggle for black civil rights and the effort to pull the United States out of Vietnam. Both movements followed a comparable evolution.

Growing dissatisfaction with government policies and a feeling that "the system" was not responding led a small number of people to take radical political action. In both movements this involved marches, seizures of buildings, violence-prone demonstrations, and a revolutionary language ("down with the establishment").

As these movements gained a degree of support among the general public, many militant leaders realized that future progress lay not in the direction of extreme tactics but in working within the system to attract even more people. Instead of staging violent confrontations with the police, the radicals redirected their energies into more conventional activities such as registering sympathetic voters or passing out campaign literature. Some activists even went so far as to shave off their beards and wear suits and ties so as not to alienate voters.

At first victories at the polls were few. Sometimes a "success" meant not losing too badly. Within a short time, however, electoral politics began to pay off. The civil rights movement succeeded in electing several black officials in the South, a few northern cities chose black mayors, and black **bloc voting** occasionally became an important and courted political force. Similarly, several antiwar candidates were successful in a variety of state and local races, and in 1972 the antiwar movement played a major role in securing the Democratic presidential nomination for Senator George McGovern.

The entry of activists into mainstream politics by means of the elec-

Civil service Civil service refers to appointed public officials chosen according to merit as determined by objectively administered exams. Civil service exams are usually written and stress technical, factual knowledge.

Bloc voting When a group sharing a common goal or characteristic all vote together.

Initiative A procedure that allows a certain number of citizens to put a policy question on the ballot for a vote.
Recall A procedure that allows a certain number of citizens to have a public official stand for reelection before he or she would normally be up for reelection.
Referendum A policy question put on the ballot by the state legislature for citizens' approval or disapproval.

toral process spared us from the possibility of large, permanently rebellious groups who felt shut out of the system. The comparative availability of elections has allowed the incorporation of many dissatisfied radicals into ordinary, day-to-day politics. Indeed, many a veteran protester such as Julian Bond or Gary Hart became members of legislatures rather than guerilla leaders plotting the overthrow of the government.

This is *not* to suggest that elections are a good way of stifling dissent. Rather, elections provide a way to bring political dissatisfaction safely

THE INITIATIVE, RECALL, AND REFERENDUM

Selecting public officials is not the only purpose of U.S. elections. Many states allow citizens to play a more direct role in government through procedures such as the initiative, recall, and referendum. The **initiative** allows citizens to propose and adopt laws by putting them on the ballot. As of 1978, intiatives are permitted in twenty-three states, the District of Columbia, and numerous cities. In November 1978, there were some forty citizen-sponsored proposals on various state ballots dealing with issues ranging from the right of homosexuals to teach in California to the control of health care costs in North Dakota (many dealt with limitations on state tax rates). Though a majority vote may approve an initiative, it may not be binding on public officials. For example, jailed San Francisco narcotics dealer Dennis Perone organized a drive to put an initiative on the ballot that would have cut off police funds used to enforce antimarijuana laws. This initiative was endorsed by 57 percent of the city's voters, but the chief of police said he will continue to enforce the state marijuana law (courts can also declare voter-passed legislation unconstitutional).

The **recall** permits voters to remove a public official from office. If opponents of an officeholder collect a certain number of signatures of eligible voters, a new election can be called. The successful use of recall is extremely rare, but it can be effective. In 1977 in Madison, Wisconsin, a local judge was removed from office after making what many women considered offensive remarks on a rape case.

Of the three techniques the **referendum,** which allows voters the right to accept or reject legislation, is the most popular. In the November 1978 elections there were some 320 referendums on various state ballots. Initiatives are put on the ballot at the request of citizens, while referendums are placed on the ballot by the state legislatures. Several states require that proposals to change the state constitution and to increase borrowing be automatically put to a vote.

into the system. A good case can be made that radicals benefited as much by electoral activity as those who worried about a revolution in the United States. To appreciate the availability of elections, just imagine what might have happened if southern civil rights protesters had been up against a system that did not allow newly emergent groups to play at obtaining political power. The result might have been greater and greater extremism and perhaps even calls for a separate black nation to be created out of a violent revolution.

Some states, like Illinois and Nevada, allow "adivsory," nonbinding referendums to be voted upon.

One famous initiative was Proposition 13, a plan for limiting property taxes. It was accepted by California voters in 1978 after a hard campaign that was marked by emotional appeals from both sides.

Much controversity surrounds the use of the initiative and referendum. Critics of these techniques claim that giving such power to citizens frequently results in confused, poorly drafted legislation. It is also claimed, on the other hand, that this power allows citizens to overcome unresponsive elected officials. For example, when California voters became angry about high property taxes and a lack of official action, they passed an initiative (Proposition 13) to limit these taxes. Without this mechanism voters would have had little recourse besides pleading with their legislators.

For a review of some of the issues before voters on initiatives and referendums, see Richard J. Cattani, "Voters Face Growing List of Decisions," *Christian Science Monitor*, November 1, 1978.

TO ENHANCE POLITICAL SOLIDARITY

Periodic conflict centering around elections draws people *together* and reinforces attachments to the political system. At first this may appear to be a contradictory argument. After all, many elections are frequently hard-fought battles in which both sides engage in mudslinging and "unfair" tactics, so we should expect elections to *increase*, not *decrease*, antagonisms. Indeed, one of the traditional arguments against elections was that they are a divisive political event which can tear society apart.

The emphasis commonly placed on the divisive effect of elections unfortunately overshadows the possibly integrative function of conflict. Sociologists have frequently observed that as long as conflict is held within certain boundaries, the combatants can feel better toward one another following the conflict. This is not unlike the situation in which a romance is improved following a good fight. Obviously, it is an exaggeration to say that *all* conflict leads to better feelings afterward. Rather, *limited* conflict may enhance attachment and heighten feelings of community.[1]

Does this apply to U.S. elections? Elections promote political solidarity in at least two important ways.

First, elections can clear the air of a lingering, troublesome issue. Differences are ever-present in society and must be tolerated, but if too many differences accumulate, the antagonisms can be destructive. By giving proponents of an issue "their day in court," elections can help end certain conflicts. Such is what happened in the 1972 election when many advocates of immediate withdrawal from Vietnam were successful in securing the Democratic party nomination for George McGovern. McGovern's decisive defeat by Richard Nixon, who advocated a more cautious approach to withdrawal, helped eliminate the immediate withdrawal option from heated debate. In short, by acting as a safety valve for sharp differences of opinion, elections may contribute to long-run moderation of conflict and help keep society united.

Second, elections can promote political solidarity by providing regular, shared experiences that reaffirm people's common political values. Periodic elections are not alone in holding the U.S. system together, but they help. This role is similar to that of high school pep rallies, proms, and other group events used to enhance "school spirit." Electoral participation in the United States is akin to a civic religion in which all participants come away with a heightened awareness and appreciation of our system of government.[2] This feeling is partly facilitated by the patriotic rhetoric employed by office seekers. Few candidates can resist such phrases as "these great United States of America" or "our visionary

---

[1] The role of conflict in promoting feelings of solidarity is described in Lewis Coser, *The Functions of Social Conflict* (New York: Free Press, 1956), Chap. 7.

[2] For a more complete analysis of how elections increase citizens' support for the political system, see Benjamin Ginsberg and Robert Weissberg, "Elections and the Mobilization of Popular Support," *American Journal of Political Science*, 22 (1978), pp. 31–55.

Founding Fathers who gave us our Constitution." Feelings of togetherness are also enhanced by the rituals following most elections—despite all the animosity of the campaign, losers customarily congratulate winners and offer whatever help is necessary in the future to make government work. It is almost unthinkable in U.S. politics for losers to attack winners publicly or to encourage their supporters to reject the electorate's verdict as final. The upshot of all the conflict, then, is that the basic agreements and shared purposes of citizens are reaffirmed.

One way to demonstrate the integrative role of elections is to compare people's votes and opinions before and after an election. Consider, for example, the amount of popular support enjoyed by the President following the election. Table 6.1 shows that despite accusations, mudslinging, and bad feelings during the presidential campaign, newly elected Presidents receive considerable public support. And—what is perhaps most significant—much of this support comes from people who probably voted against the winner. The proportion giving high ratings is always much larger than the winner's proportion of the popular vote.

President (election year)	Percentage of popular vote received by President	Percentage of citizens "approving" of the way the President is handling job (most recent poll following inauguration)
Harry S. Truman (1948)	49.6	87
Dwight D. Eisenhower (1952)	55.1	68
Dwight D. Eisenhower (1956)	57.4	79
John F. Kennedy (1960)	49.7	72
Lyndon B. Johnson (1964)	61.1	79
Richard M. Nixon (1968)	43.4	59
Richard M. Nixon (1972)	60.7	68
Jimmy Carter (1976)	50.6	66

TABLE 6.1
POPULAR SUPPORT FOR THE PRESIDENT BEFORE AND AFTER THE ELECTION

Sources: Elections data are from *The U.S. Fact Book: The American Almanac for 1977* (New York: Grosset and Dunlap, 1977), p. 452; Gallup data are reported in *The Gallup Poll: Public Opinion 1935–1971* (New York: Random House, 1971), p. 2234, and Gallup poll, release of Feb. 6, 1977.

SURVIVAL OF THE ELECTORAL SYSTEM IN THE UNITED STATES

One of the most remarkable features of U.S. political history is the persistence of the institution of elections. This may not appear impressive until one considers all of the countries that have not been able to maintain a tradition of genuine elections. Moreover, even in the United States elections have not gone unchallenged by various groups since the ratification of the Constitution. What explains this longevity?

Many historical factors help to account for the persistence of elections. These include the migration of British Royalists following the Revolutionary War, the success of early elections in attracting the support of powerful interests, and the successful incorporation of newly arrived ethnic groups into electoral politics.

Yet there is another explanation that is particularly relevant for understanding the survival of the electoral system: the idea of voting as a method for settling political questions is deeply ingrained in U.S. citizens. Little can compete in popularity with elections as a means of resolving political disputes.[3] The strength of citizen commitment to the voting process becomes clear when we examine what young children learn about elections. Even in the early grades children are knowledgeable about voting and talk about the day when they will be legally qualified to vote. Young children also view the right to vote as one of the most valuable characteristics of the U.S. political system. Indeed, the idea of free elections seems to be basic to everyone's conception of democracy.[4]

Moreover, well before children are of voting age, many of them have had extensive exposure to voting in school. As all of us know well, U.S. schools are rife with elections and electioneering to choose class president, student council representative, most likely to succeed, or recipient of the yearbook dedication. Children also become involved in adult politics despite their inability to vote. One study, for example, found that most grade-schoolers talked to their parents and friends about the presidential candidates, read about the candidates, and wore a campaign button.[5] By the time children reach adulthood, elections are a familiar and well-accepted method of reaching a collective decision.

MAJOR ARGUMENTS AGAINST ELECTIONS

Our analysis argues that elections are a useful, deeply valued mechanism of settling the difficult question of who should rule. No doubt most of us believe that elections are the best—though perhaps not perfect— mechanism for choosing leadership. Nevertheless, we should not allow our deeply instilled acceptance of elections to obscure the possible drawbacks of the electoral system. There *are* reasonable criticisms of the system that must be faced. Many antielection arguments have been put forward, but here we shall consider only two of the most important: (1) elections provide only the illusion of citizen control of government; and (2) elections discourage qualified people from seeking public office. These are not hypothetical, easily rejected arguments.

The "elections provide only illusion" argument

According to this argument, elections and campaign activity are more akin to Indian rain dances or pagan religious rites than to a method of

---

[3] See, for example, Jack Dennis, "Support for the Institution of Elections by the Mass Public," *American Political Science Review*, 64 (1970), pp. 819–835.

[4] Data on children's conception of government and the importance of voting are found in David Easton and Jack Dennis, *Children in the Political System* (New York: McGraw-Hill, 1969), pp. 113–118.

[5] Several studies in political participation among children are described in Robert Weissberg, *Political Learning, Political Choice and Democratic Citizenship* (Englewood Cliffs, N.J.: Prentice-Hall, 1974), pp. 84–92.

citizen political control. The candidates' appeals for voter support, the exhortations to vote, and all the rhetoric stressing the enormous power of the voters serve only to give the *appearance*, not the substance, of popular control. Such rituals can reassure citizens that they have control, make the ordinary person feel important, and fit well with commonsense notions of democracy. But the ultimate purpose of elections is to hide the fact that the ordinary citizen has almost no control over government.[6] One is reminded of the role played by some high school student governments: the existence of student councils provides only an illusion of student power—the real power is wielded by teachers and administrators.

Advocates of this argument support their position with a variety of facts. They note that many citizens know little about what candidates stand for or their qualifications and backgrounds. Moreover, this ignorance is encouraged by Madison Avenue-type campaigns that frequently stress physical appearance, personal style, ethnicity, and other characteristics irrelevant to crucial political questions. Thus, electoral outcomes, having been decided by ignorant, manipulated citizens, provide no clear-cut political direction. What does the fact that Jimmy Carter beat Gerald Ford in 1976 mean, for example? What collective desires were expressed in this decision? Absolutely none, would answer those claiming elections to be illusions. They would note that neither candidate had a clear issue identity, and many voters acted out of ignorance or on the basis of superficial traits.

Those who take the position that elections are illusions also claim that even if citizens did provide clear instructions to their leaders, elected officials do not possess the power necessary to implement popular demands (even if elected officials *wanted* to follow popular desires). Vast quantities of political power, the argument continues, lie in the hands of nonelected public officials, such as bureaucrats or judges, or in private hands, such as executives of large corporations or lobbyist groups.

Hence, given both mass susceptibility to symbols rather than to substance and the existence of substantial political power among nonelected officials, elections, it is argued, provide relatively cheap and therapeutic mechanisms for keeping the people happy. Citizens will think they have control, and leaders will reinforce this satisfying belief, but the truth is otherwise. Elections might thus be classified as a mass participation sporting event—one works up a sweat, has a good emotional release, and sometimes even experiences a thrill or two, but there is no lasting or significant impact. Elections are façades that hide the real exercise of political power.

Is this argument true? Undoubtedly it contains elements of truth. How much of it is true or false is a question of degree. Because the answer is complex, we shall temporarily set it aside until we complete a more elaborate analysis of voting behavior, campaigns, and the many other aspects of U.S. politics. This argument deserves a thoughtful answer, but for the moment we must withhold judgment.

<hr />

[6] Murray Edelman, *The Symbolic Uses of Politics* (Urbana, Ill.: University of Illinois Press, 1964), pp. 2–3.

The "elections discourage 'good' people from seeking office" argument

The second important argument against elections is that they do not foster the emergence of the best leadership. This belief is probably fairly popular, and it is a difficult argument to refute precisely. The most perplexing aspect of it concerns what constitutes the "best" people for the job of President, member of Congress, mayor, or justice of the peace. Do we want the smartest people in the United States? Do we want officials with some hard-to-define quality such as "leadership ability?" Despite this problem, however, the argument is sufficiently important to warrant our attention.

Those who believe that elections provide only second-rate leaders usually make the following points. First, the process of getting elected requires wheeling and dealing and even deception. U.S. electoral politics demands that leaders gain the support of diverse groups and interests. A candidate must therefore develop the skills of avoiding being pinned down on emotional issues and of managing to say contradictory things without getting caught. Integrity, high principles, and speaking plainly, the argument goes, simply have no place in electoral politics — at least for winners. Even a good person is corrupted by the electoral experience.

Another argument against elections involves the costs and benefits of a career that depends on frequent elections. Running for office is costly. Seeking public office is time consuming, and it can be financially ruinous; family life is disrupted, and one must put up with all kinds of personal abuse. Given the opportunities, and absence of hassles, in private life for intelligent, talented individuals, why should such people go into electoral politics? As a result, the argument goes, only second-raters, lacking opportunities in private life, venture into electoral competition.

Finally, it can be claimed that obtaining political office by means of election is such a demanding, exhausting process that only power-crazed individuals succeed. Normal people lack the overwhelming drive for power. Electoral politics, therefore, produces government by power-obsessed individuals, as opposed to, say, government by idealistic, high-minded leaders concerned with the public interest.

Do U.S. elections discourage high-quality political leadership? We can probably all agree that U.S. political leaders as a group are neither prime candidates for sainthood nor members of the world's intellectual elite. And surely many examples can be found of incompetent, dishonest officeholders. Nevertheless, much evidence shows that the more extreme charges against elections are untrue. While successful candidates may be gluttons for punishment and abuse, it does not seem that elected officials as a group suffer from personal disorders that significantly interfere with their jobs.[7] Nor does it appear that public officials are second-raters who could not otherwise succeed in society. To be sure, elected political leaders do not come entirely from elite universities and do not always have skills that would make them successful outside politics. Several studies have demonstrated, however, that elected leaders as a

[7] See, for example, Rufus Browning and Herbert Jacob, "Power Motivation and the Political Personality," *Public Opinion Quarterly*, 28 (1964), pp. 75–90.

group are several cuts above ordinary citizens in education and possess a wide variety of experiences and accomplishments outside politics.[8]

More important, however, many of the supposed defects of leadership attributed to elections may not be defects at all. Consider, for example, the ability to satisfy conflicting groups. Perhaps we *want* leaders skilled at compromise and conflict reduction. Politics, it is often said, is the art of the possible, and to insist on one's principles regardless of the opposition may make for martyrdom, but in U.S. society it is bad politics. Imagine the consequences if leaders were inflexible and refused to give an inch. The "failure" of electoral politics to recruit the very best intellectual leadership may not even be a failure at all, since citizens probably want leaders who are more like ordinary people, not intellectual geniuses. After all, nothing in the Constitution prohibits a highly altruistic, intellectually gifted, high-minded person from being put into office by popular acclaim. It may be that elections discourage "the very best" from public life, but it is also likely that the public does not want such individuals in public office. If citizens did, such distinguished leaders could easily be elected.

ELECTIONS: AN EVALUATION

As we describe the benefits of U.S. elections, it becomes clear that elections play a valuable role in maintaining the existing system of government. Elections help generate support for leaders and the government, legitimize the transfer of political power, and seem to drain off potentially dangerous antisystem behavior. Even one of the major criticisms of the electoral process — that elections are a fraud to pacify dissatisfied citizens — argues for its prosystem role.

It is evident that if one wants to continue existing political arrangements, one should advocate free and open elections. Elections, as we have noted, are an important vehicle of change; they allow citizens the opportunity to get rid of undesirable leaders. At the same time, they help stabilize politics despite the commotion of circuslike campaigns. These are not inherent consequences of elections; in other nations elections can contribute to increased chaos and instability. In the United States, though, elections work to stabilize politics.

What are the alternatives to elections?

Elections play a key role in U.S. politics, but it would be a mistake to conclude that elections are the only way to choose political leaders. Elections are but one of several ways of selecting leaders.

---

[8] For an interesting comparison of top political leaders versus heads of large corporations in terms of backgrounds and education, see Andrew Hacker, "The Elected and the Anointed: Two American Elites," *American Political Science Review*, 55 (1961), pp. 539–549.

Aristocracy A small non-elected group of people who rule and owe their position to birth, wealth, ability, or social position.

HEREDITARY ARISTOCRACY

One alternative is to follow the example of medieval Europe or contemporary Saudi Arabia and have an hereditary **aristocracy.** Such a system would have the advantage of continuity because leaders serve for life, the transfer of power is usually clear-cut, it would probably be cheaper than periodic elections, and it would perhaps please fans of pomp and ceremony. As a realistic political alternative, however, it is not feasible (though certain families—the Byrds of Virginia, the Lodges of Massachusetts—have been successful at holding political power over generations and constitute a "democratic aristocracy").

SELECTING OFFICIALS THROUGH EXAMINATIONS AND APPOINTMENTS

A much more realistic alternative is to select leaders on the basis of special skills determined through examinations. Instead of electing a member of Congress, we could fill the position much like a corporation hires an executive trainee. Applicants would take a written exam (per-

BUT MUST THEY BE RELIABLE AND CLEAN CUT?

Getting the best person for high political office is difficult, and many solutions have been proposed. Perhaps one of the most interesting is offered by C. Northcote Parkinson, the British political scientist and humorist. How do you get the most energetic, courageous, patriotic, experienced, popular, and eloquent person in the country? According to Parkinson, you would place an advertisement such as:

Wanted—Prime Minister of Ruritania. Hours of work: 4 A.M. to 11:59 P.M. Candidates must be prepared to fight three rounds with the current heavyweight champion (regulation gloves to be worn). Candidates will die for their country, by painless means, on reaching the age of retirement (65). They will have to pass an examination in parliamentary procedure and will be liquidated if they fail to gain 75 percent of the votes in a popularity poll held under the Gallup Rules. They will finally be invited to try their eloquence on a Baptist Congress, the object being to induce those present to rock and roll. Those who fail will be liquidated. All candidates should present themselves at the Sporting Club (side entrance) at 11:15 A.M. on the morning of September 19. Gloves will be provided, but they should bring their own rubber-soled shoes, singlet, and shorts.

haps waived for college graduates) and be interviewed, and the top candidate would become a congressional representative. Before one dismisses this possibility as absurd, one should realize that many powerful public officials in the United States are not elected but *are* chosen on the basis of written examinations and expertise in a particular area. Indeed, while we may glorify elections as *the* method of choosing leaders in a democracy, we probably have *more* nonelected than elected positions of power in the United States.

One important group of nonelected public officials are **bureaucrats,** who get their jobs through civil service examinations. Especially in recent years, at all levels of government bureaucrats have become extremely important. Some people have even complained that bureaucrats who hold their jobs for many years dominate elected leaders who typically serve for only a few years. Another group of nonelected public officials are federal and many state judges. Appointed judges' invulnerability to the consequences of the election process has been extensively illustrated by the Supreme Court's vigorous endorsement of busing to achieve school integration: polls have consistently shown public opposition to busing, and politicians have denounced the Court. But because

Bureaucrats Nonelected public officials who administer the business of government.

Parkinson points out that this strategy has several advantages:

Observe that this advertisement saves all trouble about application forms, testimonials, photographs, references, and short lists. If the advertisement has been correctly worded, there will be only one applicant, and he can take office immediately—well, almost immediately. But what if there is no applicant? That is proof that the advertisement needs rewording. We have evidently asked for something more than exists. So the same advertisement (which is, after all, quite economical in space) can be inserted again with some slight adjustment. The pass mark in the examination can be reduced to 85 per cent with 65 per cent of the votes required in the popularity poll, and only two rounds against the heavyweight. Conditions can be successively relaxed, indeed, until an applicant appears.*

If this story seems farfetched, you will be interested to know that President Richard M. Nixon began his long political career in response to a want ad in the *Los Angeles Times!* It seems that in 1946 the local California Republican organization was looking for a good congressional candidate; they placed an ad in the *Los Angeles Times,* friends of Nixon contacted him about the notice, and the rest is history.

* Reprinted from C. Northcote Parkinson, *Parkinson's Law* (Boston: Houghton Mifflin, 1957), pp. 57–58.

federal judges are appointed for life, public outcry has little impact. Perhaps the best evidence that elections are not necessarily the best way to choose leaders is the decision of many cities to replace elected officials with hired experts. Many cities have replaced popularly elected mayors with professionally trained appointed city managers who are supposed to replace "politics" with businesslike decision making.

The important point is that despite the popularity of elections in the United States, their use is not preordained. Most political systems have *not* employed elections, and even in U.S. politics many positions of political power are not filled by elections. An important question, one usually obscured by all the campaign hoopla, is why some officials are chosen by election while others are appointed or selected by written examination. In certain states, for example, positions like registrar of deeds are elected, in others they are appointed, and in yet others they are filled by regular civil servants who must demonstrate their competence on examinations. Should we elect Supreme Court Justices? Yet, few citizens question why some public officials are never elected or whether it is necessary to elect others. In short, there *are* alternatives to elections, and several alternatives have their merits and advocates.

How are U.S. elections organized?

A crucial aspect of any electoral system is how that system is organized. Organization refers to regulation of the timing of elections, who votes for what offices, and the procedures used for counting votes. All of these regulations are important even though they are frequently obscured by day-to-day events. Election rules are as important to electoral outcomes as the rules of sports are in deciding who wins and loses a game or match. As sports fans know, there is no such thing as a perfectly neutral regulation. Since participants vary in their resources and skills, a particular rule always favors one side over the other, even if it is enforced with absolute impartiality. To take one simple example, consider the fact that national elections are held on Tuesday. Sounds harmless, doesn't it? Who could possibly lose from this technical requirement? One group of potential losers are people who work Monday through Friday for hourly wages. Unless the polls are open early in the morning or late at night, such a rule puts many of these citizens at a disadvantage. Business executives or college professors, however, can easily vote during the middle of Tuesday. Holding elections on Sunday—as is done in many European nations—would probably increase turnout among working-class citizens and thus make poorer citizens more influential in politics.

We shall examine rules that determine how the desires of citizens are translated into election outcomes. Basically, we want to know whether our electoral system treats all voters equally and allows citizens to control their government. Let us examine five rules governing U.S. elections that significantly affect the translation of citizen desires into political outcomes. These five rules are: (1) staggered elections; (2) calendar-determined elections; (3) geographically defined election districts; (4) the winner-take-all system; and (5) constitutional requirements affecting the equality of votes.

STAGGERED ELECTIONS

At all levels of government—national, state, and local—**staggered elections** are the rule, so that only portions of the government are elected at any one time. At the national level, for example, only one third of the Senate is up for reelection every two years, and presidential elections fall with every other House of Representatives election. Many states have even more fragmented elections: federal elections occur in even years, state elections in November of odd-numbered years, and local elections in April of odd years (it is even more chaotic when primaries and school board elections are considered).[9]

The net results of this staggering of elections are twofold. First, citizens must frequently wait comparatively long periods to change political leadership completely. For example, if citizens suddenly wanted to throw every public official out of office, the process might take a few years (six years at the national level). Second, since different officials were elected at different times, it is possible that government will be comprised of individuals who owe their success to different issues, issues that were popular during their particular electoral campaign. Clearly, political life would be much more straightforward if all officials faced reelection at the same time.

CALENDAR-DETERMINED ELECTIONS

Suppose citizens wanted immediate government action on some major issue that suddenly dominated the political scene, but leaders ignored the clamor. What could be done? Very little until the next election. For better or worse, we are constitutionally bound by rigid, **calendar-determined election dates** no matter how pressing the issue. This is not true in nations like Great Britain where elections can be called when crucial political issues emerge (for example, Britain's entry into the Common Market). In fact, it has been argued that if we want issue-oriented campaigns, we should schedule elections when important issues arise. This would be more effective than hoping that important questions will surface in the fall of predetermined election years.

The value of noncalendar elections is well illustrated by the crisis produced by Watergate in 1974. As each new piece of damaging evidence emerged, both Congress and President Nixon became preoccupied with the possibilities of impeachment, the lack of public confidence in government, and even with the President's ability to govern effectively. In Euro-

Staggered elections The principle of not electing all officials on the same date or in the same year.
Calendar-determined election dates Specifying in advance exactly when elections will be held. This involves the number of years between elections and the dates of the elections.

---

[9] The number of states having major elections in a nonpresidential election year seems to be on the increase. Between 1920 and 1970 the number rose from twelve to thirty. See Walter Dean Burnham, *Critical Elections and the Mainsprings of American Politics* (New York: Norton, 1970), pp. 94–96.

Geographically defined electoral districts The procedure of grouping citizens into election districts on the basis of where they live (as opposed to other characteristics such as income, occupation, or social group).

pean nations, where election dates are not permanently fixed, the issue of whether a leader should be replaced is solved by holding a new election. If the United States had such a system, President Nixon could have taken his case directly to the people, received a quick answer, and Watergate would have been resolved. Instead, the Watergate crisis lingered on until enormous pressure brought about President Nixon's resignation. Unfortunately, the constitutional requirement of fixed terms means that with rare exceptions (for example, death or impeachment) a popular majority may not be able to act when it wants to act. In some states and cities voters have the legal option of instituting a petition to recall an elected official, but this process is a cumbersome one that is rarely successful.

GEOGRAPHICALLY DEFINED ELECTORAL DISTRICTS

Suppose we want a political system in which citizens choose leaders to represent them. Which citizens should elect which leaders? This may seem like a minor technical question, yet the way elected leaders are grouped with voters is crucial. Several reasonable alternative methods are possible. One is to have *all* citizens elect *all* officials. This sometimes occurs in local elections where all voters choose all members of a city council. A second alternative, one popular in university elections, is to divide citizens into groups on the basis of some common characteristic. For example, university legislative bodies include representatives of such groups as undergraduates, graduate students, faculty, and nonacademic staff. A third alternative is to divide citizens into **geographically defined electoral districts.** In campus politics this might be on the basis of the building in which one works or lives. Elections in the United States are based on such geographical divisions, with public officials representing states, countries, wards, and other units defined by physical boundaries. They do not represent economic interests nor do they represent groups of people on the basis of shared racial or ethnic heritages.

Political significance

What is the political significance of the geographical basis of elections? This method of organizing elections generally makes it more difficult for leaders to heed faithfully, or even to know, citizen preferences. The reason is that, except in rare instances, geographically defined electorates are more diverse politically than are those determined according to a common social or economic characteristic. Many congressional districts and states contain such a diversity of people and groups that it is nearly impossible for any elected official to keep everyone satisfied. Representation would be much easier, no doubt, if officials were elected by citizens who shared certain political preferences. Instead of having leaders who represent northwest Chicago, for example, we might have a leader elected by middle-class home owners of European descent.

The organization of electorates on a geographical basis does *not*, however, discriminate equally against all citizens. Specifically, citizens sharing common interests who happen to be clustered geographically are

The Illinois Twenty-first district is one of the major agricultural areas in the world (each of these 24 storage tanks holds 750 large truckloads of corn or soybeans). Farm prices and agricultural export controls are thus major issues in the district.

There are several colleges in the district, including the University of Illinois with 36,000 students. This makes government aid to higher education an issue to be heeded.

Though generally well-off, the district nevertheless contains substantial numbers of poor people. Many of these poor people are black and frequently desire policies at odds with those advocated by Edward Madigan's Republican Party.

Like much of America, the Twenty-first contains miles and miles of moderately priced suburban homes. Many of these people want cheap food, oppose extensive help to poor people, and are not sympathetic to policies advocated by many college students.

Because members of Congress are elected from geographically defined constituencies, they typically must represent a diverse group of people. In 1970, the average congressional district had 465,000 citizens. This has frequently meant that a legislator must satisfy the demands of both urban and suburban residents, blue-collar and white-collar workers, young wage earners, the elderly on social security, and many other groups whose goals may conflict. The Twenty-first Congressional District of Illinois is probably typical of the diversity that can be found when 464,693 people are grouped together. Located in east central Illinois, it is a mixture of several medium-sized cities and farm land. It also contains a major military establishment—Chanute Air Force Base. Since 1972, the Twenty-first has been represented by Edward Madigan, a moderate Republican.

FIGURE 6.1

THE IMPACT OF THREE DIFFERENT SYSTEMS OF ELECTIONS

GEOGRAPHICAL REPRESENTATION, WINNER-TAKE-ALL SYSTEM
(present U.S. system)

Division of Electorate

District 1 2 3 4 5 6

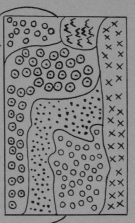

Winner O | O | · | · | O | O
(interest with most votes) in each election district

In this system, the "X" and "M" interest get no winners since neither one is a majority in any of the 6 districts. The O's get half the victories since they are a (bare) majority in 3 districts. But the O's constitute much less than half the people.

CORPORATE ELECTORS—the
electorate is divided into groups of like-minded people, and elections take place within these groups

All O interests vote together

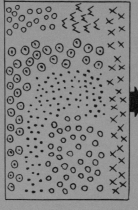

In this system, all the O's vote together, etc. Thus, the M's will vote for a fellow-M, regardless of where all the M's live. Each group may or may not be given offices in proportion to its strength in the population. Many corporate systems did not give power in proportion to a group's number in population.

PROPORTIONAL REPRESENTATION—
parties compete for votes, and party share of victories is proportional to votes received.

Electorate

Legislative body

In this system the legislative distribution of seats mirrors the overall divisions of voting within the entire nation or state. The M's thus get about 10% of the seats because they are about 10% of the population. The O's only get about 30% of the seats, since they are only 30% of the population (not half, as in the first system).

likely to fare better than citizens with the same interests who are dispersed geographically. To see how this principle operates, compare the congressional representatives accorded to farmers, a group with a strong geographical concentration, with those accorded to manual workers, a group much more dispersed. Despite their small numbers, farmers frequently receive vocal and effective representation in Congress. This is due in large part to farmer domination of many electoral districts. The more geographically dispersed manual workers, however, do not have this political clout because there are few congressional districts dominated by them.

Winner-take-all system Principle of giving victory to the candidate with the most votes and nothing to all other candidates. *Proportional representation* An electoral system in which parties have lists of candidates, voters choose a list, and legislative seats are divided in proportion to votes received by each party.

WINNER-TAKE-ALL SYSTEM

Elections in the United States, unlike those in many European democracies, operate on the principle of winner take all. The candidate with the most votes (even if not a majority) wins *everything;* those who placed second, third, or fourth get absolutely *nothing.* Three important points need to be made regarding this system. First, though the **winner-take-all system** is widely accepted by citizens, a workable alternative exists, namely, the system of **proportional representation.** The essential feature of this system is that political parties offer lists of candidates, and voters choose lists, not individual candidates. Offices, for example, legislative seats, are then awarded on the basis of the *proportion* of the vote won by each party. Suppose we have two parties—the American Apple Pie Party and the American Cherry Pie Party. In an election the Apple Pies win 61 percent of the vote; they therefore get (as closely as possible) 61 percent of the offices up for election. Under the winner-take-all system, however, the losing party has no guarantee of winning anything. Theoretically, it is possible for the losing party to get 49.9 percent of the vote in every legislative district and yet get no seats! Proportional representation, on the other hand, insures that losers get a share of the power that corresponds to their electoral strength. Proponents of proportional representation have argued that the winner-take-all system is undemocratic because many people—those voting for the loser—receive no representation.

A second point about the winner-take-all system is that it allows the election of leaders who receive less than 50 percent of the vote unless there is a run-off election. This happens when three or more strong candidates split the vote so that one candidate is victorious with less than a majority. In primaries, where getting on the ballot is comparatively simple, it is not unusual for the winner to receive 30 percent or less of the vote. Even in general elections many officeholders win with less than a majority. In the 1976 election, eight members of Congress won with less than 50 percent of the total vote of their districts. Many Presidents—for example, Harry Truman in 1948, John Kennedy in 1960, and Richard Nixon in 1968—won with less than 50 percent of the popular vote. On occasion this system results in a comparatively unpopular candidate winning. For example, in the 1970 New York Senate race a very conservative candidate (James Buckley) won with 38.8 percent of the vote when

> **"CAN A SYSTEM BE FAIR IF IT HELPS ELECT COMMUNISTS?"**
>
> Proportional representation (PR) has been tried in the United States. In 1937, for example, New York City employed the system for elections to its city council. Any group that could get even a small percentage of the total vote got a city council seat (as opposed to needing more than 50 percent in one electoral district). When several Communists were elected, the system was discontinued. Obviously, proportional representation would greatly help small minorities in getting at least some members elected (if the House of Representatives were elected by PR, only 0.2229 percent of the total vote would be needed to get one member elected).

his two opponents split the moderate and liberal vote (Buckley lost in 1976 in a two-person race). This situation of minority victories could be solved by requiring run-off elections between candidates with the highest vote totals, but except in a few instances in states and cities, this solution has not been employed.

A third important point about the winner-take-all system is that it distorts the translation of votes into political power. Generally, it exaggerates the impact of certain majorities and diminishes the representation of minorities.[10] To illustrate how this occurs, let us consider the situation of black voters trying to elect black public officials. If blacks comprise 40 percent of a city electorate and both blacks and whites vote along racial lines, what proportion of the offices do blacks win? Zero percent. The winner-take-all system is not antiblack; it discriminates equally against all groups that are less than a majority. Not only are minorities at a disadvantage at the polls, they are probably even discouraged from political action. After all, what is the point of working hard to increase one's vote from 20 percent to 40 percent if the effect is the same? Hence, groups with a small following in a geographical area have little chance of obtaining any power. Of course, in a close election the votes of a minority may be crucial and thus highly valued, but the fact remains that the winner-take-all system usually handicaps groups that lack the power to win a majority.

[10] For a more detailed analysis of this process, see Edward R. Tufte, "The Relationship between Seats and Votes in Two-Party Systems," *American Political Science Review*, 67 (1973), pp. 540–554.

Year	Proportion of votes for House candidates given to Republicans (percents)	Proportion of seats won by Republican candidates (percents)	Number of House seats "lost" by Republicans due to distortion
1960	45.0	39.8	23
1962	47.4	40.7	29
1964	42.5	32.2	45
1966	48.7	43.1	24
1968	49.1	44.1	22
1970	45.8	41.5	19
1972	47.3	44.6	12
1974	41.4	33.3	35
1976	43.8	32.9	47

TABLE 6.2
VOTES RECEIVED VERSUS CONGRESSIONAL SEATS WON, 1960–1976

Sources: Statistical Abstract of the United States, 1960, 1964, 1968, 1974, 1977, 1978.

To show how this distortion works on a national level, compare the proportion of votes won by Republican congressional candidates between 1960 and 1976 with the corresponding number of seats the Republicans actually won. Table 6.2 shows that if House seats were exactly proportional to votes received, the Republicans would have done much better in each election. The major culprit of this distortion is the winner-take-all system.

CONSTITUTIONAL REQUIREMENTS AFFECTING THE EQUALITY OF VOTES

In recent years the principle of **one man, one vote** has faced a long and largely successful legal battle. Prior to the landmark Supreme Court ruling in *Baker* v. *Carr* (1962), each state was almost completely free to decide the population and geographic shape of election districts. This discretionary power frequently led to major inequalities. In California, for example, Los Angeles County and sparsely populated Alpine County each elected one state senator. Sometimes a minority of the voters could elect a majority of the state legislature. Another common practice was called **gerrymandering.** Here a district's boundary lines were drawn to achieve a political advantage. For example, if Republicans wanted to reduce the voting power of Democrats living in a large city, election districts could be drawn so that portions of the city were combined with rural areas to dilute the Democratic city votes. Such gerrymandering sometimes resulted in oddly shaped election districts. The *Baker* v. *Carr* decision and several subsequent court decisions prohibited both unequal populations in election districts within a state (for state and national elections) and oddly defined district boundaries.

One man, one vote A principle according to which each citizen has proportionally the same power in selecting legislators or the executive. A system in which 10 people would choose one candidate and 100 people would choose another legislator would violate this principle.
Gerrymandering The drawing of election district boundaries in order to gain an electoral advantage.

THE RIGHT TO VOTE

The right of all citizens to vote is today regarded as fundamental. The Supreme Court in 1964 even ruled (*Westburry* v. *Sanders*) that the right to vote is the basis of all our other political and civil rights. Nevertheless, the electoral system has *never* allowed everyone to vote. Restrictions on who could vote have existed from Colonial times to the present.

During the pre-Revolutionary period voting was a restricted privilege. Several colonies prohibited members of certain religions (for example, Jews and Quakers) from voting, and Massachusetts even required prospective voters to have a pastor's certificate vouching for their personal character. All states had a property requirement, and some even spelled out the number of acres a person had to own. Women, blacks, and those under 21 years of age were universally excluded.

The Revolution of 1776 did not bring a dramatic relaxation of these restrictions. The most significant changes occurred in the type of property needed to qualify for the vote. Following the Revolution several states included personal property (for example, houses and livestock) or the payment of taxes, as opposed to land ownership, in their voting requirement. This was considered a step in the broadening of the electorate. Vermont, which joined the Union in 1791, was the first state to allow the vote to all men residing in the state for a year, regardless of property ownership, who were of "quiet and peaceable behavior." By 1850 most states, especially the newly admitted western states, had abolished personal property requirements for voting (and all states had abolished the land-owning requirement). The sex and age restrictions continued, though these were frequently assumed rather than written into law. In fact, during New Jersey's early years women voted, but when the state legislature realized this, it promptly legally prohibited the practice.

The trend of liberalized voting requirements did not, however, continue for long. Beginning in the 1850s, the United States experienced a massive influx of immigrants, and many eastern states responded with new voting requirements designed to keep foreigners from voting. The most successful of these measures was the **literacy test,** which required a demonstrated capacity to read and write (or, in some instances, interpret a portion of the state or federal constitution). One of the advantages of the literacy requirement was that election officials had great discretion in who "passed" or "failed" the test. Thus, native-born illiterates frequently passed while immigrants

Poll tax A fee charged for voting. Commonly used to exclude poor people from voting.

failed (such discrimination was largely limited to eastern seaboard states).

Two groups have had a particularly important place in the battle over voting rights: women and blacks. The exclusion of women from voting was a long-standing custom going back to medieval times. Though women had voted in New Jersey after the Revolution, the issue of women's right to vote did not emerge until 1848 when it was proposed at a conference on the rights of women held at Seneca Falls, New York. Women were given the right to vote in Wyoming in 1869 when Wyoming was still a territory, and in Utah and Washington soon thereafter. However, these enfranchisements were invalidated by Congress or the federal courts. When Wyoming entered the Union in 1890, it gave women the right to vote. Many western states followed its lead, and after several years of political agitation by women, the Nineteenth Amendment, granting women the right to vote, was passed in 1920.

A prospective voter analyzing a sample ballot.

The battle of blacks for the vote was far more complex. The Fifteenth Amendment, adopted in 1870, prohibited denying the vote on the grounds of "race, color, or previous condition of servitude." Nevertheless, many states, including all southern states, found numerous legal and illegal methods to overcome the amendment. The **poll tax,** a fee for voting, was widely employed (and in some states a prospective voter had to pay all fees for previous elections in order to vote in the present election). Property and literary requirements, originally employed by northern states, were adopted in the South. Since these

Felons Person convicted of a felony. A felony is a serious crime (precise definition of "serious" differs among states).

procedures did not inherently discriminate against blacks, they were upheld by the courts. Another popular method was to bar blacks from the Democratic primary, which was usually the real election because Republican opposition was usually absent. This was justified on the grounds that the Democratic Party was a private organization.

These restrictions proved highly effective in excluding blacks and were not seriously challenged until 1944 when the Supreme Court, in *Smith* v. *Allwright,* declared the all-white primary to be illegal. Beginning in 1957, however, the national government launched a major effort to insure that blacks could vote. The 1957 Civil Rights Act, for example, allowed the federal government to get a court injunction (a court order) to prevent obstruction to voting. The 1960 Civil Rights Act strengthened the right of blacks to vote by requiring the preservation of voting records. In 1964 legislation was passed to keep voting records by race and allow the Justice Department to enter lawsuits on behalf of illegally disenfranchised blacks. The Twenty-fourth Amendment prohibiting poll taxes was passed in 1964, while the 1965 Voting Rights Act provided for registration of black voters by federal examiners. The 1965 Act was readopted in 1970 as the Voting Rights Act of 1970, which also effectively barred the use of literacy tests (this Act also required that bilingual voting information be made available in voting districts with large numbers of Spanish, Asian, or Indian voters).

Compared to the past, contemporary voting requirements are nonrestrictive. Some restrictions do remain, however. Though several states once allowed aliens to vote, today they are excluded (many areas of the country have large alien populations). Idiots and the insane are disenfranchised in forty-four states. People in institutions, prisoners, and convicted **felons** are barred from voting in forty-seven states. Other criteria for disenfranchisement include a dishonorable military discharge, a history of subversive activity, refusal to take a loyalty oath, "bad moral character," and being designated a "pauper." Idaho presently excludes prostitutes, patrons of houses of ill-repute, people who "lewdly cohabit," and those whose marriages are "patriarchical, plural or celestial."

It is apparent from the historical development of the right to vote that there can be a major gap between the right of all citizens to vote and the actual administration of this right. Decisions regarding such "details" as residency, literacy, fees, citizenship, and prison records can greatly affect who wins the election. What might be described as a "simple administrative procedure" can really be a decision of considerable political significance.

This analysis of voting rights is largely adopted from William J. Crotty, *Political Reform and the American Experiment* (New York: Crowell, 1977), Chap. 1.

These court decisions do not mean, however, that unequal weighting of votes no longer exists. The most obvious inequality results from the constitutional requirement of two Senators from each state regardless of population. What this means, simply, is that citizens of states with small populations get a substantial representational bonus compared to citizens of large states such as New York and California. For example, in 1975, each Senator from Alaska, with a population of 341,000, represented 170,500 people. California Senators, however, were responsible for 20,876,000 people, or over 10 million for each Senator.

A similar, though less severe, tendency occurs in elections to the House of Representatives. Because small states must have at least one Representative, while large states get approximately what they deserve on the basis of population, once again there are inequities in the power of votes. In 1970, for example, congressional districts varied in size from 333,000 to 530,000. Hence, even though the courts have insured the one man, one vote principle within states, it is still true that congressional representation is not exactly proportional from state to state.[11]

Perhaps the clearest violation of the one man, one vote rule is the operation of the electoral college in presidential elections. Recall that a state's electoral votes equal the number of Senators (2) plus the number of Representatives. The electoral college also operates on a winner-take-all basis: the victorious candidate gets *all* of a state's electoral college vote no matter how small the margin of victory (this is not a constitutional requirement but a long-established custom). Much has been said lately about the value of the electoral college versus a direct presidential election, but the point here is that the electoral college makes the presidential votes of some citizens far more valuable than the votes of others.[12] Specifically, voters in large states such as California are courted far more strenuously by presidential candidates than voters in South Dakota or Nevada. The reason is obvious: a few thousand votes in populous states can determine the outcome of a large bloc of electoral votes. Hence, voters in these crucial large states (for example, California, Texas, Illinois, New York) loom large, not only in terms of setting campaign strategy and policy positions but also in determining who will get the presidential nomination. A candidate with weak big-state support is likely to be a loser no matter how well he or she could do in the rest of the nation.

A conclusion: the electoral system

The description given here of how elections are organized in the United States may be disturbing to some readers. Particularly for those who want elections to be a neutral mechanism that translates citizen desires

[11] *Statistical Abstract of the United States, 1977*, p. 459.

[12] For a brief review of the case for and against the electoral college, see Wallace A. Sayre and Judith H. Parris, *Voting for President: The Electoral College and the American Political System* (Washington, D.C.: The Brookings Institution, 1970).

into public policy, such features as staggered elections, unrepresented minorities, and unequal weighting of votes are serious flaws. Indeed, many sophisticated analysts who have concurred in this opinion have proposed ways to remedy these supposed defects.

The question now becomes: Is the U.S. system of elections—regardless of the outcome of specific contests—so seriously flawed that it requires a drastic change? Rather than discuss each alleged defect separately, let us offer two general defenses of the existing system. The first concerns citizen satisfaction with the existing electoral procedures, while the second emphasizes the purpose of U.S. elections.

The first defense of the electoral system is that most citizens are basically content with the present arrangements, or at least can think of no better alternative. Certainly, few people strongly believe that the system is perfect, but if one reviews both the changes that have been made and the proposals for reform that have been put forward, it is clear that there is no widespread support for fundamental change. Electoral reform efforts are rarely aimed at changing the basic structures. The successful ones have focused on such issues as the rights of blacks or of women to vote on campaign financing, not on questions having to do with the timing of national elections or the underrepresentation of geographically dispersed minorities. Perhaps the last great successful electoral reform was the establishment of direct election of Senators in 1913. Advocates of more extreme proposals, for example, proportional representation, have had a hard time finding a receptive audience, let alone any success. In short, our system may not be perfect, but it's generally what most of us want.

A second, and much more sophisticated, defense of the electoral system begins with the question: What is an electoral system supposed to accomplish? If the answer is "produce a government *that accurately mirrors public sentiment*," then indeed the existing system is highly flawed. This answer would not, however, be given by those who initially designed the U.S. electoral system. The drafters of the Constitution were not interested in maximizing popular influence in government. Essentially, the electoral system was originally designed to accomplish two goals:

1. Allow citizens to choose public officials.
2. Prevent the emergence of a tyrannical faction, whether a majority or minority.

The first goal is comparatively simple to accomplish: you merely hold elections. The second goal, however, requires considerable ingenuity to meet. As James Madison makes clear in Federalist Number 10, the possibility of a majority faction taking power, which in turn would result in tyranny, is a major problem where leaders are directly elected. If the U.S. electoral system is viewed as a solution to this problem—to prevent a single faction from dominating government—then many of its "faults" become virtues. Staggered elections, rigid terms of office, and highly diverse election districts become obstacles to potential tyrants, *not* impediments to citizen rule. U.S. elections are constitutionally *designed* to thwart the immediate and accurate transmission of voters' opinions into electoral outcomes.

Thus, one's evaluation of the electoral system depends on what one thinks the electoral system is intended to accomplish. Should it act as an accurate conduit for citizen preferences? Or should it allow citizen participation in leadership selection while hindering domination by a single faction? If we want extensive political change and are convinced that the people are behind us, then the existing electoral system is clearly a hindrance. If, however, we are satisfied with the status quo and fear sudden and drastic changes, the present system is to be preferred. It is not a question of what type of electoral system is inherently "good," but of what political values we wish to pursue.

Major questions raised

1. Why have elections? Elections are not the only way of choosing leaders, but in the United States they serve several important functions. Elections allow citizens to remove objectionable leaders, help legitimize the transfer of political power, channel political participation into "safe" activities, and promote political solidarity. They have been criticized, however, for providing only the illusion of citizen power and for discouraging qualified people from seeking public office.

2. What are the alternatives to elections? Historically, elections have not been a common method of selecting leaders. Many nations use the principle of hereditary transfer of power, and in the United States we choose some leaders on the basis of examinations or by appointment. The key question is: "Why are some, but not all, leaders elected?

3. How are U.S. elections organized? Basically, U.S. elections are organized so that several distortions occur in the way votes are translated into electoral outcomes. Practices such as staggered elections and calendar-determined elections frequently make it difficult for citizens to change leaders immediately. Other features, for example, the winner-take-all principle and the geographical basis for determining election districts, make it difficult for votes to be translated accurately into electoral decisions. This is a defect only if one views elections as a means by which citizens directly control the government. In the view of those who drafted the Constitution, however, these features were virtues, not flaws.

QUESTIONS FOR FURTHER DISCUSSION

1. It can be argued that if giving every citizen an equal chance to be elected to public office were our primary goal, the lottery would be the best method of choosing leaders. That is, everyone's name would be put into a giant hat, and the first one picked might be President, the next one hundred U.S. Senators, and so on. There would be no discrimination based on wealth, race, sex, religion, geography, or personality. Every citi-

zen would have a precisely equal chance of growing up to be President. Would such a lottery be inconsistent with democracy? Could such a system ever be justified?

2. The system of representation in the United States is based upon geography. Other nations, for example, Ireland, Germany, and Italy, have tried what is sometimes called corporate representation. Here distinct interests such as landowners or workers choose legislators who then represent these groups. In the United States, for example, blacks, who comprise about 11 percent of the population, might elect 11 percent of Congress. What would be the advantages of such a system? Who would benefit? Would you endorse this type of system?

3. Steve Chochrek is an inmate in an Oregon state penitentiary, serving time for robbery. He has filed a class action suit claiming that it is unconstitutional to deny prisoners the right to vote. Chochrek claims that the approximately 285,000 inmates in U.S. prisons could become an effective political bloc on behalf of prisoners' rights. Would you allow prisoners to vote in national elections? What about voting for judges? Would you permit prisoners to vote in local elections? What about in situations where prisons are located in small towns, so that prisoners could dominate local politics by the virtue of their numbers?

4. The following item appeared in the September 5, 1978 *National Review:*

> According to the Federal Voting Rights Act, areas that have a significant minority group that speaks a language other than English must be given ballots printed in the other language. Which is why the Federal Government, on behalf of the Lumbee Indians, ordered three counties in North Carolina to print ballots in Lumbee. The only hitch is that there is no Lumbee language. There was once, but the Indians abandoned it in favor of English when white settlers moved into the area. County officials in the beleaguered area are considering applying for a federal grant to invent a new Lumbee language and teach it to the Lumbees.

This item suggests that:
   a. North Carolina officials have a sincere interest in helping the Lumbee Indians find their linguistic roots.
   b. North Carolina officials may have friends and relatives who could be employed to invent and teach the Lumbee language.
   c. The actions of the North Carolina county officials are a dodge since federal bureaucrats have for years been communicating in Lumbee.
   d. The Lumbee Indians should claim that their original language was French and that they need a federal grant to go to Paris to relearn their lost heritage.

BIBLIOGRAPHY

Crotty, William J. *Political Reform and the American Experiment.* New York: Crowell, 1977.
   Examines several aspects of the electoral process, including voting laws, registration systems, campaign financing, party nominating procedures, and electoral reform.

Dahl, Robert. *Preface to Democratic Theory.* Chicago: University of Chicago Press, 1956.

    A theoretically oriented examination of how different electoral systems affect citizen control of government. Chapters 1 and 2 are especially relevant for comparing the present U.S. system with one designed to give people greater power over policy.

Lakeman, Enid, and James D. Lambert. *Voting in Democracies.* London: Farber and Farber, n.d.

    A comprehensive and sympathetic analysis of proportional representation. Examines electoral systems in several European nations.

Longley, Lawrence, D., and Alan G. Braun. *The Politics of Electoral College Reform.* New Haven, Conn.: Yale University Press, 1972.

    A comprehensive analysis of the origins and operations of the electoral college. Also reviews several plans for reform and their strengths and weaknesses.

Milnor, A. J. *Elections and Political Stability.* Boston: Little, Brown, 1967.

    A brief but good description of various electoral systems, their operations, and some of their consequences. Most of the analyses concerns non-U.S. nations. Also examines the relationship between electoral systems and different conceptions of representation.

Pomper, Gerald M. *Elections in America: Control and Influence in Democratic Politics.* New York: Dodd, Mead, 1970.

    A good, wide-ranging analysis of elections. Contains chapters on the controversy over having elections, the theory underlying elections, the right to vote, the role of money in politics, and elections as a method of democratic control.

Rae, Douglas W. *The Political Consequences of Electoral Laws.* New Haven, Conn.: Yale University Press, 1967.

    Though occasionally complex, this is the best and most comprehensive review of different electoral systems and their political impact. Contains a bibliography.

PREVIEW

How politically knowledge-able are voters?

We must ask two separate questions: (1) How politically knowledgeable *should* voters be and (2) How informed is the average voter? While no clear standard for high or low levels of voter knowledge exists, we can consider political acumen in terms of what elections are supposed to accomplish. If elections are intended to allow citizens a direct role in policy making, then voters must be highly informed. But if we believe that elections merely allow citizens the opportunity to choose leaders, then less knowledge is required.

As to the second question, one national study found that most people are poorly informed about political matters. On the other hand, most voters knew the positions candidates took on issues when the candidates stated their positions clearly. In many other cases, however, voters were divided on where candidates stood. Some of this ignorance cannot be blamed on citizens.

What determines how people vote?

There is no single, universally accepted explanation. Three frequently cited determinants are party affiliation, issue voting, and group identity. The party-identification explanation asserts that most people early in life acquire a loyalty to either the Democratic or Republican Party and that this loyalty predisposes voting behavior. The issue-voting explanation claims that citizens choose candidates closest to their own positions on important issues. The group-loyalty approach sees voters as members of groups, such as Catholics, and claims that people vote on the basis of these characteristics.

Do political campaigns have any impact?

Campaigns typically sway comparatively few voters. Many people make their voting choice before the campaign, campaign communications are frequently distorted or ignored, and campaign messages cannot easily overcome strong predispositions. However, because a small change in the vote can influence an election outcome, campaigns are important. Campaigns result in only a small increase in political knowledge. Many campaigns do not emphasize issue differences, the media do not always emphasize candidate policy differences, and the deluge of campaign information is overwhelming. Are campaigns fair? Wealthy interests have an advantage because of the high cost of campaigning, but one cannot buy an election. Some people argue that campaigns are unfair because advertising agencies can sell candidates as they do soap. Though considerable selling of candidates does occur, there are limits to what the public will buy.

Attempts have been made to reform campaigns—especially to place ceilings on campaign costs and donations and to finance campaigns out of public funds. Reforms are difficult to enforce, however, and some conflict with the constitutional guarantee of freedom of speech.

CHAPTER SEVEN

VOTERS, CAMPAIGNS, AND MASS MEDIA

ew political events are as well scrutinized and widely debated as national elections. Enormous amounts of money and time are also put into political campaigns. Nevertheless, despite all the attention we give elections and the involvement in them of thousands of citizens, national elections still remain a complex and frequently mysterious process. Even experienced campaigners are unsure of what affects voters' decisions or whether certain types of campaigns are more effective than others. Debate has also centered on whether voters act intelligently or are easily misled by simplistic slogans. The impact of campaign money has likewise generated considerable controversy: Can a candidate buy an election, or is money just one of several, but not decisive, factors? Answers to these questions are essential if we are to decide whether national elections are a meaningful expression of citizen preferences or just ritualistic pageants. This chapter examines the significance of U.S. elections in the light of three questions:

1. How politically knowledgeable are voters?
2. What determines how people vote?
3. Do political campaigns have any impact?

How politically knowledgeable are voters?

The question of whether the ordinary citizen is qualified to vote on crucial questions of leadership and public policy has long been raised. The Constitutional Convention debated at length whether citizens could resist the enticing slogans of unscrupulous candidates. Even today one still hears complaints that most voters are poorly trained to exercise their civic responsibilities. Two questions are involved here: (1) How politically knowledgeable *should* the average voter be and (2) How informed *is* the average voter? Let us begin with an especially difficult question — what level of knowledge is required.

NEED FOR POLITICAL KNOWLEDGEABILITY ON THE PART OF VOTERS

To evaluate the political knowledge of the average voter we need some standard by which we can measure it. Must a citizen know, for example, how a bill becomes a law or the names of all important political leaders to be considered adequately informed? Or is a general like or dislike of candidates and policies sufficient? This is an important question, because the standard we set will greatly affect how many citizens we label as knowledgeable or poorly informed.

One way of resolving this question is to focus on what we believe to be the role of elections in the United States. If we see elections as a means by which citizens can be lawmakers, then the requirements for being informed are considerable. Voters would have to be well informed on the positions different candidates take on various issues, degree of candidate commitment to these positions, and the likely consequences of alternative policy positions. A sophisticated knowledge of government operations and laws would also be essential. This conception of elections places a heavy burden on the ordinary citizen.

At the other extreme we can view the electoral process merely as an instrument that allows citizens to choose the leaders they prefer to run the government. If officials prove unsatisfactory, citizens have the responsibility to replace them. In this case the requirements for being adequately informed are much more modest. A well-informed citizen would need only a broad awareness of government policy and a general acquaintance with the views of candidates. At election time voters would be able to reward or punish officials depending on the job they had done. There would be no need for citizens to understand all of the complexities of government and public policy. The key requirement would be to be able to relate one's likes and dislikes to the electoral process.

Between these two extremes, of course, are innumerable variations. We cannot argue that one or the other (or something in between) is the best standard for judgment. Rather, we need to remember that behind such common assertions as "the average voter is incompetent" or "the genius of the ordinary citizen makes democracy work" is a standard of knowledge that depends on what elections are supposed to accomplish. If one has high expectations about elections, citizens have a high standard to meet. If one views elections more modestly, many more voters will probably be considered politically informed.

VOTERS' KNOWLEDGE OF CANDIDATES AND ISSUES

How much do voters know about the candidates and issues during a presidential or congressional campaign? Table 7.1 presents voters' responses to factual questions in 1972. These questions represent only a small number of informational items, and an incorrect answer does not absolutely prove that a person was uninformed. Nevertheless, ignorance is common, and its implications are clear. After all, how is one to cast an informed vote for a member of Congress if one does not even know who is running for that office (and remember, these results are from people who *actually voted* in 1972).[1]

TABLE 7.1
POLITICAL KNOWLEDGE OF VOTERS, 1972

Question	Percentage of voters giving correct answer
(1) How many times can an individual be elected President?	80
(2) How long is the term of office for a U.S. Senator?	34
(3) Can you remember the names of the candidates who ran for the House in this district?	55
(4) How long is the term of office for members of the House of Representatives?	37
(5) Which party had the most members in the House before the last election?	73

Source: Center for Political Studies, University of Michigan, Ann Arbor.

What about voters' knowledge of candidates' positions on important issues? This is a hard question to answer, because it is frequently impossible to determine exactly where candidates stand on controversial issues. Nevertheless, in some cases candidates have made their positions so clear that it is reasonable to ask voters how they perceive these

[1] Among nonvoters ignorance is even greater. For example, only 58 percent of nonvoters knew that a President is limited to two terms; only 19 percent knew the length of a Senator's term; and a mere 20 percent knew the names of both House candidates in their district. These data are from the 1972 American National Elections study conducted by the Center for Political Studies, University of Michigan, Ann Arbor.

views. In 1972, for example, George McGovern, the Democratic candidate for President, repeatedly emphasized his commitment to immediate U.S. withdrawal from Vietnam. Similarly, for years George Wallace had been outspoken in his opposition to school busing to achieve racial integration. What proportion of voters correctly perceived these positions? Surveys done by the University of Michigan in 1972 showed that 89 percent of a national sample correctly perceived McGovern's stand on immediate withdrawal from Vietnam, and 92 percent correctly perceived Wallace's antibusing stand. This suggests that when candidates go to great lengths to make themselves clear, voters *can* accurately perceive their positions.

But where candidates do not make their positions so clear, can voters reach a consensus on what the candidates stand for? Consider the candidates' stands on school busing in the 1976 presidential race. Among voters, 34 percent believed that President Ford favored busing, 46 percent believed that he opposed busing, and 20 percent believed he took the middle position. Perceptions of President Carter's position were also divided: 39 percent believed him to be for busing while 35 percent perceived him to oppose busing. On other important issues of the election, for example, tax policy and women's rights, many voters also disagreed on where the candidates stood.[2]

Does all this mean that the average voter is not informed? Not necessarily. First, some of this ignorance is attributable to the very nature of U.S. politics. Candidates do not always emphasize their positions on issues, and campaigns are not intended to be great educational experiences. Second, the typical voter may not possess a textbook knowledge of government, but he or she is capable of expressing specific likes and dislikes at the polls. Voters upset with economic conditions, a disastrous war, or runaway inflation can and do express these feelings in their vote. In 1932, widespread dissatisfaction with President Hoover's handling of the economy resulted in his being replaced by Franklin Roosevelt. In 1964, millions of voters clearly rejected the conservative policies proposed by Barry Goldwater, the Republican nominee. McGovern's support for immediate U.S. withdrawal from Vietnam was also widely understood (and widely rejected). Voters are perhaps like automobile buyers: few people are competent enough to judge the quality of the engineering, yet they have likes and dislikes that affect their buying decisions. In short, the average voter is somewhere between being uninformed and being a political expert — while not able to explain the minor differences between a Lincoln or a Cadillac, he or she is unlikely to buy an Edsel.[3]

[2] Data reported in the 1976 American National Election Study conducted by the Center for Political Studies, University of Michigan, Ann Arbor.

[3] The question of voter competence is much more complex than our discussion here suggests. See, for example, analyses in V. O. Key, Jr., *The Responsible Electorate* (New York: Vintage Books, 1968), Chap. 1; and Bernard Berelson, "Democratic Theory and Public Opinion," *Public Opinion Quarterly*, 16 (1952), pp. 313–330.

What determines how people vote?

Explaining voting behavior has been a popular exercise for political analysts, campaigners, and just about everyone else interested in politics. As one might expect, no single explanation has been universally accepted. In answering the question, "Why did individual X vote for candidate Y?" we shall present three different and popular explanations. Given all the elections that are held country-wide and the enormous diversity in human behavior, it is more than likely that all three theories contain elements of truth.

ARE MEN RESPONSIBLE ENOUGH TO VOTE?

The issue of whether some citizens are too poorly informed about politics to be allowed to vote frequently surfaced in the battle over extending the vote to women. Opponents asserted that women were too involved in domestic matters to be responsible citizens. They also argued that giving women the vote would encourage emotionalism in politics and destroy family life. Many women vigorously opposed these arguments. One woman—the American novelist and poet Alice Duer Miller—took the offensive in 1915 by questioning the ability of men to vote. Here are her arguments:

Why We Oppose Votes for Men

Because man's place is in the army.

Because no really manly man wants to settle any question otherwise than by fighting about it.

Because if men should adopt peaceable methods women will no longer look up to them.

Because men will lose their charm if they step out of their natural sphere and interest themselves in other matters than feats of arms, uniforms and drums.

Because men are too emotional to vote. Their conduct at baseball games and political conventions shows this, while their innate tendency to appeal to force renders them particularly unfit for the task of government.

PARTY IDENTIFICATION

Party identification Feelings of attachment and loyalty to a political party. Often compared to religious identification. Sometimes abbreviated as "party I.D."

The party-identification explanation contains three elements. First, it maintains that fairly early in life most people (between 60 and 75 percent) acquire a psychological identification with either the Democratic or Republican Party. This feeling of attachment, or **party identification,** is acquired from parents and tends to continue unchanged over a lifetime.

Second, this explanation continues, party identification acts as a powerful filter in the perception of political reality. For example, a Democratic Party identifier is likely to exaggerate the positive aspects of Democratic candidates and their policies while belittling the virtues of Republican candidates.

Third, these perceptual biases lead to consistent voting for the candidates of one's party. Democratic identifiers vote for Democrats, and Republican identifiers vote for Republicans. Such behavior may then be rationalized in terms of voting "for the man, not the party" or on the basis of issues.[4] However, the true explanation is one's deeply ingrained political party loyalty.

Is this explanation correct? Three sets of statistics support the claim that party identification significantly affects voting:

1. In 1976, 81.2 percent of all Democrats who went to the polls voted for Jimmy Carter while 86.1 percent of the Republicans who voted chose Gerald Ford. Of the party identifiers who voted, only 15.8 percent voted for the "wrong" candidate. Moreover, data for previous presidential elections show a similar pattern of party consistency.
2. Over half of all party identifiers voting in 1976 had *always* supported the presidential candidate of their party.
3. Especially at lower levels (for example, congressional elections) where information on candidates' positions is limited, party identification is a very strong predictor of people's voting behavior. In 1974, for example, 82 percent of the party identifiers supported their party's congressional candidates.

Despite these relationships, the party-identification explanation has been criticized. Some people claim that the basic assumption that party identification comes first and then determines voting is exaggerated. People do change party loyalties, the argument goes, and those who change sometimes do so on the basis of issues (for example, a Democrat who does not like Democratic policies becomes a Republican). Therefore, it is said, party identification really is not an unconscious deterministic force. Rather, issues and candidates sometimes help determine party loyalty.[5]

---

[4] A more complete description of the party-identification theory of voting can be found in Angus Campbell, Philip E. Converse, Warren E. Miller, and Donald E. Stokes, *The American Voter* (New York: Wiley, 1960), Chaps. 5 and 6.

[5] The decline of party identification and the relationship between changing parties and issue positions is described more fully in Norman H. Nie, Sidney Verba, and John R. Petrocik, *The Changing American Voter* (Cambridge, Mass.: Harvard University Press, 1976), Chaps. 4 and 5.

A delegate to the 1976 Democratic convention that nominated Jimmy Carter for President. The campaign material makes it clear that the late Mayor Richard J. Daley of Chicago gave his blessing to the Carter nomination.

A second criticism of the party-identification explanation of voting is based on the argument that, for a variety of reasons, party loyalty is becoming less common in U.S. politics. Between 1952 and 1976, for example, the proportion of Independents increased from 22 percent to 36 percent.[6] In addition, even voters who stick with their parties have increasingly crossed party lines to support a candidate of another party.[7] We find, then, that party loyalty is a good predictor of voting, but it is far from being a perfect one.

ISSUE VOTING

The issue-voting explanation may be characterized as the ideal theory for citizens in a democracy to hold because many contemporary democratic notions of politics require that citizens vote on the basis of candidates' positions on government policies. That is, citizens control government by choosing candidates who best reflect popular preferences. How many citizens make their voting decisions on the basis of issues?

This is a complex question because one may vote for a candidate on the basis of some issues yet oppose the candidate's stands on other matters. Moreover, some voters probably choose a candidate first and then justify their decision on the basis of issues afterwards. Nevertheless, let us examine the extent of issue voting in the 1976 presidential election. If the issue explanation of voting is correct, it should at least apply at the presidential level, where issues are most visible.

[6] Warren E. Miller and Teresa E. Levitin, *Leadership and Change: Presidential Elections from 1952 to 1976* (Cambridge, Mass.: Winthrop, 1976), p. 36.

[7] Nie, Verba, and Petrocik, p. 53.

What constitutes voting on the basis of issues? For our purposes, voters will be considered "issue voters" if they choose the candidate closest to their own positions on important issues. For example, if in 1976 one believed that inflation was a crucial issue, and one also believed that President Carter's position was closest to one's own position, then a Carter vote (as opposed to a Ford vote) would be an issue vote.

Table 7.2 shows that at least on the issues of taxes and school busing, most voters decided in accordance with their issue preferences. Voters concerned about taxes who believed Carter to be closer to their own position chose Carter 3 to 1 over Ford (74 percent versus 25 percent). A similar, though perhaps not so strong, pattern emerged on the issue of busing to achieve racial integration. Voters who considered the issue an important one usually sided with the candidate they believed was closest to their own position on busing. In short, though there are many exceptions, people's positions on taxes and busing have helped to predict how they would vote.[8]

TABLE 7.2

ISSUE VOTING IN THE 1976 ELECTION

Issue voting on tax policy	Voted for		
	Carter	Ford	Other
Felt taxes to be important issue and believed CARTER to be closer to their own position on taxes.	74%	25%	1%
Felt taxes to be important issue and believed FORD to be closer to their own position on taxes.	31	67	2

Issue voting on school busing	Voted for		
	Carter	Ford	Other
Felt racial issues-busing to be important issue and believed CARTER to be closer to their own position.	68%	30%	2%
Felt racial issues-busing to be important issue and believed FORD to be closer to their own position.	33	66	2

Source: Center for Political Studies, University of Michigan, Ann Arbor.

GROUP VOTING

The third explanation of voting asserts that people choose candidates on the basis of their group identity. This explanation is behind analyses of elections in terms of bloc voting—"the black vote," "the Catholic vote"—

---

[8] For a more detailed analysis of issue voting in several presidential elections, see Gerald M. Pomper, *Voters' Choice: Varieties of American Political Behavior* (New York: Dodd, Mead, 1975), Chaps. 8 and 9.

and campaign appeals to distinct groups, for example, getting out "the Jewish vote." This explanation is based on two main assumptions. First, its adherents point out that all citizens belong to identifiable groups, for example, blue-collar workers, Jews, Poles, farmers, and that they vote on the basis of these characteristics. They vote either for people like themselves, for example, blacks vote for blacks, or for candidates who best appeal to their own group interests.

The second assumption is that successful candidates put together coalitions of these groups. The classic illustration that is cited is Roosevelt's New Deal coalition, which consisted of workers, poor people, intellectuals, and certain ethnic minorities.

How valid is the group-voting explanation? Like the other two theories, it contains some truth, but here again many problems are associated with it. The best argument in its favor is that in each election a certain amount of **bloc voting** does occur. For example, in the 1976 presidential election blacks and Jews supported Carter over Ford by overwhelming margins. Similar instances of strong group voting can be found at the state and local levels. No doubt further research would uncover cases in almost every election in which groups such as union members, blacks, Catholics, or Chicanos voted more or less in unison.[9]

Nevertheless, as a comprehensive account of voting decisions the group-voting explanation is limited. For one thing, many clearly defined groups have not consistently behaved as a bloc. In presidential elections over the last twenty-five years, for example, Catholics have sometimes voted more or less together (1960 and 1964) and at other times (1956 and 1972) have been divided almost 50-50 in their voting.

A second criticism is that this theory is vague in predicting *which* groups will vote as blocs. That is, even if a group votes together in one election, it is difficult to predict whether it will *continue* to do so in future elections. On the basis of past uniformity in voting behavior one would have predicted extensive bloc voting by Jews for McGovern in the 1972 presidential election. Nevertheless, significant numbers of Jews broke ranks in the Nixon-McGovern contest. A related problem concerns voters with multiple group characteristics. Is the Catholic farmer supposed to vote like a Catholic or like a farmer? What about a middle-class black? Probably one needs to look at the specific situation, but the group explanation is usually not a reliable predictor of the specific characteristic that is likely to matter in a given election.

Overall, then, the group explanation is of limited use. In certain circumstances, for example, in an election in which the issues are closely related to group interests, it may be comparatively useful. Many elections do not offer group-related issues for most groups. More generally, however, this theory of voting is too imprecise to be helpful as a general explanation. It is frequently much easier to see group patterns in past elections than to predict group voting in coming elections.

Bloc voting A group sharing a common goal or characteristic all voting together.

[9] One detailed and influential analysis of voting using this group-characteristic approach is Kevin P. Phillips, *The Emerging Republican Majority* (New York: Doubleday, Anchor Books, 1970).

Do political campaigns have any impact?

Like many other aspects of politics, the significance of political campaigns is both hotly debated and highly complex. We shall address three general questions about the impact of campaigns:

1. How effective are campaigns in swaying voters?
2. Do campaigns inform citizens on the issues?
3. Is the existing style of electoral campaigns reasonably fair to all groups and political interests?

VOTE-SWAYING EFFECTS OF CAMPAIGNS

Judging from the enormous amounts of money, time, and energy expended on campaigns, one would think that they are a powerful political tool. Certainly, many of the advertising consultants, pollsters, and others who earn their livelihoods from them claim that campaigns can make or break candidates. And numerous stories are told of how a brilliant campaign thrust an unknown into a public office. Such claims and stories,

---

CAN PROFESSOR ANDY "BIG MIKE" ANDERSON EVER BE BEATEN?

Voters must frequently choose among dozens of unknown candidates for lower-level offices. What happens when voters have only the limited information given on the ballot to go on? Gary C. Byrne and J. Kristian Pueschel analyzed the results from 500 elections for party central committee in California between 1948 and 1970. These researchers found that the small amount of information given on the ballot about the candidates greatly affected voting. The three most important pieces of information were occupation (which appeared on the ballot), ethnicity of the candidate's name, and whether the candidate had a nickname. On the average, professors had a 74 percent advantage in votes received while real estate brokers, salespersons, and homemakers lost between 20 and 24 percent because of their occupations. Candidates with Scandinavian names usually fared best, while those with Italian names did the worst. Candidates with nicknames received an average of 78 percent more votes than would be predicted by chance!

Gary C. Byrne and J. Kristian Pueschel, "But Who Should I Vote For for Coroner?" *Journal of Politics,* 36 (1974), pp. 778–884.

however, do not address the basic question: Can many voters be swayed? On the whole, campaigns—at least at the presidential level—have only a limited impact on vote changes, but even small shifts in a close election are politically important. Let us consider some of the supporting evidence for this conclusion.

Limits on campaign effectiveness

First, a significant proportion of the electorate decides whom to support for President *before* the campaign even begins. In 1976, a survey conducted by the University of Michigan's Survey Research Center found that 33.3 percent of all voters had made their decisions before the candidates were even nominated, and 54.1 percent had decided by the end of the party nominating conventions but before the campaign. Of course, as a result of primaries some campaigning occurs prior to the nominating convention. Nevertheless, by the time the campaign effort is beginning, about half the potential audience for conversion has already committed its votes.

Second, despite expensive campaign efforts, many voters still manage to avoid direct contact with campaign communications. Exposure to the campaign on television is almost universal, but about half the U.S. public does not follow the campaign on radio or in magazines. Many undecided voters also avoid radio and magazine election coverage. In local races, where campaigns are usually less prominent and interest in politics is lower, there is even less exposure to campaign material.

Third, studies have shown that there are severe obstacles to messages having the desired impact—even if they are received. People misinterpret campaign messages, they selectively forget portions of them, or they garble them in other ways.[10] Such distorted messages may affect the voting decision, but this uncontrolled impact cannot be viewed as evidence of the power of campaigns. More important, however, studies of the effectiveness of political communications indicate that persuasive messages have their greatest effect when they deal with topics about which individuals have weak or nonexisting prior opinions. It is far more likely, for instance, that one could be convinced of life on Jupiter than of the healthful benefits of giving up sex.

The last point is extremely relevant, for rarely do voters face the campaign, the parties, and the candidates with totally blank minds. People typically hold many beliefs and opinions that can influence how they will evaluate campaign messages. A lifelong Democrat who remembers that the Great Depression began under a Republican President is probably predisposed against the Republicans' claim that theirs is the party of prosperity. Similarly, many loyal Republican businesspersons will discount a Democrat's claim that his or her party best supports business interests. It is not that such people never could be convinced. Rather, it

[10] Many studies on this point are described in Joseph T. Klapper, *The Effects of Mass Communications* (New York: Free Press, 1960). Also see Dan Nimmo, *The Political Persuaders* (Englewood Cliffs, N.J.: Prentice-Hall, 1970), Chaps. 4 and 5.

takes far more to overcome long-standing beliefs than is usually possible in an election campaign.

The limitations of campaigns are demonstrated in a study by Patterson and McClure of the impact of television on the changing images of Richard Nixon and George McGovern during the 1972 campaign. In interviews over the course of the campaign the researchers asked people how they felt about the candidates' experience, trustworthiness, and other personal characteristics. Comparing the responses of persons who had watched numerous television commercials with those of people who had watched only a few spot commercials, they found no (or very little) overall difference between the groups in the images they formed of the candidates. Those who were positive toward President Nixon to begin with became even stauncher Nixon supporters if they viewed numerous Nixon commercials. Yet, the same shift in attitude occurred among pro-Nixon viewers who watched only a few Nixon commercials. A similar pattern held for those sympathetic to McGovern — little difference existed between those who watched many or a few McGovern advertisements.[11]

The importance of campaigns

Does this mean that campaigns are a waste of time for candidates? Hardly. In the first place, much of a candidate's campaign effort is directed not at converting members of the opposition but at mobilizing his or her own supporters. Especially considering the low voter turnout in U.S. elections, merely getting one's supporters to the polls can spell victory. Therefore, the failure of a campaign to sway even a single vote does not necessarily mean the campaign failed. A campaign that got every supporter to the polls without a single conversion would be judged an extraordinary success.

Campaigns are also crucial because even though typically they sway only a small portion of the vote, the change they effect may be enough to mean victory or defeat for a candidate. Two or 3 percent of the vote may not seem like much unless one stands to lose by that amount — and then it makes all the difference in the world. The fear of coming out just short of victory is a powerful incentive for a candidate to mount a major campaign effort.

VALUE OF CAMPAIGNS IN EDUCATING CITIZENS

Defenders of extensive (and expensive) political campaigns believe that massive efforts are necessary if voters are to be equipped to make intelligent voting decisions. Without all the speeches, rallies, and media coverage, how will citizens know how to vote, they ask. How will people gain an understanding of the issues and correctly associate candidates and policies?

In general, campaigns do serve to inform voters because they convey an enormous amount of information that reaches virtually everybody in

[11] Thomas E. Patterson and Robert D. McClure, *The Unseeing Eye: The Myth of Television Power in National Politics* (New York: Putnam's, 1976), pp. 111–112.

CAMPAIGNING IN THE GOOD OLD DAYS—CHICAGO STYLE

Modern campaigns are waged largely through the media and frequently emphasize such candidate qualities as leadership ability and trustworthiness. In the "good old days" candidates to a greater extent oriented their campaigns around material benefits for the voters and utilized far more face-to-face contact. Understandably, such old-time elections could get violent, and they often attracted a criminal element. Chicago during the 1920s became famous for gangsterism in election campaigns. How bad were these good old days? Pretty bad! Connie Fletcher provides a short description of one successful politician during this era.

The gangster-politician

In 1928, John "Dingbat" Oberta was elected 13th Ward Republican committeeman and ran for state senator. Oberta had an unusual background in politics. He was a member of the Saltis-McEriane gang, had been indicted for the murder of John Foley in an early twenties bootlegging skirmish, and was wanted for bombing the home of city comptroller Charles Fitzmorris. He ran on a solid gangster platform: "There is too much money for police. I would favor slashing appropriations in that department." On February 28, 1927, Oberta appeared before superior court judge Oscar Hebel with this problem: "Every time a copper sees me, he wants to throw me in the can. They raid my campaign headquarters and everything—and all I'm trying to do is get elected for the good of the town."

The Dingbat was a forceful campaigner. He is credited with obtaining the Senate nomination by having carloads of gangsters travel from polling place to polling place on primary day, threatening election officials and voters. His opponent for ward committeeman, Felix Kucharski, filed a petition against Oberta with county Judge Edmund Jarecki on December 13, 1928. Kucharski claimed that Oberta and pals intimidated poll officials into altering tally sheets and drove Kucharski supporters away from the polls. Oberta's favorite political tactic was to drive through his ward in a car with sawed-off shotguns protruding from the windows. Dingbat used to advise opposing election officials to "take it on the lam."

Oberta's political career ended abruptly on March 6, 1930, when he was taken for a ride in his own Lincoln sedan.

Reprinted from Connie Fletcher, "Every Horse Voted," *Chicago*, November 1976, p. 124.

the country. A campaign provides voters with information about candidates' professional accomplishments, their personalities, and their lifestyles—and this includes tidbits about their families. How many of us would know about the exploits of Billy Carter and all the folk of Plains, Georgia, had it not been for the 1976 presidential campaign? Would we know about Gerald Ford's halcyon football days at the University of Michigan if the media had not enlightened us during the campaign?

Such sidelights on candidates can be important to many voters. Given the difficulty of predicting the postelection behavior of politicians, voters may be sensible to choose candidates on the basis of their personal styles and the images they convey of trustworthiness, honesty, and sincerity rather than on their positions on issues. Since many citizens want such information and find it relevant in voting, by this measure most campaigns are probably informative. To be sure, not everyone cares whether a candidate was a war hero, has a happy marriage, or is religious, but some voters want to know these things, and campaigns typically provide such information.

Informing citizens on issues

What about informing citizens of issue positions? Campaigns may be effective in displaying an aspect of a candidate's personal life, but do television commercials, speeches, billboards, and so forth, really inform citizens about issues? After all, isn't this the ultimate purpose of campaigns? Can voters use campaigns to determine who stands for what?

Unfortunately, even presidential campaigns, which are very visible indeed, do only a limited job of helping citizens discern candidates' views on issues. Voters learn something about issues in campaigns, but not a great deal. Again, the Patterson-McClure study found that people who watched many television commercials had a better knowledge of candidates' stands on issues than did those who watched comparatively few commercials.[12] Recall too that in special instances, for example, McGovern's anti-Vietnam war stand in 1972, a candidate's position is conveyed with enormous clarity. In general, however, even in presidential campaigns the U.S. electorate does not get a complete picture of the candidates' views on important issues. If campaigns are intended to provide numerous well-defined policy alternatives to voters, their purpose is not being accomplished. Recall from our analysis of voter knowledge that only on rare occasions (for example, McGovern's anti-Vietnam position) do citizens agree on where candidates stand on important issues.

Campaigns fail to define candidates' positions on issues for three major reasons. First, most candidates have an incentive to be vague. Vagueness can maximize the number of people who *believe* the candidate agrees with them. To clarify one's position on an issue might serve only to alienate potential supporters. Not surprisingly, studies have shown that in really explosive areas such as school busing, abortion, legalization of marijuana, gun control, and capital punishment, many candidates say many different things to different groups in the hope of

[12] Patterson and McClure, pp. 125–127.

THE THOUSAND DOLLAR MISUNDERSTANDING — OR, THE MEDIUM IS NOT THE MESSAGE

The ease with which issues can become garbled is well illustrated by Senator George McGovern's 1972 plan to give "everyone" a $1,000 income tax credit. His proposal was intended to increase the income of poor people. Wealthier citizens would have lost $1,000 as a function of increased tax rates. Despite McGovern's efforts at clarification, many people believed that the proposal meant that everyone would simply get a $1,000 government handout. The same kind of confusion followed Jimmy Carter's 1976 promise to increase taxes on incomes above the *median* income and lower taxes on those below the *median* income. ("Median" is a statistical term that indicates the line dividing a series of numbers into two equal parts.) President Ford, like many college students in statistics courses, misinterpreted the concept of "median." For a while he attacked Carter's program because it would raise taxes on *medium*-income people. Eventually, however, Ford acknowledged his mistake. Unfortunately, many citizens do not even know when they are misinterpreting a candidate's position on an issue. It should be obvious why in a campaign many complex questions become oversimplified or avoided entirely.

appealing to virtually everyone.[13] From a candidate's point of view this is a reasonable strategy.

Second, the news media do not always emphasize the specific issues that divide the candidates. The differences are often subtle and complex, and since neither the media nor the public see them as "newsworthy," they get little press coverage. Television, newspapers, and radio today are more oriented to reporting action-type stories than to describing in detail a candidate's stance on a government policy.[14] If specific issue positions are covered, it is usually because the media are playing up some special "angle" — for example, a Catholic candidate in a Catholic area endorses abortion. News programs and magazines that do stress issues rarely attract attention.

Finally, comparatively few citizens are motivated enough to seek out issue positions from the deluge of campaign information. It is possible, of course, for an ambitious voter who follows a campaign closely to determine exactly where each candidate stands on key issues, but few peo-

[13] One such study is Benjamin I. Page and Richard A. Brody, "Policy Voting and the Electoral Process: The Vietnam Issue," *American Political Science Review*, 66 (1972), pp. 979–995.

[14] Doris A. Graber, "Press and TV as Opinion Resources in Presidential Campaigns," *Public Opinion Quarterly*, 40 (1976), pp. 285–303.

Madison Avenue marketing At one time, most major advertising agencies were located on Madison Avenue in New York City, so that Madison Avenue came to be identified with promoting a product. Thus "Madison Avenue marketing" means to sell something through elaborate promotion, exaggeration, and media use.

ple are willing to make such an effort. Moreover, the highly motivated citizens who might expend the effort are typically so deeply committed to their own candidate that acquiring information about other candidates does not change their vote. It could even be argued that it is irrational for ordinary citizens to obtain crystal-clear information on candidates' positions on issues. Many candidates do not take definite stands on many issues (or will not publicly reveal them). Even if they did, what would they predict about their future behavior and policy? In short, given the lack of interest on the part of the voters in issue politics, there is only so much the candidates and the media can accomplish.

POLITICAL FAIRNESS OF CAMPAIGNS

A common complaint about electoral politics is that not all groups and individuals have an equal chance for public office. In particular, it is frequently alleged that the vast sums required for contemporary campaigns discriminate against poorer candidates and interests. It is also claimed that in this era of **Madison Avenue marketing** of candidates an unfair advantage accrues to candidates who can manipulate the media. Are these charges true?

MONEY AND CAMPAIGNS

An obvious feature of contemporary political campaigns is their great cost. One campaign finance expert estimates that it cost Richard Nixon and Spiro Agnew $50 million to get elected President and Vice President in 1972, while George McGovern spent $38 million in his losing effort.[15] In 1976, the campaigns of both major parties were publicly financed, but even so, much money was required in the early stages before public money was available.

Congressional, state, and local elections may be cheaper, but even here the costs are impressive. Common Cause—a public interest lobby group —estimates that in 1972 the average Democratic member of Congress spent $47,500 for reelection, compared to $47,600 for the typical Republican (and these figures included uncontested or lopsided races—where the race was close, the average winner spent $107,400).[16] Races for the Senate and governorships in large states now routinely run a million dollars or more. In 1970, Nelson Rockefeller spent nearly $9 million to win reelection as governor of New York. North Carolina Senator Jesse Helmes spent $6.7 million in his successful 1978 reelection campaign (his opponent spent $217,000). The average 1978 Senate campaign cost $900,000 (winners averaged $1.2 million)—an increase of 40 percent over 1976 figures. Clearly, then, one cannot get very far in state or national politics without substantial financial backing.

Such expenditures raise a crucial question: Does the requirement for

[15] David W. Adamany, "Financing National Politics," in Robert Agranoff, ed., *The New Style in Election Campaigns*, 2d ed. (Boston: Holbrook Press, 1976), p. 382.

[16] Adamany, "Financing National Politics," p. 383.

REPLACING FAT CATS WITH COOL CATS

It is frequently difficult to anticipate the consequences of campaign reform. Such reform may not reduce ''unfair advantage'' as much as it takes this advantage away from one interest and gives it to a different one. The 1974 Campaign Act was in part directed against business interests that have traditionally been large campaign donors. The law limited financial donations but not donations of services. Many candidates quickly realized that the free services of a famous entertainer are worth millions. Thus music stars such as the Allman Brothers, The Eagles, Joan Baez, and many others gave benefit concerts for candidates. A well-known rock star like Bob Dylan could probably raise a

Jimmy Carter poses with two members of the Marshall Tucker Band. Marshall Tucker had given a benefit concert for Carter's campaign in 1976.

million dollars for a candidate, and all of it would be legal as long as it was not a direct personal transaction. This allowance of unlimited donations of services seems to help more liberal candidates who have greater access to entertainment figures. Future presidential candidates in search of funds may have to appeal to the likes of Alice Cooper or Linda Ronstadt for support instead of to the president of General Motors.

enormous campaign war chests bias electoral politics in favor of wealthy interests? Our somewhat speculative answer is: "Yes, but not overwhelmingly so." The money requirement gives wealthy interests an advantage, but this advantage is not the same thing as domination of elections.

It is *not* true that one can automatically buy public office with massive amounts of money. Obviously, many wealthy people have been successful in politics, for example, the Kennedys and the Rockefellers. But there are also cases like the one of Richard Ottinger who used $3.9 million of his family's money in an unsuccessful try to win a New York Senate seat. In 1970, Norton Simon spent $2 million to his opponent's $637,761, but failed to capture the Republican nomination for Senator in California. And even though Nelson Rockefeller was successful in winning four terms as governor of New York, his family fortune—which could have easily financed a lavish presidential campaign—did not get him the Republican presidential nomination he so avidly sought.

Nor is vast personal wealth essential for political success. It helps to be a du Pont or a Heinz (two successful well-off politicians), but U.S. politics is not strictly a rich man's sport. Consider, for example, the financial backgrounds of recent presidential contenders such as Jimmy Carter, Gerald Ford, Richard Nixon, George McGovern, George Wallace, and Barry Goldwater. Though hardly impoverished, none originally came from very wealthy backgrounds. Their personal wealth might have appeared large to the ordinary citizen, but they were a long way from being in the multimillion dollar category. In terms of financial assets, they were much closer to successful small businesspersons than captains of industry.

We must also realize that merely because winners usually outspend losers does not necessarily mean that victory was due to the difference in expenditures. In many instances a candidate who looks like a winner will attract considerably more financial support because people would rather donate to a winner than to a loser. In fact, virtually unbeatable candidates or those with no opposition frequently receive sizable contributions, and this can give the misleading impression that the more one spends, the bigger one wins.

Finally, even though much money is required for a respectable campaign, the money need not be raised exclusively from the very rich (or "fat cats," as substantial contributors are sometimes called). Obviously, it is easier to raise vast sums from a few major sources, but it is also possible to raise millions of dollars by soliciting large numbers of small contributors. George Wallace, for example, raised 85 percent of the money for his 1968 presidential campaign ($5.76 million) from 750,000 people who gave less than $100 each.[17] Indeed, in the wake of the 1974 campaign finance regulations, which limit contributions to candidates in federal elections, campaigns based on large numbers of small contributions will probably now be the norm.

Nonfinancial resources can sometimes be substituted for financial ones. Financial difficulties can be partially overcome if supporters work for nothing and friendly groups provide free meeting places, computers, telephones, and other vital campaign requirements. Corporations and labor unions, prohibited from making cash contributions, frequently provide many campaign services with no money changing hands. Several candidates—notably Eugene McCarthy in 1968—have made great

---

[17] Adamany, "Financing National Politics," p. 393.

use of student volunteers to do everything from stuffing envelopes to campaigning door to door.

The consequences of expensive campaigns

The above considerations do not mean that money does not give an advantage to the rich. In the first place, there are enough instances of campaign contributions having actually bought desired policies to indicate that campaign money can be an important political weapon. On occasion Presidents "just happened" to appoint substantial campaign contributors to ambassadorships and other positions of power. For example, Maxwell H. Gluck, a dress-shop chain owner, was appointed Ambassador to Ceylon by President Dwight Eisenhower. Gluck had contributed $26,000 to Ike's reelection campaign in 1956. Matthew McClosky, a longtime Democratic contributor and fund raiser, was John F. Kennedy's choice for Ambassador to Ireland. President Johnson appointed Edward Clock, a wealthy Texas lawyer and confidant, Ambassador to Australia. President Nixon appointed several major contributors to diplomatic posts, the most prominent being Walter Annenberg (publisher of *TV Guide*, among other things), whom he named Ambassador to Great Britain. For many years it was alleged that there were specific prices for ambassadorships, depending on the size and prestige of the nation involved—$10,000 might be enough for Latin America, but a major European nation like France was in the $100,000 plus category.[18]

More insidious, however, is the long list of public scandals suggesting a close relationship between large campaign contributions and political favors. As with the sale of ambassadorships, it is usually difficult to show a precise connection between the donation and the benefit. In 1966, for example, top executives of the Anheuser-Busch brewery contributed $10,000 to a Lyndon Johnson campaign fund. Shortly afterward, without any explanation, a long-standing antitrust suit against Anheuser-Busch was dropped by the Justice Department.[19] During the Nixon Administration, the efforts of International Telephone and Telegraph (ITT) and the dairy industry to buy influence are well documented.[20] According to Common Cause, the American Medical Association (AMA) donated more than $85,000 to nineteen House of Representatives Commerce Committee members who supported the organization's position on a hospital-cost containment bill.[21] By no means does our government sell favors to the highest bidder. Many bribes are unsuccessful, and numerous public officials cannot be bought. It is true, however, that major contributors have had considerable success in politics.

Less obvious than outright bribery, however, are the indirect con-

---

[18] George Thayer, *Who Shakes the Money Tree?* (New York: Simon & Schuster, 1973), pp. 146–147.

[19] Thayer, p. 145.

[20] See Mark J. Green, James M. Fallows, and David R. Zwick, *Who Runs Congress?* (New York: Bantam Books, 1972), Chap. 1.

[21] Cited in "One $6 Million Man Is Enough," *Christian Science Monitor*, November 9, 1978.

sequences of the need for campaign money. Because of the ever-present need for money, candidates and their organizations must devote a great deal of time to fund raising. Especially at the beginning of campaigns, when name recognition may be low and other resources (for example, party support and government subsidies) are not yet available, lining up the money can become a major task. Even if no direct bribery occurs in this process, the need for money probably affects the candidate's frame of mind. Lest they offend potential backers, candidates must be cautious and try to please many diverse interests because no single group can usually finance an entire campaign. In addition, candidates must calculate campaign tactics in terms of money (for example, a speech to twenty-five "fat cats" is worth more than mingling with one hundred college students). Whether these subtle constraints on candidates are good or bad is a moot point, but it seems probable that much of the hectic nature of U.S. campaigns and political bargaining can be traced to the ever-present need for money. Equally important, once in office politicians must weigh their actions in terms of how they might affect future fund raising.

CAMPAIGNS AND MADISON AVENUE HUCKSTERISM

With the emergence of slick advertising techniques, the increasing reliance of campaigns on the media, and the big "hype," some people argue that candidates are merchandised like deodorant or "Star Wars." Not only does this demean the electoral process, but it greatly affects the types of candidates and issues presented to the public. Specifically, some people argue that thanks to modern advertising techniques, it is now possible to package even an unattractive candidate as a brilliant and sincere leader. The emphasis on the media also provides, according to the Madison Avenue hucksterism argument, an enormous advantage to those who come across well on television, that is, attractive people with nice smiles. The net result is that the U.S. public buys shoddy merchandise attractively packaged. Is this argument correct? While some supporting evidence exists, in general, Madison Avenue hucksterism is overexaggerated.

The evidence for the Madison Avenue hucksterism argument

One supporting fact is that the recent emergence of public relations firms whose prime function is to manage campaigns. These firms handle everything from conducting a poll to staffing a campaign headquarters to writing speeches to providing research on which issues to endorse. For better or worse, then, many candidates are in the good hands of people experienced in merchandising Alka Seltzer or Preparation H. The advertising people are joined by a vast number of political consultants who, for a fee, will advise candidates on issues, campaigning, and running their organizations.

A second piece of supporting evidence is provided by the innumerable examples of professional, well-run campaigns that have transformed unknowns into potent political personalities. One particularly famous

"*I was packaged by Candidates Limited. Who packaged you?*"
Drawing by Handelsman; © 1970 The New Yorker Magazine, Inc.

example is Ronald Reagan's successful quest for the California governorship in 1966. Reagan started with severe handicaps. Though a well-known actor, his lack of political experience was equally well known. In addition, he was widely perceived as being highly conservative in a largely liberal state. To overcome these disadvantages Reagan employed the public relations firm of Spencer-Roberts. What then occurred was almost a model merchandising campaign. Reagan's political inexperience was handled by making it a virtue, not a defect. Reagan would claim it was time for "ordinary citizens like you and me to bring some common sense thinking" to all the problems created by "professional politicians." His image was carefully nurtured to show him as youthful, vigorous, moderate, responsible, and decent, and he was scheduled to appear at numerous carefully planned dinners, community meetings, and rallies. A team of psychologists conducted in-depth interviews on Reagan's image as an "extremist" and then advised him to avoid the matter entirely and instead emphasize taxes, government spending, and morality.[22] Reagan won decisively and went on to become a major figure in national politics.

The limits of political merchandising

Does the Ronald Reagan case apply to most other elections? Does success rest completely on the right advertising campaign? Such a campaign may occasionally be victorious, but its effects should not be exaggerated. First, just as high-powered advertising campaigns for soap sometimes fail, so do some on behalf of political candidates. For every Reagan-like success story, there are ones like Sol Wachtler's, who lost his

[22] Robert Agranoff, "Professional Campaign Management," in Agranoff, pp. 54–55.

This cartoon was published in November 1974. In July 1978, Nick M. Belluso, a candidate in the Georgia gubernatorial primary, announced that he had hired a "renowned hypnotist" to cast a spell over voters during a 50-second TV commercial shortly before primary election day. (Belluso also said that if this failed, he might try "levitating" above the Peachtree Plaza Hotel in Atlanta.) The TV station (WTCG) appealed to the Federal Communications Commission (FCC) to be allowed to censor this

FRANKLY SPEAKING....by phil frank

© College Media Services, Box 9411, Berkeley Ca. 94709.

hypnotic campaign pitch on the grounds that it constituted a "clear danger to the public health and safety." Despite warnings from two psychiatrists that some viewers might go into a trance and others might become disoriented, the FCC did not let WTCG censor Belluso's commercial. In any case, Belluso lost the primary.

race for Nassau County (New York) executive despite an extensive $700,000 campaign directed by a sophisticated public relations firm.[23] If both candidates for the same office employ sophisticated marketing techniques, inevitably one set of merchandisers must lose.

Second, despite claims that advertising people will do anything for a buck, deceptive merchandising is generally frowned upon by most advertising and public relations firms. Many advertising executives stress the distinctions between actively helping a candidate and outright deception

[23] Walter Troy Spencer, "The Agency Knack of Political Packaging," in Agranoff, p. 89.

POLITICS IS FUNNIER THAN HUMOR DEPARTMENT, PART 2

A clever politician does not have to imply that his or her opponent is a Communist in order to destroy the person's reputation. Character assassination can be done with class. In his 1950 campaign for the Florida Senate seat of Claude Pepper, George Smathers let it be known that Pepper had practiced nepotism, had a sister who was a thespian, a brother who

"I have never stooped, my friends, nor will I now stoop, to the kind of vicious falsehoods, mud-slinging, and personal vilification indulged in by my opponent and his Commie pals."

Drawing by Whitney Darrow, Jr., © 1956 The New Yorker Magazine, Inc.

was a *Homo sapien,* and when in college had matriculated. Smathers won. In addition, during the election voters were reminded of Pepper's liberal voting record in the Senate by references to "Red Pepper."

to sell shoddy goods. Moreover, even if devious image making were acceptable, the ever-present danger of exposure by the press or one's opponents acts as a deterrent. Sooner or later a newly created "plastic" image will develop cracks.[24]

[24] Spencer, pp. 89–90.

Finally, even the slickest campaign cannot operate independently of the candidate, the issues of the day, and unforeseen events. Short of locking the candidate in a closet, little can be done to keep him or her out of potential trouble. The most carefully prepared speech can be read incoherently; staged events can be ruined by slips of the tongue (recall President Ford's slip in the 1976 presidential television debates to the effect that Poland was not under Soviet influence); and researchers can miscalculate the public mood. Perhaps even more important, many experienced political leaders refuse to be marketed like deodorant. Professional advertising people can offer advice, but most politicians possess their own perspectives and beliefs and are not willing to be made into a "new and improved" product.

This does not mean that clever merchandising is completely irrelevant politically. Especially with political newcomers (for example, Ronald Reagan in 1966), it may be extremely important. In close races where a few votes are crucial, an expensive, elaborate campaign might determine the outcome. On the whole, however, Madison Avenue hucksterism hardly appears to be an overwhelming threat to the integrity of the electoral process. It occurs, but it is not a dominant feature of elections.

WHY RUN WHEN YOU CAN WALK OR JOG FOR THE SENATE?

A major reason for the high cost of campaigns is the increased reliance of candidates on the mass media. In the past a politician might rely on scores of party workers, the support of friends, endorsements, or past favors such as a job or intervention in an immigration case. Today, however, the emphasis is on television, newspapers, and radio, and these can be very expensive. To overcome these costs (and state and national campaign expenditure limits), candidates have devised numerous ways to make themselves "newsworthy" and thus get free media attention.

A common tactic is to walk a lot (a strategy pioneered by Dan Walker, who was elected governor of Illinois in 1972). In 1970, Lawton Chiles walked from Pensacola, Florida, to Key West, won the Senate election, and became known as "Walkin' Lawton." Hamilton C. Horton, a North Carolina Republican, campaigned in 1978 by taking a 17-day, 218-mile journey through the fifth congressional district (he lost). Going one step quicker, Donald Shasteen jogged from one side of Nebraska to the other (471 miles) as part of his Senate election campaign (he too lost).

Working odd jobs to be a "regular fellow" is another good method of

MAKING CAMPAIGNS FAIRER

A common complaint throughout U.S. history has been that campaigns have provided wealthy interests an unfair advantage. Unfortunately, few critics have agreed exactly on what was "unfair" or who was the evil force corrupting the system. As a result, campaign reform was rare and usually very limited. Several laws were passed in the early part of the twentieth century forbidding certain corporations, such as banks, from contributing to federal election campaigns and otherwise limiting campaign contributions. Such legislation had little impact. For example, a 1940 law limiting a political committee to expenditures of $3 million a year was easily circumvented by the creation of many separate committees such as Democrats for Kennedy, Citizens for Roosevelt, and so on.

In the 1970s, however, in an effort to curb abuses, Congress toughened its stance on the sources and uses of campaign money. In 1971 and 1974, legislation was enacted that greatly affected campaign financing of federal (but not state and local) elections. The essential features are as follows.

---

getting lots of free media attention. Between mid-July and early October 1978, Edward L. Young of South Carolina worked a number of one-day jobs as part of his gubernatorial campaign (as restaurant waiter, shrimp boat worker, and cement layer, to name a few). He lost anyhow. Bob Graham of Florida went from a 3-percent rating in the polls to the Democratic nominee for governor after working at some 100 odd jobs ranging from garbage collector to grocery store bagboy (as a millionaire he hardly needed the money). He won.

Odd names can also be used to attract free publicity. When George Firestone ran for secretary of state in Florida, his campaign used the "Firestone Blimp" and the slogan "It's a good year for Firestone." In Wyoming, Hugh Binford sought the Republican Senate nomination under the name "Bigfoot" (he lost).

Such stunts represent only the most obvious ways of getting free publicity to reduce the cost of campaigning. Less obvious, but probably more common, are well-publicized investigative trips, question and answer sessions, dramatic announcements of routine information, and numerous other media "events." It seems likely that further attempts to reduce campaign spending, coupled with higher and higher media prices, will encourage more activities along these lines.

These and other incidents are further described in "Odd Jobs and Other Campaign Gimmicks," *Christian Science Monitor,* October 12, 1978.

Contribution limits

An individual may annually give up to $1,000 to each candidate for each election in which the person runs (a general election and primary count as separate elections). Annual donations by individuals of $5,000 for each political action committee and $25,000 for each national political party committee are also permitted. No individual may donate more than $25,000 in a single year. However, the Supreme Court in *Buckley* v. *Valeo* (1976) ruled that there are *no* limits on what can be spent *on behalf* of a candidate, provided the candidate does not control the funds. Nor does this reform limit a candidate's expenditure of personal funds. In other words, an ordinary citizen may organize an unlimited campaign for a favorite candidate, and rich candidates may freely use their own resources. Finally, there are no limits on the contribution of personal services to a candidate.

Government campaign subsidies

The Federal Election Campaign Act of 1974 created a Presidential Election Campaign Fund that derives its income from a voluntary income tax form checkoff that allows citizens to allocate $1 to $2 to the fund each year. This money goes *only* to presidential candidates to cover primary election expenses, the cost of nominating conventions, and general election expenses. In the primaries federal money is dispensed to match private contributions once a certain minimum amount is collected. The major parties each receive $2 million, plus adjustments for cost-of-living increases, for their nominating conventions.

Limits on candidate spending

Campaign spending limits apply only to presidential candidates. In primaries candidates have a choice: they can spend without limit or, if they accept federal subsidies, they can spend up to $200,000 or 16 cents for each resident of voting age (whichever is larger) in each state. In the general election candidates who accept public funding are limited to $20 million, plus a percentage for cost-of-living increases. Several provisions in the 1974 act, however, allow for expenditures beyond this limit—for example, state committees may make expenditures on behalf of national candidates.

Disclosures of contributions

The names and addresses of all persons donating $100 or more, as well as expenditures of $100 or more, must be reported to a six-member Federal Election Commission which monitors and enforces campaign financing regulations.

A similar reform movement is also underway at the state level. As of 1976, forty-nine states required that campaign contributions be disclosed, twenty-five states had bipartisan election commissions to enforce campaign funding rules, and twenty-two states limited the size of individual contributions. In addition, numerous states are experimenting with various means to subsidize campaigns with state money.[25]

THE IMPACT OF CAMPAIGN REFORM   Will these new regulations eliminate the "unfair" use of money in politics or reduce the role of wealthy contributors? They will probably have some effect, but a dramatic change seems unlikely. First, despite all these reforms, there are still many elections in which constraints on contributors are nonexistent or very limited. Second, there are enough special provisions and ambiguities to allow determined contributors to use their resources to advantage. Even in presidential races there are many perfectly legal ways of soliciting substantial amounts of money. A candidate might accept a loan rather than a gift with the understanding that it will not be paid back. Another way of avoiding campaign limitations is for candidates to delay declaring their candidacy, since campaign financing laws apply only to official candidates. Third, while penalties are provided for violations of the recent laws, enforcement of them is difficult. As the Watergate affair demonstrated, the in's and out's of campaign financing can be extremely complicated. Given hundreds of organizations and perhaps millions of contributors, adequate policing may be nearly impossible.

The adaptability of contributors to campaign expenditure limits is well illustrated by the recent emergence of **Political Action Committees (PACs)** among business and labor groups. Until 1971, union and corporate campaign contributions were explicitly prohibited. With the passage of the Federal Election Campaign Act of 1971, however, corporations and unions have been permitted to establish, administer, and solicit campaign funds. In 1976, amendments to the law allowed corporations and unions who do business with the government (which includes most large corporations and unions) to organize Political Action Committees (PACs). This opened a floodgate for corporate and union involvement. By November 1978, 1,700 PACs were officially registered. Though federal law limits solicitations to management and stockholders in businesses (but all members of unions) and restricts individual donations to $5,000 annually per PAC, these committees have become a potent political force. In 1976, corporate and business-related PACs donated $8.1 million. In 1978, with no presidential race, PACs spent over $60 million. The PAC Committee of the American Medical Association spent $1.6 million on the 1978 election, making it the largest single PAC (the PAC of the National Realtors Association was second with $1.1 million). Many of these PACs identify themselves by names that one would not associate with large corporations. For example, the Nonpartisan Political Action Committee, which gave $112,020 to candidates in 1978, is run by General Electric.[26]

PAC Political action committee. An organization established by corporations, unions, or trade associations to solicit and spend money for political campaigns.

[25] Herbert E. Alexander, *Financing Politics: Money, Elections and Political Reform* (Washington, D.C.: Congressional Quarterly Press, 1976), p. 189. For a more general discussion of reforming campaign finance laws, see David W. Adamany, *Campaign Finance in America* (North Scituate, Mass.: Duxbury Press, 1972), Chap. 7.

[26] For more information on PACs, see Charles W. Hucker, "Corporate Political Action Committees," *Practical Politics*, Vol. 1, May/June 1978, pp. 21–25; and "One $6 Million Man Is Enough."

Finally, vigorous government efforts to limit campaign contributions can run up against major constitutional restrictions. In the *Buckley* v. *Valeo* (1976) case, for example, the Supreme Court, relying on the First Amendment's guarantee of freedom of speech, ruled that spending one's own money on behalf of a candidate or issue could not be restricted (though direct contributions to candidates could under the Constitution be limited). Legal scholars have also speculated that limiting the expenditures of all candidates may give incumbents an advantage and thus violate the Fourteenth Amendment, which guarantees to all citizens "the equal protection of the laws." That is, since the incumbent already possesses many advantages such as a name that is generally recognized, free mailing privileges, benefits to dispense, and easier access to the media, a challenger may have to spend more just to be equal.[27] In short, eliminating allegedly unfair campaign practices can quickly collide with guarantees of political freedom to all citizens.

A conclusion: voting, campaigns, and citizen control of government

We have examined a considerable amount of material on individual voters and political campaigns. What can we make of all this information? Does it prove that U.S. elections are meaningless illusions of citizen rule? Or, on the other hand, does our analysis show that our elections are an effective means by which citizens control their destinies?

Obviously, neither argument is entirely correct. In general, voters in the United States are not well informed, do not always vote on issues, and have occasionally been manipulated by clever public relations campaigns. At the same time, however, voters can reject objectionable candidates and resist lavishly funded campaign efforts.

Perhaps the best way of characterizing individual voting and electoral campaigns is to consider them as general and imprecise mechanisms that affect the direction of government. Elections do not determine policy directly. The electoral system is biased against their playing this role, while voters are probably incapable of dealing with the complexities of lawmaking. Nevertheless, by eliminating grossly objectionable leaders and policies, voters exercise some degree of influence. Elections are much better at serving as filtering devices to eliminate unwanted candidates than they are at serving as precise mechanisms of popular control of policy making.

How one accepts this characterization depends on how one views the ordinary citizen. If the average voter is viewed as politically knowledgeable, reasonable, and involved, then the crudeness of this control mechanism is objectionable. From this perspective, U.S. politics would

[27] Some of these legal issues are discussed further in Albert Cover, "The Constitutionality of Campaign Expenditure Ceilings," *Policy Studies Journal*, Vol. 2 (Summer 1974), pp. 267–273.

be improved by giving citizens greater direct influence. On the other hand, if one believes that the average voter possesses only a limited amount of political judgment, then the limited electoral influence of voters is acceptable. After all, who wants millions of ill-informed citizens deciding government policy? Moreover, as we observed in Chapter 6, this limited role of elections is what the Founding Fathers intended. They understood the limitations of ordinary citizens and thus designed a system that would work *in spite of* uninformed voters and circuslike campaigns.

Perhaps the easiest way to answer our original question — Should elections give citizens more influence? — is to ask: Would *you* let the U.S. public make crucial decisions affecting *your* life? Whom would you trust to make key decisions affecting you — the people themselves or elected leaders?

Major questions raised

1. How politically knowledgeable is the average voter? An important prior question is: How knowledgeable should the average voter be? If you expect most citizens to be highly informed about politics, you'll be disappointed. In general, citizens have only a limited knowledge and understanding of the workings of government. Nevertheless, the level of competence may be adequate for making the types of crude choices allowed by our electoral system.

2. What determines how citizens vote? There are no simple, perfect explanations. Party identification and issues are important factors. It is also claimed that group identity plays an important role, but the evidence is less supportive for this explanation.

3. Do campaigns really have an impact? Yes, but not as much as some people claim. Campaigns are not able to sway large numbers of voters, greatly inform the public, or allow unknown incompetents to get elected. Campaigns generally have a limited impact. However, where elections are close, even a small vote shift may be crucial. For this reason campaigns are an important part of electoral politics. Numerous attempts have recently been made to reform campaign financing, but their long-term effect remains to be seen.

QUESTIONS FOR FURTHER DISCUSSION

1. A perennial problem in U.S. elections is how to handle "dirty" or "unfair" charges made against candidates. Many an officeholder has won election by suggesting that his or her opponent was "soft on communism" or "linked to the underworld," when, in fact, there was no evidence to support these damaging charges. By the time the charges are investigated and proved false, the election is part of history. Should there be some method of controlling campaign accusations *before* they are made? Should individual television stations and newspapers exercise the right to refuse advertisements that *might* contain untrue state-

ments? On the other hand, is a certain amount of "dirty politics" the necessary price for freedom of expression?

2. Election turnout is not very high in the United States. In the 1976 elections, 54.4 percent of the eligible population voted for President (in 1972 the figure was 55.5 percent). In nonpresidential years the turnout is even lower — 36.1 percent in 1974, for example. Other nations have a much better record. In a recent Albanian election only one registered voter failed to vote, and a mere three spoiled their ballots. In June 1978, the African nation of Sierra Leone had a turnout of 103 percent (*New York Times*, November 22, 1978). What might be the impact on election campaigns if the United States reached these levels of voter turnout? Would a higher turnout improve the quality of public debate over the issues? What might be the impact on the cost of running for office?

3. Many discussions of voting implicitly assume that voting on the basis of nonpolitical characteristics such as a candidate's appearance, personality, or record of church attendance is wrong, while deciding on the basis of issues is good. Can the use of nonpolitical criteria be justified? Is it wrong for someone to say, "I won't vote for candidate X because he looks tricky?" Under what conditions might nonpolitical traits be more relevant than a candidate's position on issues?

4. In order to get a driver's license one must demonstrate a minimal knowledge of driving rules (for example, what traffic signs mean). No such minimum competency rules apply to voting. Yet it could be argued that choosing leaders wisely is as important as driving a car properly. If it could be administered without bias and with the same standards for every citizen, would you endorse a minimum voter competency requirement? After all, since we require prospective citizens to demonstrate a knowledge of U.S. history and politics, why can't we expect all citizens to demonstrate their civic competency?

BIBLIOGRAPHY

Agranoff, Robert. *The New Style Election Campaigns*, 2d ed. Boston: Holbrook Press, 1976.
> An excellent collection of articles on campaigning, many of which are written by professional campaigners. Particularly relevant for information on the impact of the media.

Alexander, Herbert E. *Financing Politics: Money, Elections and Political Reform*. Washington, D.C.: Congressional Quarterly Press, 1976.
> An excellent and comprehensive analysis of money in politics written by the leading authority on the subject. Contains material on the impact of money on election victories, the various sources of campaign money, reform at the national and state levels, and the actual texts of various laws affecting campaign financing. Contains a good bibliography.

Campbell, Angus, Philip E. Converse, Warren E. Miller, and Donald E. Stokes. *The American Voter*. New York: Wiley, 1960.
> Though based on 1952 and 1956 surveys, *The American Voter* remains the most comprehensive analysis of voting behavior. The hard-cover edition in particular, though sometimes fairly technical, is a good place to begin in trying to understand the factors that affect individual voting behavior.

Key, V. O., Jr. *The Responsible Electorate*. New York: Vintage Books, 1968.
> Based upon numerous surveys conducted between 1936 and 1960, Key argues that voters do behave in a reasonable, intelligent fashion. Much of Key's analysis rests on the issue positions of those who change the party they vote for from one presidential election to the next.

Miller, Warren E., and Teresa E. Levitin. *Leadership and Change: Presidential Elections from 1952 to 1976.* Cambridge, Mass.: Winthrop Publishers, 1976.
> Based on the extensive opinion surveys conducted during each presidential election from 1952 to 1976 by the University of Michigan, the authors consider numerous issues, including the alleged decline of party loyalty, citizen perceptions of political leaders, and preferences on different public policies. Most of the book is concerned with the emergence and impact of the "new politics" of the 1960s. This "new politics" is associated with the rise of a counterculture, protests against established institutions, and rejection of repressive agents of social control.

Napolitan, Joseph. *The Elections Game and How To Win It.* New York: Doubleday, 1972.
> The author is one of the nation's foremost political consultants. This book relates his experiences in several campaigns and provides a wealth of insights into sophisticated campaigning (for example, the advantage of radio over television in reaching specific audiences). Contains a good chapter on the use of opinion polls in campaigns.

Neuborne, Burt, and Arthur Eisenberg. *The Rights of Candidates and Voters.* New York: Avon Books, 1976.
> A brief but fact-filled compilation on such issues as who can vote, who can get on the ballot, the guarantees provided by the different voting rights acts, and the content (and court interpretations) of campaign reform laws. Organized in a convenient question and answer format.

Nie, Norman H., Sidney Verba, and John R. Petrocik. *The Changing American Voter.* Cambridge, Mass.: Harvard University Press, 1976.
> A detailed, and sometimes complex, analysis of American voting behavior relying on data collected between 1939 and 1974. An especially good analysis of how voter issue orientation and party loyalty have changed over time. Also contains good coverage of how voters from different social, racial, and geographical groups have behaved in the last twenty years or so.

Niemi, Richard G., and Herbert F. Weisberg. *Controversies in American Voting Behavior.* San Francisco: Freeman, 1976.
> A collection of thirty articles examining different aspects of U.S. voting behavior. Some of the articles are fairly technical, but this book brings together some of the most current work on voting.

Patterson, Thomas E., and Robert D. McClure. *The Unseeing Eye: The Myth of Television Power in National Politics.* New York: Putnam, 1976.
> A systematic analysis of the impact of television on people's perceptions of candidates and issues. Basically asserts that television has less of an impact than is widely claimed.

Pomper, Gerald M. *Voters' Choice: Varieties of American Electoral Behavior.* New York: Dodd, Mead, 1975.
> A wide-ranging analysis of many important topics in voting behavior. Considers, for example, the role of party loyalty, social class, sex, age, and race in voting. Also deals with the concerns of voters and whether the typical voter has become more issue oriented over time. A good source of statistical information on voters across a number of elections.

Rosenbloom, David Lee. *The Election Mess: Professional Campaign Managers and American Democracy.* New York: Quadrangle Books, 1973.
> An in-depth examination of professional public experts who manage political campaigns. Argues that professional managers are not responsible to the public and are thus undermining democratic government. Contains several short case studies of professionally managed campaigns.

Thayer, George. *Who Shakes the Money Tree?* New York: Simon & Schuster, 1973.
> A well-written nontechnical review of political money in the United States from the campaign of George Washington to the early 1970s. Contains numerous behind-the-scenes stories of campaign financing.

PREVIEW

What are political parties?

U.S. political parties are comprised of three elements: citizens, party officials, and elected officeholders. Psychologically most people identify with either the Democratic or the Republican Party. The parties have no control over such affiliation, and as a result both include people of diverse backgrounds. The official party organization ranges from the smallest precinct unit through the state committee to the national committee. In principle, but not in practice, these organizations are hierarchically organized and well coordinated. The third group comprising political parties consists of elected officials like governors and members of Congress. Though this component of the party is frequently viewed as the party itself, it too is a diverse group with no power to control party membership.

Do the Democratic and Republican parties differ?

Differences between the parties exist, but they are usually moderate, and they do not extend to all issues. One difference is in the types of people attracted to the parties: Democrats tend to attract poor people, blacks, Jews, Catholics, and southerners. The GOP has its strongest support among business and professional people. One large issue—the role government should play with regard to the economy—provides the clearest illustration of the difference between the political philosophies of the parties. Differences also emerge when we examine preferences of party leaders, the policies endorsed in party platforms, and votes in Congress.

Do political parties have any impact?

Parties play a role in helping citizens decide how to vote. Though a candidate's party affiliation is an imperfect guide to his or her position on issues, in the absence of other information it allows for reasonable guessing. Parties also simplify election conflict because they identify the "ins" and the "outs." Parties provide campaign funds, technical help, and a certain number of "automatic" votes for candidates. They likewise help coordinate the actions of government officials. The tie of party loyalty helps overcome the fragmentation of political power that is created by our constitutional system. In addition, parties provide organized opposition to government policy by choosing candidates to run against incumbents and by serving as forums in which government policies can be criticized. Finally, because they contain diverse groups, provide entry into politics of new interests, and create broad electoral coalitions, parties help moderate divisive political conflict.

Should parties be abolished?

U.S. political parties are often criticized. But what would happen if there were no parties? Studies suggest that the absence of parties harms poor, less well-organized interests, encourages issueless campaigns, and makes it difficult for voters to punish or reward leaders. Of course, these consequences may be desirable to some people.

CHAPTER EIGHT

POLITICAL PARTIES

THE DEMOCRATIC WHISTLESTOP

he existence of political parties in the United States is a paradox. On the one hand, the Democratic and Republican parties have had a long and successful history. Few political parties in other countries can match their longevity. Moreover, only on rare occasions do members of other parties or those having no party affiliation win elections. On the other hand, many voters dislike political parties, and proposals have been offered to abolish or sharply curtail them. If the Democratic and Republican parties suddenly disappeared, many citizens would not feel a great loss. Why do the two parties thrive while so many people are uneasy about them? Are contemporary parties still relevant or have they outlived their usefulness? In this chapter we explore this "love-hate" relationship between the people of the United States and political parties as we consider four questions:

1. What are political parties?
2. Do the Democratic and Republican parties differ?
3. Do political parties have any impact?
4. Should parties be abolished?

Political party A group of citizens, party officials, and elected officeholders sharing a common identity.
Party identification Feelings of attachment and loyalty to a political party.

What are political parties?

What exactly do we mean when we speak of the Democratic or Republican Party? The answer is not simple, because political parties in the United States are not well-defined organizations with clearly stated goals. The Democratic and Republican parties are loose collections of ordinary citizens, party organizations, and elected officeholders. Each of these elements is an integral part of the party, yet each frequently acts independently of the others. Describing **political parties** is like the task faced by the twelve blind men who each hold a different part of the elephant. Let us briefly describe each of the three components of the Democratic and Republican parties.

CITIZENS

As mentioned in Chapter Seven, psychologically most citizens identify with one of the two major parties. In 1976, for example, about 63 percent of a national sample viewed themselves as either Democrats or Republicans, while 37 percent categorized themselves as independents or had no preference.[1] Moreover, whenever pollsters have asked questions about **party identification,** the results have indicated that most people consider themselves to be affiliated with one of the two major parties.[2] (The number of people who identify with a minor party, such as the Socialist Party, is almost infinitesimal.)

Party "membership" is entirely up to the individual. Being a Democrat is more like identifying with a religion than belonging to an organization like the Knights of Columbus or the Future Farmers of America. If one decides to be a Republican, one becomes part of the Republican Party. If other Republicans do not want you to consider yourself part of "their" party, they can do little about it.

Needless to say, some people are unhappy that others can call themselves Democrats or Republicans regardless of how these people view political issues. After all, how would you like it if you were a Democrat and the leaders of the U.S. Communist Party also publicly declared themselves to be Democrats? Since anyone is free to identify with a particular party, there is nothing the membership can do. Such a situation is not merely hypothetical. During the 1950s and 1960s many northern and western liberal Democrats were disturbed by the anticivil rights policies of southern Democrats, and while they would like to have excluded the southerners from the party, they could not.

That political parties cannot control who affiliates with them is an important point. Both the Democrats and the Republicans have frequently

[1] Study conducted by the Center for Political Studies, University of Michigan, Ann Arbor.
[2] For data going back as far as 1937 on the proportion of citizens identifying with the Democrats and Republicans, see Everett Carll Ladd, Jr., with Charles D. Hadley, *Transformation of the American Party System* (New York: Norton, 1975), p. 292.

been criticized for not taking distinct positions on issues or for trying to please incompatible interests. Yet without the right to control their own following, fuzziness on issues and conflicting viewpoints are almost inevitable. As we saw in Chapter Seven, parties rely heavily on their supporters for votes, so they must satisfy many diverse people who, entirely on their own, have decided to identify with them.

PARTY ORGANIZATIONS

Both political parties have thousands of party officials with such titles as precinct captain or county leader. Unlike the psychological identification which serves to affiliate ordinary citizens with a party, party offices have to be acquired through some specific means—one cannot simply decide to become, say, a Democratic county chairperson. Becoming a party official typically requires winning elections among either citizens affiliated with the party or fellow party officials.

The organization of political parties

In principle, party officials are organized into a pyramid-shaped organization (see Figure 8.1). In practice, lines of authority are usually weak. As one study put it, "The political party organization in the United States can best be described as a network of committees which interact and cooperate when it is to their mutual benefit."[3] Since the primary goal of the party is to win elections, party organizational structure generally follows the organization of electoral districts.

PRECINCT The most elemental component in this structure is the **precinct,** which usually has fewer than a thousand voters. The precinct organization is headed by a precinct leader who is either elected in the party primary or at a party precinct meeting or appointed by higher party officials, depending on the state. The basic job of the precinct organization is to register sympathetic voters, maximize voter turnout on election day, distribute campaign literature, and collect political information that will have a bearing on coming elections. In larger cities precinct leaders sometimes act as mediators between citizens and municipal bureaucracies.

COUNTY ORGANIZATION On the next rung up is the county organization. Considerable variation exists among states in how these officials are selected. In some states they are selected by county voters in the party primary; in others they are elected from precincts or even chosen by party convention. The county party leader, also chosen in one of several ways, depending on the state, frequently plays a major role in making patronage appointments, directing the campaign, and recruiting candidates for office. The county chairperson also usually represents his or her area at the state level. In past days when party "**machines**" domi-

Precinct The smallest administrative unit in the electoral system, frequently encompassing less than a thousand voters.
Machine At a time when a political party could control all offices in an area and could completely manipulate the vote, the party was known as a "political machine." A machine was controlled by a "boss."

[3] Frank B. Feigert and M. Margaret Conway, *Parties and Politics in America* (Boston: Allyn & Bacon, 1976), p. 138.

FIGURE 8.1

**U.S. POLITICAL PARTY
ORGANIZATION—IN
PRINCIPLE**

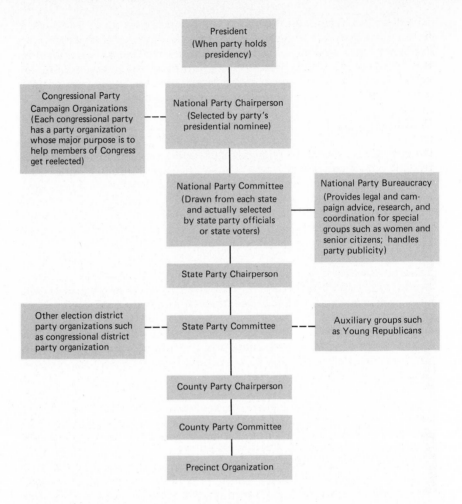

nated politics, the county party chairperson was a position of enormous power.

STATE ORGANIZATION   The third rung up is occupied by the state party committee. Again, there is wide state-to-state variation in how these organizations are constituted. Typically, state law requires that a certain number of men and women from each electoral district be represented on the state committee (county leaders and elected officials are also sometimes automatically included on state party committees). The major responsibilities of the state party chairperson include raising money, coordinating state campaign activities, maintaining party organizations, and providing a channel of communication between national and state party officials. Since states play a key role in U.S. electoral politics (even at the presidential level because of the electoral college), the state organization is usually the most important unit in party organization.

In many states several additional party organizations exist that do not fit into the pyramid-shaped organizational chart. Most parties have created special organizations to attract particular groups (for example, the Young Republicans). Other groups are created for fund-raising purposes. In several states issue-oriented wings of the state party have built a sort of party within a party to advance their causes. In 1953, for example, liberals in the California Democratic Party formed the California Democratic Council (CDC) to work on behalf of liberal causes through campaign activity, forums, and social activities. The relationship between state organizations and these auxiliary groups varies considerably from one of subservience to one in which there is conflict over resources and responsibilities.

The Democratic and Republican parties have adapted to the diversity of American society. Both parties contain numerous ethnically based local organizations, many of which have their own distinctive goals and orientations.

NATIONAL ORGANIZATION   The apex of the party organizational structure is the national committee headed by a national chairperson. Democrats and Republicans differ in the roles they assign their national committees, and these functions also change occasionally to reflect changes in party successes and electoral orientations. The basic system used by both parties is to include on the national committee a man and a woman from each state plus a certain number of party or elected officials from that state. In 1972 the Democrats substantially expanded their national committee by including people from the Young Democrats of America, Democratic House and Senate leaders, and twenty-five additional members to provide a balanced representation of Democratic voters. In principle, the national committees are selected by the presidential nominating conventions. In practice, however, the conventions ratify the choices of the state committees (here too selection procedures differ from state to state).

Though national committee members play a role in fund raising, helping in the presidential campaign, and providing a channel of communication between national and state officials, the greater part of party work is done by the national chairperson and the staff of the party's offices in Washington, D.C. The chairperson, who is selected by the party's presidential nominee, is involved in party public relations, fund raising, settling party conflicts, and coordinating patronage with the President if his or her party is in power. National committee chairpersons have differed widely in their job orientations. James A. Farley, who served the Democrats from 1932 to 1940, had a knack for developing organizational effectiveness and coordination. Leonard Hall, **GOP** chairman from 1953 to 1957, played an active role in advising President Dwight Eisenhower and worked hard at Republican public relations.[4]

The national staffs of both parties have grown enormously in the last few decades as elections have become more complex. Some of the important services they perform are researching election trends, analyzing policies advocated by the opposition, and collecting relevant material published in newspapers and magazines. They also help candidates to develop stands on campaign issues, supply candidates with information on election and registration laws, and give candidates advice on campaign techniques and the uses of the mass media. Both national organizations, through various "minority" or "ethnic" divisions, also develop programs to increase party success with blacks, Chicanos, Jews, women, and other groups.

Finally, the national party organization can exercise significant influence on the rules that are adopted for and the officials who will run the presidential nominating convention. This is especially important when a party is out of power (an incumbent President almost always sets the rules for his party's nominating convention). The importance of this power was illustrated when the Democratic National Chairperson (Senator Fred Harris) appointed Senator George McGovern to head a reform committee following the tumultuous Chicago convention of 1968. Many of the McGovern committee's suggestions for "opening up" the delegate-selection process were followed by the national committee, and these changes greatly helped McGovern himself secure the 1972 Democratic nomination.

Coordination among party groups

Despite an impressive-looking organizational chart, it would be a mistake to view party organizations as well-coordinated, disciplined armies ready to battle for victory at the polls. Only on paper do the vast number of party officials look like an impressive army. First, many official positions are unfilled. Especially where one party dominates elections, official positions in the minority party are unattractive. Moreover, in many states and cities party officials have little power, so there is little reason

[4] For a more complete description of the national committees, see Hugh A. Bone, *American Politics and the Party System,* 4th ed. (New York: McGraw-Hill, 1971), Chap. 6.

to seek party positions. Many years ago when the parties provided the essential labor for campaigns, party positions were powerful and sought after. The advent of television, however, has reduced the value of party labor, so control of the party is sometimes—but not always—not worth fighting over.

Second, party organization is less powerful than it may appear because the party lacks control over its own officials, and considerable independence exists among separate units. A county chairperson might want the local precinct captains to work hard for a particular candidate, but except in certain places (for example, Chicago during Mayor Richard Daley's leadership) enforcement power is limited. Similarly, the national committee may want a state party organization to recruit more blacks or women, but it cannot simply order this to happen. When party officials controlled numerous jobs and could dispense favors, such material rewards brought power. Unfortunately for party officials, the growth of the **civil service** and professionalism in government administration have eliminated many of the resources necessary for parties to act like disciplined armies.

A third factor that undermines tight organization is that frequently party organizations can be taken over by outside political groups. Preceding the 1972 presidential election, for example, George McGovern's supporters "captured" many established Democratic organizations by religiously attending meetings and voting as a bloc (the Republicans experienced the same thing in 1964 with Barry Goldwater's supporters). These takeovers are possible because party organizations are not private clubs where membership is decided by those who already belong. Though their regulations vary in details, all state party organizations provide for the participation of ordinary citizens in party affairs. In many states citizens elect party officials, and internal party rules can be challenged in the courts. Legally, political parties are very different from private organizations such as the Masons or Lions. By legally allowing citizen involvement in internal party decisions, the power of party officials to control their own party is weakened.[5]

ELECTED PUBLIC OFFICIALS

The third element of the Democratic and Republican parties is made up of elected public officials. When people make statements like: "The Democrats are responsible for war and inflation," or "The Republicans bring depression," they are defining the parties in terms of elected officials. At the national level are the Democrats and Republicans in the House and

Civil service The system of filling nonelected political positions on the basis of merit. Merit is frequently established by the use of objectively written tests that measure technical knowledge.

---

[5] The battle between those who claim that political parties are private organizations and those who say that party affairs ought to be open to everyone has been going on for a long time. In most other democracies internal party affairs are considered private matters. The "public" versus "private" conceptions of political parties are described further in Austin Ranney, *Curing the Mischiefs of Faction: Party Reform in America* (Berkeley: University of California Press, 1975), pp. 75–100.

Caucus Originally a meeting to make nominations for office, but now meaning a meeting of a political group.
Primary An election within a party to decide which candidates will have the party's label, or nomination, in the general elections. Also called the direct primary.
Party nominating conventions Meetings of party officials to select candidates who will run with the party label in the general election.
Open primaries Primaries with no restrictions on who can participate in the selection of the party's nominations.
Closed primaries Primaries in which one has to prove or claim allegiance to a party before one can vote in a party's nominations.

Senate. Each group has its own leadership and **caucus** that occasionally make pronouncements in the name of the national party (congressional Democrats and Republicans also have their own party campaign committees). In some situations the President also serves as a national party voice and leader. Separate state and local parties exist wherever there are legislatures or city councils elected along party lines. Hence, such diverse groups as California Republican state senators and New York City Republican councilpersons are all part of the same party, though they may have no legal links with each other. The only time some of these diverse officials get together may be at the national presidential nominating convention, but these conventions include other people as well, and thus they are not forums just for officeholders of the same party.

A party's elected public officials, like its other two elements, do not comprise a tightly organized group with a common purpose. Here too the party has difficulty deciding just who can or cannot join. Take, for example, party membership in Congress. For years there were Democrats

PRIMARIES

Before 1904 parties selected their candidates through closed meetings or conventions. Access to the selection process was usually limited by party officials. In response to widespread charges that such a selection process is undemocratic and prone to manipulation and corruption, Wisconsin in 1904 instituted the first direct **primary.** Other states soon followed, and today the primary system is the predominant method of nominating candidates in all states (some states use a mixture of primaries and **party nominating conventions**). The presidential nominating conventions are the last great holdouts of the primary system, but even here, more and more states are using primaries to select convention delegates (30 in 1976, up from 23 in 1972).

In primaries voters decide which of several candidates will be their party's official nominees for offices to be voted on in a coming election. Primaries are usually classified as "open" or "closed." **"Open primaries,"** currently used in seven states, allow voters complete freedom to choose which party's primary they will participate in. A **"closed primary"** restricts participants to party "members" (which is legally defined). Typically, to become a "member" one must declare one's membership prior to primary election day or claim past party allegiances (party officials can challenge these claims). In actual practice, however, there is little difference between "open" and

in Congress who were strongly committed to racial segregation and others who just as firmly opposed it. Democratic presidential candidates also opposed racial segregation, as did many citizens who identified with the Democrats. Nevertheless, prosegregation members of Congress were still a powerful part of the Democratic Party. Only under the most extreme and rare circumstances can a party decide to expel an elected official from party activity (and even then, expelled officials can still consider themselves members of the party that expelled them). The looseness of party membership is also evident when an occasional member of Congress decides to change parties after an election (for example, Senator Wayne Morse of Oregon shifted to the Democrats, and Senator Strom Thurmond of South Carolina became a Republican).

Wide-open (or blanket) primaries Primaries in which voters can select nominees for both parties (but for different offices).
Cross-filing The practice of a candidate running for the same office in the primaries of both parties.

THE CASE FOR STRONGER, BETTER-ORGANIZED POLITICAL PARTIES

Thus far, we have shown two things about the Democratic and Republican parties, First, neither is a single entity. Each consists of three some-

"closed" primaries. A third type of primary—one used only in Alaska and the state of Washington—is the so-called **wide-open** (or **blanket**) **primary.** In it voters can choose candidates from both parties simultaneously (though they cannot vote for two candidates for the same office).

An important issue in primaries is whether candidates can run in both Democratic and Republican primaries at the same time. All states presently forbid this practice, although it was permitted in California until 1960, and the ban has been upheld in federal court. The result of this practice—called **cross-filing**—was frequently that one candidate ended up being both the Democratic and Republican nominee for office. On general election day, voters had no choice.

Primaries have been criticized on several grounds. Voter turnout tends to be low, and primary participants are not always a cross-section of the general electorate. Thus it has been charged that primaries promote rule by unrepresented minorities. Primaries have also been viewed as weakening party organizations by depriving parties of control over their labels. On occasion candidates highly unsympathetic to party goals have "captured" the party nomination, leaving the party helpless. In 1962, for example, a strict segregationist named John Kennedy won the Ohio Democratic nomination for U.S. Representative despite the party's efforts to disown him. Finally, primaries have increased the cost of campaigning and this may give wealthy interests added political power. Nevertheless, despite these criticisms, primaries are popular.

THIRD PARTIES IN U.S. HISTORY

Though the Democrats and Republicans have dominated politics for over one hundred years, their positions have not gone unchallenged. At all levels of government other political parties have been formed, and several have had a limited degree of electoral success. Especially from the 1870s to the mid-1920s, many new parties developed in response to sharp economic fluctuations. For example, economic discontent among western farmers in the 1870s led to the creation of the Greenback Party. In 1878, fourteen Greenback members of Congress were elected, but the party soon declined. The successor to the Greenbacks was the Populist Party, formed in 1892. Drawing support largely from poor people in the southern and northwestern states, the Populist presidential candidate in that year (General James B. Weaver) won 8.5 percent of the popular vote and 22 electoral votes; the party also won three governorships and hundreds of local offices. Perhaps the last—and most successful—expression of economic discontent was manifested in the presidential candidacy of Robert M. LaFollette, who ran in 1924 under the banner of the Progressive Party. This party was an offshoot of the Republican Party, but it nevertheless attracted many voters disturbed by the conservative economic policies associated with the Republicans. Calling for an end to monopolies, the right of labor to organize, and public ownership of railroads and water power, LaFollette polled 16.6 percent of the popular vote (largely from the West and Upper Midwest).

Another important thirty-party element has been a Democratic or Republican faction that splits off from the main party, usually because of some crucial issue. When this issue passes, the splinter

what overlapping elements—citizens, party officials, and elected officeholders. Second, both parties are loose collections of diverse people that have limited control of their own members or their policies. The Democratic and Republican parties are not well-disciplined organizations clashing over well-defined issues. Political parties in the United States are fragmented and decentralized.

Not all political parties are like the Democratic and Republican parties. In fact, considering political parties in other countries, those in the United States are unique. In many political parties elsewhere in the world, membership is restricted, and all members must follow party principles or face expulsion. A member of the British Parliament who repeatedly opposed fellow party members would soon be expelled from the party. Hence, when the British vote for a party candidate, they can be

Doctrinaire party A political party more committed to maintaining the purity of its position and following than to winning elections.

movement disappears. In 1912, for example, Theodore Roosevelt, unhappy with the conservative policies of fellow Republican Howard Taft, ran against Taft as a Progressive and polled 27.4 percent of the popular vote. In 1948, the issue of black civil rights split the Democratic Party. Dismayed by the liberal policies of President Harry S. Truman, southern Democrats organized the States Rights (or "Dixiecrats") Party with Senator J. Strom Thurmond as their presidential candidate. Thurmond carried South Carolina, Alabama, Mississippi, and Louisiana, but Truman still won the 1948 election (interestingly, Thurmond won only where he was listed as a Democrat on the ballot). More recent examples of such splits was the candidacy of George Wallace in 1968 (who won 13.5 percent of the popular vote) running under the banner of the American Independent Party.

A third type of minor party is what might be called the **doctrinaire party.** These parties do not hope to win much electorally; the idea is to use the campaign to publicize a cause. There were several such parties represented in the 1976 election, though most received no public attention. The Socialist Labor Party, with the ticket of Julius Levin and Constance Blomen, is the heir to the Socialist Party. Its leaders seriously believe that the party will eventually triumph once the built-in contradictions of capitalism emerge (the Socialist Party was once a real force in U.S. politics, receiving 6.0 percent of the presidential vote in 1912 and winning numerous local offices). The American Communist Party, with the ticket of Gus Hall and Jarvis Tyner, also was on the ballot in many states in 1976. Other doctrinaire parties taking part in the 1976 elections were the Socialist Workers Party, the United States Labor Party, the People's Party, the American Party, and the Free Libertarian Party (this party actually received an electoral vote in 1972).

reasonably sure what they are getting for their vote. A U.S. citizen voting a straight Democratic ticket cannot be sure that all of the candidates will follow the same policies.

Whether the United States should have strong, centralized political parties has long been debated by political scientists. Advocates of such reorganization claim that the existence of two clearly defined parties committed to specific policies would provide voters with a more meaningful choice. Instead of facing a bewildering collection of choices, with no guarantee of what each candidate supports, the voter would choose one party over the other and, thus, knowingly choose one set of policies over another. Despite these claims, however, citizens seem to like the idea of loose, open parties that cannot force their programs on public officials.

Winner-take-all system The principle of giving victory to the candidate with the most votes and nothing to any other candidates.

DO THIRD PARTIES HAVE ANY IMPACT?

The impact of third parties on politics is difficult to determine. There has been much speculation, for example, about whether the candidacy of George Wallace in 1968 "gave" Richard Nixon his victory by taking away votes from fellow Democrat Hubert H. Humphrey. Similar controversy exists over whether Theodore Roosevelt's 1912 Progressive campaign resulted in the election of Woodrow Wilson, a Democrat. It seems likely, however, that because of our **winner-take-all system** (see Chapter 6), third parties have sometimes held the balance of power by controlling a small percentage of the vote.

It has also been argued that minor parties frequently develop new policies that are eventually incorporated by the major parties. This argument is only partially true. Sometimes the program of a minor party does eventually become established policy. For example, the 1932 platform of the Socialist Party called for:

programs of public employment for those out of work
a six-hour day and a five-day work week without reduction in wages
a comprehensive system of public employment agencies
unemployment insurance financed by the government and employers
old age pensions
health and maternity insurance
workmen's compensation and accident insurance
government aid to farms and mortgage protection for home owners.

All of these policies (except the six-hour day) were eventually made into law or have become well-established customs. On the other hand, the Socialist Party platform also called for:

public ownership of all mines, forests, oil companies, transportation systems, communications, and utilities

Do the Democratic and Republican parties differ?

A frequent criticism of the Democratic and Republican parties is that they are the same. Many citizens probably believe that it makes little difference whether a candidate is of one party or the other or whether the Democrats or the Republicans dominate a legislature. Moreover, since both parties are loose coalitions of diverse people, it would seem difficult for the parties to remain distinctive. Are the two parties different? The

Socialist campaign poster for 1904 with ticket of Eugene W. Debs and Ben Hanford. Prior to the Russian Revolution of 1917 socialism was not necessarily un-American, and Debs received considerable electoral support in his various presidential campaigns.

    public ownership of the credit and banking system
    proportional representation in elections
    abolition of the Supreme Court's power to declare legislation un-
       constitutional
    government ownership of the liquor industry.

None of these programs has been enacted or even given serious attention in recent years.

Party platforms of both major and minor parties can be found in Donald Bruce Johnson and Kirk H. Porter, comp., *National Party Platforms, 1840–1972*, 5th ed. (Urbana: University of Illinois Press, 1973).

answer is yes, they are different but not in every regard, and rarely are these differences large.

DIFFERENCES IN PARTY SUPPORTERS

The easiest way to illustrate party differences is to examine what types of citizens identify with the two parties. In general, the Democratic Party disproportionately attracts poor people, manual workers, blacks, Jews, Catholics, and southerners. The Republican Party, on the other hand, has its greatest strength among business and professional people, Protestants, high-income groups, and residents of small and medium-sized cities. There are many exceptions, of course, so neither party is the exact opposite of the other. There are, for example, many wealthy Democrats and poor Republicans. Moreover, these social-group alignments can change over time, as evidenced by the fact that until the 1930s most blacks were staunch Republicans.

Likewise, Democratic and Republican identifiers sometimes differ on important political issues. The most persistent policy differences between party identifiers are seen in the way each party views the role of the government in the economy. In 1976, for example, 41.9 percent of Democratic identifiers wanted stronger government efforts to guarantee jobs and a decent standard of living, compared to only 16.1 percent of the Republicans.[6] This pattern has existed since the days of President Franklin Roosevelt and the New Deal.

On noneconomic issues the differences are not nearly as sharp or as persistent. Race-related issues such as school busing and integration do divide the two parties, but most of this difference is accounted for by the large number of black Democrats. Party differences are well illustrated by the feelings of voters on the federal government's role in school integration: the difference between Democrats and Republicans favoring stronger efforts is 20.3 percent. However, among whites only, the difference is reduced to 11.5 percent. On foreign policy questions, for example, diplomatic recognition of the Peoples' Republic of China, or foreign aid, small differences are sometimes apparent, but they do not always show a clear pattern. In short, party identifiers do differ on many important political questions, but the most important area of disagreement is the role of government vis-à-vis the economy.

DIFFERENCES AMONG PARTY OFFICIALS

When we examine differences among party officials, for example, county chairpersons or national committee members, policy disagreements are frequently much larger.[7] Of course, given the enormous diversity and decentralization of political parties, sharp differences between the parties are easy to spot. We hardly expect a black Democratic precinct captain from Philadelphia to see eye to eye on all issues with a GOP county chairperson from rural Nebraska (probably the black precinct captain would also differ with a Democratic party official from rural Nebraska). Nevertheless, in general, issue differences between Democratic and Republican officials are sharper than those that exist between Republicans and Democrats who are merely party identifiers. For example, a

[6] Center for Political Studies, University of Michigan, Ann Arbor, 1976 Presidential Election Study. Other analyses of differences between Democrats and Republicans on economic issues can be found in Norman H. Nie, Sidney Verba, and John R. Petrocik, *The Changing American Voter* (Cambridge, Mass.: Harvard University Press, 1976), Chap. 12.

[7] Herbert McCloskey, Paul J. Hoffman, and Rosemary O'Hare, "Issue Conflict and Consensus among Party Leaders and Followers," *American Political Science Review*, 54 (1960), pp. 406–427.

JOHN HANCOCK
LOSES THE
WIZARDS' VOTE

Many subtle biases can occur in descriptions of the differences between the two parties. Sometimes the Democratic party is described as "the party of the people," while the Republicans are society's "better elements." A good historical illustration of biased descriptions comes from the 1787 governor's race in Massachusetts. The candidates were James Bowdoin, who appealed to the wealthy, and John Hancock, whose supporters were considerably less well off. Following his defeat, Bowdoin's supporters gave this analysis of the vote:

	Bowdoin	Hancock
Physicians	19	2
Clergymen	2	0
Lawyers	17	3
Independent gentlemen	50	0
Merchants and traders	295	21
Printers	8	4
Tradesmen	328	279
Laborers, servants, etc.	5	466
	724	775

Hancock's supporters then provided an alternative interpretation of the data:

	Bowdoin	Hancock
Usurers	28	0
Speculators in public securities	576	0
Stockholders and bank directors	81	0
Persons under British influence	17	0
Merchants, tradesmen, and other "worthy" citizens	21	448
Friends of the Revolution	0	327
Wizards	1	0
	724	775

Source: Massachusetts Centinel, April 4 and 7, 1787.

Party platform A set of principles and policy objectives favored by a party and its candidates in a particular election. Typically written by special committees, not by the candidates themselves.
Platform plank A statement on a specific policy which is part of the overall party platform.

1972 study of Democratic presidential nominating convention delegates (many of whom are party officials) found delegates to be much more liberal on the guaranteed annual income issue than rank and file Democrats (and recall that these Democrats are in turn more likely than Republicans to support this proposal).[8] Studies have found that Republican Party leaders are generally more conservative on economic and social issues than ordinary Republicans.

The nature of party policy differences becomes clear when we examine **party platforms** written at the national convention. Even though these platforms are never implemented completely, they are good indicators of where party activists stand on important issues. Table 8.1 compares Democratic and Republican positions in the 1976 elections.

Careful reading of these illustrative **platform planks** reveals basic party differences. For example, the Democrats clearly endorsed a strong effort on the part of the federal government to provide jobs for everyone who wants one, while the Republicans asserted that such programs would only be a "quick-fix" solution. Also note how frequently the Democratic platform mentioned increasing taxes on the rich, while the Republicans called for more tax credits for education and simplification of tax forms. On the racial equality issue, both parties firmly endorsed government action to promote equality, but the Democrats spoke of "compensatory opportunity" while the Republicans denounced a reverse quota system. Similarly, on energy both parties called for conservation and supported attempts to find new energy sources, but they differed substantially on the role of government in regulating the energy industry.

DIFFERENCES AMONG ELECTED OFFICIALS

To gain another dimension of party differences, let us consider the actions taken by political parties. Does it make much difference whether Democrats or Republicans are elected? This is a complex question, because party differences vary from state to state. To simplify our analysis, let us consider whether party makes a difference in Congress. Specifically, what happens when citizens replace a Democrat with a Republican, or vice versa? Do the constituents receive different representation when such changes occur? The answer is yes — a change in the party of one's member of Congress makes a real difference. This is well illustrated by the 1974 congressional election, which saw forty-nine Republicans replaced by Democrats and six Democrats replaced by Republicans. As Table 8.2 shows, the newly elected Democrats were much more liberal than the Republicans they replaced (the opposite was true of new Republicans). Note that the average ADA score — a measure of liberalism-conservatism in voting — of newly elected Democrats was 47 points higher than for the Republicans they replaced, a significant move in the liberal direction.

[8] Dennis G. Sullivan, Jeffrey L. Pressman, Benjamin I. Page, and John J. Lyons, *The Politics of Representation: The Democratic Convention of 1972* (New York: St. Martins Press, 1974), p. 32.

TABLE 8.1
DEMOCRATIC AND
REPUBLICAN PARTY
PLATFORM PLANKS ON
ECONOMICS AND RACE
RELATIONS, 1976

Government jobs

Democratic Platform Position on Creating Government Jobs to Solve Problems of Unemployment:

. . . The Democratic Party is committed to the right of all adult Americans willing, able, and seeking work to have opportunities for useful jobs at living wages. To make that commitment meaningful, we pledge ourselves to the support of legislation that will make every responsible effort to reduce adult unemployment to 3 per cent within 4 years. . . .

. . . Every effort should be made to create jobs in the private sector. Clearly, useful public jobs are far superior to welfare and unemployment payments. The federal government has the responsibility to ensure that all Americans able, willing, and seeking work are provided opportunities for useful jobs.

Republican Platform Position on Creating Government Jobs to Solve Problems of Unemployment:

Massive, federally-funded public employment programs . . . will cost billions and can only be financed either through very large tax increases or through ever increasing levels of deficit spending. Although such government "make-work" programs usually provide a temporary stimulus to the economy, "quick-fix" solutions of this sort—like all narcotics—lead to addiction, larger and larger doses, and ultimately the destruction of far more jobs than they create. Sound job creation can only be accomplished in the private sector of the economy. Americans must not be fooled into accepting government as the employer of last resort.

Taxes

Democratic Platform Position on Changes in Federal Tax Policy:

We pledge the Democratic Party to a complete overhaul of the present tax system, which will review all special tax provisions to ensure that they are justified and distributed equitably among our citizens.

We will strengthen the internal revenue tax code so that high income citizens pay a reasonable tax on all economic income.

We will reduce the use of unjustified tax shelters in such areas as oil and gas, tax-loss farming, real estate, and movies.

We will eliminate unnecessary and ineffective tax provisions to business and substitute effective incentives to encourage small business and capital formation in all business. . . .

We will end abuses in the tax treatment of income from foreign sources, such as special tax treatment and incentives for multinational corporations that drain jobs and capital from the American economy.

We will overhaul federal estate and gift taxes to provide an effective and equitable structure to promote tax justice and alleviate some of the legitimate problems faced by farmers, small businessmen and women, and others who would otherwise be forced to liquidate assets in order to pay the tax.

We will eliminate tax inequities that adversely affect individuals on the basis of sex or marital status.

We will curb expense account deductions.

TABLE 8.1 Continued

Republican Platform Position on Changes in Federal Tax Policy:

The Republican Party advocates a legislative policy to obtain a balanced federal budget and reduced tax rates. While the best tax reform is tax reduction, we recognize the need for structural tax adjustments to help the working men and women of our nation. To that end, we recommend tax credits for college tuition, post-secondary technical training and child care expenses incurred by working parents.

Over the past two decades of Democrat control of the Congress, our tax laws have become a nightmare of complexity and unfair tax preferences, virtually destroying the credibility of the system. Simplifications should be a major goal of tax reform.

We support economic and tax policies to insure the necessary job-producing expansion of our economy. These include hastening capital recovery through new systems of accelerated depreciation, removing the tax burden on equity financing to encourage more capital investment, ending the unfair double taxation of dividends, and supporting proposals to enhance the ability of our working and other citizens to own "a piece of the action" through stock ownership. When balanced by expenditure reductions, the personal exemption should be raised to $1,000.

Racial inequality

Democratic Platform Position on Government's Role in Achieving Racial Equality:

To achieve a just and healthy society and enhance respect and trust in our institutions, we must insure that all citizens are treated equally before the law and given the opportunity, regardless of race, color, sex, religion, age, language, or national origin, to participate fully in the economic, social and political processes and to vindicate their legal and constitutional rights.

In reaffirmation of this principle, an historic commitment of the Democratic Party, we pledge vigorous federal programs and policies of compensatory opportunity to remedy for many Americans the generations of injustice and deprivation; and full funding of programs to secure the implementation and enforcement of civil rights.

Republican Platform Position on Government's Role in Achieving Racial Equality:

There must be vigorous enforcement of laws to assure equal treatment in job recruitment, hiring, promotion, pay, credit, mortgage access, and housing. The way to end discrimination, however, is not by resurrecting the much discredited quota system and attempting to cloak it in an aura of new respectability. Rather, we must provide alternative means of assisting the victims of past discrimination to realize their full worth as American citizens.

Wiping out past discrimination requires continued emphasis on providing educational opportunities for minority citizens, increasing direct and guaranteed loans to minority business enterprises, and affording qualified minority persons equal opportunities for government positions at all levels.

TABLE 8.1 Continued

Energy

Democratic Platform on Government's Role in Solving Energy Problems:

The Democratic Party will strive to replace the rapidly diminishing supply of petroleum and natural gas with solar, geothermal, wind, tide, and other forms of energy, and we recommend that the federal government promptly expend whatever funds are required to develop new systems of energy. . . .

The Democratic energy platform begins with a recognition that the federal government has an important role to play in insuring the nation's energy future, and that it must be given the tools it needs to protect the economy and the nation's consumers from arbitrary and excessive energy price increases and help the nation embark on a massive domestic energy program focusing on conservation, coal conversion, exploration, and development of new technologies to insure an adequate short-term and long-term supply of energy for the nation's needs. A nation advanced enough and wealthy enough to send a man to the moon must dedicate itself to developing itself alternative sources of energy.

Republican Platform on Government's Role in Solving Energy Problems:

Our approach toward energy self-sufficiency must involve both expansion of energy supply and improvement of energy efficiency. It must include elements that insure increased conservation at all levels of our society. It must also provide incentives for the exploration and development of domestic gas, oil, coal and uranium, and for expanded research and development in the use of solar, geothermal, co-generation, solid waste, wind, water, and other sources of energy. . . .

Unwise government intervention in the marketplace has caused shortgage of supply, unrealistic prices, and increased dependence on foreign sources. We must immediately eliminate price controls on oil and newly discovered natural gas in order to increase supply, and to provide the capital that is needed to finance further exploration and development of domestic hydrocarbon reserves.

Fair and realistic market prices will encourage sensible conservation efforts and establish priorities in the use of our resources, which over the long run will provide a secure supply at reasonable prices for all.

We have seen that the differences between the two political parties are not extreme and do not apply to all issues. To those who prefer two sharply defined parties (perhaps liberal and conservative parties) these differences may appear trivial. Nevertheless, attempts to further separate the parties are likely to fail. For one thing, many citizens do not want highly distinctive parties. That the Democrats and Republicans may be no more different from one another than are McDonald's and Burger King is perfectly satisfactory to most of us.[9] Second, attempts to make

[9] Extensive data on this point are presented in Jack Dennis, "Support for the Party System by the Mass Public," *American Political Science Review*, 60 (1966), pp. 600–615.

TABLE 8.2

WHAT HAPPENS WHEN A DEMOCRAT REPLACES A REPUBLICAN OR A REPUBLICAN REPLACES A DEMOCRAT, ADA SCORES IN 1974 AND 1975

Where Democrats won	
Average 1975 ADA score[a] of Democrats who defeated Republicans in 1974 congressional election (49 cases)	78.5
Average 1974 ADA of the Republicans these Democrats defeated	31.5
Where Republicans won	
Average 1975 ADA score of Republicans who defeated Democrats in 1974 congressional election (6 cases)	32.7
Average 1974 ADA score of Democrats defeated by these Republicans	46.8

[a] ADA stands for Americans for Democratic Action, which is a liberal organization. These scores are based on the votes of members of Congress on key issues. The higher the score, the greater the degree of liberalism. A score of 100 indicates a perfect liberal voting record in the eyes of the ADA; 0 is a perfect conservative record.

one of the parties more distinctive have typically resulted in electoral disasters. In 1964, for example, Barry Goldwater offered his conservative followers "a choice, not an echo" and was trounced by Lyndon B. Johnson. Much the same thing happened to McGovern in 1972 when he offered a far more liberal program than is usually offered by the Democrats.

Do political parties have any impact?

Does the existence of the Democratic and Republican parties really make any difference? Even though parties are loosely organized, composed of diverse groups, and sometimes refuse to disagree on issues, having parties *does* make an important difference. Abolishing them would greatly affect many aspects of U.S. politics. Specifically, political parties in the United States play an important role in five important areas: (1) assisting citizens in voting; (2) helping candidates campaign; (3) coordinating actions of public officials; (4) providing organized opposition; and (5) moderating conflict.

ASSISTING CITIZENS IN VOTING

Chapter Seven showed that party identification is an important factor in many people's voting decisions. Most voters identify with either Democrats or Republicans, and most identifiers usually stick with their party. This is particularly true when voting for less prominent offices (for example, state senator) or when little additional information is available.

In other words, most Democrats and Republicans find party labels a convenient, time-saving method of deciding how to vote. This process is not unlike the usefulness of sticking with a favorite brand of beer: if you are a hard-core Budweiser drinker, shopping for beer is easy because there are no decisions to agonize over.

Sticking with one's party may not seem very useful. In fact, some people have argued that candidates should not be identified by party on the ballot so that citizens would be forced to judge each candidate on his or her merits. Granted, voting by party may not initially appear sensible, but further thought shows that it does have some benefits. In an ideal world in which citizens had perfect knowledge, voting solely according to political party would not occur. However, a good case can be made that, under present conditions, party voting can be useful.

To appreciate the value of party voting, imagine that you had to make twenty-five voting choices, ranging from President to county judge, and possessed little or no information about most candidates. What would you do? Under conditions of unfamiliarity and ignorance, a candidate's party label may be a *reasonable* clue to his or her stands on issues. Recall that with some exceptions the parties *do* differ in many significant ways. Thus, if you had to make reasonable guesses about candidates, guessing on the basis of party label is frequently the best bet under difficult conditions. What are the alternatives? One could vote on the basis of the candidate's sex or ethnic background, but all things considered, these are not generally as useful as party labels (what do you do in a contest between John Smith and Robert Jones?). In a world of limited knowledge, party labels can provide useful information. Of course, mistakes occur and people are sometimes misled, but compared to having no information at all, voting by party affiliation is an improvement.

Besides providing clues about candidates, parties can help voters by simplifying political conflict. That is, instead of political conflict between individual politicians, conflict is confined to a battle between Democrats and Republicans. This simplification is akin to giving athletic teams names instead of referring to them by the names of individual players. Thus, instead of saying the team of Murcer, White, Chambliss, Jackson, and so on, beat the team of Garr, Bannister, Orta, and so on, we say that the Yankees beat the White Sox. In politics we say that the Republicans took control of Congress in the last election.

Such simplification is especially useful when voters want to punish leaders. Suppose, for example, that one is upset with government policy. One effective way of expressing this discontent is to vote against the *party* in power. If the Republicans control the government, one can vote against every Republican on the ballot as a way of expressing dissatisfaction. Obviously, this strategy would be impossible if parties did not exist. And, in fact, many voters do seem to employ it. Party punishment was well illustrated in the 1974 congressional elections when many normally "safe" Republican members of Congress were defeated as a result of public outrage over the Watergate scandal. In this case it was impossible to vote against Nixon directly, but voting out other Republicans helped get the message across. For a voter who wants a simple method of distinguishing the "ins" from the "outs," parties are extremely useful.

Party machine The organizational structure of a political party that enabled the manipulation of elections.

Instead of thousands of unrelated officials we have the Democrats and the Republicans.

HELPING CANDIDATES CAMPAIGN

In Chapter Seven we saw that running for office can be extremely expensive and demanding. Fortunately, the political parties from the precinct organization to the national committee can provide help to office seekers. Without the assistance of political parties, politics would be much more of a rich person's activity.

The most useful service parties provide candidates is delivery of a minimum vote. Merely being a Democrat or a Republican insures a candidate of the votes of numerous party identifiers. Some voters are like the southern Democrats who called themselves "Yellow Dog Democrats" because they would vote Democratic even if the party ran a yellow dog for office. Most candidates probably get half or more of all their votes from these "automatic voters" at little cost and effort.

A second important way parties help individual candidates is to provide an overall ticket or team of office seekers. Thus, instead of candidates running for office all by themselves, they are part of the Democratic or Republican ticket. Running on a ticket has several advantages. First, many states allow citizens to vote a straight party ticket by making a single choice. As part of the ticket office seekers get all the votes of people who may never have heard of them but who are attracted to the ticket by other candidates. A second advantage of a party ticket (as opposed to everyone running separately) is that individuals receive the benefits of a collective campaign. Advertisements such as "Vote for Peace—Vote Republican" or appeals like "Support the Team of Governor Frump—Vote Democratic" are all directed toward electing a party ticket. Especially where funds are limited, such ticket advertising is efficient.

Third, the party organization can provide crucial services during the campaign. Even if a candidate has little contact with the actual party organization, party services are important. For instance, political parties commonly play a major role in voter registration drives and getting supporters to the polls on election day. The old-time urban **party machines** were especially famous for their vigorous registration and turnout efforts (turnout even exceeded 100 percent, since dead people voted). Perhaps only wealthy candidates could afford to hire people to do the work of getting out the vote that is normally performed by party workers.

Another form of candidate assistance generated by political parties is money. Party organizations at all levels raise money, which is then distributed to individual candidates. In 1976, for example, the Republican National Committee directly gave $3.7 million to candidates running for national office (and indirectly gave them another $1.9 million). National Democratic groups donated $3.2 million to candidates at the national level.[10] Parties can also offer numerous campaign services that many candidates cannot themselves afford. These range from tips on how to

[10] Charles W. Hucker, "Party Finances," *Practical Politics*, July/August 1978, p. 3.

campaign to information derived from public opinion polls. Occasionally this even means providing candidates with experts on the use of the media, computerized mailings, and other sophisticated techniques. Clearly, though political parties may not be as powerful as the machines of yesteryear, they are still a major assistance to candidates who lack great personal resources.

COORDINATING ACTIONS OF PUBLIC OFFICIALS

The U.S. political system is designed to thwart the consolidation of power. Rather than having one all-power leader, political power is dispersed and fragmented. Recall that the Constitution constrains the actions of public officials through the system of checks and balances and that federalism disperses power between state and national levels.

If our government intended only to prevent things, such fragmentation would be perfectly acceptable. However, in modern times all levels of government are expected to play an active political role. The discrepancy between the institutional fragmentation of political power and modern demands for stronger government thus presents a conflict. How can we maintain our basic constitutional order and still achieve the coordination among government leaders that is necessary to implement major policies?

To some extent the political parties help meet this need. That many public officials share a common party affiliation frequently provides a basis for cooperation and coordination that would not exist if there were no parties. For example, Presidents typically feel an obligation to listen to governors and mayors of their own party. And, usually, at least once a year a delegation of state and local officeholders treks to the White House to argue that "for the sake of the party" they should get federal assistance. Of course, the bond of common party membership is strongly reinforced by the importance of state and local party efforts in presidential elections (several Presidents have been elected because of vigorous efforts by state and local party organizations). Common party membership, like shared religious preferences, helps facilitate interaction among diverse officials.

Perhaps the most important of the coordinating roles performed by the parties occurs in congressional-presidential relationships. Legally speaking, because neither branch can systematically impose its wishes on the other, making public policy requires cooperation. Political parties, especially when the same party controls Congress and the presidency, frequently provide the link necessary for policy making. Presidents Kennedy, Johnson, and Carter, for instance, maintained close relationships with congressional party leaders, who in turn organized Democratic Representatives and Senators. These relationships were not always peaceful or productive, but they contributed significantly to executive-legislative coordination.[11] Even when the Congress and the President are of dif-

[11] Nelson W. Polsby, *Congress and the Presidency*, 2d ed. (Englewood Cliffs, N.J.: Prentice-Hall, 1971), pp. 144–145; and Randall B. Ripley, *Congress: Process and Policy* (New York: Norton, 1975), pp. 236–242.

THE POLITICAL PARTY AS WELFARE AGENCY

Contemporary political parties are almost entirely oriented toward electoral activities. Years ago, however, before the advent of government welfare bureaucracies, political parties sometimes played a major role in helping people in such areas as housing, employment, and recreation. These services were important means of getting people's votes. One of the best at this type of strategy was George Washington Plunkitt, a leading New York City politician around the turn of the century. Here is Plunkitt's secret of success:

What tells in holdin' your grip on your district is to go right down among the poor families and help them in the different ways they need help. I've got a regular system for this. If there's a fire on Ninth, Tenth, or Eleventh Avenue, for example, any hour of the day or night, I'm usually there with some of my election district captains as soon as the fire engines. If a family is burned out I don't ask whether they are Republicans or Democrats, and I don't refer them to the Charity Organization Society, which would investigate their case in a month or two and decide they were worthy of help about the time they are dead from starvation. I just get quarters for them, buy clothes for them if their clothes were burned up, and fix them up till they get things runnin' again. It's philanthropy, but it's politics, too — mighty good politics. Who can tell how many votes one of these fires bring me? The poor are the most grateful people in the world, and, let me tell you, they have more friends in their neighborhoods than the rich have in theirs.

If there's a family in my district in want I know it before the charitable societies do, and me and my men are first on the ground. I have a special corps to look up such cases. The consequence is that the poor look up to George W. Plunkitt as a father, come to him in trouble — and don't forget him on election day.

ferent parties, for example, under the Nixon and Ford presidencies, parties still facilitate lawmaking.

PROVIDING ORGANIZED OPPOSITION

An important element of a democratic government is the existence of organized opposition. Someone must be willing and able to criticize government policy and offer reasonable alternatives. Even popularly elected leaders are kept more honest if they know that abuses will receive immediate attention. Of course, if the opposition is too vehement and obstruc-

George Washington Plunkitt, New York City political leader, dispensing advice from the County Court House bootblack stand. Approximately the turn of the century.

Another thing, I can always get a job for a deservin' man. I make it a point to keep on the track of jobs, and it seldom happens that I don't have a few up my sleeve ready for use. I know every big employer in the district and in the whole city, for that matter, and they ain't in the habit of sayin' no to me when I ask them for a job.

And the children—the little roses of the district! Do I forget them? Oh, no! They know me, every one of them, and they know that a sight of Uncle George and candy means the same thing. Some of them are the best kind of vote-getters. I'll tell you a case. Last year a little Eleventh Avenue rosebud, whose father is a Republican, caught hold of his whiskers on election day and said she wouldn't let go till he'd promise to vote for me. And she didn't.

William L. Riordon, *Plunkitt of Tammany Hall* (New York: Dutton, 1963), pp. 27–28.

tionist, chaos may result. The problem is to provide a regularized opposition within certain bounds.

In the United States political parties are important as sources of reasonable opposition and public scrutiny. This is an extremely important role, yet parties frequently do not get much credit for their work. To appreciate the importance of this role, ask yourself how the Watergate scandal would have been investigated if after the 1972 election all leading Democrats had been banished to Siberia? Parties offer constructive opposition in two important ways: (1) they provide a forum for opponents of government policy, and (2) they provide electoral opposition to incumbent officeholders.

A forum for opponents of government policy

Whether at the local, state, or federal level, governments are forever considering policies. Naturally, many citizens disagree with government actions. One convenient outlet for this opposition is the party currently out of power. This "out" party typically sees such discontent as an opportunity to increase its own electoral strength and eventually become the "in" party. Thus, as President Carter announced his policies on energy and welfare reform, various Republicans gave speeches criticizing portions of these programs. Such pronouncements not only provide alternative viewpoints on important issues but they offer a potential rallying point for other dissatisfied individuals.

Of course, parties are not the only source of criticism or opposition. Newspaper columnists, television commentators, and soap-box orators all can criticize government policy. The political party is crucial because eventually it can provide alternative policies, and it can replace the current leadership. A popular television newscaster may attack a government policy, but he or she will probably never get a chance to enact different policies. On the other hand, when the Senate Republican leader says that Democrat Carter's farm policy is a disaster, the Republicans are promising to do a better job if they gain power. Such pronouncements are listened to with care and cannot be dismissed as one dismisses an unfavorable newspaper editorial. While anyone can speak against the government, the opposition of leaders of the out party has to be taken far more seriously than complaints of ordinary citizens.

Electoral competition

In politics, as in economics, competition is important. Just imagine a world in which only the Coca Cola Company could sell soft drinks. The product might taste awful and cost a fortune. Imagine the political scene if there were little competition for public offices. Of course, competition itself does not guarantee the emergence of great leaders who are committed to the public welfare. Nevertheless, knowing that others are interested in one's job can usually inhibit the more severe abuses of office.

In many areas of the country political parties recruit candidates for office and thus make most elections at least technically competitive.[12] Especially where an incumbent is entrenched, the local party plays a key role in getting at least someone to provide opposition. The party supports such occasional hopeless causes because running as many candidates as possible helps the entire ticket, and every so often one of these candidates wins. What is most important, however, is that without the efforts of the party, voters would frequently not have a choice on election day.

We have seen that parties can aid candidates who lack extensive personal resources. Such aid helps make the election more of a contest and makes opposition more credible. Without the votes of party members, the

[12] See, for example, Lester G. Seligman, "Political Parties and the Recruitment of Political Leaders," in L. Edinger, ed., *Political Leadership in Industrialized Societies* (New York: Wiley, 1967).

existence of a ticket, and other resources provided by the parties, the prospect of running against an incumbent would be extremely unattractive. Few citizens could afford running. Though many elections are not close, they would probably be even more lopsided without the efforts of political parties.

MODERATING CONFLICT

Because parties play an important role in providing opposition, it might seem contradictory to claim that they moderate conflict. How can they moderate conflict if they attack incumbent leaders and contribute to electoral conflict? The answer is that by providing outlets for certain types of conflicts, U.S. parties inhibit more severe and disruptive conflicts. Without parties, many of the forces that divide our society could get out of hand. In other countries parties often do not moderate conflict — look, for instance at the Italian Communist Party. In the United States, however, the Democrats and Republicans hold down sharp disagreements by (1) recruiting supporters from diverse social groups; (2) providing easy entry into politics by new groups; and (3) putting together overlapping electoral coalitions.

Diverse recruiting

We have seen that the loose, decentralized nature of parties prevents them from having a "pure" membership. If poor, illiterate, unemployed persons want to join the party of the Rockefellers, nothing can stop them. This ease of party affiliation and membership sometimes makes Democrats and Republicans hard to separate. From the perspective of political conflict, however, this overlapping of membership is crucial. In neither party do all members agree with one another on important issues. Businesspersons, for example, disproportionately belong to the GOP, yet the Republican Party cannot be the all-out advocate of businesspersons against everyone else. Because there are many Republicans who are not businesspersons, such probusiness efforts would disrupt the party. Hence, Republican enthusiasm for business interests must be somewhat subdued.

Perhaps the most important conflict moderated by the parties is that between rich and poor. In many societies the battle between the haves and the have nots ignites revolutions. In the United States, however, political parties help to contain this conflict. The Democrats could not enthusiastically come out with the slogan "Soak the rich," because many Democrats are quite rich. And since many Republicans are poor, the GOP could not campaign on the platform "Make war on poverty — bomb poor people." Politics would be far different if the parties restricted their membership to maintain their purity.

Entry for new groups

Chapter 6 indicated that elections help to channel public dissatisfaction into "safe" electoral activity. Political parties also contribute to this channeling process. Specifically, parties are sufficiently accessible that

WISCONSIN DEMOCRATS RECRUIT MY MOTHER-IN-LAW

Though political parties are important in getting people to seek political office, this role is rarely very visible. To show how this recruitment occurs, it may be useful to relate how the Wisconsin Democratic Party recruited my mother-in-law, Germaine Luther Hume, to run for county office. In 1958 Germaine Hume had no interest in politics and certainly no desire to hold public office. The local Democratic Party, however, which at the time was almost a hopeless minority, sought out Germaine Hume

RE-ELECT

Germaine Luther Hume

Register of Deeds

Calumet County
Democratic Ticket

Your Vote Of Confidence Will
Be Appreciated.

Auth., Circulated and paid for by
G. L. Hume, Chilton, Wis.

(who was not even a Democrat) and convinced her that her background would make her a fine candidate. Germaine was convinced, waged a vigorous door-to-door campaign, and was elected register of deeds. She was successful in numerous other campaigns, and as a result of efforts such as these, the Wisconsin Democratic Party eventually achieved equal footing with the once-dominant Republicans. Wisconsin voters now have a greater choice than before, and much of this choice derives from the party's efforts to get people like Germaine Hume to run for office.

almost any group of people can capture a piece of them, and even insurgent political groups can become part of "the system."

One can "capture" a party in several ways. Perhaps the easiest way is to run candidates for party leadership positions or to get all of one's supporters to attend the meeting at which these positions are filled. A different route is to run candidates in a party primary. Here again, coordinated efforts of a relatively small number of people can be successful. Both party organizational meetings and primary elections frequently draw light turnouts, and with many candidates running, a few hundred people can sometimes capture a fairly large city or county organization. Finally, many people have simply formed their own branch of the Democratic or Republican Party. In New York, Chicago, and Los Angeles during the 1960s, for example, many liberal reformers, dissatisfied with "old-fashioned" Democratic organizations, simply created new "reformed" Democratic clubs.[13]

It is quite likely that this ease of capture has prevented the emergence of numerous strong third parties. After all, why start a new party when one can play a role in an existing party? Rather than having the American Militant Black Party, we have instead the Adam Clayton Powell Democratic Club located in a black area of New York City. Practically every group that has wanted a piece of the political action has succeeded in finding a place in one of the two parties, so these groups are now part of "the system."

Overlapping electoral coalitions

A third important way parties moderate conflict is by competing for the votes of the same groups. Recall from Chapter 6 that elections are a winner-take-all affair: getting 49.9 percent of the vote usually means defeat. Under these circumstances, in order to win both the Democrats and the Republicans must put together large, diverse groups of voters. In this competition each party makes raids on the supporters of the other party.

This activity becomes clear when we examine party campaign organizations. Both the Democrats and the Republicans set up special organizations to attract members of the other party. Thus, while most blacks are Democrats, Republicans usually make a special effort to increase their share of the black vote. Democrats similarly "raid" Republican strongholds, hoping to get the few more votes necessary to reach over 50 percent. Organizations such as Republicans for Carter or Democrats for Ford were established specifically to attract opposition-party members.

The upshot is that many conflicts are blurred. To achieve victory the parties sometimes appear as if they were offering everything to everyone. To people who like to see identifiable differences between parties,

[13] The takeover of the Democratic Party in parts of New York, Chicago, and Los Angeles by liberal reformers is described in James Q. Wilson, *The Amateur Democrat* (Chicago: University of Chicago Press, 1962).

this raiding of nonsupporters is exasperating. Nevertheless, like the diversity of membership, the diversity of electoral coalitions serves as a means of moderating political conflict.

Should parties be abolished?

Though political parties in the United States are the longest lived in the world, they are not universally loved. For as long as parties have been around, a strong antiparty sentiment has also existed. Parties have been criticized as boss-ridden, corrupt, undemocratic, inflexible, wishy-washy on issues, inefficient, and so on. These accusations raise the questions: Would we be better off without political parties? Is there a new, improved product to replace the Democrats and the Republicans?

THE ARGUMENT THAT PARTIES ARE IN DECLINE

Many people feel that these questions are irrelevant because parties are gradually disappearing anyway. Several observers maintain that certain social and economic trends are eroding the bases of the two parties.[14] Four factors in particular are usually emphasized in this argument.

1. Partisan affiliation is slowly declining. More people than ever do not identify with one or the other party.
2. The role of the party in campaigning is being gradually overshadowed by professional consultants and organizations. The party machine can no longer make or break candidates.
3. Civil service and professional standards have deprived parties of the power to reward their followers with political jobs. Without such patronage to dispense, parties can no longer maintain large organizational networks.
4. Political reforms in the sixties and seventies have made it even more difficult for parties to resist capture by new groups not committed to traditional party values. Parties have become more open, but at the price of greater party conflict and disorganization.

There is considerable truth in each of these contentions. Parties have weakened and may continue to do so in the future. Nevertheless, we cannot say that the parties are dead yet. Most citizens still identify with them, and almost all candidates have a party label. Perhaps one hundred years from now they will have disappeared, but reports of their death are premature. Thus, we still face the question: Should they be abolished?

---

[14] Data based on these points and the findings of several other relevant studies are presented in Ladd, Chap. 6. Not everyone, however, accepts the fact that party attachments are declining. In particular, some analysts claim that the recent entry of large numbers of young people—who typically have the weakest party loyalties—into the electorate gives the impression of weakened parties. Warren E. Miller and Teresa E. Levitin, *Leadership and Change: Presidential Elections from 1952 to 1976* (Cambridge, Mass.: Winthrop, 1976), pp. 243–255.

The party is not over, yet. The election of Jane Byrne (pictured at right) as mayor of Chicago was interpreted by some as a defeat for the late Mayor Richard J. Daley's political machine. Byrne, however, was a protégée of Daley and received strong machine backing in the election.

POLITICS WITHOUT POLITICAL PARTIES

Perhaps the best way of answering this question is to ask what would happen if there were no parties. Would politics be improved? Would officeholders be more sensitive to the public? Would campaigns be more issue-oriented? To answer these questions we must examine two political situations in which parties are largely irrelevant. The first occurs in elections in which party labels (and certain other forms of party involvement) are prohibited. These are called **nonpartisan elections** and are fairly common at the local level in many states. The second situation is one in which everyone belongs to the same party, so the role of the party is sharply limited. This type of nonparty politics was once typical of the solid Democratic South.

Studies of nonpartisan elections and southern one-party politics have clearly indicated that for several reasons poor citizens suffer when party labels are not present. First, with no political organizations working to get out the vote, poor citizens are less likely to vote. Second, without parties to recruit candidates for office, those who do run for elections are disproportionately drawn from the middle and upper classes.[15] Third, and perhaps most important for persons who are less well off economically, policy enacted by "partyless" government tends to be biased against them. In the South for years the lack of party strength allowed "special

Nonpartisan elections Elections in which no party designations are permitted on the ballot, and other forms of party electoral participation may be prohibited.

[15] Kenneth Prewitt, *The Recruitment of Political Leaders: A Study of Citizen-Politicians* (Indianapolis, Ind.: Bobbs-Merrill, 1970), pp. 142–147.

interests" an enormous influence, because they could provide the resources necessary to campaign for elections.[16] A similar pattern is found in nonpartisan California cities where the great influence of the business community leads to officeholders who are less willing to use government to solve the problems of the poor and disadvantaged.[17] In short, without the parties to mobilize less well-off voters and to provide electoral resources, those already in positions of power do even better.

Another important consequence of not having parties is an increase in issue*less* elections. Battles between Democrats and Republicans may not be great debates over issues, but they typically have more issue content than when there are no parties. Without parties campaigns place even greater emphasis on personalities, friendships, places of residence, and other nonpolicy attributes. Candidates who are well known and are personally attractive have a considerable advantage. In addition, without parties citizens find it more difficult to vote on the basis of issues. As we noted earlier, voting by party is frequently a good strategy if one's information is limited. Where one faces many choices of candidates but does not even know what party they represent, deciding according to issues is even more difficult.[18]

Finally, observers agree that the absence of political parties makes it more difficult for voters to punish and reward leaders.[19] Recall that one advantage of having parties is that they provide clearly labeled "ins" and "outs." In 1979, for example, with Jimmy Carter as President and Democratic control of Congress, the Democrats were the ins and the Republicans the outs. Dissatisfied citizens could easily punish the ins by voting Republican in 1980. In nonpartisan and one-party politics, however, no clear in or out group usually exists. Typically, conflict involves numerous individuals with shifting alliances, so that it is hard to tell who is acting with whom. It is as if two basketball teams constantly exchanged players during a game. Because it is difficult to establish responsibility without party labels, the average voter may find it impossible to express satisfaction or dissatisfaction at election time (it would be like deciding which basketball team won).

The value of partyless politics
Whether these consequences of abolishing parties are bad or not depends on what you want to accomplish. If you are well off, well educated, and satisfied with present conditions, the absence of political parties would probably be an advantage. After all, you do not need a party to motivate you, aid your candidates, or provide information on the candidates. Perhaps for this reason much of the support for nonpartisan elections has come from wealthy, established political interests. On the other hand, if you are not well off, abolishing parties would be harmful to your

---

[16] V. O. Key, Jr., *Southern Politics* (New York: Random House, 1949), p. 305.

[17] Willis D. Hawley, *Nonpartisan Elections and the Case for Party Politics* (New York: Wiley Interscience, 1973), Chap. 6.

[18] Hawley, p. 148.

[19] Key, pp. 303–305.

cause. In many important ways political parties allow the have nots to compete more effectively with the haves. Therefore, getting rid of parties would probably "improve" politics only for certain groups.

Is there an alternative to parties that would "improve" politics for everyone equally? Probably not. Of course, many alternatives have been offered. Some people, for example, claim that stronger, more issue-oriented parties should replace existing parties.[20] Others go to the opposite extreme, arguing that for each election there should be a new set of groups competing for votes. These groups would dissolve after the election. Each of these suggestions has some attraction, but none offers an infallible solution. What is perhaps most important to understand from our analysis is that abolishing parties is not the cure-all for the problems associated with U.S. politics.

A conclusion: political parties and democracy

Political parties have been criticized on many grounds, but the most important complaint is that they subvert democracy. The fact that party officials, frequently meeting in secret, decide such questions as who will run for what office, how campaigns will be run, and what legislative programs will be pursued is typically viewed as undemocratic "back-room" politics. The undemocratic image of political parties is given considerable support by the long tradition of party **"bosses"** who ran cities and states without much public interference or scrutiny. In their heyday, bosses such as Richard J. Daley of Chicago and Carmine De Sapio of New York controlled thousands of votes, dispensed numerous economic benefits, and even decided what laws would be enforced. Through their capacity to deliver the vote, their power extended to state and national levels.

The fear of government by the Daleys, the De Sapios, and other party leaders has had a major impact on politics. The widespread practice of filling some positions with civil service bureaucrats rather than with elected officials, as well as the use of primaries, nonpolitical municipal elections, and laws regulating internal party affairs all derive from the fear of party power. Many a reformer has equated strong parties with corrupt government administered by party hacks. To weaken parties was then to strengthen good government.

Antiparty sentiment is still very much alive. Following the violence-marred 1968 Democratic presidential convention in Chicago, many citizens called for replacing established party leaders with new blood not drawn from the ranks of the party faithful. Running against the party "bosses" remains a useful campaign tactic in many areas. President

Bosses A name given to the leaders of strong party organizations (organizations were frequently called "machines").

---

[20] One recent and well-publicized call for stronger political parties can be found in David S. Broder, *The Party's Over: The Failure of Politics in America* (New York: Harper & Row, 1971), especially Chap. 11.

Carter's successful campaign for the Democratic presidential nomination relied heavily on an image of being a party outsider and thus (implicitly) a man of the people. Being closely identified as a party person is not a great asset in U.S. politics.

The frequent charge that parties are run undemocratically and therefore must be reformed rests on the key assumption that a democratically run political party means greater democracy. This assumption can be challenged. An alternative argument is that democracy depends on conflict *between* the parties, and what goes on within parties is comparatively unimportant. According to this perspective, democracies are strongest where voters are given a choice of candidates on election day and where all candidates can wage vigorous campaigns for public support. Parties offer candidates and then help the candidates campaign. So long as voters are not coerced by the parties, how parties choose candidates, how money is raised, and so on, is irrelevant. If voters do not like what a party offers, they don't support it. Just as Ford and General Motors compete for car sales, so do parties compete for voters. Democracy exists because voters have real choices, not because parties are democratically run. Ford and General Motors may be run as dictatorships, but citizens are still free to decide between a Ford and a Chevy.

The idea that competition between the parties is basic to democracy is useful for evaluating proposed reforms of U.S. political parties. It is possible, in the name of attempting to "increase" democarcy, to reform the parties out of existence. Allowing everyone to participate in internal party affairs, limiting party patronage, and weakening party control over public officials might make for more democracy to some people, but the net result might well be a reduced capacity of parties to compete for citizen support (and thus, from a different perspective, less democracy).

In short, the relationship between "democracy" and parties is complex. If one does not like parties or particular party officials, it is tempting to attack them in the name of democratic reform. We must be careful, however, not to endorse a program merely because its advocates call it democratic reform. Many conceptions of democracy exist, and at least one would see reforms such as primaries, which weaken parties, as detrimental to democracy. We should keep in mind that many of the features of parties that are viewed as undemocratic by some people (for example, control of nominations by nonelected party officials) are common in many European countries regarded as democratic.

Major questions raised

1. What are political parties? They are loose collections of citizens, party officials, and officeholders. Power in the Democratic and Republican parties is dispersed, and neither party can strictly control its own membership.

2. Do the Democratic and Republican parties differ? In general, Democrats and Republicans differ in the people they attract on many issues,

especially on the question of the role government should play with regard to the economy. However, they also overlap in their memberships and the policies they favor. At least at the congressional level, electing a Democrat over a Republican (or vice versa) does make a difference.

3. What are the consequences of having parties? Political parties perform several useful purposes: they help people make voting decisions, help candidates campaign, coordinate the actions of public officials, provide organized opposition to government, and moderate political conflict.

4. Should parties be abolished? One's answer to this question depends on one's political values. The evidence suggests, however, that U.S. political parties are most helpful to poor, less well-organized citizens.

QUESTIONS FOR FURTHER DISCUSSION

1. Both the Democratic and Republican parties have issue-oriented wings (for example, liberal Republican or conservative Democrat). On several issues, the wings of the parties overlap. For example, conservative Republicans and conservative Democrats agree that government spending should be reduced. Why not simplify things and just have two parties—one called Conservative and the other Liberal? In this way voters would have greater confidence in choosing candidates on the basis of party label. Such a system would also allow each party to offer clear choices to the electorate. Would you replace the Democratic and Republican parties with the Liberal and Conservative parties? What might be some of the costs of this change?

2. In the U.S. Congress a legislator cannot be forced to vote with fellow party members. Thus, a Democrat can vote with Republicans on every issue and still run in the next election as a Democrat. In the English political system, however, a member of Parliament (MP) who differs with party leadership can be deprived of the party label. The MP may seek reelection, but not as a member of the party. Traditionally, no matter how popular the MP might have been in his or her district, losing the party label means defeat. Should U.S. party leaders be able to say to an official, "Since you do not support our party's programs, you can no longer call yourself a Democrat (or Republican)"? Or should public officials be free to choose their party affiliation regardless of how they behave or what they believe in?

3. It has been claimed that one of the most important roles of political parties is that of "loyal opposition." That is, the party out of power has a responsibility for scrutinizing and criticizing programs of the in party. By this means citizens are kept informed and those in power are kept honest. Though the loyal-opposition notion is accepted with regard to domestic policy, some people doubt its applicability to foreign policy. They claim that opposing official U.S. foreign policy will only undermine delicate and complex dealings with foreign governments. It is argued, for example, that internal division undermined President Johnson's effort to resolve the war in Vietnam. But it may also be argued that the *lack* of a strong loyal opposition helped create the Vietnam disaster! Should

parties provide a loyal opposition on foreign policy? Are there situations when the party out of power should not criticize those in power?

4. One of the criticisms of primaries, especially open primaries, is that they allow cross-over voting. That is, Democrats vote for the Republican nominee, and vice versa. The frequent object of such cross-over voting is to nominate the weakest candidate for the other party. This then helps the candidate of one's own party. Of course, the net result may be that the two weakest candidates in the entire field face each other in the general election. What is needed to prevent cross-over voting is a stronger test for party affiliation. How would you keep Democrats out of Republican primaries, and vice versa? Would you charge a fee for participating, which would then go to the party? Should one party be allowed to exclude from its primaries members of the other party? What about one-party areas where winning the nomination of the majority party usually means certain election?

BIBLIOGRAPHY

Bone, Hugh A. *American Politics and the Party System*, 4th ed. New York: McGraw-Hill, 1971.
> A comprehensive text on virtually every aspect of U.S. political parties. Covers everything from origins of the party system through its contemporary operation. Bone also has several chapters on campaigns, voting, political participation, and interest groups.

Broder, David S. *The Party's Over: The Failure of Politics in America.* New York: Harper & Row, 1971.
> Broder covered politics for many years as a reporter. His basic argument is that our society is facing new and difficult challenges, and unless parties are reformed, we shall not be able to meet these challenges. The solution, according to Broder, is a stronger, more responsible party system.

Chambers, William Nisbet. *Political Parties in a New Nation: The American Experience.* New York: Oxford University Press, 1963.
> A detailed but clearly written description of early U.S. political parties. Unlike most other histories of the period, Chambers makes use of contemporary perspectives on parties to relate parties to overall U.S. political development. Contains "A Summary of Sources" that provides an excellent bibliography of works on early U.S. parties.

Davis, James W. *Presidential Primaries: Road to the White House.* New York: Crowell, 1967.
> A thorough examination of the history and operation of presidential primaries. Also discusses campaign strategy and what can happen to a presidential hopeful who enters a primary. Analyses are well documented with numerous examples and compilations of data.

Epstein, Leon D. *Political Parties in Western Democracies.* New York: Frederick A. Praeger, 1967.
> An extensive examination of the origins, organization, and policy roles of political parties in the United States and Western Europe. Also considers how party leaders are recruited, the impact of the electoral system on parties, and patterns of party competition. The best comparative treatment of parties available.

Feigert, Frank B., and M. Margaret Conway. *Parties and Politics in America.* Boston: Allyn & Bacon, 1976.
> The most up-to-date of the standard texts on political parties. It treats parties in a broad political context and thus examines individual voting behavior, citi-

zen communications with government, legislative behavior, different campaign tactics, and parties in the judicial branch.

Hawley, Willis D. *Nonpartisan Elections and the Case for Party Politics*. New York: Wiley Interscience, 1973.

The most systematic discussion of nonpartisanship available. Examines all the major arguments regarding nonpartisan elections. Many of these arguments are tested with data collected from 88 cities in the San Francisco Bay Area. Also presents information on the extent of nonpartisan elections throughout the United States.

Keefe, William J. *Parties, Politics, and Public Policy in America*, 2d ed. Hinsdale, Ill.: Dryden Press, 1976.

A brief but information-rich review of various aspects of U.S. political parties. Considers the characteristics of the parties, parties and election campaigns, and the role of parties in government. Concludes with a good analysis of the future of parties and possible party reform.

Key, V. O., Jr. *Politics, Parties and Pressure Groups*, 5th ed. New York: Crowell, 1964.

For many years this was the standard book on U.S. political parties. Contains excellent chapters on state parties, minor parties, the functions of parties, and party organization. Also contains extensive treatment of elections and interest groups.

Ladd, Everett Carll, Jr., with Charles D. Hadley. *Transformation of the American Party System: Political Coalitions from the New Deal to the 1970s*. New York: Norton, 1975.

Based on numerous opinion surveys, the authors describe the changing popular support for the Democratic and Republican parties. Good analyses of the role of social class, race, and region on party affiliation and voting.

Mazmanian, Daniel A. *Third Parties in Presidential Elections*. Washington, D.C.: Brookings Institution, 1974.

A concise but well-documented study of third parties. Examines the history of third parties, their policy impact, the electoral problems they face, and some of the possibilities of new third parties in the future.

Ranney, Austin. *Curing the Mischiefs of Faction: Party Reform in America*. Berkeley: University of California Press, 1975.

A knowledgeable and relatively brief introduction to the issue of reforming U.S. political parties. Considers our historical ambivalence about parties, the legal rules affecting party organization and behavior, recent reform attempts, and some of the difficulties of making parties mirror the make-up of society. Ranney is a leading academic authority on parties and also played a role in a recent effort to change the procedures of the Democratic Party.

Sorauf, Frank J. *Party Politics in America*, 3d ed. Boston: Little, Brown, 1976.

A popular text that covers virtually every aspect of U.S. parties. Covers in detail the organization of parties, their electoral role, and their function in government.

Wilson, James Q. *The Amateur Democrat*. Chicago: University of Chicago Press, 1962.

An excellent analysis of the reform movement in the Democratic Party in New York City and Los Angeles. Provides a good description of the ins and outs of contemporary big-city party politics.

PREVIEW

What are interest groups?

Interest groups take a variety of forms in U.S. politics, but all of them are collections of people acting together to influence decisions made by government. Formal organizations are the classic interest groups, and they range from the huge, well-financed U.S. Chamber of Commerce to much smaller one-person operations. Most of these groups are concerned with economic issues. A second type of group is the professional advocate. These include law firms, public relations firms, and well-connected individuals. The single-issue group is primarily concerned with mobilizing citizen support and tends to disappear once its issue fades into the background. Finally, many groups and associations devoted to nonpolitical causes can occasionally act as interest groups. On the whole, U.S. politics is very open to interest groups.

How do interest groups function?

Some groups try to sway public opinion or neutralize public opposition. Most groups attempt to influence legislation through such techniques as bribery, gaining the good will of legislators, providing legislators with necessary information, and even drafting legislation. Because the actual impact of much legislation depends on how it is interpreted, interest groups are also active in the administrative process. Groups work for the appointment of sympathetic administrators, influence administrative appointments, and even transform administrators into allies within the government. They also influence the appointment of judges and provide assistance in court cases.

How successful are interest groups?

Despite large expenditures and occasional successes, interest groups do not dominate government. Some are more successful than others. What makes for success? An organization's goals are one important factor—narrow, technical goals or ones that are socially acceptable are the easiest to advance. The opposition to one's goals also affects success. Groups that draw widespread public resistance or presidential opposition are less likely to succeed. Organizations with built-in access to the government have a great advantage.

Do interest groups undermine the public interest?

Interest groups have been widely criticized for undermining the national welfare by pursuing their own narrow goals and being more sensitive to policies favoring well-established economic interests. Interest groups can, however, be defended. On occasion less well-off citizens have won out over well-financed professionals. Also, no agreement exists on what really constitutes the "public interest." The public interest may be merely the sum total of all separate group interests, and controversy typically surrounds policies that are in the public interest. Moreover, some groups, for example, Common Cause, claim to work for the overall common good. On balance, pressure group politics seems to favor established economic interests.

CHAPTER NINE

INTEREST GROUPS AND PRESSURE POLITICS

ike political parties, interest groups are viewed with mixed feelings. On the one hand, everyone accepts the right of citizens to organize politically and to petition government. In fact, if asked how they would influence a political decision, most people would say "organize a group." On the other hand, people also believe that there is something evil about interest groups. Terms like "pressure group," "lobbyist," or "special interest" do not convey positive images, yet each is just another name for interest group. This chapter examines interest groups and their behavior through four key questions:

1. What are interest groups?
2. How do interest groups function?
3. How successful are interest groups?
4. Does the pursuit of narrow, selfish goals by interest groups harm the public interest.

Interest group A collection of people acting together to influence policy. Also sometimes called pressure group or special-interest group.

What are interest groups?

In principle, an **interest group** is easy to define. It is a collection of people acting together to influence government policy. This definition does not, however, capture the full range of interest group activity in U.S. politics. Depending on their goals and resources, interest groups take a variety of forms. In some instances these organizations will even deny that they are interest groups. Describing all the different varieties would be as impossible as describing all the diversity in North American vegetation. Nevertheless, interest groups seem to take the following general forms.

FORMAL ORGANIZATIONS

The classic interest group is a formal, permanent organization with a hired staff that advances well-defined political goals. Some groups, for example, the AFL-CIO in Washington, have impressive buildings, large, well-trained staffs, and ample resources. At the other extreme are formal organizations like the Citizens Lobby for Freedom and Fair Play that survive with minimal staffs and a lot of hustle.[1]

These groups operate at all levels of government, and their goals range from the very liberal (Americans for Democratic Action) to the very conservative (Americans for Constitutional Action). The most common type is the group designed to promote a particular economic interest. The American Hot-Dip Galvanizers Association, the National Kraut Packers Association, the Hawaiian Sugar Planters Association, the National Shrimp Congress, and the Instant Potato Products Association are typical of the several hundred such groups represented in Washington, D.C. The reason for the existence of large numbers of economic organizations is that contemporary government exercises considerable influence over businesses, so that political involvement is an economic necessity.

Many interests are represented through two or more organizations. Most business interests, for example, are represented by the U.S. Chamber of Commerce, which looks out for some 1,300 professional and trade associations and 68,000 corporations. A corporation may also support the National Association of Manufacturers, the Business Roundtable (an organization of nearly 200 business executives), and its own specialized trade organization. Just to be sure, large businesses may have their own lobbyists (Ford Motor Company, for example, has a full-time Washington staff of forty in addition to supporting a number of other organizations). Labor, likewise, has a complex representation—fifty labor unions have their own Washington organizations in addition to the AFL-CIO. This multiplicity of overlapping organizations helps explain

[1] The Citizens Lobby for Freedom and Fair Play is run by Harry and Ruth Kingman. This organization has an annual budget of $8,000, most of which comes from Harry Kingman's pension from the YMCA. The Kingmans lobby for civil rights and federal aid to education. This and other descriptions of lobbyists can be found in James Deakin, *The Lobbyists* (Washington, D.C.: Public Affairs Press, 1966), Chap. 1.

why an issue affecting one interest can bring out several different groups. For example, the debate over government regulation of national gas prices has mobilized 117 separate **lobbying** groups.[2]

PROFESSIONAL ADVOCATES

The professional advocate might be characterized as a political "gun for hire." Suppose that you and your friends are flunking out of college; rather than study harder, you decide it would be easier to get a law passed saving endangered students. Each of you could chip in a few thousand dollars to set up an association to work on your behalf. Since you need action fast and lack financial resources, however, you would probably be better off to obtain the services of a well-connected advocate, who, for a fee, would take on your case.

Where could you find such a gun for hire? The most obvious places are the politically connected law firms that are always near centers of government at all levels. In Washington, for example, the firm of Arnold and Porter has looked after the political interests of such diverse clients as *Playboy Magazine*, the Swiss Embassy, and the American Baseball League.[3] Less visible are the numerous public relations and consulting firms, which will guide you through the maze of government decision making. Many of these firms hire former members of Congress or other high-ranking officials. The least publicly visible gun for hire is the freelance political advocate (or "**influence peddler**"). Because these individuals operate in private without large staffs, not much is known about their activities. What we do know commonly emerges from scandals when these advocates are caught obtaining government favors on matters that mean a lot to some people but have little overall impact on public policy.[4]

SINGLE-ISSUE GROUPS

Whereas the previous two types of interest groups usually consist of a few individuals working near centers of power, the single-issue mass groups try to enlist thousands of supporters and openly seek wide publicity. Many of the civil rights, anti-Vietnam war, and ecology groups were of this type. These groups tend to be comparatively short-lived and lack

Lobbying To lobby means to contact officials on behalf of one's cause. The term comes from the fact that such contacts frequently took place in the lobbies of legislatures.
Influence peddler An unsavory name given to people who, for a fee, will try to get government favors for a client. Many influence peddlers prefer the label political consultant.

---

[2] "Single Issue Politics," *Newsweek*, November 6, 1978.

[3] For an excellent description of how these law firms influence public policy, see Joseph C. Goulden, *The Superlawyers* (New York: Weybright and Talley, 1971); and Mark J. Green, *The Other Government: The Unseen Power of Washington Lawyers* (New York: Grossman Publishers, 1975).

[4] One of these "influence peddlers" has provided a detailed record of his activities (Robert N. Winter-Berger, *The Washington Pay-Off* [New York: Dell, 1972]). Among the things arranged by Winter-Berger were getting the son of a very rich family out of the Marines, helping businesspeople with awkward tax problems, and covering up the arrest of a U.S. Senator in a homosexual bar. None of these activities undermine the vital national interest, and none is clearly illegal. These advocates do, however, provide great benefits for those able to afford their services.

THE CASE OF "TOMMY THE CORK" CORCORAN

In his study of Washington law firms, Joseph C. Goulden relates a classic instance of high-powered legal intervention. In the late 1960s, a tool and die company was in serious trouble with the Pentagon over defective welds in gun barrels. The Defense Department stood to gain substantial damages from the company in a rather clear-cut case. The tool and die company hired one of the best Washington lawyers—Tom "Tommy the Cork" Corcoran—to plead its case. Corcoran spent less than an hour hearing the case, made a brief call to the Pentagon, and announced that the problem was settled. "Tommy the Cork's"

Tom "Tommy the Cork" Corcoran.

bill was $10,000, which was far less than the penalties would have been for the faulty weld. The assisted company was outraged—not over the $10,000 bill but over how little effort Corcoran exerted to earn the fee.

Reported in Joseph C. Goulden, *The Superlawyers* (New York: Weybright and Talley, 1971), pp. 148–149.

strong organization. The typical pattern is for a group of citizens concerned over a specific issue, for example, saving a redwood forest from loggers, to "stir things up" by holding demonstrations, writing letters, staging boycotts, or working in political campaigns. The emphasis is on mobilizing public pressure, not on hiring professional advocates. When the issue is resolved or loses public appeal, the group may disappear.

Some people argue that because of their transitory, poorly organized nature, these "one-shot" groups are less effective than permanent organizations that can cultivate close ties with decision makers. Moreover, these single-issue groups disproportionately favor liberal causes, for example, ecology, while formal organizations tend to be used by more conservative or business interests. Therefore, liberal causes are less successful at interest group politics even though at times they mobilize tens of thousands of people. We shall have more to say later about what makes for interest group success.

"NONPOLITICAL" INTEREST GROUPS

To claim that nonpolitical groups engage in political pressure may appear to be a contradiction. This contradiction disappears, however, when we realize that there are thousands of groups whose basic purpose is nonpolitical, but which on occasion engage in political action. And because these groups receive tax advantages for being nonpolitical, this political activity must be conducted very carefully. In fact, activity on the part of these interest groups is sometimes so subtle that it is hardly viewed as political.

One of the best examples of such groups is provided by organized religions. We would not normally consider the Catholic Church in the same business as, say, the Poultry and Egg Institute of America, but both engage in lobbying. On the abortion and birth control issues in particular, the Catholic hierarchy has made its presence felt in the lawmaking process. Similarly, Jewish rabbis sometimes act as spokespeople for the U.S. Jewish community on issues pertaining to Israel. Another common nonpolitical interest group is the professional association. Organizations such as the American Political Science Association exist largely to

A group of citizens demanding better treatment for women over 45. Interests such as this one are likely to be less successful than groups advancing specific goals involving a few key people.

promote scholarly activities. Nevertheless, my $35 yearly membership fee helps support a Washington office that occasionally tells the government why we political scientists need more federal research grants or keeps us informed of relevant legislation. Even charities sometimes use their memberships and organizations to advance political causes. The United Cerebral Palsy Association, Inc., while not legally a lobby, nevertheless engages in some lobbying for federal funds for medical research.

Of course, many interests advance their causes by employing several of these methods. The black civil rights movement, for example, uses all four approaches. If a law on employment discrimination were being considered, members of Congress would probably receive mail generated by mass organizations or visits from ministers of churches with black congregations. Typically, these efforts are instigated by established organizations such as the National Association for the Advancement of Colored People (NAACP), which in turn may make use of Washington lawyers or public relations experts for portions of their campaigns.

It is obvious from this review of different types of organizations that interest group politics is a very open system. One does not need much money or a full-time organization in Washington, D.C., or the state capital to play the game. Though numerous state and federal regulations exist, these laws largely concern registration and disclosure of expenses and do not inhibit starting a group. No wonder, then, that there are thousands of groups all competing for their own goals. Is this multitude of organizations a good thing? Defenders of the present system claim that the diversity and number of groups is evidence of democratic

THE CASE OF THE ENTERPRISING TREKIES

A classic illustration of a one-shot interest organization was the massive write-the-White-House campaign organized by fans of the television series "Star Trek." Star Trek fans wanted the name of the U.S. space shuttle changed from the "Constitution" to the "Enterprise," the name of the spaceship in the television series. The National Aeronautics and Space Administration (NASA) has a firm policy of not responding to names suggested by the public. Rebuffed by NASA, the Trekies bombarded President Ford with mail for over a year, until Ford finally convinced NASA to give in to them. President Ford told James Fletcher, administrator of NASA, "I'm a little partial to the name Enterprise."

Reported in The New York Times, Thursday, September 9, 1976.

vitality. Opponents counter that the overall public interest loses out when each group uses politics solely to advance its own selfish interests. Later we will consider this question in more detail.

How do interest groups function?

All interest groups attempt to influence political decisions. However, because of differences in specific goals and resources, all do not follow the same tactics. A well-heeled organization that is pushing a single bill hardly behaves like an impoverished group dedicated to saving the world. Though most groups engage in several types of activities, we can distinguish four general interest group aims: (1) to influence public opinion; (2) to influence legislation; (3) to affect administrative decision making; and (4) to influence court decisions.

INFLUENCING PUBLIC OPINION

Group representatives understand that public opinion does not precisely determine government policy, yet they also realize that public opinion must be cultivated. At a minimum, outright public hostility to one's objectives must be softened or neutralized. Even the most powerful interests recognize that political leaders will not make unpopular decisions that could jeopardize reelection. The importance of public opinion is well demonstrated in the failure of Arab efforts to overcome U.S. support for Israel. Even if billions were spent on their behalf, Arab interests would still face an uphill fight because of widespread public sympathy for Israel.[5]

Public opinion is cultivated through a variety of strategies. A familiar example is an advertising campaign to enhance the image of an entire industry. Over the years private electric companies have placed numerous magazine ads describing the advantages of private enterprise over public ownership of utilities. Similarly, in 1973, the American Petroleum Institute spent $2.5 million for advertisements in mass circulation magazines depicting the virtues of big oil companies.[6] These campaigns are typically "soft sell" programs designed to create favorable climates of opinion. The technique is not limited to business interests. Many liberal groups such as environmentalists have used the identical methods to generate support for their causes.

[5] Recently, however, the Arabs have begun to take an interest in molding public opinion. In 1978, the Saudi Arabian government paid $65,000 to a public relations firm to take the Saudi point of view to the people. They have also hired the Washington lawyer Frederick G. Dutton, a former official in the Kennedy Administration, to help improve their image. More information on attempts by foreign interests to influence public opinion is presented in Chapter Nineteen.

[6] *The Washington Lobby*, 2d ed. (Washington, D.C.: Congressional Quarterly, 1974), p. 84.

Women lobbying legislators in the 1860s.

Less visible than advertisements in *Time* or *Newsweek* are campaigns directed toward particular segments of the public. Interest group leaders frequently reason that it is more effective to reach a few thousand opinion leaders than to appeal to millions of people through the mass media. This is especially true when the topic is not relevant to most citizens. In 1963, for example, the public relations firm of Selvage and Lee, working on behalf of the Overseas Companies of Portugal, bombarded members of Congress and thousands of influential citizens with such pamphlets as "Angola: A Challenge and Opportunity" and "Behind the Terror in African Angola." Here again, the purpose is to create an environment and public pressure generally favorable to a political cause, in this case U.S. support for Portuguese control of the African colony of Angola.[7]

INFLUENCING LEGISLATION

Because interest groups must ultimately deal with laws, sooner or later all groups must face the problem of convincing legislators. Whether the setting is a city council meeting or the U.S. Senate, a method must be found to guarantee the right decision. How do interest groups try to influence legislative votes?

[7] Deakin, p. 22.

Direct and indirect bribery

One method is the outright buying of votes. Since the "right" government decision can be worth millions of dollars to certain individuals, it is not surprising that potential beneficiaries will invest a few thousand dollars to secure that outcome. Especially in the nineteenth century, and at the state and local levels until fairly recently, outright bribery was common and perhaps even acceptable. For example, Senator Daniel Webster, widely viewed as incorruptible, received $32,000 from Nicolas Biddle for his support of the second Bank of the United States. Webster saw nothing wrong with this behavior. During the great economic expansion of the nineteenth century, whole state legislatures were purchased outright by railroad, lumber, or oil interests.[8] Payoffs were so common that it was sometimes said that an honest politician was one who, when bought, stayed bought.

In contemporary politics such systematic and blatant buying of votes has almost disappeared. One reason is that the growth of the mass media and laws pertaining to outright bribery have made such practices risky. The exposure of Tongsun Park's gifts to members of Congress on behalf of South Korean interests clearly demonstrates the risks of buying votes. Though one might on occasion buy a few votes, as a long-term strategy blatant corruption is likely to be discovered and thus backfire. It is also true that some of the old bribes are less valuable today than they were in the past. Today, a few bottles of whiskey would not buy a legislator's vote (and a truckload of bottles would arouse suspicion).[9] Even the old ploy of using call girls to sway votes has become limited because of the advanced age of many powerful legislative leaders.

Bribery has not disappeared, however. It still exists, but much of it has become so subtle that it is almost impossible to distinguish it from useful assistance. Whereas an obvious vote buyer provides a concrete payment for a specific vote, today's skillful lobbyists emphasize a more general feeling of "good will" between legislators and themselves. Such "good will" can be created in numerous ways. For instance, until 1970, Ford Motor Company leased cars to members of Congress at very reasonable

---

[8] A brief history of legislative bribery is presented in Deakin, Chap. 3. The existence of bribery is not always a result of evil interests forcing money on reluctant legislators. When money is tight, an enterprising legislator can generate it. For example, a study of the California legislature—which is relatively "clean"—describes the use of the "cinch bill." A cinch bill is legislation that would financially harm a major interest that has been less than generous in its contributions. Faced with such possible legislation, the affected interest suddenly becomes financially generous. This process is described in Larry L. Berg, Harlan Hahn, and John R. Schmidhauser, *Corruption in the American Political System* (Morristown, N.J.: General Learning Press, 1976), p. 153.

[9] Whiskey can be used in other ways than as an outright bribe. Many years ago, the night before a key vote in the House Education and Labor Committee, a labor lobbyist took Representative Carroll Kearns (R-Pa.) out drinking. The lobbyist got Kearns so drunk that he was unable to show up the next day and vote against labor. Cited in "The Swarming Lobbyists," *Newsweek*, August 7, 1978.

SWEET-TALKING THE PUBLIC

Because the public relations campaigns of many interest groups are not openly labeled as such, we are frequently unaware of them. Many magazine and newspaper stories called "news" are really part of the strategy of an interest group to mold public opinion. This is well illustrated by the tactics used by Samuel E. Stavisky in the mid-1950s on behalf of Cuban sugar interests. Stavisky's goal was to generate public pressure on Congress to increase the amount of sugar Cuba could export to the United States under a quota system. Douglas Cater, a Washington reporter, has described Stavisky's activities.

Commencing not with the politicians but with the press, Stavisky reasoned that he had a complex story to get across on a subject about which most reporters couldn't care less. He invited small groups of his former colleagues for sumptuous meals at Washington's Colony Restaurant where he discussed the subject with a former newsman's feel for the "facts" and the "angle." Assisted by a liberal expense account, he "encouraged" reporters to visit Cuba and see the problems for themselves. A few were provided with direct travel subsidies when they couldn't get their publications to finance them. One correspondent even charged off his gambling losses in Havana, Stavisky recollects.

These efforts began to pay off in a sudden spate of stories about Cuba and its sugar problems. A number bore the notation, gratifying to a reporter's ego, that they had been based on "a personal conference with President Batista." But the recurrent theme was one emphasized by Stavisky; in the words of one news column, "Whether Cubans eat or go hungry depends on the absorption in the United States market of a large portion of their sugar." A second Stavisky theme — the threat of Communist takeover in Cuba — usually followed.

Equally important to his campaign, Stavisky soon worked out a news angle that made the fate of Cuban sugar of important local interest all

rates.[10] Large corporations make their private jets available free of charge to legislators with the sudden urge to fly home. Many members of

[10] While an average citizen would pay $4,000 a year to lease a Lincoln Continental, key members of Congress paid only $750. General Motors gave even a better deal by leasing Cadillacs to high Pentagon officials for only $100 a year. These and other such favors are reported in Carol S. Greenwald, *Group Power: Lobbying and Public Policy* (New York: Praeger, 1977), pp. 80–83.

over the United States. By a meticulous IBM punch-card breakdown of shipping invoices, he was able to trace the origin of more than $400 million in U.S. exports to Cuba, according to state, city, congressional district, product, industry, and company. A steady flow of stories began to appear in small papers across the country with such edifying facts as "Cuba is the most important market for Columbia basin red beans . . ." (*Wenatchee* [Washington] *World*); "The Cuban imports are important to the industrial prosperity of Texas" (*Littlefield* [Texas] *Leader*); "Cuban Sugar Makes Possible Exports of Rice" (*Yellsville* [Arkansas] *Mountain Echo*); "Much Ohio Lard Goes to Cubans" (*Tiffin* [Ohio] *Advertiser-Tribune*). In the western tier of the North Central states, whose congressmen were considered hostile to sugar imports, the information that 708 manufacturers had sold Cuba more than $22 million of goods in a single year was treated as news by dozens of papers. Stavisky also sorted out his statistics to appeal to industry, farm, and labor publications. With a special solicitude for the American consumer, there soon appeared a number of magazine feature stories critical of the domestic sugar growers under such eye-catching titles as "Flies in the Sugar Bowl" and " 'Sugar' for U.S. Sugar Producers at the Expense of Many." When the Department of Agriculture issued a routine report with a section on "Cuba as a Market for United States Agricultural Products," Stavisky made certain that it did not suffer the ignominious fate of many such government publications.

Stavisky's office likewise stimulated a steady flow to various letters-to-the-editor, aware that this is usually the most widely read feature outside the comic pages. A special campaign was directed at labor unions, using arguments about "economic self-interest, American security, and friendship for Cuba's strong anti-communist labor movement." Despite the self-interest opposition of the AFL beet workers and the CIO packinghouse workers, their parent unions strongly endorsed Cuba's cause.

Stavisky's campaign was successful.

Douglass Cater, *Power in Washington* (New York: Random House, 1964), pp. 200–203.

Congress find it remarkably easy to obtain hard-to-get professional football or theater tickets, thanks to helpful lobbyists. What comes closest to old-fashioned bribery are campaign contributions made by lobbyists, but as long as they are reported, they are perfectly legal.

Such favors are not one-time attempts to influence specific votes. The hope is that these favors will create feelings of good will that make "hard sell" tactics unnecessary. Imagine that as a member of Congress your Washington existence has been made much easier because of the efforts of a certain corporation. In addition, thanks to weekend fishing trips or dinner parties, you have developed close personal ties with these corporate representatives. One day a bill quite harmful to the corporation is introduced in Congress. Even if you had come to Washington committed to such a bill, you might now find it difficult to support it. Is this a case of bribery, or have your personal contacts given you a new perspective?

Another method of winning influence is to pay legislators for speaking before one's group or contributing to one's publications. Providing "honoraria" for such services is perfectly legal and widely practiced. In 1976, for example, eighty-four Senators reported a total of $981,403 in the form of honoraria. Senator Herman E. Talmadge (D.-Ga.), Chairperson of the Senate Committee on Agriculture, Nutrition and Forestry, earned $25,000 in such fees, primarily from speaking to agricultural interest groups (the Senate honorarium champ is Daniel P. Moynihan, who earned $165,393.18 from speeches, but while he was a candidate for office, not an incumbent). Recent legislation, however, may curb these practices. As of January 1, 1979, the outside income members of Congress may receive from special interest groups is limited to 15 percent of a member's official salary ($8,625 on the present salary of $57,500).[11] However, as with past efforts to control outside donations, the impact of these tougher laws remains to be seen.

Supplying legislators with information

Besides subtle and not so subtle bribery, interest groups try to affect legislation by supplying information. Modern legislatures must daily deal with complex subjects. Legislators, no matter how intelligent or hard working, cannot on their own obtain all the information they need on most issues. Congress has tried a variety of methods of providing information, but these attempts have been only partially successful. At the state and local levels the problem of obtaining good information is even more severe.

Into this picture steps the interest group representative who is more than willing to supply the needed data. This is frequently done at public hearings conducted by legislative committees. For example, in 1975, hearings were conducted on bills to regulate lobbyists. Representatives from such diverse groups as the National Association of Counties, the National Wildlife Federation, the Noncommissioned Officers Association of America, and the American Conservative Union all provided needed testimony on the likely impact of different proposals.[12] When congressional committees considered energy legislation in 1977, they greatly depended on oil and gas data supplied by oil-industry associations. In other instances information is given directly to legislators and

[11] "New Ethics Codes Require More Details," *Congressional Quarterly Guide to Current American Government*, Spring 1978, pp. 11–17.

[12] "Lobbying—Efforts to Influence Government Actions," Hearings Before the Committee on Standards of Official Conduct, House of Representatives, 94th Congress, first session (Washington, D.C.: Government Printing Office, 1976).

OILING THE BIG
WHEELS OF
GOVERNMENT

One important way lobbyists conduct business is by throwing a cocktail party. It is estimated that about 1,500 such parties a year are given by Washington groups. In some instances, wining and dining can be a major weapon. For example, between 1969 and 1974, Northrop Industries hired Madame Chennault to host parties as part of their promotion of the F-5 fighter jet. A total of $160,000 was spent on these parties. Subsequently, Northrop billed the Pentagon for these expenses, listing Madame Chennault as a consultant.

Numerous other instances of lobby wheeling and dealing can be found in Carol S. Greenwald, *Group Power: Lobbying and Public Policy* (New York: Praeger, 1977), pp. 80–83.

their staffs. As a result of these efforts, many of our laws are based on data supplied by interests directly affected by the legislation.

Is it a wise idea to rely on information supplied by lobbyists? After all, such material is unlikely to be completely objective.[13] Perhaps the best answer to this question is that even biased information is sometimes better than ignorance. Certainly most legislators realize that, say, the American Medical Association may exaggerate the evils of government-sponsored health care. Then, too, legislators often receive information from different sides, so biases can cancel each other out. Thus, on transportation legislation, groups representing railroads and trucking companies can usually be counted on to supply information against each other. It is hoped that by weighing biases and conflicting testimony legislators may arrive at the truth.

Drafting legislation

The third way that interest groups influence legislation is by actually drafting legislation. Here, the line between lobbyist and legislator is nonexistent. According to some estimates, *half* of all the legislation proposed in Washington is drafted entirely or in part by interest groups.[14] As in the supplying of information, this service results from limitations

[13] Since a lobbyist has to worry about long-term relationships, it would be foolish to get a reputation for supplying inaccurate information. A study of California lobbying suggests that such information is always regarded as accurate. See Berg, Hahn, and Schmidhauser, p. 144.

[14] Deakin, p. 6.

SELLING OUT TO THE RUSSIANS

Though buying legislative votes has had a long history in the United States, the long-term impact of such bribery is not completely clear. While bribery itself is illegal and reprehensible, it need not result in disastrous public policy. This is well illustrated by events in Washington during 1868. At this time Congress was debating legislation of considerable financial value to the Russian government. The Russian minister in Washington—a Mr. Stoekl—decided to help move things along by purchasing the support of leading public figures. N. P. Banks, chairperson of the House Committee on Foreign Relations, was given $8,000 for his support. The "incorruptible" Thaddeus Stevens, a leading member of Congress, got $10,000. John W. Forney, a former public official and prominent newspaper publisher, received $30,000 to publicize the Russian cause. Two well-known Washington lawyers received $20,000. Overall, about $200,000 was spent to bribe officials and sway public opinion. In the end, Stoekl and the Russian government were successful, and the United States agreed to pay for Alaska.

Details of this scandal are reported in William A. Dunning, "Paying for Alaska: Some Unfamiliar Incidents in the Process," *Political Science Quarterly*, 27 (1912), pp. 385–398.

on congressional resources: Drafting bills usually requires expertise and time, and most legislators cannot do everything themselves. In addition, the lobbyist providing the bill will occasionally also provide the speeches in support of the bill.

Hiring former legislators

In many instances interest groups insure their access to the legislative process by hiring former members of Congress. For example, Andrew J. Biemiller, chief lobbyist for the AFL-CIO, was once a member of Congress from Wisconsin. The Tobacco Institute, which spent $4.5 million in 1977 to protect tobacco farmers from government interference, is headed by Horace R. Kornegay, a former Representative from North Carolina. The Institute's legal problems are handled by Marlow Cook, former Senator from Kentucky, and David Henderson, ex-member of the House from North Carolina. When Wilbur Mills left Congress he made a very good living advising corporations on the tax laws that he, as chairperson of the House Ways and Means Committee, had helped write.

Not only are these former legislators knowledgeable about the lawmaking process but their friendships with current members of Congress provide them with access denied to outsiders. (A frequently expressed concern is that some legislators act with an eye to becoming well-paid lobbyists while they are still in Congress.)

AFFECTING ADMINISTRATIVE DECISION MAKING

Even if an organization is successful in the legislature, its job is not over. The actual impact of a law frequently depends on its administration. Every law requires some degree of interpretation, and in many instances administrative agencies possess great discretion in formulating their own rules and regulations. Therefore, the passage of a favorable bill may merely mean that the battle now shifts to the Department of Agriculture, the Interstate Commerce Commission, or some other agency responsible for daily enforcement (lobbying is especially crucial where administrative opinion affects the prices of goods and services).

Since administrative agencies, like legislatures, are responsible for making rules, many activities of lobbyists in Congress and the bureaucracies are similar. For example, most agencies are required to hold public hearings on proposed changes in regulations, and these are attended by group representatives. Thus, when the Interstate Commerce Commission considers a change in the maximum cargo trucks can carry, representatives of the truckers, the trucking companies, highway safety groups, and the railroads all provide expert testimony on the impact of the proposed regulation. Moreover, especially when regulations are highly technical, interest groups can play a major role in the drafting process (on some topics not more than a few people in the world understand all the complexities).

Influencing administrative appointments

Several activities of lobbyists are particularly relevant to administrative agencies. One of the most important is making sure that administrative appointments are acceptable to affected interests. It would be a disaster, for example, if the airlines had to deal with hostile Civil Aeronautics Board members, so airline representatives work long and hard with Congress and the executive branch to insure the right appointments. The impact of interest groups on agency leadership was well illustrated in 1969 when the American Medical Association (AMA) successfully blocked President Nixon's nomination of Dr. John Knowles as Assistant Secretary of Health, Education, and Welfare for Health and Scientific Affairs. Despite his standing and distinguished record, the AMA, fearing that Knowles would favor public health programs at the expense of private medicine, waged a strenuous campaign that cost him the position.[15]

[15] The politics of the Knowles appointment are described in L. Harmon Zeigler and G. Wayne Peak, *Interest Groups in American Society*, 2d ed. (Englewood Cliffs, N.J.: Prentice-Hall, 1972), pp. 255–258.

Triangle relationship A mutually beneficial relationship that typically involves an interest group, a government agency, and a congressional committee.

Influencing appropriations of administrative agencies

Another means to influence administrative decisions is to use group influence on legislative appropriations. A close interrelationship often develops among interest groups, bureaucracies, and the congressional committees that help determine an agency's budget. For example, over the years veterans' groups, legislative committees dealing with veterans' benefits, and the Veterans Administration have built up a close working relationship. Each member of this **"triangle" relationship** helps the others. It is not surprising that in exchange for help to the House Committee on Veteran Affairs on next year's budget, officials in the Veterans Administration will lend a sympathetic ear to the American Legion. Such give-and-take relationships occur in virtually every federal agency, whether the policies involve education or national defense.[16]

JUSTICE AND THE NATIONAL INTEREST REQUIRE HIGHER TARIFFS ON FERROCHROMIUM

A skilled lobbyist knows how to transform a self-serving policy into one that appears to support humanitarian and patriotic goals. Consider the issue of whether the tariff on ferrochromium, a metal used to manufacture stainless steel, should be increased. In 1977, the United States imported about half its ferrochromium, most of it from South Africa, where its production cost is significantly lower than in the United States. Domestic producers of ferrochromium convinced the International Trade Commission, an independent government agency, to recommend to President Carter that tariffs on this metal be increased by 30 percent. Carter rejected the tariff increase as inflationary. Undaunted, the domestic ferrochromium producers hired Robert J. Keefe, a former top aid to the Democratic National Committee, to lobby on their behalf. By emphasizing the repressive racial policies of South Africa, Keefe sought support for the tariff increase among blacks in Congress and other influential blacks. The higher tariff was also promoted as a step toward slowing down the mounting U.S. trade deficit. Finally, Keefe invoked national defense by pointing out that without the tariff increase, the United States might become dependent on an unstable foreign nation for an allegedly key defense material. In short, the tariff issue became linked with the issues of racial prejudice, protection of the dollar, and a strong national defense.

"The Ferrochromium Caper," *Forbes,* September 18, 1978.

[16] These "triangle" relationships are described more fully in Theodore J. Lowi, *The End of Liberalism* (New York: Norton, 1969), Chap. 4.

Coopting administrators

The third method of influencing administrative decision making employed by organizations is "**cooptation.**" Here an interest succeeds in transforming a government agency into an agent for its own cause. The group not only influences a few decisions but also manages to run the entire show. Perhaps the classic case of such cooptation occurred when the railroads "captured" the Interstate Commerce Commission (ICC) shortly after its creation. Originally designed to protect the public through the regulation of railroad rates, the ICC instead became the defender of the railroads against Congress, the public, and other transportation industries.

How can a private organization capture an administrative agency? One way is to encourage the interchange of personnel. It is not unusual for a member of an interest group to become part of the government and then return to that group as a professional lobbyist. After a while, common experience and friendship result in one big happy family.[17] Interest groups also stress to administrators that they share the same basic interests and goals. The American Farm Bureau Federation owes much of its success with various Agriculture Department agencies to the selling of an "all of us farm people are in the same boat together" philosophy. In short, a possible conflicting relationship between a lobbyist and an agency is transformed into a cooperative relationship based on common purpose—as defined by the interest group.

Cooptation The process by which one interest transforms a potential enemy into an ally —though on paper the conflict may still exist.

INFLUENCING COURT DECISIONS

At first glance one would think that interest groups have little impact on the judicial process. After all, judges are well above day-to-day politics, strict canons of judicial procedures govern court decisions, and judges are not usually accessible to group representatives who want to plead their causes. Nevertheless, the formalities and apparent inaccessibility of the judicial process does not exclude interest group activities. This behavior is not always visible, but it can be as intense as efforts directed toward legislators or administrators.

Influencing judicial appointments

One important method organizations use to influence court decisions is to play a role in judicial appointments. Though judges must operate within relatively narrow guidelines, interest groups are well aware that not all judges think alike. Particularly in complex cases without clear precedents, the personal opinions of judges can be crucial. Hence, whether the appointment is a city judge or the Chief Justice of the

---

[17] This easy family feeling can sometimes get out of hand. The story is told of a Washington lawyer who was representing a trucking firm before the Interstate Commerce Commission. After a lunch at which alcohol was freely consumed, the attorney returned, took a seat in the *hearing examiner's chair,* and gaveled for order. He had to be reminded that since he had resigned from the ICC two years before, he now belonged on the other side of the table. This and other instances of such switching are found in Goulden, Chap. 5.

Amicus curiae *brief* A brief
prepared by a person or a
group not directly involved in
the legal proceeding that contains additional information.

Supreme Court, citizens whose interests could be affected frequently lobby for a sympathetic judge. Over the years some of the most publicized efforts at getting "good" judges—especially in the Supreme Court—have been made by black civil rights groups. These groups were instrumental, for example, in blocking the Nixon appointments of Clement Haynsworth and Harold Carswell, both of whom were viewed as unsympathetic to black interests. Other groups are also active in the appointment process, but because pressure is frequently applied in the early stages of the nominating process, it is hardly noticed by most citizens.

Support cases

A second important method of exerting influence is to support cases as they move through the court system. In the U.S. judicial system obtaining a legal ruling requires that a case be brought before a judge. Interest groups who are seeking legal changes are therefore always on the lookout for a case that can be used to advance their causes. Through this method civil rights groups have managed to overturn many discriminatory laws. The law requiring racial segregation of schools, for example, was overturned in 1954 in *Brown* v. *Board of Education,* a Kansas case guided through the courts by NAACP lawyers.[18] Similarly, the American Civil Liberties Union has had a major impact on politics by supplying lawyers and financial support in cases involving free speech, censorship, and religion in public schools.

Even if not a direct party to a case, an interest group can try to influence judicial decisions by supplying relevant information. The most common method is to file what is called an **amicus curiae** (friend of the court) brief. Here a group with a stake in a case can offer arguments not offered by the immediate participants. These briefs have played important roles in the outcomes of several major cases.[19] In the 1978 Bakke case involving the use of racial quotas in a California medical school, some fifty *amicus curiae* briefs were filed. Interest groups can also encourage scholarly research that might ultimately prove valuable. This strategy has become important as some judges increasingly rely on sociological research in addition to knowledge of technical points of law.

Thus far we have shown that (1) political organizations are numerous and easily formed, and (2) virtually every area of U.S. politics is open to their influence. This situation has disturbed many people. In fact, some critics suggest that interest groups ought to be severely restricted or even abolished. Before we consider this important argument, however, let us examine the crucial question of how much impact interest groups have.

---

[18] Particularly in cases involving poor people, support from interest groups may be essential if the cases are to be adequately considered. The 1954 *Brown* v. *Board of Education* case cost the NAACP over $200,000. Obviously, few blacks could afford to pursue school integration on their own.

[19] The *amicus curiae* brief has been employed with great skill by civil rights groups. Typically, the brief presents arguments that go beyond the narrow legal points in the case. The classic study of the use of *amicus curiae* briefs by interest groups is Clement E. Vose, *Caucasians Only* (Berkeley: University of California Press, 1959).

How successful are interest groups?

Do organizations such as the American Gas Association, the Young Women's Christian Association, and the American Trial Lawyers Association really have an impact on public policy? Is government behavior largely a result of the pushes and pulls of pressure groups? Most observers would probably agree that interest groups in general do have political clout, but by no means is government run by these groups. Almost all groups have some degree of success, but success does not mean domination.

ARGUMENTS SUPPORTING THE POWER OF INTEREST GROUPS

People who claim that interest groups are successful frequently point to all the money spent on lobbying. At all levels of government, business, labor, consumer, and educational groups spend tens of millions of dollars each year to advance their causes. A study by the House Subcommittee on Commerce, Consumers and Monetary Affairs estimated that in 1978

TOO MUCH SUCCESS CAN LEAD TO FAILURE

Successful lobbyists can do very well financially, but if they are *too* successful, they may eliminate their own jobs. Lobbyists are thus like doctors, who would become unemployed if they succeeded in banishing disease. This dilemma is well illustrated in a story told by James Burke, a Democratic member of Congress from Massachusetts. Over the years Burke had co-sponsored a bill to restrict imports to the United States in order to protect the troubled New England shoe industry. Burke and his co-sponsor realized that the bill had little chance of passing, but they nevertheless kept it on the legislative agenda. A professional lobbyist, however, did not realize Burke's lack of commitment and invited him to a dinner party sponsored by industries opposed to the bill. At length the lobbyist berated Burke about his bill, claiming that it would ruin the economy and bring national disaster. After the spiel Burke admitted with a straight face that perhaps his bill was a disaster and stated that he would withdraw it. Faced with the possibility of sudden unemployment, the lobbyist responded, "You wouldn't do that, would you?"

Cited in Austin H. Kiplinger and Knight A. Kiplinger, *Washington Now* (New York: Harper & Row, 1975), p. 214.

lobbyists for big business spent $1.8 million per member of Congress to advance their cases.[20] Would contributors to these groups throw their money away? Of course not, it is argued. Therefore, contributors must be getting the political results they paid for. On the other hand, the reasoning may be like that with advertising—big spenders are never sure that their expenditures do much good, but since their competitors also advertise, they are afraid to stop.

A second argument supporting the success of interest groups is based on instances of great victories. Over the years certain lobbyists have scored great political triumphs, and these are so numerous that they suggest an overall pattern of success. This is especially true at the state and local levels where business interests have sometimes dominated politics. At the national level some famous cases have been the American Medical Association's defeat of national health care legislation, the National Rifle Association's blocking of gun control legislation, and the oil lobby's defense of special tax benefits for oil producers. We have already mentioned the clear success of civil rights groups in stopping two of Nixon's Supreme Court appointments. Many of our laws are almost solely the result of vigorous interest group activity.

This argument can sound convincing, but it overlooks an equally long history of failures. For example, the enormous political success of nineteenth-century railroad interests came at the expense of powerful steamship groups. We must remember that for almost every great success there is a failure. Because these failures are rarely newsworthy, they go unnoticed, and we can easily get the erroneous impression that all groups are successful.

The crucial issue in evaluating the success of interest groups is in terms of *when* they succeed, not in terms of whether they are generally successful or unsuccessful. Specifically, what types of groups are successful, and under what conditions are they likely to be victorious? Three broad factors may determine group success: (1) the organization's goals; (2) the nature of the opposition; and (3) the organization's relationship to government.

Organizational goals
In any political struggle the likelihood of success depends in part on one's goals. Interest groups vary considerably in what they try to achieve, so some groups have a built-in head start to success. One way to characterize goals is in terms of how specific and technical they are. Some groups, for example, civil rights organizations, are committed to broad social changes in numerous areas. Other groups, especially those representing specific economic interests, may focus all their attention on one or two fairly obscure bills. Because of the crush of business faced by government and the difficulty of openly dealing with highly detailed matters, the second type of group frequently has the advantage. On some occasions these narrow groups are successful with hardly anyone realizing it. This does *not* mean, however, that groups with narrow goals have a

[20] Cited in *Mother Jones*, December 11, 1978.

greater overall impact on public policy. Even if a group like Trout Unlimited — which is dedicated to preserving trout habitats — always wins, its impact is far less than more generally oriented groups with lower success rates. In short, if a high batting average is what you want, make your group's goals specific and technical.

A second way to characterize a group's goals is in terms of their social acceptability. Your chances for success are improved when your case is accepted as proper by most people. For example, government officials, like most citizens, support the right of business to make decent profits, the right of farmers to earn a good living, and the principle of a strong national defense. Hence, lobbyists advancing proposals consistent with these principles will receive sympathetic hearings.[21] The importance of the overall acceptability of group goals is illustrated by the increased power of civil rights groups over the last twenty-five years. Prior to the 1960s, these groups faced an uphill struggle, but as the ideals of racial equality became more accepted their influence also grew. A similar battle was waged by organized labor as it sought respectability for its cause.

Nature of the opposition

Rarely do interest groups operate unopposed. Not only must groups battle each other, but other potential opponents must be avoided if success is to be achieved. Studies of lobbyist success suggest that one such opponent is the President.[22] Both in Congress and the bureaucracy the exercise of presidential leadership can frequently counter the most vigorous group advocates. This is especially true when the President's party also has a congressional majority. In this situation legislative leaders usually give priority to the President's program.

A second difficult opponent for interest groups is a concerned public. Ultimately, all legislators (and indirectly, many appointed administrators) depend on public approval for their jobs and are, thus, reluctant to violate popular desires. For this reason groups advocating relatively obscure causes do not have to deal with possible public counterpressure. Of course, an obscure issue may involve millions of dollars and have significant implications, but it still can be unknown to most citizens. Here again, the situation favors groups with narrow, technical concerns. Thus when the American Ladder Institute representative visits a legislator to discuss regulating stepladders, he or she does not have to worry that pressure from "the folks back home" will undermine the cause. Compare

[21] A major problem faced by lobbyists for such causes as homosexual rights or the legalization of marijuana is that their open association with public officials could be disastrous for the official. Imagine if representatives of homosexual organizations, like lobbyists for business, supplied legislators with weekend trips, lavish dinner parties, and handsome gifts? The public's views on controversial questions involving morality obviously hinder such organizations.

[22] In his study of Washington lobbies Lester W. Milbrath reported that according to congressional leaders, the President is far more powerful than any interest group. Of course, on many issues there may be little disagreement between the President and interest groups. See Lester W. Milbrath, *The Washington Lobbyists* (Chicago: Rand McNally, 1963), pp. 351–354.

this situation to one faced by a representative of a group arguing a position—for example, school busing—that could affect the legislator's reelection. In sum, groups that avoid public controversy probably have an advantage.

The organization's relationship to government

In principle interest groups and government are separate. In practice, however, some groups are much closer to the center of power than others. Whereas some groups are no better off than a collection of ordinary citizens, others have a natural "in" with policy makers. Perhaps the best way of getting direct access to policy making is to have one's "own" legislative committee or bureaucracy. We mentioned earlier that organizations can "capture" a government agency or develop close ties with relevant congressional committees. In this way, for example, union leaders have easy access to government through the Department of Labor or congressional committees handling labor issues.

Not all groups have such access. Women's groups have frequently complained that they do not have their "own" bureaucrats in the same way that businesspeople have "their" people in the Department of Commerce. Other groups supposedly shut out of close government contact are the consumer interest groups. These "excluded" groups argue that they cannot compete in the policy-making process because few officials share their perspectives and interests. This desire to have their "own" public officials is partly responsible for the increase in new bureaucracies. Two fairly recent examples are Housing and Urban Development (HUD), which "represents" urban blacks, and the Environmental Protection Agency (EPA), which is designed to give environmentalists access to government.

Another way interest groups can increase their chance of success is to become closely involved with the administrators of policy. The intermixing of government and interest group is well illustrated by the role of the American Bar Association (ABA), an association of lawyers that looks out for the legal profession. Unlike many other professional groups, however, it also plays a direct role in government decisions. Specifically, both at the state and national levels, the ABA's approval of judges is frequently an integral part of the judicial appointment process.[23] This mixing of public and private occurs in many other areas as well, for the simple reason that it is frequently much more efficient for the government to work through interest groups than to deal separately with each member. Obviously, a group closely connected with actual decision making stands a better chance of success than one that is a bystander.

How successful are interest groups? The answer is, "It depends." Claims that interest groups *run* government are exaggerated. Degree of success depends on many factors. The most successful groups are likely to have narrow, socially approved goals that do not mobilize public or

---

[23] For an excellent study of how the ABA can become almost inseparable from government itself, see Joel B. Grossman, *Lawyers and Judges: The ABA and the Politics of Judicial Selection* (New York: Wiley, 1965).

presidential opposition. Success is likely to be even greater if the group has a close relationship to government. This does not mean, however, that groups without these traits always fail. More important, even if they do fail most of the time, a few victories can be very important politically. Just remember that the temperance movement, which opposed the use of alcoholic beverages, had few of the characteristics of the "successful" group, yet it succeeded, for a time, in prohibiting the legal sale of liquor in the United States.

Do interest groups undermine the public interest?

Interest groups perform many valuable political services. Without such groups many opinions would not be heard; in addition, public officials frequently depend on information provided by private organizations. Nevertheless, despite these useful functions, interest group politics has been severely criticized. Some of this criticism is directed at tactics such as bribery and the interchange of government and group personnel. Much more basic, however, are criticisms claiming that interest group activity manipulates public opinion and produces policies that are not in the national interest. Therefore, the argument goes, interest group power should be sharply reduced. Is this antigroup position valid? Let us consider three specific anti-interest group claims about the distortion of public opinion and national interest.

THE ARGUMENT THAT INTEREST GROUPS ARE UNREPRESENTATIVE OF THE PUBLIC

One frequent charge against interest group politics is that not all citizens are equally represented. While all interests may have a representative or two, close inspection of the roster of organizations shows that some citizens are much better represented than others. According to one observer, when interest groups speak, they speak with an upper-class accent.[24] Business and professional interests are much better organized than the interests of ordinary people. Blacks, poor people, women, Indians, and certain ethnic groups not only have fewer organizations to advance their causes but these citizens are not very supportive of the organizations they do have. It follows, then, that much of the public is outgunned in obtaining political benefits.

Defenders of the interest group system make two counterarguments. First, one cannot equate the number of groups promoting an interest with the strength of the interest. Consider the power of organized labor. There may be thousands of business-oriented groups in Washington, but

---

[24] Detailed evidence on how interest organizations underrepresent ordinary people is presented in E. E. Schattschneider, *The Semi-Sovereign People* (New York: Holt, Rinehart and Winston, 1960), pp. 29–36.

the AFL-CIO, with its vast membership, may be as powerful as all of them combined.[25] In the 1960s, Ralph Nader almost singlehandedly took on General Motors on the issue of the safety of Chevrolet's Corvair and won! A second rejoinder to the some-interests-are-excluded argument is that even if some interests are not organized, the mere fact that they *could* become organized can be politically influential. An excellent illustration of unorganized groups suddenly becoming organized occurred when skyrocketing beef, sugar, and coffee prices resulted in coordinated consumer boycotts. Thus, even if a business group faces no organized opposition, it is constrained by the fear that pushing too hard might mobilize opposition.

THE ARGUMENT THAT INTEREST GROUP LEADERSHIP IS UNRESPONSIVE

A second attack on interest groups concerns how well group leadership truly reflects the desires of group members. Critics claim that because of their daily experiences, backgrounds, and life-styles, many group leaders lose touch with the people back home. Fifty years ago, George Meany, former president of the AFL-CIO, might have been a typical plumber, but after years of living well and dealing with national leaders, he probably no longer thinks like a regular union man. As a result of leadership losing touch, interest groups frequently do not even work for their own members. It has been observed, for example, that leadership of the American Medical Association (AMA) is not a cross section of the medical profession, and for this reason the AMA's policies are more conservative than many doctors desire (many doctors belong to the AMA, however, for practical reasons despite political differences with AMA leaders).

The counterargument is simply that such distortions are grossly exaggerated. Leaders may lose touch with members in organizations that pursue broad, diverse goals, but this is unlikely to happen in groups that are committed to specific, technical goals. And recall that such organizations are the most common. Moreover, such leader-follower disagreements are not unique to interest groups. It may be true that labor leaders

[25] It is also true that numerous small, poorly financed groups supporting the interests of less well-off people can pool their resources by forming coalitions. For example, in 1973, in response to President Nixon's budget, which cut back many welfare expenditures, 100 such groups organized as the Coalition for Human Needs and Budget Priorities. The coalition included such groups as the Sisters of Charity, the National Council of Senior Citizens, the National Urban League, and the National Welfare Rights Organizations. The activities of this coalition are described in *The Washington Lobby*, pp. 76–79. These coalitions sometimes involve strange partners. In early 1978, for example, the NAACP came out against government-mandated fuel economy standards for trucks (a position shared by the truck manufacturers). The NAACP claimed that these standards would create unemployment and strengthen foreign competition, which, in turn, would harm blacks. "NAACP Opposes Truck Fuel Code," *The New York Times*, January 13, 1978.

The president and vice president of the California Builders Association deliver mail to Senator Alan Cranston (D–California), center. Scenes such as these help all three people to demonstrate publicly that they work hard at their jobs.

lobbied for civil rights laws even though such legislation was opposed by a majority of union members, but political parties have also acted contrary to the wishes of their supporters. Even the President interprets popular desires. In short, one should not measure interest groups by higher standards than one applies to other political groups and officials.

THE ARGUMENT THAT INTEREST GROUPS UNDERMINE THE NATIONAL INTEREST

The third major charge against interest groups is that the pursuit of narrow, self-serving goals by thousands of separate people does not promote the overall national interest. That is, the nation as a whole is harmed if, say, our energy policy results from the pressures of dozens of separate groups, all of whom are striving only for their own selfish gains. Under such circumstances the welfare of the nation as a whole is ignored. What might be good for oil producers, auto manufacturers, truckers, and other organized interests separately could be a disaster nationally. Do interest groups subvert the national good by acting selfishly?

Many people would answer affirmatively. They point out, for example, that in crucial areas such as agriculture, foreign trade, and transportation, interest group activity results in hodgepodge, frequently contradictory policies: We build more superhighways while we encourage less driving; we warn against cigarette smoking yet we subsidize tobacco farming. Critics of interest group politics also claim that certain groups, for example, the AMA, sabotage policies that would benefit most citizens —for example, government-subsidized medical insurance—because of their selfish desire for financial gain.[26]

While numerous instances of "special interest" selfishness can be documented, not everyone agrees that the activities of such organiza-

[26] The AMA's thirty-year battle against government-subsidized health care is described in Richard Harris, *A Sacred Trust* (Baltimore, Md.: Penguin Books, 1969).

tions harm the general public. The activities of narrow special interests can be defended two ways. First, despite talk of a "public interest," there really is no such thing. If there is an overall public interest, it is merely the sum total of all narrow interests. What, for instance, is the public interest with regard to food prices? Consumers would say that *low* prices are in the public interest. Farmers would say that if prices are not *increased,* production will eventually decline and nobody will eat well; therefore, higher prices are in the public interest. Who can really say? The only way to decide is to let the different groups fight it out. Remember that virtually every group claims that it is working in the public interest.

A second rejoinder to the interest-groups-subvert-the-public-good

IS RALPH NADER UNSAFE FOR POOR PEOPLE?

Of all the people claiming to work for the public interest, perhaps none enjoys a greater reputation for integrity and unselfish motives than Ralph Nader. He is a tireless worker who has had a considerable impact on public policy. It has been argued, however, that Nader and other public interest lobbyists do not really work for the common good. Instead, critics claim, their programs favor the well-off, white, college-educated groups, precisely the people who support Nader, Common Cause, and the other "idealistic" groups. To evaluate this charge, consider Nader's energy proposals. Essentially, Nader wants a low-energy, low-growth economy. This would entail abandonment of nuclear power, government regulation of oil prices, development of new sources of energy (for example, solar energy), strict conservation measures, and high environmental standards for oil and coal production. Would such policies benefit everybody? Critics resoundingly answer: NO! Clearly, these policies hurt energy producers; less obvious is the assertion that they would also harm poor people. Not only would such policies make energy prohibitively expensive for poor people, the argument goes, but by stopping economic growth poor people would be frozen into their present economic positions. Social and economic advancement depends on high energy use, not energy cutbacks. Of course, Nader would oppose these claims, but the point here is that working for the "national interest" is no easy thing to define.

Further analysis of this controversy is found in Andrew S. McFarland, *Public Interest Lobbies: Decision-Making on Energy* (Washington, D.C.: American Enterprise Institute for Public Policy Research, 1976), pp. 67–77.

argument is that there *are* organizations dedicated to policies that benefit the general public. Such groups as Common Cause, the League of Women Voters, and about fifteen separate public interest groups directed by Ralph Nader are *not* in politics for their own economic gain. These public interest lobbies supposedly can act as watchdogs to insure that weakly organized interests, for example, consumers, are well represented. Because of these groups, for example, extensive legislation now exists that protects citizens from excessive pollution and unsafe products. Common Cause has been especially active in making government more open and reducing the influence of campaign contributions — two goals that would seem to benefit most citizens.

To return to our original question — Do interest groups subvert the public interest? — the answer is "Some people say yes, others say no." Evidence exists for both points of view. Nevertheless, there is considerable agreement that, in general, interest group politics works for the benefit of established groups in society. These groups have the resources to play the game. The biggest problem in answering this question definitively is agreeing on what constitutes the public interest on a particular issue. Until this question is answered, every group — no matter how self-serving its goals — will claim to be furthering the public good.

A conclusion: controlling interest groups

From the perspective of the ordinary citizen the existence of numerous interest groups presents a real dilemma. Though organizations like Common Cause and people like Ralph Nader claim to work for the ordinary citizen, much evidence suggest that the average person is at a disadvantage competing against established organizations. As we have seen, a well-financed group advancing a narrow goal is in a much better position to get its way than members of the general public. Moreover, there are difficulties associated with forming effective organizations around broad issues, for example, inflation.

Should the average citizen support laws to abolish or greatly restrict interest group activity? It has been argued that doing away with such groups would greatly further the public interest while providing all citizens a more equal share of political power. Unfortunately, this solution is not as attractive as it first appears.[27] Its major defect is that it would severely limit the political freedom of *everyone.* How would you like to be barred from forming a group to influence a government decision? Imagine a law that prohibited members of social or professional associations from speaking with public officials? Not only would such laws violate our basic freedoms but they would be practically impossible to enforce.

[27] For an excellent analysis of how interest groups might be regulated, see H. R. Mahood, "Pressure Groups: A Threat to Democracy?" in *Pressure Groups in American Politics*, H. R. Mahood, ed. (New York: Scribner, 1967).

This does not mean that interest group behavior is beyond control. Numerous laws exist affecting expenditures, public disclosures, and other important aspects of the operation of groups. These laws are primarily designed to prevent blatant abuses of power, and they have been reasonably effective. Going beyond these relatively minor restrictions, however, is difficult. Legally, we cannot say "good" groups are permitted, but "evil" ones are prohibited. In short, part of the price we pay for our political freedom is toleration of groups whose activities may be detrimental to our personal interests.

Major questions raised

1. What are interest groups? An interest group is any group of people working together to influence government. U.S. interest groups are extremely diverse and include well-financed, formal organizations, professional advocates, single-issue mass groups, and even organizations claiming to be nonpolitical.

2. What types of activities do interest groups engage in? Interest groups are found at all levels of government, and no branch of government is immune to pressure. Tactics range from outright bribery to perfectly legal favors to the supplying of necessary information. Many interest groups are more concerned with maintaining favorable political relations and "good will" than with blatant buying of influence.

3. How successful are interest groups? In general, the more obscure and technical the issue, the greater a group's rate of success. We must remember, however, that the success of one group frequently means the failure of another. Remember too that interest groups are rarely dominating forces on major issues. This is especially true when public opinion is outspoken and the President takes a strong position.

4. Does the pursuit of narrow, selfish goals by interest groups harm the overall public interest? Considerable disagreement surrounds this question. One reason for the controversy is that nobody can agree exactly on what the public interest is. The evidence seems to suggest, however, that interest group politics gives greater weight to the concerns of better-off groups in society—which may, of course, be in the public interest.

QUESTIONS FOR FURTHER DISCUSSION

1. Suppose that you are the chief lobbyist for a group fighting for tough anticorruption laws. In one state legislature a rigorous anticorruption law will soon be voted upon. The vote looks very close, and you are approached by a shady character who tells you that for $500 he can guarantee passage of your bill. This is a lot less than you had planned to spend to publicize your cause. Do you accept the offer? What if the shady character says that the $500 is not a bribe but merely expense money necessary to mobilize the anticorruption legislators? Would you pay the money to prevent the sure defeat of the anticorruption legislation?

2. One proposal frequently supported by those opposing special interest influence is complete financial disclosure by all high-ranking public officials. In fact, in 1977, both the House and the Senate passed such requirements for their members. Might not it be argued, however, that while such disclosure rules may bring about an admirable goal—reduced special interest influence—they unreasonably violate privacy? Why should public officials have less privacy than other citizens? Where do we stop? What about professors who do government consulting work or accept free lunches from book publishers? Disclosure laws are merely the first step in undermining our fundamental right to privacy. Certainly the right to privacy is more important than knowing how much a Senator earned giving speeches. Do you agree? How do you enforce such disclosure laws without creating a police state?

3. It is often said that thanks to lobbyists, no member of Congress ever has to buy his or her own lunch. This can present ethical problems. As a legislator, which of the following rules makes the most sense?
a. Accept free lunches only from lobbyists you already agree with because they will not influence you to do something you oppose.
b. Accept free lunches only from lobbyists whose causes you oppose. This will give you a chance to learn a different point of view and increase your overall knowledge.
c. Accept all lobbyists' lunch invitations, but insist that you eat at McDonald's on the grounds that such food would not influence you.
d. Refuse all lunch offers (but hint that you are free for dinner).

4. Compared to the British Parliament, the U.S. Congress is a hotbed of interest group activity. Lobbying exists in Britain, but not on the U.S. scale. The major reason for this difference is the much greater power of British legislative party leaders. Because party leaders set the legislative agenda and decide which bills pass, there are far fewer points of access for special interest groups. Would you favor strengthened legislative party leadership as one solution to counteracting pressure group power? Would this shift in power reduce the role of established economic groups?

BIBLIOGRAPHY

Berg, Larry L., Harlan Hahn, and John R. Schmidhauser. *Corruption in the American Political System.* Morristown, N.J.: General Learning Press, 1976.
A well-balanced treatment of corruption that goes beyond merely exposing it. Especially good at discussing campaign finances and the problems of controlling special interests. The book concludes with a discussion of reform and even offers some concrete proposals. Contains many examples from state—especially California—politics.

Cater, Douglas. *Power in Washington.* New York: Vintage Books, 1964.
Cater, a long-time Washington reporter, provides a detailed description of how lobbyists for foreign governments operate. *Power in Washington* also examines other aspects of government, including Congress, political parties, and the presidency. Well written and nontechnical.

Deakin, James. *The Lobbyists.* Washington, D.C.: Public Affairs Press, 1966.
Deakin spent twelve years in Washington as a reporter and presents a detailed but fascinating review of lobby activities from the early nineteenth century to the 1960s. Very good at describing the "ins" and "outs" of exercising political influence in Washington.

Goulden, Joseph. C. *The Superlawyers.* New York: Weybright and Talley, 1971.
Describes how some of the top Washington law firms and lawyers pull political strings. Contains many good stories. For example, a corporation once
asked Clark Clifford his advice on what it should do about certain tax legislation. "Nothing," said Clifford, and then billed the company $20,000. When the
company asked for a more elaborate explanation, Clifford said, "Because I
said so," and then billed the company another $5,000.

Green, Mark J. *The Other Government: The Unseen Power of Washington Lawyers.* New York: Grossman Publishers, 1975.
Green was once associated with Ralph Nader, and he takes a largely negative
view of Washington lawyers who represent business interests. Especially
good coverage of the role of high-powered lawyers in the drug laws and administrative rulings, government regulations of the food industry, auto safety
controls, airline regulations, and the broadcasting industry. Green concludes
with an interesting discussion of legal ethics and the public interest.

Greenwald, Carol S. *Group Power: Lobbying and Public Policy.* New York:
Praeger, 1977.
The most comprehensive and up-to-date text on interest group politics. Examines internal organization of groups, the techniques of lobbying, interest
groups and electoral politics, group activities in the three branches of government, and the impact of interest groups on public policy. Contains a good annotated bibliography.

Lowi, Theodore J. *The End of Liberalism,* 2d ed. New York: Norton, 1979.
A widely read book that takes a dim view of policy making through the interaction of interest groups. Lowi argues that the policy resulting from group-
dominated government is usually undemocratic and disastrous to society in
general. Several case studies from urban policy, the war on poverty, and
foreign relations are provided. Lowi would replace the existing system with
one emphasizing less administrative discretion and greater precision in law.

McFarland, Andrew S. *Public Interest Lobbies: Decision-Making on Energy.*
Washington, D.C.: American Enterprise Institute for Public Policy Research,
1976.
A good review of the rise of so-called public interest groups and the position of
groups such as Common Cause and the Sierra Club on energy policy. Also
briefly discusses whether there can be such a thing as working for *the* public
interest on a particular issue.

Mahood, H. R., ed. *Pressure Groups in American Politics.* New York: Scribner,
1967.
A highly useful collection of articles on interest group politics. Contains articles on the different theories of pressure groups as well as studies of how different groups organize and attempt to influence government.

Milbrath, Lester W. *The Washington Lobbyists.* Chicago: Rand McNally, 1963.
Based on interviews with lobbyists conducted in 1959. Emphasizes lobbyists
as individuals and describes their backgrounds, attitudes toward their jobs,
perceptions of politics, and the day-to-day nature of their jobs. Provides a good
view of the "average" lobbyist as opposed to the superlawyer or famous advocate.

Ornstein, Norman J., and Shirley Elder. *Interest Groups, Lobbying and Policy-
making.* Washington, D.C.: Congressional Quarterly, 1978.
An up-to-date and fact-filled description of lobbying in Washington, D.C. Contains a good discussion of different theories of pressure groups; reviews some
of the major lobbies and their resources; and describes various reform efforts.
The book contains three major case studies of pressure group activities that
involve an organized labor issue, clean air legislation, and the controversy
over the B-1 bomber. Contains a good bibliography.

Schattschneider, E. E. *The Semi-Sovereign People.* New York: Holt, Rinehart and Winston, 1960.

Schattschneider is interested in the general question of how citizens can control government. He views the pressure group system as a system that excludes most citizens and favors the rich over the poor. The way to defeat the pressure group system is to expand the scope of conflict.

The Washington Lobby, 2d ed. Washington, D.C.: Congressional Quarterly, 1974.

An excellent overall review of the many facets of Washington interest group politics. Contains in-depth examinations of particular lobbies such as the oil lobby and representatives of foreign nations. A good source for specific facts and figures.

Winter-Berger, Robert N. *The Washington Pay-Off: An Insider's View of Corruption in Government.* New York: Dell, 1972.

A fascinating example of "kiss and tell" journalism. Winter-Berger relates his own experiences as a wheeler-dealer in Washington for some of the best-known politicians in the United States. Names, places, and dollar amounts are all given, even when the information is highly incriminating.

Part three

Institutions

PREVIEW

How much power does Congress have?

Congressional power has waxed and waned over time. The Constitution provides Congress with several major powers, the most important and far-reaching one being the power to tax and spend. This power has been used to regulate both economic and noneconomic policies. A second important power is in foreign affairs, where Congress can declare war and regulate commerce with other countries. A third constitutionally granted power is control over commerce among the states—a power that allows vast government intervention in all our lives. Congress is also given the power to remove federal officials, including the President, from office through impeachment. Other explicit congressional powers are confirming presidential appointments to the judicial and executive branches and amending the Constitution. Finally, if no candidate receives a majority of electoral college votes, the House of Representatives, with each state casting one vote, elects the President. Given the "necessary and proper" clause, these are broad and significant powers.

Two important powers not mentioned in the Constitution have also developed over time. The power to investigate has played a role in exposing problems and placing topics on the public agenda. And through the procedure of administrative oversight Congress has influence over the vast federal bureaucracy.

What are the limits of congressional power?

The Constitution limits the powers of Congress in several ways. Congress cannot pass certain types of laws (for example, *ex post facto* laws) or limit the free exercise of speech. The very design of Congress, especially the fact that it is a two-house legislature with elections called for frequently, also checks legislative power. The most important constraints are the countervailing power of the presidency, the courts, and the principle of federalism.

What determines whether Congress passes or defeats a particular bill?

Most bills introduced never get passed. First a bill must get through committee. Success at this stage depends on the composition of the committee and the attitude of the committee chairperson. Committee chairpersons have great influence over committee agendas, resources, and the organization of subcommittees. Recent reforms, however, have been aimed at making committees operate more democratically.

The success of a bill greatly depends on the support it receives from party leaders, who make key decisions concerning which bills will be considered, when votes will be taken, and how much pressure will be exerted.

Finally, a bill is voted on by all members of the House or Senate. Because of the importance of committee decisions, the complexity of most legislation, and the enormous amount of business to be conducted, rarely is there extensive debate. However, the decision on the floor is not automatic.

CHAPTER TEN

CONGRESSIONAL
POWER

ncreasing demands have been made on the federal government in recent years. Whereas in the early history of the United States its role was limited to a few simple tasks such as collecting tariffs or coining money, today the federal government sometimes seems to be taking on all of the world's problems. At the center of much of the work of government is Congress. The 435 Representatives and 100 Senators must deal with problems that range from finding a lost social security check to deciding how much to spend on interstate highways to choosing among alternative plans for nuclear disarmament. Because Congress is unable to solve all the problems it confronts to everybody's satisfaction, it has variously been criticized as undemocratic, unresponsive, corrupt, incompetent, unrepresentative, lazy, self-serving, antiquated, miserly, and overly generous.

Unfortunately, many of these criticisms are based on an incomplete knowledge of what Congress can accomplish, how it operates, and what it has actually done. It would be unfair to hold Congress accountable for resolving a problem whose solution would require unconstitutional laws or a gross violation of accepted legislative procedure. Before we can fairly and constructively criticize Congress, we must first understand how it operates. This chapter and the next examine two crucial aspects of the ability of Congress to respond to contemporary issues: (1) the nature of congressional power and (2) the results of congressional activity and lawmaking.

Excises Taxes on commodities produced or sold within the boundaries of a country.
Tariffs Taxes on goods imported into a country.

Our analysis of congressional power addresses itself to three politically significant questions:

1. How much power does Congress have?
2. What are the limits of congressional power?
3. What determines whether Congress passes or defeats a bill?

How much power does Congress have?

The power of Congress has evolved since April 1789 when the legislative body first convened. Congress has passed through several "strong" and several "weak" periods, depending on the personalities of its leaders, the ambition of the President, the philosophies of judges, and social and economic conditions. At times Congress appeared to be running the country; at other times it seemed to be a half-useless debating society. The best place to begin our examination of Congress is to examine the explicit powers granted that body by the Constitution. Of course, these constitutional grants of power are always open to interpretation by government officials, but they remain relevant for understanding the basic framework in which Congress operates. Following our analysis of explicitly granted powers, we shall consider powers that have emerged over time.

CONSTITUTIONALLY GRANTED POWERS

The Founding Fathers were deeply concerned about legislative power. Indeed, a major reason for calling the Constitutional Convention was to restrain the actions of several radical state legislatures. As a result, the powers (and restrictions) given to Congress, unlike those listed for the presidency and the courts, are spelled out in detail. The most important of these can be organized into seven basic types.

1. Taxing and spending

Article I, section 8, clause 1 of the Constitution states: "The Congress shall have power to lay and collect taxes, duties, imports, and **excises,** to pay the debts and provide for the common defense and general welfare of the United States." The power to tax and spend is a power that has an enormous effect on both ordinary citizens and the executive branch of the government. Tax rates have a major impact on the overall economy. Many of the important decisions people make in their lives—buying a house or changing jobs—are greatly influenced by congressional taxing and spending policies. The prices of imported goods are affected by **tariffs** set by Congress. During the U.S. involvement in Vietnam, several legislators attempted to influence presidential actions by cutting off funds for the war effort. The power to tax has also been used for nonmonetary purposes. Until 1968, Congress attempted to suppress gambling by putting a special tax on it and requiring gamblers to register with the Internal Revenue Service (similar taxes were put on the ownership of machine guns and narcotics). At one time Congress tried to discourage the use of margarine by putting a high tax on it when it was colored to resemble butter. More recently, President Carter proposed a tax on gas-guzzling automobiles as a means of conserving energy. The explicitly granted congressional power over the **national debt** also deserves mention. Since a significant portion of government revenue comes from borrowed money, this power has become an important tool in controlling national spending (in fiscal 1976 the public debt of the federal government was $620.4 billion, with interest totaling $37.1 billion). With some exceptions, the courts have allowed Congress considerable freedom in taxing and spending.

National debt The total amount of money owed by the national government plus interest. Money is owed to people holding savings bonds, Treasury notes, and other such financial obligations. Also called public debt.

2. Foreign affairs

While the President may play the dominant role in foreign relations, Congress still possesses considerable power in this area. Many presidential actions involving other countries, such as waging war or providing economic assistance, require money raised and appropriated by Congress. Moreover, the Constitution grants Congress the powers to regulate foreign commerce, declare war, and call up the military to repel invasion. With the requirement that all treaties with foreign nations be ratified by two thirds of the Senate, that body is given particular power in foreign affairs.

3. Commerce

The Constitution explicitly grants Congress power in such commercial matters as regulating bankruptcies, fixing weights and measures, punishing counterfeiters, granting copyrights and patents, running the post office, and coining money. Much more significant, however, is the language in Article I, section 8, clause 3, which simply grants Congress the power to regulate commerce among the several states. Over the years this power has been used as the basis for considerable government intervention in the lives of citizens. Through this power, for example, the government has banned interstate shipping of impure foods and drugs. Current regulations of oil and gas prices, long distance telephone rates, and airline fares derive from this power over commerce (much of this power is exercised by regulatory commissions created by Congress). Important civil rights laws have also been based on this power. In the Civil Rights Act of 1964, for example, racial discrimination against blacks in hotels, restaurants, and movie theaters was banned on the grounds that it adversely affected interstate commerce.[1] There is hardly an aspect of contemporary life that remains unaffected by congressional action based on the power of Congress to regulate commerce.

[1] Congressional control over commerce has traditionally been a complex, controversial subject. For a more complete analysis, see C. Herman Pritchett, *The American Constitution*, 3d ed. (New York: McGraw-Hill, 1977), Chap. 2; and *Powers of Congress* (Washington, D.C.: Congressional Quarterly, 1976), Chaps. 9 and 10.

Impeachment A formal process that states an accusation of a crime. Under the Constitution, the House of Representatives is responsible for bringing an impeachment. *Senatorial courtesy* The custom whereby a President appointing a federal district judge has the appointment approved by the senior Senator from the state in which the judge will serve in cases when the President and Senator are of the same political party. The tradition is not always followed, and a Senator's approval does not guarantee Senate confirmation.

4. Impeachment

The Constitution grants Congress the power to remove federal officials (but not fellow members of Congress or military officers) from office through impeachment. The House of Representatives, by a majority vote, can bring about **impeachment.** By a two-thirds vote of all those present, the Senate can convict, and the official is then removed from office. This power has been used infrequently. Since 1789 only thirteen federal officials have been impeached by the House, and only four of these cases resulted in conviction by the Senate. President Andrew Johnson was impeached by the House in 1868, but the Senate failed to convict him (a Supreme Court Justice, Samuel Chase, was also impeached but not convicted). As the Watergate scandal and Richard Nixon's subsequent resignation indicated, the threat of impeachment is a powerful weapon. The mere possibility that a resolution to impeach could be introduced in the House probably deters abuses of office.

Members of the House Judiciary Committee debate the impeachment of President Richard M. Nixon, 1974.

5. Confirming appointments

In every session the Senate must confirm thousands of presidential appointments. These include cabinet and subcabinet positions, major diplomatic and military posts, all federal judgeships, and top positions on independent and regulatory boards. In 1977 the Senate confirmed a total of 54,065 of President Carter's appointments (61 nominations were withdrawn) and rejected none (most of them were military commissions). As a result of this power Senators frequently have a strong say in who gets a nomination. This is especially true in the selection of federal judges. Thanks to the custom of **senatorial courtesy,** a President appointing a federal judge to serve in a state clears the appointment with the senior Senator of his party from that state. Even with nonjudicial nominees,

Senators can influence the appointment process by threatening long and difficult confirmation proceedings. On several occasions the Senate has used confirmation hearings to embarrass the President or provide a forum for debating presidential policy. When President Carter nominated G. William Miller as chairperson of the Federal Reserve Bank in 1978, for example, many Senators used the confirmation hearings as an opportunity to discuss publicly Carter's economic program.

6. Constitutional amending

The Constitution allows amendments to be proposed by either a convention called by two thirds of all states or by a vote of two thirds of both houses of Congress. All constitutional amendments have originated in Congress, however. In fact, given the technical and legal complexities of state conventions, it is very likely that if future amendments to the Constitution are to succeed, they will first have to be considered by Congress. Adopting amendments is not a congressional power. To be adopted an amendment must be ratified by three quarters of all state legislatures or by a three-quarters vote of conventions in all states. Congress can specify which adoption process will be used, however. The Twenty-first Amendment, which repealed Prohibition in 1933, was ratified by state conventions as specified by Congress.

7. Electing the President

If no candidate for President receives a majority of the electoral college vote, the House, with each state casting one vote, then chooses the Chief Executive. The Senate elects the Vice President. Only twice—in 1801 when Thomas Jefferson was elected and in 1825 when the House chose John Quincy Adams over Andrew Jackson—has the House actually exercised this power. Nevertheless, the very existence of this possibility has had an impact on campaign strategy. For example, in 1968, George Wallace's third-party bid was partially based on the hope of throwing the election into the House. In addition, the Twentieth and Twenty-fifth Amendments to the Constitution give Congress power to settle disputes arising from presidential incapacity or resignation.

In reviewing the constitutionally delegated powers of Congress we should not forget the "necessary and proper" clause described in Chapters 2 and 3. Article 1, section 8 of the Constitution enumerates many congressional powers, including the power to borrow money, coin money, raise an army, and establish a post office. Article 1, section 8 concludes by giving Congress the power to make all laws "necessary and proper" to carry out its previously listed responsibilities. This provision gives Congress considerable freedom to pursue its legislative responsibilities. Recall that the Supreme Court ruled in *McCulloch* v. *Maryland* (1819) that Congress could establish a national bank (a power not mentioned in the Constitution) on the grounds that such a bank was necessary for Congress to carry out its explicitly granted responsibilities. Obviously, then, the formal powers enjoyed by Congress go well beyond those that are precisely spelled out in the Constitution.

"Witch hunts" **A vigorous
search for wrongdoing with the
purpose more to stir things up
than to establish guilt. The
term comes from the days
when evil was blamed on
spells cast by witches, and
eliminating evil required widespread, loosely defined inqui-
sitions.
Contempt of Congress **Knowingly obstructing the legislative
process.

OTHER POWERS

There is even more to congressional power than what is mentioned or implied in the Constitution. Over the years congressional power has grown considerably. Unfortunately, it is impossible to say *exactly* how much power Congress now possesses. We sometimes do not know the limits of congressional power until Congress actually attempts to act. Nevertheless, observers of Congress agree that nonconstitutionally defined congressional power has developed in two important areas: (1) the power to investigate and (2) the power to influence the bureaucracy.

The power to investigate

Nowhere in the Constitution is Congress given the explicit power to investigate. Nevertheless, since 1792 with the first congressional investigation of an Army disaster involving Indians, the power to investigate has played an important role in U.S. politics. Investigations by Congress have helped illuminate the inner workings of the executive branch, called public attention to major social problems, and laid the basis for much legislation (for example, automobile safety requirements and the banning of dangerous drugs). Moreover, because of the attention generated by their investigations, many members of Congress have become well known. Harry S. Truman, for example, became famous for his work on the Senate Special Committee to Investigate the National Defense Program in 1944. Richard M. Nixon first gained notoriety as a member of Congress through his investigation of alleged Communist subversion.

Most congressional investigations are businesslike inquiries that get little publicity. On occasion, however, these investigations can almost dominate national politics and have an impact far beyond Congress. In 1954 the late Senator Joseph McCarthy (R-Wis.) used the Senate Government Operations Committee's Permanent Investigations Subcommittee to search for Communist sympathizers in government. Few, if any, pro-Communists were uncovered, but McCarthy succeeded in creating a widespread atmosphere of hostility and suspicion toward those with unorthodox political ideas. This atmosphere spread well beyond Washington and frequently led to so-called "**witch hunts**" where citizens with unpopular political views lost their jobs and had their reputations damaged.

A recent illustration of the importance of congressional investigations was the inquiry into President Nixon's role in the Watergate scandal. Even before the House Judiciary Committee began its impeachment hearings, congressional committees played a crucial role in bringing to light the pattern of break-ins, wiretaps, illegal political pressures, campaign fund misuse, and obstruction of justice on the part of certain White House employees. Only after these investigations had uncovered a widespread pattern of involvement and conspiracy did the special prosecutors (Archibald Cox, then Leon Jaworski), the courts, and the House Judiciary Committee act decisively.

Along with the power to investigate, Congress has also acquired the power to hold people in **contempt of Congress** (which can, and frequently

The late Senator Joseph McCarthy (R–Wis.) conducting an investigation of the Army in 1954. McCarthy used hearings such as these to wage a well-publicized war against suspected Communists and their sympathizers.

has, resulted in short jail sentences). The Constitution does not explicitly mention this power, although court decisions have generally upheld it. Between 1789 and 1976, Congress voted 384 contempt citations, typically cases involving individuals who tried to bribe or obstruct Congress or witnesses in an investigation who failed to testify or produce requested information. Today Congress can hold a reluctant witness in contempt if a simple majority of a chamber so votes, and rarely are such motions opposed. The matter is then handed over to a U.S. attorney for presentation to a grand jury.[2] In the House Watergate investigation, for example, White House staff member G. Gordon Liddy was held in contempt and received a six-month sentence (suspended) in U.S. district court.

Influence over the bureaucracy

People sometimes assume that Congress passes laws and that the executive branch, with its vast bureaucracy, then enforces them. This is not strictly true, because Congress frequently gets deeply involved in many aspects of day-to-day interpretation and enforcement. The process of congressional involvement in the affairs of the Department of Agriculture, the Department of Defense, and the numerous other executive bureaus and departments is commonly called **administrative oversight** and represents an important means of congressional influence over public policy.

Congressional oversight usually operates through the committee system. For example, not only does the House Ways and Means Committee

[2] A more complete description of congressional power to hold people in contempt and other aspects of investigations is provided in *Powers of Congress*, Chaps. 13–16.

Administrative oversight The process by which members of Congress, especially through the committee system, monitor the performance of administrators in the executive branch.

279

Legislative veto A provision in legislation that, before an agency can make a decision, it must receive approval from one or both houses of Congress.

draft tax legislation but it also assumes some responsibility for making sure the Internal Revenue Service follows its congressionally defined goals while operating effectively. Because Congress possesses an elaborate committee and subcommittee system (see p. 287), almost all agencies must contend with congressional intervention in their management. Such intervention in the bureaucracy is not limited to legislators on the relevant committees. Especially where a constituent is in need of help, a Representative or Senator can feel free to call up a bureau official to find out what the agency is doing, make suggestions concerning how things ought to run, or remedy a specific problem.

TECHNIQUES OF ADMINISTRATIVE OVERSIGHT Congress employs a variety of techniques to shape public policy in executive bureaucracies. One means is to draft the laws governing the agency so that officials will be likely to conform to congressional desires. Such laws can include precise stipulations on agency authority, the relationships among different agencies, the lines of authority within an agency, or even the exact way an agency is to conduct its business.[3] Detailed legislation of this kind sometimes has the net effect of placing a congressional committee, not the President, in charge of an executive agency.

A second important control mechanism Congress has over the bureaucracy is the **legislative veto.** Congress can require that before an agency can make a decision it must first receive congressional approval. Before a President can reorganize the executive branch, for example, he must submit the proposal to Congress; rejection by either chamber is a veto. This is no idle threat, since between 1946 and 1966 Congress rejected twenty-one of eighty-four presidential reorganization plans. Congressional veto power can even extend to much more minor matters such as an agency's proposal to buy land or sell government-run businesses.

Yet another means of congressional intervention in executive branch policy making occurs through personnel selection. We have already seen that the Constitution allows the Senate to influence the selection of top officials, but Congress also can influence who occupies many lesser positions. By legislatively defining pay scales, job eligibility, working conditions, job security, and other features, Congress can insure that only certain types of people will fill certain agency positions.[4] Equally important,

---

[3] Leroy N. Rieselbach, *Congressional Politics* (New York: McGraw-Hill, 1973), pp. 300–301.

[4] In some instances a bureaucratic position is defined so explicitly that only a single person can fill it. Here is one such set of job requirements:

Provided further, that the vacancies created in the Judge Advocate's Department by this act, one such vacancy, not below the rank of Major, shall be filled by the appointment of a person from civil life, not less than forty-five nor more than fifty years of age, who shall have been for ten years a Judge of the Supreme Court of the Philippine Islands, shall have served for two years as a Captain in the regular or volunteer army, and shall be proficient in the Spanish language and laws.

Cited in Rieselbach, p. 310.

Congress can decide how many employees an agency can hire, a power that can very much determine what gets done within the agency. In the late 1960s, congressional opponents of black civil rights attempted to undermine enforcement of civil rights legislation by cutting back on the number of Justice Department lawyers responsible for enforcing these laws.

Finally, and perhaps most important, by controlling how much money agencies receive, Congress can frequently influence how money is spent. In some instances the threat of budgetary cuts provides leverage for influencing what policies and projects an agency will pursue. In 1978, for example, the Federal Trade Commission (FTC) proposed strict limits on television commercials for highly sugared foods directed at children. These actions did not please all members of Congress. The House Appropriations Committee approved a bill forbidding the FTC from spending funds regulating products classified as safe by the Food and Drug Administration (and sugar is considered safe). Meanwhile, a Senator threatened to cut the FTC's budget by an amount equal to money spent on investigating television commercials. Faced with this pressure, the FTC backed down from its attack. Congress can also use its power over appropriations to insure that executive agencies operate effectively. Sometimes it accomplishes this by direct investigation of an agency, but since Congress also maintains the General Accounting Office (GAO), which audits the books of federal agencies, it can serve as an overall financial watchdog.

In sum, thanks to its constitutional mandate and powers that have emerged over time, Congress can have a vast influence over public policy. Not only can Congress pass laws that affect citizens directly, but it can make its influence felt by conducting investigations or by affecting the operation of the executive branch. Nevertheless, Congress is not free to do whatever it pleases. As we shall now see, numerous limitations on congressional power also exist.

What are the limits on congressional power?

The drafters of the Constitution wanted a legislature that could act effectively in a number of areas, but they also feared that the legislative body might overstep its powers. This fear was very real: in the past, several state legislatures had become virtually unchecked in their use of power. To prevent future abuses, numerous restraints were placed on the exercise of congressional power. In addition, several limits on legislative power have developed since the Constitution was drafted. We shall consider two of the major constraining forces on congressional action: (1) constitutional restrictions and the basic design of government and (2) countervailing power of other government officials.

Writ of habeas corpus   A court order directing an official holding someone in custody to show cause for the person's detention to a court.
Bill of attainder   A law that declares a particular individual to be guilty of a crime and punishes him or her without a trial.
Ex post facto law   A law that makes a crime retroactive and has an adverse effect on the accused person.
Bicameral   A legislative body that has two components, as the Congress of the United States, made up of the House of Representatives and the Senate.
Checks and balances   The method of organizing government so that each component (the legislative, executive, and judicial branches) has some power over the actions of the other components. Also applies to relations between national and state governments.

CONSTITUTIONAL RESTRICTIONS AND THE BASIC DESIGN OF GOVERNMENT

Immediately following the explicit grants of power to Congress, the Constitution, Article I, section 9, lists numerous legislative restrictions: Congress cannot suspend the right to the **writ of habeas corpus** (a court order that requires an explanation of why a prisoner is being held) except in cases of rebellion or invasion. Nor is Congress allowed to pass a **bill of attainder** (an act declaring the guilt of a particular individual and allowing punishment without a trial) or an **ex post facto law** (a law declaring something criminal and applied retroactively). Congress is also forbidden to regulate commerce so as to give one state an advantage or to tax an article exported from one state to another. Finally, Congress cannot draw money from the Treasury except by passing the proper legislation (which in turn must be signed by the President).

The other major explicit constitutional restriction on Congress appears in the First Amendment. Congress may not pass legislation establishing, forbidding, or governing religion. It is also prohibited from abridging freedom of speech, freedom of the press, the right of peaceful assembly, and the right to petition government for a redress of grievances. These restrictions have had a long and controversial history, but we must leave the question of the meaning of the First Amendment to Chapter Sixteen.

Less obvious than these restrictions are the limitations on congressional power that derive from the very design of Congress. First, Congress is a two-house (**bicameral**) legislature. One-house legislatures existed when the Constitution was drafted, but the bicameral design was a useful solution to conflicts between large and small states over representation. The significance of a bicameral legislature is that it inhibits action, especially quick action. Getting a bill through two houses rather than one is not only more time consuming but also offers opponents two opportunities to defeat the proposed legislation.

Second, the frequency with which congressional elections are called for also works to limit the power of Congress. This is especially true for members of the House, who must run every two years. House members must devote considerable time and energy just to stay in office, a situation not conducive to accumulating vast power. Senators have six-year terms, but remember that one third of the Senate is up for reelection every two years, so both the Senate and the House must face frequent changes in personnel, another factor discouraging the accumulation of legislative power. In short, if the Founding Fathers had really wanted a strong national legislature, they would have created a one-house Congress with very long terms of office for its members.

COUNTERVAILING POWER OF OTHER GOVERNMENT OFFICIALS

A key element in the design of the U.S. government is the principle of **checks and balances.** The drafters of the Constitution believed that when political power becomes concentrated in one office or body, abuse of power is inevitable. Elaborate divisions of powers and mechanisms of cooperation must therefore exist if abuses are to be checked. The result of these checks and balances is that congressional actions are frequently constrained by the powers and actions of other public officials.

Limits imposed by federalism

The principle of **federalism** is one such limiting force on congressional power. As we saw in Chapter Three, many important state and local matters are beyond the direct reach of congressional lawmaking. Of course, the line between national powers and state powers is not precise and is always evolving, but the division remains important. Congress may be able to raise billions of dollars in taxes, declare war, and ratify treaties with foreign nations, but it cannot tell New York City how to run its garbage service. It may try to influence state and local decisions by using its taxing power or its regulatory role in commerce, but Congress cannot simply treat most state and local matters as its own domain.

Limits imposed by the courts

The judicial system also contains congressional power in several important ways. Prior to the passage of the Sixteenth Amendment in 1913, the courts thwarted congressional attempts to impose a national income tax by declaring income tax laws unconstitutional. More recently, the Supreme Court in *Grosso* v. *United States* (1968) ruled that taxes requiring citizens to admit illegal activities (for example, a tax on gambling) are unconstitutional. The constant threat of rulings of unconstitutionality and the actual interpretations judges give to laws are as important as the decisions themselves. These restraints on congressional action are well illustrated by recent court decisions on religious observances in public schools. Despite widespread support in Congress for prayers in schools, no legislative action has been taken because members of Congress know that the courts will declare such acts unconstitutional. Congress has also been frustrated by the willingness of federal courts to require busing to achieve integration; numerous legislative efforts to prevent such busing have had little impact.

The countervailing power of the President

Perhaps the most important obstacles to congressional domination of government are the President and the executive agencies. A President can simply **veto** congressional legislation, and only with great difficulty (a two-thirds vote by both houses) can a veto be overcome. Between 1913 and 1976, Presidents vetoed a total of 1,350 bills. Congress overrode these vetoes forty-nine times, for a presidential success rate of 96.4 percent.[5]

The President and the federal bureaucracy also play crucial roles in setting the legislative agenda. In the last twenty years, for example, 80 percent of all nonprivate bills originated in the executive branch. The President's legislative role is especially important in setting national spending priorities. The Budget and Accounting Act of 1921 gives the

Federalism The system in which two or more levels of government rule the same people, with each level having some independence in policy making.

Veto Latin for "I forbid." The act of a President to prevent a bill passed by Congress from becoming law. The President can be overridden by a two-thirds vote of each house of Congress.

[5] *Statistical Abstract of the United States,* 1977, p. 461.

Fiscal year   For purposes of financial administration, the government's accounting year begins on October 1 and ends on September 30. Before 1977 the fiscal year ran from July 1 to June 30. Financial information, such as revenues and expenditures, are given on a fiscal-year basis (Some states, however, use a calendar year.)

Back–door spending   Creating a program the cost of which will not be fully felt until the future. This allows the present–day Congress to avoid current expenditures by passing items on to future lawmakers.

Impoundment   The refusal by the President to spend money authorized by laws passed by Congress.

BACKDOOR SPENDING

In principle Congress holds the power to determine how much will be spent each **fiscal year.** In practice, however, Congress does not have complete control over yearly spending levels. Through a practice known as **backdoor spending** future financial obligations are created that put expenditure levels beyond the consideration of subsequent legislative sessions. In other words, Congress today is bound by financial commitments made in past sessions. In 1974, only about 60 percent of government spending was subject to yearly congressional control. Congress has lost direct fiscal control for a number of reasons. In some programs, for example, social security and veterans' benefits, vast expenditures are required by previously passed laws and are thus independent of yearly congressional review. In other cases agencies are allowed to borrow directly from the Treasury or the public. Congress can also commit future revenue by setting the interest rate on the national debt, thereby commiting billions of dollars each year well into the future. The importance of this precommitted backdoor spending is that it provides much less "free" money for use in new programs. This is similar to the situation of an individual who every month must allocate most of his or her income to previously committed fixed expenses such as rent, insurance, and installment loan payments. Of course, Congress could change these procedures, but a complete overhaul of existing practices would be required. (One advantage of backdoor spending is that it allows the present Congress to avoid taking the blame for increased government expenditures in the future.)

President the power to draw up a national budget. This presidential budget is prepared by numerous experts in the Office of Management and Budget, and the Congress is given nine months to review it. The executive branch also influences this review process, since much of the information Congress uses to evaluate expenditures comes from executive agencies.

Even if Congress passes appropriations contrary to presidential desires, the President frequently controls the actual spending. The 1950 Budget Act allows the President not to spend all appropriations in order to save for contingencies or to increase efficiency. This refusal to spend has been called **impoundment.** For example, in 1972 President Nixon refused to spend $2.5 billion appropriates by Congress for highway construction as well as $1.9 billion for national defense. In response to these actions Congress passed the Congressional Budget and Impoundment

Control Act of 1974, which contains sections limiting the President's power to impound. Specifically, if the President wants to withhold funds temporarily because an expenditure would be impractical, he can do so unless the action is overturned by a resolution of either the Senate or the House. However, if the President wishes to withhold the money permanently, congressional approval is required within forty-five days. If no legislative action is taken within that period, the President must release the funds appropriated by Congress.[6]

Presidents have also discovered that they can spend money not appropriated by Congress through a system of "reprogramming" and "transfers." In 1971, for instance, President Nixon offered $52 million worth of military aid to Cambodia despite an absence of congressional appropriations for this purpose. He accomplished this by moving money from one account to another, issuing various "loans," and declaring army equipment "obsolete" and selling it cheaply to Cambodia.[7]

Presidents have even managed to avoid the congressional requirement that all treaties with foreign governments be approved by the Senate. Instead of calling a treaty a treaty, Presidents have increasingly conducted foreign relations by making "**executive agreements**" with other nations. Between 1789 and 1974, the United States entered into 1,254 treaties, but 7,809 executive agreements were made with foreign nations during this period.[8] These agreements are not subject to Senate approval, but they appear to be as important as treaties, and the courts have interpreted them to be as legally binding as Senate-approved treaties.[9]

In sum, while Congress possesses many powers, these powers are not unlimited. The constraints placed on legislative action by constitutional prohibitions and the power of other government officials are very real. Congress can greatly influence the lives of citizens, but exercising this influence requires the cooperation of many officials outside Congress.

Executive agreement An agreement with a foreign nation signed by the President that does not require Senate approval.

What determines whether Congress passes or defeats a bill?

During every legislative session thousands of bills and resolutions are introduced, but most sink into obscurity. In the 94th Congress, which met from 1975 to 1976, for example, 21,096 bills and joint resolutions were introduced, of which 729, or 3.5 percent, actually passed.[10] Why do some bills survive? Who controls the fate of these thousands of bills?

---

[6] Further discussion of the conflict between Congress and the President over expenditures is presented in *Congressional Quarterly's Guide to Congress*, 2d ed. (Washington, D.C.: Congressional Quarterly, Inc., 1976), pp. 65, 133.

[7] Mark J. Green, James M. Fallows, and David R. Zwick, *Who Runs Congress?* (New York: Bantam Books, 1972), p. 117.

[8] *Congressional Quarterly's Guide to Congress*, p. 257.

[9] Pritchett, pp. 259–260.

[10] *Statistical Abstract of the United States*, 1978, p. 502.

To answer these questions we must examine both the tortuous path a bill must travel and the individual legislators whose powers determine whether a bill will survive. As we shall see, the *how* and the *who* of the legislative process greatly affect *what* is passed. We shall consider the process by examining the impact of three important elements in legislative decision making: (1) the committee system; (2) elected leaders; and (3) floor debates and votes.

THE IMPACT OF THE COMMITTEE SYSTEM

The first step for all legislation is its introduction to the clerk of the House or the secretary of the Senate. The bill is assigned a number and promptly printed. The Speaker of the House or the presiding officer of the

CONGRESSIONAL STAFFS

Observers of Congress have recently noticed a new and increasingly important element in legislative decision making—the professional staff. The existence of large staffs is a relatively new phenomenon. The first official recognition of the need for assistance occurred in 1885 when each Senator was authorized to employ a clerk at $6 a day while Congress was in session (the House followed in 1893, also allowing each member one clerk). A dramatic increase in staff assistance has occurred since the mid-1950s. For example, between 1955 and 1975, the total House staff increased from 3,623 to 9,951. Today, each Representative has a staff allowance of over a quarter of a million dollars, while Senators from the largest states receive close to $900,000 for their staffs.

Most staff members work at routine clerical chores—filing correspondence, answering routine letters, forwarding the complaints of constituents to the appropriate agency, and so on. Staff members also run the legislator's home office and maintain close contact with bureaucrats of particular importance to the member of Congress. The politically most important staff assistants are the professional advisers hired to help in the creation of legislation. These people frequently are lawyers or hold advanced social science degrees. Some work directly for a member of Congress while others are attached to a particular committee or subcommittee. In both situations, staffs can play a crucial role in drafting legislation, conducting investigations, writing reports, scheduling appointments, providing technical advice, and coordinating legislative-executive relationships. Senator Edward Kennedy (D-Mass.), in 1977, for example, had the use of thirty-three

Senate then assigns the bill to the appropriate committee. Getting through the committee process in both houses is a great obstacle, and most bills do not survive.

The organization of congressional committees

Congressional committees are where much of the significant legislative decision making occurs. There are four basic types of committees. The most important are the **standing committees,** which continue from session to session and deal with such key areas as tax policy, expenditures, military defense, and foreign relations. In 1977, the House had 22 standing committees (which, in turn, had 138 subcommittees), while the smaller Senate had 15 full committees and 94 subcommittees. The number and roles of standing committees are not fixed. As new issues and cir-

Standing committee A committee permanently created by House or Senate rules.

---

professional staffers drawn from his own office and various committees he chaired to assist him.

As these staffs become larger and the legislative work load heavier and more complex, some people fear that staff members will have an undue influence in formulating and passing legislation. A staff member of Senator Mike Monroney (D-Okla.) was so effective in the legislative process that he became known as "the third senator from Oklahoma." Many a proposal offered in the name of a member of Congress was, in fact, the work of his or her staff. Legislators frequently rely on their assistants to tell them how to vote when they lack the time or understanding necessary to decide for themselves. As the problems faced by Congress become even more complex, the power of staff experts will increase even more.

Professional staffs are also becoming a stepping stone to elective office. In 1978, 10 of the 77 newly elected members of Congress previously worked on legislative staffs (7 of the 10 replaced their previous bosses). Of the 535 members of Congress in 1979, 40 got their start working in Congress. One does not, however, have to start in a highly professional staff position. Over the years six congressional pages have gone on to become members of Congress — as well as one Capitol Hill elevator operator (Angelo Roncallo, R-N.Y.), two doormen (one of whom — Lyndon B. Johnson — also rose to be President), and one policeman.

For more on the role of congressional staffs, see Randall B. Ripley, *Congress: Process and Policy,* 2d ed. (New York: Norton, 1978), pp. 238–253. An excellent in-depth analysis of how a legislative staff allows a legislator to act as an expert on many subjects is given in Richard E. Cohen, "The Kennedy Staff — Putting the Senator Ahead," *National Journal,* December 3, 1977.

*Select and special commit-
tees* House or Senate committees established by resolution for a limited time or for a
special purpose. Most of these
are investigatory committees.
Joint committee A committee
composed of members of the
House and Senate, frequently
created for investigatory purposes.
Conference committee A
committee created to resolve
House-Senate differences on a
specific bill.
Hearings Sessions of committee meetings during which individuals give testimony on
proposed legislation. May be
open or closed to the general
public.
Mark-up sessions The
process by which a committee
revises a bill on a section-by-
section basis. Sometimes a bill
is completely revised and a
new version is introduced to
replace the old version. (The
new bill is called a "clean
bill.")

cumstances arise, Congress modifies its committee system to meet changing needs. For example, in the early 1970s, Congress realized that it exercised little overall review of the budget submitted by the President. To correct this situation, each chamber in 1974 created new budget committees to study and recommend changes in the President's budget.

A second group of committees are the **select and special committees** which investigate either topics of nonpermanent concern or matters considered less important. Ordinarily, these committees are not allowed to report bills for a floor vote. The Senate Watergate Committee, chaired by Senator Sam Ervin (D-N.C.), that initially looked into the Watergate scandal was a select committee. Less well known is the Select Committee on the House Beauty Shop.

A third type of committee, the **joint committee,** is comprised of an equal number of Representatives and Senators. Some of these committees, such as the Joint Economic Committee, exercise significant power. Others, such as the Joint Committee on Printing, primarily handle administrative detail. Like select and special committees, joint committees are rarely allowed to send legislation to the floor.

Finally, the most short-lived of all committees are the **conference committees.** When the House and Senate pass different versions of the same bill, a conference committee attempts to resolve the differences. These committees consist of members of both houses appointed by the presiding officers on the advice of the committee chairperson responsible for the bill (members of both political parties are represented). Delegations from each house vote as a unit, not individually. Conference committees dissolve once their reports are accepted by both houses (which is usually the case). These committees sometimes deal with more than minor adjustments. For example, in 1970, the House voted $290 million for the Supersonic Transport (SST); the Senate voted to *end* this program. The conference committee reached a "compromise" and decided on "only" $210 million for the SST.[11]

Committee procedures

Once in committee a bill goes through several stages. First, if the committee thinks the bill is at least worth considering, a **hearing** on it is held. Fellow members of Congress, lobbyists, concerned citizens, and other government officials can all testify at the hearing. Committee members then vote on the proposed law, section by section, in what is called a **"mark-up" session.** If satisfactory to the committee, the bill is reported out for floor consideration, accompanied by a summary report and supporting and opposing arguments. In the Senate, bills come up for discussion in the order they are reported out of committee.

In the House there is an extra step between committee approval and floor consideration. With only a few exceptions all bills must first go through the Rules Committee, which decides when the bill will be considered and under what conditions (for example, whether amendments

[11] Green, Fallows, and Zwick, p. 63. The SST was nevertheless eventually defeated.

"There are days, Hank, when I don't know who's President, what state I'm from, or even if I'm a Democrat or a Republican, but, by God, I still know how to bottle up a piece of legislation in committee."

Drawing by Stan Hunt; © 1977 The New Yorker Magazine, Inc.

will be permitted and how much time will be allocated for debate).[12] The Rules Committee is obviously a key point of legislative control. In 1970, for example, the Rules Committee refused to report out a bill creating an independent consumer agency, thereby killing the proposal. Such blocking actions can be overcome if a House majority, after thirty days of Rules Committee inaction, signs a **discharge petition.** Such petitions are comparatively rare, however.

This description of the passage of bills through committees does not capture the complexities of legislative decision making. The process is not always orderly or democratic, and many bills with great House or Senate support are never sent to the President. If the actual decisions of committees are to be made more comprehensible, we must examine two key aspects of the committee system: (1) who gets on crucial committees and (2) who exercises power on committees.

Committee membership

An obvious factor affecting a bill's survival is the perspective of the committee considering it. To be killed in committee almost always means legislative death, while a bill fully supported by a committee has an ex-

---

[12] Bills dealing with very specific, comparatively minor issues (so-called private bills) can bypass the Rules Committee. Likewise, bills of limited importance on which there is almost complete agreement can skip the Rules Committee. Four committees—Ways and Means, Appropriations, Veterans' Affairs, and Rules—for certain types of legislation can also bypass the Rules Committee and bring bills to the floor as "privileged business," but this is comparatively rare.

Discharge petition A motion by members of the House to require a committee to send a bill to the floor for a vote. Presently 218 House members are required to sign a discharge petition.

cellent chance of being passed by the whole House or Senate. Thus, the existence of a conservatively dominated House Ways and Means Committee is a standing roadblock to all liberally oriented tax reform. If, for example, a member of Congress were interested in enacting stronger civil rights legislation, the real battle would begin with making sure the House and Senate Judiciary Committees (which handle such matters) are sympathetic to civil rights legislation. A hostile committee would be a difficult obstacle to overcome.

Who determines who gets on what committee, and, thus, who has disproportionate influence over particular legislative domains? There is no single important determinant. At times the assignment process appears incomprehensible. As one member of Congress put it: "Assignment of committees is a mystical process. It's one of the most important things that happens to you as a legislator, and before you know what's happened to you, it's over."[13] Nevertheless, each party in each house has a special "committee on committees" to make these all-important committee assignments. In the House, for example, Democrats are assigned to committees by the Steering and Policy Committee. This twenty-four member committee is composed of the speaker of the House, the Democratic Party floor leader, and other members elected on a regional basis by fellow Democrats or appointed by the speaker. Nominations by this committee must be approved by all House Democrats. The following criteria appear particularly important in committee assignments:

Seniority. The greater one's continuous service (provided one stays in the same party), the greater the likelihood that one will get choice committee assignments. Among Senate Republicans this is the only criterion. Overall, seniority is probably the most important, but not the only, factor in assignment decisions.

Interest and experience. If one represents a district with special needs, or if one has an appropriate background, the chances of obtaining a relevant assignment are improved. Thus, a farmer from a farming district stands a better chance of getting on the Agriculture Committee than an urban lawyer. Some committees also use the criterion of geographical representation.

Acceptance by congressional leadership. Party leaders play a key role in committee assignments. Especially when it comes to appointments to important committees (for example, the House Ways and Means Committee), party leaders favor "responsible" legislators. "Responsibility" means a willingness to compromise, accept existing power arrangements, and, in general, not rock the boat. Members of Congress who flaunt their independence and push too hard, for example, Bella Abzug (D-N.Y., who left Congress in 1976), find it difficult to get ahead.

Politicking. Some members wage vigorous campaigns to get choice assignments. Lobbies will also occasionally campaign on behalf of a member of Congress. Over the years, for example, oil interests have always tried to have a Texan sympathetic to the oil industry appointed to the House Ways and Means Committee, which controls

[13] Quoted in *Ruling Congress,* The Ralph Nader Congress Report, Ted Siff and Alan Weil, Directors (New York: Penguin Books, 1977), p. 72.

tax rulings crucial to oil interests. Similar campaigns are conducted by agricultural, labor, and other interest groups.

Power in committees

Each committee holds considerable power over its domain, but within each committee not all members enjoy equal power. In particular, chairpersons of committees and subcommittees have considerable influence over committee decision making. Though some are much more democratic than others, Congress has seen chairpersons who have run their committees as if other legislators did not exist. Among the most important powers possessed by chairpersons are:[14]

Control over subcommittee membership and jurisdiction. Many committees have numerous subcommittees that make important decisions. The chair usually decides who serves on these committees, their staffs, and what bills they review. (Democratic assignments on the House Appropriations subcommittees are made by the Democratic Steering and Policy Committee.) A chairperson can greatly influence subcommittee behavior. For example, when Chet Holifield (D-Calif.), chairperson of the House Government Operations Committee, once encountered disagreement from a subcommittee chairperson on consumer matters, he simply abolished the subcommittees chaired by the disagreeable representative. However, since 1974, House Democrats have provided for all Democrats to vote on the number of subcommittees. Committee chairpersons also decide the ratio of Democrats and Republicans on subcommittees (the ratio of Democrats to Republicans on committees, however, reflects the overall party balance in each house).

Control over committee budget. Committee chairpersons decide how much money should be spent on such things as clerical help, travel allowances, legal help, and other things affecting the scope of committee and subcommittee activity. Since committee staffs realize that their jobs depend on satisfying the chairperson, they quickly learn to heed the demands of the chair.

Chairpersons determine whether a bill will receive a hearing, when the hearing is to be scheduled, and how the hearing will be conducted. Until recently the chair was unchecked in this power and abuses were common. In the early 1960s, Representative Howard Smith (D-Va.) once delayed hearings on civil rights legislation on the grounds that he had to go home to inspect a burned barn. Hearing this, Speaker of the House Sam Rayburn supposedly said that he knew Smith might do a lot of things to oppose civil rights legislation, but he did not think that arson was one of them.[15] Contemporary rules and customs require some degree of formal scheduling, and there are provisions allowing committees to overrule their chairperson, but the chair still retains considerable discretion.

[14] Our analysis emphasizes general features of committee behavior. For a more detailed analysis of committee characteristics, see Richard F. Fenno, Jr., *Congressmen in Committees* (Boston: Little, Brown, 1973).

[15] Barbara Hinckley, *The Seniority System in Congress* (Bloomington: Indiana University Press, 1971), pp. 89–90.

HOW ABOUT GETTING JOHN TRAVOLTA TO TESTIFY?

It is often said that the real work of Congress goes on in committees. Though certain procedural changes have allowed members to get bills out of hostile committees, committees still remain a major legislative force. It is in committee that most bills are drafted and amended, while the key job of legislative oversight is largely a committee responsibility.

Not all committee business, however, is of earthshaking importance. Here, for example, is a memo from the Committee on House Administration, which includes among its responsibilities the House Beauty Shoppe:

Congress of the United States
House of Representatives

NINETY-FIFTH CONGRESS

ED JONES, TENN., CHAIRMAN
JOHN H. DENT, PA.   WILLIAM L. DICKINSON, ALA.
MENDEL J. DAVIS, S.C.
JIM ABERNATHY, CLERK
225-4568

COMMITTEE ON HOUSE ADMINISTRATION
SUBCOMMITTEE ON SERVICES
105 CANNON HOUSE OFFICE BUILDING
Washington, D.C. 20515

COMMITTEE ON HOUSE ADMINISTRATION
FRANK THOMPSON, JR., CHAIRMAN

September 1, 1978

Dear House Employee:

I am happy to report the success of the first month of "specials" offered by the House Beauty Shoppe. The Subcommittee on Services maintains oversight of this operation and in conjunction with the management of the Shoppe will offer another month of price reductions in September.

September will bring the fall season and the House Beauty Shoppe will present DISCO DAZE. Every Tuesday and Wednesday, special prices will be in effect for service on hairstyles, hair coloring, and permanents. Free nail decals will be given with each manicure or pedicure at the regular price. Full details on all the specials are available by calling 225-4008.

Hours of operation are from 7:00 a.m. to 4:30 p.m., Monday through Saturday. Service is provided for Members of Congress, staff, and the general public. The House Beauty Shoppe is located in the Cannon Building, room 139, just off the main rotunda.

I hope you will be able to take advantage of the excellent service, outstanding expertise, and the September "DISCO DAZE" specials.

With kindest regards and best wishes, I am

Sincerely,

Ed Jones
Chairman

This memo originally appeared in the *Washington Monthly,* November 1978, p. 20.

Finally, chairpersons (or others chosen by them) manage the bills passed by the committee during floor debate. By running the debate over proposed legislation, a skillful chairperson can cut off opposition, ignore those who offer unfriendly amendments, and otherwise manipulate support. Chairpersons are also influential in selecting members of conference committees.

Of course, not all chairpersons use their powers to the fullest or behave like autocrats. Many run their committees in a democratic fashion despite their immense power. Perhaps one reason they continue to hold vast power is that they rarely operate against the wishes of a committee majority. On occasion, committees have risen up against chairpersons who abused their power. The House Education and Labor Committee, in 1966, successfully placed many restrictions on its chairperson, Adam Clayton Powell (D-N.Y.), after he antagonized several committee members.

How does a member of Congress become a chairperson? The answer is simple: one continues to get reelected and one remains on the same committee. When one's party is in the majority, seniority will get one to the top (for the position of chairperson, only seniority within a committee counts, not seniority within Congress in general). Only on rare occasions is the seniority rule violated, and this usually requires flagrant violations of party rules or the physical incapacity of the most senior member. One study of chair assignments made between 1951 and 1969 found that in 194 assignments seniority was violated just twice.[16] Recently, several partially successful attempts have been made to make seniority less crucial, but the principle still remains important.[17]

The political consequences of the committee system

Thus far we have shown two things about the congressional system: First, not everyone is equal when it comes to getting key committee assignments, and second, committee chairpersons frequently exercise disproportionate legislative power. What are the political consequences of this state of affairs? How does it affect the legislation passed by Congress? Does the committee system make the legislative process undemocratic?

[16] *Ruling Congress*, pp. 18–19.

[17] The largest changes have occurred among House Democrats. In 1973, the rules were modified so that all committee chairpersons had to be elected by all House Democrats in a secret ballot. After adoption of the new rule, all committee chairpersons were reelected in 1973, but in 1975 three were deposed—F. Edward Hebert (D-La.) of the Armed Services Committee, W. R. Poage (D-Tex.) of the Agricultural Committee, and Wright Patman (D-Tex.) of the Banking, Currency and Housing Committee. In 1975, Democrats also agreed to have all the subcommittee chairpersons of the powerful Appropriations Committee stand for election by all Democrats. It is unlikely, however, that these new rules will result in drastic changes, since the changes are directed at particular abuses of power, not the seniority system itself. Each of the three deposed chairpersons in 1975 was replaced by a very senior Democrat on the committee. In 1979, House Democrats did not override seniority in selecting committee chairpersons.

Safe districts Congressional districts in which a member of Congress has had little or no competition for reelection.

For many years critics of Congress claimed that both the committee appointment process and the powers of committee chairpersons encouraged misrepresentation and obstructionism. The argument went as follows: First, the seniority principle gave disproportionate influence to legislators from electorally **"safe" districts.** Typically, these safe districts were rural, conservatively oriented areas with little sympathy or understanding for such "modern" problems as civil rights, urban decay, education, public health, or tax reform. This insensitivity to modern problems was further reinforced by the fact that many legislators were quite old by the time they obtained positions of power. Second, because of Democratic supremacy in the South, the consequence of virtually continuous Democratic domination of Congress for forty years was that southern Democrats controlled the committee system. Frequently these southern Democrats teamed up with conservative Republicans to obstruct new social programs. Finally, congressional rules governing committees were oblivious to competence, so as many of these entrenched elders became victims of senility, alcoholism, or indifference to the outside world, nothing was done to replace them.

There is considerable truth to these claims. During the 1950s and 1960s elderly southerners from rural districts did disproportionately dominate the committee system. Studies of roll-call voting and other legislative actions also show that those Democrats high in seniority were less supportive of presidential policy initiatives and Democratic legislative programs than were their nonsouthern colleagues.[18] Moreover, for many years southern committee chairpersons and their allies used all of their powers to keep bills on civil rights, government-financed medical insurance, aid to education, and many other important issues from ever reaching the floor for a vote.

At the same time, however, other observers of Congress have argued that this southern, rural, conservatively oriented domination of the legislative process through the committee system is *not* predetermined. It was only the particular circumstances following World War II that allowed nontypical, obstructionist committee chairpersons to rise to power. In fact, this situation may now be reversing itself as "old guard" southerners are being replaced by nonsouthern liberals and moderates, many of whom are from urban areas. For example, the House Judiciary Committee, which during the 1950s and early 1960s was used by conservative southerners to thwart civil rights legislation, has since had one chairperson from Brooklyn, New York (Emmanuel Celler) and a second from Newark, New Jersey (Peter Rodino). Perhaps the most striking change occurred in 1973 when the House Rules Committee was "captured" by House liberals. Long a bastion of conservatives, the committee began to flood the House with liberal measures, while conservatives complained about the "unrepresentative" Rules Committee.[19]

This change is well illustrated by the material in Table 10.1, which for

[18] Hinckley, Chap. 5.
[19] Gary Orfield, *Congressional Power: Congress and Social Change* (New York: Harcourt Brace Jovanovich, 1975), p. 37.

CONGRESSIONAL CAUCUSES

The word "caucus" is frequently used in politics. Its technical meaning is a group of people who meet to nominate candidates for office or decide on a program. It is also used as a verb—"to caucus." In Congress the word "caucus" is employed to describe several groups. Most important are the Democratic and Republican caucuses in each house. These simply comprise all members of each party in each house (Republicans use the word "conference" instead of "caucus," but the difference is merely semantic). Thus, the term "House Democratic caucus" merely means all House Democrats.

In addition to these caucuses, there are several groups that call themselves caucuses or behave as caucuses. The most notable is the Congressional Black Caucus, which was formally organized in 1971. Composed solely of blacks (a white once tried to join but was rejected), it has a staff of seven and a $100,000 budget. The Black Caucus had sixteen members in 1977 and has primarily been a vehicle for expressing the black point of view outside Congress. Another ethnically oriented caucus is the Congressional Hispanic Caucus, founded in 1976. Thus far, however, its membership has been small and its actions limited.

Several other caucuses also emerged in the 1970s. The Congressional Rural Caucus, founded in 1973, claims 100 members and is interested in policies affecting rural development. The Congressional Clearinghouse on Women's Rights was founded in 1975 and presently publishes a weekly newsletter. A new group is a "blue-collar" caucus of members who once had full-time blue-collar jobs. Their goal is to watch out for the rights of working-class citizens.

Finally, members of the House sharing issue orientations have created several groups. The largest and oldest is the Democratic Study Group (DSG). Created in 1957 by liberal Democrats, it has over 200 dues-paying members, publishes several reports, maintains a large staff, and offers campaign contributions to liberal Democratic candidates for Congress. A more conservative (and smaller) Democratic House group is the Democratic Research Organization. On the Republican side are the conservative Republican Study Committee and the moderate to liberal Wednesday Group.

More information on these different groups is presented in Randall B. Ripley, *Congress: Process and Policy*, 2d. ed. (New York: Norton, 1978), pp. 227–238.

TABLE 10.1
FOUR KEY HOUSE COMMITTEES AND THEIR CHAIRPERSONS, 1978

Committee	Jurisdiction	Chairperson age, and political orientation	Chairperson's district
Rules	Determines agenda of House.	James J. Delaney (76). In 1960s and early 1970s usually took conservative positions. In 1972, after being threatened in primary, became more liberal and more sympathetic to goals of other congressional Democrats	Queens, New York, district, heavily middle class or lower-middle class, conservative homeowners. Largely Catholic. Very few blacks or Puerto Ricans. Gave Nixon 73 percent of vote in 1972; Carter received 46 percent in 1976. Described as the home of Archie Bunker.
Ways and Means	Tax legislation, social security, tariffs and trade bills, health care legislation.	Al Ullman (64). Came to Congress in 1956 as a fiery liberal, has since become more moderate. A loyal Democrat not eager to disturb the political status quo.	Eastern Oregon district economically dependent on agriculture, especially lumber, cattle, and food products. Heavily rural, virtually all white and all native born. Much sympathy for public power projects, but not enthusiastic about other liberal social measures.
Appropriations	Reviews federal budget and all other appropriations.	George H. Mahon (78). Traditionally far more conservative than fellow Democrats. Has successfully kept liberals off Appropriations Committee.	West Texas district of small towns, ranches, in general economic decline. Major cities of Lubbock and Midland are dependent on oil. Cattle, grain, and cotton also important. District is 6 percent black, 19 percent Spanish-speaking.
Armed Services	Deals with Department of Defense and military matters in general.	Melvin Price (73). Generally votes with Democratic majority and strong supporters of labor. Also a strong supporter of high defense budgets.	Downstate Illinois district, east of St. Louis, consisting of industrial towns. Considerable pollution, crime, inadequate housing, and a declining tax base. Many blacks and a large proportion of poor and low-income workers.

the four most important House committees in 1978 describes the chairpersons and their districts. Only one chairperson — George Mahon of Texas — represents the classic southern conservative, and he retired later in 1978. Two — Al Ullman and Melvin Price — are moderates who generally support the policies of the Democratic majority. Congressman James Delaney had been a very conservative Democrat for several years, but since becoming chairperson of the Rules Committee, he has responded to party pressures favoring more moderate positions. Also note that two of the four districts are highly urban.

THE ROLE OF ELECTED PARTY LEADERS

The second important element in the legislative process consists of elected party leadership. In the House this consists of a speaker, majority and minority party floor leaders, and majority and minority party whips. The Senate, lacking an equivalent of speaker of the House (the Vice President presides), has only four elected party leaders: majority and minority party floor leaders and their respective whips. As we shall see, these elected leaders, like members of important committees and key committee chairpersons, have a major say on what bills survive and become law.

Speaker of the House

Every two years the House chooses a speaker who holds important power over the legislative process. Traditionally, this is done by a straight party vote so that the Democrats, who have continuously been a majority since 1955, have chosen the speaker since that year. Democratic speakers — Sam Rayburn, John McCormack, Carl Albert, Tip O'Neil — have been among the most senior representatives, but seniority itself is not the only criterion for their selection. To win election by their party colleagues, candidates for speaker must please many diverse groups and not be considered extreme or irresponsible. Once elected, speakers usually hold office until death or retirement.

What can a speaker do? The speaker has several formal and informal powers that provide him or her with a crucial role in lawmaking.

As presiding officer of the House, the speaker decides who shall speak on what issues. Since the House is large, on any important issue there are frequently many more people wanting to speak, propose amendments, or engage in parliamentary tactics than can be allowed within a reasonable time. Obviously, then, the power to recognize one legislator and ignore another can sometimes be crucial. Similarly, the speaker is usually the final judge of parliamentary procedure. Disputes on important questions, such as the relevance of an amendment to a bill, the presence of a quorum, or the interpretation of a bill, are resolved by the speaker. Getting House passage of a bill opposed by the speaker can be a serious problem.

The House speaker also counts and announces votes. This is especially important because many votes are voice votes, and it is up to the speaker to decide which is louder, the "ayes" or the "nays." Where votes are close,

(Left photo) THOMAS FOLEY (D–Wash.), House Democratic whip.
(Middle photo) TRENT LOTT (R–Miss.), House Republican whip.
(Right photo) THOMAS P. (TIP) O'NEILL (D–Mass.), speaker of the House.

(Left photo) JAMES WRIGHT (D–Texas), House majority leader.
(Middle photo) ROBERT MICHEL (R–Ill.), House minority leader.
(Right photo) Left, HOWARD H. BAKER, JR. (R–Tenn.), Senate majority leader, and right, ROBERT G. BYRD (D–W, Va.), Senate minority leader.

(Left photo) ALAN CRANSTON (D–Calif.), assistant Senate Democratic leader (whip).
(Right photo) TED STEVENS (R–Alas.), assistant Senate Republican leader (whip).

differences can be small, and no doubt on more than one occasion a majority was declared the loser thanks to the speaker's interpretation. The speaker can also affect vote outcomes by deciding *when* to call a vote. A speaker opposed to a particular bill can hold off a vote until he or she thinks opponents on the floor outnumber supporters and then quickly call for the vote.

Another major area of speaker influence concerns the committee system. It is the speaker who assigns a bill to a committee. When the content of a bill is complex and relevant committees have different philosophies, this power can mean legislative life or death. For example, a 1963 civil rights bill based on the commerce clause of the Constitution was sent to the more sympathetic Judiciary Committee rather than to the Interstate and Foreign Commerce Committee, whose chairperson was opposed to civil rights legislation. House members of conference committees (which iron out House-Senate differences) are also appointed by the speaker in consultation with the relevant committee chairpersons. In addition, recent changes in House Democratic Party rules allow the speaker (if he or she is a Democrat) to appoint nine members of the Democratic Steering and Policy Committee, which nominates Democrats for their committee assignments (these nominations are usually, but not always, accepted by a majority of all Democrats).

Finally, by virtue of these formal and informal powers, and ability to dispense rewards, the speaker can help shape overall legislative goals. Especially when the speaker and the President are of the same party, the speaker can provide overall direction and coordination of legislative efforts. During the Carter Administration, for example, Speaker Tip O'Neill has played an important role in keeping the President's programs alive in the face of congressional opposition. Without O'Neill's willingness to talk with fellow legislators, reward friends, or expedite matters, congressional action would have fallen far short of Carter's goals.

Party floor leadership

In both the House and the Senate each party elects a floor leader (called a majority or minority leader). These party leaders are, in turn, assisted by party whips (for Senate Democrats this position is called assistant floor leader) whose main responsibilities are to marshal voting support for the party's positions. Like other members of Congress in positions of power, floor leaders are almost always fairly senior, though seniority is not strictly followed in selecting them. In general, floor leaders are moderates in their policy stands and can get along with diverse people and interests. An extremely liberal or conservative legislator unwilling to compromise and negotiate is unlikely to be elected a party leader.

The major role played by party leaders is the overall shaping of a legislative program. Not every bill that is introduced or that gets through committee can be given equal consideration by the entire membership. Priorities must be established, and appropriate strategies determined. This is especially true when House and Senate majorities, leaders, and the President are of the same party. Managing the flow of legislation involves such things as deciding when a bill is to be brought to the floor, which versions of a bill will be considered, and how a bill is to be defended or attacked.

Party floor leaders can operate through a variety of techniques. Majority party leaders, in particular, are in a good position to bestow favors to achieve their goals. A cooperative member might, for example, increase his or her chances of obtaining a favorable committee assignment or improve the odds of getting his or her bills enacted. On occasion a party leader can be helpful in reelection campaigns by making a personal appearance on a candidate's behalf or arranging an event (for example, money for a local project) to make the candidate "look good." For the most part, the use of these techniques to accomplish legislative goals depends greatly on the skill and personality of the particular leaders, not the formal powers of the office. Some, like Lyndon B. Johnson when he was Senate majority leader, are masters at maneuvering legislative programs through the congressional obstacle course. Others, especially minority leaders whose powers are limited, view their role as closer to that of traffic policemen attempting to keep order.

FLOOR DECISIONS

Having survived the committee hurdle and perhaps other attempts on its life by party leaders, a bill is put on the legislative calendar for consideration. In many ways this is the most dramatic part of lawmaking. This is also the activity most people think of when they imagine Congress passing laws—a spirited debate among orators trying to sway undecided votes while appealing to the galleries. Is this final stage of lawmaking all that significant? Or, on the other hand, is the final tally of votes a mere formality since the outcome is predetermined?

The answer to these questions is that actions on the floor prior to voting *are* frequently important, but this final stage is only one of many important stages, not *the* decisive moment. Final floor debate is important because no member of Congress can be forced to support a particular bill. The U.S. Congress is not a parliamentary-type system where a party or a prime minister has the power to dictate voting decisions. Therefore, prevote activity in Congress is frequently an important period in which votes are traded, deals made, and friendly persuasion employed. This is the stage at which party leaders and whips try to marshal their forces. In many instances the final fate of significant legislation is decided in the hour or so before the voting.

Congressional debate over proposed bills can be important, especially in the Senate, but it is rare that the vote of a member of Congress is swayed by the compelling speech of another. Several factors make speech giving less important than is popularly believed. For one, there is so much legislative business to conduct that allowing for "great debates" would slow things to a standstill. When Congress had fewer members and much less business to conduct, such debates were common. Today, however, members of the House are rarely given more than a few minutes to make their points (sometimes as little as 45 seconds), and even in

DO CONGRESSIONAL LEADERS REALLY LEAD?

In viewing the role of congressional leaders in the legislative process, we should realize that elected leaders and committee chairpersons must rely much more on persuasion and the promise of future benefits than on pure coercion. Congress is not like a private business where insubordinate employees can be fired. Even the most respected senior legislator cannot remove a colleague from office or significantly intervene in his or her election.

This situation sometimes leads to a paradox: in order to achieve the *appearance* of power, one must sometimes relinquish much of the *substance* of power. Put somewhat differently, you get things done by giving many people what they want. It was claimed, for example, that much of the great power attributed to Sam Rayburn, long-time speaker of the House, derived from his unwillingness to risk losing. Rayburn appeared to be much more powerful than he actually was because he would always join the winning side.

A more recent illustration of this approach to leadership was provided by the actions of Senator Russell Long (D-La.), chairperson of the Senate Finance Committee, which handles tax policy. Long had gained a reputation for power by helping others. For example, he helped his colleague Robert Packwood (R-Ore.) get a special tax exemption for profits from an Oregon livestock exhibition. Long also arranged for reelection support for fellow committee member Floyd Haskell (D-Col.), despite some differences of political opinion. Senator Patrick D. Moynihan (D-N.Y.), also a Finance Committee member, was given responsibility for welfare matters and was allowed to attach an amendment to a social security bill providing hundreds of millions of dollars in welfare relief to New York State. These and other numerous actions to help his fellow Senators have greatly helped Long's standing. The price of such standing, however, has been an avoidance of potentially unpopular causes. Many Senators follow Long's lead in voting, not because of threats but because Long seems to know in advance which side will win.

Obviously, this style of leadership does little to overcome the fragmentation and lack of coordination in the legislative process.

The activities of Senator Long are described in "The Power Broker: If It's Important on Capitol Hill, It Goes Through Russell Long," by Robert G. Kaiser, *The Milwaukee Journal,* December 25, 1977, Part 9, pp. 1, 3.

Filibuster The tactic of speaking for long periods in the Senate so as to delay the legislative process. Can be used by a single Senator or by a group, each of whom takes a turn speaking.

Cloture A motion to end a filibuster. Needs the support of sixteen Senators to be considered and sixty Senators to be passed.

Closed rule The stipulation that a bill cannot be amended in floor debate; thus the bill is an "all-or-nothing" proposition.

the Senate where there are no formal time restrictions on speeches pressures exist to move business along.

A related point is that many legislators are so occupied with nonfloor business, such as committee hearings or helping constituents, that floor discussions are commonly poorly attended. The 1971 Revenue Act, which cut corporate taxes by $7.5 *billion*, was passed by voice vote during lunch with only about thirty members voting.[20] It is not unusual to witness a member of Congress giving a speech to only a handful of colleagues. However, when a vote is called many others will suddenly materialize only to vote.

On relatively rare occasions debate is a crucial step in the legislative process. The Senate allows unlimited debate, so in principle a few Senators can talk forever on a subject and thus kill a bill by preventing a vote. This is the so-called **filibuster,** which can be stopped only by invoking **cloture,** a vote by sixty Senators to end debate. Prior to 1975 cloture required two thirds of all Senators present and voting. Because two thirds was a difficult majority to achieve, and because many Senators supported the principle of unlimited debate, a cloture vote was difficult and occurred only rarely. Between 1917 and 1975, of 123 cloture votes taken only 34 succeeded (filibusters against civil rights bills were especially difficult to stop).[21] Whether the new rule of sixty senators as opposed to two thirds of those present will make it easier to end debate remains to be seen.

How important is the filibuster in the Senate legislative process? Over the years it has been used with considerable effectiveness to block or weaken important legislation. For many years southern Senators used the filibuster to defeat civil rights legislation on job discrimination, lynching, and voter registration. In many instances the mere threat of a filibuster was sufficient to kill proposed civil rights legislation. It was only after seventy-four days of debate that the Senate finally managed to pass the 1964 Civil Rights Act. The filibuster is not, however, used exclusively by conservative southerners. In the 1970s, liberals employed the filibuster against the military draft system, government funding of the Supersonic Transport (SST), and antibusing legislation.[22]

Perhaps the most important factor limiting the importance of floor consideration in the legislative process is the complex nature of most legislation. Many bills would require weeks of careful scrutiny to understand them fully. Others contain so many provisions designed to deal with diverse problems that a full debate would run for days. This complexity is formally acknowledged in the House where some complicated appropriations and tax bills are reported to the floor under **"closed rules"** which prohibit any amendments (in 1973 House Democrats modified the closed-rule procedure by allowing fifty or more Democrats to suggest amendments to all other Democrats; if a majority approved, these amendments would be considered despite the closed rule). Even without

[20] Green, Fallows, and Zwick, p. 74.

[21] For a complete list of cloture votes, see *Inside Congress* (Washington, D.C.: Congressional Quarterly, 1976), p. 13.

[22] Orfield, p. 43.

a closed rule, however, writing laws on the floor of the House or Senate is difficult. For the most part, the average legislator must rely heavily on the opinions of experts, members of relevant committees, and the direction of party leaders. Few legislators are willing to oppose the judgment of a committee that has studied the question at great length, especially where committee support is strong.

THINGS ARE LOOKING UP FOR CONGRESSIONAL DEBATE

Most congressional floor discussions are not very exciting. Few members of Congress can pay close attention to the details of a complicated bill about which they know comparatively little. Nevertheless, on some occasions things come up that generate rapt attention and thought among the assembled legislators. Donald Riegle, once a Republican House member from Michigan (now a Senator), described such a situation:

On the floor this afternoon as I was reading an early edition of the *Evening Star,* I felt a nudge on my arm. It was one of my younger Republican colleagues.

"Look up there—in the third row," he said, motioning furtively toward the visitors' gallery.

Sitting there was an attractive redhead in a green dress. What my colleague was directing my attention to was the fact that one of her thighs was fully exposed. He had already tipped off several other members, all of whom were casting appreciative glances at the gallery. Some, in fact, had moved to other locations on the floor to get a better view. Thigh watching is one of the most popular diversions in the House.

From Donald Riegle with Trevor Armbruster, *O Congress* (New York: Popular Library, 1976), p. 74.

In short, floor consideration is an important legislative step, but we must also realize that before a bill ever gets to the floor many key decisions have already been made. The relevant committee or subcommittee, if it reports the bill to the floor, has undoubtedly left its imprint. Party leaders and the speaker of the House have made decisions on the bill's importance or whether a major effort should be launched to pass or to defeat it. The final floor vote is but one of several steps. This step is crucial for passage, but in most instances the basic character of the bill is not decided by members in open debate over what is best for the people of the United States.

A conclusion: assessing congressional power

We have examined the powers possessed by Congress as an institution and seen how power is distributed within that legislative body. What conclusions can we draw from our analysis? What are the political consequences of these distributions of power?

The most obvious conclusion is that Congress lacks the capacity to solve singlehandedly many of the problems that face the country. As we have seen, most of the important powers of Congress are *shared* powers. Congress cannot institute major social or economic programs without the cooperation of the executive branch, the courts, and state or local governments.

Within Congress itself power tends to be *fragmented*. Many individuals hold disproportionate power, but no one person can dictate legislation. Powerful committee chairpersons may terrify bureaucrats, treat fellow committee members like children, and obtain numerous favors for their friends, but even they must bargain and make concessions to get a bill through the long and difficult legislative process. Moreover, there is a strong bias in Congress toward moderation and compromise. Leaders lead by marshaling a consensus, not by dictating policy.

Finally, much effective congressional power is largely *negative* power. By refusing to appropriate the necessary funds or holding a bill in committee, Congress can destroy a program. However, passing the necessary legislation and the required money does not guarantee that the program will operate as intended. Presidents can refuse to spend the money, judges can place restrictions on actions, and local governments can sometimes go their own way.

Is this limited capacity for direct positive action a defect in need of a cure? If one puts one's hopes on vigorous government action as the solution to problems, then this incapacity is certainly a flaw. If, on the other hand, one believes that limits on government action are essential to maintaining a free society, then such incapacity is a virtue.

Major questions raised

1. How much power does Congress have? The Constitution provides Congress with a number of explicit powers. The most important are probably the powers to tax and spend and to regulate commerce. The power to investigate and congressional oversight of the executive bureaucracy are two other important powers not mentioned in the Constitution.

2. What are the limits on congressional power? The Constitution limits Congress by spelling out certain prohibitions and by calling for a governmental design that will impede the accumulation of power. Even more important, however, are the countervailing powers of the other two branches of government and the principle of federalism.

3. What determines whether Congress passes or defeats a bill? Decisions made by specialized committees, especially their chairpersons, have a disproportionate impact on whether a bill survives. Party leaders can also play an important role in the final outcome. Members of Congress vote on only a small proportion of all measures introduced, but this stage is also important even if few votes are changed by debate on the floor.

QUESTIONS FOR FURTHER DISCUSSION

1. The original reason for having a two-house legislature was the need to win support for ratification of the Constitution. The Senate was created to guarantee representation to small states. It can be argued, however, that this original justification is no longer relevant. The U.S. Congress, like the Nebraska state legislature, should be a one-house body. This would simplify the legislative process, lower the cost of running government, and reduce the inequities in representation created by the Senate's allotment of two legislators per state regardless of population. Would you support such a change? Does a two-house legislature still have any utility?

2. The seniority principle is the single most important (though not the only) rule governing legislative power. The longer one's continuous service, provided one does not change parties, the greater one's power. Critics claim that seniority results in power being given to nontypical legislators whose chief characteristic is their advanced age. Seniority is defended on the grounds that being a leader requires experience, and seniority means experience. If seniority does not strike you as a good method of selecting leaders, what principles would you suggest? Should elected party leaders have a free hand in making committee assignments and choosing committee chairpersons? Which interests would lose the most if the seniority principle were abolished?

3. In recent years several members of Congress have introduced various "sunset" bills (none has yet passed). Essentially, sunset laws would require that all agencies and programs automatically go out of business unless they are systematically reviewed and reapproved by Congress. The purpose of sunset legislation is to eliminate expensive programs that no longer serve any valuable function but still manage to survive through legislative inaction. Though nobody wants expensive, inefficient, and irrelevant programs, on what grounds might sunset laws be opposed? How might Congress decide that a program is no longer necessary?

4. During the early 1970s, many reforms were enacted to make Congress, especially the House, more democratic. That is, power was taken away from some individuals and more evenly distributed. Reformers believed that greater equality among legislators would produce better, more responsive legislation. However, it can also be argued that by weakening leaders and dispersing power, we would make Congress less able to act at all. Passing laws requires extensive cooperation, and without some concentrated power the likely result would be stalemate. Thus, a highly democratic legislature would be unproductive, a situation that would favor conservatives who want inaction. Do you accept the proposition that having a few strong leaders is a necessary condition

for Congress to be an efficient, productive organization? Can the existence of concentrated power in a few leaders be compatible with the principles of democracy within an organization such as the House?

BIBLIOGRAPHY

Berman, Daniel M. *A Bill Becomes a Law: Congress Enacts Civil Rights Legislation*, 2d ed. London: Collier-Macmillan Ltd., 1966.
> A brief, step-by-step history of the 1960 (and, to a lesser extent, 1964) Civil Rights Act. Provides a good sense of all the effort that goes into enacting legislation.

Bibby, John F., and Roger H. Davidson. *On Capitol Hill*, 2d ed. Hinsdale, Ill.: Dryden Press, 1972.
> Contains several case studies of Congress at work. For example, it describes the workday activities of two legislators, how party officials function, and two campaigns for office. A good blend of technical detail and journalistic "insider" descriptions of Congress.

Bollings, Richard. *House Out of Order.* New York: Dutton, 1965.
> Bollings is a long-time and influential member of Congress from Missouri. Despite his close associations with House leadership, he argues for substantial reform to help Congress face complex problems requiring rapid action. Basically Bollings favors reducing the importance of seniority and lessening concentrated power. Provides numerous fascinating stories of House politics.

Chelf, Carl P. *Congress in the American System.* Chicago: Nelson-Hall, 1977.
> A highly readable overview of Congress. Provides a good feel for individual members of Congress, their problems, and the informal side of the legislative process. Contains separate chapters on legislative rules, the committee system, and floor debate. Also relates Congress to the other branches of government and discusses possible reforms.

Congressional Quarterly's Guide to Congress, 2d ed. Washington, D.C.: Congressional Quarterly, Inc., 1976.
> Over 700 big, fact-filled pages on everything you ever wanted to know about Congress and much more. Coverage ranges from historical development of Congress, including characteristics of members and its powers, to recent reforms (to list only a few of the topics covered). Contains several bibliographies and an excellent index that allows you to find easily almost any detail about Congress (or most U.S. politics, more generally). *The* reference book on Congress.

Fenno, Richard F., Jr. *Congressmen in Committees.* Boston: Little, Brown, 1973.
> An in-depth look at twelve House committees in the period 1955 to 1966. Considers goals of committee members, limitations on committee actions, how committee decisions are made, and how committee members relate to each other.

Green, Mark J., and James M. Fallows, and David R. Zwick. *Who Runs Congress: The President, Big Business or You?* New York: Bantam Books, 1972.
> A book from the Ralph Nader Congress Project that takes a somewhat negative view of legislators. Despite this bias, the book is an excellent source for material on legislative wheeling and dealing. Has chapters on who runs Congress, lawmakers as lawbreakers, and how citizens can take action against members of Congress.

Hinckley, Barbara. *Stability and Change in Congress*, 2d ed. New York: Harper & Row, 1978.
> A comparatively brief but wide-ranging analysis of Congress. Examines legislative leadership, the committee system, the role of parties, changing patterns of influence, and several other important failures of Congress. Well documented but not technical.

Oleszek, Walter J. *Congressional Procedures and the Policy Process.* Washington, D.C.: Congressional Quarterly Inc., 1978.

> An up-to-date, detailed description of how Congress operates. Excellent source for understanding such things as how bills are scheduled, Senate and House floor procedures, conference committee procedures, and the operation of legislative oversight. Contains a glossary of legislative terms and a large bibliography.

Origins and Development of Congress. Washington, D.C.: Congressional Quarterly, Inc., 1976.

> A detailed history of Congress from colonial times to 1976. Useful for understanding origins of such legislative practices as seniority, the committee system, and lawmaking procedures. Contains a bibliography.

Powers of Congress. Washington, D.C.: Congressional Quarterly, Inc., 1976.

> A careful review of major legislative powers. Particularly strong on fiscal powers, foreign affairs, and investigative powers. Contains an extensive bibliography.

Redman, Eric. *The Dance of Legislation.* New York: Simon & Schuster, 1973.

> Redman, who spent two years working in the Senate, traces one bill—the National Health Service Bill—through the complexities of the legislative process. A well-written journalistic view of the people, maneuvers, and strategies in Congress.

Ripley, Randall B. *Congress: Process and Policy,* 2d ed. New York: Norton, 1978.

> A well-documented analysis of different aspects of Congress. Contains several chapters on the inner workings of Congress as well as on how Congress deals with other officials and the public. An extensive annotated bibliography is organized by subject matter (for example, committees, party leadership, congressional elections).

Ruling Congress: How the House and Senate Rules Govern the Legislative Process. The Ralph Nader Congress Report, Ted Siff and Alan Weil, Directors. New York: Penguin Books, 1977.

> Especially good in describing the importance of legislative rules, and their interpretations, in the lawmaking process. Has chapters on floor debating and voting, conference committees, and how the procedures of Congress should be reformed.

PREVIEW

Is Congress a cross section of the public?

If we define representation as meaning we are governed by people like ourselves, then Congress is not representative of the general public. Members of Congress tend to be older, better educated, and have higher-status occupations than most citizens. Congress is also disproportionately white and male. It can be argued, however, that this composition does not mean that the interests of the poor, the young, women, manual workers, and blacks are slighted by lawmakers.

Do members of Congress respond to citizen demands?

Most legislators engage in extensive casework—helping constituents with problems involving government. Lawmakers also provide constituents "pork-barrel" benefits such as new highways. Some questions have been raised, however, on whether such services are really benefits in the long run. With respect to legislative voting on policies, on matters that are crucial to a district, most lawmakers usually follow district opinion. However, district opinion does not play a decisive role. Reasons for legislator-district inconsistency include a lack of opinion in the district, an absence of accurate information on district opinion, the legislator's view of his or her job, and nonconstituency pressures. Many citizens are represented in Congress by legislators other than those from their districts.

Does Congress respond effectively to national problems?

Critics argue that Congress responds much too slowly, its actions are uncoordinated, national problems are viewed from a local perspective, and its members lack the understanding necessary for solving contemporary problems. Its defenders assert that Congress was never designed to solve all of our problems, speedy action is not always wise action, a piecemeal approach is reasonable for complex issues, attention to local needs makes national policies more effective, and Congress seems as capable as anyone else of solving problems that affect the country as a whole.

Should Congress be reformed? If so, how?

A prior question is: Is the public satisfied with Congress? Most citizens do not give Congress a high rating. However, as measured by the willingness of voters to reelect incumbent lawmakers, the public seems satisfied. One of the most frequently suggested reforms is to strengthen Congress in relation to the executive branch. This reform would involve increasing legislative resources and having Congress take a greater initiative in formulating policy. A more powerful Congress, however, might result in more stalemates between Congress and the President. A second reform would aim at making the operations of Congress more democratic. Such a change would probably be opposed by those who are well represented under existing arrangements.

CHAPTER ELEVEN

CONGRES-SIONAL REPRE-SENTATION AND RESPON-SIVENESS

Two current political questions that have been widely debated are whether Congress adequately represents the people and whether it responds effectively to contemporary problems. People disagree sharply in their conclusions. Defenders claim that Congress has done a remarkable job given the complexity of contemporary problems and constitutional limitations on its power. Others, like Dewey Short, a Republican from Missouri who left the House in 1957 after many years of service, described his fellow representatives as a bunch of "supine, subservient, soporific, supercilious, pusillanimous nitwits." To make matters more confusing, people disagree on the meaning of words like "representation" and "responsiveness." Does a "responsive" member of Congress support what is best for the entire nation, or do the interests of those who elected him or her come first? Can a largely all-male institution adequately represent a population that is half female? These questions sometimes seem beyond resolution. Nevertheless, the issues of congressional representation and responsiveness are important and must be considered. We shall examine four questions dealing with representation and responsiveness in Congress:

1. Is Congress a cross section of the public?
2. Do members of Congress respond to citizen demands?
3. Does Congress respond effectively to national problems?
4. Should Congress be reformed? If so, how?

Is Congress a cross section of the public?

One important (but not the only) meaning of "representation" is that decisions are made for us by people like ourselves. This notion of representation underlies the demands of some black or women's groups for more public officials who are black or female. During the 1960s, many college students stood on this definition of representation when they claimed that only fellow students, not professors or administrators, should decide matters affecting students. Using this notion of representation, we would say that Congress represents the public if members of Congress, as a group, resemble the general public.

Are national legislators typical citizens? The answer is: While considerable diversity exists among members of Congress, the House and Senate are not miniatures of the U.S. population. Compared to the general public, members of Congress are disproportionately middle class: they tend to be well educated, they usually have had high-prestige occupations (for example, law), and they have typically grown up in comfortable surroundings. In the 96th Congress, which opened on January 15, 1979, there were 270 lawyers, 156 members who had been in business or banking, 64 with backgrounds in education, and 7 with medical backgrounds.[1] The 1978 Senate contained 18 millionaires and 5 others who had close to a million dollars.[2] Racially, though the number of blacks in Congress has gradually increased, blacks are substantially underrepresented compared to their numbers in the population. Women are similarly grossly underrepresented, though the number of women elected to Congress has also increased. A disproportionate number of members also come from rural areas or small towns. The religious composition of Congress is similar to that of the United States as a whole, although among Protestants, Episcopalians and Presbyterians (both considered high-status denominations) are considerably overrepresented. Finally, the age level of members of Congress, especially those in positions of power, is significantly higher than that of the general adult population.

What is the political significance of these facts? Does the underrepresentation of manual workers, poor people, blacks, women, and young people mean that the interests of these groups are ignored in lawmaking? Would the election of more manual workers, for example, make Congress more responsive to the needs of this group of citizens? Must women elect more women if they want to obtain a larger share of government benefits?

The people who accept this argument claim that such characteristics as age or sex are closely associated with certain types of experiences and that these experiences have a direct bearing on legislative behavior. During the Vietnam war, for example, it was asserted that a 75-year-old com-

[1] *Congressional Quarterly Weekly Report,* January 20, 1979.

[2] *Congressional Quarterly Weekly Report,* September 2, 1978, presents an overall picture of congressional wealth.

mittee chairperson making decisions about expanding the war effort could not really understand the feelings of a 20-year-old male facing the military draft. Similarly, it is commonly asserted that middle-class legislators, consciously or unconsciously, place their own goals ahead of the programs desired by the poor or blacks. Therefore, the argument goes, it should come as no surprise that the preferences of the less well off, blacks, women, and the young are frequently overwhelmed in the legislative struggle.

Another point of view maintains that Congress as a whole is not typical of the general population, but that this does not mean that Congress is unrepresentative of the public. First, according to this position, there is no one-to-one relationship between a person's background and the policies he or she advocates. A rich person *can* favor policies that benefit poor people, and men frequently advocate legislation that enhances women, such as equal pay for equal work. As wealthy as Nelson Rockefeller was, as governor of New York he proposed increased aid to the poor. One cannot automatically assume that because there are no women Senators, the Senate will be insensitive to the desires of women.

Second, the argument that Congress is not a cross section of the population and therefore is unrepresentative assumes that voters want legislators who resemble themselves in terms of such characteristics as education, occupation, sex, race, and place of residence. But one can equally reasonably maintain that most voters want leaders who display greater competence than they themselves possess and, thus, choose members of Congress with elitist characteristics. After all, given the openness of the electoral system, people could choose a Congress with an entirely different set of traits. If the public wanted poor black females to pass its laws, it could elect a Congress of poor black females.

Clearly, Congress as a whole is not a good cross section of the population. Disagreement arises, however, on whether its socioeconomic makeup proves that Congress is an unrepresentative institution. On the one hand, some people argue that leaders with elitist characteristics cannot possibly express the desires of a population that largely does not share these characteristics. On the other hand, it is also plausible to claim that people of one background can act for those of a different background and that citizens sometimes desire legislative representatives unlike themselves.

Do members of Congress respond to citizen demands?

Of all the questions asked about Congress, one of the most difficult to answer is whether or not members of Congress respond to popular demands. This is a crucial question, yet like so many important political questions, it has no simple answer. Responding to citizens involves several different types of behavior. We shall examine four aspects of congressional behavior: (1) congressional casework; (2) providing legislative benefits to constituents; (3) legislative voting behavior; and (4) providing a voice for particular interests.

WOULD RECRUITING MORE POOR MEMBERS OF CONGRESS HELP POOR PEOPLE?

Congress is often criticized for its over-representation of well-off citizens. Should a greater effort be made to recruit poor people for Congress? Such a proposal assumes that those who have experienced poverty will be sympathetic to the needs of poor people. This is a big assumption. Fortunately, some members of Congress have pulled themselves up from severe poverty, so that on the basis of individual cases we can consider whether economic background and issue positions have a one-to-one relationship. One good illustration is Allen Ellender (D-La.), a Senate leader on agricultural policy who served from 1937 until his death on July 27, 1972. Ellender was born on a run-down Louisiana plantation where his parents barely made a living from farming. As a young boy he usually stayed home to help his parents instead of attending school. Prior to age 14, he averaged about four or five months of school a year. When at that age he did start school full time, he commuted by riding an old mule. He then worked his way through St. Aloysius College and Tulane University Law School.

Another example of making good despite great economic handicaps is the case of L. Mendel Rivers, who spent almost thirty years in the House until his death in late 1970. Rivers' father had a small farm and turpentine still, which were lost when he died. At age 8, Rivers and his widowed mother moved to North Charleston, South Carolina, where he milked cows and delivered papers before attending school. During the summer he worked as a laborer at the Charleston Navy Yard, a sheet metal shop, and an asbestos mill. Rivers spent two years at the College of Charleston, earned a law degree from the University of South Carolina Law School, and then entered politics where he became immensely successful.

Both Ellender and Rivers came up the hard way and relied on their own abilities. Despite these backgrounds, however, neither supported government programs to help less fortunate citizens. In fact, both usually opposed "give-away" programs in education and job training. They likewise opposed the efforts of the civil rights movement and unions to help poor people achieve a higher standard of living. Their

Senator Allen Ellender (D-La.).

CONGRESSIONAL CASEWORK

Because of the growth of government at all levels, many citizens find themselves with problems that must be resolved through contact with government officials. When in need of help, many citizens turn to their

L. Mendel Rivers at the 1970 dedication of the L. Mendel Rivers Elementary School. The school was renamed for Rivers when as chairman of the House Armed Services Committee he intervened to prevent the closing of a local Air Force base.

attitude, like those of many other self-made people, seems to have been: "I made it on my own, so can everyone else."

In short, as these two examples show, we must be cautious about assuming that people's present-day behavior derives from their backgrounds. Congress may not be comprised of poor people in proportion to their number in the general population, but electing those who experienced poverty does not necessarily mean the passage of more laws to assist the poor.

For additional information on the backgrounds and careers of Ellender and Rivers, see Drew Pearson and Jack Anderson, *The Case Against Congress* (New York: Simon & Schuster, 1968), pp. 211–222, 264–274.

representative in Washington. Sometimes **congressional casework** even extends to problems that have nothing to do with the national government or that are beyond legislative intervention (for example, collecting an insurance claim). Nevertheless, unlike with many other government officials, the location of a member of Congress is at least known, and he

Congressional casework The efforts of members of Congress to provide services and benefits to citizens.

or she is likely to be far more accessible than some nameless, obscure bureaucrat. Because contemporary Senators and Representatives represent hundreds of thousands of citizens, the daily flow of requests can frequently be overwhelming. More than one member of Congress has complained that errand running for troubled constituents takes precedence over lawmaking. As one member of Congress put it:

> A Congressman has become an expanded messenger boy, an employment agency, getter-out of the Navy, Army, and Marines, a ward heeler, a wound healer, trouble shooter, law explainer, bill finder, issue translator, resolution interpreter, controversy-oil pourer, glad hand extender, business promoter, veterans' affairs adjuster, ex-serviceman's champion, watchdog for the underdog, sympathizer for the upperdog, kisser of babies, recoverer of lost baggage, soberer of delegates, adjuster for traffic violations and voters straying into the toils of the law, binderup of broken hearts, financial wet nurse, a good Samaritan, contributor of good causes, cornerstone layer, public building and bridge dedicator, and ship christener.[3]

The list of favors and services requested of members of Congress is almost endless. For example, students (from grade schoolers to university students) are sometimes encouraged by their teachers to flood congressional offices with requests for information to be used in term papers or debates.[4] Appeals for government jobs consume much time and energy. The recent efforts of government to solve problems of poverty and pollution have predictably resulted in constituent demand for government assistance in setting up local programs in urban renewal, small-business loans, or grants for water treatment plants. Members of Congress occasionally are even asked for such nonpolitical favors as making hotel and airplane reservations, replacing china, and, in one instance, asking Vice President Richard Nixon to bring a spoon back from a visit to Russia for a constituent's spoon collection.[5]

Of course, the enormous volume of these requests makes it impossible for a legislator to handle many of these problems personally. Extensive staffs have been created to handle both casework and legislation. In 1976, depending on district size, House members were allowed a staff of up to eighteen members and a payroll of more than $225,000. Senators were allowed between $400,000 and $900,000 for staff assistance. In addition, members of Congress are given substantial allowances for telephone calls, stationery, and postage to handle this casework. Most members of Congress also maintain offices in their districts which

---

[3] Luther Patrick, "What Is a Congressman," *Congressional Record*, May 13, 1963, p. A2978.

[4] Charles L. Clapp, *The Congressman: His Work as He Sees It* (New York: Doubleday Anchor Books, 1964), p. 78.

[5] Clapp, pp. 78–79. Warren Weaver reports of an inmate in a federal reformatory who wrote his representative in order to get his burglar's tools back. Warren Weaver, Jr., *Both Your Houses: The Truth About Congress* (New York: Praeger, 1972), p. 177. Also see Morris P. Fiorina, *Congress: Keystone of the Washington Establishment* (New Haven, Conn.: Yale University Press, 1977), Chap. 7.

A BANNER DAY FOR CONGRESSIONAL SERVICE

A popular request of lawmakers is for an American flag that has flown over the Capitol. To obtain such a flag, write your representative, who will purchase it from the House stationery room. The page service will hoist it atop the Capitol and the flag will then be returned to the legislator with an official letter from the Clerk of the House certifying that it was flown over the Capitol. Normally, this service for constituents is not difficult to provide. However, on July 4, 1976 — the nation's 200th birthday — demand was especially high. Eighteen temporary flagpoles were set up, and flags were flown from all of them from 12:01 A.M. to 9:00 A.M. Some 10,471 flags were sent off to civic organizations, schools, and individuals that day.

Information on the July 4th flags comes from "Report Details Capitol Costs," *Chicago Sun-Times,* December 15, 1978, p. 70.

handle many problems without direct intervention from Washington. Paid personnel are frequently supplemented by student volunteers of interns sponsored by universities or foundations. Because most members of Congress believe that taking care of constituent needs is essential for reelection, even frivolous demands will usually receive courtesy hearings.[6] Many legislators even view providing service to their constituents as their primary responsibility. This was illustrated recently when a member of the House tried to stop the practice of allowing each member to distribute 2,000 free calendars to his or her constituents. This economy move was defeated, and Representative John Murtha (D-Pa.) explained, "Distributing these calendars is the most important thing I do."[7]

Much casework is actually encouraged by members of Congress. Some legislators seek out people with problems as a way of increasing their reputation for being concerned and hard working. One lawmaker even regularly mails out six to seven thousand invitations to postal patrons asking them to bring their problems to a town meeting run by his staff or his local office. Especially in diverse districts with a multitude of per-

[6] One member of Congress who did more than just provide an occasional service was William Barrett from southwest Philadelphia. Barrett flew home to his district *every* night and held office hours from 9 P.M. to 1 A.M., hearing people's problems on everything from marriage to money. He would sometimes see as many as 750 people a week, and he did this for 27 years. For more on Barrett, see Mark J. Green, James M. Fallows, and David R. Zwick, *Who Runs Congress?* (New York: Bantam Books, 1972), p. 216.

[7] Cited in *The Washington Monthly*, November 1978, p. 35.

"Pork" Projects authorized by Congress that provide obvious material benefits in the legislator's district. Frequently not absolutely essential. The legislation creating "pork" is called "pork-barrel" legislation.

spectives and controversies, emphasizing casework is an effective and safe way of building electoral support.[8]

Impact of casework

Does this legislative intervention have much of an impact? Can members of Congress really help ordinary citizens overcome problems with the federal bureaucracy? The answer seems to be that only about 10 percent of the problems are completely resolved by congressional help.[9] We must remember, however, that many of the requests for help are hopeless or frivolous. By the time a legislator is contacted over something like collecting military disability pay or getting a government job, a citizen probably has met failure through normal channels. When the cause appears more reasonable, and especially when the member of Congress personally intervenes, success rates are much higher. Here, perhaps, a third or half the cases are successfully resolved. It may also be argued that even where intervention on behalf of a constituent is unsuccessful, the ordinary citizen at least received official attention and now knows that somebody will listen to his or her problem.

In short, the evidence on congressional casework suggests that this is one important way people's political (and even some nonpolitical) demands are met. Of course, only a small percentage of the population ever appeals for congressional help, but it is there for those who want it. Though we may not consider a legislator's urgent telephone calls to the State Department to expedite a constituent's passport application a significant issue, such legislative representation is highly appreciated by the person involved.

PROVIDING LEGISLATIVE BENEFITS TO CONSTITUENTS

We have seen that members of Congress provide extensive personal services to their constituents. There is, however, a different kind of service that members of Congress can provide, namely, conspicuous material benefits (or **"pork"** as these benefits are sometimes called). Unlike casework, where help is given on a person-by-person basis, "pork" need not be specifically requested by constituents. Rather, members of Congress widely believe that providing visible government benefits will make people happy and will, in turn, lead to reelection. As Clarence Long, Representative from Maryland, put it: "A congressman is judged by the overwhelming mass of his constituents on the personal services he gives the home folks and the contracts he brings to the area."[10]

Pork-barrel legislation is a long-established congressional tradition. For years typical "goodies" included federally funded highways, post offices, dams, defense installations, harbor and river improvements, Army and Navy contracts, irrigation projects, and veterans' hospitals. As the government has ventured into new domains, new items have been added

[8] For more on how legislators handle casework, see Richard F. Fenno, Jr., *Home Style: House Members in Their Districts* (Boston: Little, Brown, 1978), pp. 89, 101–113, 203.

[9] Clapp, p. 87.

[10] Quoted in Green, Fallows, and Zwick, p. 234.

SENATOR YOUNG SPEAKS FRANKLY

Frank The right to use the U.S. mail without paying postage to send messages involving special business to constituents.

One important way members of Congress keep in touch with their constituents is by sending them lots of mail. All members of Congress are allowed to **frank,** or send free, letters involving official business. Because the post office has been generous in interpreting "official," many legislators take great advantage of this privilege. In 1970, for example, the 535 members of Congress managed to use the frank privilege for about 200 *million* pieces of mail.

Much of this correspondence consists of form letters of one kind or another. Some legislators routinely send congratulations to parents of newborn children or bombard their districts with monthly newsletters. Rarely, however, is a communication very personal.

One well-known exception to this pattern was Senator Stephen M. Young (D-Ohio), who served from 1959 to 1970. Young was famous for his humorous, and sometimes caustic, replies to letters sent by constituents. Once a letter protested that Mrs. John F. Kennedy had a horse transported free to this country from abroad. The constituent asked what would happen to him if *he* tried to do that. "Dear Sir," Young responded, "Acknowledging your letter wherein you insult the wife of our President, am wondering why you need a horse when there is already one jackass at your office." Another constituent wrote a strong attack on welfare recipients, labor unions, the minimum wage, Earl Warren, Nelson Rockefeller, and foreign aid, among other things. Young's reply was simple and to the point:

Dear Sir:

What else is new?

Sincerely yours,
Stephen M. Young

From *The Reporter,* Vol. 27 (1962), p. 18.

to the pork barrel. Among many others these include mass transit, scientific facilities, pollution treatment centers, job training programs, space travel facilities, and government grants to universities. Typically, legislators take considerable credit for these achievements and hope that each new building or job will pay dividends on election day.[11]

[11] The role of pork-barrel benefits in elections is further discussed in David R. Mayhew, *Congress: The Electoral Connection* (New Haven, Conn.: Yale University Press, 1974), pp. 53–57.

BUT WOULDN'T IT BE EASIER JUST TO VOTE WILKES-BARRE DRY?

Most members of Congress work hard at obtaining benefits for their districts, but such efforts rarely receive widespread attention. One exception to this pattern was former Representative Daniel J. Flood (D-Pa.), a Shakespearean actor who represented an economically depressed district centered around Wilkes-Barre, Pennsylvania. Flood is known for his colorful behavior. On occasion he has campaigned among tough coal miners wearing a top hat and a black cape and brandishing a cane. When President Ford invited Flood to a formal White House dinner, Flood showed up in red, white, and blue sneakers.

As chairperson of the House Appropriations subcommittee on health, education, and welfare, Flood can also provide more than just a good spectacle. In 1960, for example, he convinced the Army to use anthracite coal (much of which comes from his district) in 8,000 coke furnaces on West German bases. When the Army found it could save $20 million a year by converting to oil, Flood got a bill passed making such conversion illegal. Flood also used his influence to have a major interstate highway linking Montreal and New Orleans (Interstate 81) pass through Wilkes-Barre. Wilkes-Barre was also the first city to participate in the Model Cities program, which was designed to help inner-city ghettos.

Flood was at his best when Hurricane Agnes flooded much of the area in his district in June 1972. When fires in downtown office buildings could not be handled because of the absence of fire hydrants, Flood got the military to transport a fireboat from Boston harbor using a giant C-130 transport. Acting as vice-chairperson of the Defense Appropriations subcommittee, Flood ordered in forty helicopers to rescue stranded residents. The Air Force flew in emergency supplies from as far away as West Germany. Flood went on television and said: "This is Dan Flood. Today I have ordered the Army Corps of Engineers not to allow the Susquehanna River to rise one more inch." It didn't.

Flood is highly regarded. There is the Daniel J. Flood Health Center, Daniel J. Flood Elementary School, Daniel J. Flood Industrial Park, and Daniel J. Flood Elderly Center. As one coal miner constituent put it: "He's done a hell of a lot for us—and don't you forget it."

From "Watch Out for Flood," *Newsweek,* February 13, 1978; "Flood: *Dramatis Persona,*" *People,* February 13, 1978, p. 33; and George Crile, "The Best Congressman," *Harpers Magazine,* January 1975.

Representative Daniel J. Flood (D-Pa.) arrives at a 1977 Christmas ball given at the White House by President and Mrs. Gerald Ford.

Though many people, including several members of Congress, have criticized pork-barrel politics, the practice is well entrenched. According to critics, Congress will authorize money for expensive projects of dubious value largely to impress constituents. To understand why legislators are so willing to shower their districts with material benefits, one must understand two facts: first, members of Congress are forever worried about reelection, and pork-barrel politics seems a good reelection strategy; and, second, the legislative style of Congress encourages pork-barrel legislation. On matters directly relating to particular district benefits, virtually every legislator follows the rule of "I'll vote for your pet project if you'll vote for mine." This practice is called **logrolling,** and the appropriations bills containing the scores of river improvements, new post offices, and other special benefits are sometimes labeled **"Christmas tree" bills** because they contain presents for everybody.

The widespread acceptance of logrolling for the distribution of material benefits explains why everyone can usually get a piece of the action. Let us suppose that my representative wants increased federal funding for a local sewage treatment plant. To get support for this project my representative might agree to support numerous other locally oriented bills favored by fellow legislators, who in turn give their support to the sewage treatment plant. On occasion, legislators will find themselves supporting projects they actually do not want, but this is the price they must pay to get support for their own projects. Of course, there are limits to logrolling to obtain district benefits. There is just so much money available, and few legislators want to be considered wild, irresponsible spenders. In addition, more than once a President has vetoed an excessive pork-barrel appropriation bill (then, too, the threat of a presidential veto is ever present).

Criticisms of pork-barrel politics

In examining how members of Congress provide various benefits to their constituents, a key question still remains: Is pork-barrel legislation really what citizens want? Are legislators responding to citizens by providing defense contracts, new post offices, highways, and other such projects? In many, perhaps even most, cases the answer probably is yes. This is particularly true in less wealthy areas or where citizens are heavily dependent on government action. In parts of the South, for example, military installations and public works projects obtained through congressional intervention are a crucial and much appreciated part of local economies. Similarly, in western states vigorous legislative efforts on behalf of federally funded dams and irrigation projects are highly esteemed. No doubt every member of Congress, at one time or another, has made constituents happy by procuring some federally paid-for benefit.

We must not, however, exaggerate the role of pork-barrel legislation in meeting citizens demands. Each of us may appreciate the nearby interstate highways or federally funded college buildings, but we might also consider that pork-barrel legislation only *appears* to be what most citizens want. Critics of this system of distributing benefits sometimes argue that although legislatively inspired projects may have highly visible benefits, their costs are high and frequently hidden. As taxpayers, cit-

Logrolling An agreement among legislators to support each others' bills.
Christmas tree bill Legislation containing numerous provisions benefiting many members of Congress.

izens must ultimately pay for useless projects whose major purpose was to help someone get reelected. Moreover, some of these locally oriented projects are contrary to the desires of the public as a whole. A good example is the maintenance of unnecessary military bases because of congressional pressure. While such pork barreling may appear helpful to a legislator's constituents, it may squander funds needed for national defense.

In short, pork-barrel projects probably meet the desires of numerous people, but we must also realize that there are costs involved. Unfortunately, it is almost impossible to compare costs and benefits to determine whether most people get what they really want from their members of Congress most of the time. It is clear, however, that legislators do work at getting their constituents innumerable concrete benefits from government, and most citizens seem to appreciate these efforts.

LEGISLATIVE VOTING BEHAVIOR

During every session members of Congress face major choices on a wide range of policies. Typically, a legislator is called upon to decide such things as levels of defense spending, provisions of the foreign aid program, changes in tax policy, subsidies for business, and hundreds of other issues. A frequently raised question concerning these legislative votes is: Do representatives vote according to the desires of their constituents? Are national legislators conduits through which public opinion is translated into government action?

The answer to this question is: It depends. Sometimes members of Congress strictly adhere to the desires of the home folks. At other times, however, little relationship exists between how a legislator votes on bills and what his or her district prefers. When do legislators follow constituency desires? Why do many legislators choose to ignore the preferences of those who elected them? Is it wise to ignore district or state opinion on controversial political issues?

Observers of Congress have long noted that when the desires of the people at home are obvious and important, few legislators will oppose them. To do so would probably mean political suicide. For example, during the 1950s and 1960s, before the advent of large-scale voting by blacks, southern legislators vigorously adhered to the anticivil rights positions of their constituents.[12] Even southern members of Congress who privately supported many civil rights proposals (for example, Senator J. William Fulbright of Arkansas) would not risk voting against district opinion. Likewise, a legislator representing a district with large, well-organized unions will rarely antagonize these groups by supporting antiunion legislation.

Much of the strict adherence to district opinion involves legislation that directly affects economic matters. No member of Congress likes to oppose publicly the economic interests of the people who elected him or her. Even a liberal legislator will take the conservative position (and vice

---

[12] Warren E. Miller and Donald E. Stokes, "Constituency Influence in Congress," *American Political Science Review*, 57 (1963), pp. 45–56.

versa) to defend the economic well-being of his or her constituents. Senator William B. Proxmire, a well-known foe of wasting money, nevertheless staunchly defends the Wisconsin dairy industry against cheap imports (which would lower prices to consumers). Senator Edward Kennedy of Massachusetts, normally an advocate of free trade, makes an exception when it comes to protecting the local shoe and bicycle industries. In general, every state and congressional district contains interests that must be heeded. Of course, there are exceptions, but these are rare, and legislators who ignore the interests of their area do not survive for long.

That members of Congress follow their constituents' desires on certain key issues is an important fact. If they stopped doing so, the result would probably be widespread public outcries and many defeated legislators. Nevertheless, issues on which constituents feel strongly comprise only a small portion of all the matters considered by Congress. On numerous other issues there is no consistent relationship between how legislators vote and majority opinions back home. More important, this lack of consistency is pretty much accepted by most members of Congress. Why does this lack of agreement exist, and why is it tolerated?

Reasons legislators do not follow constituency opinion

One important reason that legislators do not religiously follow constituency opinion is that, on many issues, the citizens they represent do not possess clear, well-informed preferences. Each year Congress confronts hundreds of technical questions that are of little interest to many citizens. Obviously, it is impossible for a legislator to follow constituency opinion where such opinion hardly exists. Therefore, on such important but complex issues as the development of atomic fusion, a reasonable legislator votes his or her own mind or follows the advice of a trusted colleague or expert.

A second explanation for voting inconsistency is that lawmakers in Washington frequently cannot get completely accurate information on what the people back home want. A member of Congress has several means available for determining opinions of constituents. Public opinion polls using mailed questionnaires, tallies of mail on issues, trips home to talk with people, and reviews of local newspaper stories and editorials are common ways of ascertaining people's political feelings. Unfortunately, each technique is limited. Congressional opinion polls, for example, frequently have very low response rates (10–20 percent), and legislators lack the resources to conduct adequate surveys on the hundreds of issues they must vote on. Similarly, even though the mail is usually given careful attention, much of it arrives *after* an issue has been decided, and even then, letters may not faithfully reflect overall home opinion. As for frequent trips home, these may be invaluable for providing general feedback on constituency "mood," but obtaining accurate information on numerous issues in a two- or three-day visit is difficult. Moreover, the incentive for getting constituency opinion may be small because many citizens do not know how legislators vote. As one legislator put it, "There isn't one voter in 20,000 who knows my voting record except on that one thing that affects him." Another lawmaker of-

Delegate role A description of the legislative job that emphasizes strict adherence to the wishes of the people in the home district. Such a legislator sees himself or herself as a "delegate," not an independent decision maker.

fered to send any constituent a copy of his entire voting record; not one copy was requested.[13]

A third reason that members of Congress do not always vote according to the wishes of their constituents is that district opinion is so diverse that regardless of how the legislator voted, the vote could not satisfy a majority. Recall from Chapter Six that elections are based on *geographical* divisions and that geographically defined election districts frequently contain an enormous diversity of people. Consider the predicament of a California Senator. California is a diverse state whose citizens undoubtedly divide into numerous positions on almost every major political question. Following *the* position of Californians on a particular issue is typically very difficult. Not surprisingly, studies of legislative representation have found that legislator-constituency agreement is greatest where districts are relatively uniform in their preferences.[14] Unfortunately for those wanting more faithful representation, states and congressional districts tend to be fairly diverse.

The attitudes of national legislators themselves are a fourth factor contributing to imperfect agreement between legislator and district. All legislators want to serve their districts, but not all legislators define this service in terms of mechanically translating district opinion into legislative votes. In fact, a study of members of Congress in 1963–1964 found that only 23 percent saw their role as one of a **"delegate,"** whose main purpose was to transmit popular opinions to the legislature. Other members of Congress asserted that their constituents expected them to use their own judgment about what was best. Still others stated that under some circumstances they might follow district opinion; at other times they might ignore it; and sometimes they might "interpret" the political wishes of their constituents.[15]

Finally, we must remember that constituency pressures are only one of many forces that affect legislative decisions. A legislator about to cast a vote might have to weigh pressure from party leaders, fellow committee members, the President, his or her staff, outside experts, and pressure groups. In some circumstances following the lead of other legislators or the President may be essential in order to take care of constituency interests in the future. We have seen that one important method of securing district benefits is by logrolling or vote trading. A legislator may go along with the desires of others—even if they are contrary to district opinion—so that on certain really important matters he or she can cash in political IOUs. Even when there is no future payoff, a legislator may vote against district preferences because of party loyalty or support for a President's legislative program.

Because lawmakers do not always follow the majority of the people in their districts does not necessarily mean that citizens' opinions are ig-

---

[13] Fenno, p. 142.

[14] Warren E. Miller, "Majority Rule and the Representative System of Government," in *Cleavages, Ideologies and the Party Systems,* Erik Allardt and Yijo Littunen, eds. (Helsinki: Academic Bookstore, 1964), pp. 343–376.

[15] Roger H. Davidson, *The Role of the Congressman* (New York: Pegasus, 1969), especially Chap. 4.

CAN THE MAIL BE TRUSTED?

Congress is deluged with mail. One study found that in 1970 Congress received 15 *million* pieces of mail; by 1976 this figure had risen to 53 million pieces.* While legislators try to give their mail serious attention, it is frequently physically impossible to do so. Even if all the mail did receive careful scrutiny, members of Congress would still interpret these messages cautiously. For one thing, much of the mail they receive on key issues is stimulated by lobbyists, and senders may have no idea what they are supporting when they write to a legislator. For example, the back page of the *American Educator* requested that I send the following message to my Senators.**

Address to: U.S. Senator _____ ■ c/o The U.S. Senate ■ Washington, D.C. 20510

Dear Senator:	Dear Senator:
The Labor Law Reform Bill (S.1883) has my strong support. It's needed. It should be passed. Please vote for it.	The Labor Law Reform Bill (S.1883) has my strong support. It's needed. It should be passed. Please vote for it.
Name	Name
Adress	Adress
City State Zip	City State Zip

Nowhere in the entire magazine, however, was there an explanation of bill S.1883. No wonder that many members of Congress discount the meaning of such issue-oriented communications.

Even more insidious are the phony letters members of Congress receive. After all, how does a legislator know that thousands of letters were not sent by a single person under different names? This problem is illustrated by a scandal in 1977 involving mail to Congress on the Panama Canal treaty. According to Representative Romano L. Mazzoli (D-Ky.), phony letters on the treaty turned up in at least twenty congressional offices. An investigation revealed a pattern of phony letter writing on a variety of other issues as well.† This problem will probably continue, since modern technology allows an organization to send out thousands of machine-produced letters all looking very personal.

* Edmond Le Breton, "House Work Is Never Done," *The Champaign-Urbana News-Gazette,* August 28, 1977, p. 10-A.
** *American Educator,* December 1977, p. 42.
† "Report: Forged Letters Send to Congress Over Canal," *The Champaign-Urbana News-Gazette,* October 23, 1977, p. 9A.

Reelection constituency The citizens in a congressional district who supported a member of Congress in a previous election.

Primary constituency The citizens who supported a legislator in the primary election and thus constitute his or her hard-core supporters.

nored. One recent study found that members of Congress view their constituencies as complex sets of groups.[16] Besides the district as a whole, most legislators also perceive a **reelection constituency** (all people in the district who voted for the legislator) and a smaller **primary constituency** (voters who would support the candidate in the primary). A smart member of Congress knows that loyalists in the primary constituency cannot be ignored on certain issues. Satisfying this group, however, can sometimes mean taking stands that are opposed by an overall majority in the entire district. Keeping one's hard-core supporters happy can thus lead to ignoring overall district opinion.

In reviewing the various reasons for the inconsistencies between how legislators vote and constituency opinion, we can see that promoting a closer relationship would be very difficult. A large-scale effort would be required to insure that citizens have clear opinions on most contemporary issues. And making sure that these opinions are accurately conveyed to legislators would not be a simple task. Similar problems exist with respect to modifying election districts, changing the attitudes of legislators, and reducing the influence of nonconstituency factors. Considerable legislator-district disagreement is therefore likely to remain in U.S. politics.

PROVIDING A VOICE FOR PARTICULAR INTERESTS

Our discussion thus far has considered whether a legislator from a particular area represents the people in that election district. In other words, if you live in the Illinois 21st congressional district, you are represented if your particular representative does personal favors for you or votes your preferences. There is another way of considering legislative representation, however. We can ask whether citizens' opinions are represented in Congress as a whole, even if they are not expressed by their own House member or Senators. For example, suppose you favor the legalization of marijuana. Suppose also that your Representative and both your Senators strongly oppose such legislation. Does this mean that you are without representation on this issue? Not necessarily. Legislators from other areas may voice your opinion, so possibly you will receive some form of legislative representation.

Over the years representation not directly tied to a constituency has been politically important. Many citizens advocating political causes have frequently been represented in Congress by legislators not from their own districts. Long before southern blacks could vote, many northern legislators "looked out" for them. More recently, several women legislators have viewed their role not only as taking care of the citizens who elected them but also as looking out for all women. Such nondistrict orientations are not unique. A 1963–1964 study of House members found that only 42 percent considered themselves as representing their own district exclusively.[17]

The number of nonconstituency interests that members of Congress

[16] Fenno, Chap. 1.
[17] Davidson, pp. 121–126.

look out for is considerable. Some legislators defend consumer interests; others see themselves as guardians of the nation's businesses. Many House members frequently also see themselves as representing their entire states. Increased attention to ecology and natural resources has resulted in a group of legislators who express the desires of conservationists scattered across hundreds of districts. A frequent opponent of the last group are legislators from oil-producing areas who speak for oil interests in all parts of the country. Several legislators representing heavily Jewish districts look beyond their own constituencies and work on behalf of goals desired by all U.S. Jews.

An important mechanism in this type of representation is the congressional committee and subcommittee system. Many congressional committees have attached to them subcommittees organized around specific interests, for example, the cotton or tobacco industry. As we might expect, legislators with a particular concern for such areas are drawn toward such subcommittees. From these positions of institutional influence those legislators represent not only their own districts but people of other districts who share their values. For example, Walter B. Jones of North Carolina represents a poor, rural district with a large number of tobacco farms. He is also the chairperson of the Agriculture Committee's Subcommittee on Tobacco in the 95th Congress. A similar case is that of G. William Whitehurst, ranking Republican member on the Military Installations and Facilities Subcommittee of the House Armed Services Committee. Whitehurst's Virginia district is the headquarters of the Navy's Atlantic Fleet and contains major military facilities. These legislators are therefore not only in a good position to represent narrow district goals but they can also act as advocates for others with similar concerns. The many tobacco growers outside Jones's district know that they have a powerful voice in Washington.

Members of Congress have many interests so there are representatives for all kinds of causes. Whether one is concerned with health care, saving endangered animals, stopping world communism, putting religion back in public schools, outlawing abortions, or any other contemporary issue, out of the 535 members of Congress there is probably someone advocating one's preference. This does not mean that Congress as a whole is an accurate reflection of the general public. Even though legislators frequently look out for nonconstituency interests, not every point of view is expressed in proportion to its strength in the population. Though precise estimates on which viewpoints are over- or underrepresented are difficult, one can probably say fairly that organized economic and group interests receive comparatively good representation while abstract, "idealistic" causes (for example, world peace) are underrepresented.[18] Certainly it is much simpler and more rewarding to advance a cause some people care a great deal about than to fight for something that means only a little to most people. If a member of Congress decides to

[18] Speaking of representing people with special characteristics, a story is told of President Franklin D. Roosevelt. On being told that a particular Senator was a jackass, Roosevelt supposedly replied: "There are a lot of jackasses out there, and they too need representation."

take up a cause that goes beyond his or her district, it makes good sense to choose something that has concrete payoffs in the form of campaign contributions, publicity, or increased stature.

In summary, do members of Congress respond to citizen demands? The average citizen is likely to receive some representation in the form of casework, concrete district benefits, and legislative votes on issues of great district concern. In many instances representation is even provided by legislators other than those from one's own district. Nevertheless, Congress is not a perfectly representative institution. Most citizens do not have their personal problems handled by national legislators, not everyone wants district projects such as new dams, and most legislators do not follow constituency preferences on most issues. Moreover, Congress as a whole probably gives greater expression to some, particularly well-organized, demands. Just as the optimist and pessimist differ over whether the whiskey bottle is half-full or half-empty, it is easy to disagree over whether Congress does the best job possible of being a representative institution.

Does Congress respond effectively to national problems?

Every session Congress passes hundreds of bills, spends thousands of hours questioning witnesses, launches dozens of investigations, and prints tons of reports. Moreover, most members of Congress bitterly complain that the work load is too heavy and that resources are being stretched to the breaking point. Especially since World War II, Congress has become a whirlwind of activity and production.

Nevertheless, despite its hectic pace, Congress has been widely and persistently criticized for failing to respond effectively to important national problems. To many people concerned with the problems of energy, ecology, women's rights, civil rights, economic growth, international relations, prices and inflation, and the like, congressional responses have not been effective. Congress is characterized by them as "obstructionist," "ineffective," and "do-nothing." These critics view all the frantic activity of Congress as essentially ineffectual in solving the pressing social and economic problems that face the United States today.

There are those who go a step further and claim that Congress is almost *inherently* incapable of resolving contemporary problems. They argue that for Congress to become an effective institution, wholesale changes in its legislative leadership and drastic reforms in its operating rules are required. Given the obvious problems associated with having the "ins" relinquish their power voluntarily, these critics are not optimistic. Unless Congress becomes revitalized, some people predict, it will drift toward political irrelevancy and perhaps even become like the powerless British House of Lords.

Is Congress really incapable of responding effectively to the demands of modern society? Has Congress failed the people of the United States on such issues as civil rights, energy, and inflation? As with so many important and controversial questions, there is no simple answer. Whether one sees Congress as effective or ineffective depends a great deal on how one views the evidence. We will now examine both points of view.

THE CASE AGAINST CONGRESSIONAL EFFECTIVENESS

People who claim that Congress is ineffective usually point to the bills passed by Congress as proof of their contention. Rarely does either the House or the Senate take a bold, decisive approach to a major problem. In many instances no action is taken whatsoever, or what is done may be compared to offering a dying person two aspirins and a glass of water. Whether the problem is inflation or environmental pollution, critics of Congress claim that lawmaking in both houses is characterized as follows:

Congress responds very slowly. Few significant pieces of legislation receive prompt consideration. Between the time a major policy is proposed and the time it is finally voted upon, years can pass. It took over fifteen years for major health care legislation proposed during the Truman Administration to become law under the Johnson Administration. Similarly, in the 1960s, major civil rights bills languished for years in committees chaired by unsympathetic southerners. In the Senate civil rights bills were kept off the agenda by the threat of a filibuster, which would bring all Senate business to a standstill. Even when such bills did make it to final votes, they frequently were only shadows of their original versions.

Moreover, lengthy delays are encouraged by the very nature and organization of Congress. Recall from our analysis in Chapter Ten that the committee system, limitations on party leaders, and the bicameral (two-house) nature of the legislature are all factors preventing swift action. A quick legislative response requires getting majorities in several committees and subcommittees, plus cooperation from key leaders. Even if most legislators wanted quick action, the internal organization of Congress discourages a prompt response. No wonder that critics frequently describe congressional enactments as "too little, too late."

Legislative responses are uncoordinated. Congress does not confront a major problem such as poverty or energy as a single issue. Rather, the problem is broken down into various pieces, and each piece is dealt with by different legislators or committees, with differing perspectives, at different times. Take, for example, government efforts at reducing poverty. In the House of Representatives there is no concerted attack on poverty. Instead, problems of hunger are considered by a subcommittee of the House Appropriations Committee; funds for special education and employment are the domain of the House Education and Labor Committee; and taxation and social security are handled by the Ways and Means Committee. Numerous other House and Senate committees also have a "piece of the action" relating to poverty. This pattern is not unique—almost every major social and economic problem cuts across several committees and subcommittees. Confusion is not surprising when we realize that the system operates so that one committee may authorize a program, a second committee may authorize the necessary funds, and a third may be responsible for raising the funds.

Congress approaches national problems from a local perspective. Every member of Congress knows that to remain in office satisfying one's constituents is essential. A legislator who repeatedly ignores crucial district desires and seeks instead to further his or her own view of the national welfare will probably soon be looking for a job. Of course, on many issues no conflict exists between national and district interests (or most constituents may not care). Nevertheless, on occasions when narrow district interests collide with national interests, localism usually prevails. And because members of Congress accept each other's need to stay in office by keeping constituents happy, many a nationally oriented policy becomes overwhelmed by purely local considerations and is thus greatly weakened.

For example, the impact of localism on policies affecting the general public is frequently found as Congress wrestles with antipollution policy. Federal policies of these kinds, however, commonly impose economic hardships on industry. Rather than spend $50 million to clean up its waste, a steel mill might find that relocating is more economically efficient. A legislator representing the district where the mill is located faces a dilemma: the passage of antipollution legislation means hurting the economic well-being of his or her constituents. Under such circumstances many members of Congress reason that jobs are more important to their constituents than cleaning up pollution and thus try to amend the bill to allow exceptions for the steel industry. Of course, not every attempt to place local interests ahead of the national welfare succeeds, but localism remains a persistent congressional force.

Congress is ill prepared to solve major problems. Many of the problems with which lawmakers must deal are complex, involve technical details, and require careful analysis. Critics argue that Congress is ill equipped to face such issues. First, they say, legislators are not chosen on the basis of their ability to understand complex social and economic problems. Campaigning effectively requires a different set of skills than dealing with many contemporary issues. Someone with a law degree who has spent the last twenty years in politics is ill prepared to debate intelligently such matters as alternative energy programs. Second, it is pointed out, most members of Congress, as we have seen, devote a large portion of their time to nonlegislative matters. Especially in the House, where elections occur every two years, the average legislator spends considerable time helping constituents with their problems, visiting his or her district, giving speeches, scrutinizing the mail, and engaging in many other nonpolicy activities. A recent review sponsored by the House staff stated that "members have too little time to concentrate on their important policy-making responsibilities, and that the House and its committees face challenges to competent and orderly performance because of work overload."[19]

[19] Task force of the House Commission on Administrative Review, cited in Edmond De Breton, "House Work Is Never Done," *The Champaign-Urbana News-Gazette*, August 28, 1977.

As a result of these inadequacies, the argument goes, the executive branch has become the moving force in dealing with important national problems. Congress, at best, deals with comparative details while the major policy leadership comes from the President or cabinet officials. For this reason, the critics of Congress say, we frequently hear such statements as, "The President has presented his comprehensive energy program and Congress hopes to consider it in due time." Then, a few months later, we hear, "The President's program is in trouble, according to congressional leaders," followed by, "The President calls for swift congressional action and an end to obstructionism."

These four characteristics are typically offered by those who view Congress as ineffective in dealing with pressing national problems. Even defenders of Congress admit that there is much truth in these descriptions. Congress *does* take its time; problems *are* approached piecemeal; many legislators *are* locally oriented; and many members of Congress *are* ill equipped to understand sophisticated and technical policy alternatives. That Congress is ineffectual is not, however, the only conclusion one can draw from examining congressional action. It is possible to argue that Congress is effective, provided one accepts a different view of what Congress is supposed to do and with what methods. This counterargument holds that Congress cannot be held responsible for tasks it was not designed for and which may be nearly impossible anyway.

THE CASE FOR CONGRESSIONAL EFFECTIVENESS

Defenders of congressional effectiveness make the following points:

Congress was never intended to be an institution responsible for promptly solving the nation's problems. Certainly this was not the intent of those who wrote the Constitution. Indeed, as we saw in Chapter Ten, many constitutional features are designed to *constrain* legislative action. Congress is not supposed to act like a political fire department that jumps into action every time we face a crisis. If we want that type of response from our national legislature, we should instead have a parliamentary system with a single-house legislature at the instant call of a prime minister. To hold Congress, as presently constituted, responsible for decisive and extensive action is like trying to race the family station wagon in the Indianapolis 500.

Congress may drag its feet on important legislation, but this is not proof that Congress undermines the national welfare. Those who criticize Congress for lengthy delays assume that (1) the delayed legislation is widely desired and (2) such legislation represents a solution to the problem. Both assumptions are frequently false. In recent years, for example, Congress has been criticized for stalling on a comprehensive energy program, yet many of the specific proposals in the program, such as increased gasoline taxes, have little public support. Is Congress being unresponsive to national needs when it delays such proposals, or is it representing public opinion? In addition, many legislators justify lengthy deliberation on the grounds that much legislation is poorly formulated. Good legislation cannot be put together overnight and may require exten-

WHAT'S A COUPLE OF BILLION BETWEEN FRIENDS?

It is sometimes difficult to imagine the responsibilities faced by members of Congress. This is especially true in financial matters, since the government deals in sums whose magnitude is well beyond ordinary experience. Most citizens fully understand the difference between $1,000 and $2,000, but how does one give meaning to the difference between $385 million and $389 million? Such differences are as abstract as the diameter of the solar system.

Senator S. I. Hayakawa (R-Calif.) meeting with loggers who have come to Washington to protest the expansion of Redwood National Park in California.

The implications are clear: Members of Congress must decide questions for which they are ill prepared in terms of their backgrounds and knowledge. This is illustrated by the experiences of Senator S. I. Hayakawa (R-Calif.) on the Senate Budget Committee. At first, Hayakawa was apprehensive, given his lack of financial background. He soon got over his worries, however. As he put it:

The numbers you work with on this committee turned out to be very simple. You are always dealing in hundreds of millions—or billions. Therefore, when we say 1.0, that means $1 billion. Then we have .1; that means $100 million—and that's the smallest figure we ever deal with in the Budget Committee.

A member of the committee will say, for instance, "Here's an appropriation for such-and-such. It was 1.7 for 1977. So for the 1978 budget we ought to make it 2.9." So all we do is add 1.2; that's not hard. The next item is 2.5. The members discuss it back and forth, and someone says, "Let's raise it to 3.7." They look around at each other. "Everybody in favor?" "Yes, sir. Okay." So in five minutes we have disposed of 2 *billion* bucks—2 billion, not 2 million. I never realized it could be so easy. It's all simple addition. *You don't even have to know subtraction.*

From S. I. Hayakawa, "Mr. Hayakawa Goes to Washington," *Harpers,* January 1978, p. 39.

sive hearings, research, and public debate. Defenders of the cautious approach point to many of the so-called Great Society programs that were quickly passed by Congress during Johnson's Administration but that were later dropped because of their effectiveness and unforeseen expense. In August 1964, Congress, with little deliberation or investigation, overwhelmingly passed the Gulf of Tonkin resolution which authorized the President to "take all necessary measures" to stop aggression in Southeast Asia. This opened the door to a long series of military and political disasters in Vietnam.

The piecemeal approach to major social and economic problems employed by Congress is a reasonable and practical strategy given the complexity of problems it faces. Specialization and an extensive committee system are essential, to the efficient operation of Congress, the defenders maintain. Problems like employment, race relations, and economic growth are too massive to be considered by a single committee or debated as a single issue. Imagine the result if 435 members of the House, as a group, sought to develop a coherent economic policy. After initial mass confusion, everyone would probably decide to split up into smaller groups to consider different pieces. In short, a step-by-step approach with uneven and sometimes contradictory outcomes is inevitable when 435 Representatives or 100 Senators must decide major policy questions. The system may not be perfect, but it is better than any alternatives.

As for the claim that congressional localism undermines legislative capacity to solve national problems, it can also be argued that all laws designed to cure national problems must be sensitive to local variations. This is especially true, given the enormous regional and local differences that exist in the United states. We cannot always expect a program that works well in New York City to work equally well in rural Mississippi. Moreover, it is sometimes difficult to distinguish between the local and the national interest. For example, proponents of a "nationally" oriented energy conservation program have called for high, federally enforced automobile gas mileage standards to reduce U.S. dependence on foreign oil. Legislators from Detroit and other autoproducing areas have generally opposed such requirements on the grounds that they would hurt the U.S. automobile industry, damage to which, in turn, would have repercussions throughout the entire economy. Which position is in the national interest? Perhaps both.

The claim that Congress is incapable of intelligently dealing with contemporary problems can be answered by saying that Congress is just as capable as any other political body. First, many legislators are extremely well informed on important aspects of public policy. For example, few people in Washington were as knowledgeable on federal tax policy as Wilbur Mills (D-Ark.), who long chaired the House Ways and Means Committee. Remember that most legislators have spent years on specialized committees studying important national problems.

It can also be argued that frequent elections and contact with citizens provide legislators with a useful perspective on national problems. A member of Congress voting on an energy bill may not have a Ph.D. in engineering, but he or she may have a better idea of public thinking than a technical expert in the executive branch. Moreover, a legislator can turn to several sources for technical assistance. He or she can hire an adviser or consult with the staff of the Library of Congress, the Congressional Research Service, the Office of Technology Assessment, or other advisory agencies.

Finally, defenders of congressional effectiveness admit that Congress does not possess solutions to the problems of racial inequality, economic development, or any other pressing problems, *but neither does anyone*

THE INSTITUTIONAL RESOURCES OF CONGRESS

Members of Congress have long been aware that intelligent lawmaking requires vast quantities of information and technical assistance. To meet these needs, Congress has created several agencies.

The oldest and largest is the Library of Congress. Created in 1800, the Library serves both as a national library and as a source of information for members of Congress. In the mid-1970s, the Library contained some 70.5 million items (besides 17.5 million books, there were 3.5 million maps, 8.5 million photographic negatives, and millions of copies of speeches, posters, and so on). Upon request the Library will supply legislators with answers to specific questions, reading lists, legal research, reviews and analyses of material on a subject, and pros and cons of arguments. It will also provide personnel to help with hearings or write speeches. Most of the Library's huge collections are available to citizens over high school age. (It has been alleged that the Library has also written numerous college term papers and dissertations as part of legislators' casework.)

Within the Library of Congress is the Congressional Research Service (CRS), which is exclusively devoted to the needs of Congress. In 1975, the CRS employed 475 full-time specialists and answered about 2,000 questions a day from legislators and their staffs. The CRS employs experts in various fields (for example, environmental policy, Soviet economics) who provide technical advice. Through its numerous publications it provides summaries and analyses of important bills, brief reports on current topics, bibliographies, and extensive reviews of all expiring programs and areas that might be of interest to Congress in the future. The CRS also tries to estimate the impact of proposed legislation. Not all congressional requests are for complex, technical information. Once the CRS was asked to determine how the Battle of Gettysburg would have ended if it had been fought with nuclear weapons. Another congressional office called to find out how much an ounce of marijuana weighs.

else. In fact, many of these problems are so complex that no all-encompassing solution exists. Congress may be only partially successful in dealing with the problems it confronts, but partial success may be the best we can expect.[20]

[20] For a positive assessment of congressional responses to major social problems, see Gary Orfield, *Congressional Power: Congress and Social Change* (New York: Harcourt Brace Jovanovich, 1975), Chap. 4.

To oversee the expenditures of the executive branch, Congress in 1921 created the General Accounting Office (GAO). When Congress wants to know how a particular congressional financial program is operating, it turns to the GAO for information. Many GAO staffers are assigned directly to congressional committees. Several major exposés have resulted from GAO investigations. For example, improprieties involving U.S. officials in the 1974 United States-Soviet Union wheat deal were discovered by GAO. The GAO also regularly monitors federal election campaign finances, revenue sharing, and such programs as Medicare, Medicaid, foreign aid, and military-procurement contracts. In 1976 the GAO employed over 5,000 people and spent over $135 million as the watchdog of Congress.

In response to the growing importance of technology, Congress in 1972 created the Office of Technological Assessment (OTA). The OTA is especially concerned with energy, transportation, world trade, health care, minerals, the oceans, and future research. In 1976 it had a staff of 110 and a budget of $6.5 million.

Finally, the 1974 Budget Act established the Congressional Budget Office (CBO). The purpose of the CBO is to analyze the federal budget submitted to Congress by the President. With a highly professional staff of 193, the CBO issues reports assessing the assumptions and claims of the presidential budget and offers special assistance to the two congressional budget committees and the House Ways and Means Committee. In 1977, for example, the CBO issued a controversial report stating that President Carter's energy proposals overstated their claimed savings.

In short, a member of Congress has access to an enormous quantity of sophisticated talent, provided he or she has the time, energy, and desire to master the material that is available.

More on these legislative resources is provided in *Congressional Quarterly's Guide to Congress,* 2d ed. (Washington, D.C.: Congressional Quarterly, 1976), pp. 439–455, 485–499. The stories about the CRS being asked about Gettysburg and marijuana were reported in Marion Clark and Rudy Moxa, *Public Trust, Private Lust* (New York: Morrow, 1977), p. 42.

CONGRESSIONAL IMPROPRIETY

A long-standing criticism of Congress is that its members frequently are corrupt and ignore the law. Ambrose Bierce, the American humorist of the late nineteenth century, in his *Devil's Dictionary,* defined the Senate as "A body of elderly gentlemen charged with high duties and misdemeanors." Mark Twain once said that America has no native criminal class, it has Congress. Such characterizations have long been traditional.

The image of impropriety has been given support by occasional scandals and criminal convictions. Most criminal actions against members of Congress in recent years have involved accepting illegal campaign contributions or accepting money for illegally intervening on someone's behalf. For example, Representative Henry Helstoski (D-N.J.) was accused of accepting bribes for his help in immigration cases. He was defeated for reelection in 1976. A different type of case was that of Representative Allan T. Howe (D-Utah), who was convicted in 1976 of soliciting sex for hire from two undercover Salt Lake City policewomen posing as prostitutes (Howe ran after his conviction but lost in 1976).

The cases involving impropriety that do reach the courts may be only the tip of the iceberg. In response to widespread claims that Tongsun Park, a representative of the South Korean government, had given lavish gifts to as many as 115 legislators, the House conducted an eighteen-month investigation into "Koreagate" and reprimanded (the mildest form of punishment) just three members. The Senate took no disciplinary action at all. Public testimony indicates that friends of Otto Passman (D-La.) turned a $900 investment into $1.7 million in a short time thanks to his intervention in shipping U.S. grain, but no action was taken against Passman. Similarly, the Senate spent ten months investigating charges that Hugh Scott (R-Pa.) had accepted $100,000 in illegal campaign contributions from Gulf Oil. Charges were dropped just before Scott announced his retirement.

Running afoul of the law, however, does not automatically mean electoral defeat. Despite being indicted by two grand juries for perjury, bribery, and influence peddling, Pennsylvania's Dan Flood was returned to Congress in 1978. So was Charles C. Diggs, Jr. (D-Mich.), who was convicted of twenty-nine counts of mail fraud, kickbacks, and false statements prior to his victory. Two of the three House members reprimanded for the "Koreagate" involvement—Edward Roybal and Charles H. Wilson, both of California—won in 1978 by 2 to 1 margins. The third reprimanded legislator—John J. McFall (D-Calif.)—lost, however, by 5 percentage points. Another 1978 loser was Representative J. Herbert Burke, who had been convicted of disorderly intoxication and resisting arrest at a Fort Lauderdale nightclub featuring nude go-go dancers. Burke had originally claimed that in his role as a member of a House committee on narcotics control he

Four wrongdoers subsequently elected to Congress in 1978. Top left, Representative Charles H. Wilson (R.-Calif.). Top right, Representative Edward R. Roybal (D-Calif.). Bottom left, Representative Charles Diggs (D-Mich.). Bottom right, Representative Fred Richmond (D-N.Y.).

had been spying on a narcotics deal in progress. However, Fred Richmond (D-N.Y.) won with 80 percent of the vote despite admitting that he had solicited a boy for homosexual prostitution. Charges against Richmond were dropped after he agreed to seek counseling.

The overwhelming reelection of legislators such as Flood, Diggs, Roybal, Wilson, and Richmond suggests that impropriety or even a criminal conviction is only one factor influencing the way citizens view their representatives. People may, in the abstract, want a perfectly "clean" Congress, but in practice many seem to be willing to be represented by less than perfect legislators.

More on congressional corruption can be found in *Congressional Quarterly's Guide to Congress,* 2d ed. (Washington, D.C.: Congressional Quarterly, 1976), pp. 716–719; Dennis Forney, "Scandals Over Fraud, Sex and Bribes Fail to Stop Incumbents," *The Wall Street Journal,* November 9, 1978; and Peter C. Stuart, "Talmadge Ethics Case Puts Congress on Spot." *The Christian Science Monitor,* December 22, 1978.

It should be clear now why it is so difficult to say whether Congress responds effectively to national problems. Two people can differ substantially on how they view "effectiveness." If one defines effectiveness in terms of rapid and extensive action on major issues, then Congress falls short. On the other hand, effectiveness can also be defined as careful examination, cautious action, and full consideration of varying needs and interests. Measured against this standard, Congress comes out much better. Perhaps the only way this question can be answered definitely is to present Congress with legislation guaranteed to solve a major problem perfectly. The subsequent reaction would then answer our question. Of course, no such legislation now exists.

Should Congress be reformed? If so, how?

Virtually every year journalists, scholars, concerned citizens, and members of Congress themselves come out for congressional reform. And unlike many political proposals, congressional reform is something few people publicly oppose. Demanding reform of government institutions is a well-established tradition, and even a brief review of the more recent proposals and enactments would fill dozens of pages. Rather than describe innumerable proposals, we shall therefore instead address two key questions pertaining to congressional reform: (1) Are most citizens satisfied with Congress? and (2) What should be the impact of congressional reform?

ARE MOST CITIZENS SATISFIED WITH CONGRESS?

Especially in recent years political commentators have spoken of a "crisis of confidence" in U.S. political institutions. Congress, in particular, is singled out for special attention as an institution in need of greater public confidence, as evidenced by the results of several public opinion polls. Table 11.1, for example, indicates that in thirteen surveys conducted between 1963 and 1978, only in two instances (1964 and 1965) were positive evaluations of Congress in a clear majority. Most of the time, most people thought Congress was doing only a fair to poor job.

Do these figures indicate that people would like to see major changes in congressional organization and behavior? Not necessarily. First, many basic features of the congressional system are deeply imbedded in our thinking. A two-house legislature, separation of powers, the fact that legislators come from the districts they represent, the absence of strong party coercion on legislative voting, and many other features are viewed as normal, virtually unchangeable elements of U.S. politics. Advocates of major reforms, such as establishing a parliamentary system, would have to overcome enormous resistance on the part of voters. To receive widespread support reforms would very likely have to be comparatively minor. Most people would be willing to accept a change in the power of committee chairpersons; few would seriously consider abolishing committees altogether.

Year	Positive[a]	Negative	Not sure
1963	33	60	7
1964	59	33	8
1965	64	26	10
1966	49	42	9
1967	38	55	7
1968	46	46	8
1969	34	54	12
1970	26	63	11
1973	38	45	17
1974	38	54	8
1975	26	67	7
1976	22	70	8
1978	28	63	9

TABLE 11.1

PUBLIC BELIEFS ABOUT THE JOB DONE BY CONGRESS, 1963–1978

[a] The question asked was, "How would you rate the job done this past year by Congress— excellent, pretty good, only fair, or poor?" "Excellent" and "pretty good" are considered positive; "only fair" or "poor" are classified as negative.
Source: Louis Harris, "Public Rates Congress Lower Than Its Members," *Chicago Tribune,* February 6, 1978, p. 9.

A second piece of evidence indicating that most citizens are wary of wholesale change is the phenomenal reelection success of legislators. Figure 11.1 depicts the success rate for House members and Senators between 1960 and 1976; it is clear that while many citizens may rate Congress negatively, they are reluctant to punish their own legislators.

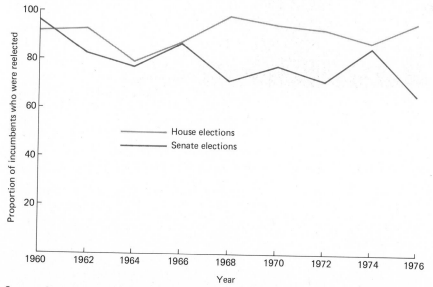

FIGURE 11.1

REELECTION SUCCESS RATES OF REPRESENTATIVES AND SENATORS, 1960–1976

Source: *Statistical Abstract of the United States, 1978,* p. 504.

Brickman, *The Washington Star.*

One would think that if citizens were that deeply dissatisfied with congressional performance, they would "fire" their legislators with greater frequency. Critics of Congress, hoping for an influx of new people to revitalize it, are likely to wait in vain.

WHAT SHOULD BE THE IMPACT OF CONGRESSIONAL REFORM?

Proposals for reforming Congress abound. It sometimes seems that everyone is for "reform," just as everyone is in favor of honesty, virtue, human rights, and good clean fun. Unfortunately, discussions of reform rarely make clear the ultimate purpose of the proposed reform. All reforms involve a change in the distribution of political power. Every reform shifts power from one interest to another. Of course, advocates of a particular reform would argue that *their* reform helps the forces of good against the forces of evil. The important question becomes, therefore, what is the political purpose behind various reform proposals? What interests win or lose when Congress is reformed? Let us briefly consider two general reform proposals and their likely consequences.

Strengthen Congress's constitutional role

Many reformers believe that Congress can no longer hold its own against the executive branch. As a result, the basic constitutional plan of checks and balances is being undermined. Congress should therefore be strengthened so it can compete more effectively against presidential domination. Specific methods of accomplishing these goals include enlarging legislative staffs, establishing more organizations to provide expert opinion, increasing vigilance over executive agencies, and reducing dependence on the executive for legislative initiative.[21] It is also argued that if it is to counter the President, Congress must make a greater effort to lead public opinion and represent the aspirations of the ordinary citizen.

Advocates of these reforms neglect to mention, however, that strengthening the constitutional role of Congress may also increase the incidence of legislative-executive deadlock. If one is mainly interested in speed of government response to issues, a stronger Congress may harm one's

[21] A more complete description of these proposals is found in Roger H. Davidson, David M. Kovenock, and Michael K. O'Leary, *Congress in Crisis: Politics and Congressional Reform* (Belmont, Calif.: Wadsworth, 1966), pp. 17–25.

cause. Of course, a Congress with greater staff resources might propose higher-quality legislation, but it seems equally likely that increased congressional vigor will encourage more frequent legislative-executive confrontations over whose policy is "better."

Make Congress internally more democratic

Chapter Ten indicated that all legislators are not equally powerful. Moreover, the abuse of power by strong legislators has a long history. Innumerable times committee chairpersons or party leaders have used their positions for personal gain or to subvert the wishes of their colleagues. In addition, the seniority system frequently rewards legislators who represent neither the positions of their fellow legislators nor those of the general public. Tyrannical power plus the seniority system, it is claimed, inevitably distort legislative democracy. Reform, therefore, must reduce power inequities and "open up" the legislative process. To accomplish these goals reformers usually advocate weakening the power of committee and subcommittee chairpersons, reducing the importance of or eliminating the seniority system, making all meetings public in order to prevent secret "deals," requiring financial disclosures of all income, and deciding all important issues by open vote with maximum participation.

At first glance making Congress completely democratic and open would seem to be a reform that everyone could favor. Nevertheless, some people believe that such reforms would weaken the legislative representation of numerous important groups. Many features of the congressional system—for example, powerful committee chairpersons—may seem "unfair," but when they are personally beneficial, one is less tempted to reform such features out of business. For example, agricultural interests have traditionally been protected by powerful congressional friends. So too have many liberals opposing school prayers, who counted on Emmanuel Celler (D-N.Y.), who was chairperson of the House Judiciary Committee for many years, to block legislation allowing prayers in public schools. Numerous other interests are also given "special" influence. Thus, while everyone opposes "unfair" power *in principle*, in practice the existing system of inequities, secrecy, and "deals" seems to provide good representation to many groups. Of course, not all citizens have their congressional protectors. Proponents of democratic reform in particular claim that less well-off interests are "shut out" by the undemocratic features of the legislative process.

Considering these and other proposed changes in the congressional system, we see that there is no such thing as a politically neutral reform. Every reform benefits some people and hurts others. What particular reform you favor depends on what policies you want. If you want a cautious approach to social problems that does not upset existing distributions of power, your idea of "reform" might be more legislative resources to fight the policies of the executive branch. On the other hand, if you desire fast and extensive congressional action, then "reform" implies weakening Congress's means to deliberate and reducing the power of conservative committee chairpersons. In short, there is no *one* reform of Congress. Behind every proposal is a desire for certain types of policies.

HOW A BILL BECOMES A LAW

1. INTRODUCTION

A legislator wanting a new law introduces this proposed legislation by putting it into the "hopper." It is given a number, is printed and is then sent to the appropriate committee.

2. COMMITTEE CONSIDERATION

Once in committee the bill may be sent to the relevant subcommittee. If the committee or subcommittee wants to consider the proposal, a hearing will be scheduled. Following the hearing will be a "mark-up" session in which the bill is examined and modified line by line, section by section.

3. COMMITTEE VOTE

Having been subject to a hearing and being examined by committee members, the committee then votes whether the bill is worthy of consideration by the entire House or Senate.

4. HOUSE RULES COMMITTEE

In the House, before a bill is sent to the floor, it usually must pass through the Rules Committee. The Rules Committee is basically charged with setting the time and terms of floor debate. (In the Senate this scheduling is done informally by elected leaders.)

5.

HOUSE OR SENATE DEBATE

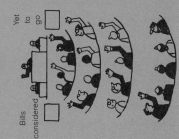

Surviving bills are sent with committee report for floor debate. Amendments may or may not be permitted and limits may be imposed on debate.

6.

HOUSE—SENATE AGREEMENT

Once a bill passes one chamber, it is sent on to the next. There it starts the process all over again, from the very beginning. If passed in identical form in both chambers, it goes to the President. If, however, different versions are passed, a conference committee is appointed to resolve these differences.

7.

APPROVING CONFERENCE COMMITTEE DECISIONS

Once the Conference Committee has reached agreement, each chamber must approve the agreement.

8.

FINALLY, THE BILL GOES TO THE PRESIDENT FOR APPROVAL.

If rejected by the President, it takes a two-thirds vote of both the House and the Senate to make the bill into a law.

Figure 11.2

A conclusion: can Congress be representative and responsive?

That Congress should be both representative and responsive is widely endorsed. However, Congress seems increasingly less able to meet those goals, and it has become commonplace to suggest ways to "improve" the law-making process. Observers of Congress have suggested everything from changing the length of legislative terms, to reforms of campaigns, to major reorganization of the committee system. Congress itself has acknowledged this dissatisfaction and has made several major changes in its rules and the makeup of its committees, and has introduced additional constraints on member behavior.

Before we accept the characterization of Congress as unrepresentative and unresponsive, we must look more carefully at these charges. In the first place, there has been a major change in our expectations regarding Congress. Fifty years ago the racial or sexual composition of Congress was not a major issue. Nor did citizens expect their legislators to formulate comprehensive programs to solve complex social and economic problems. Moreover, since the government's role in peoples' lives was more limited, legislators were not held responsible for helping citizens navigate a vast federal bureaucracy. Clearly, the standards for representation and responsiveness are now higher.

In addition, we now not only expect members of Congress to do more things more effectively, but we also sometimes expect actions that may be contradictory. While some citizens demand a prompt response to a crisis, others call for greater thoroughness in collecting information and drafting legislation. To some the disproportionately small number of blacks, women, and manual workers in Congress constitutes a problem. On the other hand, there are those who decry the trend toward narrow group representation at the expense of legislators committed to the overall national interest. What makes matters complex is that all participants in these controversies use the terms "representation" and "responsiveness" in defense of their position. For one person quick action is "responsiveness," for another extensive deliberation is "responsiveness."

What all of this shows us is that we must be cautious when we use familiar terms like "representative" and "responsiveness." People disagree on what these important words mean. The conclusion we reach on congressional representation and responsiveness greatly depends on the definitions we initially give these terms. Equally important, we must always realize that disputes over definitions are part of political conflict. If you are part of a majority it is useful to define "representation" as "following the preferences of the majority." If you are in the minority, however, you might claim that "true representation" means following the "interests, not the mere opinions" of the people (and this "interest" is what you favor). In short, the debate on congressional representation and responsiveness is likely to be ongoing. It will remain unsolved so long as these terms have multiple meanings and different groups benefit from different definitions.

Major questions raised

1. Is Congress a cross section of the public? No. Middle-class white males with professional backgrounds, older than the general adult population, are overrepresented in Congress. Disagreements arise concerning whether this misrepresentation means that the interests of poor people, blacks, women, and young people are ignored by legislators.

2. Do members of Congress respond to citizen demands? Legislators make a great effort to do things for their constituents, provide benefits for their districts, and vote the "right" way on key legislation. Citizens also receive representation from legislators they do not elect. For a number of good reasons, however, members of Congress do not follow all the wishes of their constituents.

3. Does Congress respond effectively to national problems? No, if we define effectiveness as wide-ranging comprehensive programs designed from a completely national perspective enacted into law quickly. Yes, if we think of effectiveness in terms of careful consideration, attention to local needs, and operating within constitutional boundaries.

4. Should Congress be reformed? If so, how? There is no evidence that most citizens want drastic changes despite low ratings given to Congress. Many proposals have been offered (for example, increasing the role of Congress in formulating policy), and each has its supporters, but no one reform is universally desired. The important point is that each reform helps some interests and harms others.

QUESTIONS FOR FURTHER DISCUSSION

1. How would you resolve the following dilemma? If members of Congress are to understand the problems ordinary citizens face, they should not be very unlike ordinary citizens. For example, to appreciate the impact of $2 a pound hamburger, you have to go to the supermarket and experience the shock for yourself. A luxurious life-style does not encourage understanding of most people's problems. Yet, it also can be argued that unless legislators are well paid, or even rich, they are more likely to be vulnerable to bribery. In 1979, a member of Congress earned $57,500 annually and enjoyed many fringe benefits such as subsidized meals and health care. If these benefits were reduced to make legislators more like average citizens, well-financed lobbyists would increase their power. Thus, if we paid legislators ordinary salaries to make them more like ordinary citizens, we would increase their vulnerability to favor buying. If we pay them well, they can resist such influences, yet they may acquire a new, and nontypical, perspective on life.

2. Every ten years, because of the results of the new Census, many states must redraw the boundaries of congressional districts. A question that has arisen in such situations is: To what extent should boundaries be drawn so as to maximize the number of racial, ethnic, or religious groups presently underrepresented in Congress? In other words, since blacks currently have fewer members of Congress than their numbers in the population warrant, should an effort be made to design congressional

districts so that blacks are likely to be elected? Or would you argue that such geographically concentrated groups deserve no special advantage? The only proper criteria in redistricting are equality of population and geographical compactness. Anyhow, not all underrepresented groups can increase their strength through redistricting — what about women and young people? Should redistricting efforts take into consideration the racial and ethnic make-up of Congress?

3. On several occasions critics of Congress have argued that legislative casework ought to be sharply reduced. They note that casework is an ineffective way to help citizens and, more important, that it detracts from the important policy tasks facing lawmakers. An hour spent resolving a social security foul-up is one hour less that can be devoted to examining a complex issue. Casework should be done by professionals, not elected officials. Would you endorse creating a new agency that would be devoted to handling what is now done through legislative casework? Would this benefit citizens with problems? Would this increase the amount of attention legislators give to social and economic problems?

4. One solution to making Congress better able to deal with complex national problems is to increase the length of the House term from two to four years, or even six years. Proponents of this change claim that a two-year term means almost nonstop campaigning. The result is that Representatives have short-sighted views of the job and lack the time needed for mastery of the subjects the House must face. Would a four- or six-year term make the House more effective? What incentives would then exist for legislators to involve themselves more deeply in such problems as energy conservation, foreign trade, or disarmament as opposed to preparing for the next election?

BIBLIOGRAPHY

Beard, Edmund, and Stephen Horn. *Congressional Ethics: The View from the House.* Washington, D.C.: The Brookings Institution, 1975.
Examines what members of the House themselves feel about various ethical situations such as accepting favors from interest groups, employing campaign funds for personal use, and maintaining ties with law firms while in Congress. Based on a survey of fifty House members, this study concludes that many practices considered unethical are thought to be common.

Clapp, Charles L. *The Congressman: His Work as He Sees It.* New York: Doubleday Anchor Books, 1964.
Based on discussions with members of Congress in 1959, Clapp provides a detailed but very readable description of life in Congress. Covers relations with colleagues, constituents, and interest group members. Also describes legislative procedures and what it is like to live in Washington.

Clausen, Aage R. *How Congressmen Decide: A Policy Focus.* New York: St. Martins Press, 1973.
Clausen argues that legislative voting results from a legislator's own policy perspective, constituency views, interest group pressure, and party loyalty. This argument is tested by votes on five issues — civil liberties, international involvement, agricultural policy, social welfare, and managing government. Analysis gets complex at times.

Congressional Ethics. Washington, D.C.: Congressional Quarterly, 1977.
A fact-filled but readable analysis of recent congressional scandals, attempts to institute a new code of ethics, the benefits members of Congress receive,

disciplining of legislators, and problems of campaign financing. Useful for obtaining complete and detailed information on these topics.

Davidson, Roger H., David M. Kovenock, and Michael K. O'Leary. *Congress in Crisis: Politics and Congressional Reform.* Belmont, Calif.: Wadsworth Publishing Company, 1969.
An excellent introduction to many of the issues and complexities of congressional reform. Views reform against the backdrop of what Congress is supposed to accomplish. Also reviews many of the reforms enacted in the 1960s.

Fenno, Richard F., Jr. *Home Style: House Members in Their Districts.* Boston: Little, Brown, 1978.
Intermittently for seven years Fenno traveled with eighteen members of the House as they campaigned and engaged in casework. A good insight into the variety of personalities and styles of House members. Relates the behavior of these legislators to district characteristics and their Washington responsibilities.

Fiorina, Morris P. *Congress: Keystone of the Washington Establishment.* New Haven, Conn.: Yale University Press, 1977.
Fiorina addresses the question: Why are congressional elections becoming less competitive? His answer: Congress has created new agencies with complex regulations, citizens need help with these agencies, legislators help bewildered citizens, grateful citizens reelect legislators.

Kingdon, John W. *Congressmen's Voting Decisions.* New York: Harper & Row, 1973.
Focuses on several factors affecting legislative decision making in the House: the constituency, other members of Congress, party leaders, staff, internal groups, and the executive branch. Based on interviews with House members conducted in 1969.

Mayhew, David R. *Congress: The Electoral Connection.* New Haven, Conn.: Yale University Press, 1974.
Argues that to understand the actions of legislators we must view their behavior in terms of their overriding goal of reelection. Describes many of these election-oriented activities.

Miller, Clem. *Member of the House.* New York: Scribner's, 1962.
A collection of letters from a California member of Congress to his constituents. Describes the operation of the House, the work a legislator does, the role of party leaders, and other features of the House in a very readable style. Many details are out of date, but this book remains fun reading.

Orfield, Gary. *Congressional Power: Congress and Social Change.* New York: Harcourt Brace Jovanovich, 1975.
A sympathetic view of Congress which claims that Congress is basically giving the people what they want, for better or worse. Considers some of the possible consequences of reform, how Congress is innovative, and congressional attempts to resolve problems in the fields of civil rights, education, and unemployment.

Rieselbach, Leroy N. *Congressional Reform in the Seventies.* Morristown, N.J.: General Learning Press, 1977.
Briefly examines the performance of Congress against three criteria—responsibility, responsiveness, and accountability. The author claims that Congress does not meet these criteria very well. Reform attempts between 1971 and 1975 are also examined as well as some future possibilities.

Saloma, John S., III. *Congress and the New Politics.* Boston: Little, Brown, 1969.
The author is primarily interested in evaluating Congress. Considers different ways of organizing Congress, the ability of Congress to represent citizens, and several facets of legislative effectiveness. Concludes with an interesting analysis of how Congress might have to adapt in the future.

PREVIEW

Who can become President of the United States?

Not every one can grow up to be President. The Constitution requires that a President be a natural-born citizen at least 35 years of age and have been a U.S. resident for at least fourteen years. In addition, public expectations also dictate the kinds of people who can be President. We expect Presidents to be white males who accept conventional morality; religion and ethnicity may be factors, but they are no longer crucial. A potential President must also overcome numerous electoral hurdles. One must get either Democratic or Republican Party support, put together a diverse coalition of groups and interests, and be a skilled campaigner. Critics have argued that our presidential selection process discourages great men and women from seeking the office.

How much power does the President possess?

A President's power depends to a great extent on how an individual uses the office of the presidency. The Constitution is frequently vague on presidential power. The President is commander-in-chief of the armed forces, diplomatic leader, chief legislator, and shaper of public opinion. An ambitious President can usually interpret formal powers very broadly, especially in wartime or during a national emergency. Presidents can sometimes act with considerable independence through executive orders and executive agreements.

What limits presidential power?

Though an ambitious President can probably manage an occasional excess use of power, several countervailing forces are likely to prevent systematic abuses of the office. A major countervailing force is Congress. The Senate can block presidential appointments, and Congress can refuse to enact legislation requested by the President. The powers to investigate and to impeach are also important. The courts have generally gone along with presidential actions, but there have been significant exceptions. In *United States* v. *Nixon* (1974) the Supreme Court held that the President's claim of executive privilege is not absolute—as President Nixon maintained. Members of the bureaucracy, as well as presidential aides, can also constrain the Chief Executive. They can refuse to follow orders, act in the name of the President without presidential authorization, and use their own discretion in interpreting executive directives. Finally, the general public, with its expectations regarding "proper" behavior and its power at the polls, can limit the President's freedom of action.

A continuing debate concerns whether the President has too much or too little power. If you see government as designed for limited purposes and fear potential abuses of power, then you would probably say that many modern Presidents have been too powerful. On the other hand, if you envision the President as a force who works for the benefit of all citizens, then you are likely to support extensive presidential power.

CHAPTER TWELVE

PRESIDENTS AND PRESIDENTIAL POWER

The President of the United States occupies center stage in the drama of U.S. politics. The President is, however, many things to many different people. For some the Chief Executive is a political knight on horseback riding off to do battle with evil forces in the name of the public interest—the great protector and virtuous world leader. Others, less positive, consider the President a potential tyrant capable of bringing about disaster in a quest for personal glory. They sometimes speak of the "imperial presidency," which they see as a threat to the democratic process. Still others deemphasize the importance of the office and stress that the President is only one person in a gigantic and frequently uncontrollable bureaucracy—merely the largest cog in the huge executive branch. All of these perceptions are true to some degree. The presidency is complex, and what we can say about the President depends in part on who occupies the office and what issues confront the nation. We shall examine the President and the office by seeking answers to the following questions:

1. Who can become President of the United States?
2. How much power does the President possess?
3. What limits presidential power?

Who can become President of the United States?

Many of us grew up hearing the old adage that in the United States any-one can grow up to be President. Because the backgrounds of U.S. Pres-idents have been diverse, this old saying has some credibility. Neverthe-less, on the basis of formal and informal requirements, it poorly describes reality. Most citizens have no chance to become President. Equally important, those who have the opportunity are hardly average citizens. Three major hurdles to becoming President are (1) constitu-tional requirements; (2) public expectations; and (3) electoral consider-ations.

CONSTITUTIONAL REQUIREMENTS

Article II, section 1 of the Constitution states that a President must be a natural-born citizen (that is, born a U.S. citizen) at least 35 years old and have been a U.S. resident for at least fourteen years. How many citizens are excluded by these provisions?

In 1970, 9.6 million U.S. residents were foreign born and, thus, forever barred from becoming President. During the first part of the twentieth century, when immigration to the United States was extensive, this re-striction was even more important. Of a total population of 105.7 million in 1920, for instance, 13.9 million (or 13.2 percent) were foreign born.[1] Of course, many of these foreign born came to the United States as children and were probably indistinguishable as adults from native-born citizens. Regarding the age requirement, there were, in 1975, 58.1 million citizens who could vote for the President but were too young to be President themselves.[2]

PUBLIC EXPECTATIONS

More important than the written requirements for the presidency are the public expectations concerning the kind of person the President should be. These are important factors influencing not only who wins the elec-tion but who wins the nomination. No party official wants to back a hope-less candidate, and, thus, potential candidates with the "wrong" charac-teristics are cut off at the very beginning. What sorts of people have the "right" attributes to be President?

The most obvious characteristics desired by the public concern sex and race: all serious presidential candidates have been white males. The only exceptions have been symbolic—former Maine Senator Margaret Chase

[1] *Statistical Abstract of the United States, 1977,* p. 34. Being foreign born does not exclude one from the presidency if one's parents were U.S. citizens when you were born. However, the overwhelming majority of foreign-born citizens did not have parents who were U.S. citizens.

[2] *Statistical Abstract of the United States, 1977,* p. 27.

Victoria C. Woodhull, the first woman to run for President of the United States. As the candidate of the Equal Rights Party in 1872, Woodhull advocated world government, easier divorce laws, birth control, the end of the death penalty, and an excess profits tax. She received a few thousand popular votes and spent election day in a New York City jail.

Belva Ann Lockwood, National Equal Rights Party candidate for President in 1884. She advocated social and economic equality for women (she was the first woman to argue a case before the U.S. Supreme Court). Lockwood received 4,149 votes.

Smith, who declared for the presidency in 1964, or some nominees of inconsequential political parties. While recent polls indicate that most citizens would vote for a woman or a black for President, the chances of a woman or a black becoming Chief Executive are very slim.[3]

Less obvious than race or sex, but no less important, are expectations concerning the life-style of Presidents. Voters are uneasy about individuals who challenge conventional morality or hold odd opinions. In 1968, for example, many people believed that Nelson Rockefeller's divorce and quick remarriage hurt his image as presidential material. More recently, qualms have been expressed about California Governor Jerry Brown's bachelorhood, his spartan life-style, and his interest in Oriental religion. It also helps to have been in the military. Even a presidential candidate's children must acknowledge the conventional ideals, lest people think their parents could not raise children (and, thus, could not possibly run the nation). Needless to say, unconventional characteristics such as admitted homosexuality, bizarre personal appearance, or admitted use of marijuana disqualify one for the presidency.

[3] In 1978, for example, 76 percent of the respondents in a national survey said they would vote for a woman for President if she were qualified (in 1937, this figure was only 31 percent). The comparable figure on voting for a qualified black was 77 percent. For a Jew the figure was 82 percent. Gallup poll release cited in the *Champaign-Urbana News-Gazette*, September 24, 1978. For more data on this issue, see Myra Marx Ferree, "A Woman for President? Changing Responses: 1958–1972," *Public Opinion Quarterly*, 38 (1974), pp. 390–399.

THE KNOW-YOUR-PRESIDENTS QUIZ

The lives of U.S. Presidents were once carefully studied by school children. Today, unfortunately, much fascinating information about the lives and accomplishments of our national leaders is forgotten. To acquaint you better with our heritage, we offer the following questions about U.S. Presidents (the correct answers are given below.

1. Who was the first President born west of the Mississippi?
2. Two U.S. Presidents have been engineers. One was Jimmy Carter. Who was the other?
3. Which President was frequently described as the "friend of helpless children?"
4. No American Indian has ever been President. However, one Vice President—Charles Curtis—was half Indian, since his mother was a full-blooded Kaw. Under which President did Curtis serve?
5. Only two Presidents have been Quakers (Society of Friends). One was Richard Nixon. Who was the other?
6. Which U.S. President had an asteroid named after him? What is the name of the asteroid?
7. During whose administration was the "Star Spangled Banner" adopted as the national anthem?
8. Which President received over eighty-four honorary degrees from colleges and universities after he left office?
9. Which President spoke Chinese to his wife in front of White House guests so no one would know what they were talking about?
10. Who was the Hoover Dam named after?

Answers: 1. Herbert Hoover. He was born in West Branch, Iowa.

Religion and ethnicity also play a role in limiting the pool of potential candidates, though these factors seem to be gradually losing importance. Before the 1960 election of John F. Kennedy, it was considered impossible for a Catholic to win. (Alfred Smith, a New York Catholic and Democratic nominee, was overwhelmingly defeated in 1928 by Herbert Hoover.) Religion, however, remains important, as was demonstrated by the unease of some people over President Carter's strong fundamentalist religious convictions during the 1976 campaign. Jews and Christians with unorthodox beliefs, for example, Jehovah's Witnesses, also could expect difficulty in seeking the presidency. And a 1978 Gallup poll reported that only 40 percent of the public would vote for an atheist for President. Ethnically, people of northern or central European descent

Herbert Hoover.

2. Herbert Hoover. In 1964, Stanford University honored Hoover and Thomas Alva Edison as the two greatest engineers in the history of the United States. 3. Herbert Hoover. He was also known as the "hermit author of Palo Alto." 4. Herbert Hoover. His inaugural ball was also opened by an Indian orchestra from Tulsa, Oklahoma. 5. Herbert Hoover. 6. Hervert Hoover. The asteroid was discovered in 1920 and is named Hooveria. 7. Herbert Hoover. The first Oscars were also awarded during his Administration. 8. Herbert Hoover. He also received over seventy medals and awards and about a hundred other miscellaneous honors. 9. Herbert Hoover. 10. Herbert Hoover.

Other fascinating information on U.S. Presidents can be found in Joseph Nathan Kane, *Facts About the Presidents*, 2d ed. (New York: H. W. Wilson, 1968). The story of Hoover speaking Chinese is related in William "Fishbait" Miller, *Fishbait: The Memoirs of the Congressional Doorkeeper* (New York: Warner Books, 1977).

still have the edge. At least at the national level, being of Oriental, Italian, Spanish, Middle Eastern, or eastern European origins remains a liability. This may depend, however, on how obvious these origins are—Senator Edmund S. Muskie, a candidate for the 1972 Democratic nomination, was of Polish descent, but "Muskie" is not generally viewed as a Polish name.

One important characteristic that does *not* seem to matter is family social status. Voters do not believe that Presidents must come from the most socially prominent families. Some Presidents, for example, both Roosevelts and Kennedy, did come from wealthy, prominent families, but numerous others—Truman, Eisenhower, Johnson, Nixon, and Carter —grew up in rather conventional circumstances. Nor do voters expect their Presidents to have been trained at elite schools. President Johnson received his college degree from Southwest Texas State Teachers College in San Marcos, Texas (where he worked his way through school as a janitor). President Truman did not even attend college.

ELECTORAL CONSIDERATIONS

Having reduced the pool of potential Presidents from over 200 million to a few million, we now have a group of white males, over 35, with conventional life-styles, most of whom are traditional Protestants of northern or central European descent. From here on success depends on political considerations.

Unfortunately for those people looking for the one true path to the presidency, there is no single political strategy. This was not always the case. In the past the governorship of a populous state like New York or Illinois was considered a stepping-stone to the presidency. During much of the nineteenth century success in military campaigns was an important means of getting elected President. Nevertheless, despite all the different ways of getting to the top, attaining the presidency has yet to become a completely wide-open contest. To be President an individual must pass certain difficult political tests which most citizens probably could not overcome.

Getting party support

An elementary but very important requisite for becoming President is gaining the support and endorsement of one of the two major political parties. Even presidential hopefuls without close party ties—Wendell Wilkie in 1940 and Dwight Eisenhower in 1952—must be acceptable to party leaders and proclaim loyalty to the Democratic or Republican Party. Given the importance of party identification in voting (see Chapters Seven and Eight) and the role of parties in campaigns, running as an independent for President is politically ineffective.

Obtaining party endorsement is an ordeal. Until recently it required an enormous amount of bargaining with state and local party officials for their support at presidential nominating conventions. Even such "statesmen" as Abraham Lincoln, Woodrow Wilson, Franklin Roosevelt, and John F. Kennedy had to make promises and concessions to obscure party officials in order to secure their nominations. In some instances—for example, the 1920 Republican convention that nominated Warren G. Harding—the selection has been made entirely by party officials literally sitting in smoke-filled back rooms.

Because more and more states now choose party convention delegates through presidential primaries, making the right deals during the nominating convention has become less crucial. (In 1980 about three quarters of the delegates to both the Democratic and Republican conventions were chosen in primaries.) George McGovern's (1972) and Jimmy Carter's (1976) successful use of primaries to capture the Democratic nominations showed that candidates are no longer completely dependent on back-room deals. Nevertheless, party officials are still important despite widespread use of presidential primaries. Not only do several states still allow party committees to choose convention delegates, but party organizations frequently have considerable influence in state primaries. Most primaries have low voter turnouts, and candidates possess only limited campaign resources, so the concentrated efforts of a well-organized group, such as a local party, can be the deciding factor.

Perhaps the most important consequence of the need for a party nomination is that party officials can block the nomination of a popular leader who, for one reason or another, is offensive to them. This was dramatically illustrated in 1964 when Republican convention delegates, who were far more conservative than most citizens, or even most Republican Party identifiers, overwhelmingly rejected Nelson A. Rockefeller in favor of the more conservative Barry Goldwater. This occurred despite Rockefeller's national popularity and polls showing him to be the stronger candidate against Lyndon B. Johnson. Rockefeller's moderate and liberal policy positions had so angered these Republicans that they were determined to stop him even if it meant defeat in the November election.

Putting together a winning coalition

A second hurdle to be overcome on the road to the White House is assembling a winning electoral coalition. Given the enormous social, ethnic, and economic diversity in the United States, this is a difficult task. It is a job made even more difficult by frequent conflicts within existing coalitions. For example, many recent Democratic presidential nominees have tried to keep both militant blacks and traditionally anticivil rights southern whites in the fold of the Democratic Party. Republican nominees must appeal to both conservative and moderate Republicans.

Obviously, only some people can play this game successfully. Success tends to go to moderates (some would say the wishy-washy), who are content to deal with safe generalities. Such people must also be skilled at compromise and winning the confidence of people who sharply disagree with one another. In his 1976 campaign Jimmy Carter had a remarkable capacity to appear as "one of their own" to people on different sides of issues. When confronted with what seem to be irreconcilable alternatives, for example, a stand for or against racial integration of schools, a potential President must respond with something like, "I think the real issue is *quality* education, and I am 100 percent in favor of quality education."

Campaigning for office

In the past it was possible to become President without engaging in a strenuous campaign. The campaign season was usually limited to September and October, and some successful candidates, such as Warren Harding in 1920, hardly ventured beyond their houses. The winning of votes was left to campaign managers and well-staffed state party organizations.

The situation is drastically different today. The development of rapid transportation, the constant need for exposure in the mass media, and the growing importance of numerous presidential primaries have now made campaigning more of a physical ordeal than a pleasant way of meeting ordinary citizens. Particularly for a political newcomer, serious campaigning may begin in January (before the New Hampshire primary in February) for an election in November. The would-be President must be prepared for long days, a seemingly endless succession of Holiday Inn rooms, meals eaten on the run, a severe disruption of family life, giving the same speech six times a day, six days a week, and numerous disappointments and foul-ups. No doubt, more than one potential President

THE PRESIDENTIAL CAMPAIGN CAN BE CRUEL AND UNUSUAL PUNISHMENT

Campaigning for President is grueling. Not only is it physically demanding but a candidate must always appear in command and guard against offhand remarks that could prove disastrous. In 1964, for example, George Romney's campaign for the Republican presidential nomination was all but destroyed when he casually admitted that he had once been "brainwashed" about U.S. policy in Vietnam. Recall the damage done to Carter's campaign by his candid admission in *Playboy* that in his heart he had lusted after many women.

The problems of appearing enthusiastic when one is bored, thoughtful when one is reading a prepared speech for the tenth time, and informed when one is giving a superficial response to a silly question are well described by Adlai E. Stevenson, who unsuccessfully campaigned for the presidency in 1952 and 1956. As Stevenson put it:

At least for an inexperienced candidate, I supposed we have contrived few more exciting ordeals than a presidential campaign. You must emerge, bright and bubbling with wisdom and well-being, every morning at 8 o'clock, just in time for a charming and profound breakfast talk, shake hands with hundreds, often literally thousands, of people, make several inspiring, "newsworthy" speeches during the day, confer with political leaders along the way and with your staff all the time, write at every chance, think if possible, read mail and newspapers, talk on the telephone, talk to everybody, dictate, receive delegations, eat with decorum — and discretion! — and ride through city after city on the back of an open car, smiling until your mouth is dehydrated by the wind, waving until the blood runs out of your arm, and then bounce gaily, confidently, masterfully into great howling halls, shaved and all made up for television with the right color shirt and tie — I always forgot — and a manuscript so defaced with chicken tracks and last-minute jottings that you couldn't

gave up after three months on the road and thirty-five catered banquets at which he gave the same speech and answered the same questions.

The campaign involves other costs as well. Being a presidential candidate insures that the press will dig into one's past and that political opponents will twist the meanings of one's statements. Needless to say, not everyone relishes the prospect of having one's past dug up for public display.

What types of people are most likely to survive the ordeals and pressures of presidential campaigning? Probably those with king-sized egos

follow it, even if the spotlights weren't blinding and even if the still photographers didn't shoot you in the eye every time you looked at them. (I've often wondered what happened to all those pictures!) Then all you have to do is make a great, imperishable speech, get out through the pressing crowds with a few score autographs, your clothes intact, your hands bruised, and back to the hotel—in time to see a few important people.

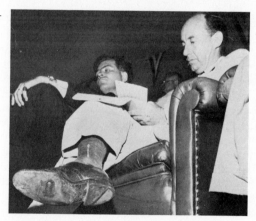

Adlai Stevenson after a whirlwind tour of five Michigan cities in 12 hours during the 1952 presidential campaign.

But the real work has just commenced—two or three, sometimes four hours of frenzied writing and editing of the next day's immortal mouthings so you can get something to the stenographers, so they can get something to the mimeograph machines, so they can get something to the reporters, so they can get something to their papers by deadline time. (And I quickly concluded that all deadlines were yesterday!) Finally, sleep, sweet sleep, steals you away, unless you worry—which I do.

The next day is the same.

Adlai E. Stevenson, *Major Campaign Speeches of Adlai E. Stevenson, 1952* (New York: Random House, 1953), pp. xii–xiii.

who are convinced that their personal mission is worth all the costs. One is tempted to state that a normal person would find the physical ordeal and the public scrutiny unbearable.

Let us return to our original question. Who can become President of the United States? Perhaps the best way of answering this question is to present a want-ad for the job. Such an advertisement would probably read as follows:

> WANTED. President of the United States. Two hundred thousand dollars a year plus many fringe benefits. Position is for four years with possibility of renewal. Must be 35, natural-born citizen, with 14 years U.S. residence. Prefer white males of western or northern European backgrounds. No weirdos, please. Should have background in compromising and convincing diverse people that you agree with everything they support. Must be approved by party officials. Willingness to travel extensively, give same speech endlessly, and receive abuse essential to job. Apply to: Democratic or Republican National Committee, Washington, D.C. We are *not* an equal opportunity employer.

TYPES OF PEOPLE EXCLUDED FROM THE PRESIDENCY

Before turning to our analysis of presidential power, let us consider one further question: Do the obstacles en route exclude the best people from the presidency? Many people answer this question affirmatively. One late nineteenth-century observer of U.S. politics even wrote a widely acclaimed essay called "Why Great Men Are Not Chosen President."[4] Certainly it is difficult to claim that Millard Fillmore, Franklin Pierce, or James Buchanan were great national leaders. It is also clear that the skills and attributes necessary to win the election are not necessarily those needed to be a good President. A superb campaigner, capable of inspiring enormous public confidence, could be a poor administrator with little interest or knack for solving problems. Remember that Warren G. Harding, generally considered one of our most inept Presidents, was elected by one of the greatest electoral landslides of all time (60.4 percent of the popular vote).

It can be argued also that by implicitly excluding women, blacks, unconventional people, and others considered to be "nonpresidential," we reduce our chances even further of finding the best-qualified person. Shortening the campaign and making it less expensive would also greatly enlarge the pool of potential Presidents.

These arguments are all reasonable, but they ignore two important points: (1) people disagree on what an ideal President should be and (2) the present method of recruiting Presidents may be the best we can do. Regarding the first point, to say that we can do better than, say, Jimmy

---

[4] James Bryce, "Why Great Men Are Not Chosen President," in *The American Commonwealth*, Vol. I (New York: Macmillan, 1906), pp. 78–85. For a rejoinder, see Harold Laski, "Why Great Men Are Chosen President," in *The American Presidency* (New York: Harper & Row, 1940), pp. 49–53.

THE VICE PRESIDENCY

The role of the Vice President is paradoxical. On the one hand, the position has little power. Under the Constitution the Vice President presides over the Senate (and votes in case of a tie). The Twenty-fifth Amendment also authorizes the Vice President and other officials to determine when a President is disabled. Presidents have rarely given their Vice Presidents major roles. Typical vice presidential jobs include chairing various commissions, traveling abroad as a presidential messenger, and publicly defending presidential actions. No wonder, then, that Harry S. Truman described a Vice President as about as useful as a cow's fifth teat.

At the same time, however, the modern vice presidency has become a stepping-stone to the presidency. In the twentieth century, six Vice Presidents eventually became President: Theodore Roosevelt, Calvin Coolidge, Harry Truman, Lyndon Johnson, Richard Nixon, and Gerald Ford.

The choice of Vice President, however, is rarely given much serious attention during the campaign. Almost always the presidential nominee selects his running mate, and convention delegates automatically approve the decision. Most vice presidential nominees are selected to balance the ticket. For example, in 1976, Jimmy Carter selected a Minnesota liberal (Walter Mondale) to counterbalance his southern background and conservative image. The choice of a running mate may also be affected by the need to keep together the party's divergent wings (for many years the Democrats nominated southerners as Vice Presidents.).

How then do we get people of "presidential timber" to accept a position that is politically inconsequential? Why should anyone give up being a Senator or governor for something that—in the words of ex-Vice President Garner—"isn't worth a pitcher of warm spit"?

For a more extensive analysis of the vice presidency, see Allan P. Sindler, *Unchosen Presidents* (Berkeley: University of California Press, 1976); and Thomas E. Cronin, *The State of the Presidency* (Boston: Little, Brown, 1975), Chap. 8.

Carter as President implies agreement on what constitutes the right attributes for the job. Do we want a President who places his principles above everything else or one who is willing to compromise? Should the President follow the law exactly or be flexible as new situations develop?

Do we want a statesman above day-to-day bargaining or a wheeler-dealer who gets things done? Until we can answer questions such as these, we do not have a standard by which to evaluate the jobs done by the people we elect.

That the present system, though not perfect, is probably the best we can do is a plausible statement if we consider the alternatives. Should we require that parties occasionally nominate women, blacks, and others previously left out of the presidential candidate pool? How would this increase the quality of the person elected? Some people have even suggested that all would-be Presidents be certified as "healthy" by a board of psychiatrists before they are allowed to run. But who chooses these psychiatrists, and what exactly is mental health? The difficulty of reforming the presidential selection process is well illustrated by the 1972 Democratic nominating convention. Following the 1968 convention, which was marked by turmoil and deep antagonisms, the nominating process was considerably "opened up," so that the 1972 convention saw an influx of groups that had previously been underrepresented in choosing the nominee. Though the 1972 nominee—Senator George McGovern—might have had more support from groups once shut out of the nominating process than the 1968 nominee (Hubert Humphrey), McGovern was, nevertheless, soundly rejected by the voters. In short, there may be a better way of getting our Presidents, but if it exists, it is far from obvious.

How much power does the President possess?

Everyone agrees that the President is the most powerful public official in the United States. There is no general agreement, however, on what powers the President actually possesses or whether certain recent actions by Presidents have been legal or illegal. Even different Presidents have viewed presidential power very differently. Some Presidents, such as William Howard Taft and Dwight Eisenhower, saw themselves as strictly limited by Congress and the Constitution. Franklin Roosevelt and Lyndon Johnson, however, believed that the presidency requires active, vigorous leadership and that the only limitations on Presidents are explicit constitutional prohibitions. Thomas Jefferson initially took the limited-presidency position, but when he became President in 1801, he was quick to make extensive use of presidential authority (as in the case of the Louisiana Purchase).

Examination of the Constitution does not clarify the problem. In the words of one expert on the presidency, the constitutional description of presidential powers "is vague, disorganized, and misleading."[5] Where the Constitution is explicit, the powers granted are comparatively

[5] Grant McConnell, *The Modern Presidency*, 2d ed. (New York: St. Martins Press, 1976), p. 18.

minor—for example, the President can grant pardons or request written opinions from heads of executive departments. Important powers, such as the President's role as commander-in-chief of the armed forces, are given no elaboration. Perhaps the broadest of all powers derives from a brief clause toward the end of Article II, section 2: "He shall take Care that the Laws be faithfully executed. . . ." This is a far different approach from the one employed to control the actions of Congress.

Nevertheless, despite this vagueness, several important presidential powers have emerged. Some of these are based on the written Constitution, others on constitutional implications and interpretations, and still others on precedent and custom. It is necessary to emphasize that no important presidential power is self-evident; much depends on how the power is used and the particular circumstances. Let us consider the power of the President in four important areas: (1) commander-in-chief of the armed forces; (2) diplomatic leader; (3) chief legislator; and (4) shaper of public opinion.

COMMANDER-IN-CHIEF OF THE ARMED FORCES

The principle of civilian control over the military is established by the Constitution's designation of the President as commander-in-chief of the armed forces. Just what the President can do in this role, however, is not clear. Not surprisingly, many Presidents have used this constitutional provision as a basis for engaging in a wide range of important political actions. As we shall see, many of the most important events in U.S. history were caused by Presidents acting as military commanders-in-chief.

Making specific military decisions

This constitutional power is most specifically used when Presidents actually make battlefield decisions. In 1794, for example, President Washington personally led an army against rebellious farmers. Lincoln also played an active military role during the Civil War. In was Truman who personally ordered the dropping of the atomic bomb in 1945. More recently, Presidents Johnson and Nixon frequently made key military decisions during the Vietnam war. Presidential influence has also been felt in the appointment of generals (all officers are appointed by the President and confirmed by the Senate). In 1951, President Truman's controversial firing of General Douglas MacArthur arose in part over whether the United States was going to expand the Korean conflict by invading the People's Republic of China.

Presidential decisions on deploying U.S. troops have also proved important. President Jefferson, for example, dispatched the Navy against the Barbary pirates when they harassed U.S. commerce. In 1854, Franklin Pierce ordered the Navy to bombard a city in Nicaragua. When Chinese rebels threatened U.S. interests in China, President William McKinley dispatched 5,000 troops to that country. More modern examples include Eisenhower's sending of 14,000 Marines to Lebanon in 1958, Kennedy's mobilization of troops during the 1961 Berlin crisis,

A RANDOM SAMPLING OF PRESIDENTIAL WIT

I had not the advantage of a classical education, and no man should, in my judgment, accept a degree he cannot read.

> — Millard Fillmore in declining a degree from the University of Oxford

That 150 lawyers [referring to Congress] should do business together is not to be expected.

> — Thomas Jefferson

Conservatism is the policy of "make no change and consult your grandmother when in doubt."

> — Woodrow Wilson

The unforgivable crime is soft hitting. Do not hit at all if it can be avoided; but *never* hit softly.

> — Theodore Roosevelt

A good leader can't get too far ahead of his followers.

> — Franklin D. Roosevelt

I took the Isthmus, started the Canal, and then left Congress — not to debate the Canal, but to debate me. . . . But while the debate goes on the Canal does too.

> — Theodore Roosevelt

A radical is a man with both feet firmly planted — in the air. A conservative is a man with two perfectly good legs who, however, has never learned to walk forward. A reactionary is a somnabulist walking backwards. A liberal is a man who uses his legs and his hands at the behest . . . of his head.

> — Franklin D. Roosevelt

You have to stand every day three or four hours of visitors [to the

Johnson's dispatching of 32,000 Marines to the Dominican Republic in 1965, and President Ford's use of military force to rescue the USS *Mayaguez* when it was seized by Cambodian troops in 1975. The two most important examples of Presidents using their powers as commanders-in-chief were the Korean and Vietnam wars. Neither of these conflicts was a congressionally declared war, but Presidents were, nevertheless, able to spend billions of dollars and commit hundreds of thousands of troops to battle.

White House]. Nine-tenths of them will want something they ought not to have. If you keep dead-still they will run down in three or four minutes. If you even cough or smile they will start up all over again.
— Calvin Coolidge

I think the American public wants a solemn ass as a President, and I think I'll go along with them.
— Calvin Coolidge

I have just received the following telegram from my generous Daddy. It says, "Dear Jack: Don't buy a single vote more than necessary. I'll be damned if I'm going to pay for a landslide."
— John F. Kennedy, 1958

When we got into office, the thing that surprised me most was to find things were just as bad as we'd been saying they were.
— John F. Kennedy

President Lyndon B. Johnson used to tell the story of Magnus Johnson, a Swede from Minnesota, who one day rose in the House and declared: "What we have to do is take the bull by the tail and look the situation in the face."

President Johnson used to say that there were two kinds of speeches. The Mother Hubbard speech, which, like the garment, covers everything but touches nothing; and the French bathing suit speech that covers only the essential points.

If Lincoln were alive today, he'd roll over in his grave.
— Gerald R. Ford

Stories from Millard Fillmore through Calvin Coolidge appeared in Caroline Thomas Hornsberger, ed. and comp., *Treasury of Presidential Quotations* (Chicago: Follett Publishing Company, 1964). The Kennedy quotes are from Bill Adler, ed., *The Kennedy Wit* (New York: Citadel Press, 1964). The two Johnson stories are reported in Bill Adler, ed., *The Johnson Humor* (New York: Simon & Schuster, 1965); the Ford quote appeared in Richard Reeves, *A Ford, Not a Lincoln* (New York: Harcourt Brace Jovanovich, 1975), p. 145.

Using the military to preserve domestic order

The President has also dispatched troops for domestic purposes. In 1894, President Grover Cleveland sent troops to Chicago to restore order during the Pullman strike. During the 1950s and 1960s, when the racial integration of southern schools threatened to become violent, U.S. troops were sent in to maintain order. Similarly, when Detroit police could no longer control the situation during the 1967 riots, President Johnson dispatched paratroopers. On many occasions the President has responded to potential violence or natural catastrophes by nationalizing state militias. This power to commandeer state troops is explicitly granted the President in Article II, section 2 of the Constitution.

Far-reaching uses of military power

Several presidents, however, have interpreted their power as commanders-in-chief to go well beyond the directing of troops. Especially in wartime, or when war is threatening, ambitious Chief Executives have exercised considerable powers, which they claimed derived from the position of the President as military head. Acting as commander-in-chief in the period between the attack on Ford Sumter and the convening of Congress, Lincoln added over 80,000 men to the armed forces, spent two million dollars in unauthorized funds, banned "treasonable correspondence" from the mails, suspended the writ of *habeas corpus*, and had people arrested for what he judged treasonable offenses. The Emancipation Proclamation, which freed over four million slaves, was issued on the basis of Lincoln's position as commander-in-chief. In 1942, when a Japanese attack on the U.S. mainland appeared to be a real possibility, President Roosevelt, fearing espionage and sabotage, initiated procedures whereby 112,000 Japanese-Americans (most of whom were U.S. citizens) were forcibly removed from the West Coast and resettled in ten inland "relocation centers." Six months *prior* to Pearl Harbor, Roosevelt, acting as commander-in-chief during an "unlimited national emergency" (which he had proclaimed), took over a strike-bound plant of the North American Aviation Company. [6]

The significance of the President's position as commander-in-chief becomes even more apparent when we realize that, except for the War of 1812 and the Spanish-American War, presidential action played a key role in the United States' entry into war. When President James Polk ordered troops into Mexico, he virtually declared war (though officially only Congress can declare war). On other occasions, for example, President Woodrow Wilson's arming of merchant ships, executive action set the stage for subsequent congressional declarations of war. The possibility that a President might order a show of military force that unexpectedly leads to nuclear warfare has crossed the minds of many members of Congress. We shall have more to say later on how Congress has tried to control the commander-in-chief.

DIPLOMATIC LEADER

In foreign affairs the President holds vast authority. Congress can impinge on his authority by reducing appropriations or failing to ratify treaties, but compared to other areas of presidential power, the President has great freedom over foreign relations.

[6] For a more complete description of presidential use of commander-in-chief powers, see Louis W. Koenig, *The Chief Executive*, 3d ed. (New York: Harcourt Brace Jovanovich, 1975), Chap. 10.

Constitutional sources of presidential power in foreign relations

This power derives from several constitutional sources. The President's position as commander-in-chief of an enormous military organization automatically makes him an important diplomatic and world leader. Theodore Roosevelt became a major force in international affairs through his deployment of U.S. military might. It was Roosevelt's use of the Marines that "solved" the diplomatic problem of obtaining the rights to build the Panama Canal. Today there is less of such blatant "**gunboat diplomacy**," but the commander-in-chief of one of the world's strongest military machines remains a major figure in international dealings.

Another constitutionally based source of power in foreign relations comes from the President's right to appoint and receive ambassadors. On many occasions this power has been used to shape overall foreign policy. In 1947, for example, President Truman, by quickly accepting the Israeli ambassador to the United States, officially "recognized" the state of Israel. This rapid **diplomatic recognition** conveyed to the world that the United States would support Israel's right to exist. Similarly, the decision to establish full diplomatic relations with the People's Republic of China and end diplomatic ties with Taiwan, made at the end of 1978, was President Carter's not Congress's. The restoration of normal relations with Cuba would also depend on presidential action.

The appointment of an ambassador can be a significant policy choice. President Carter's appointment of Andrew Young as ambassador to the United Nations clearly signaled an increased concern for third world nations. The political orientation of the U.S. ambassador to the Soviet Union is likewise considered a message regarding presidential policies vis-à-vis Russia.

Another constitutionally derived power concerns the President's role in treaty making. Though the Senate must ultimately approve all treaties, it is the President who initiates and negotiates treaties. As the Senate-President debate over the Panama Canal treaty in 1977 and 1978 well illustrated, the President usually sets the terms and the time of debate (a President can delay sending a treaty to the Senate until the chances of passage are high). With a few major exceptions, for example, the Covenant of the League of Nations, the Senate has endorsed presidential action. Even if the Senate resists, however, the President can act through **executive agreements.** Some of President Johnson's most important commitments to South Vietnam in the 1960s were secret executive agreements between him and the President of South Vietnam and were, thus, beyond congressional control. As pointed out in Chapter Ten, the courts have treated these executive agreements as virtually identical to Senate-confirmed treaties.

The need for quick action and presidential power

These constitutionally defined roles are, however, only the beginning of contemporary presidential involvement in world affairs. The threat of nuclear holocaust, the speed at which international events move, and an almost endless succession of crises have demanded extensive presidential attention to foreign relations. Whereas a revolution in an obscure Af-

Gunboat diplomacy The show of military force to achieve diplomatic objectives, especially against smaller nations. The term derives from the past practice of having the Navy shell cities to teach leaders a lesson or to obtain an agreement.

Diplomatic recognition The establishment of full diplomatic relations with a nation. Significantly affects trade relations between the countries and facilitates travel by citizens to the other country.

Executive agreement An agreement with a foreign nation signed by the President that does not require senatorial approval.

"Pocket" veto When a President does not sign a bill and Congress adjourns within ten days (excluding Sunday); thus the bill does not become law. *Item veto* The power to veto only a part of a bill. This power is possessed by some governors but not the President.

rican nation was once a strictly local matter, it may now be viewed as the source of a potential confrontation between the big powers. Consequently, Presidents increasingly find themselves acting as world-wide trouble shooters on behalf of the people of the United States. The President is now "responsible" for peace in the Middle East, committed to keeping communism at bay in Africa and Latin America, and looked upon as the leader of the free world. What is important here is the widespread expectation that when a crisis occurs, even if it is in Timbuktu, the U.S. President must respond.

CHIEF LEGISLATOR

We sometimes view Congress as the lawmaking branch of government and the executive branch as the law-enforcing arm. In reality, the division is less clear. As we saw in Chapter Ten, through investigations and congressional oversight legislators can influence the administration of laws. It is also true that the President has considerable power over lawmaking. In fact, some observers argue that modern Presidents virtually dominate the making of laws. How can the Chief Executive enact legislation? Has the President's power encroached upon congressional responsibilities?

Affecting legislation through the veto power

One prerogative that enables the President to strongly influence lawmaking is explicitly granted in the Constitution—the veto power. Presidents can veto bills in two ways. First, they can simply refuse to sign a bill, in which case the bill is returned with an explanation to Congress, where a two-thirds vote of each house is necessary to override the veto. Second, a Chief Executive can use the **"pocket" veto.** According to the Constitution, the President has ten days (excluding Sundays) to decide on a bill. If the ten days pass and the President has not signed, the bill automatically becomes law. If, however, Congress has adjourned during this period, the bill cannot be sent back to that legislative body. Then after ten days the bill is "pocket vetoed." Between 1913 and 1976, there were 1,350 presidential vetoes, of which 552, or 59.1 percent, were pocket vetoes (only 49 of these regular vetoes were overridden by Congress).[7]

Not only does the veto power affect which bills become law, but the threat of veto can determine actual legislative content. Presidents are not shy about telling legislators what they will accept. Hence, many a bill is modified in advance to avoid a presidential veto. Congress is not completely defenseless, however, against a threatened veto. Unlike many state governors, the President lacks an **item veto,** or the power to veto a portion of a bill and accept the rest. The presidential veto is an all-or-nothing weapon. Congress will sometimes take advantage of this situation by including in a bill the President much desires various provisions

[7] *Statistical Abstract of the United States, 1977*, p. 461.

the President opposes. To get what they want Presidents frequently accept the entire package.

Proposing legislation to Congress

A second way the President acts as legislator is by actually proposing legislation. This mixing of legislative and executive roles is traditional in U.S. politics. As President, Thomas Jefferson personally drafted legislation creating a national university, protecting harbors, changing tariffs, and establishing a naval militia. Jefferson also campaigned vigorously for his bills.[8] Of course, most of the bills that originate in the executive branch are not personally drafted by the President. Through a process known as **central clearance** the Office of Management and Budget which is under presidential direction controls the flow of legislative proposals from executive departments (for example, the Department of Commerce) to Congress. These proposals represent the President's legislative program. This program is usually conveyed to Congress through House and Senate leaders of the President's party. It has been estimated that between 50 and 80 percent of all bills considered by Congress carry the stamp of the executive branch.[9]

Central clearance The procedure by which legislation desired by officials in the executive branch must be approved by the President or his advisers before the request is sent to Congress.

Power over the budget

But the President's legislative role involves more than merely bombarding Congress with bills. In 1921, Congress passed the Budget and Accounting Act creating the Bureau of the Budget with a director appointed by the President. With this legislation the President assumed chief responsibility for preparing the federal budget. The influence of the Chief Executive over expenditures was further enhanced in 1970 when President Nixon replaced the Bureau of the Budget with the Office of Management and Budget (OMB) and placed it more directly under presidential control. An essential feature of this change was to make officials responsible for budgetary decisions, which greatly determine the legislative agenda, work almost completely at the discretion of the President.

Naturally, Congress must approve the budget and is fully capable of making changes in it. Nevertheless, this initial formulation of federal expenditures is an important lawmaking mechanism. The President has more staff resources, more detailed knowledge, and more time than Congress in the battle of the budget, so presidential priorities frequently dominate. Presidents can also achieve their policy goals by hiding or disguising budget items. When President Roosevelt wished to keep the atomic bomb project a secret, hundreds of millions of dollars were budgeted for "Engineer Service, Army" and "Expediting Production," and no members of Congress became suspicious.[10] Presidents Johnson

[8] Louis Fisher, *Presidents and Congress* (New York: Free Press, 1972), p. 53.

[9] Fisher, *Presidents and Congress*, p. 54.

[10] Fisher, *Presidents and Congress*, p. 112. A more detailed analysis of presidential control over expenditures is presented in Louis Fisher, *Presidential Spending Power* (Princeton, N.J.: Princeton University Press, 1975).

and Nixon likewise avoided congressional interference by hiding money for the Vietnam war effort. Given an incredibly large and complex budget, many legislators are simply willing to trust the President.

Power over how legislation will be enforced

Presidents also determine the content of laws through their decisions concerning how laws will be administered. Even President Taft, a believer in strict legal interpretations, acknowledged the importance of administrative discretion when he said, "Let anyone make the laws of the country, if I can construe them." The Chief Executive affects the administration of laws in several ways. The power of appointment allows a President to select people who share his views on running the federal bureaucracies. President Nixon, for example, had a great impact on the Justice Department without expending much effort because he chose his old friend John Mitchell as Attorney General. In the area of budget making, the President can reward administrators who make the "right" decisions and punish those who don't. Given that so many of the government regulations which affect our lives are decisions originating in the executive branch, the power over administration is crucial.

The President also acts as lawmaker when a law passed by Congress delegates to the President considerable discretion under certain circumstances. For example, the Federal Pay Compatibility Act of 1970 allows the President, without congressional approval, to raise the pay of federal employees to match salaries in private industry. Many laws that regulate foreign trade frequently give the President authority to adjust tariffs, within limits, as the occasion arises. Perhaps the most important laws providing legislative power to the President concern wartime or national emergencies. For example, because of laws already on the books, during wartime the President can restrict travel, institute martial law, take over the transportation system, and seize private property without first consulting Congress. Similar laws provide vast discretionary power during peacetime emergencies (the President used such authority to deal with a 1970 national postal strike).

The use of executive orders and proclamations

Finally, Presidents can make law by issuing **executive orders** or proclamations. In many instances the President is merely acting to fill in the details of a previously enacted law. Such "details" can be significant, however. Many Presidents have used executive orders to achieve civil rights objectives—such as banning job discrimination—because they knew that Congress would never pass such laws. By executive order President Kennedy established an Equal Employment Opportunity Commission that had far more power than a similar agency established by an act of Congress (the new agency could cancel any government contract if the contractor was guilty of racial discrimination). In 1907, Theodore Roosevelt, by proclamation, increased the national forest land by 43 million acres (about the combined area of New York, New Jersey, Connecticut, and Massachusetts). The ease with which executive orders and proclamations can be issued has made them popular means of lawmaking. Between 1907 (when they were first numbered) and 1971, Presidents have issued some 11,615 executive orders.[11]

SHAPER OF PUBLIC OPINION

As Chief Executive of the United States the President is the center of much attention. Almost everything the President does or says is reported, conveyed to millions of citizens, and widely discussed.[12] It is almost impossible to escape from mass media accounts of presidential activity. Moreover, in their early school days most citizens learned respect for the office of the presidency and automatically look to the President for leadership and reassurance. Especially in times of crisis or uncertainty, we expect the Chief Executive to lead the way. Even in normal times presidential pronouncements are considered more authoritative than statements of ordinary politicians.

Methods of influencing public opinion

As a result of this visibility, and the respect that citizens have for the office, the President exerts a strong influence on public opinion. More than newspaper editors, television commentators, or even college professors, Presidents can shape public thinking. The President's capacity to put a topic on the public agenda has much to do with this. For example, poverty has always existed in the United States, but it was never as prominently discussed as when Lyndon B. Johnson focused presidential attention on the subject in 1964. President Carter has likewise used his leadership position to heighten the public's awareness of world-wide human rights. For years the black civil rights movement depended on sympathetic Presidents to remind the public that racial discrimination, poor housing, and the like, were pressing national problems.

Presidents also influence public opinion by formulating the terms of public debate. The ability to define the policy choices is sometimes as important as the actual choice. This was strikingly illustrated by President Johnson's handling of the debate over U.S. involvement in Vietnam. The war between North and South Vietnam, prior to extensive U.S. intervention in 1965, could have been characterized as purely a civil war or as an ethnic-religious dispute. Evidence exists for both characterizations. Once the United States became heavily committed militarily, however, President Johnson successfully defined the war as one between the free world led by the United States and world communism. Opponents of U.S.

---

[11] Fisher, *Presidents and Congress*, pp. 50–52.

[12] An excellent description of how Presidents communicate to the general public is presented in Elmer E. Cornwell, Jr., *Presidential Leadership of Public Opinion* (Bloomington: Indiana University Press, 1965). The importance of effective communication to the public is perhaps underlined by President Ford's hiring of Bob Orben, a $40,000 a year joke writer who once worked for Jack Paar and Red Skelton.

involvement were thus burdened with the implied stigma of being Communist sympathizers. Counterclaims that the war did not represent the United States versus the Communists made little headway against Johnson's definition of the debate.

A third form of presidential influence over public opinion involves the President's capacity to change people's opinions. Most people not only look to the President for leadership but also believe that the President is highly competent to make the right decision. After all, the President has access to all kinds of information, can employ numerous expert advisers, and is aware of all the complexities of issues. Under such circumstances it is tempting to accept the President's position as one's own.

The President's impact on public opinion

How successful is the President in affecting the opinion of ordinary citizens? Table 12.1 indicates public opinion on nine issues *before* and *after* presidential action. In each case more people agreed with the President after he had taken a public stand than before the public stand was announced. For example, before President Nixon's May 1969 announce-

TABLE 12.1

THE IMPACT OF PRESIDENTIAL ACTIONS ON PUBLIC OPINION

Date	Presidential action	Poll results	
July 26, 1963	Kennedy announces nuclear test ban treaty	Before:	73 percent favored
		After:	81 percent favored
August 18, 1963	Kennedy appeals for tax cut from Congress	Before:	62 percent favored
		After:	66 percent favored
May 2, 1965	Johnson tells of Gulf of Tonkin incident and explains his Vietnam policy	Before:	42 percent positive on LBJ Vietnam policy
		After:	72 percent positive on LBJ Vietnam policy
January 31, 1966	Johnson announces resumption of bombing of Vietnam	Before:	61 percent favored
		After:	73 percent favored
March, 1968	Johnson announces end to bombing of Vietnam	Before:	40 percent favored
		After:	64 percent favored
June 7, 1968	Johnson endorses stronger gun-control legislation	Before:	71 percent favored
		After:	81 percent favored
May 14, 1969	Nixon announces phased troop withdrawals from Vietnam	Before:	49 percent favored
		After:	67 percent favored
April 30, 1970	Nixon announces invasion of Cambodia	Before:	7 percent favored
		After:	50 percent favored
June, 1971	Nixon announces 90-day price and wage freeze	Before:	50 percent approved
		After:	68 percent approved

Source: "Public Service Time for the Legislative Branch," Hearings Before the Communications Subcommittee of the Committee on Commerce, 91st Congress, second session, pp. 20–21. June 1971 data are reported in *Gallup Opinion Index,* August 1971.

ment of phased withdrawal of troops from Vietnam, 49 percent of those polled favored this policy. After the announcement 67 percent favored troop withdrawal. Note also the dramatic turnabout in public support for the 1970 U.S. invasion of Cambodia—only 7 percent favored invasion before Nixon's action, compared to 50 percent afterward.

Although the President's impact is strong, we should not jump to the conclusion that public opinion is clay in the hands of the President. The Chief Executive usually has the greatest influence on issues that are completely new or have little direct bearing on people's everyday lives— for example, the invasion of Cambodia. When citizens hold strong opinions on issues, say forced busing of children to achieve racial integration, the President's impact is much smaller. Recent polls suggest, for example, that President Carter's efforts to convince the public of an energy crisis have been unsuccessful. Recall that as the facts of the Watergate scandal emerged, President Nixon had little success in convincing the public of his innocence.

The figures in Table 12.1 also raise an interesting and important problem with regard to the manipulation of public opinion. On the one hand, we expect the President to inform the public. We want Presidents to hold press conferences, give public speeches, and be candid about their actions. Yet this very openness can shape—intentionally or unintentionally—public opinion. Not surprisingly, then, Presidents have frequently been accused of manipulating public opinion for their own advantage. During the 1930s, for example, Roosevelt's opponents claimed that the President's "fireside chats" over the radio were not neutral descriptions of public policy but attempts to undermine Republican opposition. During the Vietnam war President Johnson's dramatic, well-publicized television pronouncements during prime time viewing hours were sometimes criticized as blatant attempts to increase his popular standing. Obviously, it is difficult for Presidents to strike a balance between their obligation to keep the public informed and their inclination to use the presidency as a platform from which to manipulate public opinion.

What limits presidential power?

We have seen that contemporary Presidents can exercise enormous political power. Indeed, use of presidential power is likely to increase as the federal government gets larger and world crises necessitate even more rapid executive action. The actions of President Nixon and his aides in connection with the Watergate scandal dramatically called our attention to the issue of whether Presidents have become too powerful. The fact that Nixon was able to secretly bomb Cambodia, employ illegal wiretaps in the name of national defense, use the Internal Revenue Service to harass political enemies, and engage in other questionable acts illustrate the difficulty of checking abuses of presidential power. Has the Chief Ex-

The President is a major force in Congress, yet our constitutional system requires that the President persuade, not command, in dealing with Congress. Here President Ronald Reagan wines and dines three top Republican Senators.

ecutive become too powerful for a democratic society? Do we now have an elected king?[13]

One basic answer to this question is that while Presidents can act with considerable freedom, important constraining forces exist. These constraints cannot stop every abuse of office, but they probably prevent a widespread and unchecked pattern of abuse. Three factors are particularly crucial: (1) the countervailing power of Congress and the courts; (2) the role of the presidential staff and the executive bureaucracies; and (3) public opinion.

THE POWER OF CONGRESS AND THE COURTS

As our analysis of congressional power showed, the constitutional system allows each branch of government some power over the others. Recall that the Senate must confirm many presidential appointments.

[13] When the Constitution was ratified it was widely believed that the President would eventually come to behave like a monarch. Edmund Randolph of Virginia believed that a single Chief Executive would be "the foetus of monarchy." To Patrick Henry the presidency was a "squint towards monarchy." Thomas Jefferson argued that once elected, a President would serve for life. Even after Washington became Chief Executive, the presidency was viewed as a type of kingship. This came out immediately following Washington's inauguration when a decision had to be made on how to address the President. Vice President John Adams suggested "His Most Benign Highness." A Senate committee opted for "High Highness, the President of the United States of America and Protector of the Rights of the Same." After much debate, agreement was reached on "President of the United States."

HOW A PRESIDENT BECOMES A KING (IN HIS OWN MIND)

George E. Reedy, one-time press secretary to President Johnson, has argued that the nature of the presidency can easily transform an ordinary person into a regal leader convinced of his own infallibility. Just being President can encourage a person to magnify his own importance and power. The process begins with the electoral victory, which is interpreted as a special calling and a public affirmation of one's virtues. Such thinking is reinforced by the way the individual finds himself treated as President of the United States. Every facility and comfort is made available to the Chief Executive. Jets, yachts, limousines, plush weekend retreats, special guards, elaborate dinners, all attest to the President's importance. Even old friends treat the President like a royal personage. Everyone waits until the President speaks. Chief Executives are addressed as "Mr. President," people hang on their every word, and few people risk disagreeing with them. Since their jobs depend on keeping the President happy, staff members indulge the Chief Executive's every whim. Strange requests are honored so frequently that after a while they no longer seem strange. Effective staff members can shield the President from bad news and insulate him against disturbances such as demonstrations or angry members of Congress.

Unless Presidents make a special effort, according to Reedy, they can soon lose touch with reality. Proposals that would be rejected as unintelligent in a basic political science course are accepted as gospel when uttered by the President to his loyal staff. Disagreement with the President is easily interpreted as disloyalty, and a "disloyal" staffer can lose all influence or be banished. Surrounded by official grandeur and people who cater to their every wish, Presidents may gradually fail to understand why a reasonable person disagrees with them or opposes their programs.

For a further analysis of how the presidency can corrupt the President, see George E. Reedy, *The Twilight of the Presidency* (New York: World Publishing Company, 1970), especially Chaps. 1, 6, and 12.

The vast majority of these appointments are confirmed, but on occasion one is rejected, and the President has no recourse. We have seen that President Nixon's efforts to appoint two southern conservatives—Clement F. Haynsworth, Jr., and G. Harrold Carswell—to the Supreme Court were unsuccessful despite great presidential pressure on many Senators. From time to time Congress has used its confirmation power to paralyze the executive branch. During the last year of President John Tyler's Administration, for instance, the Senate rejected nominations for four cabinet members, four Supreme Court Justices, two ambassadors, and fifty-nine lesser officials.[14] Often the mere possibility of Senate rejection is enough to stop the President. Supposedly, when Spiro Agnew resigned as Vice President, Nixon wanted to appoint ex-governor of Texas John Connally to replace him. Nixon was convinced however, that Connally would never get Senate approval, so instead he nominated Gerald R. Ford.[15]

Congress can also limit presidential power by refusing to consider or pass legislative proposals originating in the executive branch. To appreciate the power of Congress, consider Lyndon B. Johnson's legislative success rate in 1965. Johnson had won a landslide victory, he had overwhelming Democratic majorities in both houses, and he was a past master at congressional bargaining — yet 31 percent of his legislative proposals never became law. Other Presidents, especially when Congress was dominated by the opposing party, have done much worse. Following his landslide victory over McGovern in 1972, the Republican Nixon made 183 requests of the Democratic Congress and had 57 (31 percent) approved.[16]

A third way Congress can check presidential power is to pass specific legislation regulating presidential action. In the wake of the Vietnam war, when Presidents frequently acted without congressional authorization, several laws were enacted to reduce the chances of future Vietnams. In 1973, Congress passed the War Powers Resolution, which requires the President to explain to Congress within 48 hours why U.S. troops have been sent abroad, limits the time troops can remain abroad to 60 days unless Congress again gives its approval, and allows Congress to withdraw these troops after 60 or 90 days (depending on circumstances), regardless of presidential action.[17] In the 1976 Arms Export

[14] H. G. Gallagher, "The President, Congress, and Legislation," in Thomas E. Cronin and Rexford G. Tugwell, eds., *The Presidency Reappraised*, 2d ed. (New York: Praeger, 1977), p. 273.

[15] Richard Reeves, *A Ford Not a Lincoln* (New York: Harcourt Brace Jovanovich, 1975), p. 39.

[16] These data are reported in Congressional Quarterly, *Nixon: The Third Year of His Presidency* (Washington, D.C.: Congressional Quarterly, 1972), p. 52; and *Congressional Quarterly Weekly Report*, January 19, 1974, pp. 99–106. We must emphasize, however, that the outcomes of President-Congress conflicts can be complex. This is well illustrated in the story of Theodore Roosevelt's battle with Congress in 1907 about sending the U.S. fleet (known as the Great White Fleet) around the world. Congress refused to appropriate the necessary money. Roosevelt did, however, have enough money to send the fleet *halfway* around the world, which he did. Congress was then faced with the choice of leaving the U.S. Navy stranded somewhere in Asia or appropriating the extra money. Congress gave in, and the Great White Fleet was able to come back home.

[17] The War Powers Resolution of 1973 is described in greater detail in *Congressional Quarterly's Guide to Congress*, 2d ed. (Washington, D.C.: Congressional Quarterly, 1976), pp. 279–283.

Control Act Congress gave itself the right to veto a President's decision to sell more than $7 million worth of arms to foreign governments. Similarly, the 1976 International Security Assistance Act states that no military or paramilitary aid may be given to Angola unless Congress specifically authorizes such assistance by law.

The congressional power to expose through investigation is a fourth legislative check on executive power. During the 1960s, when President Johnson gradually escalated U.S. involvement in Vietnam, the Senate Foreign Relations Committee, chaired by J. William Fulbright, provided a visible forum for opponents of presidential actions. Though foreign relations are usually considered the domain of the President, seventeen House and fourteen Senate committees have some jurisdiction over foreign policy. During the Watergate scandal it was congressional investigations of President Nixon's involvement with the Watergate break-in and other abuses of power that eventually brought about his resignation.

The final legislative restraint on presidential power is impeachment. The Constitution states that the House by a majority vote can bring about impeachment and that the Senate by a two-thirds vote can convict and thus remove a President from office. Only one President—Andrew Johnson—has ever been impeached, but the Senate fell one vote short of convicting him. President Nixon would probably have been the second President impeached (and probably the first convicted) had he not resigned in August 1974 just prior to the House vote. Obviously, the threat of impeachment is irrelevant to everyday President-Congress interaction, but like the death penalty for murder, it does not have to be frequently employed to be an effective deterrent.

Court limitations on presidential power

Compared to Congress, the courts have been far more willing to give the President free reign. Especially when the President acts in the capacity of commander-in-chief or chief of state or exercises administrative discretion over the executive bureaucracy, the courts have usually upheld presidential action. The judicial branch has even generously interpreted the President's power to issue executive orders and proclamations. On the whole, the burden of proof has been on those challenging presidential authority, not on the President.[18]

Nevertheless, in key situations the courts have decisively blocked presidential action. One important case involved President Truman's 1952 seizure of the steel mills in order to head off a strike. Truman argued that since we were at war in Korea he could, as commander-in-chief, act to prevent a national emergency. In its landmark decision, *Youngstown Sheet and Tube Co.* v. *Sawyer*, the Supreme Court ruled that since there was no official declaration of war and since Congress had not specifically legislated such action, the President had overstepped his authority. The Court admitted that Truman may have had a good

[18] Glendon A. Schubert, *The Presidency in the Courts* (Minneapolis: University of Minnesota Press, 1957), especially pp. 347–354.

Executive privilege The right of the President, or those designated by the President, to refuse to provide information to, or appear before, a legislative committee or court. Derives from the principle of separation of powers and from custom.

practical reason for seizing the mills, but protection against tyrannical power overshadows the needs of the moment.

A more recent and highly dramatic President-Court confrontation occurred over President Nixon's claim of **executive privilege** in refusing to release various White House tape recordings and documents in connection with the Watergate affair. When congressional committees, the Watergate special prosecutor, and judges in several Watergate-related cases requested this material as evidence, Nixon refused. The President claimed that records of his confidential conversations were protected by the principle of executive privilege. To allow other branches of government access to this material, Nixon claimed, would effectively destroy the separation of powers and weaken the presidency. He argued that the principle of executive privilege was well established by the actions of numerous other Presidents. However, the Supreme Court in *United States* v. *Nixon* (1974) ruled otherwise and ordered the tapes and documents released. The Court stated:

> Neither the doctrine of separation of powers, nor the need for confidentiality of high level communications, without more, can sustain an absolute, unqualified, presidential privilege of immunity from judicial process under all circumstances.

The release of these tape recordings made Nixon's resignation almost inevitable. The Court acknowledged, however, that the principle of executive privilege has a constitutional basis. Especially when military, diplomatic, or sensitive national security issues are involved, complete confidentiality is protected. When no such issue is involved, presidential records may be requested in criminal cases.

THE ROLE OF THE PRESIDENTIAL STAFF AND EXECUTIVE BUREAUCRACIES

No matter how energetic or conscientious a President is, he must still exercise power with the help of others (see Figure 12.1). Over the years the presidential staff and the staffs of the executive bureaus (for example, the Department of Defense) have grown considerably. This staff ranges from close personal advisers (for example, President Carter's Hamilton Jordan) to institutionalized bureaucracies within the White House (for example, the Council of Economic Advisers). Some Presidents, such as Eisenhower and Nixon, have organized their staffs along tight lines of authority where each person has specific responsibilities. Others, such as Franklin D. Roosevelt and John F. Kennedy, allowed looser lines of authority and responsibility.

Presidents need extensive staffs if they are to deal effectively with the business of government. No individual can sort through tons of daily information, see thousands of people, manage a complex legislative program, prepare multibillion dollar budget estimates, and devise solutions to pressing national problems. Presidential staff members such as Sherman Adams (Eisenhower), Ted Sorensen (Kennedy), Bill Moyers (Johnson), and H. R. Haldeman (Nixon) are extensions of the President and thus can multiply the Chief Executive's power. Without all the special

OF MICE AND PRESIDENTS

The problem of managing the bureaucracy one time surfaced as President Carter's battle against White House mice. When two mice scampered across Carter's office, the General Services Administration (GSA), the federal building housekeeping agency, was ordered into action. Its efforts were less than 100 percent effective, however, since one mouse had got into a White House wall, died, and filled the Oval Office with a terrible stench. The GSA was again called to the rescue. It now claimed that since it had previously disposed of all mice within the White House, the new dead mouse must be an "outside" mouse, and thus the responsibility of the Interior Department, which maintains White House grounds. The interagency deadlock was finally broken when Carter called officials of both agencies to his office to smell the dead mouse.

Perhaps the real reason for the deadlock was not a bureaucratic jurisdictional dispute but had to do with getting a better mousetrap. At about the same time that Carter was trying to get rid of White House mice, the federal government had drawn up specifications on how to build a mousetrap. The specs ran to 20,000 words on 700 pages and weighed 3.3 pounds. With the usual delays in building government projects, cost overruns, and so on, the lack of quick action was understandable.

aides, advisory councils, and the like, a President would be overwhelmed.

How staff members limit presidential power

At the same time the presidential staff and the heads of executive agencies can greatly inhibit the exercise of presidential power. As many a President realizes upon becoming Chief Executive, it is one thing to order something and quite another to have it done. President Truman put it nicely when he described what would happen to Eisenhower when he took office: "He will sit here and he'll say, 'Do this! Do that!' *And nothing will happen.* Poor Ike—it won't be a bit like the Army! He'll find it very frustrating."[19] How can people legally obligated to follow presidential directives frustrate presidential power? Can't the President fire people who refuse to carry out orders? Wouldn't such insubordination outrage people?

[19] Quoted in Richard E. Neustadt, *Presidential Power* (New York: New American Library, 1964), p. 22.

PRESIDENT RONALD REAGAN AND CABINET GOVERNMENT

Since Dwight Eisenhower Presidents have not made extensive use of cabinet officials. Some Presidents, such as Lyndon Johnson, involved themselves directly in the activities of cabinet-level departments. Richard Nixon relied heavily on close appointed aides and bypassed cabinet officials. President Ronald Reagan, however, is strongly committed to cabinet government. Under such a government the President would set broad policy goals, and it would be up to cabinet officials, in close consultation with the President, to implement these general objectives. Here are brief profiles of some of the key people in the Reagan cabinet.

RICHARD S SCHWEIKER Secretary of Health and Human Services. Born June 1, 1926, in Norristown, Pennsylvania. Served in the Navy during World War II, graduated from Penn State, and then for ten years worked in his family's ceramic tile business. Elected to the House in 1960; elected to the Senate in 1968 where he gained a reputation as one of the most liberal Republican Senators. (He was one of the few prominent Republicans who spoke out against U.S. involvement in Vietnam.) Long interested in health care legislation, Schweiker sponsored bills to combat cancer, diabetes, black lung disease, sickle cell anemia, and lead paint poisoning. In his unsuccessful 1976 bid for the Republican presidential nomination, Reagan announced Schweiker to be his choice as Vice President well before the nominating convention. Soon afterward Schweiker became much more conservative in his voting, although he attributes this change to a gradual evolution becoming more visible. He is generally regarded as well briefed on health care matters and is strongly committed to improving the nation's health programs, especially those involving the private sector. According to one staff aide, Schweiker has a knack for sensing a coming trend and getting out front early.

ANDREW L. LEWIS, JR. Secretary of Transportation. Born November 3, 1931, in Philadelphia. Graduated from Haverford College and Harvard Business School. Has worked for a number of large corporations, frequently as a "Mr. Fixit" charged with restoring troubled firms to financial health. Most recently was a consultant to a number of banks and investment groups. Lewis has been long active in Republican politics in Pennsylvania (he lost a bid for the governorship in 1974). Ran several campaigns for his neighbor and close friend Richard S. Schweiker. Ran Gerald Ford's 1976 campaign and served as deputy chairman of the national Reagan-Bush committee. Though considered outspoken and opinionated, he is nevertheless regarded as a savvy politician good at mending fences.

WILLIAM FRENCH SMITH (*left*), Attorney General. Born August 26, 1917, in Wilton, New Hampshire, grew up in Boston, but has lived his entire adult life in Los Angeles working for a prestigious law firm. Graduated from the University of California at Berkeley and Harvard Law School. Until his appointment as Attorney General had direct political experience other than his service on the California Board of Regents, which supervises higher education in the state (he was appointed by Governor Reagan). Besides being a highly regarded, well-paid labor lawyer, he has served on several corporate boards and has been active in civic affairs (he is also the former director of an organization that provided legal assistance to poor people in Los Angeles). For the past fifteen years Smith has served as Ronald Reagan's personal attorney and close friend and adviser. Smith played an influential role in getting Reagan into politics and helped raise money for his campaigns. His personal appearance gives one the impression of the quintessential lawyer—impeccably dressed, with white hair and courtly manners. He is frequently described as a tough conservative, but one who is willing to listen and be flexible. Smith characterizes himself as a true liberal—one who would keep the exercise of power at the lowest possible level. He believes that government should interfere as little as possible in such matters as civil rights, civil liberties, and regulating businesses.

CASPAR W. WEINBERGER (*right*), Secretary of Defense. Born August 18,1917, in San Francisco, California. Graduated from Harvard and Harvard Law School. Military experience began in 1941 as a buck private ditch digger; finished the war as a captain on General Douglas MacArthur's staff. Elected to the California state assembly in 1952 as a Republican but supported liberal programs. Unsuccessful in his bid for higher office in California, but continued to work in California government (he also wrote newspaper columns and hosted a TV talk show). Served as Governor Reagan's finance director in 1968. Came to Washington, D.C., in 1969 as chairman of the Federal Trade Commission, moved over to the Office of Management and Budget, and then became Secretary of Health, Education and Welfare. Built a strong reputation as a dedicated budget cutter while at OMB and became known as "Cap the Knife." Nevertheless, he has consistently advocated large military expenditures. Universally regarded as a first-rate lawyer and a highly intelligent man who can quickly get to the heart of complex issues. Weinberger is also widely admired for his personal warmth and humility. Much of his power comes from his long-standing close friendship with Ronald Reagan, and he also serves the President as a more general adviser.

FIGURE 12.1

**THE EXECUTIVE OFFICE
OF THE PRESIDENT**

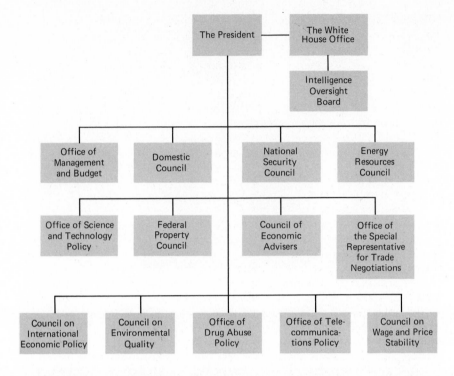

Presidential directives or preferences sometimes come to nothing because they are simply ignored by advisers or cabinet officials. Presidents make hundreds of decisions, and it is impossible for them to make sure that every command is implemented. In many instances they do not even know if an order is followed or ignored, so disobedience may pose little risk. An aide to President Roosevelt described the situation this way:

> Half of a president's suggestions, which theoretically carry the weight of orders, can be safely forgotten by a cabinet member. And if the president asks about a suggestion a second time, he can be told that it is being investigated. If he asks a third time, a wise cabinet officer will give him at least part of what he suggests. But only occasionally, except about the most important matters, do presidents ever get around to asking three times.[20]

A more recent illustration of "subordinates" operating contrary to explicit presidential orders occurred shortly after Gerald Ford became President. Casper Weinberger, the Secretary of Health, Education and Welfare originally appointed by Nixon, had proposed certain changes in welfare regulations. President Ford objected to these changes and told Weinberger to come back with an alternative. In two months Ford had forgotten the incident, but Weinberger had gone ahead and implemented the changes despite explicit presidential orders to the contrary.[21]

[20] Quoted in Neustadt, p. 49.
[21] Reeves, p. 127.

Presidential power can also be reduced by staff actions when lesser officials begin to make important decisions in the President's name. No President can literally make every decision that must be made in the executive branch. To free themselves for important questions, Presidents will delegate authority. Sometimes so much authority is delegated, or close advisers become so power hungry, that it can be difficult to determine who is really in charge. Sherman Adams, Eisenhower's chief of staff, frequently decided major policy questions so as not to "bother" the President. During Nixon's last months in office, when he spent much of his time dealing with Watergate, many people believed that his chief of staff—Alexander Haig—was actually acting as President on many day-to-day matters. In fact, when Ford succeeded Nixon, he found it difficult to break the hold Haig maintained on White House decision making.[22]

We must also realize that in many situations a presidential directive is not a military order but an attempt to persuade a subordinate. One leading expert on presidential power has, in fact, described presidential power as the *power to persuade,* since presidential orders are rarely self-activating.[23] A White House aide to President Kennedy put it this way: "Everyone believes in democracy until he gets to the White House and then you begin to believe in dictatorship. Every time you turn around, people just resist you, and even resist their own jobs."[24] The need to persuade is especially relevant when the official ordered to do something is deeply opposed to the order and is well regarded by Congress or the bureaucracy. Under such circumstances Presidents must make sure that they get more than just lip service to their requests, since the threat of removing such advisers for insubordination is not very credible. This problem is well illustrated by the relationship of both Presidents Nixon and Ford to Secretary of State Henry Kissinger. Because of his diplomatic triumphs, Kissinger's standing was so high that it was nearly impossible for either President to order him to pursue policies he opposed (and firing him would have resulted in public outrage). Members of the executive branch, for example, former FBI Director J. Edgar Hoover, can become so well established that Presidents must almost plead for their help, though technically the President can remove them from office at any time.

Finally, presidential directives may come to nothing because they must pass through so many bureaucratic hands. Each special adviser, cabinet member, undersecretary, assistant secretary, and so on, has an opportunity to "interpret" the directive. The end result can be frustrating. As one-time Eisenhower aide Emmet J. Hughes put it: "The sheer size and intricacy of government conspire to taunt and to thwart all brisk pretentions to set sensationally new directions. The vast machinery of national leadership—the tens of thousands of levers and switches and gears—simply do not respond to the impatient jab of a finger or the angry

---

[22] Reeves, pp. 124–125.

[23] Neustadt, p. 23.

[24] Cited in Thomas E. Cronin, "Everyone Believes in a Democracy Until He Gets to the White House . . .: An Examination of White House-Departmental Relationships," *Law and Contemporary Problems,* 35 (1970), p. 575.

THE PRESIDENTIAL MULTIPLE-CHOICE EXAM

One very important way the presidential staff influences presidential decisions is by organizing the information given the President. A skillful aide, who desires a particular decision, can subtly bias the information to make the staff member's own position look more attractive. Perhaps the only way to guard against this is to have different aides provide their assessments independently. Not only is this time consuming, but such overlapping of administrative responsibilities can create confusion and conflict.

Below is one example of how a key decision is organized by the presidential staff. This particular memo is one of *fifteen* such memos given to President Ford on August 14, 1974, and deals with the future of a controversial agency initiated under Lyndon Johnson's Great Society program.

MEMORANDUM FOR THE PRESIDENT

FROM: KEN COLE

SUBJECT: OEO COMMUNITY ACTION PROGRAM

Background:

The Nixon Administration, from 1969 on, considered direct Federal support of the Community Action Program inappropriate. They first considered folding this program into Urban Community Development Revenue Sharing, but that option was subsequently dropped. The budgets for 1974 and 1975 then proposed termination of OEO and Community Action.

Key Facts:

The Congress is considering bills which would either continue Community Action in a new, separate agency, or transfer it to HEW. (A transfer bill has passed the House 331-53.) State and local officials across the political spectrum strongly support Community Action as a Federal program. The Community Action appropriations authorization expired June 30, 1974, and the program currently operates under a Continuing Resolution. The basic authorization for the program itself expires June 30, 1975.

Current Position:

The Administration has proposed a bill to discontinue the program and authorize HEW to oversee the orderly phase-out of Community Action activities in 1975.

Options:

1. Support the House bill which would eliminate OEO and transfer Community Action to HEW.

Pro— This would recognize the strong House sentiment for Community Action.

Con— Would probably rule out future chance of phasing out Community Action.

2. Support the House bill when an amendment providing Executive reorganization authority to break up Community Action within HEW at the end of 12 months.

Pro— Would give you an opportunity to reassess the situation after one year.

Con— It could be both difficult and unwise to move this program twice in such a short period of time.

3. Support Gaylor Nelson's proposal for a 12-month extension of OEO with reorganization authority to at the end of the year.

Pro— Would put the issue to rest for now and give us the opportunity for a better deal next year.

Con— Would continue a crippled OEO for 12 months with the possibility Community Action would end up in HEW after all.

4. Indicate support for Javits' proposal for an independent community action agency within the Executive branch.

Pro— Would be recognizing support for Community Action.

Con— Such an agency could be more difficult to phase out than an HEW program.

5. Maintain opposition to any legislation to continue Federal support of Community Action.

Pro— Would be consistent with philosophy that Community Action is more properly a State/local program and save the Federal Government over $300 million.

Con— Veto may not be sustained.

Staff Views:

Ash	Option 5—maintain our current position of opposition "I don't have $300 million."
Timmons	Option 5—maintain opposition.

Recommendation:

I recommend we maintain opposition—for time being—we can always switch later.

Decision:
Option 1. ____
Option 2. ____
Option 3. ____
Option 4. ____
Option 5. ____ (Recommended by Ash, Timmons, Cole)

As in almost every other case, Ford went along with the options recommended by his advisers.

Source: Richard Reeves, *A Ford, Not a Lincoln* (New York: Harcourt Brace Jovanovich, 1975), pp. 78–80.

pounding of a fist."[25] We shall have more to say about bureaucratic responsiveness in the next chapter.

In short, the bureaucratic apparatus that allows the President to operate effectively also constrains the "Chief Executive's actions. An adviser can actually veto presidential decisions, and the President might never know it. As one top aide to President Ford described part of his job: "My job is to protect the President from himself. I'm here to override him if that's necessary."[26]

PUBLIC OPINION

We have seen that the President can play a major role in shaping public opinion. Also recall from our analysis in Chapter Four that public opinion is frequently ignored by government decision makers. In light of these considerations, why should a President worry about adverse public reaction? Wouldn't a rational President say: "The public be damned, they can't decide what I can or cannot do." Yet public opinion is a factor limiting presidential action, though it is a less obvious one than a hostile Congress or an uncooperative bureaucrat.

Public expectations about presidential behavior

One important, though subtle, way public opinion constrains the President concerns the high expectations most citizens have regarding "proper" presidential conduct. The President is more than just the chief public official. A President is also the head of state and as such supposedly above day-to-day politics. We expect Presidents to act with fairness, behave in a dignified manner, uphold the traditional moral virtues such as a belief in God, and, in general, be worth emulating. Considerable effort is spent maintaining this image (for example, newspaper reporters do not report unpleasant personal habits of Presidents), and Presidents accept the obligation of being "statesmen," not politicians.[27]

By being on a public pedestal, the President cannot always do the things other less exalted leaders can do (or, at least, do them publicly). In some instances the President may find it convenient to let the Vice President engage in "unpresidential" activities. During President Nixon's first term, Vice President Agnew played the role of the President's "heavy," as he vehemently attacked opponents of Nixon's policies. The same speeches coming directly from the President would have been a cause of great concern, because we do not expect the head of state and symbol of national unity to call enemies an "effete corps of impudent snobs" or "unwashed hippies."

[25] Quoted in Thomas Cronin, *The State of the Presidency* (Boston: Little, Brown, 1975), p. 170.

[26] Reeves, p. 120.

[27] What should be reported about the personal lives of Presidents has become a thorny issue. Should a reporter write about a Chief Executive's extramarital love life? One interesting solution to the problem of protecting the President's image was found for Warren Harding. A favorite Harding activity was taking in the girlie show at Washington's Gayety Burlesque. To avoid embarrassment, a special box was built that concealed the President from public view.

The importance of these high public expectations became clear during public reaction to Nixon's Watergate-related tape conversations. Much of the public outcry was directed at the "unpresidential" behavior of Nixon—his use of profanity, racial and ethnic slurs, petty vindictiveness, and open contempt for other officials. These actions are not uncommon in politics, but citizens were upset that their *President* acted in such an uncouth manner. Even some of Nixon's admirers turned against the man who seemed to be bringing disrespect to the presidency. In short, the respect the President possesses is both a political advantage and an obligation that limits freedom.

The fear of electoral punishment

Public opinion also constrains the President much more directly—through the power of voters at the polls. A first-term President, in particular, must pay attention to opinion poll results as the reelection campaign nears. Controversial or unpopular proposals may thus be offered early, in the hope that voters will eventually forget them, or be held off until after the election when the consequences of presidential unpopularity will be less severe. To ignore public opinion until just prior to election day would be almost unthinkable. President Carter's frequent consultations with pollster Patrick Cadell attest to the importance Presidents place on keeping a constant watch on shifts in public thinking.

Public opinion is also important to second-term Presidents who do not have to worry about reelection. Certainly no President wants to go down in history as having been an object of widespread public disdain. Even a thick-skinned President will probably try to avoid sinking too low in opinion polls so as not to bring electoral disaster upon fellow party members in state and congressional races. During President Nixon's last months in office, when his popularity was at its ebb, some of the pressure for resignation came from fellow Republicans who argued that his unpopularity would mean widespread electoral retribution against all Republican candidates in the upcoming 1974 congressional elections. A second-term President also realizes that a low standing increases the chances that the opposing party will capture the White House—hardly an attractive possibility for most Presidents.

Public opinion and presidential prestige

Finally, high regard in public opinion polls not only makes a President feel good but can also enhance a Chief Executive's prestige. Since a President's power to persuade partially rests on his personal prestige at a given moment, the importance of this factor cannot be discounted. A highly popular, well-respected President will find it easier to convince others of the value of a program and the legitimacy of certain actions. Government officials find it difficult to resist a leader who enjoys overwhelming public confidence. Partly for this reason, many Presidents have their greatest legislative successes at the beginnings of their terms when their public popularity is at its highest.

On the other hand, when public opinion starts to run heavily against a President, as was the case in the last year of Johnson's Administration, presidential power can erode. Members of Congress can vote against the

President's program without fear of electoral punishment. Indeed, opposing the unpopular President may be good politics. Top aides and members of the White House staff may resign or disassociate themselves from the President's policies rather than be linked to an unpopular Chief Executive. Bargaining with foreign nations may become more difficult if

PRESIDENTIAL SUCCESSION

Since George Washington, eight Presidents have died in office, at least three others may have been unable to perform their duties due to health problems, and five others have been objects of unsuccessful assassination attempts. Thus the rules for presidential succession are important. Article II, section 1 of the Constitution provides that in case of presidential death, resignation, or other inability to discharge the duties of office, the Vice President shall assume the President's duties. The Constitution states that Congress may provide for succession beyond the Vice President, but no "next-in-line" sequence is specifically mentioned.

The question of who becomes President if both the President and Vice President die or cannot serve has been resolved four different ways in U.S. history. Legislation passed in 1792 called for the presidency to devolve on the president pro tempore of the Senate and then the speaker of the House. After the speaker, the electoral college would reassemble and choose a President for a full four-year term. This act was never used. In 1886, new legislation provided that the presidency would go to cabinet officers beginning with the Secretary of State. In 1947, the line of succession was changed again— speaker of the House, president pro tempore of the Senate, followed by cabinet officers beginning with the most senior department (State, Treasury, and Defense, in that order are the three most senior). Present rules of succession after the Vice President are spelled out in the Twenty-fifth Amendment (ratified in 1967). This amendment solves the matter of succession by providing that there will always be a Vice President. When a vacancy in the vice presidency occurs, the President nominates a Vice President who takes office following confirmation by a majority vote of both houses of Congress. When Spiro Agnew resigned as Vice President in 1973, President Nixon used this procedure to make Gerald Ford Vice President. When Nixon resigned and Ford became President, the procedure was again employed to make Nelson A. Rockefeller Vice President.

foreign leaders assume that the President, because of a low standing, cannot deliver on promises or get the public to accept an agreement. Clearly, then, what the public thinks about presidential performance matters, though there may be no one-to-one relationship between what the public wants and what the President does.

The problem of deciding precisely who is President under what circumstances is exemplified by the possible presidency of David Rice Atchison. March 3, 1849, was the last day in office of President James K. Polk. His successor, General Zachary Taylor, was supposed to take office the next day, which was Sunday. However, for religious reasons Taylor refused to be sworn in on a Sunday and insisted that the ceremony be delayed until Monday. Hence, for all of Sunday, March 4, 1849, there was no President. Under the law, the president pro tempore of the Senate, who was David Rice Atchison, automatically became President. Neither Atchison himself, nor legal historians, could be certain whether Atchison is really our twelfth president or not.

David R. Atchison, President of the United States for March 4, 1849.

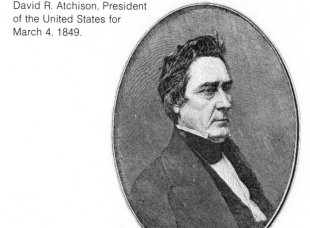

The Atchison story appears in David Wallechinsky and Irving Wallace, *The People's Almanac #2* (New York: Bantam Books, 1978), pp. 178–180.

A conclusion: does the President have too much or too little power?

Over the years a running debate has gone on over presidential power. When Franklin Roosevelt took vigorous actions in dealing with the Great Depression, many people claimed that the presidency was showing signs of becoming a monarchy. A few years later, when the less active Dwight D. Eisenhower was President, experts on the presidency spoke about ways to make Presidents more effective and stronger national leaders. President Nixon's actions, such as the secret, unauthorized bombings of Cambodia and illegal break-ins, again reawakened interest in the question of presidential power.

Obviously, there is no simple answer. Nor is it likely that people will ever be able to agree on such a complex, controversial issue. Though we cannot resolve the matter, we can at least lay out some of the basic reasoning underlying the two different points of view. Essentially, people disagreeing on whether the presidency should be made stronger or weaker usually differ in their opinions of what political risks are worth taking and the likely benefits of making changes. Let us first consider the case for greater constraints on executive power.

People who are fearful of executive power and desirous of additional constraints usually argue that the possible abuses of presidential power are not worth the alleged benefits of having strong Chief Executives. These critics typically make the following points:

1. Our basic constitutional order is not designed to have an all-powerful leader responsible for comprehensively dealing with every national problem. To allow Presidents greater and greater power for this purpose is to undermine a form of government that has been successful in preventing tyranny.
2. Even if we did grant Presidents more increased powers, why should their actions be more intelligent or more effective than, say, actions initiated by Congress or state governments? Presidents, like everyone else, can make mistakes. Moreover, why put such a great political burden on a single person?
3. Even if the President did come up with better programs to solve national ills, there is still no guarantee that the programs would be implemented effectively. Problems of bureaucratic foul-ups, insubordination, staff incompetence, and the like, are probably incurable. Legal grants of more power would not solve these problems.
4. Therefore, we would only increase the risk of abuses of office while not appreciably improving the national welfare. A more powerful President could get away with more excesses, such as illegal wiretapping of political opponents or irresponsible foreign adventures, but we would be no closer to solving such enduring problems as inflation, world conflicts, energy shortages, racial tensions, and pollution. Greater concentration of power is not an automatic solution to anything, and it invariably brings grave risks.

Yet many people see a strong President as a necessary response to the numerous (and growing) problems of the contemporary world. In response to the above arguments, they claim:

1. The likelihood that a stronger, more vigorous President would try to run the country by personal whim is grossly exaggerated. Certainly an occasional abuse of power will occur—as in the past—but given our political tradition, the institution of free elections, and the countervailing power of the other branches of government, widespread and persistent patterns of abuses are unlikely. The real lesson of Watergate is *not* that Presidents can overstep their limits but rather that such abuses are uncovered and corrected.

2. The core issue underlying whether presidential power should be expanded or reduced concerns policies, not the corrupting influences of greater power. Specifically, vigorous uses of presidential power have traditionally (though not exclusively) been associated with promoting *liberal* causes. For example, Franklin D. Roosevelt used his power on behalf of programs like social security and prounion legislation. President Lyndon Johnson took full advantage of presidential prerogatives on behalf of civil rights and antipoverty programs. This tendency is understandable, because the President, more than any other political official, must represent all the people, not just well-organized interests.

3. To constrain the President further is to constrain the one individual most capable of helping the ordinary citizens, who cannot influence congressional committees, hire public relations experts, or employ expensive lawyers to argue their cases. The President, more than anyone else, can be the defender of underrepresented groups such as young people, the poor, and minority groups.

4. The real choice, therefore, is not between possible excesses of power and no excesses of power but between a government responsive to the needs of ordinary citizens and a government incapable of redressing social and economic inequities. Conservatives fear a stronger executive because of the liberal policies that would be enacted. The fear of tyrannical power is merely a convenient and respectable way of opposing these policies.

Both positions have considerable merit. One's own position in this debate should probably depend on one's satisfaction with the current balance of political power. If one is doing well under the existing system, why take a chance by giving more power to the Chief Executive? Who needs a powerful, energetic leader to correct the problems of society? The worry over abuses of power is, of course, less relevant to, say, poor blacks, who look to the government to solve their economic problems. The system of checks and balances and other inhibitors of decisive action only perpetuate a not very satisfying status quo.

Major questions raised

1. Who can become President of the United States? In principle, any native-born citizen 35 years or older. In practice, however, the pool of available Presidents is heavily biased toward male, white, Anglo-Saxon Prot-

estants with conventional life-styles. Individuals who cannot get party approval or withstand the rigors of campaigning are also excluded.

2. How much power does the President possess? On the basis of constitutional provisions and custom, the President has considerable power in the areas of controlling the military, exerting diplomatic leadership, initiating legislation, and shaping public opinion. Much of the actual power of Presidents, however, depends on how Chief Executives use their authority and the resistance they encounter on the part of other officials.

3. What limits presidential power? The major checks on presidential power are the other two branches of government, the roles of staffs and the bureaucracy in presidential decision making, and public opinion. Whether one believes that the President is too constrained and not given sufficient powers probably depends on what one values most—the absence of possible abuses of office or vigorous leadership to solve national problems.

QUESTIONS FOR FURTHER DISCUSSION

1. The President of the United States performs two jobs that are frequently separated in European nations. Like the Queen of England, the President is the head of state—he receives foreign dignitaries, presides over important ceremonies (for example, throwing out the first ball on opening day of the baseball season), and otherwise represents the United States. Like the British prime minister, the President is responsible for formulating political programs, supervising the administration of huge bureaucracies, and otherwise acting as a politician. It has been claimed that these two roles are too much for one person. Moreover, both would be better served if two different people, with different skills and personalities, were chosen for these jobs. Should the United States have a separate "head of state" who would be above daily politics and relieve some of the burden on the President? How about a distinguished citizen, elected for a single ten-year term, who is acceptable to Democrats, Republicans, and almost everyone else?

2. The public expects Presidents to lead, yet our constitutional system does not give the President much power to coerce a reluctant Congress. As a result, vigorous presidential leadership has frequently required the use of threats against unsupportive legislators. President Lyndon Johnson, for example, might "persuade" a member of Congress by threatening to close all military bases in that individual's district, reroute a new interstate highway away from the district, or otherwise use government programs to the legislator's disadvantage. Johnson was criticized for such actions, but he did manage to get many programs through Congress. President Carter, however, seems reluctant to use such techniques. As one Carter aide put it, "Nobody is afraid he's going to get smashed if he messes with the President." At the same time, Carter has been criticized for his lack of legislative effectiveness. If you were President, and the success of your legislative program depended on persuading a few members of Congress, how far would you go? Would you merely argue the merits of your program? wine and dine them at the White House? offer to modify your program slightly in return for their

votes? hint that there were many district benefits you could get for these legislators? let it be known indirectly that the Justice Department might look into their campaign finances?

3. Close aides of the President sometimes acknowledge that they disregard presidential directives when these directives are not what the President "really" wants or are issued in a fit of anger or while intoxicated. What is an aide's responsibility when the President starts to issue orders that *might* reflect a reduced capacity to think effectively? Should an aide protect the President during a period when the Chief Executive is overly tense or physically impaired? Or is an aide's responsibility to the people of the United States, not the President, so that the aide should alert others to the President's possible deficiency, even if it embarrasses or weakens the President?

4. Traditionally, the selection of the vice presidential nominee by the presidential nominee has been a last-minute, sometimes confused process. Given the growing importance of the vice presidency, should voters play a greater role in the selection process? Should there be primaries for the vice presidency? Should presidential candidates name their running mates before the party nominating conventions (as did Ronald Reagan in 1976)? Or should the matter be completely up to the presidential nominee?

BIBLIOGRAPHY

Barber, James David. *The Presidential Character: Predicting Performance in the White House*, 2d ed. Englewood Cliffs, N.J.: Prentice-Hall, 1977.
   Barber argues that a person's basic character will shape his actions and policies once he achieves the presidency. The two key components of character are level of activity and enjoyment of political life. Several presidencies are analyzed in terms of the basic character of the President. President Carter claims to have been greatly influenced by this book, and the second edition contains a brief analysis of Carter's early development and political career.

Cronin, Thomas E. *The State of the Presidency.* Boston: Little, Brown, 1975.
   A popular and well-written text covering virtually all the important features of the contemporary presidency. Topics treated include presidential power, limits on the presidency, the role of advisers and departmental heads, the Vice President, and numerous reforms of the presidency. Contains a bibliography.

Cronin, Thomas E., and Sanford Greenberg, eds. *The Presidential Advisory System.* New York: Harper & Row, 1969.
   Contains twenty-nine articles dealing with various aspects of advising Presidents. Articles cover different types of policy (for example, advice on economics and science), the use of outside experts, and what can be done to improve the quality of advice.

Cronin, Thomas E., and Rexford G. Tugwell, eds. *The Presidency Reappraised*, 2d ed. New York: Praeger, 1977.
   Contains seventeen articles dealing with various aspects of recent presidencies. Many of the articles deal with the issue of whether we now have an "imperial presidency" and how the presidency should be changed. Contains a bibliography.

Fisher, Louis. *President and Congress: Power and Policy.* New York: Free Press, 1972.
   A detailed and clearly stated review of presidential and congressional power and conflicts between the two branches. Examines both the legal basis of

presidential-legislative relationships and actual decisions in such fields as economic policy, national defense, and tariffs. Useful for placing current conflicts in historical perspective.

Fisher, Louis. *Presidential Spending Power.* Princeton, N.J.: Princeton University Press, 1975.
A detailed examination of a key presidential power from 1789 to President Nixon. An important book for understanding why funds appropriated by Congress are not also spent according to the desires of Congress.

Griffith, Ernest S. *The American Presidency: The Dilemmas of Shared Power and Divided Government.* New York: New York University Press, 1976.
An overview of the presidency and its place in the U.S. political system. Begins with the White House staff and moves on to the cabinet, policy making, Congress, the President and political parties, the President and the mass media, and the problems of the modern presidency.

Hargrove, Erwin. *Presidential Leadership: Personality and Political Style.* New York: Macmillan, 1966.
Examines the personalities and actions of six presidents—Theodore Roosevelt, Taft, Wilson, Hoover, and Eisenhower. Emphasizes how each President's personality and skills shaped the presidency.

Kessel, John H. *The Domestic Presidency: Decision-Making in the White House.* North Scituate, Mass.: Duxbury Press, 1975.
Based on interviews with members of President Nixon's Domestic Council, this book offers a systematic analysis of how one part of the executive office of the President operated. Covers recruitment of the Domestic Council staff, communications within the White House, and how the President uses agencies like the Domestic Council. Analysis occasionally gets technical.

Neustadt, Richard E. *Presidential Power.* New York: Wiley, 1960.
A classic analysis of presidential power that emphasizes the President's need to persuade, not command. Good analysis of conditions under which presidential directives are most likely to be followed. Most of the book considers decisions made before 1960, but arguments are still relevant.

Rather, Dan, and Gary Paul Gates. *The Palace Guard.* New York: Warner Books, 1975.
A well-written description of White House politics during President Nixon's first term. Provides an excellent picture of key aides such as H. R. Haldeman and John Ehrlichman, as well as an inside view of White House power plays and conflicts.

Reedy, George E. *The Twilight of the Presidency: An Examination of Power and Isolation in the White House.* New York: World Publishing, 1970.
A reporter and former press secretary to President Johnson, Reedy emphasizes the problems faced by a President trying to keep things in perspective. He argues that we could end up with a dangerous, mentally unbalanced President.

Reeves, Richard. *A Ford, Not a Lincoln.* New York: Harcourt Brace Jovanovich, 1975.
Reeves is a former chief political correspondent of the *New York Times.* He provides a penetrating analysis of both the Ford style and how the Ford White House operated. Excellent for understanding how personalities and day-to-day incidents affect the presidency. Contains several "insider" stories of Washington wheeling and dealing.

Rossiter, Clinton. *Constitutional Dictatorship: Crisis Government in the Modern Democracies.* New York: Harcourt, Brace and World, 1963.
Deals with the important question of how a democracy can survive when circumstances call for dictatorial leadership. Rossiter compares the U.S. experiences in the Civil War, World War I, and World War II with experiences of France, Great Britain, and Germany. Good insight into the full powers of the President in a national crisis.

Schlessinger, Arthur M. *The Imperial Presidency.* Boston: Houghton Mifflin, 1973.

Analyzes the growth of presidential power from the drafting of the Constitution to U.S. involvement in Vietnam. Particularly interested in the President's war powers. Also considers whether foreign policy making can be done democratically, the need for secrecy in decision making, and the future of the presidency.

Sorensen, Theodore C. *Decision-Making in the White House.* New York: Columbia University Press, 1963.

Sorensen was Special Counsel to President Kennedy and thus writes from experience. The complexities of decision making are illustrated with several specific examples. Particularly good at describing the limits of presidential decisions and the difficulties of advising the President.

Wildavsky, Aaron, ed. *The Presidency.* Boston: Little, Brown, 1969.

A large (48), diverse collection of articles on the presidency. Articles cover such topics as public expectations about the President, the nature of presidential power, presidential relations with the press, and the President and the courts.

PREVIEW

What is the federal bureaucracy?

The term "bureaucracy" refers to both a way of doing business and a large number of federal government organizations engaged in prescribed tasks. The bureaucratic approach is characterized by (1) a clear division of labor; (2) hierarchical authority patterns; (3) specified job qualifications; and (4) objective administration of rules. Bureaucratic organizations are primarily designed to accomplish goals rather than attend to the specific problems of individuals, and therefore bureaucratic procedures are sometimes viewed as cold and impersonal.

The government organizations that comprise the federal bureaucracy employ some 2.8 million people. They are not organized according to an overall, clear-cut pattern. The Executive Office of the President consists of fourteen agencies and operates at the discretion of the President. The twelve cabinet-level departments include the largest bureaucratic organization in government. Executive agencies range enormously in size. The regulatory commissions are not directly under presidential control.

Why has the federal bureaucracy grown so large?

The federal bureaucracy is huge. Some major reasons for the continuing increase in personnel are a growing U.S. population, domestic and international crises, demands for new government agencies, and the desire of many public officials to increase their power by adding more employees. One reason for the proliferation of paperwork is that we now expect government to resolve complex social and economic problems. Increased red tape also results from a concern for legal due process in administration. Red tape frequently derives from the best of intentions.

Is the federal bureaucracy effective?

Conservatives have called the bureaucracy wasteful, and liberals have characterized it as dehumanizing. Yet the federal bureaucracy has been successful in many areas, especially in technical tasks. There also has been relatively little corruption, and most citizens are satisfied with their experiences with government agencies. Where tasks have been complex or involve difficult social problems, however, success has been more limited.

Does the existence of a large-scale bureaucracy pose a threat to democratic government?

It has been alleged that bureaucrats are responsive to political leaders since political leaders cannot replace civil servants who oppose their policies, that bureaucrats can obstruct policies and can even implement their own goals. It is also claimed that a strong bureaucracy, when used by an unscrupulous leader, can impinge on our freedom. Despite occasional abuses, widespread use of the bureaucracy for oppressive purposes seems unlikely. Bureaucrats can resist pressure to act illegally, abuses can be appealed in the courts, coordinating extensive illegal action is difficult, and the public would be outraged.

CHAPTER THIRTEEN

THE FEDERAL BUREAUCRACY

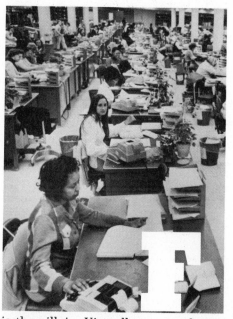

ew political words have as negative a connotation as "bureaucracy." Whereas reformers once emphasized pressure groups as the source of political evil, today the bureaucracy is the villain. Virtually every politician—Democrat or Republican, conservative or radical—promises to do something about the bureaucracy. Nobody has ever been criticized for being too hostile toward "faceless, bumbling bureaucrats and their red tape." Nevertheless, despite all the opposition, the federal bureaucracy continues to grow. Each year sees the birth of new agencies with new regulations, with few old agencies ever going out of business. When President Carter ran for office he spoke of "the horrible bloated bureaucracy," yet in his first eleven months in office 18,476 people were added to the federal payroll. Moreover, the impact of the bureaucracy on people's lives seems to be increasing. Indeed, almost everything of consequence is regulated by a government agency. How can there be so much opposition to an institution that continues to thrive? Is the bureaucracy like an incurable disease? This chapter examines four questions that relate to these issues:

1. What is the federal bureaucracy?
2. Why has this bureaucracy grown so large?
3. Is the federal bureaucracy effective?
4. Does the existence of a large-scale bureaucracy pose a threat to democratic government?

What is the federal bureaucracy?

Most people understand little about the structure and operations of the federal bureaucracy. Yet reform is impossible unless we know what needs to be reformed. What do we mean by "bureaucracy?" Actually, there are two distinct meanings of this term. The first refers to a way of conducting business, whether in government or in private enterprise. We have this meaning in mind when we say things like "This university or social club is run bureaucratically." The second use of "bureaucracy" refers to a nonelected government organization that is engaged in some set of specific tasks, for example, the Department of Defense. To understand the problems of bureaucracy, we must understand both of these meanings.

BUREAUCRACY AS A WAY OF DOING BUSINESS

Any large task, whether it is waging war or cleaning city streets, can be approached in several ways. For example, we could ask for volunteers who would all decide their own activities and hours of work. Or we could create a bureaucracy to coordinate the job. Scholars who have described the bureaucratic approach to problem solving agree that this approach has the following characteristics.

A clear division of labor

A large endeavor is broken down into a series of specific tasks, and each person is responsible for a particular task. An alternative would be for everyone to do a little of everything: In such a system two people might be doing one job while another job is ignored. In football, for example, a defense is "bureaucratized" when it has designated positions such as left outside linebacker or right defensive end instead of eleven players milling around in hopes of stopping the opposing team.

Hierarchical authority patterns

Each person fits into a chain of command, and orders are conveyed through established channels. The organization of positions looks like a pyramid, with one chief who gives orders to, say, three assistants, who in turn direct twelve aides, and so on. This is in contrast to a system in which everyone has an equal say or leadership changes with the task to be performed. The organization of a football team, with a hierarchy ranging from head coach to offensive coordinators to line coaches to player-captain, illustrates the bureaucratic authority pattern. Another classic example is the Army.

Specified job qualifications

Since each job in a bureaucracy is a cog in a large organization, the job occupant must have special expertise and qualifications. One could not pluck just anyone off the street and expect him or her to be, say, the safety officer for the federal left-handed monkey wrench standards bureau. Typically, bureaucrats are chosen by written examination or specified previous experience. Bureaucratic jobs usually turn into long careers where advancement is on the basis of merit.

Objective administration of rules

Each official follows written rules that are uniformly applied regardless of personal feeling. Personal discretion or use of criteria irrelevant to the decision at hand are minimized or eliminated. Emphasis is on the application of predetermined, publicly known rules and regulations; making up new rules as situations arise is not encouraged. Therefore, everyone knows what to expect, and previous decisions are part of a written record. Certain professional football teams, for example, have adopted this bureaucratic approach by instructing their players to follow certain practices under specified conditions rather than improvise.

Of course, these four characteristics do not apply entirely in each and every bureaucracy. Just as every football play is not executed as it appears in the play book, so on occasion does a bureaucracy violate a rule. On the whole, however, these four characteristics describe the organizations we call bureaucracies.

What is the significance of the bureaucratic approach to getting something done? Here we get a glimmer of why the bureaucracy is sometimes viewed unsympathetically. Basically, an organization that embodies bureaucratic traits can simultaneously be efficient and unpleasant in its human relations. Things may get done, but not everyone likes all the regulations or enjoys being treated impersonally.[1]

Especially in large organizations such as those found in the federal government, the virtues of hierarchical authority and fixed, objective rules are self-evident. Imagine trying to run a major government program with nobody clearly in charge. What would happen if, say, thousands of officials in the Social Security Administration all used different rules in dispensing benefits? Obviously, without a reasonably high degree of bureaucratization, modern governments would disintegrate into chaos. Max Weber, a German sociologist, argued that compared to any other way of doing business, bureaucracies are more precise, faster, less ambiguous, more knowledgeable, more unified, generate less conflict, and cost less in material and personnel.[2]

Unfortunately, if one wants instant action and personalized treatment, the bureaucratic approach can cause problems. Bureaucracies exist to

[1] Students of professional football are well aware of this occasional contradiction. The Dallas Cowboys are perhaps the most bureaucratized of all professional teams, and they are consistently among the most efficient. Nevertheless, many of their players complain about the impersonality of the Cowboy "system." Clearly, maintaining an effective organization and at the same time keeping people happy presents problems.

[2] Max Weber, "Essay on Bureaucracy," in Francis E. Rourke, ed., *Bureaucratic Power in National Politics*, 3d ed. (Boston: Little, Brown, 1978), pp. 85–96.

handle large numbers of cases in an orderly, predetermined way. They are not geared to treating the special problems of individuals. Many a troubled student has suffered through the university's bureaucratic system hearing: "We handle only missing grades here, not transcripts"; "That's not my job, go see Dean Fat over in 221 Admin"; or "Petitions to waive the language requirement can be approved only by Vice-Chancellor Frump, and you must file forms HP-59, TX-58, and HP-165 in triplicate." When dealing with the federal government such problems can be far worse. We shall have more to say about these bureaucratic problems.

BUREAUCRACY AS SPECIFIC ORGANIZATIONS

The people of the United States elect 535 national legislators and one President, who in turn choose nine Supreme Court Justices. This is only the tip of the federal iceberg. In addition to these policy makers, there were, as of January 1976, some 2,857,472 paid civilian employees in the federal government,[3] the vast majority of whom worked in the executive branch. This, then, is the size of the thing called the bureaucracy. What do these 2.8 million people do?

For people who like neat organizational charts, there is no simple graphic description of the federal bureaucracy. Government agencies have grown rapidly over the years—in both size and numbers—as different officials have taken different approaches to government organizations. No wonder, then, that agency roles sometimes overlap, or that one agency is relatively independent while a similar bureau is firmly under direct presidential control. For reasons of space we can consider here only a few of the major bureaucratic organizations.

Executive Office of the President

Perhaps the most logical place to begin in describing the bureaucracy is with the presidency. Immediately surrounding the President is the *Executive Office of the President,* which might be considered the President's "personal" bureaucracy. It is here that the Chief Executive has the greatest leeway to eliminate or create new agencies as the need arises. In 1977, there were fourteen separate agencies with staffs of 1,836 people and budgets totaling $73 million. Among the most important of these were the Office of Management and Budget (OMB). The basic purpose of OMB is to help the President prepare the federal budget. Its responsibilities also include coordinating government programs, promoting man-

[3] *Statistical Abstract of the United States, 1977,* p. 249. Confusion sometimes occurs regarding the terms "executive bureaucracy" and "federal bureaucracy." We use the term "federal bureaucracy" to mean all the agencies and employees of the national government. The "executive bureaucracy" is used by people referring to departments explicitly under presidential direction (for example, the Department of Defense). However, in some respects this is a misleading term, because Congress does play a significant role in the operation of agencies such as the Department of Defense. Moreover, other agencies, especially the independent regulatory commissions, are not controlled directly by either the President or Congress.

agerial efficiency in government, and monitoring the legislative proposals made to the President by the heads of agencies and departments (the practice of central clearance—see Chapter Twelve). An OMB director with strong presidential support can wield tremendous power. Jim McIntyre, OMB Director under President Carter, had played a vigorous role in reducing federal agency budget requests, and agency heads knew that without McIntyre's support the President would not agree to their budgetary requests.

A second important agency within the Executive Office of the President is the National Security Council (NSC). Comprised of the President, Vice President, Secretaries of State and Defense, director of the Central Intelligence Agency (CIA), chairman of the Joint Chiefs of Staff, and the assistant to the President for national security, the NSC advises the President with respect to integrating domestic, foreign, and military policies to safeguard national security. (The NSC and the President also oversee the CIA.) The Council of Economic Advisors consists of three members and provides overall advice on economic programs. Less well known are the Council on Environmental Quality, the Federal Property Council, the Office of Drug Abuse Policy, and several other agencies.

The Executive Office undergoes changes as new issues arise. In 1970, for example, President Nixon created the Domestic Council to provide overall coordination of domestic programs. In response to the energy shortage in 1974, President Ford created the Energy Resources Council as part of the Executive Office of the President.

Cabinet-level departments

The next ring of agencies surrounding the President includes the thirteen *cabinet-level departments*. These are: State, Treasury, Interior, Justice, Agriculture, Education, Commerce, Labor, Defense, Health and Human Services, Housing and Urban Development, Transportation, and Energy. Originally there were only three—State, Treasury, and War (later re-

DAVID A. STOCKMAN, Director of Office of Management and Budget. Born November 10, 1946, in Texas. Youngest person ever to hold this position. Grew up in St. Joseph, Michigan, and graduated from Michigan State University, majoring in history. As a teenager he became involved in conservative causes; briefly became more radical while at Michigan State and returned to the conservative fold while at Harvard Divinity School. Served as an aide to Congressman John Anderson in 1970 and successfully ran for Congress from Michigan in 1976 (and was re-elected in 1978). In the House he attracted attention due to his intellectual abilities, flair for dealing with numbers, capacity for long hours, and devotion to conservative economic policies. As a member of Congress Stockman opposed many of Carter's energy proposals and the government bail out of Chrysler (his home state's largest employer) but supported the Equal Rights Amendment. The core of his philosophy is a commitment to the free market economy and sees his job at OMB as one of producing growth through economic policy. High taxation and excessive regulation of business are the main causes of a lack of growth, according to Stockman.

BUREAUCRACIES DO NOT DISCRIMINATE ON THE BASIS OF PERSONAL APPEARANCE

One of the virtues of modern bureaucracies is that everyone is treated alike. Apparently, as the following story indicates, this also applies to pigs.

BOB WELKOS (AP)

GOLCONDA, Nev.—The holder of Social Security number 530-80-4623 is a pig—in fact a drunken pig.

Waterhole Ike never works; has dozens, if not hundreds, of offspring, and spends a good deal of his time lolling in the mud.

Every morning he waddles into Mark Cowley's cafe-tavern—Waterhole No. 1—in this town in northern Nevada, and drinks beer from a 5-gallon bucket.

"He's all right until about 10:30 a.m. and then he comes in, has his drink and he's in hog heaven," Cowley said. "It uncurls his tail."

After a drink, Waterhole Ike listens as Cowley reads him letters from around the state.

Cowley heads a syndicate that promotes the pig. He already has sold about 1,000 shares of stock in the porker at $1 each. If a thoroughbred horse can be syndicated, said Cowley, so can a pig.

"The racehorse, Secretariat, was syndicated and worth I don't know how many millions," Cowley said. "And he had trouble performing stud service."

So far, that's not been a problem for Waterhole Ike. He charges $25.

Waterhole Ike's story began about two years ago, when Cowley and eight of the patrons in his bar formed the syndicate. All the money collected was put in a cigar box.

When the syndicate outgrew the box, Cowley decided to open a savings account for the pig. But the savings and loan firm needed a Social Security number for the account holder to report interest for taxes, so Cowley applied for a card.

"Everything I put on there was the truth," Cowley said. "His mother was Go-Pig-Go, and his father was Three Stars. He was born on May 1, 1974.

named Defense)—but as government grew, additional cabinet-level departments were added (the Department of Education is the last addition). These departments represent some of the largest components of the federal bureaucracy. In 1976, for example, the Defense Department employed 1,023,255 *civilian* workers and spent $92.8 billion. Health, Education and Welfare employed "only" slightly over 148,000 people and took $127 billion out of the 1977 federal budget. The Depart-

Waterhole Ike has breakfast.

"Down at the bottom where it says signature, I wondered what to do, since everybody knows a 2-year-old pig can't write," he said. "So I wrote 'Waterhole Ike by Mark Cowley.' "

The Department of Health, Education and Welfare sent Waterhole Ike a Social Security card and Cowley gave the number to the bank.

"I went to the welfare people and told them I knew this guy who couldn't work because he is an alcoholic and he has 10 dependents.

"The welfare department was going to give him $650 a month. I even almost got him into the alcoholic rehabilitation program. As far as the government is concerned, he's just the same as you or I."

Waterhole Ike got a letter the other day from his bank.

"The letter said he is now eligible to borrow from $2,500 to $25,000 or more at any of their statewide offices," Cowley said.

"Syndicated Swine Gets Social Security Number," *Champaign-Urbana News Gazette,* March 15, 1978.

ment of Labor is the smallest of these giants and employed some 15,418 people in 1976.[4]

The expression "the President's cabinet" conveys an image of the President and all of his department heads gathered to discuss overall national policy. This image is misleading, however, because rarely are

[4] *Statistical Abstract of the United States, 1977,* p. 249.

A meeting of the Carter Cabinet.

cabinet members among the President's closest advisers and trusted confidants. Cabinet members are frequently appointed because of their special abilities or ties to groups associated with the department (for example, the Secretary of Labor always has close links with organized labor). In many instances cabinet members are more oriented to their bureaucracies than to the President who appointed them. Presidential attempts to meet regularly with the entire cabinet to discuss national problems are rarely productive. Both Eisenhower and Carter began their presidencies with talk of "cabinet government" but soon discontinued regular full cabinet meetings because they found them cumbersome. Particular cabinet officials can be highly influential with the President, but the cabinet as a group of twelve officials acting together has little power.

Executive agencies

A third type of federal bureaucracy is the *executive agency*. These agencies do not enjoy cabinet status, but the larger ones are important. In 1976, the Veterans Administration employed over 219,000 people. Other well-known agencies in this group are the National Science Foundation (NSF), the Central Intelligence Agency (CIA), the Commission on Civil Rights, and the Consumer Product Safety Commission. Some executive agencies are legally established as government corporations and are intended to be run along more businesslike lines (though they are still responsible to the President). The U.S. Postal Service, once a cabinet-level department, is the largest of these government corporations. Others are the Tennessee Valley Authority (TVA) and the Federal Deposit Insurance Corporation (the familiar FDIC seen on bank advertisements). In some instances the government and universities or private industry are involved in cooperative ventures with the federal government, for example, the Oak Ridge National Laboratory and the Rand Corporation.

Independent regulatory commissions

Furthest removed from direct presidential influence are the *independent regulatory commissions.* These include the Federal Trade Commission (FTC), the Securities and Exchange Commission (SEC), and the Civil Aeronautics Board (CAB). Essentially, these commissions are charged with regulating industries that are near-monopolies (the Federal Communications Commission oversees the telephone industry) or areas of public trust (for example, the SEC regulates the stock market). Members of the boards of these commissions are nominated by the President and confirmed by the Senate, but unlike other bureaucrats, they cannot be fired by the President. Terms can be very long (up to fourteen years) and do not overlap, so a new President has to live with many appointments made by his predecessors.

Before exploring why bureaucracies have grown as extensively as they have, one misconception about federal agencies and their employees should be cleared up. Many people automatically think of a bureaucrat as a pencil-pushing paper shuffler who sits in Washington thinking up new, incomprehensible federal regulations. Like many stereotypes, this one is much exaggerated. First, in 1975, only about 14.4 percent of all federal employees worked in the Washington, D.C., metropolitan area.[5] Second, many government workers are highly trained technical specialists, not just paper pushers. Thousands of physicians, veterinarians, engineers, biologists, architects, and the like, are "bureaucrats." Many others are blue-collar and unskilled workers. Finally, numerous government workers do not fit the stereotype of bureaucrat, yet they are very much part of the bureaucracy. How many of us would consider an FBI agent, a forest ranger, an airport flight controller, or the county agricultural extension agent a faceless paper-pushing bureaucrat?

In short, when we say "bureaucracy," we mean both a way of doing business and specific organizations of government. If we accept the idea that large government is responsible for a wide variety of tasks, the bureaucratic solution is probably the most effective—though not perfect—system for getting results.

Why has the federal bureaucracy grown so large?

The federal bureaucracy has grown considerably since the ratification of the Constitution. When President Washington took office the entire federal bureaucracy consisted of about 350 people. Even after the hiring of

[5] *Statistical Abstract of the United States, 1977,* p. 252.

innumerable Revolutionary War veterans, worthy men in need of jobs, and friends and relatives of government officials, there were still only 2,100 federal employees in 1801. If early Presidents had hired bureaucrats at the ratio of public servants to population that we now have, the United States would have begun with a public payroll of some 45,000.[6]

THE GROWTH OF THE FEDERAL BUREAUCRACY

Public employment at the federal level, however, soon became a growth industry. Especially after Andrew Jackson's election in 1828, a government job became a major way of rewarding supporters for electoral help. Even Abraham Lincoln was not above adding to the public payroll as a means of getting congressional support for his programs. By 1901, the executive branch employed 256,000 persons, and by 1930, over 580,000. In 1976, the figure was over 2.8 million (the number of employees, though not the cost, has remained relatively stable since 1960, however). The payroll for all these executive branch employees was nearly $40 billion in 1976 (or about 12.5 cents of every federal dollar spent).[7]

Number of employees and expenditures do not, however, capture the psychological impact of the federal bureaucracy. Consider that the regulations issued by all the hundreds of agencies now run to more than 50,000 printed pages a year. More than two *billion* forms must be filled out and submitted to the federal government each year. This comes out to ten forms for each man, woman, and child in the United States (there are more than 5,000 different federal forms a citizen might have to complete). One federal agency supposedly had issued enough documents to make a stack seventeen feet high (remember, we are excluding state and municipal paperwork).[8] Some 164 federal regulatory agencies have jurisdiction over hospitals, and it is estimated that it costs hospitals $35 per patient to comply with their rules.[9]

For businesspeople and others who are self-employed, the burden of federal forms can be staggering. A firm with fewer than fifty employees must submit between seventy-five and eighty reports a year to various agencies. The chairman of the board of a large drug company claimed that his firm prepared 27,000 government forms a year at a cost of $5 million. He also asserted that more company time was spent filling out

[6] Herbert Kaufman, "The Growth of the Federal Personnel System," in The American Assembly, *The Federal Government Service*, 2d ed. (Englewood Cliffs, N.J.: Prentice-Hall, 1965), pp. 7–8.

[7] *Statistical Abstract of the United States, 1977*, p. 249. Though in the long run the federal bureaucracy has experienced gigantic growth, in the last thirty years the largest growth in public employment has occurred at the state level. In 1950, there were some 2.1 million federal employees and about 4.3 million state and local employees (a 1 to 2 ratio). By 1976, the federal payroll had increased by 726,000, but states and cities had added 7.88 million employees (a ratio of about 1 to 4.3).

[8] Herbert Kaufman, *Red Tape: Its Origins, Uses, and Abuses* (Washington, D.C.: The Brookings Institution; 1977), p. 7.

[9] Cited in the *National Review*, February 17, 1978, p. 196.

forms than on cancer and heart disease research combined.[10] It is estimated that private industry now spends between $25 and $32 billion in filling out federal forms (a cost that naturally is passed on to consumers).[11] The requirement that the Federal Highway Administration file an environmental impact statement prior to road construction, for example, has added 18 million extra pages to the agency's yearly work load.[12] Universities too must employ large staffs to answer federal inquiries about employment practices, the composition of student bodies, how government research money is spent, and so on.

In addition, the nature of the requested information is frequently exasperating. Many businesspeople, in particular, complain that they cannot see the relevancy of numerous regulations and forms. Some have even complained that the mountain of useless paperwork is a conspiracy to drive them out of business. Redundant and contradictory rules and regulations also add to the psychological burden of having a huge bureaucracy. What should you do if one federal agency prohibited inquiries about race on job application forms while another required records of job applicants by race in order to monitor racial discrimination?[13] How do you react if you, like the Scottdale Savings and Trust Company of Scottdale, Pennsylvania, answer questions on a government report with "none," only to have the report returned with the request that "-0-" be used instead of "none"?[14] Such experiences, no doubt, give concrete meaning to the statistics showing the emergence of large-scale government bureaucracy.

REASONS FOR BUREAUCRATIC GROWTH

How has such a situation come about? The rapid growth of executive agency staffs and the proliferation of bureaus is relatively easy to understand. Obviously, sizable population increases account for part of the bureaucratic growth. A nation of 215 million people cannot be run by the same number of officials who ran a country of 50 million. Compounding this increase in size is a dramatic change in the nature of contemporary life. Thanks to technology, we now face complexities undreamed of a hundred years ago. As a result, agencies such as the Office of Science and Technology, the Civil Aeronautics Board, the National Aeronautics and Space Administration (NASA), and the National Science Foundation have come into existence. The launching of communications satel-

[10] Kaufman, *Red Tape*, p. 8.

[11] "Federal Paperwork: A Small-Businessman's Nightmare," *New York Times*, March 20, 1978.

[12] Hearings, Subcommittee on Investigations and Oversight, Committee on Public Works, House of Representatives, 92nd Cong., 1st sess., June 22, 1971.

[13] Another interesting contradiction is provided by the Occupational Safety and Health Administration requirements that (1) construction site vehicles have back-up alarms, and (2) construction site employees wear earplugs to keep out noise.

[14] Cited in "Federal Paperwork: A Small Businessman's Nightmare."

Cold War An expression used to describe the state of tension and antagonism between the United Sates and the Soviet Union.

lites or the regulating of atomic energy, for example, requires some degree of government involvement.

The **Cold War** with the Soviet Union and a succession of world crises have also contributed to bureaucratic increases. In the wake of World War II, a sizable Defense Department became an accepted fact. New agencies have also emerged in response to the continued conflict between the United States and the USSR. These include the Central Intelligence Agency, the Arms Control and Disarmament Agency, the U.S. Information Agency, and even the Peace Corps, which is designed to generate good will abroad. Wars in Korea and South Vietnam have also helped maintain a large Veterans Administration.

Domestic economic crises have likewise contributed to the swelling of the government payroll. During the depression of the 1930s, President Franklin D. Roosevelt added over 100,000 federal jobs in his first year in office to combat unemployment and economic stagnation (by 1940, Roosevelt had nearly doubled the number of federal employees). Many of Roosevelt's Great Depression remedies have been extended (for example, social security) as people have accepted the idea that the federal government has a responsibility to help citizens in many different areas. Whereas the ill, the neglected, the retired, and the disabled once had to depend on family or charity to survive, the federal government now administers a vast number of assistance programs. Similarly, victims of earthquakes, storms, floods, and other catastrophes are now considered at least the partial responsibility of the national government. Once the government bureaucracy commits itself to resolving some hardship, it is difficult to withdraw such assistance. Temporary assistance can easily come to be viewed by those aided as an inalienable right to a benefit.

A fourth reason for bureaucratic growth involves the relationship between citizens and different agencies. As we saw in Chapter 9, which examined the behavior of interest groups, many bureaucracies develop close relationships with citizens and groups, who are usually referred to as an agency's clientele. For example, the Office of Education in the Department of Health Education and Welfare had a close supportive relationship with state superintendents of education. On occasion the existence of one such clientele relationship encourages the creation of countervailing clientele bureaucracies. If businesspeople can have "their" people in the Department of Commerce, labor people can have "their" supporters in the Department of Labor. Recent proposals for a Department of Consumer Affairs are based upon the belief that ordinary citizens need advocates in government to oppose industry-oriented bureaucrats.

Finally, once established, some agencies experience strong internal pressures for expansion. Especially since power and prestige within government are frequently measured by size, many high agency officials constantly try to add a few more bodies to their domains. This aggrandizement is frequently encouraged by the budgetary process in government—last year's expenditures are accepted as a "given," so one might as well take the offensive and demand more. The strategy of more, more, more can become addictive as even more people are needed to supervise

CAN FEDERAL STANDARDS FOR SAFE ELECTRIC CHAIRS BE FAR BEHIND?

The willingness of the federal government to regulate virtually everything apparently knows no bounds. This particular story begins with government attempts to reduce the importation of Mexican narcotics to the United States by supplying Mexico with herbicides to kill marijuana and opium plants. One of these herbicides was Paraquat. In 1977 and 1978, Mexican marijuana heavily contaminated with Paraquat entered the U.S. market on a large scale. Since smoking Paraquat-tainted pot can cause serious lung damage, counterculture entrepreneurs began selling Paraquat testing kits to insure consumer safety.

Unfortunately for the consumer, many of these kits were useless because equipment was improperly calibrated and reagents were impure. Naturally, disgruntled citizens began complaining to the Department of Health, Education and Welfare about this shoddy merchandise. Federal officials were disturbed by the potential danger caused by defective contaminated-dope detector kits. Said one official at HEW, "I guess we're going to need federal guidelines so that people can use an illegal substance safely."

Neal Travis, "Paraquat Tests Go All to Pot," *New York Magazine,* June 5, 1978, p. 6.

Red tape A common expression for what appears to be needless and unnecessarily complex regulations. The term comes from the old English practice of tying legal records together with red ribbon.

or coordinate those previously hired (and more and more time is spent merely dealing with internal organizational problems).

GROWTH IN RED TAPE

These factors help us to understand the growth of the executive bureaucracies. What about the dramatic increases in **red tape** in recent years? Why, for example, did Dow Chemical Company have to spend $186 million in 1977 to comply with federal regulations—a jump of 27 percent in one year?[15] Is the federal bureaucracy run by a bunch of clerical sadists who get their kicks by dreaming up new and more confusing regulations? Or are federal officials so incompetent that everything has to be done at least twice? Though a few clerical sadists and incompetents may exist, the major reason for the proliferation of red tape is that red tape is primarily designed to create efficiency and to protect citizens. This statement only appears to be a contradiction. What ends up as red tape usually starts out with the best of intentions.

[15] Cited in "Federal Paperwork: A Small Businessman's Nightmare."

"More rules and regulations!"

Courtesy of Mobil Oil.

To understand why good intentions can easily lead to hundreds of detailed and obscure forms to be filled out, we must understand two things about the contemporary national government: (1) it is responsible for innumerable highly complex tasks, and (2) we expect it to function in accordance with laws and standards of fairness. Herein lies the source of much of the blizzard of red tape.

Preventing harm before it occurs

Take, for example, the problem of consumer protection. In the old days if you found a rat in your peanut butter, your response would be to stop buying that brand of peanut butter. If the rat bit you, you might take the company to court and sue for damages—a long, costly, and generally inefficient solution. Such was the nature of the free enterprise system—consumer beware, period.

Today, however, we expect to be protected against such evils *before* they occur. We want the government to guarantee in advance that we will find no surprises in our peanut butter. This responsibility may require a small army of federal officials, armed with forms, to monitor the production of peanut butter in hundreds of factories. Manufacturers, of course, would have to comply with dozens of rules regarding plant sanitation, method of production, security of storage and shipping facilities, and the like. Meanwhile, the Food and Drug Administration might conduct an investigation into whether eating too many rats causes cancer. Also, the Federal Trade Commission might consider whether it is deceptive to advertise peanut butter mixed with rats as "peanut butter with whole natural protein."[16] More and more complex rules and regulations are clearly the alternative to "let the buyer beware."

[16] Though our illustration is an exaggeration, the Food and Drug Administration does indeed regulate such matters. For example, 10 ounces of popcorn may contain up to one rodent hair or one rodent pellet and still not legally be considered contaminated. On the other hand, the fig paste in fig newtons may contain 13 insect heads per 100 grams and still be allowed.

The extent to which government now attempts to thwart evil before it happens is staggering. The national government requires that loan contracts be written in plain English language so that borrowers will not be misled; rules and regulations stipulate how clothing is to be labeled with washing instructions; and standards exist governing the kinds of claims manufacturers can make about their products. A few years ago the Federal Trade Commission prohibited the Campbell Soup Company from putting marbles in soup bowls for television commercials. The Campbell people were worried that the television viewer could not see the vegetables, so they added marbles to bring the vegetables closer to the surface. The practice was deceptive, according to the FTC, and was not allowed. Perhaps Campbell should have offered a condensed marble-vegetable soup.

HOW TO BE A CREATIVE BUREAUCRAT

What separates the merely good bureaucrat from the great bureaucrat? According to James H. Boren, the humorist and student of bureaucratic ways, it is the artistic use of words. The expert bureaucrat has a certain creative flair for making complex something that is simple. A rank beginner might reject a proposal by writing, "I recommend that this proposal be rejected." No style, obviously. A more experienced official would say, "On the basis of the documented report of the committee, I recommend the proposal be rejected." Better, but still a long way to go.

A true creative artist, however, would offer:

While the initial study committee has made a skillful and in-depth analysis of the alternative resources mixes as they relate to the proposal in question, the optimal functions as reflected by the committee's thematic projections would suggest a nonaffirmative response if the executive office were forced to make an immediate decision. In view of the paramount importance of the multivious aspects of the proposal, it is my recommendation that a special task force be created with the assigned responsibility of appropriately developing sound administrative options to the proposed implementation decision. Reliable and tested administrative procedures would enhance the practicality of the proposal and add to it the incremental viability factors essential for the type of creative innovation that functions within established guidelines.

James H. Boren, *When in Doubt, Mumble* (New York: Van Nostrand Reinhold, 1972), pp. 7–8.

Due process of law The principle that government cannot act arbitrarily in depriving citizens of life, liberty, or property. Such deprivation must follow prescribed procedures and allow the individual to defend himself or herself.

Insuring that government operates fairly

To appreciate how the need to operate legally and fairly spawns red tape, consider the problem of providing social security benefits for disabled citizens. If benefits are due a disabled person, we want to make sure that those legally deserving aid receive it. We also want to stop officials from giving away public money to their friends under the guise of aiding the disabled. To make sure the program uniformly works as intended by Congress and the President, many details must be spelled out. In fact, within the social security program it takes *fifteen* pages of rules and regulations just to define "disability." The rules even state exactly what is meant by "blindness" and exactly how it is to be measured ("usual perimetric methods, utilizing a 3 mm. white disk target at a distance of 330 mm. under illumination of not less than 7 foot-candles").[17] Without such clarity some disabled person might be unfairly refused benefits or a nonblind person unfairly given public aid.

Another way the desire to be fair generates red tape is the requirement that bureaucracy operate according to **due process.** This means that decisions must be made in accordance with set procedures and that those affected must be allowed to participate. An example of the absence of bureaucratic due process would be if you suddenly received a mysterious set of government rules regulating your business that had been devised without notice to you and without your having been consulted. The principle of due process is fundamental to our system of justice and is a major bulwark against dictatorial government action. It also can generate delay, confusion, and red tape by the yard.

An increasingly common illustration of red tape generated by regard for due process is provided by the environmental impact studies that now must be conducted on many major building projects. In the old days if the state of Illinois wanted to build a dam on the Dirty River, the project basically involved engineering and financing problems. Today, however, in order to be fair, the dam builders must first conduct extensive studies on the impact of the dam on the environment, ascertain the preferences of local citizens, and in other ways "give people their say" in the project. Moreover, to avoid possible trickery, the types of studies, timing of public hearings, nature of reports to be filed, and so on, are all spelled out in administrative guidelines. The costs of avoiding possible unfairness are lengthy delays and a mountain of paperwork. To some people the costs may be worth the end result; others might disagree.

Due process in the bureaucracy also means the opportunity to review decisions. That is, if you feel you were wronged you can appeal your case and get a second (or third or fourth) evaluation. This provision is intended as a check on possible abuses or poor judgment. Because a decision may ultimately be reviewed, an agency must keep extensive, detailed records, have explicit rules governing the review process, spell out the rights of all parties, and make sure that no rule or regulation is ambiguous or contradictory. All of this means protection for the citizen, but it also is very confusing to the outsider.

[17] Kaufman, *Red Tape*, p. 38.

"IN CASE OF FIRE, PROCEED IMMEDIATELY TO THAT PORTION OF A MEANS OF EGRESS . . ."

Perhaps the most exasperating aspect of bureaucratic procedure is the obtuse language that is often used in communications. Everything has to be spelled out in boring, overly complex detail. Here, for example, is the definition of "exit" used by the Occupational Safety and Health Administration (OSHA). An "exit" is:

that portion of a means of egress which is separated from all other spaces of the building or structure by construction or equipment as required in this subpart to provide a protected way of travel to the exit discharge.

An "exit discharge" in turn is defined as:

that portion of a means of egress between the termination of an exit and a public way.

A "means of egress" is:

a continuous and unobstructed way of exit travel from any point in a building or structure to a public way and consists of three separate and distinct parts: the way of exit access, the exit, and the way of exit discharge. A means of egress comprises the vertical and horizontal ways of travel and shall include intervening room spaces, doorways, hallways, corridors, passageways, balconies, ramps, stairs, enclosures, exits, escalators, horizontal exits, courts, and yards.

Not all definitions are as complicated, however. OSHA tells us that "Hazards are one of the main causes of accidents. A hazard is anything that is dangerous."

Reported in Murray L. Weidenbaum, "The Cost of Overregulating Business," *Tax Foundation's Tax Review,* August 1975, pp. 34–35.

The need for extensive information

The need for information is yet another reason for the quantities of regulations and red tape that stem from federal agencies. To deal effectively with complex issues, as we expect our government to do, requires large amounts of information. Thus, farmers must fill out forms describing their planting, businesspeople must provide payroll information, and so on. Without such data how would the government know whether its economic policies are working? One important lesson of the depression of the 1930s was that social problems cannot be correctly analyzed without substantial amounts of citizen-supplied data. This principle applies to

> ## "BUT WHAT ABOUT 'ALL OF THE ABOVE' OR 'NONE OF THE ABOVE?' "
>
> Government forms are sometimes highly complex in order to ensure that requests for information will be precisely understood. The need to be exact is well illustrated by the case of a young job applicant who filled out Form 57, which was once required for government employment. The question was: "Do you favor the overthrow of the Government by force, subversion, or violence?" The applicant, obviously experienced with undergraduate multiple choice examinations, answered: "violence."
>
> Cited in Norval Morris and Gordon Hawkins, *The Honest Politician's Guide to Crime Control* (Chicago: University of Chicago Press, 1970), p. 55.

noneconomic issues as well. Suppose the government is committed to abolishing sex discrimination in employment. Holding government responsible for this task requires considerable paperwork, because both the degree of progress and possible problems must be identified. Otherwise we would have no way of determining whether government claims about its successes are true or false. Holding government accountable—a widely approved goal—generates forms and regulations.

In short, if we want our government to protect us against poorly designed automobiles, act with care in disturbing the environment, or keep "welfare chiselers" from getting money, specific, detailed rules and regulations are required. Moreover, people must be hired and forms designed if we want the process to operate according to strict guidelines with ample opportunity for citizen participation. The need for information makes for even more paperwork. To return to our original question of why so much bureaucracy and red tape, the answer seems to be that people want it. Of course, nobody wants *all* the government agencies and millions of rules. Rather, each person wants only a few more officials and a few more regulations. It all adds up, however.

Is the federal bureaucracy effective?

Many citizens who disagree on numerous political issues share a negative image of "big government," especially big bureaucracy. Some conservatives, for example, assert that huge federal agencies waste taxpayer's money, move at a snail's pace, and create more problems than they solve. They argue that problems involving energy, housing, transportation, and agriculture, to name just a few, should be left to free enterprise, which could do a better job faster and less expensively. Even worse, they believe the federal bureaucracy undermines the capacity of people to do things themselves and, thus, will eventually destroy the nation.

Many liberals and radicals also see big bureaucracy as ineffective. In addition, they maintain that the bureaucratic process itself is dehumanizing and unresponsive to social needs. Huge Washington-based bureaucracies such as the Department of Health, Education and Welfare turn their employees into mere cogs in giant machines, more worried about petty rules and job security than about helping people. Such organizations, critics claim, must be made more sensitive to human needs or replaced by smaller, community-based organizations.

BUREAUCRATIC SUCCESSES

Whether or not the federal bureaucracy works effectively is a tough question. Because the government in Washington has created thousands of agencies in charge of tens of thousands of separate programs, a single answer is impossible. Certainly there are many agencies with excellent records of public service. A familiar example is the Internal Revenue Service (IRS), which manages to collect almost $300 billion in taxes cheaply and with comparatively little citizen outrage. Of course, citizens complain about high taxes and complex tax forms, but given the enormous job it faces, the IRS has performed an essential function well. Similarly, between World War II and the war in Vietnam, the Selective Service System was highly effective in raising a large military force. Here again, bureaucratic organization managed to do a competent job despite enormous problems and opposition.

Government bureaucracies have also had a long history of success in highly technical projects. It was government agencies that built the world's first atomic bomb, constructed the massive interstate highway system, brought electricity to millions of rural Americans through the Rural Electrification Administration, and with the Apollo program put a man on the moon. Much of our extensive system of ports, canals, dams, bridges, airports, and scientific laboratories were created by federal, state, and local bureaucracies. Considerable quantities of highly useful research has been conducted or initiated by bureaucracies such as the National Science Foundation, the National Institute of Mental Health, and similar agencies.[18]

[18] For example, a recent study sponsored by the National Heart, Lung, and Blood Institute found that chicken soup is good for colds. The report called chicken soup "efficacious upper respiratory tract infection therapy." The soup used in the study, which was advertised as "just like homemade," came from the Epicure Market in Miami Beach. Reported in "Mom Knows—Chicken Soup," Chicago Sun-Times, June 13, 1978.

Merit system The hiring and advancement of government workers on the basis of demonstrated ability and accomplishment.

It is also widely acknowledged that the federal bureaucracy is relatively free of the deeply rooted corruption so characteristic in bureaucracies in many other nations and in some states and communities. Federal bureaucrats do not buy their jobs and then make up the expense by taking bribes. Nor typically do they use their powers to punish their political enemies and reward their friends. It would be unthinkable, for example, if Republicans in the Social Security Administration used their positions to deny benefits to Democrats. Of course, some scandals occur, but despite all the opportunities for corruption, surprisingly little has taken place.[19] Moreover, thanks in part to the **merit system,** civil servants tend to be well educated and qualified for their positions. In 1977, almost 12 million people inquired about government jobs and 1.7 million applied, but only 151,614 were selected.

LIMITS ON BUREAUCRATIC EFFECTIVENESS

Critics of the federal bureaucracy can, of course, counter these virtues with numerous stories of bureaucratic bungling. Especially in tryng to correct deeply rooted social problems, federal bureaucracies have experienced many failures. The Justice Department, despite enormous expenditures and many special bureaus, task forces, experimental programs, and research projects, has met with only limited success in reducing the crime rate. Similarly, the Medicare program, once believed to be the solution to health-care problems, has generated huge cost overruns, driven up the price of medical care, and been the source of numerous scandals and frauds. Many of the antipoverty programs enacted as part of President Johnson's Great Society program have become models of poorly administered, wasteful programs with meager accomplishments. Agencies designed to protect citizens (for example, the Environmental Protection Agency) have been accused of exhibiting "waste, bias, stupidity, concentration on trivia, conflicts among the regulators, and worst of all, arbitrary and uncontrolled power."[20]

The Oakland project as a case study

The dark side of the federal bureaucracy was well illustrated when the federal government, in particular the Economic Development Administration of the Department of Commerce, decided to help Oakland, California. In the 1960s, Oakland was a city with a large poor black popula-

[19] For an analysis of some recent corruption in the General Services Administration, see Christina Kenrick, "Housecleaning at the GSA," *Christian Science Monitor*, November 3, 1978. Most of this GSA corruption involved employees who received kickbacks from firms doing business with the government or used government material for personal gain.

[20] Murray L. Weidenbaum, "The Cost of Overregulating Business," *Tax Foundation's Tax Review*, 36 (August 1975), p. 33. A more general analysis of bureaucratic effectiveness is found in Robert C. Fried, *Performance in American Bureaucracy* (Boston: Little, Brown, 1976), especially Chap. 6.

tion, high unemployment, and a deteriorating economic base—conditions which at that time were frequently associated with urban riots. On April 29, 1966, the Assistant Secretary of Commerce in charge of the Economic Development Administration (EDA) announced a $23.3 million plan to build various projects in Oakland to create 3,000 jobs for previously unemployed people. Government, the business community, and local residents were all to be involved, and hopes for success were high.

As described by Jeffrey L. Pressman and Aaron Wildavsky, the best of bureaucratic intentions plus $23.3 million can produce more frustrations than accomplishments.[21] First, many key decisions had to be approved by several layers of bureaucracy, and this caused considerable confusion and delay. For example, when one Oakland business wanted to initiate a job-training program, it had to pass through eight separate and time-consuming bureaucratic reviews (this involved three separate federal agencies, and they ultimately disagreed over the plan).[22] Second, participants in the project frequently disagreed over priorities. Whereas black leaders emphasized creating new jobs, business interests stressed economic improvements. These differences in priorities were understandable given the scope of the Oakland project, but they fostered inaction. Finally, the desire to maximize participation and consultation frequently meant that nobody had the power to force action. Officials in Washington, local bureaucrats, community leaders, local elected leaders, and Oakland businesspeople all had some influence, but no single person or group could force a solution. Not surprisingly, then, after three years and thousands of meetings, hundreds of memos, and millions of dollars, a grand total of only twenty jobs for minorities were created.[23]

What does the Oakland experience tell us about the performance of the federal bureaucracy? Many lessons have been learned from such failures, but perhaps the clearest is that success is most likely where the bureaucratic goal is unambiguous. When a bureaucracy is devoted to one goal—even an expensive one—the chance of success is likely to be higher than when three or four goals must be accomplished simultaneously. To see how this works, let us consider briefly various solutions to slum housing which show that as the criteria for success become increasingly complex, effectiveness becomes more difficult to achieve.

Resolving increasingly complex problems

Imagine a largely black inner-city slum. If our goal were only to build decent housing for the fewest dollars, our task would be relatively simple—contractors would bid on the project, and we would accept the lowest bid. This was the traditional way slums were cleared in the 1950s, and success, as measured by living units for each dollar, was usually high.

[21] Jeffrey L. Pressman and Aaron Wildavsky, *Implementation* (Berkeley: University of California Press, 1973).
[22] Pressman and Wildavsky, pp. 45–47.
[23] Pressman and Wildavsky, p. 4.

BUREAUCRATIC EFFECTIVENESS: THE CLIENT'S VIEW

An important measure of bureaucratic effectiveness is public satisfaction with agency service. It would be hard to claim bureaucratic effectiveness if people who use government services received poor treatment. To ascertain public satisfaction with bureaucratic services, Robert L. Kahn and his associates asked a sample of 1,431 adults about their experiences in seven areas: employment, job training, compensation for work-related accidents, unemployment compensation, medical care, public assistance, and retirement benefits. How badly did these bureaucracies do?

Contrary to the image of bureaucracy as inept, 69 percent of the respondents reported satisfaction with their experiences. Only 14 percent were very dissatisfied. The highest levels of satisfaction were with retirement benefits, the lowest levels with health care. People did not enjoy all the necessary paperwork, but most did not complain about it, either. Overall, only 13 percent of the respondents claimed that they were treated unfairly.

Age and race seemed to make a difference in level of satisfaction. Young people and blacks were more likely to report dissatisfaction, though clear majorities of both groups were satisfied.

What is especially interesting is that 71 percent of all people who had had experiences with the federal bureaucracy said their problems had been solved, but only 30 percent believed that government agencies did a good job of taking care of people's problems. Obviously, many people must view their own experiences as exceptional.

Robert L. Kahn, Barbara A. Gutek, Eugenia Barton, and Daniel Katz, "Americans Love Their Bureaucrats," *Psychology Today*, June 1975, pp. 66–71.

Then things became more complex. Agencies charged with rebuilding slums were given the added responsibility of creating a good environment for the new housing. Attention had to be given to recreation and shopping facilities, protection against crime, proximity to transportation, and so on. Being successful became more difficult.

The redevelopment agency now had to consult with the people moving into the new housing on what they wanted. Designers had to be found who could meet these complex needs within budgetary constraints. In many instances the housing developer became responsible for the "human ecology" of the project—the ratio of blacks to whites, the ratio of middle-income to lower-income residents, number of children allowed, and so forth. Success now included filling up the buildings with the "right" types of occupants and building the "right" type of dwelling. Failure could occur if whites refused to live near blacks.

Today, an agency charged with this responsibility would face still another problem—finding contractors with sufficient numbers of black employees to work on the project. This very well could involve instituting special training programs or going to court to enforce hiring agreements, both of which would mean costly delays. The agency must also be prepared to comply with Environmental Protection Agency standards, another potential source of increased expense and added delay. Of course, all during the project various affected groups and citizens would be given ample opportunity to object to agency plans.

Obviously, it is much easier to be effective if you want only to construct good, inexpensive buildings than if you want to provide a good environment, with the right balance of tenants, that meets the needs of the community and that helps further minority employment. Compared to building such housing, developing the atomic bomb appears simple. In sum, federal bureaucracies *can* be effective, but we must be less optimistic when federal agencies are given complex, deeply rooted problems to solve. Unfortunately for those who prize effectiveness, as government moves into more difficult areas (for example, crime prevention and poverty) and bureaucracies are held accountable for more, and sometimes contradictory, goals, effectiveness will probably decline.

EFFICIENT INEFFICIENCY

Bureaucratic efficiency without concern for the specifics of a situation can sometimes result in gross injustices. Take the case of an elderly woman from Mississippi who received an overpayment of $146 in her social security check. She reported the error to the local social security official, who suggested putting the extra $146 in the bank while he investigated the situation. Ten months passed and the woman's bank balance grew to $1,400. At this point she received a notice from Medicaid, which is run by the Social Security Administration, ending her government aid. With a bank balance of $1,400 she had too much money and thus failed to quality for the program.

Reported in *Playboy*, May 1976.

Spoils system The practice of filling government positions with one's political supporters, almost regardless of their qualifications or their previous performance. From the expression, "To the victor belongs the spoils."

Does the existence of a large-scale bureaucracy pose a threat to democratic government?

As we have seen, the federal bureaucracy is open to many criticisms. The most serious question, however, concerns the compatibility of huge bureaucratic organizations and democratic government. Even defenders of bureaucratic efficiency are uneasy when this issue is raised. This unease usually takes two forms. First, there is a concern that bureaucrats will be *unresponsive* to popularly elected officials. Bureaucrats will frustrate the popular will as expressed by the President and Congress. Second, there is a fear that the massive bureaucracy, in the hands of an unscrupulous leader, would pose a serious threat to our political freedom. This fear derives from observation of the cases of Nazi Germany and the Soviet Union where the extensive apparatus of government became a key instrument of tyrannical dictators. Are these fears realistic? Let us consider each argument separately.

BUREAUCRATIC RESPONSIVENESS TO ELECTED LEADERS?

Those who worry that huge bureaucracies will frustrate the policies of elected leaders usually make the following points.

1. Elected leaders are not free to choose many subordinates who make important decisions. In the nineteenth century all administrative positions were filled by elected officials. This was under a **spoils system** in which victorious candidates rewarded their supporters with government jobs. However, beginning with the Pendleton Act (Civil Service Act of 1883), an increasingly large number of government jobs have been filled on the basis of merit, as determined by competitive examinations administered by the Civil Service Commission. Thus, newly elected officials committed to new programs are "struck" with the "old" bureaucracy. Replacing officials protected by civil service is nearly impossible. When Carter was elected President in 1976, for example, he could replace only 2,000 top government administrators. Sometimes it is hard to replace appointed officials — the terms of regulatory commission members, for instance, frequently do not coincide with presidential terms, and they cannot be fired.
2. Permanent administrators are much more knowledgeable about agency policy making than are political appointees. Higher civil servants have spent years learning the ropes and are, thus, indispensable to the political appointees who come and go every two or three years. It is not surprising, then, that officials appointed by the President frequently complain that their ambitious plans are resisted by civil servants who explain that "we don't do it that way here," or "based on my eighteen years of experience, this program will not work." A common result is that the political appointee

with a new perspective is gradually converted to the agency status quo.

3. Permanent bureaucrats and political leaders frequently have divergent perspectives on policy implementation. The President may, for example, appoint a Secretary of Agriculture committed to innovative policy and quick, dramatic results. To the career civil servant, however, such vigor and innovation constitute a disruption in long-established ways of getting things done. Because new rules and regulations must be learned and new pressures handled, and because uncertainty is increased, the new policies are resisted. In addition, many permanent civil servants have long-established relations with **agency "clients,"** and these further contribute to divergent perspectives. For instance, several recent Presidents have been frustrated in their attempts to change the Veterans Administration because many senior civil service administrators are much more sympathetic to the veterans they serve than to a President who desires a new policy.

4. Finally, the size and technical complexity of the federal bureaucracy undermines control (see Figure 13.1). An outsider, even the President of the United States, is frequently at a loss to know what is actually being done. The incomprehensibility of much bureaucratic language, the diffusion of responsibility, and the secrecy of decision making can easily create a situation in which political leaders can be insulated from the administration of laws. For these reasons sometimes years elapse before the true nature of a public program is known, and by that time much of the damage or inefficiency has already taken place.

Agency "clients"   A group having a close relationship with a particular government agency.

Elected leaders' control over the bureaucracy

Are these charges true? Is the federal bureaucracy pretty much beyond the control of elected leaders? Elected leaders do possess significant — though far from complete — influence over the operation of federal bureaucracies. This is particularly true when elected leaders make a major effort to influence the operations of a bureau. When the work of an agency is deemed acceptable or of low priority, elected officials typically conceded to civil servants a relatively free hand. However, when a member of Congress or the President takes a strong interest in the way a program is administered, several important mechanisms to control the bureaucracy are available.

The most basic way elected officials can control bureaucratic behavior is through the budgetary process. Both the President and Congress can threaten to punish an unresponsive agency or reward a cooperative one financially. We saw in the discussion of congressional oversight in Chapter Ten that Congress closely monitors much bureaucratic behavior and that no official wants to incur the displeasure of the legislators.[24] The

[24] The role of Congress in controlling bureaucracy is more fully described in Norman John Powell, *Responsible Public Bureaucracy in the United States* (Boston: Allyn & Bacon, 1968), especially pp. 49–70.

FIGURE 13.1
THE COMPLEX NETWORK OF GOVERNMENT: OFFICE OF EDUCATION (HEW) LINKS WITH OTHER AGENCIES.)

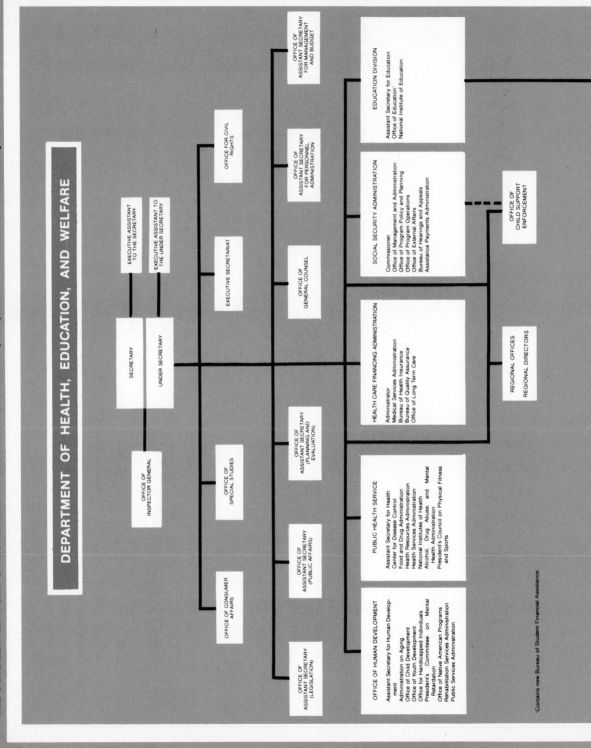

DEPARTMENT OF HEALTH, EDUCATION, AND WELFARE

SECRETARY

UNDER SECRETARY

EXECUTIVE ASSISTANT TO THE SECRETARY

EXECUTIVE ASSISTANT TO THE UNDER SECRETARY

OFFICE OF INSPECTOR GENERAL

EXECUTIVE SECRETARIAT

OFFICE FOR CIVIL RIGHTS

OFFICE OF ASSISTANT SECRETARY FOR MANAGEMENT AND BUDGET

OFFICE OF SPECIAL STUDIES

OFFICE OF ASSISTANT SECRETARY (PLANNING AND EVALUATION)

OFFICE OF GENERAL COUNSEL

OFFICE OF ASSISTANT SECRETARY FOR PERSONNEL ADMINISTRATION

OFFICE OF CONSUMER AFFAIRS

OFFICE OF ASSISTANT SECRETARY (PUBLIC AFFAIRS)

OFFICE OF ASSISTANT SECRETARY (LEGISLATION)

EDUCATION DIVISION
Assistant Secretary for Education
Office of Education
National Institute of Education

SOCIAL SECURITY ADMINISTRATION
Commissioner
Office of Management and Administration
Office of Program Policy and Planning
Office of Program Operations
Office of External Affairs
Bureau of Hearings and Appeals
Assistance Payments Administration

HEALTH CARE FINANCING ADMINISTRATION
Administrator
Medical Services Administration
Bureau of Health Insurance
Bureau of Quality Assurance
Office of Long Term Care

PUBLIC HEALTH SERVICE
Assistant Secretary for Health
Center for Disease Control
Food and Drug Administration
Health Resources Administration
Health Services Administration
National Institutes of Health
Alcohol, Drug Abuse, and Mental Health Administration
President's Council on Physical Fitness and Sports

OFFICE OF HUMAN DEVELOPMENT
Assistant Secretary for Human Development
Administration on Aging
Office of Child Development
Office of Youth Development
Office for Handicapped Individuals
President's Committee on Mental Retardation
Office of Native American Programs
Rehabilitation Services Administration
Public Services Administration

OFFICE OF CHILD SUPPORT ENFORCEMENT

REGIONAL OFFICES
REGIONAL DIRECTORS

¹Contains new Bureau of Student Financial Assistance.

FIGURE 13.1 Continued

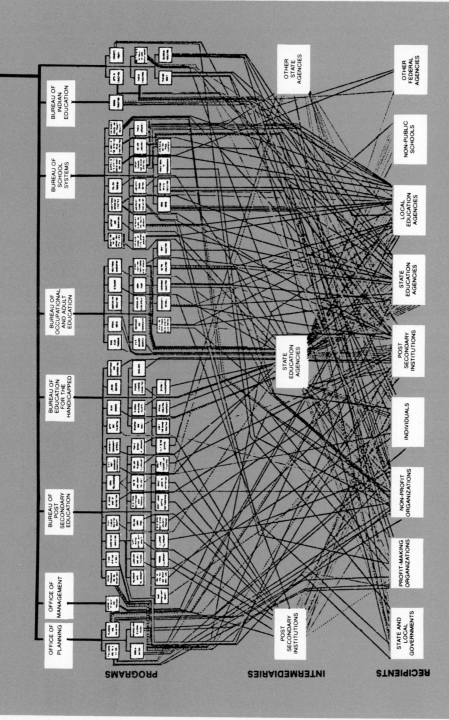

PROGRAMS

INTERMEDIARIES

RECIPIENTS

President's use of the budget was well illustrated by Nixon's treatment of many of Johnson's Great Society antipoverty programs. President Nixon disapproved of the administration and staff of the Office of Economic Opportunity, but instead of trying friendly persuasion, he simply curtailed its activities by depriving it of necessary funds. Such "lessons" are carefully noted by other agencies.

A second important method for controlling bureaucracies is reorganizing existing agencies and creating new ones. Suppose a President is elected on a program of vigorous enforcement of civil rights legislation. Once in office the President summons the heads of relevant agencies and demands dramatic action. "No way," explains the appointed agency head, "the permanent staff will never cooperate." Moreover, depriving them of their operating funds would not work because inaction is what they want anyhow, and they really cannot be fired. What can the President do? A common solution is to create an entirely new agency staffed

PRESIDENT CARTER AND CIVIL SERVICE REFORM

The spoils system was greatly criticized for putting politically connected incompetents on the public payroll. The merit system was supposed to eliminate such problems, but instances of incompetence in the bureaucracy still exist. And because of all the elaborate procedures that protect government employees, it is sometimes difficult to fire an unsatisfactory worker. For example, one agency fired a messenger for threats and abusive behavior. He filed suit that he was being discriminated against on the basis of age (he was 48); not until three years later was he finally dismissed. No wonder, then, that in fiscal 1977 only 226 federal employees, out of a work force of 2.8 million, were fired for inefficiency. In many instances it is easier to keep an incompetent on the job than to implement the elaborate procedures necessary to fire the person. One case has been reported involving an individual earning around $40,000 annually who has not shown up for work in six years. His superiors know about this behavior, but they allow it because his showing up for work would only make matters worse.

For reasons such as these President Carter made civil service reform a high priority. After extensive bargaining with members of Congress and representatives of government employees, Carter's civil service reform was enacted into law on October 13, 1978. The essential features were:

1. The Civil Service Commission, which previously administered

by people committed to the President's program. This is what President Johnson did on a grand scale when he created the new cabinet-level Department of Housing and Urban Development in 1965. Alternatively, both Congress and the President can redefine an agency's responsibility so that a particular program will be administered by more sympathetic people. Over the years, for example, different Presidents have emphasized different agencies for the enforcement of civil rights legislation. Given the size and complexity of government, it is usually possible to find several different agencies that could administer the same program.

A third control mechanism involves enacting very precise legislation that allows little administrative discretion. Elected officials realize, of course, the impossibility of providing for every situation and, therefore, usually give bureaucrats room for interpretation. In key policy areas, however, almost every contingency will be anticipated. This is especially evident in tax laws, where Congress and the President have tried to en-

---

personnel policy, was replaced by two new agencies. The Office of Personnel Management would set pay scales, selection procedures, and other aspects of U.S. government personnel policy. The Merit System Protection Board would be the highest board of appeal for employee grievances.

2. Managers now have more freedom in firing imcompetent employees. However, employees still enjoy substantial job protection (they have the right to an attorney in an extensive appeals process).

3. A group of top civil servants, called the Senior Executive Service (SES), was created. These 8,000 officials can receive substantial cash bonuses for their work, but they enjoy less job security than before, and they can be more easily transferred within or between agencies.

4. Merit pay must be clearly earned in middle-level positions instead of being given almost automatically.

5. The right of civil service employees to join unions is established by law (this right previously existed on the basis of executive order).

6. Reprisals are prohibited against employees who publicly expose violations of the law (sometimes called whistle-blowing).

The stories of civil service inefficiency are reported in Raymond Coffey, "Our Civil Service: A Shield for Incompetents," *Chicago Tribune*, May 28, 1978. For the details of President Carter's civil service reform, see "Congress Approves Civil Service Reforms," *Congressional Quarterly Weekly Report*, October 14, 1978, pp. 2045–2050.

sure that no minor official in the Internal Revenue Service will be able to create tax policy as he or she goes along. Similarly with military expenditures, bureaucrats are frequently greatly inhibited by precise legal restrictions.

The role of political appointees in shaping agency behavior is also important. This is especially true when inaction rather than action is desired. For example, when President Nixon took office in 1969 the Justice Department was working on several large antitrust cases. Taking the cases to court required the approval of the Attorney General, and Nixon's appointee – John Mitchell – decided that his department would not vigorously pursue judicial decisions. This stance was perfectly consistent with Nixon's policies, but if it hadn't been, Nixon would have had difficulty forcing Justice Department lawyers to initiate litigation.[25]

Finally, the overall professionalism of administrative officials contributes to the proper execution of the decisions made by elected officials.[26] The overwhelming majority of federal officials do not view themselves as petty tyrants responsible for independently making public policy. Most bureaucrats, like most citizens, accept the primacy of laws enacted by Congress and signed by the President. Such laws may be needlessly complicated or confusing, but they are not ignored. Moreover, the principle of following congressional or presidential intentions is reinforced by civil service professional organizations and procedures for career advancement. An administrator who suddenly believes that he or she is the law and interprets rules in blatantly contrary ways will probably soon be seeking new employment.

Disagreement among leaders over controlling the bureaucracy

The four factors we have described only facilitate control over the bureaucracy by elected leaders; they do not guarantee tight control. Members of Congress and the President are continuously attempting to control the bureaucracy, and success has varied considerably. One important reason for occasional failures is that elected leaders disagree among themselves concerning what bureaucracies ought to do. For many years Presidents have had numerous failures in "ordering" the Department of Defense to close unnecessary military bases. This failure, however, can also be interpreted as congressional success in getting the Defense Department to keep these bases open to help the local economy. Congress and the President frequently differ with one another (and many members of Congress differ among themselves), and since the bureaucracy must ultimately please everyone, confusion and occasional rule bending is to be expected.

[25] This tactic was also used to block the Department of Health, Education and Welfare from forcing the racial integration of public schools. See Gary Orfield, *Must We Bus? Segregation and National Policy* (Washington, D.C.: The Brookings Institution, 1978), pp. 280–281.

[26] Francis E. Rourke, *Bureaucracy, Politics, and Public Policy*, 2d ed. (Boston: Little, Brown, 1976), pp. 177–179.

BUREAUCRACY AS A THREAT TO POLITICAL FREEDOM

Whereas the first fear of bureaucracy concerned its unresponsiveness to elected leaders, the second is based on the opposite contention. That is, some people believe that the federal bureaucracy can be an effective instrument through which an unscrupulous leader can tyrannize citizens. Agencies created for the public good can also be used for evil purposes. The essential elements of this argument are:

1. Because of the growth of government, the federal bureaucracy plays a major role in people's lives. Increasingly, bureaucratic decisions affect where we live, what we see on television, where we go to school, what we eat, how we travel about, and how we earn a living. Much of this influence is taken for granted and not even noticed by most people.

2. Some of the world's most oppressive political systems, for example, Nazi Germany, were not administered by bloodthirsty thugs but by ordinary "decent" citizens just doing their jobs. An important lesson of modern dictatorships is that a large bureaucracy staffed by people who merely follow orders is an effective means of political control.

3. The long-standing Cold War against communism, plus the more recent concern over the growing incidence of crime, have created an atmosphere tolerant of bureaucratic excesses in the name of "national security" or "law enforcement." In fact, we have already seen that leaders can use the bureaucracy to stamp out political opposition. President Nixon, for example, employed several government agencies to punish his enemies and to cover up the Watergate break-in. Lyndon B. Johnson also used such tactics to suppress opposition to his Vietnam war policy.

4. In short, as more and more agencies are created and as more and more areas of our lives come under bureaucratic supervision, we come closer to realizing a dictatorship. When such a dictatorship arrives, it will be mislabeled as a benevolent government committed to making life "better" and "safer."

Limits on the dictatorial use of the bureaucracy

Is this fear realistic? What would prevent a President and a willing Congress from using the considerable array of government agencies to institute a virtual dictatorship? Experience suggests that an unscrupulous official—even the President—could get away with some abuses of the bureaucratic system, but it would be exceptionally difficult to transform most federal agencies into a coordinated instrument of political oppression. Put somewhat differently, the existing system is susceptible to hit and run abuses, but such abuses can be checked before they encompass the entire system.

Perhaps the most powerful impediment to the systematic abuse of the bureaucratic system is the fragmentation of national political power. The systematic misuse of the bureaucracy would require the cooperation of hundreds of administrators, and such coordination is usually difficult to achieve under any circumstances (even for positive purposes). Sup-

Plaintiff The person who initiates a legal action to collect damages.

pose that one day a President decides to use the full power of the government to crush the militant feminist movement. Among other things, the President plans to have the Internal Revenue Service audit tax returns of feminist leaders, have the Federal Communications Commission review the broadcasting licenses of sympathetic radio stations, use the FBI to harass feminist groups, and demand that the Department of Health, Education and Welfare stop funding projects favored by the feminist movement (to cite only a few possible actions). Moreover, the President threatens that unless action is taken immediately, heads will roll and budgets will be slashed.

No doubt some of the administrators involved would object to the President's scheme. Thanks to the constitutional system of checks and balances, plus various established customs, however, they would not be powerless to resist the President. Agency chiefs could complain to members of Congress, who could then use their powers to protect the agency against presidential threats. Recall that many federal bureaus have well-developed relations with congressional committees and that these relationships are frequently immune to presidential pressure. Congress might also create a special committee to investigate alleged presidential abuses or threaten to hold up other programs until the matter is cleared up. A mere handful of legislators can cause an enormous commotion if they put their minds to it (and this can occur even when the supersecret Central Intelligence Agency is involved).

Bureaucratic abuse of power can also be attacked through the federal court system. The Administrative Procedure Act of 1946 allows citizens damaged by arbitrary or unsupportable actions of federal administrative agencies to bring their cases to court. Over the years the courts have gradually broadened their definition of who can bring legal action against government decisions. Environmentalists in particular have taken advantage of this change to stop federal agencies from damaging the environment.[27] There are limits to judicial recourse, however. In the Supreme Court case *Laird* v. *Tatum* (1972), an effort to stop Army surveillance of civilian political activity was thrown out of court when the judges in a 5 to 4 vote ruled that the **plaintiffs** themselves had not directly sustained any harm. In general, a judicial remedy is most available when one has been directly harmed.

The public can also provide an impediment to the extensive misuse of bureaucratic power. In particular, widespread public exposure of congressional or presidential bureaucratic misuse can be devastating. Many people were incensed when President Nixon's use of the Internal Revenue Service against his enemies came to light. Such damaging exposure is especially likely when attempts of misuse are extensive and numerous people are involved. Public exposure of wrongdoing is also more likely in the wake of the Freedom of Information Act of 1966 (and a 1974 amendment). This act allows ordinary citizens access to government records except for matters involving national defense, confidential personal ma-

[27] C. Herman Pritchett, *The American Constitution*, 3d ed. (New York: McGraw-Hill, 1977), pp. 134–135.

REGULATORY ENFORCEMENT VERSUS CONSTITUTIONAL RIGHTS

As the efforts of the federal government to regulate business have increased, many businesses have decided to fight back. In most instances, the businesses have not questioned the goals of government regulations—job safety, reduced pollution, and so on, rather, they are opposing the methods used by agencies to achieve these goals. The basic issue is whether government investigators can look into company operations even when they have no specific complaint or suspected violation in mind. Can the Environmental Protection Agency (EPA) send investigators out to the local Buick plant to request records, inspect smokestacks, and talk to workers (at considerable cost to the company) merely to insure compliance with federal rules even if they are not looking for anything in particular? Companies argue that such "fishing expeditions" violate their constitutional protection against unreasonable searches and seizures, their right to privacy, and their right to legal due process.

Several such conflicts are now in the courts. For example, when the EPA sent a team of engineers with cameras to investigate a Dow Chemical complex at Midland, Michigan, Dow refused to admit them without a **search warrant.** Rather than obtain such a warrant (which would require it to specify what it was looking for), the EPA chartered a plane and flew over the Dow plant, taking extensive, detailed pictures. Dow then went to court charging invasion of privacy, unreasonable search, and denial of due process. The court issued an **injunction** impounding the EPA's films until the case is settled. Similar actions against alleged "fishing expeditions" have been taken by General Motors, Chrysler Corporation, Burlington Northern Railroad, and F. G. Barlow—a 63-year-old plumber from Pocatello, Idaho, who chased a government inspector out of his shop for not having a search warrant (Barlow's actions were upheld by the Supreme Court).

These conflicts are described further in Leonard M. Apcar, "Business Backlash, More Companies Bar Regulatory Agencies from Factories, Files," *Wall Street Journal,* January 22, 1979.

Search warrant   A court order allowing searches by government officials which specify what is to be searched, when, and what the searchers are looking to find.
Injunction   A court order that can require an individual to take an action or not take an action. Violations are punishable by fine or imprisonment.

terial, and law-enforcement files. Denial of access can be challenged in the courts. Despite numerous bureaucratic attempts to hide possible abuses of office, this act has been instrumental in exposing and deterring misdeeds.

Finally, there is the nature of the bureaucracy itself. A potentially dictatorial president (or legislator) would know from experience that getting 100 percent cooperation from thousands of separate officials would be a difficult task. Presidents (and legislators) must persuade, not order; presidential orders are often ignored; and subordinates sometimes "interpret" directives. Moreover, thanks to the civil service system and the independent power bases of nonelected administrators, insubordinate officials cannot easily be removed. The importance of the power to obstruct was dramatically illustrated when President Nixon attempted to use the FBI against his political enemies. Nixon's plan called for ignoring many of the legal restraints on wiretaps, mail intercepts, burglaries, and other hostile acts against radicals. FBI Director J. Edgar Hoover's refusal to cooperate in effect killed the scheme. The President and his staff could do little about this insubordination.[28]

Does, then, the existence of a large bureaucracy pose a threat to democratic government? The answer seems to be that it could pose such a threat and that on occasion it has been detrimental to democratic government, but for the present we should not be overly worried. Elected leaders can exercise a significant degree of control over bureaucrats, and various internal features of bureaucracy do limit the misuse of bureaucratic power. We must realize, however, that this state of affairs may not continue. It is entirely possible that the government bureaucracy may gradually become an irresponsible, oppressive power into itself.

A conclusion: bureaucracy and U.S. politics

As we have seen, it is easy to oppose big, inefficient bureaucracies that ensnarl us in needless red tape. How can any reasonable person advocate inefficiency or needless red tape? Yet we must realize that there is another side to the story. Big bureaucracy is not an evil, like the plague or pay toilets, which everyone should enthusiastically oppose. Before we get carried away we must realize that the federal bureaucracy, with all its forms, petty regulations, incomprehensible communications, and the like, may be an unavoidable cost of accomplishing certain goals. More important, the costs may be well worth the results to some people.

Consider the plight of someone committed to solving complex, deeply rooted problems, such as racial inequality, misuse of the environment, or discrimination based on sex. In many instances the only real choice is between inaction and government bureaucratic action that *might* solve the problem. The environmentalist does not want hundreds of forms and millions of pages of paperwork, but he or she wants an ecologically disruptive dam even less. Nor does the consumer advocate want to pester businesspeople with seemingly endless new regulations, yet this

[28] John Dean, *Blind Ambition* (New York: Simon & Schuster, 1976), pp. 34–38.

may be the necessary cost of getting safe products. Big bureaucracy and red tape are thus comparable to the unpleasant side effects of a medicine — as long as the benefits outweigh the costs, take the medicine.

We should also realize that calls of "down with the bloated bureaucracy" are usually vague about where reductions ought to occur. Every once in a while a high official will suggest closing thousands of rural, highly inefficient post offices. The typical response is indignant outrage on the part of the residents of these communities, many of whom are supporters of the principle of bureaucratic cutbacks. Veterans, likewise, decry plans to close underutilized veterans' hospitals. Obviously, one person's essential government service is another's bloated bureaucracy. Political leaders are, therefore, prone to move cautiously despite speeches calling for drastic action.

Another point to remember is that it is frequently much easier to oppose the way a program is administered than to oppose the goals of the program. A person in business, for example, finds it much easier to complain about stupid rules and bureaucratic gobblegook than about the protection of consumers from deceptive business practices. The same person, however, might be outraged if the government decided to abolish all the complicated forms regulating welfare payments since he or she probably believes that recipients cannot be trusted to do the right thing without stringent bureaucratic controls. Of course, this person may have a real case against government overregulation, but we must always look behind such simplistic slogans as "down with the bureaucracy."

We have seen that managing the federal bureaucracy involves many complex, and sometimes contradictory, issues. It is filled with paradoxes. We want the bureaucracy to treat everyone equally, yet we get upset if our personal circumstances are ignored. We want fairness, yet we complain about too many explicit rules and regulations. We want the federal bureaucracy to be responsive to elected leaders, yet we fear that if it were too responsive it could become a dictatorial tool for an unscrupulous leader. Perhaps we should create a Bureau of the Bureaucracy to look into these problems.

Major questions raised

1. What is the federal bureaucracy? "Bureaucracy" refers to both a method of doing business and a large number of organizations that do the work of the federal government. As a way of doing business, bureaucracies emphasize a clear division of labor, hierarchical authority patterns, prescribed job qualifications, and administrative objectivity. Bureaucratic agencies are the organizations that do the work of government. They grow because of their comparative effectiveness in dealing with large-scale problems. By 1976, the federal bureaucracy employed 2.8 million persons.

2. Why has the bureaucracy grown so large? Population increases, technological developments, and growth in government responsibility have contributed greatly to bureaucratic growth. Attempts to solve complex problems in a fair, equitable manner have helped generate enormous quantities of red tape.

3. Is the federal bureaucracy effective? It has been relatively effective in many areas, especially in projects that involve a single, clear goal. The bureaucracy is also comparatively free of corruption, and most of its clients seem to be satisfied. However, when agencies attempt projects with numerous, complex goals, success is less likely.

4. Does the existence of a large-scale bureaucracy pose a threat to democratic government? Critics of big bureaucracy fear that bureaucrats (1) will ignore the policies of elected leaders or (2) will be the willing tools of dictatorial leaders. On occasion, both of these fears have been temporarily realized. However, because of various controls over the bureaucracy, we are still a long way from government for and by bureaucracy.

QUESTIONS FOR FURTHER DISCUSSION

1. What if you created a group called Citizens Against Bureaucracy and tens of thousands of people offered their time and money to your cause. You realize, of course, that bureaucracy will not go away merely by having big rallies against it. You need a long-term battle plan. Do you create special task forces (for example "citizens concerned about bureaucratic inefficiency"), appoint aides possessing particular knowledge of bureaucratic faults, and formulate a precise plan of attack on bureaucratic methods? How might you effectively organize thousands of citizens who share an opposition to bureaucratic solutions to social problems?

2. Some people argue that the "merit system" of selecting high public officials does not really give everyone an equal chance. Basically, civil service merit requirements for top positions only reinforce the dominant position of certain social and economic groups. This bias is confirmed by several studies demonstrating that women, blacks, Chicanos, and members of other minorities are underrepresented in the top ranks of the federal bureaucracy. Would you argue that the government has a responsibility to insure that all groups are fairly represented in the upper levels of government agencies? Should the merit concept be broadened to include such attributes as special empathy for disadvantaged citizens or experience in community organizations? Or should merit continue to mean specialized training and skills as reflected in examination scores or college degrees? In other words, what attributes should define merit?

3. One major reason incompetent civil servants remain on the public payroll is that firing them can take almost forever. The story is told of a supervisor who tried to fire a typist who was repeatedly and unexcusably absent from work. Only after 18 months of threats and actions did she resign "for reasons of health." Meanwhile, the supervisor received a "poor" rating in his job performance because of the extensive amount of time he expended trying to fire the incompetent typist. He was fortunate because the typist could have considerably prolonged the process by tak-

ing her case to the Federal Employee Appeals Authority, then to an arbitration board, and then to the Civil Service Commission itself. Given these problems, what would you do if you were the supervisor? Tolerate the illegal absences of the typist because it doesn't pay to take any action? Give the typical tough assignments in the hope she'll get the message and leave? Give her a glowing letter of reference and recommend promotion to some other department? Try to get her fired even if it means possibly ruining your own career?

4. A recently developed method of limiting bureaucratic growth and encouraging efficiency is zero-based budgeting (ZBB). Under the present system of budgeting only new programs, not existing programs, are questioned and scrutinized. Under ZBB, however, all expenditures—new and established—are extensively reviewed. The basic purpose of ZBB is to force agencies to justify all expenditures. Though the intent of ZBB is admirable, what might be some of the negative consequences of this reform? If you were a power-hungry bureaucrat intent on expanding your agency, how would you deal with ZBB?

BIBLIOGRAPHY

Fried, Robert C. *Performance in American Bureaucracy*. Boston: Little, Brown, 1976.
>
> An extensive analysis of the performance of the bureaucracy at the national, state, and local levels. Uses three standards for judging performance: adherence to legal rules, responsiveness to the political community, and effectiveness in getting the job done. Numerous chapters examine the internal and external constraints on bureaucratic performance. Concludes with an analysis of possible reforms.

Hummel, Ralph. *The Bureaucratic Experience*. New York: St. Martins Press, 1977.
>
> Designed as a practical guide to bureaucracy, the book argues that bureaucracy is a new way of organizing social life. Analyzes the special psychology of the bureaucracy, its language, its exercise of power, and how bureaucracy might be controlled. One of the few books on the subject written from the perspective of the person confronted with a bureaucracy.

Kaufman, Herbert. *Red Tape: Its Origins, Uses, and Abuses*. Washington, D.C.: The Brookings Institution, 1977.
>
> A clearly written book that provides an explanation and possible cure for the problem of bureaucratic red tape. Kaufman is a recognized expert on bureaucracy, and though brief, this book contains numerous illustrations of red tape in action.

Krislov, Samuel. *Representative Bureaucracy*. Englewood Cliffs, N.J.: Prentice-Hall, 1974.
>
> Examines several aspects of bureaucracy through the question of are they representative. Consider the growth of modern bureaucracies, the problem of staffing them with ordinary citizens, and the various roles played by bureaucracies. Also briefly analyzes bureaucracies in other nations such as India and Canada.

Levitan, Sar, and Robert Taggart. *The Promise of Greatness*. Cambridge, Mass.: Harvard University Press, 1976.
>
> A data-rich analysis of one of the greatest bureaucratic undertakings in U.S. history—the Great Society Program of the 1960s. The author analyzes several programs, including health care, compensatory training, and civil rights, and

concludes that these efforts were generally successful. Nontechnical despite extensive use of statistical information.

Mosher, Frederick C. *Democracy and the Public Service.* New York: Oxford University Press, 1968.
> Examines the background and orientation of administrative officials from the perspective of democratic government. Contains chapters on how the U.S. civil service system evolved, the role of professionals in government service, and different questions of merit and morality in administration.

Peters, Charles, and Michael Nelson, eds. *The Culture of Bureaucracy.* New York: Holt, Rinehart and Winston, 1979.
> An interesting collection of journalistic articles that takes a somewhat suspicious view of bureaucrats. Articles include "Nothing Fails Like Success," "Dumping $2.6 Million on Bakersfield," and "Delivering the Mail: We Did It Once and We Can Do It Again."

Powell, Norman John. *Responsible Public Bureaucracy in the United States.* Boston: Allyn & Bacon, 1967.
> A clearly written, balanced introduction to understanding the bureaucracy. Begins with the meaning of the bureaucratic approach and its operation and then shows how bureaucrats interact with groups outside of government. Contains a good chapter evaluating the performance of the bureaucracy and its responsiveness.

Pressman, Jeffrey L., and Aaron Wildavsky. *Implementation.* Berkeley: University of California Press, 1973.
> An in-depth case study of how one Washington-formulated program actually worked in Oakland, California. A good insight into all the problems that can befall a bureaucracy when it tries to solve a long-standing, complex economic and social problem.

Ripley, Randall B., and Grace Franklin. *Congress, the Bureaucracy, and Public Policy.* Homewood, Ill.: The Dorsey Press, 1976.
> A comprehensive analysis of how Congress attempts to control the bureaucracy. Contains several studies of policy areas such as the war on poverty, Medicare, revenue sharing, and defense policy. Concludes with a general perspective on policy making in U.S. politics.

Rourke, Francis E. ed. *Bureaucratic Power in National Politics,* 3d ed. Boston: Little, Brown, 1978.
> Contains 29 diverse articles dealing with various aspects of bureaucracy. Especially relevant for material on the exercise of bureaucratic power, how this power might be reformed, and whether this power can be controlled by citizens.

Sayre, Wallace S. ed. *The Federal Government Service,* 2d ed. Englewood Cliffs, N.J.: Prentice-Hall, 1965.
> Five articles by experts on the bureaucracy dealing with such issues as administering the civil service system, the operation of the patronage system, and the relationship between the bureaucracy and elected public officials.

Seidman, Harold. *Politics, Position, and Power: The Dynamics of Federal Organization,* 2d ed. New York: Oxford University Press, 1975.
> Seidman spent many years inside the Washington bureaucracy and writes of the battles among agencies, Congress, and the executive branch. He argues that they are not battles over increased efficiency, progress, or reform; each change is designed to help one interest against others.

United States Government Manual. Washington, D.C.: Office of the Federal Register, National Archives and Records Service, General Services Administration, 1978.
> Provides 835 fact-filled pages on what federal agencies do, their top personnel, and where one can obtain information on these agencies (telephone numbers are provided). Invaluable resource in trying to make sense of the national bureaucracy. Periodically updated.

Weidenbaum, Murray L. *Business, Government, and the Public.* Englewood Cliffs, N.J.: Prentice-Hall, 1977.

An up-to-date and authoritative review of government regulation. Looks at consumer regulations, automobile production, job safety, environmental protection, as well as some of the different techniques of regulation. Contains several case studies and a good bibliography on government regulations.

Woll, Peter. *American Bureaucracy*, 2d ed. New York: Norton, 1977.

A thorough but nontechnical overview of the bureaucracy. Good coverage of power and limits of federal agencies, the operation of administrative law, and the relationship of bureaucrats to Congress and the President.

PREVIEW

<hr>

What is the federal court system, and how does it function?

Beyond creating the Supreme Court, the Constitution is vague about the judiciary. The organization of the federal court has changed several times. Presently its major elements are federal district courts, Courts of Appeal, the Supreme Court, and specialized courts such as the U.S. Customs Court. Court jurisdiction is set both by the Constitution and by Congress. Especially where constitutional issues, acts of foreign nations, or issues of federal law are involved, cases are handled in federal courts. Federal judges are appointed by the President and confirmed by the Senate. For federal district judgeships, political connections and support are necessary. Almost all appointed judges are members of the President's political party. A potential federal judge must also meet legal training and ethical standards. Much debate centers around the question of whether justice is compromised in a system in which politics plays a large role in judgeship selection.

How do Supreme Court Justices decide cases?

Few cases appealed to the Court receive extensive review. A case is considered if it raises important legal issues, if lower courts have given conflicting opinions, or if lower-court decisions conflict with previous Supreme Court decisions. Getting to the high Court also requires much time and money.

One explanation of how Supreme Court Justices approach voting is that they mechanically compare the Constitution and the case. Usually, however, cases are too complex for this approach. Following precedent is another possible explanation, but if precedent were clear, the case would probably not have reached the Court in the first place (and precedents can conflict). The attitudes of Justices are good predictors of how they vote. Judges are not free to enact their personal biases into law, however. Finally, the interactions of the nine Justices can affect the final decision.

What has been the political impact of the Supreme Court?

The Court can affect public policy through its power to declare laws and executive actions unconstitutional. It can also reinterpret existing legislation. Recently, lower courts have actually administered schools and hospitals.

The Court has been accused of being an instrument of the ruling classes. Particularly in the last half of the nineteenth century, the Court vigorously protected dominant capitalist interests. At other times—especially during the Warren Court (1953–1969)—the Court has played a strong role in protecting less powerful groups.

The judicial system is limited. Only issues in specific cases are considered. Too, the courts are reluctant to address controversial "political questions." The courts also lack an independent means to insure compliance. Finally, both Congress and the President can affect federal court jurisdiction, how court orders will be enforced, the legislation to be redrafted, and the fate of constitutional amendments.

CHAPTER FOURTEEN

THE SUPREME COURT AND THE JUDICIAL SYSTEM

ompared to Congress and the President, the judicial branch of government seems to be the weakest partner. Unlike Congress, it lacks the broad constitutional power to legislate in many important areas. Against the executive bureaucracies and contemporary presidential power, the federal courts appear almost overwhelmed. Moreover, the appointment of judges and much of what they can do are determined by the legislative and executive branches. Nevertheless, despite these handicaps, the court system has been able to hold its own. In fact, certain critics of the federal judiciary have asserted that judges have now become too powerful. Especially in sensitive matters involving racial and economic policy, federal judges—not elected officials—are making and enforcing public policy. This chapter examines three questions dealing with the role of the federal court system in the political process:

1. What is the federal court system, and how does it function?
2. How do Supreme Court Justices decide cases?
3. What has been the political impact of the Supreme Court?

FIGURE 14.1

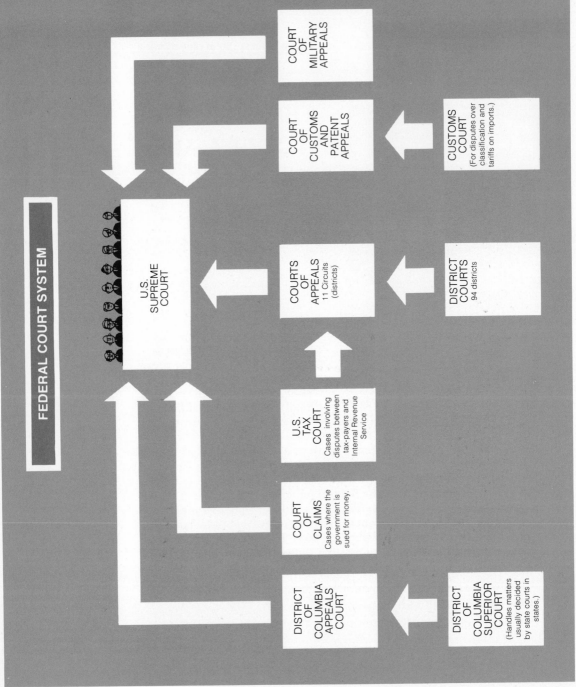

FEDERAL COURT SYSTEM

U.S. SUPREME COURT

COURT OF MILITARY APPEALS

COURT OF CUSTOMS AND PATENT APPEALS

CUSTOMS COURT
(For disputes over classification and tariffs on imports.)

COURTS OF APPEALS
11 Circuits (districts)

DISTRICT COURTS
94 districts

U.S. TAX COURT
Cases involving disputes between tax-payers and Internal Revenue Service

COURT OF CLAIMS
Cases where the government is sued for money.

DISTRICT OF COLUMBIA APPEALS COURT

DISTRICT OF COLUMBIA SUPERIOR COURT
(Handles matters usually decided by state courts in states.)

What is the federal court system, and how does it function?

Despite the importance of the courts in politics, even well-informed citizens know little about the judicial system or the names of very many judges. Since federal judges do not run for office and since many of their activities are technical, the relative obscurity of the judiciary is to be expected. Only on rare occasions, for example, when the Supreme Court makes an unpopular decision, does the judicial process receive widespread scrutiny. To better understand how the federal judicial system operates, let us consider three basic aspects of that system: (1) the federal court system; (2) federal court jurisdiction; and (3) the selection of judges.

THE FEDERAL COURT SYSTEM

The federal government now includes a large, complex court system (Figure 14.1), although the Constitution does not specify how the federal courts are to be organized. The Constitution simply says, in Article III, section 1, "The judicial power of the United States, shall be vested in one Supreme Court, and such inferior Courts as the Congress may from time to time ordain and establish." There is no mention of Supreme Court size or of the size and number of lesser courts. The first Congress dealt with this vagueness in the Judiciary Act of 1789. This act formally created the first Supreme Court, thirteen district courts (one for each state), and three circuit (or appeals) courts presided over by one district court judge and two Supreme Court Justices.

The development of the judicial system
This was only the first of several versions of the federal court system. The most obvious changes have been in the size of the Supreme Court. The original Court had six justices. The number dropped to five between 1801 and 1807, rose to seven between 1807 and 1837, increased to nine between 1837 and 1863, reached a high of ten between 1863 and 1866, fell back to seven between 1866 and 1869, and has remained at nine since 1869. The last major effort to change the size of the Court was in 1937 when President Franklin D. Roosevelt, angry over decisions by conservative Justices, proposed to add new Justices when those then serving reached the age of 70.

The largest growth in the federal judicial system has occurred below the Supreme Court level. Immediately beneath the Supreme Court are the United States Courts of Appeals. Since 1977, the United States and its territories have been divided into eleven **judicial circuits,** with one court in each circuit. Depending on the work load, between three and fifteen judges are assigned to each Court of Appeals (there are ninety-seven judges in all). One Justice of the Supreme Court is also assigned to each one for purposes of general supervision. Usually cases are tried by

Judicial circuit A geographical area, frequently including several states, over which a court has jurisdiction. The term derives from the days when judges traveled from town to town dispensing justice. These towns constituted a circuit.

John Marshall, Chief Justice of the Supreme Court, 1801–1835.

three-judge panels, though on special occasions all the judges in a judicial circuit sit on a case.

The courts that bear the brunt of the federal judicial work are the district courts. Each state, plus Washington, D.C., and the Commonwealth of Puerto Rico, has at least one federal district court, and some of the larger states have four. These federal district courts have between three and twenty-seven judges each. Congress, in 1968, created the Judicial Panel on Multidistrict Litigation, which provided for seven federal judges that can be temporarily transferred to a single district for pretrial proceedings involving cases that cut across district lines.

The Supreme Court, the Courts of Appeals, and district courts comprise the basic elements of the federal court system. Additionally, there are several special courts. In 1855, the United States Court of Claims was established to decide claims against the U.S. government. A typical case in this court might involve a defense contractor suing the government for unpaid bills. A second special court is the United States Court of Customs and Patent Appeals. As its name indicates, it handles disputes involving patent ownership and certain laws regulating customs duties. A third special court is the United States Customs Court, which is composed of nine judges and deals mainly with questions involving tariffs. If you imported a wool work of art (which is duty-free) and the customs agent believed it to be a mere rug (on which there is a duty), you could take your case to the Customs Court. For court-marshaled military personnel there is a fourth type of special federal court, the United States Court of Military Appeals. Finally, a student who disagrees with the Internal Revenue Service's disallowance of a tax deduction of $250 for Friday afternoon beer as a "necessary and ordinary occupational expense" can seek redress in the United States Tax Court.[1]

[1] Another class of federal courts exists where there is no state court system, that is, in Washington, D.C., and U.S. territories. These courts handle matters usually left to state courts, such as criminal cases involving local laws or civil actions (lawsuits).

Staff and work load of federal courts

Associated with each of these courts are various officials who assist in judicial administration. The major aides of the Supreme Court are the clerk, the reporter of decisions, the marshal, .and the librarian. Since 1971, the nonjudicial duties of the eleven Courts of Appeals have been administered by a circuit executive (general judicial matters are discussed once a year in a judicial conference of all circuit and district judges). The federal district courts, which actually conduct trials, have larger staffs, with each consisting of a clerk, a U.S. marshal (who carries out court orders but is formally employed by the Justice Department), one or more U.S. magistrates, bankruptcy referees, probation officers, court reporters, and clerical aides. In 1976, the entire federal judicial system employed 10,825 people (compared to 2.8 million employees in the executive branch and over 37,000 in the legislative branch).[2]

In view of the comparatively small size of the federal judicial system, the courts have borne an enormous case load. In 1975, the Supreme Court considered 2,708 cases (though most were not considered in depth). The Courts of Appeals considered many more cases. In 1975, the circuit courts faced 16,658 cases and managed to resolve 16,000 of them (between 1960 and 1975 the number of appealed cases quadrupled). Yet this is nothing compared to the case load of the district courts, which in 1975 handled over 158,000 cases, of which 19,236 ultimately required trials (a 100 percent increase over 1960).[3]

FEDERAL COURT JURISDICTION

What makes a case a "federal case"? What determines whether a case will reach the Supreme Court? These are important questions, because *who* decides a case and according to *what* rules can have a major bearing on *how* a case is decided. During the 1960s, for example, many civil rights lawyers sought to have their cases tried in federal rather than state courts in the hope of getting more sympathetic treatment. Whether a case becomes a federal case is largely prescribed by the Constitution and by acts of Congress regulating federal court jurisdiction.

Article III of the Constitution describes the domain of the federal, as opposed to state, courts. A case can become a federal case depending on the types of law it involves or who is involved in the case. Regarding the *type of law* involved, an issue enters the federal system when:

1. *The Constitution itself is involved.* If you challenge a federal or state law on the explicit grounds that it violates the Constitution, you may have a federal case.
2. *Laws and treaties enacted by the federal government are involved.* If Congress has made the importation of heroin illegal and you are caught importing it, you go directly to federal court. This is one of the most common reasons for a case going to federal court.

[2] *Statistical Abstract of the United States, 1977,* p. 249.
[3] *Statistical Abstract of the United States, 1977,* pp. 167–169.

Original jurisdiction The authority of a court to hear a case when it first begins. If a court can hear a certain type of case only after it first is heard by another court, it has appellate jurisdiction. Some courts have both types of jurisdictions, depending on the case; other courts are limited to only one type of jurisdiction. *Consul* An agent acting on behalf of a foreign government charged with administrative responsibilities.

Less common are cases involving treaties with foreign nations or with Indian tribes.

3. *Cases involve admiralty and maritime jurisdiction.* These involve crimes committed on the high seas or other navigable waters as well as maritime-related commercial transactions.

The Constitution also gives the federal courts jurisdiction when certain *types of people* are involved. Specifically, a federal court can become involved when:

1. *The U.S. government is a party in the case.* If the government is suing a private citizen or is being sued by an individual for damages, the case is tried in federal court.
2. *Controversies arise between two or more states.* This would include, for example, cases in which the agency of one state was polluting water that flowed into a second state. Here, and in other instances in which a state is involved, the Supreme Court has **original jurisdiction** (the case goes directly to the Supreme Court).
3. *Civil (as opposed to criminal) controversies arise between a state and citizens of another state.* In the *Georgia* v. *Pennsylvania R. Co.* (1945), for instance, the state of Georgia in federal court sued twenty railroads for price fixing, even though these railroads were not located in Georgia. However, the Eleventh Amendment generally forbids citizens of one state to sue a different state without the permission of the state (but states can sue citizens).
4. *Conflict arises between citizens of different states.* If a citizen of New York sues a citizen of, say, New Jersey (or a corporation chartered in New Jersey), one of the parties can request that the trial be held in federal court. However, in the key decision in *Erie Railroad* v. *Tompkins* (1938), the Supreme Court ruled that federal courts must follow appropriate state (not federal) law in such circumstances. A large proportion of federal cases involve this jurisdiction.
5. *Cases involve foreign states and citizens.* If a recognized foreign government sues a U.S. citizen, or a state sues a foreign citizen, or if a foreign and U.S. citizen are involved, the case, at the request of one of the parties, is decided in federal court.
6. *Cases involve ambassadors, ministers, and consuls.* Under international law ambassadors and ministers representing foreign governments are exempt from U.S. jurisdiction (**consuls** are not exempt). Nevertheless, a foreign ambassador suing a U.S. citizen would take the case to the Supreme Court, which has original jurisdiction in such matters.

The Constitution, also allows the other two branches of government to regulate court jurisdiction much more precisely than does the Constitution. In 1845, for example, Congress explicitly expanded the jurisdiction involved in "admiralty and maritime jurisdiction" to include *all* navigable waters in the United States. In the Judiciary Act of 1925 Congress gave the Supreme Court considerable powers of discretion in accepting cases appealed from the lower courts. The Administrative Procedures Act of 1946 allowed decisions made by many regulatory and executive agencies to be appealed in federal courts. In 1958, Congress sought to

THE SOLICITOR GENERAL

A key figure in the U.S. judicial system is the Solicitor General. This individual—the chief lawyer for the U.S. government—decides, with a staff, which cases involving the government will be appealed to the Courts of Appeals or the Supreme Court, the position the government will take in a case, and how a case will be presented both orally and in the written briefs. Since the government cannot appeal each and every decision, the Solicitor General plays a major gate-keeper role. Recently, when a lower court ruled against the Defense Department in an award of back pay in a racial discrimination case, the Solicitor General decided that the decision did not warrant an appeal (only about a third of the cases in which the government loses are appealed to the Supreme Court). However, when a lower court ruled that the Food and Drug Administration could not investigate defectively designed medical equipment, a decision was made to appeal. It was the Solicitor General, with staff help, who shaped the government's position in the Bakke case. They are the ones who represent the government before the Supreme Court.

Under President Carter the Solicitor General was Wade H. McCree, Jr., a graduate of Harvard Law School. McCree was elected a judge in Detroit in 1954 after several years of private legal practice. In 1961, he became a federal district judge, and in 1966 he was elevated to the Court of Appeals. He spent a total of twenty-three years as a judge prior to being named Solicitor General. McCree is assisted by a staff of eighteen lawyers, all of whom were in the top 2 percent of their graduating law school classes.

Wade McCree. By custom the Solicitor General appears before the Supreme Court dressed in a morning coat.

Civil suit A legal dispute between individuals or corporations in which one person seeks court intervention. This is different from a criminal case, in which the government prosecutes for a violation of law.

reduce the number of cases in the federal system by requiring that a **civil suit** between citizens of different states involve at least $10,000 before it can be tried in federal court (cases involving worker compensation laws are also excluded from federal courts).

Federal-state jurisdiction relationships

Thus far, the jurisdiction of the federal system is relatively clear. What occasionally makes the situation complex is the relationship of the federal courts to the state courts. To understand the federal court-state court relationship, we must enumerate three points. First, Article VI, paragraph 2, the so-called supremacy clause of the Constitution, makes federal law supreme. Where state law conflicts with federal law, judges (federal and state) must enforce federal law. Second, where no such conflict exists, state law, as interpreted in state courts, is supreme. Federal courts are not superior to state courts in the sense that federal judges can tell state judges how to interpret nonconflicting state laws. There is no superior-inferior relationship between the two systems. Third, state judicial decisions can be appealed in the federal system only where disputes involve federal law or the Constitution. Under such circumstances the appeal must proceed through the state court system before it can be taken directly to the Supreme Court (bypassing the lower federal courts). On the whole, Supreme Court Justices are cautious in reviewing cases appealed from state courts.[4]

SELECTION OF FEDERAL JUDGES

Who can become a Supreme Court Justice or a district or circuit judge? The formal requirements for these positions are simple: nomination by the President and confirmation by a Senate majority. There are no age, training, or residency requirements (you must live within the jurisdiction of your court when in office, but not before). There are, however, several informal criteria, the most important of which concern political associations, legal training, and "judicial temperament."

Political requirements

All federal judges must satisfy certain political requirements. Being of the same political party as the President is very important. Ninety percent or more presidential appointments have come from the ranks of the President's own party. Even a President such as Dwight Eisenhower, who was not widely regarded as a strong party man, nevertheless drew 94.8 percent of his judicial appointments from the Republican Party.[5] A second political requirement, especially important for federal district judges, is created by the custom of *senatorial courtesy*. According to this

[4] Getting from a state court into the federal system involves several complex issues. For a more complete discussion of this process, see C. Herman Pritchett, *The American Constitution*, 3d ed. (New York: McGraw-Hill, 1977), pp. 118–119.

[5] The role of political parties in the selection of judges is described more fully in Richard J. Richardson and Kenneth N. Vines, *The Politics of Federal Courts* (Boston: Little, Brown, 1970), pp. 68–70.

custom the senior Senator of the President's party from the state in which the appointment is to be made usually – but not always – has veto power over the appointment. For example, if President Reagan wishes to fill a district court judgeship in Illinois, he must negotiate the nomination with the senior Republican, Charles Percy. Where there are no Senators of the same party, the President has a freer hand.

Philosophical agreement between the President and the prospective nominee is a third important political consideration. This is a particularly crucial factor in Supreme Court appointments, since these judicial decisions can have a major impact on public policy. In 1971, President Nixon, consistent with his pledges to make the Supreme Court less liberal, appointed two judicial conservatives – Lewis F. Powell, Jr., and William H. Rehnquist. Unfortunately for Presidents, however, their expectations are not always realized. President Eisenhower appointed Earl Warren Chief Justice in 1953 believing him to be conservative and was subsequently gravely disappointed when Warren led the Court in a highly active and liberal direction.

However, in 1978 President Carter sought to place greater emphasis on merit as opposed to political connections. Before Congress created 152 new federal judgeships, the President issued an executive order creating a merit commission to recruit candidates for circuit courts (another executive order called for merit panels to recommend candidates for district judgeships). As things worked out, considerable state-to-state variation occurred in how merit panels were run, and some states did not cooperate at all (or members of Congress manipulated the panels). A major goal of Carter's reform – recruiting more minorities and women – has not been successful despite suggestions that merit panels be composed of some women and members of minorities. (Despite this action on behalf of merit, only two of Carter's sixty-six judicial appointments have been Republicans).[6]

A fourth political consideration is whether or not a judicial nominee has outraged a significant political group. In most instances nominees grossly unacceptable to important groups are eliminated in the initial screening process by the Attorney General. For example, it is unlikely that a lawyer known for his or her outspoken antilabor views would survive Senate confirmation hearings, so that the very nomination of such an individual would be unlikely.

Legal training

Federal judges must also meet certain standards of legal training. At one time graduating from law school was not a requirement – of all the federal district judges sitting in 1930, 46.2 percent did *not* have law degrees.[7] Today, however, a law degree is not only essential, it must come

[6] For more on Carter's merit plan, see "Report Card on Judicial Merit Selection," *Congressional Quarterly Weekly Report*, February 3, 1979, pp. 189–194.

[7] Richardson and Vines, p. 74. Many of these judges did have some legal training, however. Most states once allowed a prospective lawyer to "read law" (work for a lawyer) as a method of qualifying for a law degree. Many judges thus learned their law through on-the-job training rather than in law school.

Judicial temperament A general collection of attributes relating to morality, impartiality, and skill which make a person suitable for being a judge.

from a recognized, established law school. This was illustrated in the conflict over President Kennedy's nomination of Francis X. Morrissey to a district judgeship. Strong objections were raised when it was discovered that Morrissey's law degree came from a three-month extension course (nevertheless, he was approved by the Senate Judiciary Committee, but ultimately withdrew).

One type of legal training that is not required is previous experience as a judge. In some European nations becoming a judge in a high national court involves a long career in the legal system. This is not the case in the United States, where less than half of appointed federal judges have had previous judgeship experience.[8] Many federal judges are drawn from political life or are lawyers who were active in political campaigns. Some Presidents have even appointed law school professors as judges.

Judicial temperament

The third broad requirement—"**judicial temperament**"—is perhaps the most difficult to define. At a minimum this means being a law-abiding, upstanding citizen. This issue is usually settled in the preliminary stages of the nomination process by an FBI investigation. Nominees with criminal records or problems that might compromise their positions, for example, alcoholism or excessive gambling, are quickly eliminated.

Other important traits—impartiality, prudence, legal knowledge, ethics, and propriety—are more difficult to ascertain. The American Bar Association (ABA), through its Committee on the Federal Judiciary, has increasingly played an important role in making these evaluations. Since 1947, this committee has been rating judicial nominees as "not qualified," "qualified," "well qualified," and "exceptionally well qualified." Presidents have accepted the ABA's recommendations, though both Eisenhower and Kennedy nominated several judges evaluated as "not qualified." (In some instances an "unqualified" rating depends on a technicality. For example, when President Kennedy nominated a 64-year-old woman, she was declared "unqualified" simply because the ABA committee had a rule opposing the appointment of anyone 64 or older.)

It is important to realize that "impartial ratings" such as these may conceal political biases. One of the most distinguished Supreme Court Justices of all time—Louis Brandeis—was bitterly opposed by almost the entire organized legal profession when he was nominated in 1916. He was called "unqualified," but the opposition was largely based on Brandeis' liberal philosophy (and some people would say his Jewishness as well). For many years the ABA was dominated by established lawyers who found it relatively easy to say that a nonestablishment nominee somehow lacked "judicial temperament" or "impartiality."[9] Of course, such biases are not limited to conservatives—liberals in the ABA can question the "ethics" of candidates sympathetic to business interests.

[8] Richardson and Vines, pp. 75–78.

[9] For an excellent description of how the American Bar Association screens prospective judges, see Joseph C. Goulden, *The Benchwarmers: The Private World of the Powerful Federal Judges* (New York: Weybright and Talley, 1974), pp. 39–74.

The consequences of how judges are selected

What are the political consequences of the recruitment of federal judges? Are the best people selected? Are federal judges an unrepresentative political elite? Unfortunately, it is much easier to describe the characteristics of federal judges than to determine the consequences of these traits. We know that judges tend to come from high social-status families, have usually had the benefits of prestige colleges and law schools, are older, and are usually white males. In recent years, especially because of the appointments of Democratic Presidents, more people of lower-status origins, women, blacks, and other "nonestablished" types have become federal judges, though much of the upper-status character remains.[10]

The most difficult question concerns the impact of politics on the recruitment process. Getting on the federal bench is closely tied to politics. We do not have a civil service review procedure that impartially selects judges. Some people have argued that judges chosen on political grounds cannot possibly be fair and impartial. Moreover, unfairness is reinforced by the unrepresentative nature of the federal judiciary—judges not only play politics but because of their high-status backgrounds, they usually tend to play politics in the same (conservative) direction. This is a complex and crucial question, but we must delay our answer until we discuss the impact of court decisions.

How do Supreme Court Justices decide cases?

Every year many key policy issues raised in court cases ultimately find their way to the Supreme Court. In the last thirty years the nine Justices have made landmark decisions in the areas of civil rights, criminal justice, religious freedom, and presidential power. What determines how the Justices arrive at their decisions? Do they carefully follow the law, or do they base their decisions on personal opinion or scientific studies? Two separate questions are really involved here. The first concerns what particular cases will be examined by the Court. Only a small portion of cases appealed to the Court are ever given serious consideration, so this step is crucial. The second question is: Once a case is on the agenda, what influences the outcome? Let us begin by considering which cases are considered by the Supreme Court.

GETTING TO THE SUPREME COURT

In 1975, 2,708 cases were taken to the Supreme Court. Most of these were dismissed entirely or quickly decided on technical or narrow considerations. Only 178 were actually put on the agenda for more serious

---

[10] Sheldon Goldman and Thomas P. Jahnige, *The Federal Courts as a Political System* (New York: Harper & Row, 1971), pp. 64–70. As of 1979, of some 500 federal district and Appeals Court judges, there are twenty-seven blacks and thirteen women (two of whom are also black).

The Supreme Court. Front row, left to right: Byron R. White, William J. Brennan, Jr., Chief Justice Warren E. Burger, Potter Stewart, and Thurgood Marshall. Back row, left to right: William H. Rehnquist, Harry A. Blackmun, Louis F. Powell, Jr., and John Paul Stevens.

JUDICIAL PROPRIETY

Appointed for life, all federal judges can be removed only through impeachment or conviction for a criminal offense. Only rarely are judges removed from office due to **impropriety.** Among Supreme Court Justices, one—Samuel Chase in 1804—was impeached by the House, but he was not convicted by the Senate. Justice Abe Fortas resigned in 1969 under charges of misconduct and impropriety, although no criminal charges were ever brought. At the lower level seven judges have been impeached and three convicted. The last federal judge to be impeached and convicted was Halsted Ritter in 1936. Four judges have been indicted for criminal behavior and two have been convicted.

It is not always easy to tell when actions taken against a judge for alleged misconduct are really directed against the individual's unpopular decisions. This problem surfaced in 1970 when several Republican members of Congress attempted to impeach Justice William O. Douglas. Appointed to the Court in 1939, Douglas has been an outspoken liberal advocate on and off the bench. He has also had a controversial private life, especially as he has had several marriages to women considerably younger than himself.

Led by Representative Gerald Ford, some members of Congress

Impropriety **A fancy word for improper behavior.**

review.[11] Why does one case make it through while dozens of others do not?

Cases can be placed on the Court agenda in one of two basic ways. First, the Constitution or laws passed by Congress give certain cases a right to Court consideration. Recall that cases in which a state is a party or cases that affect ambassadors, public ministers, and consuls fall under the original jurisdiction of the Court. In 1975, eleven cases came to the Court under this original jurisdiction. Congress has also specified that certain types of cases—particularly cases in which lower courts have ruled that federal laws were unconstitutional—receive a Supreme Court review as a matter of right (though the Court can readily dismiss such an appeal).

Most cases, however, do not involve original Supreme Court jurisdiction or laws declared unconstitutional. For these appeal cases from the lower courts, Supreme Court Justices can exercise considerable discretion. Basically, if four Justices of the Court think a case is "special and

[11] *Statistical Abstract of the United States, 1977*, p. 167.

---

called for the impeachment of Douglas on the grounds of judicial misconduct. Among other things, they claimed that his book—*Points of Rebellion*—justifies possible violence against the establishment and thus "violates standards of good behavior." Douglas had also written an article for *Evergreen Review,* which appeared in an issue that also contained photographs of nude women. Moreover, Ford and others claimed that Douglas showed "gross impropriety" when he failed to disqualify himself in a magazine obscenity case after previously accepting money from the same publisher for an article on folk singing. Douglas was also accused of illegally and unethically accepting money from a foundation. Upon investigation, all charges were dismissed and impeachment proceedings were never begun.

The Douglas case shows that it may be difficult to separate genuine "impropriety" from trumped-up charges designed to intimidate judges. What if a judge owns a few hundred shares of Ford Motor Company and Ford is a party to a suit? What if the judge and one of the lawyers in a case belong to the same country club and once met socially? In 1974, Congress tried to specify just when judges should disqualify themselves, but given the complexities of investments, previous legal associations, and friendships, finding a completely impartial and disinterested judge may be impossible.

More on the issue of judicial impropriety is presented in *The Supreme Court: Justice and the Law,* 2d ed. (Washington, D.C.: Congressional Quarterly, 1977), pp. 36, 42, 49.

Writ of certiorari A court
order requesting a lower court
to send a case up for review.

important," it will be reviewed by the entire Court (the technical name
for agreeing to review the case is granting a **writ of *certiorari***). Cases most
likely to be reviewed are those in which two federal Appeals Courts have
rendered opposing decisions; cases in which a federal Appeals Court has
decided on a new and important question of law; or cases in which a federal court has made a decision that appears to conflict with a previous
Supreme Court decision.[12] Most requests for writs of *certiorari* (usually
80 percent or more) are rejected, so for all intents and purposes (though
not technically) the previous decision stands.

To receive a full hearing from the Supreme Court, however, more is
needed than just meeting these technical requirements. Time and
money are also necessary. A case commonly takes between two and five
years to get to the Supreme Court (and not everyone has this much pa-
tience).[13] Costs for minimal items, such as copies of records, can add up
to thousands of dollars. When lawyers' fees for the necessary prior trials
are included, the bill can easily go over $100,000. Not surprisingly, then,
those who take their cases to the Supreme Court tend to be either the
government itself or citizens with access to expensive legal help. Only
rarely do we find instances such as that of a Louisville, Kentucky,
handyman who took his $20 local police court fine directly to the Su-
preme Court and won a unanimous reversal (*Thomas* v. *Louisville*
[1960]).

DECIDING A CASE

When the Supreme Court reviews an important case speculation often
arises over the legal justification of the ultimate decision (which sometimes can be as important as the decision itself). Numerous theories
claim to explain eventual outcomes. Some stress the people making the
decisions, others emphasize the technicalities of the case involved, while
other explanations stress the political climate of the day. Most of these
theories have an element of truth in them, but no single explanation has
proved to be complete. Let us briefly consider some of the more popular
explanations of judicial decision making and their supporting evidence.

The Constitution as the guiding standard

Perhaps the simplest explanation is that judges decide what is right or
wrong by mechanically comparing the facts of the case with the Constitution. In *United States* v. *Butler* (1936), for example, Justice Owen J.

[12] Pritchett, p. 98. There is, however, one additional, though rarely used, way a
case can receive Supreme Court review. Through a process called certification, a
difficult, complex case can be sent to the Supreme Court by the appellate courts
without the involved parties themselves appealing it. This usually happens only
once a year, however.

[13] Samuel Krislov, *The Supreme Court in the Political Process* (New York:
Macmillan, 1965), p. 41. On occasion, however, where a pressing national issue is
involved this process can be speeded up considerably. The case of *United States* v.
Nixon (1974), involving tapes of White House conversations, took only about two
months from start to finish.

Roberts stated that the one duty of the judicial branch was "to lay the article of the Constitution which is involved beside the statute which is challenging and to decide whether the latter squares with the former." Thus, if you wanted to know whether the Supreme Court was going to overturn, say, reverse discrimination in favor of blacks in jobs, you would simply consult the Constitution.

This explanation may satisfy some people, but it has many drawbacks. First, even where the Constitution is fairly explicit, reasonable people may disagree over what it means. For example, the Constitution explicitly gives Congress the right to regulate commerce between the states, yet one of the lengthiest debates in constitutional law concerns the meaning of "interstate commerce." Second, in many important instances the Constitution is vague or says nothing. We saw in Chapter Ten, for example, that congressional power to investigate or oversee executive bureaucracies is not mentioned in the Constitution. What does a Justice do if a case involves an investigation conducted by a congressional committee?

The explanation that rests on mechanical application of the law is also problematical when it is applied to nonconstitutional statutes. On occasion judges have sought to interpret a law precisely, only to find that Congress had drafted a vague law. A classic instance was the Sherman Anti-Trust Act, which never provided clear definition of the key term "monopoly."[14] Such vagueness can be intentional and necessary, because in complex areas Congress may realize that spelling out all the details may be impossible. Another problem is that Congress may have enacted contradictory laws. On various occasions, for example, Congress has passed laws promoting economic competition (the Clayton Anti-Trust Act) and legislation restraining vigorous competition (the Robinson-Patman Act). Such conflict is to be expected with tens of thousands of laws on the books.

Precedent

Another explanation of judicial decision making emphasizes the role of precedent. Like English law, U.S. law operates on the principle of **stare decisis** (let the decision stand). The principle of *stare decisis* means that if two essentially similar cases arise, the decision on the second case should be in accordance with the principles of the first. A different system is **code law**—a judge applies a written code to a particular case without regard to previous decisions in comparable cases. Thus, since U.S. law is based on *stare decisis*, and since judges are trained to follow precedent, a Supreme Court Justice confronted with a new case will simply make a choice consistent with decisions in previous comparable cases.

As an explanation of routine court decisions, this is a good account.

---

[14] Walter F. Murphy, *Elements of Judicial Strategy* (Chicago: University of Chicago Press, 1964), p. 14. The problem is compounded because many important legal terms, for example, "due process," mean different things to different people.

Stare decisis Latin for "let the decision stand." The principle that court decisions should follow precedent.
Code law A form of law in which judicial decisions are based on interpretations of the law without regard to previous court decisions.

THE PUBLIC FACE OF THE COURT

Though most of the work of the Supreme Court is settled in private, on occasion, on important cases, the Court hears arguments from lawyers. These public proceedings are not like the familiar courtroom trial. There are no witnesses, and Justices can and do play an active role in questioning lawyers. Especially when an important, long-awaited case is to be heard, the drama can be intense.

The workings of the Court were observed closely by J. Harvie Wilkinson, III, who was a law clerk to Justice Lewis F. Powell, Jr., during the 1971 and 1972 terms. Here is Wilkinson's firsthand description of arguments before the Court:

It is on days of oral argument that the Supreme Court is most alive. The small first-floor cafeteria becomes a hub of activity, with its swarms of tourists and dark-suited lawyers huddling intently at their tables. Members of the press, perhaps John MacKenzie, of the *Washington Post,* or Fred Graham, formerly of *The New York Times* and now with CBS, might stroll through. Occasionally, Solicitor General Griswold would appear, bedecked in formal tux and tails. Eating breakfast there, I would sometimes be interrupted by friends dropping by and wanting to know what seats in the courtroom were available that day.

The courtroom itself, where argument takes place, is elegant in its simplicity. It is of clean, rectangular composition, somewhat higher than it is wide, and ringed about with twenty-four columns of Italian marble. It is imposing but at the same time sufficiently intimate to give dialogue between counsel and Court a conversational tone, not one of formal debate. Institutions of government, even in a democracy, require an aura of drama and ceremony, and the Supreme Court, on a day of argument, is no exception. The courtroom is a theatrical creation, with its high, ornate ceiling, its bench of rich, deep mahogany behind which are the high-backed black leather chairs of the Justices and the red velvet curtain

---

When it comes to Supreme Court decisions, however, *stare decisis* is only partially relevant. One reason is obvious—if a decision consistent with precedent could have been easily made, the case would probably not have reached the Supreme Court in the first place. One factor that helps get a case before the Court is an absence of clear precedent, so we cannot expect judges to follow the *stare decisis* rule in such instances.

For several other reasons precedent is not always precisely followed. A complex case may involve numerous, sometimes conflicting, precedents.

from which they emerge, black-robed, promptly at 10:00 A.M., as the marshal bangs his gavel and announces solemnly,

> The Honorable, the Chief Justice, and the Associate Justices of the Supreme Court of the United States. Oyez! Oyez! Oyez! All persons having business before the Honorable, the Supreme Court of the United States, are admonished to draw near and give their attention, for the Court is now sitting. God save the United States and this Honorable Court.

Again the gavel falls, the Justices and all others take their seats, and the day's business begins. . . . Argument at its best is an illuminating and rapid-paced exercise, at its worst pedantic and unprofitable, sending spectators and judges alike into bouts of drowsiness. Argument before the Court can also take a most unpredictable bent, such as when one celebrated lawyer, after several evasions, finally answered, "I don't know, your honor," to a question on a cricial fact of his case; or when an Assistant Attorney General from a Midwestern state failed to cite, when asked, a single federal precedent for his position; or, more pleasantly, when a young, green-looking attorney still in his twenties gave a plucky argument in the face of stiff questioning by the Justices in a significant search and seizure case.

I never sat long in that courtroom, however, without recognizing that effective oral arguments before the Supreme Court of the United States demand the very best from a lawyer. Personally, he has to communicate candor and directness, confidence but not arrogance, and, in the case of the great advocates, an appropriate touch of humor and eloquence. Intellectually, he needs a determined instinct for the jugular of his case, and the agility of mind to take advantage of play as it develops, to synchronize the questions of the Justices with the logic and momentum of his own argument. Model appellate advocates are exceedingly rare; when one does perform, it is a thing of exquisite grace and power, a view of a master artist at work.

J. Harvie Wilkinson, III, *Serving Justice: A Supreme Court Clerk's View* (New York: Charterhouse, 1974), pp. 31–34.

Which of these past cases is the most relevant? In other instances doubts may be raised regarding the relevancy of a precedent to a new issue. Can one apply a precedent based on steamship travel to an airline case? Is copying a book on a Xerox machine the same as reproducing it on a printing press? On occasion Justices may simply reject precedent as no longer relevant to contemporary values. Overall, *stare decisis* cannot be ignored where clear precedent is overwhelming, but judges cannot rely on it entirely.

"Do you ever have one of those days when everything seems un-Constitutional?"

Drawing by Joe Mirachi; © 1974 The New Yorker Magazine, Inc.

Attitudes of Justices

A third major approach to Supreme Court decision making emphasizes the attitudes of the Justices. This explanation contends that (1) every Justice, consciously or unconsciously, holds an opinion on controversial issues and (2) cases before the Court are usually complex and ambiguous, so that inevitably personal preferences influence decisions. Thus, Justices predisposed to a procivil rights position will—perhaps unconsciously—be more easily convinced to rule in favor of that position. Of course, Justices might claim complete objectivity and impartiality and would support their decision with evidence and judicial precedent.

Do Supreme Court Justices vote their personal opinions? Much evidence suggests that they do, though this is not proof that the law and precedent are entirely disregarded.[15] Observers of the Court note that most Justices follow a highly predictable pattern in certain types of cases. For example, Justice William O. Douglas, who served the Court for over thirty years, consistently supported liberal free speech and civil rights positions. These positions were also widely advocated by Douglas in his public speeches and writing. On the other side were Justices like John Marshall Harlan, who could almost always be counted on to take a conservative perspective. Other Justices have displayed more complex behavior: on some types of cases (for example, civil rights) they may

[15] Two books that examine the role of Justices' attitudes in their decision making are Glendon Schubert, *Judicial Policy-Making* (Chicago: Scott, Foresman, 1965), Chap. 5; and David W. Rohde and Harold J. Spaeth, *Supreme Court Decision Making* (San Francisco: Freeman, 1976), Chap. 7.

have consistently chosen the liberal position, while on cases involving different issues (for example, national security) they have endorsed a moderate or conservative position. Such consistency, plus other non-Court statements, strongly suggest an adherence to an underlying disposition.

It would be a mistake, however, to claim that Justices use their powers to advance their preferences in complete disregard of the law. Cases in which the votes of the Justices are publicly identified constitute only a small fraction of the cases reviewed by the Court. Usually the Justices — liberal, moderate, and conservative — essentially concur in their legal interpretations so cases are quickly decided without publicity. A Justice's personal values are important, but they are actually relevant only when a case cannot be decided on clear legal grounds. Equally important, even when legal grounds are unclear, Justices hold strong professional standards regarding what is "fact" and what is "interpretation." Differences usually occur over nuances; this is not the same thing as basic disagreements over reality. As for the charge that this means we have government by people and not by law, the response is that a certain degree of personal bias is probably inevitable. Ignoring one's own values in those rare instances when a case is complex and without much precedent is probably impossible.

Group interaction of Justices

A final point regarding how Justices decide cases concerns the interactions among the eight Associate Justices and the Chief Justice. Observers of the Court claim that we cannot fully understand the behavior of the Court unless we consider the interaction of these nine individuals as they decide cases. Justices usually circulate draft opinions to elicit reaction, hold meetings to discuss differences, and otherwise act as a group rather than as nine isolated people. The Chief Justice plays a particularly important role in this group activity because by custom he or she has the right to speak first (which can set the tone of the discussion) and to decide who will write the majority opinion if he is in the majority (this is frequently important because Justices who vote together may differ on the reasons for their votes).

Viewing the Court as a small group is not intended as an overall explanation of judicial voting. Rather, it helps us understand why decisions are not always the sum total of each individual Justice's initial intention. In other words, a Justice may believe a case should be decided in a certain way, yet because of social pressure eventually change his or her mind. Examination of the private papers of several Justices has shown that judges can behave just like ordinary people trying to get their way in a group decision. Some will use flattery and friendliness toward their colleagues to win over potential opponents. Outright vote trading can occur — one Justice will go along with a colleague in one case in return for a similar consideration on another case. Even a Justice in the minority on a case can affect the majority decision by threatening to write a strong dissenting opinion unless certain changes are made in the written opinion of the majority. In extreme cases Justices can threaten

Judicial review The power of a court to declare legislative and executive actions unconstitutional and thus null and void.

to air their differences in public. In short, the nine Supreme Court Justices do not operate as isolated individuals. Like any group working on a common goal, there is give and take, accommodation, and bargaining.[16]

How, then, do Supreme Court Justices decide cases? Many factors—legal statutes, precedents, the political values of the Justices, and group interaction of the Justices—are relevant, but their importance varies at different stages of the legal process. If a case involves clear-cut laws and has ample precedent, it is unlikely to get to the Supreme Court. The outcome of cases that are fully considered by the Court hinge to a great extent—but not entirely—on the personal viewpoints of individual Justices. A judge's values may predispose him or her in one direction where the conflict is close, but no judge would claim that black is white. Finally, on such matters as writing the opinion, the size of the majority—and even the actual justification of the decision—the social interactions of the Justices themselves can be important.

What has been the political impact of the Supreme Court?

A perennial question of U.S. politics concerns the political impact of the Supreme Court. For some people the Court is the weakest of the three branches of government, capable only of making high-sounding but unenforceable pronouncements. To others the Court is an overzealous meddler beyond the reach of Congress, the President, or public opinion. To understand the impact of the Court, let us consider three aspects of Court behavior: (1) the means by which the Court can affect public policy; (2) the goals the Court has sought to achieve; and (3) the limits on the political impact of the Court.

HOW CAN THE COURT AFFECT PUBLIC POLICY?

The majority of judicial decisions have little impact beyond the immediate parties involved. On rare occasions, however, judicial action has far-reaching implications for large numbers of citizens. In the last thirty years, for example, the Supreme Court has had a profound impact on our educational system, the administration of criminal justice, and the quality of our physical environment. How has the Supreme Court made its presence felt?

The power of judicial review
One important way the court affects policy is through its power of **judicial review.** Judicial review is the power of a court to declare both national and state laws (and executive actions) unconstitutional. The capacity to declare an act of Congress or a state law null and void is such an important power of the Supreme Court that it deserves special attention.

[16] Murphy, Chap. 3.

The question of who ultimately interprets the laws—the executive, the legislative, the judiciary or the people—is an old, and perhaps insoluble, problem of English law. The framers of the Constitution inherited this problem and, for a while, attempted to resolve it. James Madison, for example, proposed to the delegates at the Constitutional Convention that the President and a "convenient number" of Supreme Court Justices form a council that could veto congressional legislation. This plan and similar ones were defeated, and the whole matter was conveniently avoided by not including in the Constitution anything about who has final say in questions of constitutionality.

Here the matter stood until 1803. The question of who is the "ultimate" constitutional interpreter began to be resolved during the last week of President John Adams term (February 24 to March 4, 1801) when he appointed forty-two justices of the peace for Washington, D.C. However, Adams' Secretary of State John Marshall neglected to make out and deliver the formal notifications of appointment before leaving office. When Thomas Jefferson became President on March 4, 1801, he ordered his Secretary of State (James Madison) not to deliver the forty-two appointments. William Marbury and three other frustrated appointees, under section 13 of the Judiciary Act of 1789, petitioned the Supreme Court for a **writ of mandamus** to compel Madison to deliver the commissions. The case of *Marbury* v. *Madison* (1803) thus came before the Supreme Court, led by Chief Justice John Marshall (who had been appointed by John Adams and who had caused the problem in the first place).

The Court had several reasonable alternatives before it. On technical grounds it could have claimed that it lacked jurisdiction and, thus, throw out Marbury's claim. Or the Court could have ruled that Madison's withholding of the commissions was illegal and that Marbury deserved his justice of the peace commission. Instead, through a lengthy piece of legal reasoning, Marshall wrote that section 13 of the Judiciary Act of 1789 and Article III of the Constitution (listing the Supreme Court's original jurisdiction) were in conflict. Therefore, reasoned Marshall, it was his duty to declare section 13 unconstitutional.

Some legal scholars and judges view this claim that the Supreme Court can declare laws unconstitutional of dubious merit. For example, many of the legislators who drafted the Judiciary Act of 1789 were once delegates to the Constitutional Convention itself, so it is hard to argue that Congress consciously passed an unconstitutional act. Moreover, twice before the Court had issued writs of *mandamus* without questioning the constitutionality of the 1789 act. Even if section 13 were clearly unconstitutional, there was no logical reason for the Court to assert that it could declare *any* law unconstitutional. The Court could claim the power of judicial review only on matters affecting the judicial branch of government. Nevertheless, though the reasoning in *Marbury* v. *Madison* is controversial, the custom of judicial review is now firmly embedded.[17]

Writ of mandamus A court order to a private individual or government official requiring some action to be taken.

[17] For a sampling of the arguments surrounding judicial review, see Archibald Cox, *The Role of the Supreme Court in American Government* (New York: Oxford University Press, 1976), pp. 9–16.

A Supreme Court decision can say far more than just what party won. The particular type of decision given and the divisions within the Court can both be important. Confronted with a major constitutional issue, the Court can dispose of the case in several different ways. It can ignore it by refusing to review it (which allows the decision of the previous court to stand). If the case is reviewed, the Court may decide the case on the narrowest technical grounds possible and thus, for the moment, sidestep the constitutional issue. If the Court does deal with the constitutional question, it may limit the impact of its decision to the immediate parties to the case. Or, on rare occasions, it may confront the "big" question directly and in terms of its broad implications.

The margin of victory can also be important. A 5 to 4 decision may not be the same as a 9 to 0 decision. In the 1954 *Brown* v. *Board of Education* decision, for example, the fact that the Court ruled 9 to 0 against state-required school segregation was a clear sign that the decision was a firm one. Had the Justices divided 5 to 4, and some of the majority wrote separate opinions partially disagreeing with their colleagues, the victory for civil rights groups would have been weakened. Opponents of the *Brown* ruling would have been encouraged to file a new suit in the hope that a slight change in facts would yield a different outcome.

A demonstration in San Francisco, July 2, 1978 protesting the Supreme Court decision requiring the University of California Medical School at Davis to admit Allan Bakke, a white student who has claimed reverse discrimination.

All the complexities of decision wording and the final vote majority is well illustrated in the Bakke case (*Regents of the University of California* v. *Bakke*). This case began when Allan Bakke, a white male, in 1973 and 1974 applied for admission to the medical school of the University of California at Davis. He was rejected both times. During this time the medical school maintained 100 openings, but 16 of these slots were reserved for "disadvantaged" groups—blacks, Chicanos, and Asians. Because Bakke's academic record and letters of recommendation were better than those of many students admitted in the "disadvantaged" category, Bakke believed that he had been discriminated against on the basis of his race. Citing the equal protection clause of the Fourteenth Amendment and Title VI of the 1964 Civil Rights Act (which prohibited discrimination on the basis of race in programs receiving federal funds), Bakke filed suit in the state courts of California. The state court ruled in favor of Bakke, but did not order him admitted to medical school. The university appealed to the California Supreme Court. Bakke again won, and the university appealed to the Supreme Court. In early 1977, the Court agreed to hear the case. On Wednesday, June 28, 1978, to a packed house, the Court gave its decision on Bakke. The essential elements were:

> Four Justices (Stevens, Burger, Stewart, and Rehnquist) ruled that the Davis medical school policy of setting aside sixteen positions for nonwhites violated the equal protection clause of the fourteenth amendment and Title VI of the 1964 Civil Rights Act.
> Four Justices (Brennan, White, Marshall, and Blackman) asserted that the use of race was permissible in such situations as admission to medical school.
> One Justice (Powell) agreed with the first group that the Davis program, by use of racial characteristics, violated the Fourteenth Amendment and the 1964 Civil Rights Act.
> On the question of using race as *one* factor in school admissions, however, Justice Powell sided with the second group.
> The net result of the decision, therefore, was (1) Bakke was admitted to medical school (the California Supreme Court decision was upheld); (2) the Davis program was declared illegal; and (3) the use of race (as one, but not the only, factor) in school admissions was upheld by the Court (overturning part of the decision made by the California Supreme Court).

A total of six separate written opinions were given in this case. The opinion written by John Paul Stevens (joined by Potter Stewart, William Rehnquist, and Warren Burger) saw the conflict as one between two litigants—Bakke and the University of California—not as a clash of constitutional philosophies. Moreover, Stevens explicitly stated that his opinion on the Bakke case applied only to the Davis program and to no other school or program that treats blacks differently than whites.

In short, by their written opinions and the nature of division (a sort of 4-1-4 split), the Justices gave a victory to Allan Bakke but did not launch a broader attack on all special programs designed to help disadvantaged citizens. The same pro-Bakke outcome, but with a strong opinion by a unanimous Court based on the illegality of using any racial characteristics under any circumstances, would have been a very different type of decision.

For more on the Bakke decision, see Allan P. Sindler, *Bakke, DeFeFunis, and Majority Admissions: The Quest for Equal Opportunity* (New York: Longmans, 1978).

Self-incrimination Evidence given by a person that reveals criminal actions. The Fifth Amendment states that persons cannot be compelled to give evidence against themselves.

Statute A law enacted by a legislature (a legislature can also pass resolutions, but these are not statutes).

Separate but equal doctrine The principle maintaining that blacks were not being deprived of their legal rights by being separated from whites as long as the facilities provided them were equal to those of the whites.

Equal protection clause A portion of section 1 of the Fourteenth Amendment which states "No state shall . . . deny to any person within its jurisdiction the equal protection of the laws."

The controversial basis of judicial review has not inhibited the use of this power by the Court. Between 1789 and 1978, the Court struck down 136 provisions of federal law and almost 800 state laws as unconstitutional.[18] Some of these decisions were well publicized and involved important policies. For example, in the famous *Dred Scott* v. *Sandford* (1857) case congressional prohibition of slavery in portions of territory belonging to the United States was declared unconstitutional. Similarly, an 1894 legislative attempt to introduce a national income tax was struck down. In 1918 and 1922, efforts to ban child labor were voided. Between 1935 and 1936, the Court held that twelve New Deal laws violated the Constitution. More recently, the Court struck down the Marijuana Tax Act (and related laws), which required dope dealers to register with the Internal Revenue Service and pay a tax on their sales (*Leary* v. *U.S.* [1969]). Such registration and tax, declared the Court, was **self-incrimination** and, thus, violates the Fifth Amendment.

Reinterpreting existing statutes

The use of judicial review may be likened to a boxer's big knockout punch. It is not the only weapon available to the Court, however. Equally effective, though less dramatic, is the Court's power to create policy through new interpretations of existing law. The Court may "discover" that a particular section of the Constitution or **statute** governing one class of policies now encompasses additional policies, so that acts believed to be legal may become illegal, or vice versa. A famous, but by no means unique, illustration of this interpretive power occurred in the *Brown* v. *Board of Education* (1954) case in which the Supreme Court outlawed state-imposed racial segregation in schools.

In the 1896 case of *Plessy* v. *Ferguson* the Court had ruled that a state could require racial segregation in public facilities (specifically railway cars) provided that the facilities, though separate, were equal. State-imposed racial segregation, the Court ruled, did not necessarily amount to discrimination. Gradually, however, this **"separate but equal" doctrine** came under legal attack. Finally, in the 1954 Brown decision, the Court ruled that the particular Kansas law requiring segregation was unconstitutional. More important than the declaration of unconstitutionality, however, was that the Fourteenth Amendment was now interpreted to apply to cases involving racial segregation. It is not likely that the framers of the Fourteenth Amendment had school segregation in mind when they drafted the **"equal protection" clause.** This new interpretation of this clause served as the basis for a drastic change in policy that eventually went well beyond segregated schools. The Court discovered that an amendment that had been on the books for eighty-six years (from 1868 to 1954) now banned state-imposed segregation in public schools.

Court administration of institutions

In recent years the Court has gained political impact by use of a third mechanism: administering public institutions. For the present this in-

[18] P. Allan Dionisopolous, "Judicial Review in the Textbooks," *DEA News*, no. 11 (Fall 1976).

volves only the federal district courts, but such actions occur with the knowledge and endorsement of the Supreme Court. To understand how a federal judge can become a hospital or school administrator, consider the case of *Wyatt* v. *Stickney* (1972). The story began with a suit in federal court charging that the care received by patients in Bryce Hospital (run by the state of Alabama) was so poor that it violated their constitutional rights. The judge agreed and issued detailed orders to remedy the problems. Among other specifications the judge ordered that "thermostatically controlled hot water shall be provided in adequate quantities and maintained at the required temperature for patient or residential use (110 degrees F at the fixture) and for mechanical dishwashing and laundry use (180 degrees F at the equipment)."[19] Not only had the federal judge become the chief administrator of Bryce Hospital but indirectly he had superseded the Alabama state legislature in issuing bonds and levying taxes.

Similar actions have occurred in Detroit and Boston over the racial integration of public schools. Faced with uncooperative local officials, federal judges have taken the initiative in deciding such matters as school district lines, classroom racial mixture, school staffing, extracurricular activities, and the length of permissible student travel time. For a while a Detroit district court found itself in charge of Detroit schools as well as fifty-three school districts in the suburbs with approximately 750,000 students. (This action was reversed in a 5 to 4 Supreme Court ruling in 1974 because the suburban districts had not violated the Fourteenth Amendment.[20])

SUPREME COURT GOALS

A frequent question in U.S. political history has been: What is the court trying to accomplish? Depending on the popularity of its most recent decision, people have answered with everything from "ruin the country" to "save America." Nevertheless, transcending these momentary reactions has been a more enduring debate over the basic political role of the Court. At the heart of this debate is the question of the involvement of the Court in the political process. Two largely opposing positions can be distinguished.

The Supreme Court is the guardian of freedom

The basic argument here is that because Justices serve for life the Court is above day-to-day politics. Thus, the Court can uphold the rights of the weak against the strong, protect the unpopular against the orthodox, and prevent the majority from tyrannizing the minority. Proponents of this view say that it is the Supreme Court that has guarded our basic freedoms by protecting the Constitution from those who would undermine it.

[19] Cited in Cox, p. 97.
[20] Cox, pp. 82–83.

The Supreme Court is merely another instrument of the ruling class

This position emphasizes the role of personal values and recruitment in judicial policy making. One does not usually get to the Supreme Court by challenging the powers that be. Supreme Court Justices inevitably reflect the values of the most powerful forces in society and are thus committed to the preservation of the status quo. If, for example, business interests dominate society, the Court will protect these interests in the name of "freedom," "liberty," and the like.

Which of these two contentions is correct? The most reasonable answer seems to be that neither description is completely valid for the entire history of the Court, but during some historical periods one description has been much more accurate than the other. In particular, the second position—the Court acts on behalf of dominant interests—had considerable validity until the 1950s, when the first contention seemed to become more accurate.

That the Court has aligned itself with powerful interests for most of its history is unquestioned by scholars who have examined this issue. Robert G. McCloskey, for example, in *The American Supreme Court*, notes that the early Court, largely under the direction of John Marshall (1801–1835), labored long and successfully on behalf of established commercial and property interests. Marshall had been a staunch Federalist (as opposed to being a Jeffersonial Republican) and as such was committed to a strong national government and the sanctity of property and contracts. In several landmark decisions, for example, *McCulloch* v. *Maryland* (1819) and *Dartmouth College* v. *Woodward* (1819), Marshall achieved important victories on behalf of established Federalist interests.[21]

When Chief Justice Marshall died in 1835, and with the Populist-oriented Andrew Jackson in the White House, wealthy interests feared that the end had come. As Chief Justice the President appointed Roger B. Taney, who joined four other Jackson appointees already on the Court. Those who hoped that the Court would now favor ordinary citizens and more democratically oriented state legislatures were disappointed. While the Taney Court did not act with the vigor of the Marshall Court, it nevertheless continued to uphold the rights of property and the supremacy of the national government. Even the one notion dearest to the hearts of wealthy interests—the sanctity of contracts—was upheld by the Jackson appointees.[22]

---

[21] Robert G. McCloskey, *The American Supreme Court* (Chicago: University of Chicago Press, 1960), Chap. 3. In *McCulloch* v. *Maryland* Marshall established the broad authority of the national government under the "necessary and proper" clause of the Constitution (Article I, section 8, paragraph 18). In the Dartmouth case Marshall established the principle of strong protection of vested rights and broadened the meaning of the contract clause (Article I, section 10 prohibits states from passing laws "emparing the obligation of contracts").

[22] McCloskey, p. 84.

The end of the Civil War in 1865 marked a turning point for the Supreme Court. Two major social problems emerged that brought the Court into contact with difficult legal questions. The first involved the plight of freed slaves. Immediately following the Civil War the Thirteenth, Fourteenth, and Fifteenth Amendments to the Constitution (and several civil rights acts) were enacted to help blacks obtain political equality. The end of southern Reconstruction placed many of these newly won rights in great jeopardy. The reaction of the Court was essentially to avoid the problem. Laws calling for outright and flagrant racial discrimination were struck down, but indirect segregation (which was just as effective) was usually tolerated. In a number of interpretations key provisions of the Fourteenth Amendment and other civil rights laws were emasculated.[23]

This strategy of judicial avoidance did not, however, apply to the other great issue of the day—the control of capitalism. The post-Civil War era saw a rapid expansion of industry accompanied by numerous attempts on the part of the states and the federal government to control private enterprises. Little by little, precedent by precedent, the Court became the defender of **laissez-faire,** the principle that government should not interfere with or regulate business. As more and more regulatory attempts were made, the Court "discovered" new ways to protect unrestricted capitalism.

When states tried to regulate railroad rates, the Court ruled that the national government is supreme in matters involving interstate commerce, so such regulations were illegal. Between 1877 and 1886, fourteen separate instances of state regulation were nullified. More important, the Supreme Court gradually began interpreting section 1 of the Fourteenth Amendment (no state can deprive a person of life, liberty, or property without due process of law) to mean protection not only of persons but of property from government control (*Allgeyer* v. *Louisiana* [1897]). In *Santa Clara County* v. *Southern Pacific Railroad* (1886) the Court even ruled that corporations are "persons" and are entitled to full protection of the Fourteenth Amendment. In some instances the Court had to stretch the law considerably to protect free enterprise. In 1895, for example, it ruled that the Sherman Antitrust Act, intended by Congress to prevent monopolies, did not forbid manufacturing monopolies because manufacturing was not an interstate business.[24]

The underlying bias in favor of established interests remained pretty much intact between the 1890s and 1936. As already mentioned, it was during this period that the Court voided attempts to institute a personal income tax and to ban child labor. The Court also struck down state attempts to set minimum hours and wages as part of its overall attack on the **"welfare state"** and "creeping communism." The civil rights of blacks remained a judicial nonissue, and the Court maintained a cautious stance on the right of free speech. Perhaps the only major decision

Laissez-faire The economic doctrine that the economy operates best with no government intervention. Literally means "hands off!"
Welfare state A society in which all basic human needs—housing, health, food—are provided through government action. The government is responsible for everyone's welfare.

[23] McCloskey, pp. 120–121.
[24] McCloskey, pp. 124–128.

of this era in support of free speech was a 1925 ruling that the **due process clause** of the Fourteenth Amendment protects free speech from state encroachment.[25]

Writing in 1943, the historian Henry Steele Commager drew this conclusion regarding the record of the Supreme Court:

> [T]he record . . . discloses not a single case, in a century and a half, where the Supreme Court has protected freedom of speech, press, assembly, or petition against congressional attack. It reveals no instance [save one possible exception] where the court has intervened on behalf of the underprivileged—the Negro, the alien, women, children, workers, tenant farmers.[26]

In 1937, in a series of close decisions, the Court reversed much of its long-standing opposition to government regulation of the economy. In many respects this date also marked a new era in Court policy. Especially as Roosevelt appointees began replacing previous Justices, the Court began to reexamine some of the previously avoided questions regarding civil rights, free speech, criminal justice, and the rights of employees in labor disputes. The Court had yet to become the great protector of the oppressed, but it was no longer the champion of the economic establishment.

The Supreme Court is the guardian of freedom

If the first argument described above—the Court as the protector of personal freedom—has any validity, it received its strongest support during the period when Earl Warren was Chief Justice (1953–1969). The changes brought about by the Warren Court were monumental, particularly in three areas: (1) political equality; (2) civil rights; and (3) free speech and free association.[27]

POLITICAL EQUALITY Laws requiring a fee to vote (poll tax) or property tax payments were struck down. The principle of "one man, one vote" was extended to congressional, state, and local legislative districts so as to prevent a minority of citizens from electing a majority of legislators (*Gray* v. *Sanders*, 1963, and other cases). The Court also held that a state

[25] It is significant that some of the major "victories" for free speech during this era actually resulted in the conviction of the speaker. For example, in the *Gitlow* v. *New York* (1925) case a Communist was convicted for "criminal anarchy." That the Fourteenth Amendment protects free speech against state action was an offhand addition to the decision.

[26] Henry Steele Commager, *Majority Rule and Minority Rights* (New York: Oxford University Press, 1943), p. 55.

[27] A more complete description of the decisions of the Warren Court can be found in Philip B. Kurland, *Politics, the Constitution, and the Warren Court* (Chicago: University of Chicago Press, 1970).

legislator could not be denied a seat solely because the legislature objected to the individual's political views.

CIVIL RIGHTS   The Warren Court outlawed state-enforced racial segregation in public schools. In other decisions it outlawed racial discrimination in public facilities such as swimming pools, parks, means of transportation, and courthouses. The Court, in 1967, ruled that state laws forbidding racial intermarriage are unconstitutional (*Loving* v. *Virginia*, 1967). The Warren Court also took vigorous actions to prevent unreasonable delay or sabotage in the implementation of civil rights rulings.

FREE SPEECH AND FREE ASSOCIATION   The Court extended the meaning of "free speech" to include "symbolic speech" such as the burning of a U.S. flag and the wearing of a black armband to protest the war in Vietnam. The Court also took steps to protect people using their right of free speech from economic retribution. For example, it ruled that a teacher could not be fired for criticizing the local school board. Local ordinances limiting demonstrations were overturned. Laws making it a crime to be a Communist were made virtually inoperable. State-required "**loyalty oaths**" were declared unconstitutional. Newspapers were given considerably more freedom in what they could say about public figures.

Loyalty oath A declaration made under oath that an individual has never, nor will in the future, act to overthrow the U.S. government.

This review only skims the surface. (Landmark decisions in the area of criminal justice are described in Chapter Fifteen.) Many of the decisions of the Warren Court, especially those dealing with enforced desegregation and the rights of dissenters, were highly unpopular. In some localities putting up "Impeach Earl Warren" billboards became a growth industry. Much of the establishment was profoundly upset by this "irresponsible" behavior, which was supposedly undermining the Constitution. For some conservative extremists it was all part of a Communist plot. Through all of this, of course, the Supreme Court simply stated that it was correctly interpreting the Constitution and not waging a war for public approval. Defenders of the Court argued that at last the United States had a Court more committed to freedom than to the sanctity of wealth and private enterprise.

Was the Warren Court doing the right thing while the post-Civil War Court was wrong? Should future Justices look back to the Warren Court as the golden era of the Supreme Court? These questions bring to the surface some of the dilemmas we face in evaluating Court decisions. In the abstract we want the Court to defend unpopular minorities, yet many people are outraged when this occurs. We want the Court to be impartial and "above" politics, yet the refusal of the Court to heed Congress or the President generates hostility. We want the Court to uphold the Constitution, yet it should be "responsive" to social and economic changes. Obviously, until we can all agree on precisely what it should be (an unlikely possibility), we cannot say conclusively whether the Court is fulfilling its proper role. All we can say is that the Court has varied in how it has interpreted its role.

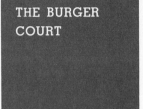

THE BURGER COURT

The Warren Court, with its philosophy of judicial activism on behalf of blacks, accused criminals, people advocating greater freedom of expression, and other such causes, was frequently attacked by conservative leaders. Richard M. Nixon, in his 1968 presidential campaign, promised to appoint Justices who would not "coddle" criminals, smut peddlers, or political radicals. Nixon declared that "we need a court which looks upon its function as being that of interpretation rather than breaking through into new areas." Nixon was elected President and had an opportunity to transform the Supreme Court through several new appointments. Shortly after taking office he named Warren E. Burger to replace Chief Justice Earl Warren. In 1970, Harry A. Blackmun was appointed, and in 1972 Lewis E. Powell, Jr., and William H. Rehnquist were appointed. Almost half the Court was Nixon-appointed, and three liberal Justices—Warren, Fortas, and Black—were gone.

Did this "Burger Court" turn back the clock and follow the principles of the conservative courts of the late nineteenth century? No. Many hopeful conservatives were disappointed. At the same time, however, those who looked to the Court for new and activist solutions to contemporary problems were also disappointed. The orientation of the Burger Court may be described as cautious maintenance and some extension of the Warren Court principles, but no ventures into new territory. Its decisions have tended to be consistent with those of the Warren Court, but it has rejected the role of aggressive protector of the disadvantaged.

In the area of civil rights, for example, it further broadened the right of blacks and other minorities to attend integrated schools. In *Swann v. Charllotte-Mecklinburg County Board of Education* (1971), by a 9 to 0 vote, the Court recognized the use of busing, racial-balance ratios and gerrymandered school districts to eliminate state-imposed segregation in southern schools. In a 1976 decision by a 7 to 2 vote the Court ruled that a racially segregated private school that refused to admit blacks violated the 1866 Civil Rights Act. Previously the Court had ruled that in order to receive some state aid, private schools could not practice racial discrimination. A 9 to 0 decision in 1973 held that a community recreation association could not run a swimming pool as a private club in order to exclude blacks. In several decisions the Court also moved to give greater legal protection and opportunities for compensation to people who had been victims of racial discrimination in employment.

Chief Justice Warren E. Burger, appointed by President Richard Nixon in 1969.

The Burger Court also extended constitutional protection of free speech. In 1970, in an 8 to 0 vote, it invalidated a law that prohibited an actor from wearing a military uniform in a production unfavorable to the military. A law making it a crime "to treat contemptuously" the U.S. flag was invalidated as too vague (the case had arisen when a man wore the U.S. flag on the seat of his pants). In two separate 1976 decisions the Court held that attorneys could advertise routine legal services and a state could not ban advertisements for contraceptives. In a highly publicized 1971 decision the Court upheld the right of newspapers to publish the "Pentagon Papers" (a top secret government report on U.S. military involvement in Vietnam) despite government claims that publication compromised national security. In early 1979 the Court ruled that even remarks made in private between individuals are protected by First Amendment guarantees of free speech (*Givran* v. *Western Line Consolidated School District*).

The Burger Court also significantly advanced the cause of women's equality. By a 9 to 0 vote in *Phillips* v. *Martin Marretta Corp.* (1971) the Court struck down employment discrimination against women merely because they have young children—hiring policies must be the same for both men and women. A 1971 decision also overturned a state law automatically giving fathers preference over mothers as executors of son's estates. Mandatory five-month pregnancy leaves in schools were struck down as a violation of the right to due process. In *Stanton* v. *Stanton* (1975) the Court held that states cannot set different ages for when males and females become adults. Several Court decisions also gave women greater choice in whether or not to have abortions.

(Continued on page 464)

(Continued from p. 463)

In many other situations, however, the Burger Court stopped well short of the positions advocated by liberal activists. In *Milliken* v. *Bradley* (1974), for example, in a 5 to 4 vote the Court ruled that school districts that have not engaged in segregation cannot be ordered to be part of a multidistrict court-ordered integration plan. A 5 to 3 vote in 1971 held that equal protection of the laws is not violated if a community votes to ban a low-income housing project (*James* v. *Valtierra*). A number of opinions were given that also uphold the right of whites to bring suits if landlords or employes practice reverse discrimination. While the right to abortions was enhanced, the Court refused to order state Medicaid programs to pay for abortions. A 1978 decision held that the Federal Communications Commission can prohibit the use of offensive language on radio programs even if the language is not "legally obscene" and is protected in another medium. In *Zurcher* v. *Stanford Daily* the Court gave the police the right to raid newspaper newsrooms without warning to search for evidence of crimes.

In short, the Burger Court on numerous occasions has acted to protect many important rights and freedoms. It has not, however, viewed itself as a self-appointed vigorous defender of the oppressed. In several instances it has purposely avoided issues that could have opened the door to new judicial controversies. The Court can be characterized as a cautious defender and extender of our freedom, not a force for dramatic change.

More on the personalities and decisions of the Burger Court can be found in *The Supreme Court: Justice and the Law,* 2d ed. (Washington, D.C.: Congressional Quarterly, 1977), pp. 31–123.

WHAT LIMITS THE IMPACT OF THE COURT ON PUBLIC POLICY?

Given the considerable leeway Justices have in reaching decisions, and given the near impossibility of removing a Supreme Court Justice simply on the basis of unpopular decisions, one might ask: What is to stop an ambitious Court from dominating politics? After all, Justices do not have to worry about reelection, getting campaign support, or disgruntled constituents. What prevents government by the Supreme Court? Three important checks limit the power of the judicial system and the Supreme Court: (1) the types of issues the judicial system will or can consider; (2) the lack of enforcement power; and (3) the power of Congress and the President.

TYPES OF ISSUES FEDERAL COURTS WILL OR CAN CONSIDER

The contemporary Congress and the President, as we saw in Chapters Ten to Twelve, can involve themselves in almost any subject imaginable. Congress, for example, through its powers of investigation, legislation, or debate, could, if it desired, deal with the question of life on Mars. The President, likewise, can focus on almost any topic of interest. This is not the case with the judicial system. Unlike the other branches of government, the federal courts are greatly limited in the scope of their action. In part this results from constitutional and congressional controls over court jurisdiction. In addition, however, certain doctrines and customs further limit the involvement of the Court. Understanding these doctrines and customs is enormously helpful in understanding why courts sometimes appear to do little to resolve pressing legal issues.

Courts cannot consider hypothetical cases

An important restriction that federal courts impose on themselves is exclusion of **"moot"** cases from consideration. That is, judges will not decide on a case unless the consequences are real. This was illustrated in a suit over a New Jersey state law requiring that Old Testament verses be read in school. The Supreme Court refused to make a ruling on the grounds that the case was moot because the child whose parents brought suit had already graduated from the school. More recently, a crucial case testing reverse discrimination—*DeFunis* v. *Odegaard* (1974)—was dismissed because the law student claiming discrimination had graduated by the time the Court was to hear the case. In criminal cases, however, the Supreme Court has been somewhat less stringent in applying mootness.[28]

Moreover, unlike some state supreme courts, the U.S. Supreme Court will not offer advisory opinions on the constitutionality of proposed legislation. President Washington once asked for such an opinion and was refused. Thus, an unconstitutional statute can be on the books forever unless it generates an actual Court case.

Court cases must have real consequences

The courts have also shown an unwillingness to confront cases where no harm to an individual has occurred. This was exemplified in a series of decisions regarding the constitutionality of a Connecticut law prohibiting the use or sale of birth-control devices. In one case (*Poe* v. *Ullman* [1961]) a physician claimed that his liberty and freedom were unconstitutionally being restricted. A married couple also claimed in the suit that the woman's health and well-being were being jeopardized by the ban on contraceptives. The Supreme Court, nevertheless, refused to decide the case on the grounds that the Connecticut law was not being enforced, so there was no real or immediate threat of prosecution. (Ultimately, in

Moot cases Hypothetical cases or those in which a decision would have no impact on the people involved.

---

[28] Samuel Mermin, *Law and the Legal System—An Introduction* (Boston: Little, Brown, 1972), p. 180.

Political questions Issues which the Court claims should be decided by legislators or executives, not judges.

1965, the Court did rule the law unconstitutional, but only after it had been enforced.)

A closely related principle employed by the Court is that for a person's claims to be heard damage must have been done to him or her personally, as opposed to having been done to all citizens. Suppose that in the interests of better national health all citizens are required to eat eight ounces of government-supplied organic wheat germ every day. Like most normal people you prefer Hostess Twinkies to wheat germ, so you bring suit claiming that not only is your good tax money being wasted but that your body is suffering great harm. Unless you can prove that this law has caused you or some specific class of people (as opposed to all citizens) harm, your case will not be considered. At least at the federal level, merely having your tax money wasted does not allow you to challenge government action in a court of law.[29]

Courts will not consider "political questions"

Another self-imposed Court restraint is the tradition of refusing to deal with "**political questions.**" On several important occasions the Supreme Court has refused to become involved on the grounds that it would be improperly imposing its views on questions better left to the executive or legislative branches. Such questions have sometimes involved whether the President acted correctly in recognizing a foreign government or whether military action such as the war in Vietnam was legal. In the nineteenth century the Court refused to rule on whether the executive branch had honored its treaty obligations with the Indians. No hard and fast line separates nonpolitical from political questions, and much seems to depend on the climate of political opinion. For example, in *Colegrove* v. *Green* (1946) the Court used the political-question doctrine to refuse to rule on population inequalities in congressional districts. Sixteen years later, in *Baker* v. *Carr* (1962), it changed its mind and declared such inequalities unconstitutional. Overall, the practice of avoiding political questions appears to be a convenient way of bypassing complex, difficult issues. As one federal judge put it, "[political questions] encompass all questions outside the sphere of judicial power" (*Velvel* v. *Johnson* [1968]).

Courts have limited power over their agendas

Finally, it is the nature of the judicial system that courts have little power to place specific cases and issues on their agendas. Courts can only decide cases that someone else brings to them, though on occasion a Justice might hint about decisions on a hypothetical case. The Justice Department, in the executive branch, handles the government side of

[29] Recently, the courts have allowed "class action" suits to be filed. That is, an injured individual can sue on behalf of a group of people who have been similarly harmed. In most instances, however, the class of people involved must be fairly well defined. A group of people cheated by a company might be permitted to sue, but not a group of taxpayers upset over U.S. foreign policy. These kinds of suits are described further in Pritchett, pp. 132–133.

cases, and, thus, influences such key questions as to what cases to take to the Supreme Court, which arguments to make, and whether a decision will be appealed. The Solicitor General of the Justice Department is especially important in this process because he or she chooses the government-involved cases that will be appealed to the Court and when. In short, a federal judge wishing to rule on a particular case may have to wait years before the right case in the right context comes up (if it ever does).

LACK OF ENFORCEMENT POWER

A second major factor limiting their power is the fact that federal courts —including the Supreme Court—possess little enforcement power. It is one thing to declare a behavior illegal and quite another to ensure that the ruling will be complied with. Ultimately, whether court decisions are carried out depends on the actions of other public officials or the general public. Perhaps the classic statement regarding judicial dependence was President Andrew Jackson's famous remark: "John Marshall has made his decision, now let him enforce it."

Lower courts can ignore Supreme Court decisions

Noncompliance with court decisions can occur in a number of ways. Once a doctrine is stated by the Supreme Court, lower-court judges can simply ignore it. This blatant defiance by judges themselves was well illustrated in the early 1960s when the Court banned mandatory religious observances in public schools. Though the decision of the Court was unambiguous—for example, no Bible readings permitted—many state court judges refused to adhere to it (perhaps contending that a Bible reading is in the area of history and not religion).[30] Similarly, some law-enforcement officials have responded to decisions protecting accused criminals by reinterpreting Court rulings or ignoring them altogether.[31]

Supreme Court Justices make every attempt to present their written opinions in a clear, unambiguous fashion in order to encourage compliance with them by lower-court judges. On occasion a Justice has even employed personal persuasion or flattery to encourage compliance. Sometimes pressure can be brought through the Judicial Conference of the United States, an annual meeting of the chief judge of each circuit, one district judge from each circuit, and the chief judge of the court of claims, with the Chief Justice of the Supreme Court presiding. The most forceful means of controlling lower-court judges is to overturn their decisions. No judge likes to be overruled by higher authorities, and being overturned repeatedly can cause a loss of prestige within the legal community.

[30] George Allen Tarr, *Judicial Impact and the State Supreme Courts* (Lexington, Mass.: Lexington Books, 1977).

[31] Donald L. Horowitz, *The Courts and Social Policy* (Washington, D.C.: The Brookings Institution, 1977), especially Chap. 6.

Courts cannot review all violations

The difficulties of obtaining compliance are especially severe where thousands of people and millions of small decisions are involved. A judge may rule that racial or religious discrimination in apartment rentals is unconstitutional, but monitoring all such situations is virtually impossible. The enforcement of school desegregation orders in the South was particularly susceptible to this type of problem. The Court would issue one order after another, yet officials ranging from school principals to governors to Senators (and even the President occasionally) would conspire to maintain segregation. In some instances this was accomplished by withholding funds for enforcement or making misleading claims regarding compliance.

POWER OF CONGRESS AND THE PRESIDENT

A third major constraint on the actions of the Supreme Court is the power of the other two branches of government. An angry Congress or President can take several measures. Recall that the appellate jurisdiction of the Supreme Court is set by the President and the Congress, not the Constitution, so that it can be modified to strip the Court of its ability to hear certain types of cases. In the late 1950s, for example, congressional anger over Court decisions regarding "subversive activity" led to proposals to prohibit Court jurisdiction in such cases (the effort failed). When the Court operates in ill-defined areas, an upset President and Congress can pass legislation that greatly constrains judicial interpretation on the part of the Justices. On civil rights issues, for example, many of the Court's enforcement options have been reduced by specific laws.

On at least one occasion Congress has pressured the Supreme Court through control of the salary of the Justices. In 1964 Congress voted a pay raise of $7,500 for all federal judges, but because many members of Congress were feeling unsympathetic toward the high Court, Supreme Court Justices received only a $4,500 pay raise.

Also recall that it is the President and the Senate that choose Supreme Court Justices and, though it may take a few years, a contrary Court can be brought into line. President Nixon's use of the appointment power well demonstrated this mode of control. In the space of three years Nixon appointed one Chief Justice and three associate Justices and was, thus, able to bring the Court closer to his own moderate-conservative philosophy. Sometimes a change of one or two votes can have a major impact on the direction of the Court.

Finally, a President or Congress confronted by a Supreme Court that insists on its own policies can frequently legislate around the Court. In some instances this has meant two or three attempts at passing laws before success occurs. In 1920, for example, the Supreme Court invalidated an act that required employers to compensate dock and harbor workers injured on the job. In 1922, Congress again passed a compensation bill for workers, and again the Court struck it down. In 1927, Congress tried a third time, and this time it succeeded. One or two new

Justices, a few technical changes in the law, and a change in political atmosphere can sometimes make a big difference.

The most extreme way of overcoming the Court is the passage of a constitutional amendment. This strategy has succeeded twice in U.S. history. When the Court ruled that a state could be sued in federal court by a citizen of a different state, Congress and the states passed the Eleventh Amendment prohibiting such action. When the Court refused to rule the income tax constitutional, the result was the Sixteenth Amendment. In recent times unpopular decisions on prayers in public schools, abortion, and school busing have instigated campaigns for constitutional amendments.

To come back to our basic question: What has been the impact of the Supreme Court? One conclusion we can draw is that the Supreme Court and the federal judiciary *cannot* dominate the political process. Despite an occasional unpopular decision, we have never had government by judiciary. At the same time, however, the courts are not rubber stamps. Numerous instances of judicial defiance of Congress and the President have occurred on such important issues as tax policy, civil rights, freedom of speech, and political equality. Overall, it appears that the court system has had its greatest impact when it has acted in cooperation with the other branches of government.[32] If the executive branch vigorously enforces its rulings, and Congress cooperates, judges can appear to be very powerful. This was demonstrated in the mid-1960s when all three branches of government made a concerted effort to advance black civil rights. On the other hand, where disagreements occur, the judicial system is greatly constrained. It will not be rendered powerless, but its impact beyond legal interpretation will be limited. In sum, the courts can probably reinforce the directions taken by the other two branches, but the judicial branch itself cannot be a great policy innovator.

A conclusion: the Supreme Court and the judicial system

We have seen that the judicial system is an important part of the political process. Judges may wear black robes, base their actions on obscure technical principles, and claim impartiality, but they are not neutral computers processing law into court rulings. Federal judges are chosen on political grounds, and their decisions can have major political ramifications (many of which are intentional).

Nobody disputes the political character of judicial decision making. Considerable conflict surrounds the question of how politically involved the courts *ought* to be. Should the courts shun great political controversies whenever possible? Or is it the duty of the court system to resolve conflicts over such controversial issues as abortion, private sexual be-

[32] Robert A. Dahl, "Decision-Making in a Democracy: The Supreme Court as a National Policy-Maker," *Journal of Public Law*, 6 (Fall 1957), pp. 279–295.

"OK TEAM, LET'S GO OUT THERE AND WIN AN INJUNCTION FOR THE GIPPER!"

A larger and larger number of disputes are finding their way into courts. Matters once settled privately now seek judicial solutions, and the trend is increasing. This new use of courts was nicely illustrated in a 1977 case involving an Illinois high school basketball game.

A basket by a Walther Lutheran High School player at the half-time buzzer was disallowed by the referee. Unfortunately, the official scorekeeper forgot to remove this disallowed basket from the score. Eventually, Walther Lutheran won the game 67-66 and was preparing to face the next team in the tournament. The defeated team, St. Michael, protested, but the Illinois High School Association allowed the final score to stand. Illinois Circuit Judge Joseph M. Wosik issued an injunction to stop the tournament and then negotiated an agreement in which the second half of the disputed game was to be replayed with new referees, a new scorekeeper, and a new timer (with no spectators permitted).

The implications for sports are considerable. Perhaps future teams will have a coach, captain, and team lawyer. Instead of the coin flip before a football game to decide who will receive the kick-off, officials will read players their legal rights. This statement is not so far-fetched. Recently, following a particularly violent incident, a professional hockey player filed assault and battery charges against an opponent.

The Illinois high school basketball case was reported in *The Daily Illini*, March 4, 1977, p. 36.

havior, discrimination practices by ordinary citizens, and the like? In one form or another, this debate has been going on since the early days of the Republic.

It is probably impossible to settle the conflict objectively. Each side has several persuasive arguments. Those claiming that judges should maintain a low political profile (sometimes labeled the **judicial-restraint** position) believe that involvement in controversial issues brings the judicial process into disrepute. The power of judges derives from their adherence to the law, and when they go beyond narrow legal interpretation they lose their special standing. Moreover, the argument continues, judges are less qualified to make public policy than elected leaders. Nor are judges politically accountable for their actions at election time. And even if they were well qualified, deciding such questions as racial mixtures of school classrooms is not the constitutionally prescribed role of judges. The use of constitutional interpretation as a foundation for policy making can only undermine the very Constitution judges are sworn to uphold.

To the defenders of **judicial activism** in policy making, the above arguments are irrelevant. The Constitution, they argue, must be adapted to contemporary situations if it is to maintain its relevance. Without such adaptation, the Constitution becomes merely an historical document. And why should today's problems be governed by the dead hand of the past? Merely because the Constitution does not mention school busing, for example, does not mean that judges cannot mention school busing. Moreover, there really is no such thing as "abstract" law. Since one cannot separate law from its social context, judges must deal with economic and racial factors in their decisions. It would be a dereliction of judicial duty, for example, to claim that a poor and a rich person are equally "free" to hire a first-rate lawyer. In dealing with social and economic realities judges must become involved with broader, more controversial questions.

If we cannot resolve this conflict, at least we can understand why most (but not all) people tend toward one side or the other: one's stance depends on whether one favors or opposes the judicial outcomes. When economically conservative judges used the Fourteenth Amendment to protect free enterprise from government regulation, businesspeople applauded, and proregulation people protested that Supreme Court Justices should stick to a narrow interpretation of the law. When later Justices employed the same provision to protect black civil rights in public accommodations, many businesspeople accused the Court of going too far. Considerable evidence exists that neither interpretation is consistent with the intentions of those who drafted the amendment.[33] Perhaps the moral of all this is: beware the people who claim the sanctity of judicial decisions; they have possibly just won their case.

Judicial activism The philosophy stating that judges should play a large role in dealing with controversial social and economic questions. Decisions should address broad issues, not just the statutes.

Major questions raised

1. What is the federal court system, and how does it function? The three basic elements of the court system are the district courts, circuit courts, and the Supreme Court. The cases handled by these courts are defined in the Constitution and by laws passed by Congress. Most cases involve violation of federal laws or suits between citizens of different states. The appointment of federal judges is made on the bases of political consideration and legal background.

2. How do Supreme Court Justices decide cases? Cases that have relatively clear precedents or do not raise important legal questions are unlikely to receive Court attention. Of the cases reviewed by the Court,

[33] Raoul Berger, *Government by Judiciary: The Transformation of the Fourteenth Amendment* (Cambridge, Mass.: Harvard University Press, 1977), Chap. 1.

decisions are usually based on the political values of the Justices. This does not mean, however, that Supreme Court Justices have a completely free hand.

3. What has been the political impact of the Supreme Court? The Court has a variety of weapons at its disposal, perhaps the most important of which is its power to declare a law unconstitutional (judicial review). Except for the period when Earl Warren was Chief Justice (1953–1969), the Court has usually reinforced the values of dominant interests. However, numerous checks exist on Supreme Court power that prevent it from dominating the political process.

QUESTIONS FOR FURTHER DISCUSSION

1. A persistent controversy in the selection of Justices of the Supreme Court concerns how representative the Court should be of the general public. Before the appointment of Thurgood Marshall many civil rights leaders were outspoken in their call for a black Justice. More recently, calls have come for the appointment of a woman to the Court. In the past a tradition existed for at least one Justice to be Jewish (for example, Brandeis, Cardozo, Frankfurter, and Goldberg). If you were President, how much weight would you give to social, ethnic, or sex characteristics of Supreme Court appointees? If two candidates are equally qualified, and one is female, would you appoint the female on the grounds that the Court should, if possible, reflect the make-up of the population?

2. In the past judges were expected to be legal technicians. A good legal education, therefore, was considered appropriate training for judgeships. Today, however, a judge must frequently know more than just the law. In a school desegregation case, for example, a judge must know how to interpret complex statistical information regarding the existence or effects of segregation. A judge may even be called upon to issue orders to professional educators on how to run schools. In suits over environmental pollution a judge may face a bewildering (and conflicting) array of biological and chemical findings. Professional economists have frequently complained that judges have done great harm as a result of their faulty understanding of modern economics. How might this problem of technical expertise be handled? Expand legal training to include courses in economics, statistics, the environment, and the like? Create a system of specialized courts staffed by judges with the relevant expertise? (For example, we now have special tax courts to deal with the complexities of taxes.) Or are we expecting too much of the judicial system in having judges administer schools, decide safe levels of air pollution, and so on? The problem of expertise should be solved by letting legislatures and executives decide such matters because they have access to the appropriate resources.

3. During almost every session of Congress a debate centers around whether some proposed legislation is constitutional. Laws on government aid to church-affiliated schools was one such issue where legislators repeatedly had to guess what the Supreme Court might eventually rule. Moreover, a case takes years to get to the Court, and in the mean-

while an unconstitutional law is in force. Should the Constitution be amended so that Congress can ask the Supreme Court whether proposed legislation is constitutional before it is enacted? Wouldn't such a procedure reduce the burdens on the judicial system by settling the issue of constitutionality before a case goes into the system?

4. If one believes that democratic government requires that all leaders be accountable to the public, does it not follow that federal judges—from district to Supreme Court—ought to be elected? What could we do if five Supreme Court Justices systematically outraged the public? Would not such behavior constitute tyrannical rule by an unaccountable elite? Can the practice of appointing judges for life be squared with the principle that all public officials must be accountable to the public?

BIBLIOGRAPHY

Abraham, Henry J. *The Judicial Process*, 3d ed. New York: Oxford University Press, 1975.
> An interesting comparison of the U.S. judicial system with those of England and France. Examines such things as differing conceptions of law, how court systems are organized and administered, how judges are recruited, and different approaches to the policy of judicial review.

Becker, Theodore L., and Malcolm M. Feeley. *The Impact of Supreme Court Decisions*, 2d ed. New York: Oxford University Press, 1973.
> A collection of diverse articles dealing with what happens after the Supreme Court decides. The articles consider such topics as the actual enforcement of the Court's ban on school prayers, the effect of reapportionment orders in state politics, and how decisions on the rights of criminals affect local public behavior. Also contains articles on the general issue of how courts can help implement their decisions.

Berger, Raoul. *Government by Judiciary: The Transformation of the Fourteenth Amendment*. Cambridge, Mass.: Harvard University Press, 1975.
> A careful analysis of how the Fourteenth Amendment was created and eventually interpreted. Berger asserts that the meaning of this amendment has been greatly distorted by modern judges and that this rewriting of our Constitution poses a threat to democratic government.

Cox, Archibald. *The Role of the Supreme Court in American Government*. New York: Oxford University Press, 1976.
> A very brief but excellent introduction to the types of issues considered by the Supreme Court. Especially relevant for questions dealing with protection of liberty and the Court's attempt to promote equality. Also examines the complex tasks that the judicial system has taken on.

Goldman, Sheldon, and Thomas P. Jahnige. *The Federal Courts as a Political System*, 2d ed. New York: Harper & Row, 1976.
> A step-by-step analysis of the federal court system. Covers the legal role of the courts, the recruitment of judges, the impact of Congress and juries, how judges decide cases, and the consequences of these decisions.

Goulden, Joseph C. *The Benchwarmers: The Private World of the Powerful Federal Judges*. New York: Weybright and Talley, 1974.
> A journalistic and highly readable account of the lower federal court system. Presents several case studies of successes and failures of the system. Very good at describing the behind-the-scenes politicking for federal judgeships and the particular problems faced by federal judges trying to resolve lengthy,

complex cases. Concludes with a good treatment of the problem of making judges publicly responsible for their behavior.

Krislov, Samuel. *The Supreme Court in the Political Process.* New York: Macmillan, 1965.

A brief but wide-ranging analysis of the Court which emphasizes its political aspects. Begins by describing how Justices are appointed, goes on to explain how cases get on the Court's agenda, and then deals with how Justices decide cases. The role of the Court in the political system and some of the important decisions are also examined.

Kurland, Philip B. *Politics, the Constitution, and the Warren Court.* Chicago: University of Chicago Press, 1970.

An in-depth review of the decisions of the Warren Court. Kurland argues that these decisions have greatly strengthened the national government, but at a major cost to both the Court and the government. Increasingly, the Court must rely on force to implement its decisions, and these decisions have created expectations that the government may not be able to satisfy.

McCloskey, Robert G. *The American Supreme Court.* Chicago: University of Chicago Press, 1960.

A well-regarded history of the Court that emphasizes the power of judicial review. Places the Court's key decisions in their historical and political context. Very useful for providing clear, nontechnical descriptions of legal doctrines and cases. Contains a detailed bibliographical essay on Court history and major events.

Murphy, Walter F. *Elements of Judicial Strategy.* Chicago: University of Chicago Press, 1964.

Using the private papers of numerous past Justices, Murphy attempts to describe how Supreme Court Justices actually operate. He describes how Justices influence each other, how they attempt to influence lower-court judges, and many of the limits on the behavior of Justices. Murphy sees judges as reasonable people employing the best strategy available to obtain their goals.

Pritchett, C. Herman. *The American Constitution,* 3d ed. New York: McGraw-Hill, 1977.

A clearly written, well-organized analysis of the Constitution and its interpretation. Superb coverage of Court rulings on property rights, equal protection of the law, freedom of association, and many more issues. If you want to know what the Supreme Court has done in an area, this is a valuable book.

Richardson, Richard J., and Kenneth N. Vines. *The Politics of Federal Courts: Lower Courts in the United States.* Boston: Little, Brown, 1970.

A systematic overview of lower federal courts. Concentrates on the selection of lower-court judges, how they decide cases, and the relationship between lower courts and the Supreme Court. Points out the role of political factors in judge selection and decision making.

Rohde, David W., and Harold J. Spaeth. *Supreme Court Decision Making.* San Francisco: Freeman, 1976.

A scientific and sometimes technical approach to the activities of the Supreme Court. Examines the role of judges' values in decisions, how precedent is treated, the process by which Justices are appointed, who has access to the Court, and how opinions are drafted, among other things.

Scigliano, Robert. *The Supreme Court and the Presidency.* New York: Free Press, 1971.

Examines the conflict and cooperation between the President and the Supreme Court throughout U.S. history. Scigliano argues that the framers of the Constitution intended the Court and the President to counterbalance Congress, especially the House. Analyzes various presidential successes and failures in dealing with the Court. Contains a bibliography.

The Supreme Court: Justice and the Law, 2d ed. Washington, D.C.: Congressional Quarterly, Inc., 1977.

An excellent and comprehensive treatment of the Supreme Court. Describes the organization of the federal court system, the judicial work load, and recent relations between the Court and the other two branches of government. Especially helpful are brief descriptions of recent important decisions and biographies of the current Justices. An appendix contains much factual information, such as a complete listing of everyone who served on the Court since 1789 (with terms) and a list of all federal laws declared unconstitutional. Contains a glossary of common legal terms and a bibliography.

Wilkinson, J. Harvie III. *Serving Justice: A Supreme Court Clerk's View.* New York: Charterhouse, 1974.

The author served as a clerk to Justice Lewis R. Powell, Jr., and presents an informative and informal view of how the Supreme Court operates. Describes some of the personal habits of Justices and the role of clerks and other assistants in helping to decide cases.

PREVIEW

What are crime, law, and justice?

These concepts are defined through the political process. A crime is an intentional violation of criminal law. Law is a government-formulated rule enforceable in the courts. Criminal law is an action against the public order. Civil law regulates disputes between individuals. Laws are spelled out in statutes, rules of administrative agencies, and judicial decisions. Some people claim the existence of higher, or "natural law," as well. The role of law in society is widely debated. Justice is the most complex of the three terms. One definition emphasizes equal application of the law. Utilitarians define justice as the equal application of laws that, on balance, benefit society. Justice as the following of specific procedures is a third definition. Finally, justice can be defined as making the procedures and punishment fit specific circumstances.

Is the U.S. system of criminal justice fair?

This question involves police behavior, the rights of suspected criminals, and unequal sentencing. The police have been criticized for enforcing laws selectively, using illegal tactics, and discriminating against minority groups. Some of this criticism may be exaggerated, and some of these behaviors are reasonable considering many of the situations the police must face.

Suspected criminals enjoy many rights. Police are limited in their searches for evidence, and several rules constrain police investigations. The accused must be promptly charged with an offense, has a right to reasonable bail, cannot be forced to give testimony against himself or herself, has a right to a lawyer and a speedy jury trial, and following trial cannot usually be tried twice for the same crime. An experienced criminal can sometimes go free by manipulating all of these guarantees.

Discrepancies exist with respect to sentences and punishments received by different individuals. Judges can usually exercise sentencing discretion. White-collar criminals frequently receive comparatively light sentences while blacks are more likely to receive the death sentence for capital crimes. However, no clear pattern of sentencing discrimination exists against any group. The practice of plea bargaining has been criticized because it can result in crimes being lightly punished.

Is the U.S. system of justice effective in stopping crime?

The U.S. crime rate is high, and it has been rising. Official figures underestimate the extent of crime because many crimes go unreported. The police are generally unsuccessful in apprehending criminals, and relatively few criminals go to jail. Many crimes are committed by repeaters. Attempts to correct this situation have proved of limited value or difficult to implement. A major constraint in combating crime is that such efforts may conflict with a free and open society.

CHAPTER FIFTEEN

THE POLITICS OF CRIME AND JUSTICE

When people think of "politics" they usually have in mind such things as elections, legislative debate, presidential actions, and the like. Rarely do people conceive of crime, police, jails, and other issues related to law enforcement as being a part of the political process. Nevertheless, decisions affecting the treatment of muggers are as political as legislative actions regulating election laws. Both involve the use of government authority and force to control citizen behavior. In fact, in terms of relevance for the average citizen law enforcement involves some of the most important contemporary political questions. Especially during outbreaks of violent crime, "law and order" can be the most emotional and divisive issue on the political agenda. The politics of crime and justice affects all government officials—from county sheriff to President—and entails one of the most basic purposes of government, the protection of life and property. This chapter examines three questions concerning the politics of crime and justice:

1. What are crime, law, and justice?
2. Is the U.S. system of criminal justice fair?
3. Is the U.S. system of justice effective in stopping crime?

Crime An intentional action that violates criminal law.

What are crime, law, and justice?

People rarely give much thought to the meaning of the words "crime," "law," and "justice." And for most day-to-day purposes it is not essential to examine these words very closely. However, understanding the role of politics in the law-enforcement process requires that we analyze these terms more fully. Words like "justice" have no self-evident, obvious meaning. Indeed, deciding what is or is not justice is not all that different from a legislature deciding how much money to spend on, say, agricultural subsidies.

CRIME

What is a crime? Basically, in the United States a **crime** is an intentional (as opposed to an accidental) action that violates criminal law.[1] This is a simple, widely accepted notion of crime, but this definition contains two elements worth elaborating. First, in the United States a crime involves some intentional *action.* In his 1976 *Playboy* interview President Jimmy Carter admitted that in his heart he lusted after many women, but so long as this happened only in his heart, no crime was committed. According to some religious laws, just *thinking* about a crime makes one as guilty as actually committing a crime, but fortunately for President Carter and many other citizens, criminal thoughts do not constitute a crime.

The second important point is that criminal *law* defines a crime. This is crucial. You may believe that a person's actions are vile, disgusting, and dangerous, yet without a law prohibiting these actions there is no crime. Nor does violation of customs, morality, or ethics mean that a crime has been committed.

This legalistic notion of crime is comparatively new. For most of recorded history no criminal law existed that specifically defined crimes. Crimes were defined by unwritten tradition or in religious scriptures (for example, the Ten Commandments). Interpretations and punishment of crimes were essentially a private matter. If someone made off with your new fur pelt and you felt wronged, you might get revenge by stealing that person's fur pelt. Such unwritten definitions of crime were troublesome as society grew larger, and a formal legal code of crimes gradually emerged. Interestingly, the first formally defined crimes were crimes against the king. With time "crimes against the king" were extended to "crimes against the king's subjects."

A related question is the definition of a criminal. In our system of justice a criminal is someone who has been *convicted* of a crime.[2] This is not, however, the only reasonable definition. We could, for example,

[1] For a good analysis of different conceptions of crime, see Richard Quinney, *The Problems of Crime* (New York: Dodd, Mead, 1975), pp. 3–19.

[2] There is no consensus, however, on when one's status as a criminal ends. From some perspectives one is no longer a criminal after one has "paid one's debt to society." However, in terms of the loss of certain rights criminal status is frequently defined for a lifetime, regardless of how long one has been out of prison.

define a criminal as anyone who has *committed* a crime. Under this definition almost everyone is a criminal, because most people have committed such petty crimes as speeding, loitering, jaywalking, littering, and so on. Millions of citizens are also guilty of the more serious crimes of fornication, driving while intoxicated, or using illegal drugs but have never been apprehended or convicted. Defining "criminal" is not just an exercise in semantics. Being a "criminal" can entail the loss of important rights, for example, the right to vote in some states, and affect employment possibilities.

LAW

In our system, a **law** is a rule formulated by a government body and enforceable in a court of law. Society has many rules and regulations, but most of them are not laws. For example, a college fraternity may require pledges to wear suits and ties to dinner, but violations cannot be dealt with by the courts. It may be social custom to excuse oneself after burping, but this is not a government edict. Thus, laws—like crime—result from political decisions.

Criminal and civil law

U.S. law is usually divided into two basic types: criminal and civil. A **criminal law** defines an action as a crime and specifies a penalty. Serious crimes are called felonies and less serious ones are labeled misdemeanors (the precise line between these varies from state to state). In principle, all criminal actions are against the public order. If Smith assaults Jones, the government (not Jones) will prosecute Smith. In contrast, under **civil law,** the government provides a code regulating conduct for settling disputes between private persons. For example, if Jones buys a car from Smith and the car suddenly falls apart, Jones may sue Smith for damages under provisions of state civil law regulating contracts and liability. Because civil law sanctions are less severe than criminal law punishments, civil law standards of proof are less demanding.

The distinction between criminal and civil law is not always clear. This is well illustrated in the continuing conflict over auto safety regulation. Suppose that as a result of a mechanical failure you have an accident resulting in personal injury. Also suppose that this failure resulted from the very design of the automobile, for example, poorly engineered brakes. Some auto safety advocates such as Ralph Nader claim that the manufacturer should be charged with *criminal* violations because the firm knowingly endangered human life. The auto companies, however, have argued successfully that such disputes should be settled between themselves and car owners, without government playing a part. A similar conflict occurs in pollution laws—is a polluting industry to be stopped by a civil suit or treated like an individual who is trying to murder people by poisoning the water supply?

The sources of law

In addition to the criminal-civil law distinction, another frequent distinction in the analysis of law concerns the source of law. The laws gov-

Law A rule formulated by government and enforced in the courts.
Criminal law A law defining an action as a crime and specifying a penalty.
Civil law A code formulated by the government for settling disputes between individuals in the courts.

Statute law Laws enacted by legislatures and executives.
Administrative law Rules issued by administrative agencies as part of the implementation of their legal responsibility.
Case law Interpretations made by judges regarding the meaning of statutes or administrative rules that guide subsequent judicial decisions.
Common law A collection of rules and principles based on judicial custom in medieval England.
Natural law Laws that exist apart from written law or legal custom, that derive from God, the nature of the universe, or some other higher authority.

erning our behavior originate from a variety of sources. The most important type of law in the United States is **statute law.** These are the laws enacted by legislators and executives, and unless declared unconstitutional by the Supreme Court, statutory law takes precedence over all other law. A second type of law is **administrative law.** Administrative agencies are sometimes given considerable discretion in implementing laws approved by Congress and the President. This discretion is exercised by the issuance of various rulings. For example, a Federal Communications Commission ruling proclaiming that television stations cannot show explicit sex on the air is an administrative law. A third source of law is **case law,** or "judge-made," law. All laws must be interpreted to meet different situations, and under the rule of *stare decisis* (let the decision stand) the decision made by one judge guides subsequent judicial decisions. Many of the rulings on civil rights (for example, *Brown* v. *Board of Education* [1954]) are instances of case law.

A fourth type of law is **common law.** Common law derives from the codification of judicial decisions based on local custom in medieval England. Today common law serves more as a set of principles in judicial procedures than as a body of enforceable statutes. Much of common law has been incorporated into statutory law and judges' decisions. The use of common law principles was exemplified in the trial of Charles Manson, the leader of a California drug-oriented commune who was charged with the murder of several people (including actress Sharon Tate). During the trial Manson suddenly held up a newspaper that he had smuggled into the courtroom carrying the headline "Nixon Says Manson Guilty." Manson's lawyers then argued that a new trial was necessary because the headline would prejudice the jury. Relying on the common law principle that "one should not benefit from one's own harmful actions," the judge ruled against a new trial. (Manson was eventually convicted.)

The last type of law is **natural law.** Unlike the previous forms of law, natural law is not a written body of rules, nor is it enforceable in the courts. Basically, many philosophers have argued that certain laws that transcend human laws exist in the universe. In some instances these natural laws have been claimed to be the laws of God; other natural law theorists have stressed the inherent nature of human beings, or society. The familiar inalienable rights of life, liberty, and the pursuit of happiness described in the Declaration of Independence derive from natural law (that is, these rights cannot be taken away since they exist independently of government actions). More recently, civil rights leaders such as Martin Luther King claimed that racially discriminatory laws were unjust and required disobedience because they were not rooted in eternal law and natural law."[3]

The role of law in society

Though the distinctions between types of law are not always clear, the source of law has been less controversial than the social *role* of law.

[3] Martin Luther King, *Why We Can't Wait* (New York: Harper & Row, 1963), pp. 84–85.

Specifically, considerable debate exists over *what* should be covered by law, regardless of whether the law is statutory law, administrative law, case law, or another type of law. There are two basic positions in this debate. The first claims that the proper role of law is to prevent individuals from harming others. Law exists to prevent and punish crimes such as murder, theft, assault, and rape. Law should not interfere with private, socially harmless conduct. Adherents of this position would decriminalize such behaviors as drug abuse, homosexuality, drunkenness, gambling, distributing pornography, bigamy, prostitution, and sexual acts between consenting adults. Society, the argument goes, has no right to regulate purely personal behavior.

Proponents of this position also assert that such decriminalization would be enormously beneficial. The most obvious benefit would be to concentrate scarce law-enforcement resources on preventing serious crimes. Instead of wasting their time locking up drunks or seizing pornographic films, the police could focus on violent crimes. Decriminalization of personal behavior might also increase respect for the law. Using law to punish widespread activities, such as gambling and prostitution, transforms police from upholders of public safety into detested enforcers of unpopular rules. It is also argued that such police activity encourages the growth of organized crime because it forces citizens to deal with criminals to obtain narcotics or place bets (and organized crime, in turn, encourages police corruption). Finally, the criminalization of many personal behaviors may in fact help perpetuate these behaviors. Labeling homosexuals, gamblers, prostitutes, and drug users as criminal deviants separates them from the social mainstream and forces them into subcultures that reinforce these behaviors.[4]

Can the criminalization of prostitution, drug abuse, or drunkenness be justified? There are those who answer "yes." First, these defenders of a wider role of law claim that the distinction between "purely personal" and "socially harmful" actions is not precise. Take, for example, the law requiring motorcyclists to wear helmets. Some motorcyclists view this law as an infringement of their personal control over their private behavior. However, the courts have usually ruled that helmet laws benefit the public because they prevent injuries and spare the state the potential burden of supporting the families of motorcyclists who are killed. It can also be argued that certain personal behaviors, though not socially harmful themselves, invariably lead to socially harmful situations. Drunken people only harm themselves, but a large number of congregating drunks might lead to widespread violence. To prevent public violence one must limit individual intoxication.

The most basic argument for legal control over personal behavior concerns the right of citizens, acting through government, to preserve society. What would happen, the argument goes, if alcoholism, drug addiction, homosexuality, illicit sex, and obscenity were allowed to flourish? The probable result would be the disintegration of the family, the work ethic, and a sense of community. Society would likely sink into a semi-

---

[4] Norval Morris and Gordon Hawkins, *The Honest Politician's Guide to Crime Control* (Chicago: University of Chicago Press, 1969), Chap. 1.

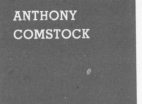

ANTHONY COMSTOCK

The classic instance of law being employed to impose morality involves the long and notorious career of Anthony Comstock. Comstock waged a forceful campaign against what he called "the sewer mouth" of society. First, as leader of the New York Society for the Suppression of Vice and then as special agent of the Post Office Department, Comstock personally forced his moral code on society. Between 1879 and 1913 he was personally responsible for the arrest of 3,600 men, women, and children for obscenity and immorality. Between March 1872 and February 1874 Comstock seized 130,000 pounds of "bad" books, 194,000 pictures and photographs, and 60,300 "articles made of rubber for immoral purposes, to be used by both sexes."

Comstock's notion of obscenity was very broad. Virtually anything that hinted at nudity, gambling, excessive violence, contraception, abortion, or situations that could contribute to these vices was vehemently attacked. In 1913, for example, he had a street vendor arrested for selling picture postcards depicting people dancing the turkey trot and the tango. Many classic works of art were attacked as lewd. Comstock's major concern, however, was protecting the morality of youth. To Comstock, nearly all light fiction and popular journalism corrupted. Juvenile delinquents were described as "schoolboys crazed by the accursed blood-and-thunder story papers." Crime resulted from "criminal reading."

Comstock's puritanical morality frequently was written into law. In 1873 he showed members of Congress choice pornographic items he had seized in order to combat smut. Congress responded by passing tougher antiobscenity legislation, and Comstock was appointed special agent to the Post Office to help enforce these new rules (which he did with a vengeance). These efforts drew the support of several very wealthy citizens, and soon many states had their own "Comstock laws." In the hands of sympathetic law-enforcement officials, with the encouragement of local Societies for the Suppression of Vice, these statutes were frequent and provided effective mechanisms for enforcing puritanical standards.* In New York, for example, it was illegal to sell, own, lend, show, advertise, or give away any "obscene, lewd, lascivious, filthy, indecent or disgusting book, figure or image, drawing, or writing paper" (none of these terms were defined). The federal statute on obscenity carried a minimum penalty of six months of hard labor in a penitentiary. For years these laws made it virtually impossible to buy contraceptives or even openly describe methods of birth control, let alone purchase "lewd" literature.

The Comstock movement, plus Comstock's own writings on the evils of pool halls, nudity, and popular fiction, are described more fully in Anthony Comstock, *Traps for the Young,* edited by Robert Bremmer (Cambridge, Mass.: Belknap Press, 1967).

Comstock's vehement antinudity campaigns were frequently the butts of cartoonists and humorists. Here is one anti-Comstock cartoon.

"Your Honor, this woman gave birth to a naked child!"
The Masses, September 1915, p. 19.

* Despite many changes in public morality, some of the Comstock-inspired laws and principles have managed to survive. Comstock was especially worried about pool halls as corruptors of youth. In 1978, the supreme court of Maine ruled that pool halls were not inherently evil. The case involved an Augusta, Maine, establishment that had lost its city license due to disturbances outside the lounge. The Maine superior court ruled that closing the pool hall was permitted due to the "harmful tendencies" of such an establishment. The supreme court, however, ruled that pool halls cannot be singled out from other establishments such as bowling alleys.

barbarian state committed solely to the pursuit of physical pleasure. Government has an obligation to maintain existing social institutions and, thus, requires the punishment of those who violate moral codes.

Both of these views on the role of law have appeal. Certainly the police should concentrate on serious crimes and not interfere with our personal (harmless) vices. At the same time, however, most citizens would also agree that the community must be protected. The matter is further complicated by disagreements over what constitutes a crime against society and what is a purely personal behavior. Which is a greater threat to our way of life, homosexuality or unsafe automobiles? Perhaps the only conclusion we can reach is that the debate will continue for a long time.

JUSTICE

"Justice" is a complex, elusive, yet highly relevant concept in U.S. politics. Unfortunately, unlike crime and law, there is no one, simple definition of justice. Justice to one person may be glaring injustice to another. What do we mean when we say things like "blacks cannot get justice in the United States," or "his trial was a travesty of justice?" To evaluate our system of law obviously requires some more specific notion of justice.

Numerous definitions of justice exist, but let us briefly describe four conceptions particularly relevant to the U.S. legal system: (1) justice as equal application of the laws; (2) utilitarian justice; (3) justice as proper procedure; and (4) personalized justice.

Justice as equal application of the law

The core notion of this definition is that if all people who break the same law are treated identically, justice takes place. Judgments are made impartially, regardless of race, age, sex, religion, or other personal characteristics. Injustice occurs if, for example, whites get lesser penalties than blacks for breaking the same laws. If there are differences in treatment, they must be explicitly justified on the basis of law. For instance, an adult and a child might receive different penalties for the same crime *if* the law provides for such a distinction. Similarly, if legally permitted, a first offender might receive different treatment than a repeater.

This definition stresses the nonarbitrary, almost mechanical, application of law to specific cases. It does not, however, consider the possibility that the law itself is unjust. What if a law prohibited women in public places after 10 P.M. without a male escort? Would precise equal enforcement of this law constitute justice? Many women no doubt would answer "no," because the law itself is unjust. To Marxists, the entire system of U.S. justice is inherently unjust on the grounds that all laws (unjustly) allow capitalists to exploit the working class. Hence, a worker automatically loses no matter how impartially he or she is treated by an unjust law.[5]

[5] This point of view is expressed in Richard Quinney, *Class, State, and Crime* (New York: Longmans, 1977), Chap. 1.

IF COOKIES ARE A MISDEMEANOR, WOULD A PIZZA BE A FELONY?

One consequence of living in a society possessing a great many laws is that you can get arrested for what appears to be perfectly normal behavior. For example, Lawrence E. Wallick was taken to court for eating a chocolate chip cookie in public. This was nothing, of course, compared to Ruth Bushnell, who was apprehended eating a crumb cake. Another citizen was discovered, blatantly and in full public view, holding a glass of water. All three had to defend themselves in court against these serious charges.

These actions resulted from an Ocean Beach, New York, ordinance banning eating in public or carrying open food containers on the walks or beaches. The only exception was an ice cream cone, which was considered too all-American to be banned.* Moreover, this ordinance has been on the books for several years and has regularly been enforced. Its purpose is to reduce litter in the village, and offenses are punishable by a $25 fine.

Irvin Molotsky, "A Cookie-Muncher Winds Up in Court," *New York Times*, August 14, 1977.

* However, a year later ice cream cones were also banned. Since the town's ice cream store is across the street from the police station, enforcement has been easy. When a police sergeant was asked about cracking down on public ice cream eaters, his reply was, "We don't make the laws. We enforce them." Irvin Molotsky, "Ice Cream Joins Cookies on Town's Proscribed List," *New York Times*, June 18, 1978.

Utilitarian justice Where laws, which bring about the greatest good for the greatest number, are enforced equally.

Utilitarian justice

Utilitarianism was a popular philosophical orientation, especially in England during the first half of the nineteenth century. Its basic premise was that all laws should seek to maximize the greatest good for the greatest number. In other words, a law that benefited many people at the expense of a few was preferable to a law that benefited a few at the expense of many. **Utilitarian justice** consisted of two requirements. First, laws should be applied equally. This is the principle described in our first conception of justice. Second, laws must incorporate the principle of the greatest good for the greatest number.[6] The utilitarian notion of justice thus allows for unjust laws.

In using this utilitarian notion of justice one must consider both the

[6] Hugo A. Bedau, "Justice as Classical Utilitarianism," in Carl J. Friedrich and John W. Chapman, eds., *Justice, Nomos VI* (New York: Atherton Press, 1963), pp. 288–289.

Procedural due process No precise definition exists, but the term is usually taken to mean judicial procedures that involve the accused being informed of the charge, an open inquiry into the charge, and a judgment after a trial.
Personalized justice Fitting the judicial procedure and punishment to the specific circumstances of each crime.

equality of a judicial decision and the impact of the decision on society. Injustices can occur either from arbitrary interpretations of "good" laws *or* by impartial applications of "bad" laws. This utilitarian conception remains relevant for contemporary analyses of justice. Some ecology advocates have, for example, claimed that certain laws regulating private property are unjust because they result in widespread pollution and, thus, social harm. Court decisions proclaiming racial integration of public schools have sometimes been described as "just" on the grounds that all society will eventually benefit from a reduction of segregation.

The problem with utilitarian justice concerns deciding *which* laws further the greatest good for the greatest number. Take the case of private property versus a clean environment. Environmentalists would assert that laws allowing individuals complete freedom with their property are unjust. Justice would prevail if the rights of others to live in a clean environment were given greater weight. The property owner, however, would claim that without the sanctity of private property, society would fall into anarchy—a fate far worse than dirty air. Who decides which position represents the greatest good for the largest number of people?

Justice as proper procedure

A third notion of justice emphasizes the *way* a decision is reached, as opposed to whether everybody receives equal treatment or whether the law promotes the public welfare. In many respects this justice-as-proper-procedure is one of the cornerstones of our legal system.

Typically, adherents of this position assert that justice requires that citizens charged with criminal offenses be promptly informed of these charges, have a right to reasonable bail, have ample opportunity to defend themselves in open court, and be judged by a jury of their fellow citizens. In civil proceedings comparable rules, for example, the right to call witnesses or request relevant material, exist to insure that each party has a fair chance. Many of these requirements come under the heading of **procedural due process,** a concept that has never been defined exactly but that is usually taken to mean no punishment without prior inquiry and trial. In other words, if you are innocent of a crime but were seized by the police, secretly tried without your knowledge, and somehow acquitted, an injustice would still have taken place because certain procedures were not followed.

This notion of justice can be controversial, especially when someone is caught in the act of committing a crime but is set free by a judge because proper procedures were violated. When the crime is horrendous and the violated procedures fairly technical, the public is frequently outraged. Nevertheless, setting the alleged criminal free despite overwhelming evidence of guilt is consistent with the notion of justice.

Personalized justice

All three previous conceptions of justice have one element in common: they require strict adherence to an explicit set of rules (for example, equality of treatment, proper procedure, due process). **Personalized justice,** on the other hand, views each case as unique and, therefore, requires an individualized response. Punishment and procedure fit the person and situation, not the crime. Two people may commit identical crimes, but because of special, complex circumstances in each case, a jury or judge might render two different decisions. Moreover, personalized justice may be informal—since there are no stipulated rights or procedure, no two cases may be handled alike. Justice exists when the judicial outcome fits well with the special facts of each case.

For many years the juvenile justice system operated under the rule of personalized justice. If a 10-year-old was caught stealing hubcaps, a judge might have given the offender a good lecture and sent the child home. A different judge with a different 10-year-old hubcap thief might have called in the parents to give the child a good beating. In a third hubcap heist a judge might have informally discussed the matter with teachers and people in the community and then "sentenced" the child to a day of picking up playground trash. Few records were kept, no particular procedures were followed, but the outcome was "just" if everyone seemed to think that each hubcap bandit was punished fairly.[7]

The principal drawback of this system of justice is the potential for abuse. A prejudiced judge might view blacks differently from whites, and blacks would have little recourse. "Irrelevant" characteristics, such as style of dress or hair length, might determine the outcome of a case. In many cases differences among judges were so great that getting the right judge made all the difference in the world. For these reasons personalized justice has been under attack in the juvenile courts. In general, while the idea of justice tailored to the needs of each situation has much appeal, it has not enjoyed much popularity in the U.S. legal system.[8]

What should be clear from our analysis of crime, law, and justice is that there is much room for interpretation and maneuver. It makes a crucial difference to each of us what is defined as a crime, how far law will be extended, and what standard of justice will be employed. Such decisions are political in nature. Crime, law, and justice do not mysteriously come into existence. These concepts may derive from our religious and moral tradition, but in the final analysis they are the result of actions taken by public officials.

---

[7] Personalized justice was also popular in the West during the nineteenth century when trained judges were few in number. In one case a prospector was found guilty of murder, but his friends on the jury decided it should be up to the prospector to decide the punishment. The prospector got stone drunk, climbed a tree, put a noose around his neck, tied the other end to the tree, waved goodbye to his friends, and jumped.

[8] Personalized justice has not completely vanished, however. Recently a federal judge in California sentenced an automobile dealer guilty of importing cars without proper pollution equipment. Rather than impose a fine or put him in jail, the judge sentenced the dealer to 100 hours of "voluntary" service in a government environmental agency. Clearly, this was a customized punishment not optional with every criminal. The incident was reported in the *Wall Street Journal*, June 13, 1978, p. 1.

Is the U.S. system of criminal justice fair?

Handling crime in a free society presents many perplexing problems. The criminal justice system must balance the need to control crime with the principles of personal freedom and fairness. Jailing without trial all suspicious people might substantially reduce crime, but this solution would be unacceptable to most of us. On the other hand, giving criminals all the advantages may well destroy the basis for civilized society. People also disagree on what should be the proper balance and standards of fairness. How much crime is tolerable in a free society, and how fair does one have to be to be "fair"? To answer these difficult questions we shall examine three aspects of the criminal justice system: (1) the role of the police; (2) the rights of suspected criminals; and (3) unequal sentencing. Though we probably cannot reach a precise conclusion concerning fairness, we can at least familiarize ourselves with the key issues in the controversy.

THE ROLE OF THE POLICE

Any consideration of the criminal justice system must begin by examining the role of the police. Who comes to trial and under what circumstances are greatly influenced by police actions. Moreover, the highest standards of justice can come to naught if the police choose to disregard them. The important question, then, is: To what extent do the police enforce the law equally and impartially? How much consistency exists between how the law ought to be enforced and actual enforcement?

Because there are thousands of separate law-enforcement agencies at all levels of government, it is impossible to reach a conclusion that applies equally to all of them. What may be common practice in big-city Gotham may be rare in Smallville. Nevertheless, numerous studies of actual police behavior suggest the following conclusions regarding the fairness and equality of police enforcement of the law.

Enforcing all laws equally

First, not all laws are enforced. Some crimes are openly tolerated, while others are severely punished. For example, statutes outlawing certain types of heterosexual acts are generally ignored, while laws prohibiting comparable homosexual practices are much more likely to be enforced. Frequently the police have been accused of being indifferent to rape unless it involves the rape of a white woman by a black man.[9] Differences in police treatment of alcoholism versus dope use have also been frequently observed. Studies indicate that police exert unequal effort in solving crimes. In many large cities the theft of private property is given comparatively little attention unless the stolen object is an au-

[9] Susan Brownmiller, *Against Our Will: Men, Women and Rape* (New York: Bantam Books, 1976), pp. 408–412.

The Whipping-Post and Pillory at New Castle, Delaware. Such public punishments were intended to deter would-be offenders. They were also a common form of public entertainment.

tomobile. There are also considerable variations from area to area in the attention given different types of crime.[10]

Second, police frequently ignore certain procedural rules regarding the administration of justice. As it is sometimes put, police break the law in order to enforce it. In some instances this involves falsifying records or planting false evidence, such as illegal drugs, in order to "get" a suspect the police could not otherwise arrest. Moreover, despite clear rules prohibiting unnecessary violence and brutality in police work, many members of the police force still employ these tactics. To justify such brutality police will sometimes carry "throwaways," that is, guns or knives that are planted on the suspects as "proof" that the use of force was necessary.[11] Police will also sometimes tap phones, intercept mail, and eavesdrop on suspected criminals without proper authorization.

Third, police do not always treat citizens equally. In particular, blacks, Chicanos, Indian-Americans, and "deviant" groups (homosexuals, hippies) are sometimes singled out for special scrutiny or harassment. Racial prejudice seems especially common in police departments, and this affects everything from how police speak to blacks to judgments concerning the seriousness of an offense.[12]

[10] Herbert Jacob, *Justice in America: Courts, Lawyers, and the Judicial Process*, 3d ed. (Boston: Little, Brown, 1978), pp. 170–171.

[11] Rodney Stark, *Police Riots: Collective Violence and Law Enforcement* (Belmont, Calif.: Focus Books, 1972), pp. 64–65. Also see Jerome H. Skolnick, *Justice without Trial: Law Enforcement in a Democratic Society* (New York: Wiley, 1966), pp. 227–228.

[12] Several studies on this point are summarized in Melvin P. Sikes, *The Administration of Injustice* (New York: Harper & Row, 1975), pp. 12–20.

Moreover, such prejudice seems to be encouraged by the very nature of police work. As one police officer put it:

> Pretty soon you decide they're all just niggers, and they'll never be anything else but niggers. It would take not just an average man to resist this feeling, it would take an extraordinary man to resist it, and there are few ways by which the police department can attract extraordinary men to join it.[13]

Defending unequal law enforcement

Does this mean that there is something profoundly wrong with the role of the police in the judicial system? Perhaps, but there are explanations. The above description levels serious charges against police behavior, but in many instances such behavior is understandable or even desirable.

First, the incidence of brutality, the planting of evidence, and illegal surveillance should not be exaggerated. When exposed these practices usually receive wide publicity, but blatant violations are rarely standard operating procedure. Most important, much of the prominence of these activities derives in part from contemporary efforts to eliminate them. The courts have recently taken many steps to prohibit excessive force and intimidation, so police behavior once viewed as normal is now singled out for harsh criticism. When such police practices as the "third degree" (beating confessions out of prisoners) were more common, few objections were raised.

Much of the unequal enforcement of laws inevitably follows from the huge number of laws on the books. If every law were enforced, most citizens would be in jail. Every police officer must exercise discretion, and discretion is frequently based on ease of enforcement, extent of citizen cooperation, seriousness of the crime, and community standards. Disorderly drunks and prostitutes may be given more police attention than an unapprehended rapist, for example, because drunks and prostitutes are more easily apprehended. In addition, more people may be disturbed by the public presence of drunks and prostitutes. If people really want equal enforcement of all laws, they should either greatly increase the number of police or sharply reduce the number of acts that are classified as crimes.

As for the charge that police break the law in order to uphold it, many police officers would assert that some slippage is inevitable if criminals are to be caught. Members of a police force are sometimes in great physical danger, and the need for quick action prevents them from carefully observing each and every rule. Many believe that the obligation to deter crime and apprehend criminals is a higher obligation than to observe picayune rules. Even if they were fully committed to following proper procedure, this may be a practical impossibility given the backgrounds and training of most officers. Criminal laws can be very complex and

---

[13] Quoted in James Q. Wilson, *Varieties of Police Behavior: The Management of Law and Order in Eight Communities* (Cambridge, Mass.: Harvard University Press, 1968), p. 43.

subtle, but most police force members are not college educated, nor are they trained to view their work from a lawyerlike perspective. A frequent police complaint is that those who make the laws—legislators, judges—don't have to apprehend dangerous criminals.

Finally, as for the charge that police discriminate against the poor, blacks, Chicanos, and the like, while some of this is true, much of it is really good police work, not unfair treatment. For example, in many cities young black males have a higher crime rate than young white males. Thus, an officer who stops and interrogates more black males views this action as justifiable and rational. To an outsider such behavior is discrimination and harassment, but to the officers involved it merely represents doing a good job. The police do not stop elderly people in search of narcotics, not because they like elderly people but because experience has taught them that they can better spend their time stopping hippy types. Moreover, what may appear as abusive or discourteous to middle-class sensibilities may be essential in dealing with criminals. Being polite to criminals is taken as a sign of weakness, not respect.

In short, police behavior may not always be in accord with the highest standards of fairness, but some—not all—of these discrepancies can be defended. At the heart of the problem is a conflict between effective crime control and respect for rights and proper procedure. We shall return to this conflict later.

THE RIGHTS OF SUSPECTED CRIMINALS

The rights of suspected criminals have been an important political issue since the adoption of the Constitution. The Constitution itself contains numerous provisions regarding criminal law. For example, Article I bans bills of attainder and *ex post facto* laws and forbids suspension of the writ of *habeas corpus* except in emergency situations. The Fourth, Fifth, Sixth, and Eighth also spell out major safeguards of individual liberties. Criminal law is extremely complex and controversial, and interpretations are always changing, but the following briefly outlines some of the major rights enjoyed by suspects. Let us begin with the initial police contact.

Freedom from unreasonable searches

A basic right of a U.S. citizen is freedom from overenthusiastic police who will stop at nothing to get evidence of criminal behavior. This fear of surprise, midnight raids in pursuit of wrongdoing led to the Fourth Amendment, which bans "unreasonable searches and seizures" and requires that search warrants be specific and be based on "probable cause." What, however, is "unreasonable?" How specific must a search warrant be? Are all police limited by the Fourth Amendment?

The easiest of these questions is the last one, which concerns the scope of the Fourth Amendment. Originally, prohibition against unreasonable searches and seizures applied only to federal actions, so the states were bound only by the broader requirement of due process stated in the Fourteenth Amendment. In 1949, however, the Supreme Court in *Wolf* v.

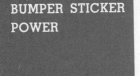

BUMPER STICKER POWER

The use of extraneous characteristics in police law enforcement was dramatically documented in a study involving bumper stickers. F. K. Heursenstamm, an instructor at California State College in Los Angeles, selected 15 of his students to participate in an experiment. Each of these 15 (who commuted to school) attached a vivid orange and black bumper sticker reading BLACK PANTHER to his or her car. During this period the militant Black Panthers had been involved in several shoot-outs with the police, and a number of policeman had been killed. The 15 students were equally divided among whites, blacks, and Chicanos and had a variety of appearances ranging from hippie to straight. All had exemplary driving records, and all made a special effort to obey the law. The cars were carefully checked for defective equipment.

Within two hours after the start of the study one student received a ticket for "incorrect lane change." The tickets started coming in rather quickly for such offenses as "following too closely," "driving too slowly in high-speed lane of freeway," "excessive speed," "making unsafe lane change," and "driving erratically." In 17 days the participants received a total of 33 traffic citations. Citations were given regardless of race, sex, ethnicity, or personal appearance. When the study concluded, relieved drivers went straight to their cars and quickly removed the BLACK PANTHER bumper stickers.

The moral of the story is that it may be wise to put a "Support Your Local Police" sticker on your car.

F. K. Heursenstamm, "Bumper Stickers and the Cops," *TRANS-action*, 8 (February 1971), pp. 32–33.

Colorado ruled that the provisions of the Fourth Amendment were applicable to state courts.

In general, contemporary interpretations hold that citizens and their possessions, such as houses or automobiles, can be searched if (1) the individual being searched consents, or (2) the search is part of a lawful arrest, or (3) there is a warrant for the search. Thus, if you are stopped by the police and they ask to search you and you agree, the search is legal. If you are running down the street carrying a couch claiming to be a psychiatrist on a house call and are arrested by a police officer, he or she can then legally search you for weapons or other stolen merchandise. Finally, if the police believe that you have stolen goods in your apartment, they can request a search warrant from a judge to search your property within a specified period to look for particular merchandise.

In practice, of course, things can get complicated, and numerous rules exist to handle the different contingencies. For example, police with a warrant are normally required to announce themselves before conducting a search, but if this announcement could jeopardize the case (for example, illegal drugs can be flushed down the toilet), **"no-knock" entry** may be permitted. The courts have also upheld **"stop-and-frisk" laws** that allow police to search people legally if there is a reasonable suspicion of wrongdoing even if no arrest occurs. The advent of electronic surveillance has also added complexities to the meaning of properly authorized searches. Originally these techniques were not covered by the Fourth Amendment. Gradually, however, the courts have held that wiretapping and the like must be justified in advance and be strictly limited (however, recording conversations with devices concealed in one's clothing has not been ruled as wiretapping or an intrusion of privacy).[14]

The legality of a search is a crucial question because the courts have ruled that illegally obtained evidence cannot be used in court. This **"exclusionary rule"** was first applied by the Supreme Court to federal cases in 1914 (*Weeks* v. *United States*). In the landmark case of *Mapp* v. *Ohio* (1961), the Supreme Court in a 5 to 3 vote ruled that the exclusion rule applied equally to federal and state courts. Since then many cases have been dismissed when the defendant successfully argued that the evidence was obtained without a proper search warrant or without the permission of the defendant.

Rights prior to trial

A second set of rights possessed by a suspect pertains to the period after arrest but prior to trial. What can you do after being taken to the police station? One important right is the right to be promptly informed of the charges against you. The police cannot legally lock you up for a few weeks while they decide what crime you committed. Federal statutes require a charge to be made "without unnecessary delay," while state regulations vary from "promptly" to as long as 72 hours in Georgia under some circumstances.[15] If, as sometimes happens, you are not promptly charged with a crime, you can file a writ of *habeas corpus*, which requests a judge to hold a hearing to inform you of the charge (or otherwise change the conditions of your confinement).

The Supreme Court has recently taken vigorous action to protect suspects during the pretrial period, especially during police interrogation. The most well known of these court actions are the so-called **Miranda rules** (from the *Miranda* v. *Arizona* [1966] decision). In the Miranda case the court held that suspects must be told that they have a right to remain silent, that anything they say may be held against them, and that they have a right to counsel prior to or during police interrogation (if the sus-

"No-knock" entry Allowing police entry without an announcement when such an announcement might jeopardize obtaining the sought-after evidence.

"Stop-and-frisk" laws Laws allowing police to stop and search citizens for a reasonable suspicion of wrongdoing, even if no arrest occurs.

Exclusionary rule The principle that evidence obtained illegally cannot be used in court.

Miranda rules Judicial ruling stating that persons arrested have the right to remain silent; they must be informed that anything they say can be held against them and that they have a right to counsel.

[14] Many of the legal complexities of electronic surveillance are described in C. Herman Pritchett, *The American Constitution*, 3d ed. (New York: McGraw-Hill, 1977), pp. 439–442.

[15] Oliver Rosengart, *The Rights of Suspects* (New York: Discus Books, 1974), pp. 76–79.

Grand jury A body of citizens who hear the evidence against the accused and decide whether the evidence justifies a trial.

Bail Money put up by the accused to insure his or her presence at a future trial. If the person fails to show up ("jumps bail"), the money is forfeited to the court.

pect cannot afford a lawyer, one is appointed). In 1972, the right to counsel was even extended to misdemeanors or petty offenses where imprisonment was possible. (The court has held, however, that a lawyer need not be present at every stage of the process, for example, during a line-up or in grand jury testimony.) In general, confessions obtained through the use of physical or psychological coercion have been thrown out of court.

Finally, in all federal cases, but only in about half the states, a person must be indicted by a **grand jury** before he or she can be tried. Grand juries usually number between twelve and twenty-three people and are basically charged with ascertaining whether there is enough evidence of a crime to warrant a full trial. Grand juries are supposed to prevent time-consuming trials based on flimsy evidence or trials that could be used to embarrass defendants. If a reasonable amount of evidence exists, the grand jury votes to indict, or issues a "true bill."

The right to bail

Between arraignment and trial most suspects have the opportunity to post **bail.** Posting bail means that the defendant gives the court a certain amount of money (determined by the judge within certain guidelines), which will be forfeited if the defendant does not show up for trial. Since the bail can be high, for example, $20,000 or more, most defendants make use of a bail bondsman who puts up the money in exchange for a fee (usually 10 percent). The Eighth Amendment guarantees only that bail will not be "excessive," so a defendant has no constitutional right to bail. Federal courts and some states will deny bail in capital cases or when the defendant has previously fled to avoid prosecution. Because "excessive" is a difficult word to define, the bail system has occasionally been used to incarcerate people without a trial. One study found that judges required a bail of $200,000 for rioters during some of the urban disturbances of the 1960s.[16] A group of civil rights workers in Americus, Georgia, were once charged with "attempted insurrection," which was a capital offense and thus not subject to bail.[17] Such abuses led to the Bail Reform Act of 1966, which allows the release of suspects in federal courts on their own recognizance or unsecured bond unless there is a reasonable suspicion that they will not show up for trial.

Rights during the trial

In the trial itself the defendant has several other important rights. The Fifth Amendment provides that persons shall not be forced to give testimony against themselves (self-incrimination). This has always applied to federal cases, and in 1964 in *Malloy* v. *Hogan* the principle was ex-

---

[16] Jerome H. Skolnick, *The Politics of Protest* (New York: Ballantine Books, 1969), pp. 300–308.

[17] Cited in Andrew Overby, "Discrimination in the Administration of Justice," in Norman Johnston et al., *The Sociology of Punishment and Correction,* 2d ed. (New York: Wiley, 1970), p. 246. Overby also describes the technique of "pyramiding" bail – a defendant is charged with numerous minor offenses so the total bail required is considerable.

tended to state courts. Essentially, the prosecution must be able to prove its case without the cooperation of the suspect. There is, however, a way to pressure a defendant into testifying: a prosecutor can request that a defendant be granted immunity from prosecution; failure to testify can result in being held in **contempt of court.** (This tactic is used to get small-time criminals to testify against bigger criminals.)

Another key right during a trial is the right to a lawyer. The Sixth Amendment provides that defendants in all criminal trials shall enjoy "the Assistance of Counsel for his defense." Nevertheless, this right was slowly implemented. Until 1938, it applied only to federal cases involving crimes with a death penalty. In 1938, the right to counsel, even if the defendant could not afford one, was extended to all federal, but not state, trials. Gradually, however, the Supreme Court held that under various special circumstances state courts must provide a defense lawyer. Ultimately, in the famous case of *Gideon* v. *Wainwright* (1963) the Supreme Court held that representation by counsel was constitutionally required in all criminal cases.

A third important trial right is the right to a jury trial (guaranteed in the Constitution itself and by the Sixth Amendment). This guarantee has been viewed, however, as a "valuable privilege," not an absolute requirement, so a defendant can waive a trial by jury. The courts have also ruled that jury trials are not constitutionally required for minor offenses. For many years the right to a jury trial applied only to federal issues, but in 1968 this right was extended by the Supreme Court to state criminal trials. Much of the debate over juries has involved their composition. Numerous defendants have claimed that trial by jury is meaningless unless jurors are a reasonable cross section of the community. By and large the courts have accepted this argument and have voided convictions in cases where certain types of people were systematically excluded from jury duty. This was especially important in the South where blacks were frequently convicted by all-white juries.

If tried before a jury, a defendant usually has the protection of the **unanimity rule**—each juror has to vote conviction for the prosecution to convict. Since there are usually (but not always) twelve jurors, this is an important safeguard to insure that the evidence for conviction is beyond a reasonable doubt. In recent years, however, the Supreme Court has upheld guilty convictions by less than unanimous votes (for example, 9 to 3 and 10 to 2) for state, but not federal, cases. The unanimity rule derives from common law, not the Constitution, so further weakening of it is possible in the future.

The Sixth Amendment also provides several other important rights during the trial. The trial must be "speedy and public," so a prosecutor cannot drag a trial on for years if he or she has no real case, nor can the trial be conducted in secret.[18] The defendant also has the right to con-

Contempt of court Disobedience of a court order or interference with the functioning of a court. May be a criminal or civil offense and is punishable by a fine or imprisonment.

Unanimity rule The custom derived from common law requiring that all jurors must vote for conviction for the accused to be judged guilty.

---

[18] There is no precise definition of a "speedy" trial. In *Barker* v. *Wingo* (1972) the Supreme Court stated that no inflexible definition of "speedy" can be given. Relevant considerations include reasons for the delay, the length of the delay, the behavior of the defendants, and the harm caused by the delay.

Double jeopardy Being put on trial twice for the same offense. The expression comes from the Fifth Amendment, which states that no person shall "be subject for the same offense to be twice up in jeopardy of life or limb."

front and cross-examine witnesses. The prosecutor cannot normally introduce written testimony from witnesses to prevent the defendant from challenging the person directly. A defendant can also have the court compel favorable witnesses to testify on his or her behalf (in both federal and state courts).

Rights after the trial

What about rights *after* the trial? Here, the most important one is the Fifth Amendment ban on **double jeopardy.** That is, the government cannot try a person twice for the same crime (thus, the government cannot appeal an acquittal). Prior to 1969, the ban on double jeopardy applied only in federal cases. In *Benton* v. *Maryland* (1969), by a 6 to 2 vote, the Supreme Court held that this ban also applied to the states. There are some exceptions, however, to the ban on being tried twice for the same crime. A convicted individual can waive this right and demand a new trial. If the jury cannot reach a decision, there may be a second trial. Or if a conviction is overturned on appeal, the government may request a new trial on the original offense. In some state courts (but not in federal courts, generally) a defendant who has committed several crimes can be tried separately for each crime, even if one act resulted in all the crimes (for example, mass murder).

Another important protection is the Eighth Amendment's ban on "cruel and unusual punishment." This prohibition has been applied in several instances. For example, when punishments have seemed overly severe for the crimes committed, they have been struck down as cruel and unusual. A California law sentencing drug addicts to ninety days in jail for merely being addicts illustrates this type of judicial "overkill." Death by torture or slow dismemberment would also be voided as unconstitutional.[19]

The major recent use of the Eighth Amendment has concerned the death penalty. Is electrocution, hanging, or gassing inherently "cruel and unusual?" In 1972 in *Furman* v. *Georgia* the Supreme Court struck down the Georgia death penalty as cruel and unusual. However, of the five-Justice majority, three said that the cruel and unusual aspect was not the death penalty itself but rather the *unevenness* of its application. The two remaining Justices believed that capital punishment is, by its very nature, barbaric and uncivilized. Following the Furman decision, numerous states reinstituted the death penalty but with new, tighter procedures granting less discretion. In 1976, the Supreme Court in *Gregg* v. *Georgia*, by a 7 to 2 margin, again held the death penalty not to be inherently cruel and unusual.

[19] Present-day punishment is mere inconvenience compared with some past practices. One popular technique in medieval France was quartering. To put the victim in the proper frame of mind, the person's limbs might be burned. Then, each arm and leg would be attached to a rope, which, in turn, would be attached to a strong horse. The horses might give short jerks or pull hard in four different directions until the limbs came off. If this did not do it, the executioner would finish the job with a hatchet, put all the limbs together, and burn them.

Our analysis of the rights of suspected criminals has included an impressive number of important rights (and there are many more we have not mentioned). Some people, in fact, argue that a suspected criminal is too well protected. The experienced criminal in particular quickly learns how to manipulate "the system," so the police must resort to illegal tactics if the public is to be protected. But it is also argued that many of these rights exist more on paper than in the real world. For example, the courts require that a lawyer be provided for those who cannot afford one, yet these lawyers are commonly inexperienced, overworked, and uninterested in their clients. Their presence only gives the *appearance* of fairness. The law may guarantee a jury trial, but it is well known that juries (especially grand juries) are disproportionately white, middle-class, and older, while criminals tend to be disproportionately black, poor, and young.

UNEQUAL SENTENCING

Our analysis of the fairness of the criminal justice system has thus far examined police behavior and the rights of suspected criminals. Our final concern is the punishment received by convicted criminals. In many respects this is the "bottom line" of the long process that began with an arrest. The police can be scrupulously fair and all the prisoner's constitutional rights carefully observed, but an unfair sentence makes the previous steps irrelevant. Determining "fair" punishment for a crime is difficult, yet this is a crucial issue that deserves close attention.

The relationship between crimes and sentences

Perhaps the easiest place to begin is to look at the sentences associated with different types of crime. Here, the question is whether the punishment fits the crime. In general, more serious crimes are punished more severely, but there are many exceptions to this rule. To appreciate the occasional inconsistency between a crime and its punishment, consider the following:

> In Iowa one can get five years in jail for beating a dog or horse, but only three years for immoral sexual behavior with a child.

> Also in Iowa, forging a check carries a maximum sentence of ten years while manslaughter has an eight-year maximum.

> Destroying a house in Colorado by fire can get you twenty years in jail. But if you use explosives, the maximum is only ten years.

> In California the maximum penalty for breaking into a car and taking the glove compartment contents is fifteen years. Stealing the entire car, however, could get you only ten years in jail.[20]

[20] These illustrations are drawn from Sue Titus Reid, *Crime and Criminology* (New York: Holt, Rinehart and Winston, 1976), pp. 416–417.

Indefinite sentences Sentences stating a maximum and a minimum penalty, allowing the judge to choose the exact sentence.

The significance of such discrepancies is that they allow a judge to impose grossly inappropriate sentences while still being perfectly within the law. Many crimes also carry **indefinite sentences,** that is, sentences with maximums and minimums, but for which the judge determines the precise penalty. Thus, a judge who wants to "throw the book" at a defendant can sometimes apply the maximum sentence for a crime that is usually given a much lighter sentence. On more than one occasion this was done to "get" southern civil rights activists, who broke what appeared to be "minor" laws. For example, Otis Johnson, a civil rights advocate in Houston, Texas, was given a thirty-year prison term for possession of marijuana.[21] Similarly, many laws on the books specify fairly severe prison sentences (for example, five years in jail) for certain common sexual practices, and every so often they are fully enforced. Such action is outrageous but legal.

Another common criticism regarding sentencing is that judges can differ enormously in how they punish very similar crimes. That some judges dispense tough sentences and others give lenient ones is a fact

[21] Sikes, p. 101.

THERE OUGHT TO BE A LAW AGAINST SILLY LAWS

U.S. legislators have traditionally shown a willingness to legislate on almost every conceivable topic. The inevitable result has been a proliferation of strange laws that can only bewilder and amuse the average citizen. Fortunately, most of these inane rules are now off the books or no longer enforced. Here are some choice examples of silly laws.

In Ashland, Wisconsin, it is illegal to play marbles for keeps.

Taking a bath in Boston requires a written prescription from a doctor.

In Nogales, Arizona, it is illegal to wear suspenders.

Your right to grow as tall as you want is legally protected in Louisiana.

Taking pictures of a rabbit from January to April is illegal in Wyoming unless you have a license.

Singing out of tune is illegal in North Carolina.

All males must grow a beard if they live in Brainerd, Minnesota.

Moscow, Idaho, prohibits riding a tricycle on the sidewalks.

In Wisconsin at least two thirds of an ounce of cheese must be served with a meal costing 25 cents or more.

well known to criminal lawyers. This situation was dramatically illustrated in two 1960 Fort Worth, Texas, fraudulent check cases. One man cashed a $58.40 check. He has no prior record, was out of work, and needed money to feed his family. He received fifteen years in prison. A second man, in similar circumstances, cashed a fraudulent check for $35.20. A different judge gave him thirty days in the clink.[22]

White–collar crime Crime typically committed by middle–class people. Involves fraud, income tax evasion, and other such behavior rather than violence or theft of personal property.

Characteristics of defendants and sentences received

Many judges have also been accused of being far more lenient in punishing "**white-collar**" **crime** than offenses involving violence or theft of personal property. In his study of federal judges Joseph C. Goulden found that during a six-month period in the New York City system only five of the ten people convicted of income tax evasion were put in prison, and even then the average stay was two months (the average amount evaded was $24,000). Well-paid executives in Wall Street firms are frequently given comparatively small fines when they are caught in illegal transactions involving millions of dollars. Goulden concludes that

[22] Cited in Reid, p. 418.

It is illegal to kiss in Riverside, California, unless both parties have first wiped their lips with carbolized rose water.

Inserting pennies in your ears is against the law in Hawaii.

Santa Ana, California, makes it a crime to swim on dry land.

In Gary, Indiana, it is against the law to go to the theatre within four hours of eating garlic.

No dog is allowed within 10 feet of a fire hydrant in Sheridan, Wyoming.

A Connecticut law gives beavers the legal right to build a dam.

In Quitman, Georgia, it is illegal for a chicken to cross the road.

Under Oregon law a dead juror cannot serve on a jury.

Massachusetts makes it illegal to put tomatoes in clam chowder.

Citizens of South Carolina are legally required to carry guns with them when they attend church on Sunday.

Idaho prohibits fishing for trout from the back of a giraffe (nor can you buy a chicken after dark without the permission of the sheriff).

Mistreating an oyster is against the law in Baltimore, Maryland.

Minneapolis, Minnesota, makes it illegal to drive a red automobile (and if you double park you may be put on a chain gang and fed only bread and water).

These and many other such laws are reported in Barbara Seuling, *You Can't Eat Peanuts in Church and Other Little Known Laws* (Garden City, N.Y.: Dolphin Books, 1976).

Capital offense A crime punishable by the death penalty or life imprisonment.

whereas well-educated, high-status judges have no problem giving harsh sentences to "hardened criminal types," they apply very different standards for "better" people who resemble the judges themselves in terms of social background.[23]

Perhaps the most serious criticism of sentencing behavior concerns inequalities based on race and socioeconomic status. In particular, it is frequently alleged that blacks and poor people receive harsher punishments than white or middle-class citizens. Is this true? The evidence from numerous studies provides some proof for this contention, but there is no general one-to-one relationship between a criminal's race or social class and the severity of punishment.[24]

One area in which there is a relationship between the defendant's race or class and the sentence received is for **capital offenses**, that is, crimes punishable by the death penalty or life imprisonment. Especially in the South, a black is much more likely to receive the death penalty than a white convicted of the same crime. Overall, between 1930 and 1965, 3,856 executions took place. Blacks comprised about half of those executed for murder and 92 percent of those executed for rape.[25] Several studies of southern states show that while blacks are frequently executed for killing whites, the opposite has never occurred.[26] Parallel findings emerge when we examine socioeconomic status—poor people are more likely to be executed than wealthy people.

When we move beyond capital offenses the picture becomes more complex. Variations in sentencing occur, but it is not always a simple case of blacks and poor people being treated more harshly. One important factor is the victim. One study of sentences in robbery and burglary cases found that blacks victimizing other blacks received more lenient sentences than whites victimizing whites or blacks victimizing whites.[27] It has also been observed that police frequently ignore many violent crimes involving only blacks (but they will make arrests if whites commit similar crimes). The general rule seems to be that if you want to avoid harsh punishment, victimize someone of lower social status than yourself, and if you are black, victimize other blacks.

The criminal record and other legal circumstances of the person being

---

[23] Joseph C. Goulden, *The Benchwarmers: The Private World of Powerful Judges* (New York: Weybright and Talley, 1974), pp. 104–105.

[24] A third attribute that appears to make a difference in the sentence received is the sex of the accused. Though the data on this question are limited, the overall conclusion seems to be that women are treated more leniently than men. According to a study done in California, except for property crimes women are less likely to be convicted, or, if convicted, are less likely to go to prison. These and other differences in sentencing are described in Jacob, pp. 186–188.

[25] Thorsten Sellin, "Executions in the United States," in Thorsten Sellin, ed., *Capital Punishment* (New York: Harper & Row, 1967), pp. 32–33.

[26] Several of these studies are described in Overby, p. 269.

[27] The impact of the victim's race on sentence received is considered more fully in John Hagan, "Extra-Legal Attributes and Criminal Sentencing: An Assessment of a Sociological Viewpoint," *Law and Society Review*, 8 (Spring 1974), pp. 369–373.

sentenced are also relevant because judges will give more severe sentences to repeaters. Analyses of black-white and poor-wealthy differences in sentences received indicate that many (but not all) of the discrepancies in sentences can be explained by purely legal differences between defendants.[28] That is, a black may receive a stiffer sentence than a white for the identical crime, not because he or she is black but because he or she may be a repeated offender. Overall, blacks and poor people do receive longer sentences, but in most instances this is justifiable on purely legal grounds.

Plea bargaining in sentencing

One final aspect of sentencing that deserves attention is the widespread practice of **plea bargaining.** Plea bargaining occurs when the prosecutor and the defense attorney (or the defendant) agree on a deal in which the defendant will admit guilt on a lesser charge in exchange for the dropping of a more serious charge. For example, an armed robber who, in the process of committing a robbery, commits the separate offenses of first-degree robbery, grand larceny, assault, carrying a dangerous weapon, and third-degree assault might plead guilty to third-degree assault if the prosecutor offered to drop the other, much more serious, charges. The judge must approve this deal, and if he or she objects, the prosecutor and the defense attorney must renegotiate it. One famous case of plea bargaining occurred in the case that led to the 1973 resignation of Vice President Spiro Agnew. The government had collected extensive evidence of Agnew's guilt on many bribery, conspiracy, and income tax evasion charges but made an agreement with Agnew to forego a full prosecution if he would plead no contest to a single charge of income tax evasion.[29]

Plea bargaining has been bitterly attacked. Numerous instances exist where people guilty of serious crimes are convicted of much less serious crimes, with the result that they are soon back on the streets. The idea of a rapist getting six months in jail after pleading guilty to petty larceny (which was incidental to the rape) offends almost everyone. It is also claimed that plea bargaining results in innocent people being convicted of crimes. Many an innocent person has been convinced that it is far easier to plead guilty to a minor offense and pay a small fine or receive probation than to try to prove his or her innocence in a full-blown jury trial. In fact, an innocent person who insists on a trial may be warned that this will only anger everyone and that a conviction will bring a really stiff sentence.

The major argument in favor of plea bargaining is that without it the judicial system would be completely overwhelmed. As it is, the courts are flooded with thousands of cases and long delays, but if every case went to

Plea bargaining Negotiations between the prosecutor and the defense attorney (or defendant) in which the prosecutor offers to drop a more serious charge in return for the defendant's pleading guilty to a lesser charge. Such an agreement must be approved by the judge.

[28] Hagan, p. 378.

[29] An excellent and fascinating step-by-step description of this negotiation is provided in Richard M. Cohen and Jules Witcover, *A Heartbeat Away: The Investigation and Resignation of Vice-President Spiro T. Agnew* (New York: Viking, 1974), Chap. 14.

trial, the entire system would cease functioning. Plea bargaining at least allows judges and prosecutors to concentrate on the most serious cases. Negotiated sentences can also be justified on the grounds that trials are unnecessary when guilt is well established. Trials are designed to establish proof of wrongdoing, but many criminals are apprehended during the commission of the crime, so establishing guilt is not a problem. Finally, supporters of plea bargaining claim that certain types of offenses are better handled without trial. Especially in cases involving young first offenders or people with psychiatric disorders or in those involving embarrassing information (for example, incest), matters are better resolved through private negotiation than public trial.

The fairness of sentencing

Two conclusions are warranted about the fairness of sentencing. First, we must be careful not to exaggerate the amount of unjust punishment. Tens of thousands of sentences are dispensed every year, and it is easy to find a few gross miscarriages of justice (for example, thirty years in jail for possession of marijuana). Moreover, grossly unfair sentences can be appealed, and on occasion have been set aside. Judges are not absolutely free to dispense whatever punishment they want, and there is a growing pressure in the legal profession to standardize punishments across states and to reduce judicial discretion.

Second, there really is no single standard of "fairness" to guide our evaluation. For example, do we conclude that much unfairness exists because people who committed similar crimes received different sentences? From this perspective evidence that characteristics of the victim, characteristics of the defendant, variations by judge, and the like, make a difference "proves" the system to be unfair. On the other hand, if we believe that fairness results from fitting the punishment to the crime on an individual-by-individual basis, such variations are to be expected. After all, would it be fair to give a young first offender and a hardened professional criminal identical sentences? We also have to decide from whose perspective we should consider fairness – the criminal's, the victim's, or society's. It can be argued that if certain types of criminal behavior get out of hand, using particularly harsh punishment to make "an example" of someone is "fair" from society's point of view. What about the costs to the victims of crime? Is it fair to punish only the offender and ignore the suffering of the victim? Some people claim that fairness must involve some form of compensation to the victim, not just punishment of the criminal. Clearly, then, establishing fairness is no simple procedure.

Is the U.S. system of justice effective in stopping crime?

Of all the political issues associated with crime and justice, the most explosive involves reducing crime. On several occasions in recent years "law and order" has been a paramount election issue. Presidents, gover-

SHOULD POOR PEOPLE RECEIVE STIFFER PRISON SENTENCES?

In examining the sentences given to criminals we must distinguish between abstract standards of fairness and what may be good for society as a whole. Treating poor people and rich people alike if they have identical situations (for example, same crime committed, previous record, same age, and so on) may be "fair," but it may be poor social policy. In fact, Peter H. Aranson in "The Optimal Length of Prison Sentences" suggests that shorter sentences for the rich may be in the interest of society.* He argues that because the rich contribute more to the well-being of society, taking them out of circulation for lengthy periods harms everyone. Moreover, it can also be argued that a short prison sentence to a "respectable" middle-class person is equivalent to a longer sentence to a poor person, since the stigma of imprisonment is much greater for middle-class people. Indeed, merely being tried for a crime can completely ruin the reputation of a businessperson, lawyer, doctor, or professor and make it impossible to practice his or her profession.

It is also likely that many of the conclusions drawn from scientific and rational studies of crime may run contrary to our traditional standards of fairness. For example, what if scientific research showed that blacks are statistically more likely to commit crimes after release from prison (perhaps due to problems of finding employment)? Should we then be less willing to grant parole to blacks? Such possibilities indicate that more scientific research may not solve many of the difficult questions involving crime and justice.

* Paper presented at the annual meeting of the American Political Science Association, New Orleans, Louisiana, September 4–8, 1973.

nors, and mayors have campaigned against "coddling criminals" and "too lenient courts," and many of these anticrime candidates have won elections. Yet this emphasis has done little to stem the crime rate. Can anything really be done about the crime rate?

AMOUNT OF CRIME

The best place to begin our analysis of the criminal justice system is with the amount of crime committed in the United States. Since 1930, the FBI has been issuing its *Uniform Crime Reports*, which show the number of "serious" crimes, as defined by the FBI, known to the police (these include murder, forcible rape, robbery, aggravated assault, and various

Clearance rate A police term referring to the proportion of crimes for which a person has been convicted. One arrested person who confesses to a thousand crimes thus "clears" a thousand crimes (but the accused may not be convicted).

property theft crimes). These figures are collected by local police using FBI guidelines. In 1976 there was a total of 11.3 million serious crimes known to the police, of which slightly less than a million were of a violent nature. On a per capita basis this comes to 5,266 crimes for each 100,000 citizens.[30] Keep in mind that we are dealing only with "serious" crimes. Excluded are such crimes as fraud and embezzlement, prostitution, arson, gambling, drug violations, and various sexual offenses. Not only is there a lot of crime, but in the last fifteen years the rate of crime has almost consistently risen. For example, in 1960, the rate of serious crimes for each 100,000 people was 1,887; by 1975, it had risen to 5,285.[31]

To appreciate the magnitude of crime in the United States compare our statistics to those of other economically developed nations. In 1973, the U.S. homicide rate for males was 15.5 for each 100,000 people. In Canada the figure was 3.2, England 1.0, France 1.1, West Germany 1.5, and Japan, 1.6. Mexico, however, had a homicide rate for males of 23.8 for each 100,000 (but females in the United States committed more homicides than their Mexican counterparts).[32] London, which is about the same size as New York City, had 113 murders in 1972. New York City—which is not the most murder-prone U.S. city—had 1,700. London had 3,000 robberies compared to 78,000 in New York. London had 150 rapes; New York had 3,300. No wonder many Europeans are fearful of visiting the United States.[33]

Even these figures do not describe the extent of crime in the United States since they include only *reported* crimes. Because people believe that the police will do nothing, are afraid of retribution, or feel the crime might embarrass them (for example, being robbed while soliciting a prostitute), many crimes go unreported to the police. To determine the "true" extent of crime, in 1974 the Law Enforcement Assistance Administration (LEAA) conducted a survey of 200,000 citizens in eight cities. Overall, the study found that there were about twice as many crimes actually committed as were reported to the police. For instance, for every reported rape there were 2.1 rapes not reported (however, a similar 1965 study reported a ratio of approximately 3.5 to 1 of unreported to reported rapes).[34]

What proportion of these crimes is successfully resolved by the police? Do the real-life Kojaks and Barrettas always get their man or woman? Figure 15.1 reports the "**clearance rate**" for serious crimes reported in the FBI *Uniform Crime Reports.* "Clearance rate" refers to the proportion of crimes in which there is a person arrested for that crime. As Figure 15.1 shows, the clearance rate drops sharply as we move from

[30] Federal Bureau of Investigation, *Uniform Crime Reports*, 1976 (Washington, D.C.: Government Printing Office), p. 35.

[31] *Statistical Abstract of the United States, 1977*, p. 153.

[32] *Statistical Abstract of the United States, 1977*, p. 159.

[33] These figures are cited in Ernest van den Haag, *Punishing Criminals: Concerning a Very Old and Painful Question* (New York: Basic Books, 1975), p. 163.

[34] These and several related studies of the "true" incidence of crime are reported in Reid, pp. 55–56.

The fear of crime.

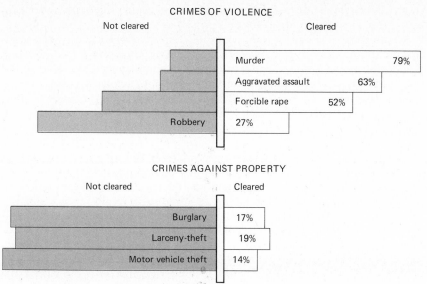

FIGURE 15.1

CRIMES CLEARED BY ARREST, 1976.

murder (79 percent) through robbery (27 percent) to motor vehicle theft (14 percent). Recall that since crimes against property comprise the majority of all reported serious crimes, these figures show that, overall, most crimes do not result in arrest. The successes of television and movie police, who always get their man or woman, are exceptionally misleading.

An even more discouraging picture emerges when we examine what happens to those who are arrested. Figure 15.2 shows, in general, that in 1976 a third of those arrested are eventually convicted; another third are sent to juvenile court; and another third are either acquitted or are still awaiting trial. But these figures can be very misleading, because being

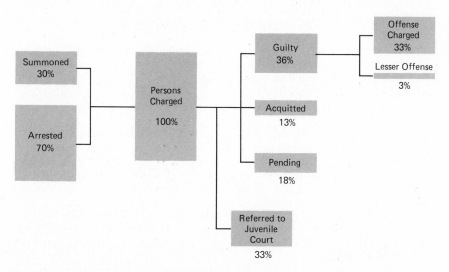

FIGURE 15.2

DISPOSITION OF PERSONS CHARGED, 1976.

found guilty does not always result in punishment. In many instances the guilty person is given probation or a suspended sentence or is placed in a nonpunitive rehabilitation program. For example, out of more than 100,000 felony arrests in New York City a year, only about 4,000 persons eventually spend a year or more in prison. Perhaps most disturbing is the fact that most of these convicted felons are soon back in circulation (the average time actually served in prison is less than 26 months).[35]

REVOLVING-DOOR JUSTICE

The last situation has led to the frequent charge that our system is one of **revolving-door justice.** Criminals see arrest as unlikely and incarceration as an occupational inconvenience, since they rarely spend much time in jail. In fact, a skillful manipulator can sometimes avoid jail altogether. In New York City one suspected thief and forger was arrested and freed on bail seventeen times in two and a half years and was never even tried for a crime. In this situation much of the crime can be caused by people who have passed through the system more than once. It is estimated that in New York State 80 percent of all solved crimes are committed by repeat offenders.[36]

To show how this system works, let us consider the case of Joseph Holloway. In 1971 Holloway robbed an elderly couple at knife point. He was jailed, and while in jail he also confessed to a rape-burglary. In August 1972 he was given four to twelve years for these crimes. In 1972 he was placed in a work-release program, and he promptly committed two armed robberies. Three years later he was paroled and committed four more armed robberies (two involved sexual abuse of the victims). He was apprehended in 1976, and in 1977 he was sentenced to ten to twenty-one years in prison. Due to a legal technicality, he will be a free man in 1981. The treatment Joseph Holloway received is by no means unique, and such actions exasperate many citizens and leaders.[37]

MAKING THE CRIMINAL JUSTICE SYSTEM MORE EFFECTIVE

Much has been written, but no clear consensus exists on whether the system can be made more effective. Many solutions have been proposed, and some have been tried on an experimental basis, but few people are optimistic. In fact, some social critics assert that high levels of crime are virtually built into the very nature of our society. Racism, unequal eco-

---

[35] Nicholas Scoppetta, "Getting Away with Murder: Our Disastrous Court System," *Saturday Review,* June 19, 1978, p. 11. Many experts claim that only 1 percent of the people who commit crimes ever go to jail. This figure is much lower than FBI or local police department figures because of the large number of unreported crimes. See Gary F. Glenn, "Crime *Does* Pay," *The Police Chief*, January 1976.

[36] Scoppetta, p. 12. Data from other cities showing comparable patterns are presented in James Q. Wilson, *Thinking About Crime* (New York: Basic Books, 1975), pp. 165–166.

[37] Cited in Scoppetta, p. 13.

nomic opportunity, and poor living conditions breed crime, and unless the fundamental problems of our socioeconomic system are eliminated, rampant crime will continue. For some critics the only solution is replacing capitalism with socialism. Other observers do not believe that the poverty-leads-to-crime assertion is factually correct. Specifically, during the 1960s the United States, including blacks and other minorities, experienced considerable economic progress and opportunity, yet crime skyrocketed. If anything, crime seems to be associated with more money and more social progress. Moreover, socialistic countries such as the Soviet Union also seem to be experiencing increased crime, so crime is not entirely a capitalist disease.

Another view of crime, also emphasizing its inevitability, sees the character of the population as the principal cause. Specifically, young people (age 11–25) have traditionally been crime prone (particularly young males). Following World War II the United States experienced a massive "baby boom," and as these postwar children began reaching adolescence in the early 1960s, crime increased dramatically. During the sixties and early seventies, the 11–25-year-old group comprised about a quarter of the population yet accounted for about 75 percent of those arrested for serious crime.[38] Cities were especially hard hit, given the large numbers of poor black youths, an especially crime-prone group. Thus, the only real solution is time. Eventually, as rambunctious youths mature and the birthrate declines, crime will likewise recede.

Many of us do not want to wait fifteen to twenty years for crime to decline, however. One frequent proposal to reduce crime now focuses on rehabilitating criminals through such techniques as psychological counseling, job training, work-release programs, halfway houses, and education. Though some programs seem to work fairly well with certain types of people, the overall evaluation of rehabilitation efforts is fairly pessimistic.[39] Especially where "hard-core" criminals and repeated offenders are involved, rehabilitational efforts have produced meager results. It has proved very difficult to take people who have spent years being criminals and transform them with a few months of therapy or vocational education.

Increasing police effort

Would a major "war on crime" help? Certain efforts in this direction have shown promise, but no automatic relationship exists between police effort and crime reduction. For example, in 1965, after two years of dramatic increases in night-time New York City subway robberies, the mayor increased the subway police force from 1,200 to 3,100. Each train

---

[38] Reid, pp. 58–59. According to the FBI, in 1975 those under 25 accounted for 95.5 percent of all criminal homicides, 77.0 percent of all robberies, 85.2 percent of all burglaries, and 84.6 percent of all motor vehicle thefts.

[39] Wilson, pp. 168–170. For an extensive bibliography of rehabilitation studies, see Charles H. Logan, "Evaluation Research in Crime and Delinquency: A Reappraisal," *The Journal of Criminal Law, Crimonology and Police Science*, 63 (1972), pp. 378–387.

and each station had a police officer from 8 P.M. to 4 A.M. Crime declined in general for two years and then started increasing again. By 1970, the overall subway crime rate was *six* times the 1965 rate or the rate before the extra police were added. Robbers simply avoided the heavy evening police shift and concentrated on daytime travelers. On the other hand, other programs, such as "Community Sector Team Police Program" (COMSEC) in Cincinnati, have had some success against crime by reorganizing police work.[40]

Simply adding more police does not solve the problem. Many violent crimes occur between people who know one another as well as in non-public areas. Thus, the police do not usually become involved until after

[40] These and similar studies are reviewed in Wilson, pp. 86–94.

SOME CRIMINALS GIVE CRIME A BAD NAME

One factor that helps police control crime is the inept behavior of many criminals. Not all criminals are the masterminds sometimes depicted on television and in the movies. Here, for example, are some incidents from the files of the Chicago Police Department.

One klutzy stick-up man waved his sawed-off 12-gauge shotgun around a South Side cleaners, holding his hostages at bay until the weapon accidentally fired while he was holding the muzzle and blew his left little finger across the room. Howling in pain, he fled with a used portable TV and ten dollars in cash. Police recovered the pinkie, fingerprinted it, and placed it in cold storage in the Cook County morgue while they searched for the rest of the thief.

In the bank robbery business, the trade that made Dillinger famous, one should not leave calling cards. But an inexperienced robber did just that in a downtown bank by writing his holdup note on the back of one of his own personalized deposit slips, which, of course, was imprinted with his name and address. The FBI reached his home before he did.

A burglar broke into a West Side apartment in the middle of the day, stacked the TV, stereo and other valuables by the front door for easy removal, and, apparently tired from his efforts, took a snooze on the living room couch. He was discovered fast asleep when the lady of the house returned home. Her screaming did not awaken him. The police did.

Another apartment burglar almost stumbled across the place's lone resident, an old man, who was lying asleep on the couch. Only he wasn't asleep. He was dead. Heart attack. His revelation was too much for the burglar, who screamed so loud that the neighbors called the police. He

the crime is committed (and prosecution is difficult in these cases). A similar problem occurs in thefts—by the time the police arrive the trail is cold. Professional thieves are also very adept at getting rid of "hot" merchandise that could imcriminate them. Stolen automobiles can be turned into untraceable parts within hours, for example. For this reason the police have increasingly emphasized such prevention measures as burglar alarms, the engraving of names on valuable objects, better locks, and the like. Police work is also greatly hampered by uncooperative citizens, especially in black communities—a problem that will not be solved by adding more police. Finally, many of the root causes of crime, for example, family disintegration and the rebellious youth culture, are beyond the resolution of daily police work. Overall, adding more police may help under certain conditions, but it is not the ultimate solution.

---

begged the police to charge him with something—anything—as long as they didn't stick him with a murder rap.

A young flashy dresser held up a West Side liquor store, but, as he fled down the sidewalk, he tripped over his own two-toned platform shoes with five-inch heels, twisted his ankle, and fell in a heap to the pavement. Before the slightly dazed crook could crawl away, two police officers gleefully caught up with him and snapped on the handcuffs.

Three gunmen hijacked an interstate truck on a tip that it contained a special shipment of gold. Only they hijacked the wrong truck. Instead of gold, the truck's cargo area held close to 1,000 cases of brand new, ready-for-installation toilet-seat covers. FBI agents, tipped off a few days later that somebody in Chicago was trying to fence a truckload of hot toilet-seat covers, soon flushed the bandits out.

The attempted robbery of a North Side liquor store might have been successful if the chief gunman had not been confined to a wheelchair. An accomplice was rolling the gunman out the door as the police arrived. After quickly appraising the situation, the accomplice fled on foot, leaving his charge to pump away furiously at his wheels. A swift patrolman quickly grabbed the would-be fugitive's chair handles and wheeled him back into custody. The accomplice was caught a few blocks away.

Few crooks can surpass the guy who successfully held up a clothing store for about $1,000 and, by the time police caught up with him the next day, had invested the entire haul in lottery tickets. His total winnings? About $30. As the cops were taking him away, he reportedly protested, "The lottery is fixed!"

Clarence Page "Keystone Crooks," *Playboy,* March 1978, p. 22.

An electric chair—originally invented as a more humane method of execution.

The role of punishment in reducing crime

Perhaps the most widely discussed issue in crime reduction concerns the role of punishment. Many people have argued that the only language criminals understand is heavy punishment. Reducing crime can be accomplished by increasing the costs of being a criminal. Two distinct issues are involved here. The first involves the *severity* of punishment. That is, do we sentence a murderer to five or ten or twenty years in jail? Many medieval laws were exceptionally harsh insofar as the death penalty was used for a large number of offenses. There has been a general trend in the United States to make criminal penalties less severe, however.

Increasing the severity of punishment is relatively easy—a legislative act is all that is necessary. Most analysts agree, however, that severity by itself usually has no significant effect on the crime rate. This was illustrated in a Pennsylvania effort to reduce rape, following several well-publicized, brutal rape cases. The *minimum* penalty for rape, which resulted in bodily harm, was increased to fifteen years, and the *maximum* penalty was increased from fifteen years to life. However, one study of rape in Philadelphia found that the increased penalties had no deterrent effect on rape.[41]

This does not mean that severe penalties have no impact. A second important aspect of punishment is its *certainty*, that is, the probability that one will actually get caught and be punished. Many studies have found that increasing the *certainty* of punishment does reduce crime. A high certainty of punishment *coupled* with severe penalties can be very detrimental to crime.[42] Imagine if the automatic penalty for exceeding the 55 mile per hour speed limit were one year in jail and the probability of being caught were one out of two every time one violated the law. Only fools would break such a law.

Certainty of punishment is more difficult to achieve than severity. You must first apprehend the culprit—no easy task, especially in crimes against property. Perhaps the most promising method of increasing certainty of punishment is to set automatic prison sentences for serious crimes. That is, regardless of circumstances, a convicted rapist will get, say, ten years in jail. The practices of suspended sentences, probation, parole, plea bargaining, and other means by which prison can be avoided would be forbidden. The argument is that persistent criminals will eventually be caught, and if they know *for sure* that apprehension means a nonnegotiable stiff sentence, they will choose different professions. Of course, such a system might mean that a punishment is inappropriate to the person committing the crime; for example, someone who could

[41] Barry Schwartz, "The Effect in Philadelphia of Pennsylvania's Increased Penalties for Rape and Attempted Rape," *The Journal of Criminal Law, Criminology, and Police Science*, 59 (1968), p. 514. Also see Charles R. Tittle, "Crime Rates and Legal Sanctions," *Social Problems*, 16 (1969), pp. 409–423.

[42] For reviews of the impact of certainty of punishment on the crime rate, see Wilson, pp. 174–179. The most comprehensive review of studies on both the severity and certainty of punishment is found in Franklin E. Zimring and Gordon J. Hawkins, *Deterrence: The Legal Threat in Crime Control* (Chicago: University of Chicago Press, 1973).

benefit from rehabilitation would be treated exactly the same as an incorrigible hard-core criminal.

THE DIFFICULTIES OF REDUCING CRIME

Is, then, the system effective? The answer seems to be "no." In 1974, a total of $14.95 billion was spent on law enforcement by various governments in the United States. This compares with $3.35 billion in 1960. During this same period over a quarter of a million police were added at the state and local levels.[43] And, as we saw, crime rose sharply during this period. Of course, one could argue that spending more on crime allowed more crime to be detected, but this could not explain why citizens reported more crime.

Can rampant crime be stopped? Here we face really difficult political choices. Experience has shown that almost every type of crime *can* be drastically reduced *if* one is willing to bear the costs. For example, China once suffered from widespread opium addiction, but the problem was solved by making addiction a capital offense and executing thousands of addicts. Opium addiction is no longer a problem. Years ago city police controlled thefts by keeping poor juveniles out of wealthy neighborhoods because "they had no business being there." Such practices are now politically unacceptable to most people. Even the sharp reduction of homicides could be accomplished if that were our only goal. The banning of handguns, stricter controls of alcohol, preventive detention of homicide-prone individuals, and the automatic death penalty for all homicides would each make a big difference, but each of these measures is politically difficult to achieve.

The real issue of effectiveness, then, is how we navigate between our concerns for freedom and our desire to eliminate crime. A totally effective criminal justice system may be incompatible with a free society. And a totally free society would probably not last long unless people were reasonably well protected from crime. Obviously, this is not an easy conflict to resolve.

A conclusion: the politics of crime

It is tempting to view crime and justice as the struggle of good against evil, the good guys versus the bad guys. Certainly this is the approach embodied in the mass media and one shared by many politicians ap-

---

[43] *Statistical Abstract of the United States, 1977*, pp. 164–165. Of course, some of this resource commitment was not wisely allocated. For example, the Law Enforcement Assistance Administration developed a new type of patrol car that featured a multiple spark-discharge ignition, hand-held voice/digital terminal, heads-up display, audio recorder, wide-angle periscope review mirror, tire sensor, brake-wear sensor, microcomputer, digital cassette reader, and a visual indicator to show whether the siren was on. A prototype cost $2 million, but the whole project was abandoned.

pealing to voters. Unfortunately, while this perspective may have high entertainment value and provide much righteous indignation, it is of little use in helping us understand the debate over crime and justice.

We have argued throughout this chapter that crime and justice are basically political questions. Our standards of "crime," "fairness," "due process," and the like, may derive from religion or philosophy, but it is the political process that gives these standards their concrete meaning. As in other political conflicts, interests compete to have their perspectives incorporated into government decisions. Operators of theaters showing pornographic movies publicly claim that police should be tracking down murderers, not interfering with their freedom of speech. Big-city property owners want "wars" on mugging, prostitution, and smut peddlers, not on building-code violations.

The political nature of crime becomes apparent when we compare "street crime" — homicide, burglary, assault — with white-collar crime — fraud, embezzlement, tax evasion, price fixing. Campaigns against crime are almost always directed at crimes likely to be committed by lower-class individuals. Moreover, the legal procedures for the two different types of crimes frequently (but not always) vary. A mugger will be picked up by the police, held for investigation, interrogated, and perhaps convicted. A persistent mugger will probably spend a couple of months in jail. On the other hand, a company that violates consumer-protection laws will face proceedings in civil court, executives will rarely face jail, and the fine (if there is one) will usually be small (and can be charged as a business expense and passed on as a price increase to consumers).

The irony of this difference in treatment is that white-collar crime may be far more pervasive and costly than street crime. It is estimated, for example, that between 25 and 40 *billion* dollars of reportable income goes untaxed each year. Securities frauds cost the public between 500 million and a billion dollars a year. The scope of tax cheating is well illustrated by what happened in 1964 when banks and corporations were required to report to the federal government interest and dividend payments to depositors. When people learned that the government knew of their earnings, there was a 45 percent increase in the reporting of this type of income.[44]

Unfairness is not necessarily caused by bias. The very system itself may be organized to give one side an advantage over the other. Suppose you buy a "guaranteed" used car from "Honest Bob — where money talks and nobody walks." After a week the car collapses from exhaustion; you stop making payments and demand your money back. Even if the process is completely impartial, the deck is stacked against you. You have the burden of proving deception. Since you signed a valid contract and have defaulted, "Honest Bob" can have the sheriff attach your wages. The best you can hope for is to break even and get your money

[44] A more complete analysis of white-collar crime is found in *The President's Commission Report on Law Enforcement and Administration of Justice, Task Force Report: Crime and Its Impact — An Assessment* (Washington, D.C.: Government Printing Office, 1967), pp. 102–109.

back. The worst that can happen to "Honest Bob" is that he will get to sell the car again. As the law now stands you cannot send "Honest Bob" to jail for cheating.

We are *not* arguing that the legal system is a conspiracy against the poor and defenseless. Especially in recent years many changes have occurred to help poor people obtain lawyers and receive fair trials.[45] Rather, our claim is that those with political power have used this power to define the meaning of crime, judicial procedures, punishments, and the like, to their advantage. This is no more evil than these interests using their resources to get a tax break or other special protection. When General Motors lobbies to make violations of auto safety regulations a civil, not a criminal, matter, it is playing politics in the same way as are individuals who pressure government to decriminalize marijuana.

Major questions raised

1. What are crime, law, and justice? A crime is an intentional action that violates the law. Law is a government-formulated rule enforceable in the courts. Little agreement exists on the meaning of justice, but the most common conceptions emphasize equal application of the law, the social utility of the law, proper procedure, and appropriateness of the punishment to each situation (personalized justice). All three terms are concretely defined in the political process.

2. Is the U.S. system of criminal justice "fair"? The existing system of justice provides suspected criminals with a large number of rights at all stages of the process. However, numerous discrepancies exist between the ideal and actual practice. The police may use illegal tactics and enforce laws selectively. Rights, such as the right to a lawyer, may be of little value to a poor person. Judges can also be inconsistent in their sentencing behavior.

3. Is the system of justice in the United States effective in stopping crime? Despite major anticrime efforts, the crime rate continues to rise. Moreover, police do not solve most serious crimes, and many criminals quickly pass through a system of revolving-door justice. Improvements may be difficult. The most perplexing problem involves the conflict between the preservation of a free society and the need to preserve the public order. Many solutions to crime violate our sense of personal freedom and thus are politically unacceptable.

QUESTIONS FOR FURTHER DISCUSSION

1. Recently, to keep comparatively minor disputes out of the court system, the federal government created an experimental program of "neighborhood justice centers." Each center has four or five full-time staffers and two to three dozen mediators drawn from the community.

[45] Jacob, pp. 237–239.

Their purpose is to settle disputes between customers and merchants, between landlords and tenants, and family squabbles. In operating these centers, what type of law should be followed? Should mediators enforce appropriate state and local law? Or, on the other hand, should decisions be based on the standards of justice within the particular community? Or should the resolution of a dispute be based solely on what is acceptable and fair to the involved parties? What if the decision is considered fair to everyone in the neighborhood center but conflicts with state law?

2. In the nineteenth century England solved the problem of what to do with hardened criminals by shipping many of them to Australia. Life in Australia was usually preferable to rotting in an English jail, and English society was spared many criminals. What about the United States setting up such a colony for unreformable criminals on some remote, presently uninhabited island? Residents would have complete freedom and would be guaranteed necessary amenities, but they would not be allowed to return to the United States. Wouldn't this be more humane than incarcerating people in overcrowded and sometimes barbaric prisons?

3. Almost everyone acknowledges that there ought to be a balance between the right of society to protect itself and the rights of individuals to be free from government interference and surveillance. Recent court decisions have generally prevented the government from vigorously pursuing criminals. For example, when a car repeatedly circled the same area, the police became suspicious and stopped it. The driver had an arrest warrant outstanding against him, and the car was searched. The police found bullets, an unregistered loaded revolver, an unregistered sawed-off shotgun, and shells for the shotgun. Though convicted in the trial court, the conviction was thrown out on appeal because the search was not based on a crime that had been committed. The police could have acted legally only if (1) the guns had been prominently displayed, or (2) a crime had been committed and there was "probable cause" that the individual had been involved. In other words, the police cannot search for evidence before a crime is committed. If you were the judge of this case, how would you balance society's right to be protected against freedom from overzealous policing? What behavior or evidence would unambiguously allow the police to make a thorough search even if no crime had been committed?

4. Considerable debate has occurred over what is "cruel and unusual" punishment. When a San Bernardino, California, pornographic movie house owner was fined and jailed, the judge added in another penalty: he was sentenced to watch twenty hours of X-rated movies. Can this punishment be considered "cruel and unusual"? If the case were appealed on these grounds, what evidence could be presented?

BIBLIOGRAPHY

Becker, Howard S., ed., *The Other Side: Perspectives on Deviance.* New York: Free Press, 1964.
    Contains seventeen articles that examine the role of deviance in society. Several articles are valuable for showing the relationship between social norms and the criminalization of certain activity. Includes articles such as "The Social Integration of Queers and Peers."

Chevigny, Paul. *Police Power: Police Abuse in New York City.* New York: Vantage Books, 1969.

> A critical view of police practices in New York City. Numerous cases and incidents are described in support of the author's argument. Concludes with an analysis of what can be done to eliminate abuses.

Editorial Research Reports on Crime and Justice. Washington, D.C.: Congressional Quarterly, 1978.

> A balanced and well-documented analysis of topics such as international terrorism, computer crime, violence in public schools, prisons, and drug policy. Contains several bibliographies.

Eisenstein, James, and Herbert Jacob. *Felony Justice: An Organizational Analysis of Criminal Courts.* Boston: Little, Brown, 1977.

> Based on extensive investigation in three cities from 1972 to 1973, this analysis raises questions about many widely believed aspects of the criminal justice system. Very good for describing courtroom behavior, the role of bargaining in trials, and what actually happens to those convicted.

Jacob, Herbert. *Justice in America: Courts, Lawyers, and the Judicial Process,* 3d ed. Boston: Little, Brown, 1978.

> An excellent overview of the U.S. legal system. Views the courts from a political perspective and covers everything from the staffing and organization of courts to the role of interest groups in the judicial process. Cites many studies of the judicial system.

Mitford, Jessica. *Kind and Usual Punishment: The Prison Business.* New York: Knopf, 1973.

> A strong attack on the U.S. prison system and how it is administered. Argues that many prisoners are systematically mistreated, underpaid for their work, and sometimes even used as if they were chimpanzees in medical research (to list a few of the many charges). Concludes with an analysis of possible reforms.

Morris, Norval, and Gordon Hawkins. *The Honest Politician's Guide to Crime Control.* Chicago: University of Chicago Press, 1969.

> Basically argues that much of our crime problem results from criminalization of socially deviant behavior. Good coverage of rehabilitation efforts, juvenile delinquency, and psychiatric defense of criminal behavior. Contains many specific recommendations to combat crime.

Quinney, Richard. *Class, State and Crime: On the Theory and Practice of Criminal Justice.* New York: Longmans, 1977.

> Presents the Marxist interpretation of crime and justice in a capitalistic system. Argues, for example, that crime results from the very nature of capitalism and that the existing criminal justice system is basically a capitalist enterprise. Style is theoretical and uses a heavy amount of Marxist terminology.

Reid, Sue Titus. *Crime and Criminology,* 2d ed. New York: Holt, Rinehart and Winston, 1979.

> A well-written, comprehensive overview of crime and justice. Covers everything from the meaning of law to conditions in prison. Excellent source of findings from specialized studies of crime.

Sikes, Melvin P. *The Administration of Justice.* New York: Harper & Row, 1975.

> A highly critical review of the criminal justice system. Especially good at documenting how minorities fare poorly in the hands of police, judges, and juries. Contains a bibliography, and charges are supported with detailed data from numerous studies.

Van den Haag, Ernest. *Punishing Criminals: Concerning a Very Old and Painful Question.* New York: Basic Books, 1975.

> The author is a well-known conservative philosopher, but the arguments made in the book rest on extensive factual evidence. Considers a wide variety of topics relating to crime—the nature of justice, the purpose of punishment,

and the various alleged causes of crime, to name but a few. A stimulating and original book.

Wilson, James Q. *Thinking About Crime.* New York: Basic Books, 1975.
A collection of interesting essays dealing with several important topics in crime control. Argues that many of the old arguments about crime, for example, poverty causes crime, are untrue. Examines how different groups of professions view crime and how this perspective affects their policy recommendations. Also discusses heroin addiction, the death penalty, and some possible cures for crime.

Wright, Erik Olin. *The Politics of Punishment: A Critical Analysis of Prisons in America.* New York: Harper & Row, 1973.
An analysis of U.S. prisons written by an ex-student chaplain at San Quentin prison. Argues, for example, that rehabilitation is only a façade for punitive prison custodial practices and that prison authorities operate outside the law. Good description of life inside San Quentin and Soledad prisons.

Part four

Policy

PREVIEW

What are rights? A right is a legal or moral claim to some benefit. Rights differ from privileges, which can be more easily restricted. The line separating rights and privileges is not always clear. One view holds that for a right to exist it must be spelled out in the Constitution or in law. A different approach claims that rights exist independently of written law—they derive from natural law or our own conscience. Deciding who has what rights raises several key issues. Should everyone have equal rights? Are some rights more fundamental than others? What is the government's responsibility for implementing rights? Finally, who resolves conflicts over rights?

What political rights do citizens possess? Several rights are viewed as fundamental in U.S. politics. The right to free speech is guaranteed in the First Amendment, but this guarantee is not absolute. Problems include defining "speech" and who can limit speech. Some types of speech are not protected by the First Amendment.

Freedom of the press is also spelled out in the First Amendment. The freedom of radio, television, and films is more limited than that of newspapers or magazines. No prior restraint of the press is permitted unless justified by exceptional circumstances, and newspapers have considerable freedom in what they can say about public figures.

While freedom of association is not spelled out in the First Amendment, it has been viewed as a corollary of freedom of speech. Freedom of association has frequently conflicted with the need to protect national security.

The religious freedom guarantee of the First Amendment involves the establishment of a state-supported religion and limits on the exercise of religion. The courts have recently become more lenient in defining religion, but when religious behavior (not beliefs) is in conflict with the law, the law prevails.

Equal protection of the laws means that the laws must apply to all citizens equally. This doctrine has helped blacks and women achieve equality. However, the Supreme Court has allowed people to be treated differently under certain circumstances.

What sustains our rights? One argument is that our rights require strong support among citizens for their survival, yet studies show that many citizens do not support many rights. The argument that political activists help maintain our freedoms does not explain why the rights of blacks and women were violated for so long without much public outcry. Finally, evidence exists that our rights may not be strongly entrenched. Government has occasionally violated our rights, and constitutional provisions are little protection against the behavior of private individuals.

CHAPTER SIXTEEN

CIVIL
LIBERTIES AND
THE POLITICS
OF RIGHTS

n many ways the political history of the United States is the history of conflict over rights. The Revolution, the writing of the Constitution, the battle over slavery, and the contemporary struggle of women and blacks for equality have all involved the rights of citizens. Compared to conflicts over monetary gain, however, those concerned with political rights have sometimes been abstract and confused. We may be willing to fight to the death for "our constitutional rights," yet many of us only vaguely understand what we would be fighting for. How many people could list five constitutionally protected rights? More generally, how many of us really understand what rights we possess? While most citizens value their rights highly, few have thought much about the rights they possess, the bases of these rights, or whether their rights have any real meaning in contemporary society. Our analysis will, therefore, address three important questions regarding rights:

1. What are rights?
2. What political rights do citizens possess?
3. What sustains our rights?

What are rights?

Essentially, a **right** is a legal or moral claim on some benefit.[1] All U.S. citizens automatically enjoy certain rights simply because they are citizens. In contrast to rights are **privileges.** Whereas rights can be ignored or violated only under unusual circumstances, a privilege is a benefit that can be given to some citizens for a limited time and is more easily taken away. For example, a fair trial is a right, but a veteran's pension or a license to practice medicine is a privilege granted by the government. These privileges can be withdrawn or extended at the discretion of the government. A college student, for instance, has a right to be treated fairly by his or her instructor. However, the opportunity to make up an exam is usually considered a privilege that *may* be granted by the instructor.

DEFINING OUR RIGHTS AND PRIVILEGES

The distinction between a right and a privilege does not, unfortunately, get us very far in determining what specific benefits are rights. Why, for example, is free speech a right while a social security pension is only a benefit? The distinction between rights and privileges is sometimes fuzzy. In fact, some privileges have been transformed into rights (for example, having a lawyer defend you in court is now a right, but it was once merely a privilege). One way to separate rights from privileges is to define rights as benefits explicitly guaranteed to citizens in the Constitution and in laws made in accordance with the Constitution.

The Constitution and statutes as sources of rights

According to this view, citizens possess many different types of specifically stated rights. Recall from Chapter Fifteen that we have several important rights regarding criminal justice. The Constitution provides for the right of *habeas corpus* (the right to a court hearing to show cause for detention), the right to a speedy and public trial, the right to due process of law, and the right to protection from cruel and unusual punishment. Other rights, called **civil liberties,** protect the individual from arbitrary government interference. Most of these civil liberties are stated in the first ten amendments and include protection against government abridgement of free speech, government censorship of the press, and government restrictions on the right to assemble peaceably. Civil liberties – which prevent government action – are sometimes (but not always) distinguished from **civil rights.** Civil rights, like civil liberties, protect citizens from the harmful actions of others. However, civil rights usually go two steps further. First, they protect citizens from other citizens (besides protecting citizens from government). Second, they provide for a govern-

[1] Like most key political terms, "rights" has many different meanings. For a more philosophical discussion of rights, see Richard E. Flathman, *The Practice of Rights* (Cambridge, England: Cambridge University Press, 1976), especially Chaps. 1–4.

mental remedy to correct the harm that is done when these rights are violated. For example, the 1964 Civil Rights Act forbids citizens to discriminate against other citizens in public accommodations on the grounds of race, color, religion, and national origin. The act also authorizes the federal government to bring suits to accomplish this goal.

Rights not stated in specific laws or the Constitution

Defining the rights of citizens in terms of specific laws or judicial interpretations is only one approach. A second perspective rejects the notion that rights are specifically given to citizens by the government. This position holds that certain rights exist independently of governmental guarantees. The rights possessed by citizens are *natural* rights given to human beings by God (or some higher authority other than government). As John Dickinson, a writer of the Revolutionary period, put it: "Our liberties do not come from charters; for these are only the declaration of preexisting rights. They do not depend on parchments or seals; but come from the King of Kings and the Lord of all the earth." Though this position has a long intellectual history, no agreement exists on what constitutes natural rights. In the Declaration of Independence Jefferson suggested that natural rights include the right to life, liberty, and the pursuit of happiness. Other writers have included religious freedom, the right to disobey unjust laws, and freedom from arbitrary searches as natural rights beyond the reach of government.

Though the natural rights argument received its strongest support during the colonial period, it remains a politically relevant idea. Many groups have claimed basic rights to engage in certain behavior, not on constitutional or statutory grounds but on natural law or "self-evident" grounds. When southern civil rights activists consciously violated racial segregation laws in the 1960s, many asserted that higher natural law gave them the right to disobey unjust laws. More recently, some advocates of legislation allowing abortion have argued that women have the inherent right to do with their bodies as they please. Neither the Constitution nor any statute mentions freedom over one's body, but such omission may not invalidate this right if one accepts the natural-right argument. Obviously, the lack of agreement on natural rights can lead to claims, counterclaims, and much disagreement. How would you respond if your friendly local finance company told you that they have a natural right to charge you 25 percent interest on your loan? Would you counterclaim that you have a natural right to pay 3 percent interest?

EQUALITY OF RIGHTS

Spelling out the precise rights of citizens is only one of the issues associated with rights. Even if we all agreed on what rights we possess, several important problems would remain to be solved. One major issue is whether everyone should enjoy identical rights. At first glance the answer for most people would be "yes." In concrete situations, however, many would be willing to make exceptions. For example, should the right to take part in the political process be extended equally to children and

THE RIGHT TO YOUR NAME

Your right to call yourself whatever you want is long established under both common law and in the existing legal system. The only general restriction is that name changes cannot be used to defraud (for example, you could not call yourself "Marlon Brando" to help your film career). The issue of name changes has recently received attention because of the desires of many women to keep their original name after marriage or to make their names less sexist (for example, one woman changed her name from Zimmerman to Zimmerperson). All states except Hawaii (and the Commonwealth of Puerto Rico) allow women to keep their maiden names, though this may involve some legal paperwork.*

Like most other rights, however, this right is not absolute. As Michael Herbert Dengler, a short-order cook and ex-teacher, is learning, you cannot call yourself a number. Dengler is legally trying to rename himself 1069 (or "One-Zero" to his friends). When he lived in North Dakota he took his cause all the way to the state supreme court, but lost. 1069 has since moved to Minneapolis, Minnesota, to renew the legal battle. So far his campaign has had mixed results. The state of Minnesota and the telephone company have refused to accept 1069 as Dengler's name. He does, however, have a social security card and a checking account in the name of 1069.**

* The legal rules governing name changes are given in Susan C. Ross, *The Rights of Women* (New York: Discus Books, 1973), pp. 348–356.
** The case of 1069 is reported in "He Says He's 'One-Zero,'" But Court Is Unconvinced" *New York Times*, November 27, 1977, p. 33.

mental incompetents? Should citizens of foreign countries permanently residing in the United States have the same voting and political participation rights as U.S. citizens? Should psychopaths enjoy the constitutionally protected right "to keep and bear arms"? We can see that depriving some people of rights supposedly guaranteed to everyone may occasionally be justified. It is difficult, however, to say whose rights may be justifiably abridged.

THE ISSUE OF WHICH RIGHTS ARE MORE FUNDAMENTAL

A second problem concerning rights is whether some rights are more "untouchable" or more fundamental than others. Are some rights so basic that they can never be abridged, while others can be violated under certain circumstances? Article I, section 9 of the Constitution, which guarantees the right to a writ of *habeas corpus,* also specifies that this right may be suspended when the public safety is endangered during rebellion or invasion. Some people would also argue that the right to free speech guaranteed in the First Amendment is more fundamental to our liberty than the right to bear arms described in the Second Amendment. Conservatives have sometimes claimed that the right to private property (which is not explicitly mentioned in the Constitution) is the most fundamental of all human rights and, thus, takes precedence over every other right.[2]

The issue of which rights are more fundamental than others usually surfaces when different rights conflict. The area of national security, in particular, has involved repeated conflicts between the right of government to protect the nation and the personal freedom of citizens. Perhaps the most famous of all such conflicts occurred in early 1942 when 112,000 people of Japanese ancestry (70,000 of whom were U.S. citizens) were forcibly relocated from the West Coast and part of Arizona to isolated areas on the grounds of military necessity. Many citizens lost their homes and businesses and lived under strict regimentation, all without due process guaranteed under the Fifth and Fourteenth amendments. In 1944, the case of *Korematsu* v. *United States,* a divided Supreme Court ruled that military necessity made such gross violation of rights acceptable. One dissenting Justice charged, however, that military necessity was never proved, and even if it had been demonstrated, such necessity did not override constitutional guarantees.

Manzanar, California, one of the several "relocation" camps established after the outbreak of World War II for people of Japanese ancestry (including those who were U.S. citizens).

[2] For an excellent brief discussion of the Supreme Court's effort to resolve the issue of which rights are most fundamental, see Henry J. Abraham, *Freedom and the Court,* 2d ed. (New York: Oxford University Press, 1972), pp. 58–62.

The black civil rights struggle has also raised numerous questions concerning which rights are more fundamental. The Civil Rights Act of 1968, for example, prohibited discrimination on the basis of race, color, religion, or natural origins in the sale or rental of housing. Many property owners believed that such laws violated their more basic right to do with their property as they pleased. Black civil rights leaders countered these claims by asserting that the right to live wherever one could afford to was more basic than property rights. This conflict between control of one's property and freedom from discrimination was illuminated in a series of events in California in 1964. Prior to 1964, California state laws prohibited racial discrimination in private dwellings of more than four units. In 1964, an amendment to the state constitution giving property owners "absolute discretion" over renting or selling their property was overwhelmingly approved by voters in a referendum. Both the California Supreme Court and the national Supreme Court ruled, however, that the amendment was void because it gave state approval to discriminatory behavior. In other words, given a choice of owner control over property versus banning discrimination, most California voters preferred owner control. The courts, however, gave greater emphasis to ending racial discrimination.

THE GOVERNMENT'S RESPONSIBILITY TO IMPLEMENT RIGHTS

A different type of issue involves the government's responsibility in implementing the rights of citizens. Recall that a right is a claim to a benefit. For example, if you are arrested you have a right to a lawyer. Does this merely mean that you can have a lawyer if you want one? Or must the government supply a lawyer free of charge? Or, going a step further, does this mean that the lawyer supplied by the government must satisfy your personal standards on what constitutes a good lawyer? All three positions are consistent with possessing a "right to legal counsel." A similar ambiguity has occurred concerning what a woman's right to an abortion means. Does this right imply that the government must provide or finance the abortion, or does it only permit an abortion?

The question of how far government should go to make sure people get their rights has generated widespread controversy. For some people the existence of rights is meaningless without a strong effort to implement them. What is the meaning of free speech, they might ask, if those with unpopular ideas cannot gain access to the mass media to present their ideas? Nor would a right to equal pay for equal work be more than a paper right without tough government enforcement. The classic example of such "paper rights" prevailed in the South, where for many decades blacks were prevented from voting despite several constitutional and statutory guarantees. If mere paper guarantees were sufficient, the Soviet Union would probably be the world's foremost free society.

The question of just how far the government must go in protecting rights has emerged on the issue of equal opportunity to education. Virtually everyone accepts the principle that all groups should have an equal right to education. But what if blacks, women, or other groups are less able to enter colleges and professional schools? Does the presence of comparatively few women in medical schools mean that the right of women to equal opportunity has been abridged? Some people would answer "yes" and therefore propose government action to make schools accept a larger proportion of women. Such efforts frequently take the form of **affirmative action programs** where schools must make an extra effort to recruit women, blacks, or members of other groups. Critics of this reasoning argue that so long as schools do not overly discriminate against women, blacks, or others as a group, their rights have not been infringed. To go beyond nondiscrimination is to practice **"reverse discrimination,"** which violates the rights of individuals not given special treatment.

Affirmative action programs Programs in which an extra effort is made to recruit women, minority group members, or other members of groups previously discriminated against.

Reverse discrimination The condition under which those who formerly did the discriminating are now discriminated against. Typically practiced against white males.

RESOLVING CONFLICTS INVOLVING RIGHTS

Obviously, deciding who has what right under what condition is difficult and perhaps even impossible. Almost any action can somehow be justified on the grounds of some right. Drug addicts might, with some justification, argue that they have the right to do anything with their bodies. Opponents of drug use can claim that society's right to self-protection and survival takes precedence. Who should decide such conflicts? Who determines, for example, whether viewing pornographic movies is a state-regulated privilege; a right, but one secondary to other rights; or a fundamental right that can never be abridged?

The Supreme Court as interpreter of rights

What about the Supreme Court as the final interpreter of our rights? If one believes that our rights consist solely of those claims enumerated in the Constitution (and related legislation) and that the Supreme Court is the final arbitrator of the Constitution, then this approach makes sense. Nevertheless, while the Court does exercise considerable power over rights questions, its power to interpret the Constitution does not automatically make it the ultimate interpreter of our rights. First, the Constitution *itself* says that it does *not* contain all the rights of citizens. According to the Ninth Amendment, "The enumeration in the constitution, of certain rights, shall not be construed to deny or disparage others retained by the people" (these "others" are subject to controversy). Hence, even if the Court were the final arbitrator of the Constitution (and many people would deny this claim), our rights are not limited to those cited in the Constitution.

Second, in deciding cases involving what is or is not a fundamental right, Supreme Court Justices have disagreed among themselves over what makes a right "fundamental." This was exemplified in a case involving education. In *San Antonio Independent School District* v. *Rodrigues* (1973) the Court rules in a 5 to 4 vote that education is *not* a fundamental right. The majority held that since education is neither implicitly nor explicitly guaranteed in the Constitution, it cannot be considered "fundamental." The minority observed, however, that in the past the Court had ruled that several nonconstitutionally listed rights, for example, the right to appeal criminal conviction, are "fundamental" rights. In short, a one-vote margin prevented education from becoming a "fundamental right," and the Justices themselves acknowledged that no clear guidelines existed to resolve this dispute. (The right to public welfare was ruled not fundamental by a 6 to 3 vote in 1970.)

Public officials as interpreters of rights

If the Supreme Court cannot settle the controversies surrounding rights, can elected national and state officials? In effect, this is what frequently happens, because the actual meaning of many rights is concretely defined by national and state laws. We all may have the constitutionally guaranteed right of assembly to petition our government, but many crucial aspects of this right (for example, the definition of "peaceful") are decided by elected officials. The resolution of conflicts over rights by giving the government the power to decide them may be a practical solution, but it ignores one basic problem. The purpose of numerous rights is to protect individuals *from* government action. To give government the ultimate power over deciding our rights is like giving foxes the power to

WHAT CAN BE A HIGHER RIGHT THAN SMOKING IN AN AIRPLANE?

Establishing one's rights can sometimes be costly. Here is the case of John McAward, who paid $250 for standing up for his rights.

Checking in at Boston's Logan Airport for a flight to New York City, McAward was told there were no available seats in the nonsmoking section. He had a right to such a seat, he insisted, so the gate agent allowed him on board to see if some arrangement could be worked out. As the plane started taxiing down the runway, McAward took a seat on the tobacco side of the SMOKING/NO SMOKING sign and asked a flight attendant to move the sign. No way, said the smokers already seated on that row. So McAward got up and headed for the cockpit. A flight attendant told him not to stand while the plane was moving down the runway, but McAward refused to take a violation of his rights sitting down.

The plane returned to the terminal, and McAward was ordered off. "The only way I'm leaving is if you place me under arrest," he said. The airline obliged and called the state police. McAward told the judge: "I felt I was entitled to what the Federal Government says I'm entitled to—a nonsmoking seat." But the judge fined him $250 for interfering with a flight crew.

TIME, July 24, 1978.

regulate the chicken coop. How would we react if we saw the following announcement: "Your government, being the final judge of citizens' rights, hereby decides that such rights exist only to the extent that they do not interfere with our efficiency and vital national interests as we define them." Many of us would claim that such government action violates our rights.

The people as interpreters of rights

Finally, a long tradition exists that sees the people themselves as the ultimate guardians and interpreters of their rights. The people may allow government to administer these rights, but this does not mean that the rights are surrendered. When the government enforces civil rights laws, for example, it is acting on behalf of the people; it is not giving the people something they do not have. If the government violates these rights, the people may justifiably overthrow their government.

The idea that the people are the ultimate interpreters of their rights underlay the American Revolution. In resolving problems of interpretation and conflict, however, this argument provides little guidance. How can society operate if each individual decides on his or her own such questions as what right takes precedence in a conflict, or whether everyone will have identical rights. Nor would putting such questions to a vote necessarily solve the problems. A majority vote may extend or restrict a privilege, but many people would claim that it cannot define an inalienable right because an inalienable right exists regardless of the actions of others. It is also argued that a right has little real meaning if it can be abolished by a simple majority of citizens. Obviously, the whole issue of defining rights is highly complex and is unlikely to ever be resolved conclusively.

Let us return to the original question of what is a right. In the abstract there is no problem of definition—a right is a claim on a benefit (for example, free speech, a fair trial, protection from racial discrimination). However, giving rights concrete meaning raises several unsettled questions. The most important lesson we can draw is that rights do not automatically fall from the sky, nor are they chiseled in marble. To obtain a right requires considerable political effort. The right of blacks to attend racially integrated schools may now seem "self-evident" and "natural," but throughout most of our history the idea was rejected as unrealistic or dangerous. In short, getting one's rights established as "fundamental" is no easy task, because every claim can be met with numerous counterclaims and arguments.

What political rights do citizens possess?

We have seen that political rights are surrounded by complex issues. Nevertheless, several important rights are widely viewed as "fundamental" in U.S. politics. We shall briefly describe five rights that constitute key safeguards of our political freedom: (1) freedom of speech; (2) freedom of the press; (3) freedom of association; (4) religious freedom; and (5) equal protection of the laws. We shall see that even though these rights are deeply entrenched, they are not immune to many of the problems previously described.

FREEDOM OF SPEECH

The First Amendment states that "Congress shall make no law . . . abridging the freedom of speech. . . ." At first glance this prohibition seems clear—no law means no law. Nevertheless, despite this appearance of clarity, only a few people—most notably Supreme Court Justices Hugo Black and William O. Douglas—have taken this "no law means no law" (frequently called the **absolutist position**). In actual practice this right has been limited, and free speech has generated a multitude of interpretations, doctrines, and unresolved questions.

The meaning of "speech"

A good place to begin our understanding of this right is to consider the meaning of "speech." What, precisely, comes under the heading of speech? Scholars have frequently distinguished three types of speech that may be protected by this constitutional right. The most obvious is called **pure speech.** This is the peaceful expression of ideas before an audience that has voluntarily chosen to listen. If you give a speech entitled "Students: The Oppressed Minority" before the International Downtrodden Association, you are engaging in pure speech, and your actions are protected by the First Amendment.

However, what if you and ten thousand of your sympathizers decide to picket the university, carrying posters that say such things as "Professors Are Finks?" Are you engaging in speech? Since you are *communicating* your ideas, this has been interpreted as constituting a form of speech (even if a word is never spoken). This action is sometimes called **speech plus.** Since your behavior goes beyond mere speech, however, your actions can be subject to various restrictions that would not apply to pure speech. For example, the Supreme Court has ruled that such "speech" cannot obstruct traffic, block sidewalks, or endanger public safety.

Defining "speech" becomes more troublesome when we enter the realm of what is usually called **symbolic speech.** Here, action is taken by manipulating symbols to express one's opinion. During U.S. involvement in Vietnam such symbolic expressions included burning draft cards, pouring blood on draft board records, and defacing the flag. The Court accepted some of these actions as exercises in free speech but rejected others. In *Tinker* v. *Des Moines School District* (1969) the Court ruled that wearing black armbands to protest the war in Vietnam was within the bounds of freedom of expression. The burning of draft cards, however, was rejected as an expression of an idea. Likewise, a 1972 Supreme Court decision held that public nudity by itself does not constitute a form of protected communication.

A member of the Young Lords, a Puerto Rican group similar to the Black Panthers, marches in a New York City Puerto Rican Day parade in 1970. The Supreme Court has interpreted acts such as flag burning as "symbolic speech."

Who can limit free speech?

A second important aspect of free speech concerns *who* cannot make laws abridging free speech. The First Amendment states only that *Congress* shall make no law. There is no mention of what states, local governments, or private individuals can do. The right of states to limit free speech was made explicit in the case of *Barron* v. *Baltimore* (1833) in which the Supreme Court ruled that the first ten amendments did not apply to the states unless explicitly indicated. In other words, a state or city could prohibit "unpopular" speech, limit free speech to approved ideas, and otherwise limit free expression with impunity. However, in 1925 (*Gitlow* v. *New York*) the Court decided that free expression is a "fundamental" right and thus is protected from state (and local) infringement.

Speech not protected by the First Amendment

A third aspect of freedom of speech involves the types of speech that are *not* protected by the First Amendment. Could you in your speech to the International Downtrodden Association say *anything* that comes into your mind? The answer is a clear "no," despite our guarantee of free speech. The Court has repeatedly held that obscenity is not protected expression. Of course, it is difficult to define "obscene." If your speech was little more than a summary of the plots of pornographic movies you had recently seen, you might be in trouble, despite your claim that such information helped you communicate your position. Sexually explicit language in the context of an attempt to communicate an idea, however, would probably be protected. In 1971 in *Cohen* v. *California* the Court overturned the conviction of a Vietnam War protester for disturbing the

Fighting words Language that clearly encourages a fight. Such language is not protected as free speech.

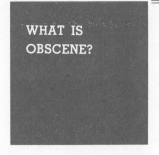

WHAT IS OBSCENE?

One of the most difficult issues associated with the right to free speech concerns obscenity. There are two key questions involved. First, should obscene material be protected in the same way that nonobscene material is protected? Second, what precisely is meant by "obscene"? In actual practice the first question has caused few problems. Most — but not all — judges and legal scholars accept the principle that the community acting through government has the right to censor obscene speech, pictures, and written material that might undermine moral standards. The Supreme Court explicitly endorsed this position in 1957 (*Roth* v. *United States*), but this principle of a distinction between obscene and nonobscene speech has long been implicitly accepted.

The second question — what is meant by "obscene"? — has never been adequately answered and perhaps will remain unresolved. Several legal definitions have been offered, but none has proved very useful. Some, such as that provided in the U.S. postal regulations, merely define "obscene" in terms of words like "filthy," "lewd," or "lascivious." This hardly solves the problem because one must then define "lewd." A second strategy has been to define obscenity in technical, scientific language. For example, several state laws read like anatomy textbooks in spelling out what parts of a woman's breasts can be exposed without being "obscene." Unfortunately, this approach ignores the overall social or artistic context of the material. If these rules were strictly enforced, most museums would be put out of business. Nineteenth-century laws frequently defined obscenity in terms of physiological reaction — an obscenity stimulated disgust or impure sexual thoughts. It could be argued, however, that repeated exposure to obscenity would reduce such improper stimulation to zero.

peace by wearing a jacket emblazoned with "F――k the Draft." The Court held that while stirring the emotions, the expression was nevertheless "pure speech" and thus was to be protected.

A second type of speech not protected by the Constitution is speech involved with what the Supreme Court calls **"fighting words."** Fighting words are a clear invitation to a brawl. They are not necessarily the same thing as controversial or insulting language. This principle was established in the 1942 case of *Chaplinsky* v. *New Hampshire*. The defendant, Chaplinsky, had caused a public disturbance by, among other things, calling the Rochester, New Hampshire, city marshall "a God-

Prurient Tending to excite lasciviousness; a restless craving for something.

The last twenty-five years have seen several legal definitions applied to allegedly obscene books and movies. In the Roth case the Court ruled that material is obscene if it, taken as a whole, appeals to the **prurient** interest of the average person applying contemporary community standards. Subsequent decisions elaborated the notion of "patent offensiveness" and absence of redeeming social value spelled out in Roth. Not unexpectedly, these criteria lacked the precision to settle the issue decisively. In the *Miller* v. *California* (1973) case the Court tried again to clarify the definition of "obscene." This decision defined "community standards" as meaning local or state standards. "Patently offensive," according to the Court, had to be specified in the law (for example, depicting masturbation as opposed to "filthy behavior"). Finally, to be obscene a work, taken as a whole, had to lack serious literary, artistic, political, or scientific value.

The criteria of the Miller decision may be more specific, but the decision is still a long way from a precise answer. For example, does the hard-core pornographic movie *Deep Throat* have artistic value? Can it be shown in some cities but not others because its message is consistent with some but not all community standards? How are these "community standards" to be measured? For the most part, the courts and the police have come to tolerate almost anything as nonobscene. The major exceptions are pornography involving children and offensive public advertising of X-rated movies. The vagueness of "obscenity" has even allowed major respectable corporations to become involved with "dirty" books and magazines. For example, the magazine *High Society,* edited by pornographic movie star Gloria Leonard (*Misty Beethoven* among others), is far more sexually explicit than *Playboy;* it is similar to the well-known and highly controversial *Hustler* magazine. *High Society* is distributed by the Fawcett Company. Fawcett is owned by CBS, which in turn, owns Holt, Rinehart, and Winston. Holt, Rinehart and Winston is the publisher of this book.

damned racketeer." Under a state law he was convicted of calling someone "offensive or derisive" names in public. This conviction was upheld on the grounds that such fighting words could bring an immediate breach of the peace. However, the Court has since applied the principle quite narrowly. For example, in a 1972 case the Court overturned the conviction of a man who called a policeman a "son of a bitch" and otherwise threatened him with violence. The Court ruled that the Georgia law under which he was convicted was too broad.

In general, the conflict between the right to free speech and the need to protect public order has been a troublesome constitutional issue. In some

Clear and present danger test The principle stating that free speech can be limited if the speech could bring about serious harm.

instances even a dull academic speech given by a dull professor in a dull three-piece suit can inspire riots (for example, a talk sponsored by the psychology department on the relationship between race and intelligence).[3] What makes this issue especially troublesome is that by acknowledging the need to maintain order, anyone willing to cause a public disturbance can exercise veto power over another person's right to free expression. In the late 1960s and early 1970s a few individuals were, in fact, frequently successful in preventing public debates on controversial issues such as Vietnam or South African racial policy merely by threatening disruptions.

Especially since the black civil rights movement of the mid-1960s, when the "fear of violence" was frequently used to prevent rallies and marches, the Supreme Court has had stringent rules allowing the abridging of free speech because of the expectation of violence. Such abridgement has been tolerated only where (1) more was involved than just "pure speech" (for example, occupying a building), (2) the state or local law authorizing the abridgement was specific, and (3) the likelihood of public disorder was demonstrably clear. The willingness of the courts to protect free speech in the face of potential violence was illustrated when the American Nazi party organized several Chicago demonstrations in the summer of 1978. Despite the fear of Chicago city officials that riots might occur (and many explicit threats of violence came from anti-Nazi groups), the Court upheld the right of Nazis to march.

Different rules regulating the exercise of free speech

Over the years judges and scholars have attempted to bring order to all the diverse rules governing the exercise and abridgement of free expression. Several general principles have been suggested. One well-known principle is the so-called "**clear and present danger**" **test** formulated by Justice Oliver Wendell Holmes in the *Schenck* v. *United States* (1919) case. This case involved the mailing of material to men subject to the draft during World War I urging them to resist induction into the army. Holmes and the rest of the Court ruled that this section was not protected free speech. The basic question, according to Holmes, was whether words would quickly and directly bring about an evil that Congress could prevent. Thus, falsely shouting "fire" in a crowded theater is not permissible because it would immediately result in a highly dangerous panic.

A second position that attempts to bring logical order to limitations on free speech emphasizes the "reasonableness" of legislatively imposed restrictions. The basic presumption is that a restriction, for example, that demonstrators cannot block automobile traffic, is acceptable if a "reasonable man" would accept such limitations. In practice this doctrine allows legislatures vast discretion in abridging free speech. Only when restrictions are clearly arbitrary or unreasonable are they to be struck down.

Finally, some Supreme Court Justices have formulated what has been

---

[3] For a description of such an event, see R. J. Herrnstein, *I.Q. in the Meritocracy* (Boston: Atlantic Monthly Press, 1973), especially the Preface.

called the **preferred position** of free speech guarantees. Basically, it is argued that freedoms involving speech, the press, and religion are more fundamental than other freedoms because they provide the basis of all of our liberties. Thus, they can be infringed only under extreme conditions. As Justice Wiley B. Rutledge put it in *Thomas* v. *Collings* (1945): "Only the gravest abuses, endangering paramount interests, give occasion for permissible limitations."

These three positions (and several variations) have all received substantial support from respected judges and scholars. Nevertheless, no general doctrine has succeeded very well. Each may seem appropriate for certain cases and in certain historical periods, but none provides a clear guide across a multitude of circumstances. Moreover, each ultimately rests on interpretations of ambiguous terms. For example, how "clear" must a danger be before it is a "clear and present" danger? What if two supposedly reasonable people differ on what is "reasonable"? Even if freedom of speech enjoys a preferred status, under what precise condition can it be abridged? Obviously, while free speech is a crucial right and its existence is unchallenged, considerable leeway exists in its actual interpretation.

Preferred-position doctrine The principle that free speech, freedom of the press, and freedom of religion are basic freedoms and thus can be limited only under extreme circumstances.

FREEDOM OF THE PRESS

Like free speech, freedom of the press is expressly protected by the First Amendment. And as was true for free speech, the interpretation of this protection is not simple. The first question concerns the types of activities that are covered by freedom of the press. Obviously, newspapers, books, and magazines are covered. In a 1938 decision the Supreme Court extended this protection to handbills. The troublesome area concerns the modern mass media—radio, television, and films. Is the CBS evening news with Walter Cronkite to be treated as equivalent to the *New York Times* (even when they use the identical material)? Is a documentary motion picture about slum conditions protected in the same way a written description is?

Limits on radio, television, and films

In general, the answer to these questions is "no," although the Supreme Court on several occasions has protected the freedom of these media. What separates radio, television, and the movies from newspapers and magazines? In the case of the broadcast media, the Court has viewed their operations as a *privilege* granted by the government, not a right. For technical reasons everyone cannot be allowed to transmit radio or television signals. By allowing a small number of people to engage in this activity, the government has granted them a privilege. As with all government-granted privileges, the government can justifiably set rules and regulations regarding the exercise of this privilege. Through the Federal Communications Commission (FCC) the government imposes rules that prohibit cigarette and hard liquor commercials, nudity, and offensive language and stipulate required amounts of "public service" broadcasting. There are also regulations regarding fairness in political campaigns. To many radio and television people such rules impinge on basic freedom; to the FCC they are necessary to insure "public responsibility."

The technical reasons that require broadcasting to be a privilege, not a right, do not apply to films. For many years, however, the courts held that movies were not a forum for the expression of ideas and thus could not be compared to newspapers or books. In a 1915 case the Court ruled that films were entertainment and subject to tight regulation in the same way that circuses or burlesques could be censored. This perspective stood until 1952 and the *Burstyn* v. *Wilson* case, which recognized the information role of films. In this and subsequent related decisions the Court extended some (but not complete) First Amendment protection to movies. Essentially, films *can* be censored prior to showing, but the burden of proof is on the censor (not the filmmaker), and there must be a quick judicial remedy for appeals.

Freedom enjoyed by books and magazines

Just how much freedom do magazines and books enjoy? Can the *Daily Planet* publish anything? Despite the importance of this question, guidelines were never correctly spelled out until 1931 and the *Near* v. *Minnesota* decision. This case involved a Minnesota weekly newspaper that had been legally prevented from publishing on the grounds that its malicious and scandalous attacks on city officials were a public nuisance. In a 5 to 4 decision the Court held that this public nuisance law was a violation of the First Amendment. Chief Justice Charles E. Hughes, speaking for the majority, reaffirmed the crucial doctrine prohibiting **no prior restraint** of publication. Freedom of the press does not mean that newspapers can do anything. Rather, punishment can occur only *after* publication, not before. The doctrine of no prior restraint is deeply rooted in English common law. Without this principle government officials could easily censor newspapers with arguments about what *might* happen if something were published.

Justice Hughes did, however, stop short of saying that prior restraint was never permitted. He specified four exceptional situations when prior censorship was permissible: (1) military necessity; (2) obscenity; (3) incitements to violence; and (4) the protection of private rights. In several subsequent cases the Supreme Court employed these standards to provide considerable leeway to newspapers printing controversial material. Perhaps the toughest case involved the publication of the so-called *Pentagon Papers* by the *New York Times*, the *Washington Post*, and other newspapers in June 1971. The *Pentagon Papers* were part of a Department of Defense study (classified as "secret") of U.S. involvement in Vietnam and contained some highly sensitive and embarrassing military information (for example, reports of early secret raids against North Vietnam that were officially denied). These documents were made available to the newspapers illegally, and the government sought to block publication on the grounds of national security (the war in Vietnam was still in progress). In a 6 to 3 vote the Supreme Court ruled that the government had not proved its claim of military necessity and thus had not met the "heavy burden" needed to justify prior restraint.

Besides having the benefit of the no prior restraint principle, newspapers also have considerable freedom in what they can say about public figures. Historically, the First Amendment has been interpreted to exclude **libel** from its protection. Libel is defamation of character (false statements that are malicious) in print or by other visual means (**slander** involves only oral defamation). Libel can be punished as a criminal offense or privately through civil suit. The laws regarding libel also have deep roots in English common law and are generally considered important for the existence of civil society. What happens if a newspaper calls a public official a "bumbling jackass who ought to be shipped off to Russia where he belongs"? Is such defamation of character protected by the First Amendment? Or can the publisher be prosecuted for libel?

These questions remained largely unresolved until the landmark case of *New York Times Co.* v. *Sullivan* (1964). This case involved an advertisement placed in the *New York Times* by a black civil rights group critical of the treatment blacks received in Montgomery, Alabama. The *Times* was convicted of libel by an Alabama court, and damages of $500,000 were awarded the Montgomery police commissioner. The Supreme Court, however, overruled this decision on the grounds that free and open communication is an essential right, and the exercise of this right can include vehement, caustic, or unpleasant attacks on government officials. And even if such attacks involve inaccuracies, they are still not necessarily libelous, the Court maintained. To require absolute accuracy in a public debate, ruled the court, would virtually eliminate all public discussion. Action could be taken against a newspaper for printing malicious falsehoods about public officials *if* such statements were known to be false and there was a total disregard for the truth (even then, however, the burden of proof is on the official being attacked).

Limits on free expression in newspapers

On many other occasions, however, the Supreme Court has constrained the power of newspapers. The *New York Times* case provided protection against libel actions from public figures; a private citizen defamed by a newspaper or magazine can still collect substantial damages. When *Time* magazine erroneously called a divorcee an "adulteress," it was taken to court and had to pay damages of $100,000 (*Time, Inc.* vs. *Firestone* [1976]). Moreover, on numerous occasions the Court has upheld the banning of obscene books and magazines. Recall that the definition of "obscenity" has undergone change, but the principle that obscenity (however defined) is not constitutionally protected generally remains unchallenged. The circulation of newspapers and magazines can also be controlled through the use of postal regulations. Though the Court has struck down laws allowing postal employees to open and read other people's mail, it has not ruled that the use of the mails is protected by the First Amendment. Thus, as it did in the Espionage Act of 1917, the government can legally make unmailable newspapers or other printed material urging treason, insurrection, or forcible resistance to the law.[4]

[4] An excellent discussion of postal censorhip is presented in Jay A. Sigler, *American Rights Policies* (Homewood, Ill.: Dorsey Press, 1975), pp. 89–91.

Libel   The making of false statements in print attacking someone's character.
Slander   The making of false statements verbally attacking someone's character.

Shield laws Laws allowing reporters to withhold information in legal proceedings in order to protect their sources of information.

Gag orders Court orders preventing reporters from describing court proceedings. Used to prevent publicity that might hinder an important trial.

Perhaps the most controversial restraint on newspaper freedom concerns the confidentiality of reporters' news sources. Some journalists maintain that if they can be forced to reveal their sources their ability to pursue the truth will be seriously hampered. In addition, government access to their private information will transform the news media into an investigative arm of the government. As of July 1978, twenty-six states have accepted this argument and have enacted so-called **shield laws** that allow reporters the right to withhold information in legal proceedings. At the federal level, however, reporters are treated like any other citizens who might have information regarding criminal behavior (this principle was clearly stated in the case of *Branzburg* v. *Hayes* [1972]). Many reporters have chosen to defy this principle, and between 1972 and 1978 about forty reporters were held in contempt of court for refusing to provide information (and more than a dozen went to jail).[5]

Finally, the freedom of newspapers has been abridged when such freedom has conflicted with a person's right to a fair trial guaranteed by the Sixth Amendment. In several cases the Supreme Court has reversed convictions where intense pretrial newspaper coverage made it virtually impossible to select unbiased jurors. New trials have also been ordered where reporters have overly affected judicial proceedings by publicizing evidence, confessions, and comments by lawyers and witnesses. In extreme cases involving controversial issues, judges have issued so-called **gag orders** that prevent newspapers from even mentioning certain trial-related facts. One such gag order forbidding reporters to mention a confession for eleven weeks was struck down by the Supreme Court, but the principle of prior restraint by judges was accepted, though it must be clearly justified (*Nebraska Press Association* v. *Stuart* [1976]).

FREEDOM OF ASSOCIATION

Unlike free speech and freedom of the press, freedom of association does not rest on an explicit constitutional guarantee. Nevertheless, the Supreme Court has held that this right is a natural corollary of the right of free speech and the right of assembly. Especially where controversial issues are involved or one's goals are ambitious (for example, equality for all women), associations with like-minded citizens are essential. What would be the value of free speech if those who share an idea could not legally associate with one another?

Freedom of association and national security

Like many of our rights, freedom of association becomes less absolute in actual practice. In particular, how do you balance the right of association with the government's right to protect itself from secret organizations that would overthrow it by violent means? What if you and your friends organized a small group that engaged in weapons training, met secretly, prepared papers on how to poison reservoirs, and engaged in antigovern-

[5] "Courts and the Process of News Gathering," *New York Times*, July 28, 1978.

ment propaganda? Could the government make your mere presence at these gatherings illegal without violating your freedom of association? What if you claimed that you were not actually attacking the government, that you were talking and thinking about the possibility of such action, but there was no subversive action?

Questions such as these have surfaced periodically since World War I when the threat of a secret Communist conspiracy (directed by the Soviet Union) became very real for many people. The reaction of courts at both federal and state levels was frequently to limit freedom of association in the name of national security. In *Whitney* v. *California* (1927) the Supreme Court upheld the conviction of Charlotte Anita Whitney who merely participated in a meeting that established the Communist Labor Party of California. Her conviction was based on a California law that made it a crime to belong to an organization that advocated, taught, or aided and abetted criminal **syndicalism.** Merely belonging, regardless of one's actions, was a crime.

Subsequent Court decisions, however, placed greater emphasis on actually committing a subversive act than on being associated with a subversive group. In 1940 the Alien Registration Act of 1940 (widely known as the Smith Act) was passed. The act made it a crime to belong to any organization that advocated the overthrow of the U.S. government, *regardless of what an individual said or did.* In effect, merely belonging to the Communist Party became a federal crime. The constitutionality of this statute was upheld in *Dennis* v. *United States* (1951) by a 6 to 2 vote. A further attack on the Communist Party was launched with the Internal Security Act of 1950. This act (commonly known as the McCarran Act) required that all subversive organizations register with the government. Once registered, organization members had to identify their public messages as subversive propaganda, they could not hold nonelective federal offices, they were forbidden to apply for or to use a U.S. passport, and their right to work in defense plants was curtailed.

During the 1940s and 1950s most states also required their employees (including teachers) to sign "loyalty oaths" affirming that they had never been a Communist or otherwise plotted the violent overthrow of the U.S. government. The purpose of such oaths was not to prevent subversives from getting government jobs (a true subversive would lie). Rather, any employee who had at some time been associated with a Communist-run organization, but who signed the oath to get the job, could at any time be charged with perjury (lying under oath). The oaths virtually gave a hunting license to anti-Communists who would investigate the backgrounds of public employees in search of some past association with one of the many supposed Communist-dominated organizations popular during the 1930s. (And many of these groups were never publicly identified as **"Communist fronts"** until years after their creation.)

Gradually, however, the Supreme Court began to restrain government efforts to make it a crime to be associated with the Communist Party. In the key decision of *Yates* v. *United States* (1957) a Court majority held that advocating an abstract doctrine is very different from directly promoting unlawful actions. The Smith Act, according to the Court,

Syndicalism The philosophy calling for the worker ownership of all industry. This is to be brought about by strikes, terrorism, sabotage, and violence. Once closely associated with communism.

Communist fronts Organizations run by Communists, but not openly known as Communist organizations.

Criminal conspiracy Two or more people meeting to plan an unlawful act or otherwise engage in unlawful behavior.
Theocracy A government based on religious law in which power is held by church officials.

could make only direct advocacy of unlawful actions illegal; advocating an abstract doctrine (for example, the inevitable collapse of capitalism) was protected by the right of free speech. Several subsequent Court decisions further weakened the Smith Act, and in the 1969 case of *Brandenburg* v. *Ohio* the whole idea of guilt by (Communist) association was thrown out. A similar fate befell the Internal Security Act of 1950 as the courts ruled that having to declare oneself a Communist, which was automatically a crime, violated protection from self-incrimination guaranteed by the Fifth Amendment. The scope of loyalty oaths was also reduced by the Supreme Court. In a 1967 decision, for example, it held that membership in a subversive organization was punishable only if there had been a "specific intent" to further the illegal aims of the organization.

Other limits on freedom of association

The anti-Communist laws of the 1940s and 1950s are largely gone or are greatly weakened today. Nor is there much "witch hunting," where those with past Communist associations are publicly exposed and punished. Nevertheless, this does not mean that one is completely free to associate with anyone. It still remains a serious crime to commit "**criminal conspiracy**," that is, with one or more people to agree to commit an unlawful act or a lawful act through unlawful means. Because criminal conspiracy usually involves secrecy, normal rules of evidence for proving guilt are usually relaxed. On several occasions the charge of criminal conspiracy has been a useful government weapon to prosecute individuals who have been associated with unpopular groups. In 1968, for example, several anti-Vietnam war leaders were prosecuted for criminal conspiracy following the widespread disorders of the Democratic presidential nominating convention in Chicago. The government argued that the defendants had conspired to create disorder. The defendants counterclaimed that the disturbances were unplanned and that the conspiracy charge was merely a means of punishing those associated with the antiwar movement. In general, the government has had little success convicting antiwar activists of criminal conspiracy, but the threat of going to court merely because one is publicly identified with some group remains real.

RELIGIOUS FREEDOM

The issue of religious freedom is perhaps the oldest controversy in U.S. history. Indeed, it was the oppression of religion that was largely responsible for the colonization of North America. By today's standards religious freedom may not seem like an important right. We must remember, however, that a **theocracy**—government by the church—can be one of the most oppressive types of government, since no aspect of one's life would be beyond its reach. The right of religious freedom is spelled out in the Constitution in two places. Article VI bans religious qualifications for public office, and the First Amendment states that "Congress shall make no law respecting an establishment of religion, or prohibiting the free exercise thereof. . . ." As in other First Amendment freedoms, the meaning of this guarantee is not self-evident.

This First Amendment right involves two separate though related provisions: (1) no national laws can "establish" a religion, and (2) no laws can limit free exercise of religion. Since each provision has involved somewhat different sets of issues, we shall consider them separately. Let us begin with the meaning of free exercise of religion.

Secular regulation rule The principle stating that the Constitution does not protect religious activities—only beliefs—and such activities are subject to the law. However, the courts can make exceptions to the application of laws to religious activities.

Free exercise of religion

When the Constitution says that no law can abridge one's religious practices, does this mean that a person can do *anything* he or she wants so long as it is "religious" in nature? The first issue raised by this problem concerns the definition of "religion." Many people disagree sharply over what constitutes a religion. Can a philosophy reject the existence of God and still qualify as a religion? Does a religion need more than one person, or can each person claim adherence to his or her unique brand of religion?

In the nineteenth century the Supreme Court held a restricted view of what constituted a religion. In the *Davis* v. *Beason* (1890) decision the court stated that "The term 'religion' has reference to one's views of his relations to his Creator, and to the obligation they impose of reverence for his being and character, and of obedience to his will." Under this definition many contemporary religions, especially those with a mystical orientation, would not qualify for constitutional protection. More recent decisions, however, have emphasized the right of people to define religion for themselves. In 1963, for example, the Court ruled that the Black Muslims were a bona fide religious organization, not a political and racist organization as prison authorities had argued. In several decisions affecting the right to refuse military service on religious grounds, the Court interpreted religious beliefs as being identical to ethical or moral beliefs. There are limits, however. In a recent case the Church of the New-Song, founded by two prison inmates, did not win court recognition as a legitimate religion. Perhaps its religious requirements of steak and sherry meals, monthly fruit baskets, and movies had something to do with this rejection.

A second issue in the "free exercise" guarantee concerns what happens when religious practices collide with the general rules of the community. Could you claim, for example, that your religious beliefs forbid you to take difficult midterm exams and that being punished for this behavior is a violation of your constitutional rights? More generally, do religious practices enjoy some special protection not enjoyed by the identical actions performed in a nonreligious context?

Over the years the courts have attempted to resolve these problems through the use of what has been called the **secular regulation rule.** This rule holds that the free exercise provision does *not* provide a constitutional basis for an exemption of behavior from regular laws. The right to hold unorthodox *beliefs* is absolute; the right to engage in unorthodox *behavior* can, however, be limited. An exemption *may* be provided, but a religious group cannot make a constitutionally protected claim to this

High-wall perspective The doctrine calling for a sharp line between government and religion.

right. This conflict surfaced in the case of *Wisconsin* v. *Yoder* (1972), which involved the refusal of old-order Amish parents to send their children to school past the eighth grade despite the state's compulsory education law. The Amish claimed that additional education would undermine their traditional religious values. The court supported the Amish parents and agreed that in this particular instance religious beliefs could override state law.

In other instances resolving the conflict between the laws that supposedly apply equally and special religious practices has been much more difficult. The Supreme Court on several occasions had to decide whether members of the Jehovah's Witnesses could be forced to salute the flag in school despite their religion's ban on worshiping "graven images." In a 1940 decision the Court ruled that a compulsory flag-saluting requirement did not infringe on the freedom of religion. Three years later the Court reversed itself and held that no child could be forced to salute the flag against his or her religious conviction. Other religious activities permitted by state and federal courts include the right not to serve on a jury, the right not to stand during the playing of the national anthem, and the right of Navajo members of the North American Church to use peyote in their rituals. However, where religious principles might result in death (for example, the Jehovah's Witnesses refuse blood transfusions because of the biblical prohibition against "eating blood"), the courts have usually ruled against religious practices (especially when the life of a child is in danger).

The establishment of religion

Besides guaranteeing the free exercise of religion the First Amendment prohibits government from establishing a religion. Disagreement exists on exactly what is meant by "establishment." Some people view "establishment" as the creation of an official, government-financed church. In Great Britain the Anglican Church is the official Church of England, and high church officials receive government salaries. Others go much further and view "establishment" as any government support of religious institutions, regardless of whether benefits apply equally to all religions. Advocates of this position (including Thomas Jefferson) have called for a "high wall" between church and state. According to the first view of "establishment," a government policy of providing free prayer books to all religions would be permissible so long as an official prayer book was not required. From the **"high-wall" perspective**, however, this would violate the First Amendment because it would be using public money to promote religion.

In principle, Congress, the President, and the courts have endorsed the second, or "high-wall," position. In practice, however, disagreements have occurred over the exact boundary line between church and state. It is sometimes almost impossible to separate benefits given to churches from laws pertaining to the general population. For example, public money provides churches with such elementary services as police and fire protection, sidewalks and highways, and many other benefits (consider the complexities if churches had to have their own separate water and sewage systems). Moreover, religious practices are so deeply embedded in our lives that exorcising them completely would be almost impossible. Imagine the outcry if Congress did away with military chaplains or the "In God We Trust" motto on coins.

The major area in which the "establishment" principle has generated legal problems is in government aid to religious schools. The "high-wall" doctrine says no aid to religion, but religious schools engage in an important public function (education) in addition to their religious activities. Is it constitutionally possible to aid the purely educational aspect of these schools without aiding the religious part as well? The Supreme Court has generally given a very limited "yes" answer to this question. In several decisions the Court has ruled that states can lend textbooks to children in parochial schools on the grounds that children, not schools, benefit from such loans. However, laws allowing religious instruction in schools, public money for religious school guidance and record keeping, and state subsidies for parochial school teachers have been overturned (standards have been less strict for public money going to religious colleges, however).

Perhaps the strongest action taken by the Supreme Court to maintain the "high wall" occurred in 1962 and 1963 when, in two separate decisions, mandatory religious prayers and Bible reading in schools were declared unconstitutional. Subsequent lower-court decisions have banned even mild, nondenominational prayers. In the *DeSpain* v. *DeKalb County School District* (1967) the United States Court of Appeals ruled that the poem "We thank you for the flowers so sweet; we thank you for the food we eat; we thank you for the birds that sing; we thank you for everything" was unconstitutional. Research on the actual practices of schools, however, indicates that prayers and Bible readings are still popular despite the judicial decisions.[6]

EQUAL PROTECTION OF THE LAWS

The idea that all citizens should be equal before the law is well established in U.S. history. The Declaration of Independence affirms this belief in the statement "All Men are Created Equal." This equality before the law means that laws apply to all citizens equally unless there is a clear reason for a distinction (for example, a law setting a minimum age for holding a driver's license). This principle is made explicit in the Fourteenth Amendment, which prohibits states from making or enforcing laws that deny any person equal protection of the laws. The Supreme Court in the decision of *Bolling* v. *Sharpe* (1954) held that the guarantee of equal protection of the laws applies to the federal government as well through the due process clause of the Fifth Amendment.

[6] See, for example, Richard B. Dierenfield, *Religion in American Public Schools* (Washington, D.C.: Public Affairs Press, 1962); and Kenneth M. Dolbeare and Philip E. Hammond, *The School Prayer Decisions* (Chicago: University of Chicago Press, 1971).

Meaning of equal protection of the laws

Like many other important rights, the equal-protection-of-the-laws guarantee has generated controversy and divergent interpretations. Many of those who drafted this provision of the Fourteenth Amendment immediately following the Civil War intended it to protect newly freed blacks and all other citizens from discriminatory laws regarding property and commerce. (Some states had made it illegal for blacks to buy or sell property or to engage in certain businesses and occupations.) Post-Civil War legislation, based on the Fourteenth Amendment, took a broad view of this guarantee and prohibited racial segregation in hotels, schools, theaters, and means of transportation. Unfortunately for blacks, however, in 1883 the Supreme Court took an extremely narrow view of "equal protection of the laws." In effect, the Court stripped the federal government of any direct power to enforce legal equality.

From the 1880s to the 1950s the equal-protection clause did little to prevent states from enacting highly discriminatory laws. Southern states in particular (but not exclusively) enacted so-called **Jim Crow laws** that legally required racial segregation in schools, transportation, housing, entertainment, restaurants, and many other areas. Such laws were not judged a denial of equal *legal* protection because they (supposedly) represented *social* distinctions. So long as blacks had more or less equal facilities, the state was not denying them their rights (the "separate but equal" doctrine). The courts also believed that Jim Crow laws reflected the attitudes of citizens and that the Fourteenth Amendment was not intended to regulate private moral values (even if these "private values" were state enforced).

Modern interpretations of equal protection of the laws

Beginning in the early 1950s the equal-protection-of-the-laws doctrine became the basis of a renewed attempt to eliminate racial discrimination. At first the issue was whether or not separate facilities were, in fact, equal facilities. In the case of *Sweat* v. *Painter* (1950), for example, the Supreme Court ruled against a Texas action that had established a grossly inferior law school for blacks rather than open to blacks the University of Texas Law School. The reasoning was largely (though not completely) pragmatic—the black law school had fewer professors and law books. The most devastating blow to the separate but equal doctrine came in the *Brown* v. *Board of Education* (1954) decision that overturned state-enforced school segregation on the grounds that segregation generates feelings of inferiority among children and is, therefore, inherently unequal.[7]

The equal-protection-of-the-laws provision, however, has broader implications than civil rights. In 1962, for example, in the historic *Baker* v. *Carr* decision, the Supreme Court ruled that state laws allowing legislative districts of unequal population could be challenged as a de-

---

[7] Court action against state-required racial discrimination is described more fully in C. Herman Pritchett, *The American Constitution*, 3d ed. (New York: McGraw-Hill, 1977), Chap. 27.

nial of the Fourteenth Amendment's equal-protection clause. The "one-man, one-vote" decision (and subsequent elaborations) has produced major political changes. No longer can election districts representing a small portion of the population of a state elect a majority of the legislature. Nor can state legislative houses be based on factors other than population — all state and local legislatures must be based on the "one-man, one-vote" rule. At the federal level the equal-protection clause has been interpreted to mean that congressional districts must be of approximately equal population and that all votes must count equally in Senate primaries.

The Fourteenth Amendment's equal-protection guarantee has also recently been employed in the battle for women's rights. In 1971, for example, the Court overturned an Idaho law that required a male to be chosen to administer estates when a male and female were equally qualified for the job. Shortly afterward the Court also ruled that a male dependent of a member of the armed forces was entitled to the same benefits as a female dependent. A federal court in New York ruled that McSorley's Old Ale House — a well-known drinking establishment — could not continue its old custom of refusing to serve women. The court held that since McSorley's was licensed by the state, the laws of New York were being used to deny equal protection. All-male state universities must admit women if they offer courses not available at other state colleges accessible to women.[8]

Limits on the equal-protection principle

The right to equal protection of the laws is a crucial right that extends to virtually every aspect of our lives. Nevertheless, like all other rights it is not unlimited. The principle does *not* guarantee that all citizens will receive equal treatment. One important limitation on the guarantee of equal protection is that it applies only to government regulation, not private conduct. A federal or state law prohibiting women from being doctors would undoubtedly be declared unconstitutional. However, if citizens refused to visit women doctors, such action would be purely private and thus beyond the scope of the equal-protection principle. Of course, the line between private and government involvement can be difficult to distinguish. For example, in 1964 the Supreme Court ruled that a private amusement park practicing racial discrimination violated the Fourteenth Amendment because the segregation was enforced by an off-duty sheriff who wore his badge.

Even if the discrimination directly results from federal or state laws, there is still no guarantee that strict equality will be enforced. Laws treating the rich differently from the poor, blacks differently from whites, women differently from men, and so on, *can* be consistent with the equal-protection principle. Over the years the Supreme Court has elaborated two doctrines that have allowed laws to make distinctions

[8] The application of the equal-protection principle to the rights of women is considered in more detail in Susan C. Ross, *The Rights of Women* (New York: Discus Books, 1973), Chap. 1.

EQUAL PROTECTION 1, YANKEES 0

The equal-protection-of-the-laws provision of the Fourteenth Amendment has been used to strike down a variety of discriminatory rules. One recent application concerned whether or not women reporters should be allowed into the men's locker rooms of athletic teams. Though the National Hockey League allows female reporters in its locker rooms, commissioner Bowie Kuhn has forbidden the practice in major league baseball. Women reporters have argued that such restrictions unfairly hinder their work because male reporters have interview opportunities they do not possess. To achieve equality of access, *Sports Illustrated* reporter Melissa Ludtke brought suit to be admitted to the New York Yankee locker room. The U.S. district judge ruled in her favor on the grounds that since the facilities at Yankee Stadium were owned by New York City, keeping Ms. Ludtke out was a violation of her constitutional rights to due process and equal protection of the laws (the ruling applies only to Yankee Stadium, however). The Yankees unsuccessfully argued that allowing women reporters to see naked men would harm the "image of baseball as a family sport." The judge ruled that if modesty was a problem, privacy could be protected by the use of towels or curtains. Incidentally, the Yankee team had overwhelmingly voted to allow female reporters into their locker room prior to the court decision.

"Judge Orders Yankees To Open Locker Room to Women Reporters, *The Champaign-Urbana News-Gazette,* September 26, 1978."

among groups of citizens—"reasonableness" and "suspect classification."

REASONABLE EXCEPTIONS TO EQUAL PROTECTION OF THE LAWS Under the reasonableness standard the key question concerns whether the legislature had a reasonable purpose in passing a law. This criterion has frequently involved an attempt to protect women and children from alleged evils. For example, in 1948 the Court upheld a Michigan law prohibiting women from being bartenders unless they were wives or daughters of proprietors (*Goesaert* v. *Cleary*). The Court argued that since women bartenders cause "moral and social problems" and since states have the right to prevent such problems, discriminatory legislation is permissible. Needless to say, the difference between what is reasonable and what is unfair discrimination is not always clear. Perhaps for this reason the reasonableness approach to departure from the equal protection of the laws is no longer popular.

Suspect classification exceptions to equal protection of the laws

The second, and currently popular, doctrine is that of "**suspect classification.**" Here the Court has ruled that if race, sex, or wealth is explicitly taken into account in the law, the law must be scrutinized carefully to see if equal protection is being denied. Such scrutiny involves asking two questions: (1) does the law accomplish an important purpose? and (2) is the suspect classification necessary to accomplish its purpose? In 1974, for example, the court upheld a Florida law granting widows, but not widowers, a $500 property tax exemption. The majority held that helping those who had lost a spouse was a legitimate state action, and making a distinction on the basis of sex was necessary to provide financial help to those who needed it the most. On the other hand, the Court overturned a Florida law prohibiting interracial sex on the ground that specifically singling out sex between blacks and whites was unnecessary to the legislative goal of promoting sexual decency.

Suspect classification The legal doctrine holding that if a law distinguishes among citizens on the basis of race, sex, or wealth, it must be closely scrutinized to make sure that this classsification is necessary to accomplish a reasonable goal.

Freedom of speech, freedom of the press, freedom of association, religious freedom, and equal protection of the laws are among the most important rights enjoyed by U.S. citizens. We must emphasize again, however, that the rights of citizens go well beyond these rights. To describe completely all rights enjoyed by all citizens would require several volumes.[9] Another point worth repeating is that rights are not clearly stated dictums etched in stone for all eternity. As we have seen, even rights that are constitutionally spelled out can be interpreted very differently. Moreover, important rights are added — and subtracted — all the time. In 1964, for example, Congress, on the basis of its constitutional power to regulate commerce, prohibited discrimination against blacks in hotels, motels, restaurants, theaters, and employment. Prior to this act few people would have viewed the commerce power as relevant to civil rights. In short, getting "one's rights" may sometimes involve a long political struggle.

What sustains our rights?

We have seen that citizens possess a long list of important rights. Remember, however, that it is one thing to have an abstract right but quite another to enjoy the right in actual practice. Many a dictator has claimed that his people are completely "free" because the constitution protects everyone's fundamental rights. In analyzing the rights of citizens we thus face a crucial question: What keeps our rights real instead of meaningless paper rights? What prevents, say, the right of free speech

[9] Among the important rights of citizens that we have not considered are consumer rights, the right to government services, the right to citizenship, rights involving housing, the right to privacy, the right to travel, and the right to death. Several of these rights (and many others) are discussed in Norman Dorsen, ed., *The Rights of Americans* (New York: Pantheon Books, 1970).

GROUPS IN THE PROCESS OF SEEKING THEIR RIGHTS.

The right of farm workers to higher wages and better working conditions has been an ongoing battle in the last twenty years. A prominent advocate of farm workers has been Cesar Chavez, shown here protesting the policies of United Brands (which markets Chiquita Bananas).

Senior citizens demonstrate for their rights.

A demonstration of handicapped citizens. The right of the disabled or handicapped to such things as equal access to public buildings has become a major issue.

from being transformed into the right of free speech to say approved things at the appropriate time and place?

CITIZENS AS GUARDIANS OF RIGHTS

One possible answer is the people themselves. It has been argued that all rights are meaningless unless ordinary citizens are willing to defend them. If the government decides that since Republicans are an endangered species they ought to be given preferential treatment (for example, five votes each), the surest check on such abuse is for citizens to punish electorally those who made these unconstitutional laws. If the local police decide that controversial speakers will be forced to leave town, citizen outrage at such violation of the First Amendment is much more meaningful than a lengthy and costly court battle. Advocates of this position believe that the lack of popular support for fundamental rights was responsible for several countries (for example, Germany in the 1930s) becoming dictatorships despite strong written protections of rights.

This argument undoubtedly has some truth to it. It is difficult to imagine the survival of the free exercise of religion if most citizens deeply believed that only one true faith exists and that everyone should accept it. Nevertheless, to claim that the people themselves are the primary protectors of their basic rights is probably an exaggeration. In the last twenty-five years several public opinion polls have asked citizens about their support for important rights, and the overall results do not show overwhelming support. Table 16.1 depicts typical findings from these surveys. Note that only 62.3 percent of the population would allow some-

Group	Percent that would allow speech in community	Percent that would allow person to teach in college	Percent that would allow book by person in library
People opposed to churches and religion	62.3	38.8	58.6
People who believed that blacks were genetically inferior to whites	58.6	40.8	61.0
An admitted Communist	55.5	38.8	55.3
An admitted homosexual	61.8	49.3	55.3

TABLE 16.1

PUBLIC SUPPORT FOR RIGHTS OF CONTROVERSIAL GROUPS, 1977

Source: National Opinion Research Center, University of Chicago. The respondents were a cross section of the U.S. population.

one opposed to religion to speak in their community (and only 38.8 percent would allow such a person to teach in college). A significantly large minority would keep books written by Communists and homosexuals out of public libraries. In general, studies of attitudes toward the rights of others suggest that people's feelings toward a group greatly influence their willingness to extend basic, constitutionally protected rights to that group. In other words, you may believe in the right of free speech, but if you oppose communism, a good chance exists that you would oppose letting a Communist speak freely.[10]

POLITICAL ACTIVISTS AS GUARDIANS OF RIGHTS

A second explanation for survival of our rights emphasizes the commitment of well-educated, politically active individuals to our fundamental rights. This argument goes as follows. Studies show that well-educated, politically active citizens are much more likely to uphold the right of free speech, the right of free association, and other important rights.[11] These citizens occupy important leadership positions both in and out of government. Besides public officials, this category includes newspaper editors, civic leaders, and supporters of organizations such as the American Civil Liberties Union that pay special attention to the possible violations of rights. Because of their relatively important positions in society, their pro-rights orientations have greater weight in policy making. These individuals act as guardians who can alert the public to government abuses as well as check the occasional intolerances of less enlightened citizens.[12] Whereas the first argument emphasizes the role of the average citizen in maintaining our rights, this one says that it is the "elite" (that is, well-educated, powerful citizens) who protect our rights.

This second argument has had considerable popularity. Its principal advantage is that it reconciles the apparent contradiction between the existence of many rights and only lukewarm (or negative) public support for these rights. Nevertheless, though this view may be correct, it remains to be completely verified. While there is little doubt that well-educated, politically involved citizens are more likely to endorse important rights, the translation of this verbal endorsement into concrete action has rarely been demonstrated. Recall that for decades black Americans were systematically denied equal protection of the laws (as are many women today), but there was little complaint from the majority of public officials, civic leaders, newspaper editors, and other so-called guardians of our rights. Only when blacks themselves forced the issues did this elite show much concern. Critics of this position maintain that

[10] Evidence for this is presented in David G. Lawrence, "Procedural Norms and Tolerance: A Reassessment," *American Political Science Review*, 70 (1976), pp. 80–100.

[11] For example, Samuel A. Stouffer, *Communism, Conformity, and Civil Liberties* (New York: Wiley, 1955).

[12] Robert A. Dahl, *Who Governs?* (New Haven, Conn.: Yale University Press, 1961), Chap. 28.

such indifference was typical. To be sure, these "guardians" do play some role in protecting our rights, but to claim that they vigilantly guard against each and every abuse is a gross exaggeration.

THE ARGUMENT THAT OUR RIGHTS ARE NOT WELL PROTECTED

A third, and quite different, response to the question of what sustains our rights is that our rights are *not* well sustained. Put bluntly, for most citizens and during most periods many of the rights that are enjoyed *are* paper rights. After all, merely because the Supreme Court declares that a specific government abridgement of a right is illegal does not necessarily mean that one can now freely exercise this right. This argument does not claim that we live in an oppressive dictatorship with no rights whatsoever. Rather, there is a significant gap between our actual rights and our "abstract" rights. This assertion can be supported on two different grounds.

The lack of protection from private abuses of our rights

First, many of the rights widely accepted as "fundamental" concern citizens protection *against* government action. The Bill of Rights (the first ten amendments) prevents government abridgement of speech, requires that government provide a speedy trial, and prohibits government viola-

---

GIVE 'EM HELL HARRY!

The issue of what rights are real and what rights exist as little more than paper rights brings to mind the story about the GI and the Russian soldier who found themselves in the same foxhole when the U.S. and Russian armies were linking up during the closing months of World War II. After celebrating their meeting the two soldiers got around to discussing the virtues of their respective countries.

"In the United States," proclaimed the G.I., "we have complete freedom."

"Same is true in Russia," answered the Russian.

"In the United States we have so much freedom that anyone can say anything he wants to," bragged the soldier.

"Same is true in Russia," answered the Russian.

"Why in the United States, we have so much freedom that I can stand in front of the White House, shake my fist, and say at the top of my lungs 'Harry Truman is an S.O.B.' "

"Same is true in Russia," answered the Russian, "I can stand in front of the Kremlin, shake my fist, and say at the top of my lungs 'Harry Truman is an S.O.B.' "

tions of due process. Such protections, though important, do not deal with *private* violations of citizens' rights. Such violations can be as oppressive as government actions. For example, the Supreme Court may protect a newspaper from government censorship. However, for most newspapers a threat from a major advertiser to the effect that if certain things are printed the advertising will go elsewhere is far more relevant.[13] You may have a perfect right to advocate the benefits of international communism, but in many communities you would pay the price by losing your job and many of your friends. The government cannot force you to attend church, but community pressure may accomplish the same thing.

The deprivation of basic rights through the actions of private individuals poses a difficult problem. On the one hand it may be tempting to extend many of our rights to such private matters. For example, we could make it a crime for advertisers to censor newspapers by threatening to remove their ads. In fact, the courts have been moving in this direction when they have prevented public employees from being fired because of public, nonjob-related statements. On the other hand, do we want further government interference in our private lives? Do we want a law that would require careful monitoring of speeches made by controversial adherents of obnoxious philosophies? Such government "protection" of our rights may present a far greater potential danger than private violations. Moreover, giving the government the obligation to interfere with so much private conduct could lay the groundwork for an oppressive police state.

The capacity of modern governments to violate our rights

The second argument supporting the view that our rights are not very well protected concerns the actions of the government. It is claimed that even where there are strong legal protections of rights, modern governments can get away with extensive violations. In part this results from modern technology. When the Bill of Rights was drafted government action against free speech was comparatively open—if you made a public speech you could be locked up or fined. Private behavior was pretty much beyond the reach of government. Today, however, sophisticated electronic surveillance techniques, computers capable of maintaining millions of records, and extensive intelligence networks have made government abuse much more difficult to detect and to stop. The willingness of public officials to violate our rights has also been reinforced by the continued threat of Communist subversion and other threats to law and order such as those provided by militant political groups.

---

[13] The debate over sexual violence on television has recently generated several efforts at private censorship. For example, Rev. Donald Wildman and his National Federation for Decency have launched a campaign against ABC-TV outlets in thirty cities because of ABC's "sexually oriented" programing. Wildman hopes to reduce ABC's audience by 3 percent a month. This would cost ABC some $60 million a year.

The precise extent of government abuse of our rights is impossible to measure. We do know, however, that on numerous occasions the government overstepped the fine line between a legitimate concern for preventing subversion and impinging on fundamental rights. For example, the FBI has long kept political intelligence files on thousands of citizens without authority from Congress or the President. This was in addition to the legal security index set up in the 1950s to identify citizens who could be politically dangerous during a national emergency. A total of 26,174 people were at one time listed on this index (and much of this information is still kept despite the repeal of the original law in 1971). Moreover, since 1939 the FBI has compiled over 500,000 dossiers on citizens with dangerous ideas. During a fifteen-year period the FBI admitted carrying out 2,370 "dirty tricks" against foreign and U.S. citizens. Of course, many of these actions were legitimate attempts to protect national security, but in many other instances there was little evidence of a threat.[14]

Frequent objects of FBI actions were ordinary citizens who happened to get involved with unpopular (but probably not dangerous) causes. Consider the case of Maude Wilkinson, the daughter of a Methodist minister who joined a student affiliate of the Socialist Workers Party to protest U.S. involvement in Vietnam. Mrs. Wilkinson was teaching four-year-old black children in Washington, D.C., when the FBI sent an anonymous letter to the school superintendent about her "in order to protect the D.C. school system from the menace of a teacher who does not have the interests of the children or the country at heart." This particular effort did not succeed, but the FBI employed a similar tactic when Mrs. Wilkinson took a teaching job in Austin, Texas. This time she was fired. When she took a new job with the Human Opportunities Commission, the FBI again tried to get her fired.[15]

Another government agency that has been used against those with unpopular political beliefs is the Internal Revenue Service (IRS). The IRS is responsible for collecting taxes, and, unlike other government agencies, it can *legally* investigate *any* citizen without a warrant and without solid knowledge that a crime has been committed (it also has the power to obtain records on its own authority). The ability of the IRS to "get" people is considerable. Intensive analysis of tax returns can result in heavy financial assessments, criminal charges, and a considerable cost of time and

[14] David Wise, *The American Police State* (New York: Vintage Press, 1978), Chap. 9. The FBI's concern with comparatively harmless groups is illustrated by the great effort the bureau has expended to harass the Socialist Workers Party (SWP). The SWP, a Marxist-oriented group with about 2,500 members, is more an intellectual anachronism and debating society than a revolutionary group. Nevertheless, over a thirty-eight-year period the FBI used some 1,600 informants to spy on the party, burglarized the New York office of the SWP at least ninety-two times between 1960 and 1966, and compiled some eight million documents concerning party activity. In all this time the FBI has yet to catch a member of the Socialist Workers Party in a single violent or illegal act.

[15] Wise, p. 316.

effort. Organizations can lose their tax-exempt status, which means that donations are no longer tax deductible (which, in turn, will reduce donations). Like the FBI and the Central Intelligence Agency (CIA), the IRS maintains a large investigative staff (and these agencies frequently share information).

The basic purpose of IRS investigations is to uncover tax cheating, and targets of investigation are supposed to be chosen according to the amount of money that can be recovered. Nevertheless, this power has occasionally been used for other purposes (for example, the notorious gangster Al Capone went to jail for tax evasion, not murder or bootlegging). In the 1950s, the IRS increasingly began using its power to punish individuals with unpopular ideas. Between 1955 and 1958, the IRS had two full-time special agents scrutinize the financial, public, and personal affairs of Reuben G. Lenski, an alleged member of the Communist Party (the IRS case against Lenski was dismissed in court).[16] Under President John F. Kennedy the IRS formed a special "strike force" to investigate eighteen right-wing (and one left-wing) groups. During the 1960s seventy-two black civil rights leaders had their taxes audited to embarrass and to distract them. The most ambitious IRS effort was the creation of the Special Service Staff (SSS), specifically designed to investigate political groups. The SSS existed between 1969 and 1973 and maintained financial and political files on 8,585 individuals and 2,873 organizations (well-known people in the SSS files included New York Mayor John Lindsay and Nobel Prize winner Linus Pauling, while organizations ranged from the Ku Klux Klan to the National Student Association).[17]

Stories such as these can be multiplied. The Watergate scandal revealed that government sponsorship of illegal break-ins, wiretaps, and "enemies lists" had become increasingly common. Even the respected (and hardly radical) journalist Joseph Kraft had his telephone bugged, while CBS correspondent Dan Rather's house was burglarized and his files ransacked.[18] Even though such actions can be defended as isolated exceptions or reasonable mistakes, they probably inhibit many citizens from fully utilizing their rights. After all, why take a chance by joining an unpopular group or getting involved in a demonstration when such action *might* get one on a list of subversives (and one would never know it). Suppressing free speech and the right of freedom of association does not require that every speaker or organization be punished. A few dozen well-publicized abuses of power can provide millions of citizens with a powerful and long-lasting lesson.

But let us return to our original question of what sustains our rights. Obviously, something more is involved than just putting them down on paper. More is also required than affirmation by the Supreme Court. What this "more" is, however, is not precisely known. Perhaps wide-

---

[16] Morton H. Halperin et al., *The Lawless State: The Crime of the U.S. Intelligence Agencies* (Harmendsworth, England: Penguin Books, 1976), p. 190.

[17] Halperin et al., pp. 196–203.

[18] Wise, pp. 166–168.

spread public indifference or apathy may protect those with unpopular ideas. People who do not like newspapers to print certain stories may not care enough to make a fuss. Nor would government officials care enough in most instances to punish the offender. This explanation, however, like the two presented previously, is plausible though far from conclusively demonstrated. We should emphasize again that in asking how our rights are sustained we may be focusing on the wrong question. More basic is the question of what rights we *really* possess. This is a difficult question to answer because one cannot say for sure until one actually tries to use one's rights. The right of free speech or free association may be quite real provided it is not pushed too far or it does not threaten the status quo.

A conclusion: the politics of rights

It is tempting to analyze rights from a philosophical or legalistic perspective. One could discuss the distinctions among different types of rights, the origins of rights, and whether some rights are more basic than others. Many descriptions of the rights enjoyed by citizens do, in fact, take this philosophical or legalistic approach. We argue instead that rights are basically no different from other benefits (money, status) obtained through the political process. To treat rights as one might treat abstract religious doctrine is to misunderstand the meaning of "right."

To appreciate the political nature of a right consider the evolution of rights regarding education. In the eighteenth century when philosophers vigorously debated the issue of inalienable rights, human rights, and the like, the right to an education at public expense was nowhere mentioned. Education was a privilege available only to those would could afford it. If you insisted that twelve years of publicly supported education was a right no different from the right of private property, you would have been a prime candidate for the lunatic asylum. The Declaration of Independence, the Constitution, the Bill of Rights, and other early statements of our rights make no mention of education.

In the twentieth century public education has emerged as a right, as opposed to a privilege, of U.S. citizens. Legal scholars did not discover that education was an accidentally overlooked right. Rather, various interests successfully asserted claims to government-supported education. A privilege for a few wealthy citizens slowly became a privilege for a larger number, which, in turn, became a right for all citizens. Nor has this process ended with universal, publicly supported education. Some people today claim that the right to education should include a right to a college education, a right to a high-quality education, a right to a vocationally relevant education, as well as a wide variety of rights within the educational process (for example, open hearings in disciplinary actions). Some of these demands may become basic rights; others may disappear without a trace.

The moral of the transformation of education from a privilege to a right is clear: if you want something, demand it as a right. If possible, claim that the right is "implicit" in the Constitution, history, or the nature of the universe. Once this right is widely recognized, assert that anything undermining it would also undermine the foundations of our political system. Through such tactics women have won the right to abortion, workers the right to join unions, and many students the right to publicly funded college educations.

Major questions raised

1. What are rights? A right is a legal or moral claim on a benefit. Unlike a privilege, a right can be abridged only under unusual circumstances. Considerable controversy exists over what our fundamental rights are, the relative importance of different rights, the role of government in enforcing rights, and who ultimately decides who has what rights.

2. What political rights do citizens possess? Among the most important constitutionally guaranteed rights that we enjoy are freedom of speech, freedom of the press, freedom of association, religious freedom, and the right to equal protection of the laws. Few people, however, believe that these rights are without limitations, and enormous differences of opinion exist on how they are to be interpreted. In addition, our rights are not fixed; many a privilege has been transformed into a right.

3. What sustains our rights? While agreement exists that rights on paper are by themselves insufficient, experts disagree on what makes our rights "real." The support of our rights by ordinary citizens and advocacy of better-educated, comparatively more influential citizens are two possible explanations. It has also been argued that a significant gap exists between our paper rights and the rights we actually enjoy.

QUESTIONS FOR FURTHER DISCUSSION

1. Rights such as freedom of speech or the right of association are considered political rights. Increasingly, many people argue that these political rights have little value unless accompanied by social and economic rights. That is, the right to free speech means little if the person making the speech has no protection against economic or social sanctions. Therefore, some people argue, American citizens will not enjoy meaningful political rights until they possess such rights as a guaranteed income or a right to a college education. Does the exercise of political rights ultimately depend on such economic guarantees of equality?

Would freedom from economic retaliation protect an individual who makes a highly unpopular speech? Would a policy of equalizing economic resources violate the rights of citizens to earn as much money as they wish? Can a poor person have the same right of free association as a rich person?

2. Most of the controversies surrounding the First Amendment's guarantee of freedom of religion have concerned whether or not government can assist religious schools. Government involvement with actual religious practices has been comparatively rare (and most of these have entailed refusal by members of a religion to follow a law). Recently, however, especially in light of incidents such as the mass suicide in Guyana of members of the People's Temple, greater attention has been focused on the specific practices of certain religious cults. Several people have complained that cults brainwash their members and destroy their personalities. Worse, some cults may even be training people to be assassins or to commit suicide on the orders of their religious leaders. Is there some point at which the government can reasonably interfere with the practices of a religious organization? Are some practices harmful to society even if all members of a religious cult accept them of their own free will? How should the government distinguish between a strange but not harmful group and a strange but possibly harmful organization?

3. One major argument for laws restricting or prohibiting pornography is that pornography is harmful to society. Suppose that a study showed that pornography was *not* socially harmful to any significant extent. Since the community is no longer protecting itself from an evil, is it still possible to justify antipornography laws?

4. What if the majority of citizens wanted major restrictions on First Amendment freedoms? For example, they wanted a law making it illegal to advocate any form of government other than a democracy. Which right comes first — the right of a majority to live under the laws they want or the right of a citizen to advocate unpopular ideas? Can a nation be democratic yet deny its citizens many freedoms so long as these denials are desired by the majority?

BIBLIOGRAPHY

Abraham, Henry J. *Freedom and the Court: Civil Rights and Liberties in the United States.* 2d ed. New York: Oxford University Press, 1972.
> A detailed analysis of our rights approached from the perspective of important judicial decisions. Particularly relevant for understanding due process of law, freedom of expression, conflicts over religion, and the quest for racial equality. Contains a bibliography.

Cowan, Paul, Nick Egleson, and Nat Henloff. *State Secrets: Police Surveillance in America.* New York: Holt, Rinehart and Winston, 1974.
> A critical analysis of government spying on ordinary citizens. Describes how the government infiltrates radical organizations, the use of modern surveillance technology by the FBI, and how grand juries are being used to harass dissenters. Several of these charges are supported by official government documents.

Cranston, Maurice. *What Are Human Rights?* New York: Taplinger Publishing Company, 1973.

A philosophically oriented (but very useful) analysis of questions associated with rights. Considers, for example, the definition of a "human right," the relationship between rights and morality, how rights are justified, and various specific rights such as the right to property. An appendix contains several major documents dealing with human rights.

Dorsen, Norman, ed., *The Rights of Americans: What They Are—What They Should Be*. New York: Pantheon Books, 1970.

A wide-ranging collection of essays dealing with almost every conceivable right. Included are the right to housing, the right to special treatment, the right to publish, the right to use alcohol and drugs, and many more rights not usually examined in books on rights.

Levine, Alan H., and Eve Cary. *The Rights of Students*, rev. ed. New York: Discus Books, 1977.

A brief but precise analysis of the rights that are supposed to be enjoyed by high school students. Covers such issues as personal appearance, the use of corporal punishment, discrimination, access to school records, and obtain ng a diploma. Information is given in a question and answer format.

Miller, Arthur R. *The Assault on Privacy: Computer, Data Banks, and Dossiers*. Ann Arbor: University of Michigan Press, 1971.

A well-documented examination of how private industry and government collect and use information on citizens. Describes how federal agencies share information, how credit information is used, and the use of electronic surveillance. Concludes by considering proposals for protecting individual privacy.

Reitman, Alan, ed. *The Pulse of Freedom: American Liberties, 1920–1970s*. New York: New American Library, 1975.

A collection of essays on freedom and repression during various periods of American history. Covers such topics as the black civil rights movement in the 1920s, the repression of radicals following World War I, the McCarthy investigations of the 1950s, and religion in public schools.

Ross, Susan C. *The Rights of Women*. New York: Discus Books, 1973.

A useful compilation of the rights of women and relevant court decisions. Presents the major federal laws dealing with sex discrimination. Has separate chapters on employment, education, the media, crime, abortion, divorce, and several other matters of special interest to women.

Sigler, Jay A. *American Rights Policies*. Homewood, Ill.: Dorsey Press, 1975.

A good overall review of many of the rights possessed by Americans. Considers free speech, freedom of the press, religious freedom, and the rights of such groups as blacks, women, Indians, and the mentally disturbed. Concludes with an analysis of how rights are imp emented.

Spicer, George W. *The Supreme Court and Fundamental Freedoms*, 2d ed. New York: Appleton-Century-Crofts, 1967.

A legally oriented approach to the rights enjoyed by Americans. Reviews the history of present-day rights policies and then examines civil rights, freedom of speech, religious freedom, problems of political and social equality, and the balance between national security and personal liberty.

Tussman, Joseph. *Government and the Mind*. New York: Oxford University Press, 1977.

Tussman is a philosopher, and in this book he deals with several of the most difficult and complex problems associated with the limits of individual freedom. Though a strong supporter of free speech, Tussman argues that the very nature of society and open discussion acquires firm limits. Free speech exists only where penalties for abuse are reasonable.

Wise, David. *The American Police State: The Government Against the People.* New York: Vintage Press, 1978.

A well-written journalistic account of how the FBI, the CIA, the IRS, and other government agencies have abused their powers. Provides names, dates, and a blow-by-blow account of many illegal operations against well-known citizens.

PREVIEW

What is the nature of private government?

In the United States much power resides in private organizations such as colleges, corporations, labor unions, and religious bodies. Some people argue that these organizations should be run democratically. They assert that undemocratic organizations are in compatible with a democratic political system, democracy in private organizations is as important as democracy in government, internal group democracy supports democracy more generally, and freedom within groups benefits individual development. Others point out that while democracy within private organizations may be valuable, it should not be required. Private associations and corporations lack the coercive power of government, and dissatisfied people can leave. Therefore, free speech and other freedoms do not need government protection. People may also freely choose to belong to undemocratic organizations.

What is the relationship between public and private power?

The assumption that public officials hold ultimate political power has been questioned by those who say that a nonelected elite rules. This power-elite view holds that all societies are comprised of pyramidlike institutions, with the most important one today being the economic sector.

Several types of evidence support this view: the corporate backgrounds of government officials, the taking of corporate jobs by ex-government officials, the activities of elite financial foundations, the use of bribery, and manipulation of the mass media to choke opposition. A key element in the power-elite perspective is the concept of "nondecision." The power elite, it is pointed out, can keep issues off the public agenda so that threats to its domination never surface.

The power-elite argument has been widely criticized. Not all members of the elite advocate policies favorable to elite interests, nor do they all desire the same policies, though they may share broad goals. Further, evidence of actual domination by a power elite is limited. The concept of nondecision has also been criticized because it is too loosely employed and people do not always disagree. Finally, the elitists assume that there must be someone in charge, but this need not be true.

An alternative perspective is pluralism, which sees society as composed of diverse groups all with some resources; policy results from the interplay of numerous interests. No one group dominates, but in the short run government dominates private groups. This approach has been criticized for putting too much emphasis on small decisions and ignoring the major forces that control the overall directions of society. Neither perspective has been conclusively proved.

CHAPTER SEVENTEEN

NONGOVERN-MENT POWER AND ECO-NOMIC ELITES

receding chapters have focused on officials holding *public* positions of power. Some officials, for example, members of Congress, are elected, while others, for example, federal judges, are appointed, but all are ultimately responsible to the public. Government in the United States exercises considerable power, but power is not restricted to government officials. Many important decisions affecting millions of people are made by private individuals who do not hold public office. The president of General Motors makes decisions that have important political and economic consequences, yet the general public has little—if any—control over who becomes president of General Motors. In fact, the heads of large corporations such as General Motors, American Telephone and Telegraph, or EXXON may exercise more power over U.S. citizens and public policy than most prominent public officials. Hence, to understand politics we must look beyond the actions of leaders who occupy public positions. We must examine the activities and political impact of private organizations—sometimes called private governments. Specifically, we seek answers to two related questions:

1. What is the nature of private government?
2. What is the relationship between private and public power?

Private governments Organizations that proscribe rules for members. These rules are not enforced by the police or by the court system.

What is the nature of private government?

All human beings are constrained by numerous rules and regulations. Without prohibitions against certain behavior, for example, murder, society would soon disintegrate. Many rules are formulated through the political process. Recall that it is through politics that societies define crimes and their punishment. Most constraints, however, are formulated by private individuals rather than by legislatures or bureaucracies. We all remember how our parents regulated our early behavior regarding where we could go, whom we could associate with, what we could eat, and our bedtime hours.

For adults some of the most important rules and regulations originate in large bureaucratic organizations sometimes referred to as **private governments.** In many ways these organizations are like separate nations within a nation. They have a defined membership (citizens), specified rules (laws), penalties for violations of rules (sanctions), and mechanisms of review and enforcement (courts and police). Perhaps the only characteristic of nationhood the private governments do not possess is the capacity to employ large-scale physical force (and some organizations such as the Mafia even have this capacity.)

COLLEGES

Private governments take a variety of forms and differ in their impact on people's lives. One type of private government that readers of this book should be well acquainted with is the college or university. In 1975, 9.9 million students were enrolled in various colleges (7.7 million of these in state-supported institutions).[1] Though colleges have substantially relaxed their control over students' lives in recent years, the average student still remains under many college-imposed constraints. Frequently college administrators tell you where you can live, limit how much noise you can create, determine whether you can have liquor in your room, require you to eat dormitory food, limit visitations with members of the opposite sex, and regulate your use of automobiles. Some colleges go a few steps further and have student dress codes, rules regarding off-campus political activity, requirements regarding religious observance, rules governing sexual conduct, and, in at least one instance, mandatory regulations regarding student weight (Oral Roberts University).[2] Such constraints are in addition to academic requirements for graduation.

[1] *Statistical Abstract of the United States, 1977*, p. 117.

[2] Oral Roberts University has been sued by the American Civil Liberties Union on behalf of four students who were placed on probation because of weight problems. This action has not deterred the university, however. Recently it extended the weight standard to faculty.

CORPORATIONS

A second important type of private government is illustrated by the companies that employ millions of citizens. Large corporations in particular may make demands on their employees that would be labeled tyrannical if such actions were taken by government. An investigation of the giant Dupont Company, for example, found that employees advocating the "wrong" political viewpoints were harassed, ostracized, or given unpleasant tasks.[3] The same study found strong company pressure on its employees to "volunteer" money or time to certain Dupont-approved charities. Consider the case of a research manager working for a large company who repeatedly spoke out against what he believed to be his company's superficial efforts to comply with antipollution laws. First, his space in the company parking lot was cancelled. His name was then "accidentally" removed from the company building directory. His requests to attend professional meetings were "lost" or buried under red tape. His superiors demanded that he rewrite his technical reports, and his staff and research allowances were drastically cut. Eventually, he quit and moved to another city.[4]

"I've called you in here, Brodie, because the way you've been dressing lately seems a little too casual for the comptroller of this firm."

Reproduced by special permission of PLAYBOY Magazine; copyright © 1979 by Playboy.

[3] James Phelan and Robert Poze, *The Company State* (New York: Grossman, 1973), pp. 61–62.

[4] David W. Ewing, *Freedom Inside the Organization: Bringing Civil Liberties to the Workplace* (New York: Dutton, 1977), p. 6.

CONTEMPORARY CORPORATIONS COMPARED TO THE THIRTEEN ORIGINAL STATES

The sheer size of modern corporations is sometimes difficult to grasp. In fact, many U.S. companies have more employees than some nations have citizens. To appreciate how the United States has grown from an economic system of small-scale enterprise to one of large organizations, compare the populations of the thirteen original states in 1790 to the number of employees "governed" by the thirteen largest corporations (in terms of labor force).

State	Population (1790)	Company	Number of employees (1978)
Virginia	692,000	American Telephone	984,000
Pennsylvania	434,000	and Telegraph	
North Carolina	394,000	General Motors	839,200
Massachusetts	379,000	Ford	506,500
New York	340,000	Sears Roebuck	472,000
Maryland	320,000	General Electric	401,000
South Carolina	249,000	International Tel	379,000
Connecticut	238,000	and Tel	
New Jersey	184,000	IBM	325,500
New Hampshire	142,000	General Telephone	213,500
Georgia	83,000	and Electronics	
Rhode Island	69,000	K-Mart	213,300
Delaware	59,000	J. C. Penney	211,000
Total	3,583,000	Mobil	207,700
		F. W. Woolworth	203,200
		U. S. Steel	166,800
		Total	5,112,700

Source: 1790 Census figures are from *Historical Statistics of the United States, Colonial Times to 1970,* Part 1, U.S. Department of Commerce Bureau of the Census, pp. 24–36. Corporate data are from *Forbes,* May 14, 1979, pp. 310–311.

In large corporations being an executive can mean building a whole life-style around company demands. Many companies once discouraged divorces among their executives on the grounds that it "looked bad" or showed an inability to manage one's affairs (now, however, some companies see divorce as a plus because it eliminates unproductive family obligations). Informal—though effective—rules frequently exist regarding dress, hair length, where one lives, and how one furnishes one's office. It is even alleged that the characteristics of one's spouse can have a major bearing on promotion because executives must frequently interact socially (an ambitious employee will thus marry the "right" mate to further his or her career). One major U.S. corporation once sent wives of executives to charm school. The impact of corporations on people's lives can sometimes be witnessed directly when hairy, unkempt college students suddenly get haircuts to go with their new three-piece suits when the recruiters from IBM or Mobil Oil arrive on campus. According to the head of planning for General Electric's international group, a modern corporation is a "virtual dictatorship" where an executive spends twelve hours a day in a democracy (mostly when he or she is asleep) and twelve hours a day in a "totally autocratic society."[5]

Closed shops An agreement between management and unions which requires that all people hired must be union members.

LABOR UNIONS

A third type of private government with substantial impact on people's lives is labor unions. In 1974 slightly over 20 million workers (26.2 percent of the nonagricultural work force) were members of unions.[6] In many localities it is the union that decides who can work and in what trade. One could not, for instance, go to Hollywood and simply apply for work as a film cutter, lighting technician, or even a driver in the motor pool. These positions are carefully controlled by strong unions. One must first get into the union, and this can be very difficult. Especially in the high-paying construction industry, failure to get a union card just about excludes one from employment as a plumber, electrician, or carpenter in many cities.

Labor unions can also determine how much work an individual can perform and the tasks he or she is permitted to do (and through its seniority rules, who gets fired first). A union bricklayer is permitted to lay so many bricks a day, and if an electrical obstacle is encountered in this work, an electrician must be called in. Some states allow "**closed shops**" in which all workers must join the union. Many unions also require their members to contribute to union health and pension plans or other union-

[5] Cited in Richard J. Barnet and Ronald E. Muller, *Global Reach: The Power of the Multinational Corporation* (New York: Simon & Schuster, 1974), p. 54. For years one of the most personally demanding corporations was IBM. Employees were governed by strict codes that specified shirt color (white only), suit color (dark), hair length (short), and general demeanor (subdued). Executives were required to live in certain areas and only in conventional types of houses. Smoking and drinking were discouraged, and public intoxication was cause for immediate dismissal even if it occurred on one's own time. Employees were also required to attend numerous company social functions, frequently sing the company anthem "Ever Onward," and recite prayers led by the official IBM chaplain. These requirements are further described in William Rogers, *THINK: A Biography of the Watsons and IBM* (New York: Stein and Day, 1969).

[6] *Statistical Abstract of the United States, 1977*, p. 384.

sponsored projects. And like corporations, unions can encourage their members to "volunteer" time and money to worthy causes (as defined by union leadership).[7]

PROFESSIONAL ORGANIZATIONS

Many professions also possess large organizations that act as private governments (there were an estimated 2,100 professional and learned societies in 1978).[8] Some of these organizations merely facilitate communication and information collection among their members. Others, however, provide detailed rules and regulations regarding permissible behavior. For example, the code of ethics of the American Medical Association, which represents 190,000 doctors, forbids doctors to own drug stores or advertise their rates. Similarly, until a recent Supreme Court decision many state bar associations had established a minimum fee schedule, and lawyers who charged less risked being officially called unethical (mandatory fees and commission rates also existed in the real estate business). Certified public accountants (CPAs) likewise belong to a professional organization that defines accepted accounting practices and sets minimum fees.

In many instances these professional private governments can exert their influence through the government itself. This happens when members of a profession—doctors, lawyers, accountants, barbers, real estate brokers, well diggers, egg graders—convince the state or local government that their profession requires special skills and ethical standards and therefore should be officially licensed. Of course, who knows more about appropriate standards than the professional association itself, so the association usually controls the membership of these licensing bodies. Thus, an individual lawyer who violates professional standards can also risk violating state or local law because the professional association controls these laws.[9] This use of state law to enforce professional standards was illustrated in a case involving Don Finley, a barber in Boca Raton, Florida. In 1973 Finley offered a new service in his barber shop—shaving women's legs (at $5 a leg). The leg-shaving business boomed, and many men came around for haircuts in order to catch the action. Unfortunately for the enterprising Mr. Finley, the state licensing board for barbers prohibited leg shaving because it was not explicitly allowed in barber shops.[10]

[7] For a more comprehensive picture of union power over its members, see Derek C. Bok and John T. Dunlop, *Labor and the American Community* (New York: Simon & Schuster, 1970), especially Chaps. 3–5.

[8] *National Trade and Professional Associations of the United States and Canada and Labor Unions*, Craig Colgate, ed., 13th annual edition (Washington, D.C.: Columbia Books, 1978), p. 6.

[9] For an excellent analysis of how professional organizations help to set state law, see Corrine Lathrop Gilb, *Hidden Hierarchies: The Professions and Government* (New York: Harper & Row, 1966).

[10] *National Trade and Professional Associations*, p. 11.

RELIGIOUS BODIES

The final type of private government we shall consider is the religious organization. In 1974 over 132 million people were official members of some 332,465 U.S. churches.[11] Many more identified with religious organizations though they did not belong to a church (admitted atheists or agnostics are very rare). As is true for professional organizations, there is great variation in how these private governments affect the lives of their members. For many citizens belonging to a church merely means attending Sunday services or swimming in the temple's pool.

For others, however, the commitment is more demanding. The Church of Jesus Christ of Latter-Day Saints (Mormons) requires its followers to donate 10 percent of their yearly income to the church and to spend two years doing missionary work (there were 2.7 million Mormons in 1974). The Orthodox Jewish religion requires its adherents to follow strict rules regarding working hours, diets, eating utensils, sex, prayer, personal hygiene, and numerous other aspects of daily life. The Amish, perhaps the most demanding religious group, not only regulate daily behavior but also forbid such "modern" practices as driving automobiles, using zippers, collecting interest on savings accounts, receiving social security benefits, and going beyond eight years of formal education.

THE CASE FOR DEMOCRACY IN PRIVATE ORGANIZATIONS

In discussing private governments one issue that frequently emerges concerns the amount of democracy *within* these organizations. We all agree that citizens should have some say in government, through institutions such as elections, and that officeholders should be accountable to the people they serve. Advocates of a position sometimes called **internal group democracy** or participatory democracy argue that the same democratic principles that guide the relationship between citizens and government should also guide the relationship between, say, citizens and employer or religious body.[12] Advocates of internal group democracy usually make the following arguments.

First, if the United States is to call itself a democracy it cannot have within it numerous institutions that are undemocratic. It would be misleading to call a society democratic if corporations, unions, religious organizations, and t1e like, were administered in authoritarian ways and citizens had no recourse but to accept decisions handed down by leaders. Democracy should apply not only to purely political matters but to economic and social relations as well.

Second, on a day-to-day basis democracy within a company or school can be far more important than in the more distant government. Consider the problems encountered by someone with an unorthodox life-

Internal group democracy The position that the internal life of private organizations ought to be run in accordance with maximum possible member participation according to democratic rules. Also called participatory democracy.

[11] *Statistical Abstract of the United States, 1977*, p. 47.

[12] For more on the idea of participatory democracy, see Terrence E. Cook and Patrick M. Morgan, eds., *Participatory Democracy* (San Francisco: Canfield Press, 1971).

style who works for a corporation that demands conventionality. Typically, this employee is confronted with a "take it or leave it" offer—conform or lose your job. With few exceptions an employee has no legal right to challenge company rules or to seek court protection if his or her constitutional rights are violated.[13] While an employee may enoy the right to protest U.S. foreign policy or vote to replace an incumbent President, without provisions for democracy within private organizations he or she can do little about being fired because of an unconventional life-style (or any other irrelevant attitude or behavior). Advocates of internal group democracy argue that democracy is most important in areas that directly affect people's lives, especially employment.

The entrance to the Rockefeller family estate in Pocantico Hills, New York. This 3,500-acre spread has its own golf course and several mansions for various members of the Rockefeller family. It is spectacular; someone once commented that this is the way God would live if he had the money.

A third defense of democracy within private government argues that democratic experience is necessary for the survival of a democratic political system. How can we maintain a democratic political system if citizens live and work in undemocratic schools, associations, businesses, and churches? Democratic private organizations, by providing citizens an opportunity to take part in important close-to-home decisions, build appreciation of the democratic political process. Holding fraternity or professional group elections and running meetings democratically also provide skills that can easily be generalized to "real-world" politics.

Finally, some advocates of group democracy go on step further and

[13] Ralph Nader, Mark Green, and Joel Seligman, *Taming the Giant Corporation* (New York: Norton, 1976), pp. 180–183. Though federal courts have thus far refused to apply the First Amendment to behavior within private organizations, some workers can seek court help if their right to free speech is violated. A 1974 lower federal court decision held that the First Amendment does apply if the company is deeply involved in government work. Several recent federal laws also protect employees in some industries (for example, coal mining) if they file complaints with a federal regulatory agency.

claim that participating in decisions affecting one's life is beneficial psychologically.[14] For example, a worker who has no voice in job decisions is more likely to feel alienated and hostile than one who can help shape the rules. Moreover, taking part in rule making is intellectually stimulating and can broaden one's horizons. Not only are these attributes inherently worth pursuing, but as companies such as Texas Instruments and Corning Glass have discovered, work-place democracy can dramatically increase productivity. In one instance Texas Instruments reduced the production time on certain radar equipment from 138 hours to 32 hours after assembly workers started to be involved in production decisions.[15]

THE CASE AGAINST INTERNAL GROUP DEMOCRACY

The arguments for internal group democracy have considerable appeal, and several political groups exist to further these goals. Nevertheless, assertions that private governments *must* be made more democratic have been criticized. The thrust of these arguments is that democracy in private organizations is not *essential* to our political system. The issue is not whether such democracy is good or bad, but whether it should be *required*. Many people who accept arguments about the beneficial results of democracy within private governments will also argue that the costs of implementing such a system would outweigh the benefits.

Critics of internal group democracy argue that private organizations lack the coercive power of the government. Compare the consequences if you refuse to pay a fine assessed by a private organization versus one assessed by the government. In the case of the private organization the worst thing that can happen is that you get thrown out of the organization. Refusal to pay a government-assessed fine can, however, mean going to prison or having property seized and auctioned off by a U.S. marshal. Similarly, IBM may require you to get a haircut, shave your beard, and wear a tie, but this is minor compared to what the government can make you do (for example, send you overseas to fight a war). Because the sanctions available to private organizations are limited, the protection provided by democratic procedures is less important. Put somewhat differently, only when private governments can make life or death decisions or seize our possessions would democratic safeguards such as popular elections be essential.

A related point is that one can always leave a private organization. If life in a giant corporation becomes oppressive, one can quit and earn a living growing wheat germ. Unlike the national government, unions, churches, and professional societies cannot force their members to maintain membership. The American Medical Association has a considerable impact on doctors, but many doctors do not belong to the AMA, and a member can always resign if he or she disagrees with association

[14] See, for example, Arnold S. Kaufman, "Human Nature and Participatory Democracy," in Carl J. Friedrich, ed., *Responsibility* (New York: The Liberal Arts Press, 1960).

[15] Cited in Morton Mintz and Jerry S. Cohen, *Power Inc.* (New York: Bantam Books, 1977), pp. 567–568.

PRIVATE INDUSTRY AS BIG BROTHER

In recent years the Supreme Court has acted vigorously to limit excessive government intrusion into people's private lives. Stringent requirements exist regarding such activities as wiretaps, illegal searches, and forced confessions. At the same time many companies have been moving in the opposite direction.

Faced with growing employee crime, the stealing of trade secrets, and sabotage, corporations have sharply increased the screening and surveillance of their workers. A 1974 survey conducted by the *Harvard Business Review* found, for example, that 39 percent of the firms used electronic surveillance in high-risk areas, 46 percent used "package checks," and 24 percent searched their employees' lockers. Currently, about 500,000 workers are required to take polygraph (lie detector) tests. These tests, plus the more common written "personality tests," are frequently designed to uncover attitudes and activities not necessarily related to job skills. This can include questions about personal debts, drug and drinking habits, gambling, religious activities, reading habits, travel, or even sexual activities. On occasion personal data dredged up by these tests are sold to other companies or credit agencies who for a fee make their files accessible.

In almost all instances submitting to these tests is a prerequisite to getting the job. Government protection from such policing activities

policy. A union plumber upset with union restrictions can in many areas still work as a nonunion plumber. In a real sense this capacity to leave (or "voting with one's feet") provides a democratic check on the power of private governments.

Finally, since people can *freely* choose the organizations they join, they have a right to belong to nondemocratic organizations. What if some people decide that they *like* a religion which tells them what to do or think without group discussion or in which there is no leader accountability through elections? What if workers want their bosses to act in an authoritarian way? Should these individuals be required to democratize their organizations? In many areas of life it is up to the individual to decide how much democracy he or she wants, so that it can be argued that an undemocratic private government is not incompatible with personal freedom.

These arguments only touch the surface of a lengthy and long-standing debate. We have not considered, for example, some of the technical

Security guard at Loeb Rhoads Hornblower & Co., Wall Street stock and bond brokers in New York City, keeps watch on TV monitors.

is slight. Presently, only seventeen states restrict or prohibit lie detector tests in employee screening, and almost everything else is legal. Of course, if the government tried some of these techniques people would screa n "police state" or "totalitarianism."

These and other corporate surveillance practices are described more fully in Peter Schrag, "Confess to Your Corporate Father: Does Your Boss Know What You Do When You're Alone?" *Mother Jones,* August 1978, pp. 56–60.

issues such as how a large corporation could be run democratically and effectively. Nor have we discussed what might happen to society if we all actively engaged in the politicking that complete internal group democracy would require. Our basic p rpose here has been to point out that much of the power wielded in the United States is exercised in private organizations, and considerable differences of opinion exist concerning whether this power should be exercised democratically.

What is the relationship between public and private power?

Of all the questions regarding private and public government, the most important and controversial one concerns the power of one over the other. Do certain private organizations dominate the government in

Washington? Preceding chapters of this book have assumed that Congress, the President, and judges are ultimately responsible for political decisions. This assumption has been challenged, and if it is false, our attention to legislative policy making, Supreme Court politics, and the like, has been misplaced. After all, why study these decision makers if they have little real power over what happens? The fact of private government domination would also raise serious questions about U.S. democracy. What is the value of elections or political parties if the real decision makers are not elected or not dependent on public opinion?

The contention that real power in our society does not lie in the hands of government officials has received support from many scholars. These scholars argue that legislators or even Presidents may make various day-to-day decisions, but ultimate power is in the hands of a comparatively small group who control the overall direction of society. This **power elite,** as it is frequently called, is usually unknown to the general public or even the political leaders it controls. Unlike politicians, the power elite shuns publicity and will deny that it possesses a disproportionate amount of power. Thus, discovering this group and its actions is very difficult, and mention of it is likely to be treated with skepticism by people who unthinkingly accept the preeminence of elected political leaders.

THE NATURE OF THE POWER ELITE

Despite the popularity of the power-elite argument, there is no precise consensus on the membership, the operations, or the goals of this elite. Scholars with different perspectives and techniques of analysis have reached somewhat diverse conclusions on this subject. Nevertheless, many who have examined the issue accept the following general arguments:[16]

1. Society is built around different hierarchically organized institutions. The political system, the economic system, and the military are the three most important institutions in our society. In nations like Spain and Italy the Roman Catholic Church is a key institution, but in the United States no religious organization occupies a comparable position. These institutions are pyramid-shaped: a few people are at the top and many more are near the bottom. In the economic sector, for example, at the top are the highest executives of giant corporations such as EXXON or International Telephone and Telegraph (ITT). Near the bottom are thousands of smaller people. Power derives from access to or control of these institutions, not money or status all by itself. A famous basketball player may earn $500,000 a year and drive a Rolls Royce, but he

[16] Our description of the power-elite argument is drawn largely from C. Wright Mills, *The Power Elite* (New York: Oxford University Press, 1959); G. William Domhoff, *Who Rules America?* (Englewood Cliffs, N.J.: Prentice-Hall, 1967); and G. William Domhoff, *The Higher Circles: The Governing Class in America* (New York: Vintage Books, 1970). We should reemphasize, however, that there are several different versions of the power-elite argument. Our description stresses areas in which there is considerable agreement.

has much less power than Alden W. Clausen, chief executive of BankAmerica Corporation with its $82 billion in assets and 73,000 employees.

2. People at the top of these institutions typically share an overall perspective and purpose. This unity of outlook does not necessarily derive from an explicit plan, frequent meetings, or an elaborate conspiracy. Even if such scheming occurs, it is not essential. Rather, top leaders share common high status and have had similar educational and social experiences, and these help to create common perspectives. Equally important, getting to the top requires certain skills and attributes, and, as a result, those who make it tend to have many things in common. If one believes in unlimited free expression, opposes nuclear weapons, and thinks that social programs deserve priority over a strong national defense, one is unlikely to become a four-star general. Hence, we find top military personnel agreeing on such policies as strong leadership, a nuclear deterrent, and high levels of defense spending. Differences of opinion do occur, but they are over details (for example, missiles versus manned bombers), not overall policy.

3. In different societies and at different times within societies one institution has tended to dominate the others. During much of the medieval period the Roman Catholic Church was the most powerful institution in European society. Several contemporary South American nations are dominated by the military. The United States has undergone numerous changes in elite domination. The early Republic saw the ascendency of a political elite composed of such men as Washington, Adams, Jefferson, and Madison. In the twentieth century, however, it is argued that the economic elite has come to prevail in U.S. society. Because of the growth of industry, plus the heightened concentration of wealth through mergers and trusts, the giant corporations now call the shots. The recent rise in the multinational corporation has further contributed to this domination. A multinational corporation like ITT can easily use its international operations to avoid taxes, circumvent antimonopoly laws, and in general resist government regulation. Power now lies in the hands of corporate leaders like Clifton C. Garvin (EXXON), Walter H. Page (J. P. Morgan and Company), or Thomas A. Murphy (General Motors).

4. This economic elite rules its own interests. Its basic goal is the preservation of the capitalist system, which allows for the accumulation of enormous wealth and social privilege. On occasion, when the stability of this system is threatened, subservient political leaders are allowed to make concessions to those less well off. Programs such as Medicare, public housing, or civil rights for blacks are little more than crumbs from the table and do not alter domination by the economic elite. Even programs designed to reduce the wealth of the elite, for example, the progressive income tax, are manipulated to achieve contrary results.

This, then, is the basic argument offered by those who believe that nongovernment power predominates in our society. It is an argument, however, not proof. Proving that the economic elite, not government officials, controls public policy is difficult. Recall that powerful private individuals supposedly avoid notoriety and would deny their influence. Nevertheless, advocates of the power elite argument have amassed considerable evidence in support of their claims. Each piece of evidence may not be conclusive proof, they believe, but the totality of the evidence points in the direction of elite domination.

HOW BIG IS BIG?

How big are the giant corporations such as Texaco, Ford, or IBM? One more way of appreciating their size is to compare them with entire countries. The top five U.S. companies in terms of total 1976 sales are listed below together with several foreign nations and their gross national product (gross national product, or GNP, is the total monetary value of all goods and services sold in one year).*

Nation or corporation	GNP or sales (1976) in billions
Japan	$550.2
Germany (West)	451.7
France	346.2
Italy	163.2
Sweden	74.1
EXXON	48.6
General Motors	47.2
Austria	40.4
Denmark	37.4
American Tel and Tel	32.8
Norway	30.2
Ford	28.8
Finland	28.3
Texaco	26.5
Greece	23.4

* Excluded from this analysis is the U.S. marijuana industry. According to the Federal Drug Enforcement Administration, Americans spend about $48 billion a year to import, distribute, and buy marijuana. This puts pot in the same league as EXXON and ahead of Austria in terms of dollar flow.

National GNP figures are from the *Statistical Abstract of the United States, 1978*, p. 900. Figures on corporate sales are reported in "The Forbes Sales 500," *Forbes.* May 15, 1977, p. 157.

CAPITOL GAMES

© 1976 Los Angeles Times. Reprinted by permission.

SUPPORT FOR THE POWER-ELITE ARGUMENT

One important type of supporting evidence concerns the corporate backgrounds of high government officials. Specifically, many high government officials are former executives of giant corporations or Wall Street law firms; when they finish their government work they return to the business world. For example, among modern secretaries of state John Foster Dulles, Dean Acheson, Christian Herter, and Cyrus Vance have all had strong ties with the economic elite. The Department of Defense has also drawn numerous high officials from private industry and Wall Street law firms. In fact, two heads of huge corporations were made secretaries of defense—Charles Wilson of General Motors and Robert McNamara of Ford. The Treasury and Commerce departments have likewise traditionally drawn top personnel from corporate management. Large corporations have also supplied Presidents with many of their foreign policy advisers—men like Clark Clifford, Averell Harriman, and John McCone. According to one study, of ninety-one individuals who were in important foreign policy positions between 1940 and 1967, seventy came from big business and high finance.[17]

The domination of big business and closely associated law firms can even be seen in the appointments made by President Carter. Despite Carter's frequent campaign pledges to bring new life to Washington and to return government to the people, many high-ranking appointees hold close corporate ties. For example, three cabinet-level officials—Cyrus Vance (Secretary of State), Harold Brown (Secretary of Defense), and Patricia Harris (Secretary of Health, Education and Welfare)—were directors of IBM. Kenneth S. Axelson, Deputy Secretary of the Treasury, once worked for the Grumman Corporation, a giant aerospace contractor. W. Graham Clayton, Jr., Secretary of the Navy, was president of Southern Railway Company and is a director of J. P. Morgan and Morgan Guaranty Trust. Griffin B. Bell, former Attorney General, once represented IBM in Atlanta (in Los Angeles IBM was previously represented

[17] Richard J. Barnet, *The Economy of Death* (New York: Atheneum, 1970), p. 88.

WHO BELIEVES IN THE POWER-ELITE ARGUMENT?

The idea that a small, cohesive group of unaccountable individuals controls the United States has appealed to very different types of people. Scholars who have advanced this idea have usually been sociologists with left-wing or Marxist politcal philosophies. Indeed, the idea of domination by an economic elite fits with the Marxist assertion that economic power (ownership of the means of production) determines all other aspects of society from art to politics. Other scholars who are not Marxists sometimes find the power-elite argument useful as an explanation of why major reforms are thwarted. Overall, academics sympathetic to the power-elite argument usually endorse such proposals as higher taxes on the rich, nuclear disarmament, guaranteed employment for everyone, and strict government measures to abolish racial and sexual discrimination in private employment.

Outside of academic life, however, the power-elite argument is frequently advocated by the extreme right wing. These people oppose programs such as the progressive income tax, the minimum wage, disarmament, welfare, and antidiscrimination laws. For these right-wingers it is the eastern liberal power elite that is responsible for the gradual Communist takeover of the United States. What makes this shared perspective especially interesting is that both left-wing academics and right-wing advocates usually identify the same people and institutions as the true (evil) powers. Here, for example, is how Robert Welch, founder of the ultraconservative John Birch Society, characterized the elite: "the powerful elitist groups run by the Rockefeller family, reaching into the giant multinational corporations, the mass media and the Establishment think tanks, and commanding leverage over the economy, politics, and public opinion of these United States."* The Council on Foreign Relations, viewed by left-wing academics as the embodiment of the conservative status quo, is viewed by right-wingers as intent on destroying U.S. national sovereignty, subverting the U.S. Constitution, and facilitating Soviet world conquest, all leading to the control of the United States by a Socialist-dominated world government.**

* Quoted in Robert Drury, "For What It's Worth: Right Wings Over America," *Crawdaddy*. September 1978, p. 18.
** Kent and Phoebe Courtney, *America's Unelected Rulers* (New Orleans: Conservative Society of America, 1962).

by Warren M. Christopher, Deputy Secretary of State). Secretary of Energy Charles W. Duncan is the ex-president of Coca Cola. Many of Carter's appointees also have close ties to prestigious Wall Street and Washington law firms.

Putting its people in key government positions is not the only way the economic elite can shape policy making. Since ex-government officials are rewarded with lucrative positions, they soon realize that if they want to do well, they do not alienate the corporate elite. For example, when Henry Kissinger left government office one of his new activities was that of highly paid consultant to Goldman, Sachs and Company, a large Wall Street investment banking firm.[18] Bryce Harlow, a close adviser to Presidents Eisenhower and Nixon, went to work for Proctor and Gamble after leaving government. Nicholas Katzenbach, former U.S. Attorney General under President Johnson, found a job at IBM. Between 1971 and 1975 almost half (48 percent) of all commissioners in government regulatory agencies who left took jobs with the regulated industries or law firms doing business with these industries.[19] The most blatant cases of going from government to well-paying corporate positions occur in the Department of Defense. Thousands of retired top defense department officials now work for Lockheed, North American Rockwell, Boeing, and other defense contractors.[20]

The role of private foundations

The economic elite has also created numerous private foundations and research organizations which supply government with ideas and technical advice. One such organization is the Council on Foreign Relations (CFR), founded in 1921 and dedicated to informing people about foreign affairs (it publishes the prestigious journal *Foreign Affairs*). Much of the financial support for the council comes from large corporations such as Gulf Oil and the Rockefeller and Carnegie foundations. An important function of the CFR is to bring government officials, business people, scholars, and military leaders together for informal, off-the-record discussions of foreign policy issues. Frequently, books and papers follow these discussions which are widely read and discussed within government. According to political writer Joseph Kraft, council activities have played a major role in shaping the U.N. charter, laying the groundwork for the Marshall Plan, which helped Europe recover economically after

[18] Kissinger's work for Goldman, Sachs (for which he is paid more than $100,000 a year) requires him to put in only three days a month. A major part of Kissinger's job consists of eating lunch with big-time customers. Kissinger is also taking the company's intensive course in financial management. "Kissinger Style Suits Wall Street," *New York Magazine*, July 31, 1978, p. 6.

[19] Data cited in "Serving Two Masters: A Common Cause Study of Conflict of Interest in the Executive Branch" (Washington, D.C.: Common Cause, 1976), p. i.

[20] Data collected by the nonprofit public interest Council on Economic Priorities found that between 1969 and 1973, 1,406 Department of Defense officials accepted jobs with defense contractors after leaving government. Cited in "Serving Two Masters," p. 58.

World War II, and shaping U.S. policy toward NATO. Many government officials, for example, Henry Kissinger and presidential adviser McGeorge Bundy, began their public service careers through the Council of Foreign Relations.[21]

The CFR is only one of many such groups. The federal government has long made use of the RAND Corporation, founded after World War II as an Air Force "think tank." Started in part with Ford Foundation money, it has maintained close ties to large corporations through its board of trustees (about half the trustees have come from corporations such as Hewlett-Packard or Monsanto, while the others were university administrators or physicists). Not surprisingly, in light of its origins and corporate ties, RAND has been criticized frequently by radicals for giving intellectual and technical support for policies that favor well-established interests. RAND studies have concerned such topics as guerrilla warfare, nuclear deterrence, U.S.-Soviet relations, energy policy, the implications of technology, and many other important political issues.[22]

The use of material rewards
In addition to the interchange of personnel and private study groups such as the Council on Foreign Relations, economic elites are not above the use of material incentives to dominate public officials. In some instances this simply involves dispensing envelopes stuffed with cash in return for specific favors. It is difficult to estimate how much out-and-out bribery occurs, but recent Watergate-related investigations suggest that corporate bribery was widespread and involved many millions. Between 1960 and 1974, for example, Gulf Oil spent $5.4 million on illegal political contributions. This money supposedly went to such prominent leaders as Lyndon B. Johnson (as Vice President-elect in 1960), Representative Wilbur Mills (D.-Ark.), Senator Henry Jackson (D.-Wash.), Senator Hugh Scott (R.-Pa.), and several others.[23] Recent and more stringent rules prohibiting corporate political contributions have been largely circumvented through the use of political action committees (PACs). These are organizations set up and run by corporations, but the money comes from voluntary gifts from employees or anyone else. In 1976, business-oriented PACs donated $6.9 million to congressional candidates in general elections.[24]

Recall, however, from our analysis of interest group techniques in Chapter 9 that such cash contributions are only part of the bribery picture. Many large corporations provide free airplane trips, tickets to sport-

[21] The role of the Council on Foreign Relations is described further in Domhoff, *The Higher Circles*, Chap. 5.

[22] During its first twenty-five years RAND produced some 13,000 publications, sponsored over 2,000 articles in professional journals, and was responsible for about 175 books produced by commercial or university publishers. About 20 percent of this total is classified under Department of Defense security regulations. *RAND: 25th Anniversary Volume* (Santa Monica, Calif.: RAND, 1973), p. 1.

[23] Mintz and Cohen, *Power, Inc.*, pp. 178–180.

[24] Charles W. Hucker, "Corporate Political Action Committees," *Practical Politics*, May/June 1978, pp. 21–25.

PRESIDENT CARTER AND THE TRILATERAL COMMISSION

While the Council on Foreign Relations may have been the preeminent private foreign policy advising body in the 1950s and 1960s, the Trilateral Commission presently occupies that position. This private organization was created in 1973 by David Rockefeller, chairman of the Chase Manhattan Bank (1977 assets: $53.18 billion). Its purpose was to promote cooperation and understanding among the United States, Japan, and Western Europe. Its approximately 240 members drawn from business, academic, and political circles meet about once every nine months to discuss common social and political problems. Sponsors such as the Ford Foundation and the Rockefeller Brothers Fund provide most of its financial support. Other income comes from individual donations, corporate gifts, and investment income. Its budget from mid-1976 to mid-1978 was $1,180,388.

Most of the recent prominence of the Trilateral Commission has resulted from President Carter's extensive use of fellow commission members. Before he became President he consulted with sixteen Trilateral members. On taking office almost every top foreign policy position has been filled by people drawn from the commission. Besides Carter, top Trilateral people include Vice President Walter Mondale, National Security Adviser Zbigniew Brzezinski, Secretary of State Cyrus Vance, former Secretary of the Treasury Michael Blumenthal, Secretary of Defense Harold Brown, and former U.N. Ambassador Andrew Young. In all, seventeen Trilateral members were appointed to high government positions.

President Carter admits that much of his education on international affairs comes from his experience on the Trilateral Commission. He himself described this experience as "a splendid learning opportunity." The President's close association with National Security Adviser Brzezinski derives in part from Brzezinski's position as Carter's mentor in Trilateral affairs. Carter's Trilateral experience also served as an excellent opportunity for him to show corporate and media leaders that he was informed and serious, not a rustic yahoo.*

* President Carter may value highly his Trilateral experience, but not everyone is as positive in their evaluations. As Lieutenant Robert Stark, national president of the Fraternal Order of Police, addressing the annual police appreciation dinner of the Wheeling, West Virginia, Lions Club said: "Don't get me wrong. I'm not saying all public officials are bad. But . . . our leaders are leftists, communists, homosexuals, violent agitators, and members of the Trilateral Commission." Quoted in *The Progressive*, January 1979, p. 13.

President Carter's relationship to the Trilateral Commission is described further in William Greider, "Trilateralists To Abound in Carter's White House," *The Washington Post*, January 16, 1977; and "Trilateral Commission: How Influential?" *U.S. News and World Report*, May 22, 1978, pp. 74–75.

Nondecision The continuation of a policy without a conscious decision or discussion.

ing events, weekends at plush resorts, and the like, to political leaders. These favors are not in exchange for specific services but are intended to create a feeling of good will between the political leader and the business providing the favors. Corporations see such actions as a long-term strategy necessary to create a positive atmosphere, which would make cash payments and other crude influence techniques unnecessary.

The elite use of the mass media

Finally, defenders of the power-elite position argue that the existence of modern, all-pervasive mass media allow the giant corporations (which control the media) to defeat any attacks on themselves whether from government or private citizens. The nonelite newspapers, magazines, radio, and television stations that challenge elite domination may lose their advertisers and quickly go bankrupt. Large corporations like EXXON or General Motors use the media to sell elite domination through "institutional" advertisements depicting how they are helping to make the United States a better and safer place in which to live.[25] It can even be argued that by endlessly bombarding the public with ads for new, bigger, and better consumer goods, for example, the home donut factory, the elite uses the media to create a materialism that reinforces its position. Such materialism is not only profitable—just when you thought that the 10-quart slow cooker was the ultimate appliance along came the electric hot dog maker—but the illusion is created that things are getting better and better thanks to private industry.

Elite power and nondecision

A key element in the elite argument is the concept of "nondecision." Essentially, a decision is a *conscious* act either to change something or to leave it unchanged. People are *aware* of making a choice. A **nondecision**, however, is when a situation continues without a conscious choice being made. A nondecision may involve the continuation of an existing policy with little debate. Or an issue may be kept off the public agenda by the elite without public debate over what should be done. Unlike decisions, nondecisions attract little attention, discussion, or controversy. The idea of nondecisions is important to the elite argument because it is through nondecisions that the economic elite exercises its greatest power.

To illustrate how nondecisions work, let us look at the policy of private ownership of U.S. energy resources. Obviously, keeping companies such as Texaco, Atlantic Richfield, and Standard Oil of California in private hands is essential if the economic elite is to maintain its predominant position (the top ten oil companies alone had total profits in 1977 of $9.85 billion). It could be reasonably argued, however, that government ownership of energy production is essential in a period of shortages and sharply increasing prices. In fact, several nations such as Mexico reached this conclusion years ago and took over all private companies. Nevertheless,

[25] Some of these tactics are described more fully in Fred R. Harris, "The Politics of Corporate Power," in Ralph Nader and Mark J. Green, eds., *Corporate Power in America* (New York: Grossman, 1973).

The board of directors of an investment company at work. Advocates of the power-elite argument believe that many key national decisions are made in surroundings such as these.

this alternative is rarely given serious political attention in the United States. Despite some talk of greater regulation of energy industries by government, the basic issue of energy ownership is not debated. Private ownership is thus a nondecision, and people who raise the issue might find themselves in trouble. Proponents of public ownership of oil might have difficulty finding a good job in private industry, their arguments would be ignored by the national media and political leaders, and the idea would be dismissed as unrealistic or un-American by "responsible" officials in the energy industry. Of course, it would be difficult to show that the elite explicitly killed off the plan because the proposal never emerged in the first place in the form of a clear yes or no choice.[26]

For many people this theory of domination by an economic elite has considerable appeal. It helps to explain why many pressing social and economic problems remain unsolved despite the enormous wealth in the United States. Why, they ask, are many inner-city areas allowed to rot while suburban areas experience rapid growth? The answer is that the giant corporations, insurance companies, and banks have found it more profitable to invest in suburban growth and have used their power to prevent programs to help inner cities. Power-elite domination also helps to explain our national obsession with fighting communism and our Cold War mentality. Anticommunism, the argument goes, helps maintain a highly profitable defense establishment. Ending the Cold War would channel money away from the elite and into such programs as income subsidies and better health care for the poor.

THE ARGUMENT AGAINST THE EXISTENCE OF A POWER ELITE

Not everyone is convinced that there is a nongovernmental elite that dominates public policy. Nobody denies that there are individuals with enormous economic and political power and that the United States is a land of large corporations. Critics of the power-elite argument believe, however, that the political impact of these individuals and corporations

[26] For a further discussion of nondecision see Peter Bachrach and Morton S. Baratz, "Decisions and Nondecisions," *American Political Science Review*, 57 (1963), pp. 632–642. Also see Raymond E. Wolfinger, "Nondecisions and the Study of Local Politics," *American Political Science Review*, 65 (1971), pp. 1063–1079.

Capital gains tax A tax on the profits made from selling things like land, buildings, or stock. Capital gains tax rates are generally lower than income tax rates for wealthy individuals.

does not add up to elite domination. General Electric, Ford, and U.S. Steel are powerful, but to claim that such companies collectively run the United States is a gross oversimplification. The economic-elite argument has been attacked on several specific grounds.

First, to show that many public officials have corporate affiliations is not by itself proof that as government officials they automatically advance corporate interests. This can happen, but people can also change, and it is not unusual to find businesspeople critical of certain aspects of corporate policy (for example, insensitivity to social problems). The absence of a one-to-one relationship between background and policy was illustrated in the strong opposition of Michael Blumenthal, former Secretary of the Treasury under President Carter, to liberalization of the **capital gains tax.** Blumenthal was once president of the Bendix Corporation, yet in 1978 he vigorously opposed a tax measure that would be enormously valuable for businesses like Bendix, Blumenthal characterized the capital gains tax as tax relief for millionaires and spoke against it on numerous occasions.

A second attack on the power-elite argument concerns the claim that members of the elite share common goals. At a general level this is no doubt true—like all citizens, members of the economic elite accept policies such as a strong national defense, economic growth, and the sanctity of private property. However, when we examine more specific policy choices elite unity frequently breaks down. For example, when the federal government decided to rescue Lockheed from financial collapse, no cheers came from Boeing or McDonnell-Douglas, despite the fact that all three companies are supposedly part of the same economic elite. Besides competition within industries (General Motors versus Ford) competition exists across industries. On tariff issues, for example, most agricultural interests support free trade while electronics manufacturers want greater protection from cheap imports. Rarely, if ever, can the economic elite act with common purpose.

The economic-elite argument has also been criticized on the grounds that this domination has never been adequately demonstrated. Advocates of the elite-domination argument can rarely point to more than a few elite-inspired decisions. Even then, these decisions are so general, for example, encouraging the creation of NATO, that it is virtually impossible to show that one group of the many involved coerced the government into accepting its policies. In such cases it is equally plausible that government officials convinced economic leaders, with the economic leaders then attempting to marshal public support for government-determined policies.

If anything, the record seems to demonstrate that government has exerted more power over the economic sector than vice versa. In the last twenty years the federal government has forced corporations to accept numerous policies they have bitterly opposed. These include more stringent pollution regulations, strengthened consumer-protection laws, prohibition against discrimination in hiring, more emphasis on employee safety, and numerous other expensive and cumbersome government regulations. That companies successfully defeated the more extreme versions of these measures is certainly not proof that private power won out over government. Moreover, these government-imposed rules came at a time when corporate power has become increasingly concentrated and when profits, assets, and other indicators of corporate strength are at an all-time high.

Criticisms of nondecision

The concept of nondecision has also come under attack. First, critics say that it is frequently employed so loosely that it can never be disproved and is therefore not very useful. For example, it is sometimes argued that the economic elite who control oil, natural gas, and coal resources prevent the full utilization of "free" energy such as solar power or wind power. This is accomplished by making little financial investment in new technology, buying controlling interests in solar and wind power companies, and manipulating public opinion against these new energy sources. As a result, our overwhelming dependence (on elite-controlled) fossil fuel continues as a nondecision. Critics of nondecision assert that this type of argument is like blaming all evil on "mysterious dark forces" that can never be seen. Rather than examine important decisions to see who won and who lost, all objectionable decisions are instead conveniently blamed on the power elite. If it turns out that oil companies had no direct role in the failure of a solar-energy project, it can still be asserted that they really did, but it was by means of a well-concealed conspiracy.

A second criticism of the nondecision argument concerns whether nondecisions occur when people disagree over important issues. Suppose that every Friday you and your friends have beer and a mushroom pizza. Also suppose that you are the only one who wants mushroom pizza; everyone else would rather have anchovies or chopped liver. If your preferences predominate without any discussion or conflict, you have used your power to create a nondecision—that is, mushroom pizza is automatically ordered despite other people's dislike for it. On the other hand, if everyone shares your mushroom craving, you really have exercised no power. To show that one person (or group) has power over another person (or group), one must show that people differed on what they wanted.

When advocates of the economic-elite position point to important nondecisions they rarely—if ever—determine whether the elite wanted something different from what everyone else wanted. Perhaps the main reason the elite is so successful in maintaining the capitalistic system is that it has no opposition from either the government or ordinary citizens. Similarly, a large defense budget may be good business for big corporations, but it can also be good business for government leaders and the millions of workers who benefit from this spending. To assert that we have capitalism or large defense budgets because of elite-enforced nondecisions is to claim power when power was not employed.

The final criticism of the elite position concerns the implicit assumption within this argument that *somebody* must have final power in society. Recall that elitists see society as comprised of key institutions—the economy, the military, and so on—with each organized like a pyramid.

Pluralist One who sees society as composed of numerous conflicting groups with no one group dominating the others. Policy results from bargaining among interests.

This perspective automatically leads elite-oriented researchers to ask: Who is at the very top? They may have differences of opinion (for example, corporate presidents versus very wealthy families), but they assume that *somebody* ultimately has final authority. This assumption can be challenged, however. It is equally plausible that in complex modern societies no one person or group controls a significant share of power. Power may be fragmented, with hundreds of interests holding "a piece of the action." To ask "Who's at the top?" is to ask a highly misleading question. The first and most important question is: Is there anyone at the top?

Thus far we have seen that the elite position can be criticized on several grounds. A fair question is whether critics can offer a better alternative analysis of the relationship between private and public power. If the economic elite does not dominate government, what then is the relationship between private power and government?

THE PLURALIST ALTERNATIVE

Another school of thought, commonly called the **pluralist,** is very different from the elite perspective.[27] Unlike elitists, pluralists see society as comprised of a multitude of loosely related, frequently conflicting groups. There is no one economic sector, for example. Rather, there are hundreds of companies organized into dozens of trade associations. Pluralists also place greater weight on ethnic, racial, and religious groups. Membership in these groups frequently overlaps—we have Catholic wheat farmers advocating high wheat prices and Catholic bakers interested in cheap wheat. Thus, it is difficult for a group to act cohesively across numerous issues because members feel pulls in different directions. For example, two wealthy businesspeople may support the same economic policy, but if one is Protestant and the other is Jewish, they might disagree on U.S.-Israel policy.

Pluralists also believe that politically relevant resources are also widely dispersed. The financial resources available to the economic elite are not the only chips in the game. Money can be countered by large numbers of people voting together, persuasive arguments, threats of violence, passive resistance, boycotts, and many other techniques. Moreover, those with lesser resources can win if they use their resources skillfully. If money were the only factor in winning, how could you explain the electoral defeats of numerous well-financed candidates? More important, if concentrated economic resources were all powerful, how are the remarkable accomplishments of the poorly financed black civil rights organizations or the women's movement to be explained?

[27] As was true for the elite-domination position, there is no single pluralist perspective. We emphasize arguments that most pluralists would generally accept. Some of the major pluralist arguments can be found in David B. Truman, *The Governmental Process,* 2d ed. (New York: Knopf, 1971), especially Chap. 16; Robert A. Dahl, *Who Governs?* (New Haven, Conn.: Yale University Press, 1961), especially Chaps. 27–28; and Nelson W. Polsby, *Community Power and Political Theory* (New Haven, Conn.: Yale University Press, 1963), especially Chaps. 6–7.

According to the pluralists, public policy emerges from the interplay of group conflict, not elite domination. Differences are resolved through bargaining. No single group can dictate policy in one area for long, and certainly no elite group is capable of dictating policies in several different areas. Obviously, not all groups are equal players, and some interests consistently do better than others. However, inequality does not mean that some interests always win while others always lose. For example, for years the oil interests were considered an extremely powerful group that virtually "owned" parts of the government. In 1975, however, the oil industry (except for small producers) lost an enormously beneficial tax provision, the 27.5 percent oil-depletion allowance. In addition, "loser" groups can sometimes be transformed into winners through skillful organization. Consider the impact Ralph Nader and his associates have had in making once lowly consumer interests a force in national politics.

Another key element in the pluralist argument is that powerful interests can frequently offset one another. Who, for instance, can be counted on to protect the public from price gouging by the giant steel companies? One such "protector" is the giant automobile companies that need cheap steel to keep their prices competitive with German and Japanese imports. Recall from our analysis of interest groups in Chapter 9 that on most important issues different organizations are in conflict with one another. Such balancing of pressure does not guarantee perfect equality of power, but it does prevent one interest from consistently imposing its preferences.

According to the pluralist perspective, there is rarely a clear hierarchical relationship between government and private organizations such as corporations or labor unions. Government does not systematically control nongovernment power centers, or vice versa. Instead, nongovernmental organizations and government usually share considerable power, with neither having dictatorial control. Consider the relationship between large labor unions and government. On the one hand, government exercises broad power over union affairs. Through legislation the federal government has told union officials how to run union elections, how to keep financial records, and what antimanagement practices they can use. On the other hand, antiunion people have frequently alleged that government is under the thumb of big-time labor. They argue that labor leaders have automatic access to Presidents and members of Congress. They also note that many powerful Democratic politicians are heavily indebted to labor for their campaign support and that labor leaders handpick top government officials who set labor policy.

If sharp conflicts do occur between governmental and nongovernmental power, it is the former that usually prevails – at least in the short run. The government's power to coerce people through fines or imprisonment is decisive. When the federal government decided that auto pollution had to be reduced, top auto executives protested vehemently, but they gave in rather than face heavy fines. In the long run, however, private organizations have the opportunity to work at changing objectionable governmental policy. Auto manufacturers can lobby to repeal tough auto-emission regulations, contribute money to sympathetic congressional candidates, or sponsor public relations campaigns to mobilize public opinion against "excessive and expensive pollution equipment that contributes to the energy crisis."

The elitist criticism of the pluralist approach

Needless to say, proponents of the power-elite argument do not view the pluralist approach as a better analysis of U.S. politics. They admit, however, that pluralism has a degree of validity when it comes to comparatively minor, day-to-day political decisions, for example, whether the social security tax will be increased 6 percent instead of 7 percent. However, advocates of the power-elite position fault pluralists for ignoring the overall pattern of benefits in our society. The pluralist is like the naive roulette player who claims that he or she can win because he or she is treated just as fairly as any other player—not realizing, of course, that the unseen house maintains the edge. The rules of the game are stacked against the person in the long run. For the advocates of the elite position, the contemporary economic elite is like the gambling house—it sets the rules and provides occasional "victory" to foster the illusion of real power.

RESOLVING THE POWER-ELITE-PLURALIST DEBATE

Our discussion of whether private organizations dominate the government has only scratched the surface of a long-standing and highly complex debate. As in many lengthy debates, fundamental differences exist regarding how key terms are defined and measured. Advocates of the elite argument tend to view money, institutional position, and social standing as indicators of "power." Pluralists, however, view these as mere resources that *may* lead to power. Power to the pluralists can be found only in actual decision making as people try to affect policy decisions. Hence, when pluralists and elitists argue over who has the power in the United States, they are usually talking about different things. Similar differences of opinion occur over what is an "important decision," deciding who really won in a conflict, and almost every other aspect of analysis. For example, does the sudden increase in oil prices (and oil company profits) truly indicate the existence of elite domination? Pluralists and elitists would probably give different answers, because each would approach the question from a different perspective.

Which position comes closer to the truth? Experts differ, but we can at least note that the pluralist position is supported by more direct evidence. Major points in the pluralist approach, such as conflicts among groups, the dispersion of politically relevant resources, and the importance of government in decisions, have been well documented. In contrast, many of the elite arguments rest on more indirect evidence. For example, to show that the economic elite shares basic goals, elitists amass information to demonstrate the similar social backgrounds of corporate leaders. Rarely are the leaders themselves interviewed or their actions observed firsthand. Advocates of the elite position have had particular difficulty in showing how major government decisions are concretely controlled by elites. At best they have shown that elite members were involved with these decisions, but involvement does not necessarily mean control. Of course, an elite of nongovernmental individuals may in fact control government, but for the present this is more an assertion than a proven conclusion.

To return to our original question: What is the relationship between private and public power? Many people believe that the United States is presently dominated by a nongovernmental elite comprised of leaders of giant corporations and related financial institutions. This elite dominates government through a variety of techniques ranging from the interchange of personnel to outright bribery. Its power is frequently realized through nondecisions that maintain existing arrangements beneficial to elite interests or that keep policy alternatives off the public agenda. Pluralists, however, reject the main idea that government is dominated by private power. They see no one private interest as being able to dictate to all others. Moreover, at least in the short run, the government's power is sufficient to enforce its will over any giant corporation or bank. In the long run these actions may be reversed. This reversal of a particular policy, however, does not prove that government is wholly dominated by a unified economic elite.

A conclusion: private power

The issue of nongovernmental power raises one of the most complex and perplexing conflicts in U.S. politics. Our discussion so far has largely concerned the possibility that private governments may dominate the lives of citizens either through private regulation or a more encompassing power elite. But there is another issue that must be addressed which involves private government: the right of the individual to do as he or she pleases versus the obligation of the government to promote the common interest by exercising its powers. While most people would worry over the existence of vast unaccountable private power, preventing the exercise of such power raises several controversies. Everyone agrees that some government control over private activities is essential, but just how far should this intervention go? Should the federal government prohibit the local Lions Club from discriminating against women or blacks? Should employers be required by government to give their employees an hour for lunch and ten free trips to the bathroom per day? We now have extensive federal regulations on job safety, but can this regulation logically be extended to cover what workers eat in the company cafeteria?

Some people fear that growing government intervention in private organizations—whether small social clubs or General Motors—will ultimately lead to the loss of our political freedom. While government intervention may begin with the highest goals, for example, banning the economic exploitation of children, it can open the door for future abuse. Yesterday it was preventing child exploitation; today it is health and safety rules; tomorrow it will be the rigid quotas for the hiring of minorities and the handicapped. At each stage there is less personal choice and more government orders. For opponents of government intervention, the drawing of a sharp line between public and private decisions represents a key bulwark against an evil, overzealous government.

The question of government intervention can, however, be posed very differently. We can ask: Should decisions with important public consequences be made by private individuals who are not publicly accountable? Should decisions regarding whether we use oil, coal, or atomic power be made in the boardrooms of EXXON or Mobil Oil? Should our social commitment to equality be administered by the personnel officers of profit-oriented private companies? Such decisions involve key public choices, and many people believe that they should be resolved solely by government. The government may not always make the best decisions, but public officials are at least accountable for their actions and can be removed through elections. The president of EXXON has no obligation to the general public and cannot be removed by ordinary citizens for his blunders.

Obviously, we face a dilemma. On the one hand, many of us fear and resent government intervention in what we consider nongovernmental matters. Professors complain about stupid government rules undermining the university. Businesspeople complain that they can no longer run their businesses as they want. Social organizations resent government stipulations concerning whom they must admit or serve liquor. On the other hand, where broad public issues are involved, we expect government to intervene on behalf of the common good. If universities refused to admit qualified female or black applicants, many of us would call for government intervention in the private affairs of universities.

In many ways whether or not we accept government intervention in private organizations depends on what we consider to be an issue with significant public impact. This is a highly controversial question. Under present civil rights law, for example, a hotel's refusal to rent rooms to blacks is a public issue. An oil company's decision to import more foreign oil rather than seek new domestic sources, however, is presently a private decision. This situation is complicated by the fact that millions of seemingly "private" decisions can have a public impact; for example, if every restaurant refused to serve blacks, blacks would find it impossible to travel. Unfortunately, there are no self-evident answers regarding what is a strictly private organization and how far government intervention ought to extend.

Major questions raised

1. What is the nature of private government? All citizens are subject to nongovernmentally set rules and regulations in schools, occupations, social organizations, and religious groups. A major question is whether such power should be exercised democratically. Proponents of internal group democracy claim that this would make the United States more

democratic and benefit everyone. It is argued, however, that while such democracy is desirable, it is not essential in our political system.

2. What is the relationship between private and public power. Some people argue that private power dominates government through the existence of a nonaccountable economic elite. While government officials run our daily affairs, this elite controls more fundamental decisions. Pluralists argue, however, that no single group dominates. Power is dispersed, and at least in the short run the government cannot be controlled by large corporations and other elite groups.

QUESTIONS FOR FURTHER DISCUSSION

1. Making large corporations "accountable" to the public has been a major issue in recent years. Those who speak for large corporations claim that they are already publicly accountable in two ways: (1) anyone can buy stock in a company, and since stockholders ultimately control a company, the public sets corporate policy; and (2) a corporation can be punished for its actions by consumers who can refuse to purchase its products. People like consumer advocate Ralph Nader claim that such "accountability" is nonsense. To make corporations such as General Motors or Gulf Oil truly accountable, representatives of the general public committed to the overall public interest should be on decision-making boards of large corporations. Which approach seems more effective in making large corporations more sensitive to the needs of the public? Is either proposal likely to be effective? Is the only solution public ownership of big companies? Is public accountability possible at all? Is *public* accountability of *private* companies a contradiction in terms?

2. The line between private and public matters frequently becomes a matter of debate in university regulation of fraternities and sororities. If a group of students, with its own money, purchases a house so as to establish a society to worship Keg, the Milwaukee deity of joy, should the university have any say over these matters? Does a university have the right to tell people how to run their nonuniversity lives even if actions do not affect the university? What if the Keg worshippers refused to allow women in their ranks but the university was state supported and the state had a law forbidding discrimination against women where state funds are involved? Can the university say that since Keg worshippers attend a state-subsidized university, and since the state prohibits discrimination based on sex, students are therefore governed by this antidiscrimination rule? Would it make a difference if the university were privately owned but some students received state scholarships? What if no state money were involved? Could the university still set policy for the Keg worshippers?

3. Defenders of the power-elite argument frequently claim that one major mechanism of elite control is the early indoctrination of citizens. As children, most of us were taught that big business is concerned with ordinary people and is responsible for the wonders of American civilization. Communism and socialism were portrayed as evil and un-American. As a result of this early learning, adults by "free choice" accept capitalist domination of society as the best policy. What evidence exists that the economic elite manipulates early education to reinforce its domination

of society? Have you yourself been manipulated? Might not the manipulators convince you that you have not been manipulated?

4. If you were elected President of the United States on a platform of reducing the power of large corporations in government, which strategy would you follow to achieve your goal:

a. Refuse to appoint anyone to a policy-making position who has worked for a large corporation or is a lawyer that handled work for a large corporation.

b. Appoint people with corporate backgrounds but insist that they break all financial connections with their companies and agree not to work for them after leaving government.

c. Appoint people with corporate backgrounds who have been critical of undue corporate influence over government. These appointees, better than anyone else, understand how corporations work and how they influence government.

d. Given a choice among equally qualified people, appoint the person most prominently associated with a major corporation (for example, Henry Ford II). The actions of this official will attract so much scrutiny that it will be impossible to advance corporate economic interests.

BIBLIOGRAPHY

Barnet, Richard J., and Ronald E. Muller, *Global Reach: The Power of the Multinational Corporation.* New York: Simon & Schuster, 1974.
> A journalistic but well-researched analysis of several major multinational corporations. The authors tend to be unsympathetic to the behavior of these corporations and present several cases of what they consider to be abuses of power.

Dye, Thomas R. *Who's Running America*, 2d ed. Englewood Cliffs, N.J.: Prentice-Hall, 1979.
> Describes top leaders in business, politics, the mass media, and civic associations. Analyzes how these leaders got to the top, the relations among them, and how they make public policy. Especially useful for good biographical sketches of leaders.

Domhoff, G. William. *The Higher Circles: The Governing Class in America.* New York: Vintage Books, 1971.
> Advances the argument that the United States is ruled by people from the upper social class. Considerable information on the people in the upper class is presented, and three chapters show how key foreign and domestic decisions are influenced by upper-class people. Concludes with a detailed rejoinder to the pluralistic argument on political power.

Ewing, David W. *Freedom Inside the Organization: Bringing Civil Liberties to the Workplace.* New York: Dutton, 1977.
> A clearly written analysis of personal freedom inside private companies. Provides many examples of how freedom is restricted as well as recent legal developments in employee recourse. Provides several suggestions on how to balance the principles of free speech with economic productivity.

Gilb, Corrine Lathrop. *Hidden Hierarchies: The Professions and Government.* New York: Harper & Row, 1966.
> A well-documented study of how the professions such as law and medicine control their own members and set policy in public areas. Describes how these private governments gained control of their fields, the interplay between professions and politics, and some of the consequences of having private governments set public policy.

Mills, C. Wright. *The Power Elite.* New York: Oxford University Press, 1959.
A highly influential book which claims that the United States is ruled by military and corporate leaders who work behind the scenes. Most of the book describes members of the military-industrial elite and how they rose to power. Though extensively criticized, *The Power Elite* is far more than a crude conspiracy theory of political power. Deserves to be read by those interested in the elitist-pluralist debate.

Mintz, Morton, and Jerry S. Cohen. *America, Inc.: Who Owns and Operates the United States.* New York: Dell, 1971.
Argues that the large corporation rules the United States. Presents numerous incidents that illustrate how big business has exerted its influence over government and provides the names of the culprits and the nature of the wrongdoings. Concludes with specific recommendations for correcting the pattern of widespread corporate abuses of power.

Mintz, Morton, and Jerry S. Cohen. *Power, Inc.: Public and Private Rulers and How To Make Them Accountable.* New York: Bantam Books, 1977.
A lengthy and diverse analysis of power inside and outside governments. Extensive documentation of government secrecy, abuses of power by public officials, corporate bribery, abuses of public trust by professional organizations, and other seamy aspects of U.S. politics.

Nadel, Mark V. *Corporations and Political Accountability.* Lexington, Mass.: Heath, 1976.
Addresses the important questions of the relationship between government and the large corporations. Examines how corporations influence government and what can be done to limit excessive influence. Well documented with numerous illustrations and data from government studies.

Nader, Ralph, Mark Green, and Joel Seligman. *Taming the Giant Corporation.* New York: Norton, 1976.
A critical analysis of the modern big corporation. Considers how large corporations affect our lives, who controls the corporation, how power is exercised over company employees, and why the marketplace cannot stop corporate misdeeds. Argues that regulation by the national government—not the states—would help "tame" irresponsible companies.

Prewitt, Kenneth, and Alan Stone. *The Ruling Elites: Elite Theory, Power, and American Democracy.* New York: Harper & Row, 1973.
A brief but very useful analysis of the long debate over whether society is always elite dominated. Covers the role of elites in early American history as well as more recent evidence of elite power. The elite-pluralist debate is described, and the existence of current American elites is discussed in detail.

Polsby, Nelson W. *Community Power and Political Theory.* New Haven, Conn.: Yale University Press, 1963.
Though largely concerned with the exercise of power at the local level, Polsby's analysis applies more generally to the debate between elitists and pluralists. Many studies showing elite domination are reviewed and criticized. Particularly useful for spelling out the pluralist view of political power.

Ridgeway, James. *The Closed Corporation: American Universities in Crisis.* New York: Ballantine Books, 1969.
Documents the growing close association between corporate power and large universities. Shows how university professors make lots of money through business connections and how universities help the government wage war. Presents much evidence on how universities are "used" despite their claims of being above economic gain or political conflict.

Rodgers, William. *THINK: A Biography of the Watsons and IBM.* New York: Stein and Day, 1969.
A fascinating and not always favorable history of the emergence of IBM. Especially useful for providing a picture of how a corporation can mold thousands of employees into a single product, all with the same dark suits, white shirts, and short haircuts.

PREVIEW

How does government affect the economy?

First, the government influences the economy through its policies that encourage economic development. Taxes and subsidies are a second source of impact. Federal taxes take almost a third of the gross national product (GNP), and they can affect many noneconomic behaviors. Important subsidies include cash payments, reduced tax liability, and low-cost loans. Regulations, a third form of government impact, not only affect prices but also influence who can compete economically and what goods and services are available. Government consumption of goods and services also affects the economy. Finally, the government itself plays a direct economic role as a producer of goods and services.

What are the economic goals of government?

Many mechanisms of government economic intervention are used to promote moderate growth of the GNP. Full employment is a second basic goal, though this is not interpreted to mean zero unemployment. A third objective of government economic policy is a low inflation rate. Until the late 1960s, high inflation was not a serious problem, and contemporary economists differ on what is an "acceptable" inflation rate and how it is best treated. Maintaining a private enterprise is a fifth major government goal even though recent administrations have taken many actions that limit business and industry. Finally, many government programs are designed to preserve the large middle-class population in the United States.

Conflict often occurs over goal priorities—economic growth versus a low inflation rate, for example. Disagreements also occur over how to reach goals. The trade-off between purely economic aims and humanitarian objectives can also cause conflict. Differences among experts and problems of implementing economic policy further contribute to conflict.

The problems of formulating economic policy are illustrated by President Carter's anti-inflation programs. Despite the severity of the problem, his anti-inflation policies were constrained by other goals, especially maintaining prosperity and keeping social welfare programs.

Has the federal government become too involved in the economy?

The government's extensive economic involvement has come under attack in the last few years. Critics such as Milton Friedman assert that individual freedom and economic efficiency would be increased if government played only a limited economic role. This perspective has been criticized for ignoring the power of wealthy interests to dominate society unless they are restructured by government. Moreover, history shows that complete free enterprise can lead to economic disaster. The conflict between unrestrained capitalism and extensive state intervention is unlikely, however, to ever be decisively resolved.

CHAPTER EIGHTEEN

GOVERNMENT AND THE ECONOMY

t was once customary to draw a sharp line between "politics" and "economics." Especially for early twentieth-century conservatives the mixing of politics and economics was viewed as somehow un-American or socialistic. Even today many people are unaware of the close connections among their jobs, the overall economy, and government action. The fact is, however, that politics and economics in the United States have traditionally been closely intertwined. No economic decision is completely divorced from politics. Such economic factors as the value of the dollar, interest rates, the use of courts to enforce agreements, private property, and the types of economic activities permitted ultimately derive from political decisions. Moreover, some of the most heated political conflicts involve economics. Few issues can galvanize citizens to action as quickly as increased taxes or the elimination of their government subsidies. This chapter examines three important questions dealing with the relationship between politics and economics.

1. How does the government affect the economy?
2. What are the economic goals of government?
3. Has the government become too involved in the economy?

How does the government affect the economy?

In contemporary society virtually every government action has economic consequences. President Carter's concern for world-wide human rights, for example, may have repercussions on U.S.-Soviet trade. Similarly, government requirements that airplanes provide no smoking sections may reduce the income of North Carolina and Virginia tobacco farmers. Although almost every government action has some economic consequences, we can distinguish among five different types of government economic involvement: (1) promoting economic development; (2) taxes and subsidies; and (3) regulation; (4) government consumption; and (5) government-owned enterprises.

PROMOTING ECONOMIC DEVELOPMENT

The obligation of the government to further economic development can be traced back to pre-Revolutionary times. Colonial governments frequently employed such techniques as tax incentives, government loans, land grants, and monopolies to encourage prosperity. Part of this early government commitment to the economy was spelled out in the Constitution. In Article 1, section 8, Congress is given the right to coin and to regulate money, to establish post offices, to punish counterfeiting, and to issue patents and copyrights to protect inventors and authors. Section 9 of Article I also encourages growth by prohibiting taxes on exports and laws giving one port preference over another.

The most important contribution to economic development made by the early national government was providing a stable and orderly commercial environment. Without a recognized currency, enforceable, uniform laws regulating business transactions, a sound credit structure, and freedom from banditry and piracy, the economy would have been reduced to primitive local barter. In fact, it was the near-collapse of commerce under the Articles of Confederation that led to the stronger Constitution. From the perspective of complex, modern government economic policy, standardizing the currency across different states, providing a reliable national postal system, and protecting U.S. ships from pirates may seem simple. However, establishing these basic conditions was a major contribution essential for subsequent growth.

Having achieved the basic political framework in which the economy could develop, nineteenth-century federal and state governments turned to more ambitious proposals. At the urging of Secretary of the Treasury Alexander Hamilton, the federal government instituted a tariff policy designed to protect newly created industries from foreign competition. Many states made major financial commitments to bridges, roads, harbors, reservoirs, and railroads, all major prerequisites for economic development. Between 1815 and 1860, for example, more than $136 million was invested in canals. Some, like the famous Erie Canal in New York (which cost $7.1 million), were spectacular successes. Others, like

The Union Pacific construction train in 1868. The federal government played a major role in encouraging the building of railroads in the nineteenth century.

the $16.5 million Pennsylvania Main Line Canal, were complete failures.[1] To encourage the building of a transcontinental railroad the national government gave the railroad companies 131 million acres of land (and the states added 48 million more). A strong steamship industry was also promoted.

Another important economically related contribution was a system of free public education. To appreciate the role of education in economic development, imagine an economy in which most people are illiterate, simple skills such as bookkeeping are almost unknown, and research is a luxury. Partly as a result of increasing business demands for skilled, literate help in the late nineteenth century, state and local governments sharply increased their spending on public education. In 1862 the federal government, through the Morrill Act, provided states with nearly eleven million acres of land for the support of colleges (the so-called **land-grant colleges**) to teach engineering, agriculture, and home economics (and this was just the beginning of federal support for higher education). These universities have produced thousands of the trained personnel essential to our economy.

Modern government economic assistance

In today's economy virtually every enterprise owes some debt to the government for early financial and technical assistance. For example, the independent family farm reaps enormous benefits from government-sponsored agricultural research, extensive networks of government-paid county extension agents, and government-funded interstate highways and waterways that allow national distribution of products. Many of the commodities that make U.S. agriculture so admired were originally designed and tested in state-supported agricultural experimental stations. Each year the federal government spends hundreds of millions ($486 million in fiscal 1976) on research on new hybrid corn, pest control, soil erosion, fertilizers, animal management, and the like.[2] The benefits of such research are usually given away free as part of government's contribution to the general welfare.

Land-grant colleges Colleges established under the provisions of the Morrill Act of 1862. The federal government granted land to the states for colleges to teach agriculture, engineering, and home economics.

[1] Douglas C. North, *Growth and Welfare in the American Past* (Englewood Cliffs, N.J.: Prentice-Hall, 1966), pp. 99–103.
[2] *Statistical Abstract of the United States, 1977,* p. 569.

WHAT IS A BILLION DOLLARS?

Analyses of the economy are usually in terms of billions of dollars. Since most people do not regularly deal with billion-dollar quantities of money, a figure such as $2.68 billion has little concrete meaning. In the United States a billion is a thousand million, or, in numbers, 1,000,000,000 (in Great Britain and Germany, however, a billion is a million million). To give this figure meaning in everyday terms, suppose you received one dollar a minute, every day, seven days a week, with no interruption starting the moment Christ was born. When would you reach your first billion? The answer: at 2:21 A.M. on April 14, 1901. Merely counting this billion at the rate of one dollar a second, eight hours a day, five days a week (with no vacation) would take 133.5 years.

Adapted from "What's in a Billion?" in Philip M. Stern, *The Rape of the Taxpayer* (New York: Random House, 1972), p. 3.

Another industry that would not have survived without the encouragement of government during its lean early years is the airlines industry. Acting on the grounds that airline service would help the general welfare, the federal government provided extensive subsidies for airmail service. Much of the airlines' overhead, such as airport facilities, navigation assistance, weather reporting, pilot training, and the design of new equipment, were business costs heavily underwritten by government. Today the federal government plays a comparable role in bearing a major portion of the start-up costs for such new endeavors as solar energy, the extraction of minerals from the sea, satellite communications, and numerous other expensive technologies.

The *principle* that government ought to create an environment permitting economic development is reasonably clear. In *practice*, however, the distinction between a contribution to overall economic well-being and an unfair advantage given a special interest is not always clear. Consider the Jones Act of 1920, which required that all commerce between U.S. ports must travel in U.S. ships built in U.S. shipyards. Is this a case of government "helping" two industries in the same way the government "helped" in the building of roads and canals? Or is it true, as some critics believe, that the Jones Act results in higher shipping costs while preserving obsolete transportation and construction techniques? Would our economy benefit if our merchant fleet and ship-building capacity all but disappeared because of cheaper foreign competition?

In sum, the U.S. government has long played a facilitating role in economic development. Without such government "overhead" contributions as physical security, public transportation, enforceable rules and regulations, public education, research and development, a postal service, and a currency people accept, much of the present-day economy would simply not exist. This role of government is so well established that we sometimes hardly notice it.

TAXES AND SUBSIDIES

Besides providing an environment conducive to economic development, the national government also plays a more direct economic role through its tax and subsidy policies. These policies involve far more than just taking money from some people and giving it to others. Taxes and subsidies can be a powerful influence on people's work habits, where they live, what they eat, how they travel, and virtually every aspect of their lives. For most citizens government taxes and subsidies represent the most obvious and direct way the government affects their economic conditions. Let us begin by considering the impact of taxes.

Taxes

It is sometimes said that if the colonists thought that taxation without representation was bad, they should see taxation *with* representation. In 1975, national, state, and local governments collected a total of $455.1 billion in taxes. Almost a *third* of the **gross national product (GNP)** — the market value of all goods and services produced in a year — went for taxes. Of this total $278.7 billion (62.6 percent) was taken in by the federal government.[3] If this bite looks large, keep in mind that in many European countries an even greater proportion of all money eventually goes for taxes. In the Scandinavian nations of Denmark, Sweden, and Norway government extracts about 45 percent of the GNP in taxes.[4]

TYPES OF FEDERAL TAXES   At the federal level the largest single source of tax revenue is the individual income tax (43.3 percent of all federal revenue in 1975). When originally instituted in 1913, the federal income tax had a very low maximum rate (2 percent) and applied only to comparatively wealthy citizens. Things have changed dramatically since then. In 1974, over 83 million individual tax returns were filed.[5] A single person with a taxable income between 0 and $500 would be in the 14 percent tax-rate bracket. At $100,000 this rate reaches the maximum of 70 percent. There are two important principles governing how much income tax one pays. The first is that the rate of taxation is **progressive** — the greater the income, the greater the proportion of income going to taxes. Millionaires are not only supposed to pay more taxes, they are also supposed to pay a greater proportion of their income in taxes. Some taxes, for example, sales taxes, are called **regressive** because the propor-

Gross national product The market value of all goods and services produced in a year.
Progressive taxation The principle that as income increases, the rate of taxation also increases. The rich pay more absolutely and proportionately than the poor.
Regressive taxation The principle that as income increases the rate of taxation decreases. A sales tax of 5 percent on food and clothing would be regressive because rich people spend proportionately less on food and clothing than poor people. Thus, a smaller proportion of their income goes to this tax.

[3] Joseph A. Pechman, *Federal Tax Policy*, 3d ed. (Washington, D.C.: The Brookings Institution, 1977), p. 2.
[4] Pechman, p. 342.
[5] *Statistical Abstract of the United States, 1977*, p. 239.

Federal tax returns at the Philadelphia Internal Revenue Service Center.

tion (but not necessarily the amount) of money going to taxes generally declines as income increases.

The second important principle is that taxes are adjusted to individual circumstances. Two people earning identical incomes do not always pay identical income taxes. Allowances are made for such factors as family size, age, medical expenses, charitable contributions, interest on loans, union dues, business losses, and occupationally related expenses. While such "individualization" of income taxes is widely accepted in principle, much debate centers on what are "**loopholes**" and what are "legitimate" allowances. We shall have more to say regarding this question.

Most of us are also familiar with a second form of individual taxation: payroll taxes. There are several kinds of payroll taxes, with social security being the most important (other payroll taxes include unemployment compensation and various railroad-related programs). In 1976, payroll taxes generated $86.5 billion in federal revenue (31.0 percent of all federal tax revenue), making it the second most important source of federal revenue after the individual income tax. The social security program, the largest of these payroll taxes, taxes both the employee and the employer. In 1979, the rate was 6.13 percent on the first $22,500 of an employee's wages (employers must contribute as well). About 90 percent of all people in paid jobs are covered by social security and are thus eligible for old-age and disability benefits, survivor's insurance, and medical coverage (Medicare). When initially enacted in 1935, the social security program was designed to operate like private insurance—that is, eventual benefits were tied to previous contributions. However, because of the massive increase in the cost of benefits, social security is now simply a government program through which money from one group of citizens is transferred to other citizens.

The third most important source of federal tax revenue is the corporation tax. In 1975, corporate taxes contributed $42.6 billion to federal revenue. Like the personal income tax, the corporate income tax is computed on all income after deducting various expenses necessary to doing business (salaries, new equipment, rent, advertising, and so on). However, the rate of corporate taxation is much less progressive. In 1979, the first $25,000 of profit was taxed at 17 percent; the next $25,000 at 20 percent; and between $50,000 and $75,000 at 30 percent. The vast bulk of corporate income is taxed at the maximum rate of 46 percent, the rate when profits exceed $100,000. This is a substantial tax, but economists are divided on who ultimately bears the burden of this tax. Some argue that it is merely passed along through higher prices to the general public. Others claim that a corporation's shareholders bear this burden, while still others assert that it is the corporation itself. The evidence so far remains inconclusive.

The last type of tax we shall describe is the excise tax. Here the federal government collects either a flat fee or a percentage every time a particular item or service is purchased. The most familiar excise taxes are on alcohol ($5.4 billion collected in 1976), gasoline ($4.2 billion), tobacco ($2.4 billion), and telephone service ($1.9 billion). Overall, in 1976, $16.9

Loopholes A common expression describing the provisions of the tax code that allow wealthy people to avoid heavy taxes. Implies that this avoidance is unfair.

NONTAXABLE PERKS

One complex aspect of the income tax concerns the meaning of income. For the most part income is defined in terms of money received in the form of salary, interest, or dividends. To the average citizen this definition is appropriate. For many corporate executives and higher-income people, however, cash income is only a portion of the benefits they receive from their employment. Many companies provide their higher-paid employees with company-paid benefits (or "perks," shortened from "perquisites," as they are called) that are not reported as income. These perks frequently allow employees to live much better than their salaries would allow. Recently, the Internal Revenue Service has attempted to tax these perks, but resistance has been strong. Some of the more common ones enjoyed by corporate employees are:

Season boxes for sporting events and free theater tickets

Free trips on company planes to resorts

Company-paid country club memberships

Free use of company-maintained vacation homes

Free use of company-maintained swimming pools, tennis courts, squash courts, and other recreational facilities

Subsidized meals in company dining rooms

Free residences and hotel accommodations.

Though these perks benefit only a small portion of the public and help raise everyone's taxes, Congress has shown a reluctance to crack down on them. One possible explanation is that Congress itself is perhaps the all-time champ when it comes to tax-free perks. Members of Congress enjoy such perks as limousines, discount haircuts and shoeshines, transportation and meal reimbursements, free parking, free day-care facilities, the use of secretaries for personal work, free picture framing, and many other "free" benefits.

---

billion was raised through excise taxes. Over the years many diverse items have been subject to federal excise taxes, for example, playing cards, musical instruments, records, photographic film, and candy. In general, this type of tax is regressive, especially since most of the revenue generated comes from such popular items as gasoline, alcohol, and cigarettes.

Value-added tax A sales tax collected at each stage of the manufacturing process. To the consumer the tax appears as part of the price and thus is not obvious.
Subsidy Economic assistance given in exchange for a specific economic behavior.

ADMINISTERING TAXES   The billions of dollars raised through taxation can be generated in several different ways. To paraphrase a well-known expression concerning cats, there are many ways to skin a taxpayer. Several European governments, for example, use the **value-added tax.** This is a sales tax on a commodity at each state of manufacture. It is a regressive tax, and its real cost is hidden in the high purchase price. Most states and communities also rely more heavily on regressive property and sales taxes.

Equally important, a great deal of discretion exists concerning how the various taxes will be administered. Congress and the President may agree that a progressive income tax is preferable to an excise tax, but the actual operation of the income tax can be controversial. Decisions on tax rates, the legal definition of "income," what constitutes a legitimate business expense, when taxes must be paid, and dozens of similar questions are major political issues. Seemingly technical questions can be of enormous financial consequence. For example, a persistent tax-related question is: What is a business? Until a few years ago gentlemen farmers who owned a few pleasure horses might declare themselves a business and legally deduct all horse expenses from their personal incomes. Congress eventually decided that the public should not underwrite gentlemen farmers and their pleasure horses and required that to be a genuine business one must show a profit at least twice in seven years.

Tax regulations can also motivate certain types of actions. Consider how the income tax encourages people to buy their own homes. If you rent an apartment, the landlord's mortgage interest and property taxes are part of your rent. However, if you own your dwelling, you can deduct mortgage payments and taxes from your taxable income (this can reduce your monthly payment considerably). A $400 a month house payment may thus really cost you only $325 thanks to provisions of the tax code (but a $400 apartment rent costs you $400). Sometimes tax rules can encourage what appears to be foolish behavior. For instance, for the rich giving away rather than selling used clothing can make greater economic sense. An old suit given to the Salvation Army is deductible from one's income tax as a charitable contribution. The value of the deduction may be greater than the cash value of the suit. A poor person, however, would be better off to sell the suit because a $100 donation is merely worth $14 in tax deductions compared to the $70 value received by someone earning $100,000 or more.[6]

Subsidies

The federal government both giveth and taketh away. Through taxation it taketh and through subsidies it giveth. A **subsidy** is economic assis-

[6] To determine the cash value of a deduction simply multiply the deduction by your income tax rate. Thus, a $500 charitable deduction is worth $350 to a millionaire in the 70 percent tax bracket. Put somewhat differently, this $500 donation costs the millionaire only $150. However, a person in the 14 percent tax bracket receives only a $70 benefit by giving away $500 to charity. Partly for this reason the wealthy can afford to be extremely generous.

tance provided by the federal government to the private sector in return for some specific economic behavior. This may involve positive action, for example, a company hiring inner-city youths, or foregoing certain behavior, for example, not planting soybeans. In 1975, it is estimated that the national government spent some $95 billion on subsidies. This figure is a conservative estimate because it excludes subsidies given through regulatory policies or through direct government purchases of goods and services (both of these are described below).[7]

Capital gains tax A tax on the profits made from selling things like land, buildings, or stock. Capital gains tax rates are generally lower than income tax rates for the very wealthy.

TYPES OF SUBSIDY PROGRAMS How and to whom does the federal government give away $95 billion? Subsidy programs take several forms. The most obvious is the direct cash payment, and in 1975, $12.3 billion was given away in this manner. The major areas of direct cash subsidies were education ($5.0 billion); job training ($3.3 billion); housing ($1.7 billion); and agriculture, health, and transportation ($0.6 billion each). A typical recipient in this group is the work-study program, which provides part-time employment to college or vocational students, especially those in financial need. These student workers cost the U.S. Treasury $250 million in fiscal year 1975.

A second common form of subsidy is a reduction of tax liability. If the government wants to encourage the construction of rest homes for overworked college students, for example, it might reduce taxes for companies that build student rest homes. Tax-relief subsidies cost the government $59.7 billion in 1975, with the greatest benefits going to commerce (for such things as tax credits for buying new equipment) and housing (the largest item here was $4.5 billion for interest deductions on home mortgages). The most controversial tax-reduction subsidy is the **capital gains** tax, a tax on the profits of buying and selling. Existing capital gains regulations are highly complex, but their overall effect is to reduce the tax burden on money earned on the buying and selling of property, stocks and other securities, artworks, or other investments compared to money earned as salary or interest. For example, if you made a $50,000 profit on selling a house in 1979, the profit would be taxed at a 28 percent rate. The same amount as salary would be taxed at 49 percent. Since most citizens do not regularly buy and sell property or stocks, this tax is largely relevant to wealthy businesspeople. The purpose of the capital gains tax is to encourage new enterprises, but some people assert that it largely gives a tax break to businesspeople at the expense of those on salaries.

A third method of providing subsidies is lending people money at below-market interest rates on guaranteed loans. Much of this program involves the government's providing low-interest, long-term financing for particular groups such as the elderly or the poor. Other programs in-

[7] "Federal Subsidy Programs," Subcommittee on Priorities and Economy in Government of the Joint Economic Committee (Washington, D.C.: Government Printing Office, 1974), p. 1. All information on subsidies cited here is from this report unless otherwise noted.

THE THREE-MARTINI LUNCH STRIKES AGAIN

One type of business deduction that periodically generates controversy is the business lunch. Former President Carter strongly attacked the "three-martini lunch," calling it a rip-off of the average taxpayer. Opponents of this tax deduction point out that if ordinary people have a lunch, they get no government benefits. However, if executives from two corporations chat about business over lunch at an expensive French restaurant, one of them can pick up the check and write it off as business entertaining. For a person in the 70 percent tax bracket a $50 lunch for two really costs only $15. The difference between $15 and $50 is made up indirectly by all the other taxpayers.

Lobbyist at work. Meals such as this one are indirectly subsidized by all taxpayers.

The existence of this allowance has spawned a whole industry of overpriced restaurants that cater to business executives who write off their meals. After all, a $25 lunch can be made digestible if the government is giving you a 50 percent discount. Moreover, many people will find excuses for conducting business over lunch, since nonbusiness lunches are more expensive.

volve loans to farmers and agriculture-related facilities such as schools, resource-conservation programs, and recreational facilities. In 1975, these loans and loan guarantees cost the taxpayer $2.9 billion.

Finally, the government annually gives away, or sells at below market value, numerous commodities and services. In 1975, the federal government spent almost $6 billion on food through such programs as food stamps and school breakfasts and lunches. Large amounts of medical services, especially to veterans and poor people, were also given away. Less obvious were government-sponsored airport projects, free postal services, gifts of surplus property, and waste-disposal plants for rural areas. The total 1975 bill for this government generosity was $20.2 billion.

Needless to say, anytime $95 billion is given away controversy arises. Many subsidy programs have been bitterly criticized. On the basis of studies of different programs, the report of the Joint Economic Committee, Subcommittee on Priorities and Economy in Government, concluded that "many subsidies do not work well economically, they are often directed at outmoded or nonexistent objects, they redistribute income to the affluent, and in too many cases their costs far exceed their benefits to society as a whole." On the other hand, subsidies may be the only means — however inefficient — to accomplish certain goals. Programs like food stamps, emergency loans to farmers, free medical services for the poor, tax breaks for homeowners, and the like, may waste some money, but without such measures more people would go hungry, many would lack adequate health care, and the home building and real estate industries would suffer. As with many other issues, one's perspective depends on whether one is receiving a subsidy or paying taxes to support one.

REGULATIONS

A third means by which the government affects the economy is through regulations. In some instances regulation is direct, for example, government-approved airfaires. In most cases, however, the impact is indirect, for example, safety standards that raise the prices of microwave ovens. Issuing rules and regulations governing economic behavior is only one of several possible control mechanisms. If safe automobiles were your goal, you might place a high tax on unsafe cars. Or you could provide a subsidy to manufacturers of safe automobiles. A more extreme solution would be for the government itself to build and sell safer cars. Nevertheless, regulation has become increasingly popular as a tool affecting the marketplace.

Federal economic regulations have always existed, but until recently they were usually fairly general. The nineteenth-century government coined money, set standard weights and measures, and provided certain minimal banking procedures but stopped well short of telling people how to run their businesses. Beginning in 1887 with the creation of the Interstate Commerce Commission (ICC), which was designed to regulate railroad rates, the federal government has played a more vigorous regu-

Monopoly A condition in which one firm exercises exclusive control over a good or service and thus is able to set prices without regard to supply or demand.

latory role. The ICC was followed by a number of other regulatory agencies, for example, the Federal Trade Commission (FTC), which, like the ICC, regulates specific industries. Since the mid-1960s, several new government regulatory agencies have been created. Unlike the ICC, FTC, and other established industry-specific regulators, new agencies such as the Consumer Product Safety Commission can involve themselves in almost any aspect of the economy, not just a single industry.

Federal regulatory efforts have grown dramatically in recent years. In fiscal 1974 these efforts cost the government about $1.9 billion; in two years this figure was almost $3 billion. Almost 9,000 new employees were added to regulatory agencies during the same period.[8] Much of this growth was a response to new laws. In 1972, for example, Congress passed the Federal Water Pollution Control Act designed to end pollution of navigable waterways. This was followed in 1973 by the Safe Drinking Water Act. Other new areas of legislative concern have been noise pollution, hiring the handicapped, boat safety, eliminating lead in paints, and rules governing interstate sale of land.

Economic impact of government regulations

One obvious economic impact of these regulations concerns the goods and services available to the public. Since the advent of regulations numerous products and firms have simply disappeared. The Food and Drug Administration, in particular, has played a vigorous role in removing dangerous products from the market. The removal of cyclamates from diet soft drinks and red dye number 2 from food are two well-known actions. The Consumer Product Safety Commission has taken off the market items ranging from unsafe toys to chromosome-damaging aerosol adhesive sprays. Even heavy industry has been affected. Because of more stringent water-pollution standards, many iron foundries have closed rather than absorb the huge cost of antipollution controls.

A related impact of regulation concerns the extent of competition in the economy. The U.S. economy is not characterized by completely free competition. Government regulations frequently create **monopoly**-like situations that maintain high prices. Suppose you organize Kamakazi Fast Freight to ship merchandise between New York and California. You estimate that you can charge half the going rate and deliver in half the usual time. Thanks to numerous ICC rules, however, your chances of ever getting going are virtually zero. Not only do you need an ICC permit to get into operation (which is difficult to obtain), but the ICC requires that you charge the same rates as everyone else and that your drivers not work longer hours than anyone else. Economists agree that government maintenance of such monopolistic practices represents a "hidden tax" on the general public.

In other areas, however, the government acts against monopolistic practices. The Sherman Anti-Trust Act of 1890 was the first major government step against monopoly and was directly responsible for the 1911

[8] Murray L. Weidenbaum, *Business, Government, and the Public* (Englewood Cliffs, N.J.: Prentice-Hall, 1977), p. 19.

dissolution of John D. Rockefeller's Standard Oil Company. The Sherman Act led to the creation of Sohio (Standard Oil of Ohio), EXXON (Standard Oil of New Jersey), Mobil Oil (Standard Oil of New York), Chevron (Standard Oil of California), and several other companies instead of one giant Standard Oil. This was followed in 1914 by the Clayton Act, which prohibited other monopolistic practices, such as one person being a director of two or more competitors or charging different custom-

COLLECT DIRTY AIR AND BECOME RICH

Government regulations sometimes have unexpected and peculiar consequences. One such instance occurred following the passage of the Clean Air Act of 1970 and amendments to this act in 1977. The purpose of the act was to reduce air pollution, but one of its consequences was to make dirty air highly valuable. The paradox occurs as follows. The law allows the building of new polluting installations in an area already heavily polluted, *provided* the new polluter finds a way of reducing the overall pollution in the area. For example, when Standard Oil of Ohio (Sohio) wanted to build oil-storage facilities off the coast of Long Beach, California, it had agreed to install $120 million worth of antipollution equipment in a southern California Edison electric plant. This equipment would more than offset the Sohio pollution so the overall air quality would improve.

What makes this situation interesting is that different types of pollution vary in their control costs. It is cheaper, for example, to reduce a given amount of air pollution from oil-storage tanks than from auto-assembly plants. Hence, it makes economic sense for the car plant to reduce the pollution at the oil-storage tanks rather than at its own facilities. Of course, a smart oil-storage tank owner might want to *charge* the auto-assembly plant for the right to clean up its dirty air. In fact, in four California counties gas stations and dry cleaners are selling their dirty air to corporations who wish to locate in their vicinity. Some people have even become dirty-air brokers, arranging deals between existing polluters and new industries. A large quantity of easily cleaned dirty air may now be worth millions of dollars. Soon we may see the day of dirty-air moguls or court cases over the theft of valuable dirty air. Unscrupulous operators might even try to pass off not-so-dirty air as the real thing.

A further analysis of the wheelings and dealings in dirty air is found in "Dirty Deals," *Forbes*, April 3, 1978, pp. 32–33.

ers different prices without an economic justification. Several important antimonopoly acts have been passed since 1914, and many of the giants of U.S. industry — IBM and General Motors — have been taken to court for their monopolistic business practices.

The economic impact of government regulations of monopolies is hotly debated. Foes of monopolies assert that monopolies maintain artificially high prices, encourage inefficiency, and inhibit innovation. Perhaps even worse, giant monopolies can become a law unto themselves and, allegedly, threaten democracy. Defenders of monopolies point out, however, that large firms generally spend more — absolutely and proportionately — on research and technical innovation.[9] Only a giant like General Motors can afford to spend tens of millions of dollars on automotive research. In nations like Japan huge monopolistic corporations are encouraged because of their more efficient contributions to the national welfare.

Government-imposed regulations can also add substantially to the cost of products (and these increased costs have repercussions on investments, inflation, and employment). The best-known, but not the only, example of this process is the increased cost of automobiles as a result of safety and antipollution requirements. For example, between 1968 and 1974, the addition of seat belts, head restraints, exhaust controls, and the like, added $350 to the average car. In 1974, the total cost for this required equipment was $3 billion. The addition of the catalytic converter in 1975 raised these costs even further. One study estimated the annual cost of these converters at $11 billion (General Motors spent about $100 million to develop and test them). Recalls mandated by the Environmental Protection Agency or the National Highway Safety Administration have become increasingly more expensive.[10] In 1977, a record 14.3 million vehicles were recalled at a cost of at least $150 million.[11]

Increased automobile costs provide only one of hundreds of examples. In 1974, the Employee Retirement Income Security Act was passed, requiring that 90 percent of all private pension plans be rewritten (the average cost to employers rose 10–15 percent, and as a result many smaller companies dropped pension plans entirely.)[12]

The Department of Agriculture has also gotten into the act by setting minimal standards for processed food. For example, if you sell "poultry chop suey" it must contain at least 4 percent chicken. The sharp operator, however, could slice the chicken requirement in half by offering "chop suey with poultry" (2 percent chicken required). Recall from our analysis of bureaucratic red tape in Chapter Thirteen that large companies spend tens of millions of dollars complying with various federal regulations (one estimate of these costs in 1976 was $65.5 billion).[13]

---

[9] For a defense of monopolies, see Joseph A. Schumpeter, *Capitalism, Socialism, and Democracy* (New York: Harper, 1950), Chap. 8.

[10] Weidenbaum, pp. 47–54.

[11] Bob Tamarkiss, "Recalls — The Costs Soar," *Forbes*, July 10, 1978, p. 79.

[12] Weidenbaum, p. 79.

[13] "The Government: Mighty Engine of Inflation," *U.S. News and World Report*, April 17, 1978.

OLIGOPOLY IN BEER: A CASE STUDY

Most college students are familiar with the terms "monopoly" (control of a market by one firm) and "oligopoly" (control of a market by a few firms). However, textbook descriptions of monopolistic or oligopolistic activities usually refer to processes and products beyond the experience of most students, for example, aluminum smelting, hydroelectric generators. A student may ultimately pay higher prices because of limited competition, but he or she rarely gets a chance to see monopolistic or oligopolistic practices up close.

One exception is the beer industry. The U.S. beer market has traditionally had a few large companies—Anheuser-Busch, Schlitz, Pabst, Coors, and Miller—and hundreds of much smaller local breweries (for example, Genesee, Jax, Iron City, Lone Star, Brew 102, Utica Club, and Huber, to name just a few). These smaller companies survived through customer loyalty and slightly lower prices. While a six-pack of Budweiser might go for $1.89, a locally made beer might sell for $1.69. On occasion, however, a beer shopper might see one of the big national beers selling for a bargain price, say, $1.39. The local brewer cannot even make and ship beer at this low price (the national brewer can well afford this low price because the rest of the country is still paying $1.89 a six-pack). In many instances this cheaper "premium" beer can wipe out the local brewer (why pay 30 cents more for local beer than for Miller or Budweiser?). When the local brewer goes bankrupt, the price of the national beer rises, and there is one less competitor to worry about. For this reason local beers have been rapidly disappearing from the scene.

Obviously, this situation can pose a problem for the smart beer buyer. Do you buy national beers at special prices and risk the possibility of future oligopoly (and higher prices)? Or do you buy local beer to prevent oligopoly (but pay a higher price in the short run)?

For a description of these and other monopolistic practices, see Morton Mintz and Jerry S. Cohen, *America, Inc.: Who Owns and Operates the United States?* (New York: Dell, 1971), especially pp. 144–147.

We are not suggesting that the costs generated through government regulations necessarily harm the economy. Many people would argue that a few billion dollars a year spent on auto safety to save lives is well worth it. We are merely pointing out that almost every time the government makes a new requirement affecting what we can buy or how businesspeople should behave, there are repercussions in the economy.

GOVERNMENT CONSUMPTION OF GOODS AND SERVICES

Besides collecting billions of tax dollars and making economic rules and regulations, the government itself is the number one spender in the economy. In fiscal 1977, the federal government had a budget outlay of $401.9 billion, and this bought a lot of paper clips, rubber bands, atomic-powered aircraft carriers, supersonic jet fighters, and much more. Many industries, especially in national defense, exist solely to sell things to the government. The extent to which government purchases affect the economy sometimes staggers the imagination. For example, the Polaris missile carried in submarines involved some thirty *thousand* contractors and subcontractors in its development and production. Putting Neil Armstrong on the moon took 300,000 workers in forty-eight states.[14] The survival of many communities depends on government purchases or government payrolls.

Government purchases are, however, far more than just another set of orders for goods or services. By virtue of its size and power the government can have a much broader economic impact. On several occasions companies doing business with the government have been required to pursue some noneconomic policy, such as banning racial discrimination in hiring, buying goods made by the blind, or establishing facilities in areas of high unemployment. During the Vietnam war, defense contractors were prohibited from using ships that had visited Cuban or North Vietnamese ports. The government has considerable discretion in many of its purchases, and this can generate intense political conflict. For example, between 1965 and 1970, the United Farm Workers union led by Cesar Chavez called for a nationwide boycott of California grapes. Under pressure from grape growers, the Defense Department, however, decided that soldiers needed more grapes and thus bought up large quantities of boycotted grapes.

One of the most important, but least known, government purchasing programs involves the U.S. stockpiles of strategic and critical materials. Beginning in 1946, the government began purchasing goods to insure that in case of a one-year war fought simultaneously in Europe and Southeast Asia we would not be unprepared. These reserves are considerable (a market value of $7.43 billion in 1975) and include some commodities as antimony, bauxite, chrome, industrial diamonds, silver, tin, tungsten, jewel bearings, and feathers (1.6 million pounds of them in 1974). Because items in this stockpile can easily be adjusted, the government can affect the prices of many key industrial goods through its purchases or sales. During July–December 1974, for example, the government sold to industry over $67 million worth of zinc, $39 million worth of lead, and $141 million worth of other commodities.[15]

[14] Cited in Lloyd D. Musolf, *Government and the Economy* (Chicago: Scott, Foresman, 1965), pp. 102–103.

[15] These figures are reported in Office of Preparedness, General Services Administration, "Stockpile Report to the Congress," July–December 1974.

GOVERNMENT-OWNED ENTERPRISES

Besides setting economic policy in the private sector, the federal government itself operates many businesses. In fact, in several instances the government competes directly with private industry. For example, in 1975, the national government owned 188 million acres of forest land, and the timber cut on this land was valued at $368.4 million.[16] Large quantities of government land were also leased or lent free for grazing and mining. What the government charges for its timber, for example, can have a major impact on what lumber companies like Boise-Cascade or Georgia-Pacific charge for their products.

Most government-owned enterprises are organized as special agencies or corporations to perform certain tasks. The best-known and largest is the U.S. Postal Service, which had 680,000 employees in 1976. Several companies such as United Parcel Service (UPS) and Greyhound compete with the post office, but thanks to various court rulings the post office has maintained its monopoly on the direct delivery of first-class mail. A second well-known government corporation is the Tennessee Valley Authority (TVA), which sells electricity to cities and industries located in the Tennessee River basin.

The Postal Service and TVA are only two of many government-run businesses. Several agriculturally related companies such as the Commodity Credit Corporation and the Federal Crop Insurance Corporation exist to provide services ranging from grain-storage facilities to farm loans. Housing is another area of government business involvement. Many citizens have been able to buy homes because the Federal Housing Administration guaranteed their mortgages. In the transportation area the government operates the Panama Canal, the St. Lawrence Seaway (jointly owned with Canada), and various other waterways. Through COMSAT the government, in conjunction with private companies, runs a communications satellite system. The government is even in the sugarcane business through its Virgin Islands Corporation.

These government enterprises can have an economic impact well beyond their immediate activities. Postal rates, for example, can spell life or death to magazine publishers and mail-order companies. Similarly, the Federal Housing Authority's policies on how houses must be built and located has had a far-reaching impact on the construction and real estate industries. The *threat* of government ownership can also have a major impact. At the height of the 1974 energy crisis, for example, the possibility of government ownership of refineries and pipelines was

---

[16] *Statistical Abstract of the United States, 1977,* pp. 676–679. Perhaps less well known than federally owned forestland is the Lone Star Beefhouse in Washington, D.C. This bar and restaurant features topless dancers and is run by the Federal Property Resources Service of the General Services Administration. Unlike many other federal operations, it makes money—$11,000 in the first six months of 1978. The government obtained the establishment when it took over the assets of a Transportation Department clerk who stole more than $850,000 in government funds.

openly discussed, in part to pressure oil companies to reduce prices. Such threats of government takeovers are not completely idle; in 1970, for example, in response to discontinuations of railroad passenger service, the federal government took over this service through Amtrak.

What are the economic goals of government?

We have seen that the federal government can affect the economy in many different ways. We did not, however, consider the overall goals sought through this intervention. What does the government hope to accomplish through taxation, subsidies, regulations, and the like? Basically, almost all public officials — whether Democrats or Republicans — have been committed to five broad goals (1) moderate growth of the gross national product (GNP); (2) full employment; (3) low inflation; (4) a strong system of private enterprise; and (5) preservation of the middle class. Let us briefly consider the specifics of these goals and the government's successes and failures.

MODERATE GROWTH OF THE GNP

We are deeply committed to economic growth. A major measure of this growth is changes in the GNP. The GNP is the dollar value of all goods and services produced in a year. In 1976, this was a little over $1.7 *trillion* dollars (or $7,903 per man, woman, and child). Over the long haul the GNP has grown substantially both in absolute volume and on a per-person basis. Between 1950 and 1975, as measured on constant (noninflated) dollars, the GNP per capita increased by a factor of 3.7. Between 1910 and 1975 the U.S. economy, as measured by constant dollars, grew at an average annual rate of 2.9 percent (which, given compounding, has meant an increase from 150 to 1,500 million). Put in more personal, direct terms, the average citizen has progressively added to his or her economic goodies — television sets, cars, vacations, housing, and food.

This long-term trend, however, masks considerable yearly variation. Not every year brings a better house or a Cadillac instead of a Chevrolet. Between 1973 and 1975, the true value of the GNP *declined* by an average of 1.8 percent a year.[17] Thus even with all our knowledge of economics and array of government economic powers, setbacks can still occur. Moreover, many citizens have become envious of the growth rates of other nations. While in the United States the per capita GNP grew at a 3.3 percent rate during the 1960s, the rate in Japan was 9.3 percent and in Italy 4.8 percent.[18]

[17] *Statistical Abstract of the United States, 1977*, p. 395.

[18] Cited in Edwin G. Dolan, *Basic Economics* (Hinsdale, Ill.: Dryden Press, 1977), p. 103.

FULL EMPLOYMENT

At least since the passage of the Employment Act of 1946, the federal government has had a major responsibility for seeing that all citizens who want to can find work. The government's commitment to jobs has recently been broadened to include eliminating employment disparities between social and ethnic groups. At least since the end of World War II, U.S. employment levels have been relatively high. Unemployment rates during this period have run between 2.5 percent and 6 percent, though at times, for example, 1975 and the beginning of 1976, the figure has exceeded 8 percent. Unemployment among blacks during the post-World War II period has usually been twice the rate for whites (in 1975, the rate for whites was 7.8 percent compared to 13.9 percent for blacks and other minorities).[19]

This commitment to "full employment" does not really mean a commitment to zero unemployment. In fact, most officials are willing to accept 4 percent or 5 percent unemployment as the equivalent of full employment. Why not seek zero unemployment? First, most unemployment is usually of relatively short duration (ten weeks or less), and this type of unemployment can be more efficiently solved by unemployment insurance programs. Also, much of this short-term unemployment is almost inevitable because it involves construction industry lay-offs in bad weather or variations in seasonal work such as fruit picking. Finally, zero unemployment would not necessarily reflect a healthy economy. If the economic situation really worsened, many people would become discouraged and give up looking for work. Thus "unemployment" would appear to decline (many black teenagers are not included among the unemployed because they have given up looking for work). Conversely, during boom times many people not usually in the labor force, such as students or housewives, seek work, and these new workers can become unemployed at the slightest cooling of the economy. For these reasons achieving full employment can be highly complex.

LOW INFLATION

Inflation is the process by which a commodity or service increases in price without increasing in real value. This means that the value of your money is reduced. If a one-pound loaf of bread goes from 50 cents to a dollar in a year, the inflation rate for bread is 100 percent. There are several different statistical measures of inflation, but the most popular is the Consumer Price Index. This index, computed by the Department of Labor, is based on the average price of consumer goods purchased by urban wage earners (about 400 goods). Changes in the Consumer Price Index reflect expenditures for ordinary, basic commodities such as housing, food, and transportation.

Following the Korean War (1952) until the mid-1960s, inflation was not a major problem in the United States. Between 1953 and 1966, only

---

[19] *Statistical Abstract of the United States, 1977*, p. 361.

DUNAGIN'S PEOPLE

"Our figures show that to maintain a middle-level standard of living, a family needs an upper-level income."

DUNAGIN'S PEOPLE by Ralph Dunagin, Courtesy Field Newspaper Syndicate.

twice (1957 and 1958) did inflation much exceed 2 percent a year (a figure considered by economists to equal "stable" prices). In the late 1960s, however, prices began to soar. Between 1971 and 1975, in particular, prices increased at an annual rate of 7.4 percent. The Bureau of Labor estimated that an urban family of four on an "intermediate budget" had to spend $9,076 to survive in 1967. By late 1974, this figure had risen to $14,333, an increase of 58 percent.[20]

Economics is much better at describing how and why inflation occurs than in providing a simple cure. Traditionally, most explanations of inflation have been called **demand-pull theories.** That is, the demand for goods exceeds the supply, so prices rise accordingly. If, for example, the public suddenly wanted only steak, not hamburger, steak would become more expensive because the short-term supply of steak is limited. More recently economists have also spoken of **cost-push inflation.** Here some element in the cost of a product increases prices even if demand remains constant. If unions, management, foreign supplies (as in oil prices), and others involved in production raise their prices, inflation will occur if these prices stick.

A high rate of inflation affects people very differently. It especially hurts those on fixed incomes or people who cannot quickly adjust their incomes to meet higher prices. A $75-a-week pension might have seemed adequate in 1944, but by today's standards its value has eroded enormously. On the other hand, had you borrowed $50,000 in 1944, inflation acts to your advantage because you are now repaying the loan in much less valuable dollars (a 1944 dollar had 3.4 times the purchasing power of a 1976 dollar).[21] Even if your salary keeps pace with the inflation rate, it can cost you; the higher your income, the greater proportion of it goes to taxes because the federal income tax rate increases as income increases.

Though a low rate of inflation is a major government goal, differences occur over what is an "acceptable" rate. For example, President Carter

Demand-pull theory of inflation The explanation of inflation that emphasizes the demand for goods and services outstripping supply, so prices rise.

Cost-push theory of inflation The explanation of inflation that emphasizes the higher prices caused by the higher cost of an element of production.

[20] *Statistical Abstract of the United States, 1977,* p. 443.
[21] *Statistical Abstract of the United States, 1977,* p. 432.

initially proposed a 4 percent inflation rate as the goal of his Administration. Compared to inflation rates for much of the post-World War II period, this rate seems high to many people. Even at an annual rate of 4 percent the dollar would lose about half its purchasing power every ten years.[22] Whether 4 percent is the minimum that can be expected under existing conditions is a difficult and controversial question.

A STRONG SYSTEM OF PRIVATE ENTERPRISE

The government may play an important role in the U.S. economy, but virtually all leaders accept the principle that the government itself should not dominate the economy. Government may provide necessary "overhead" facilities, for example, highways and post offices, and act as a referee in the marketplace sometimes, but key decisions on prices, products, and production are supposed to be made by private individuals, not the government. Perhaps the most fundamental feature of our system is private ownership of enterprises, ranging from the small family farm to industrial giants such as General Motors or Dupont.

As with so many general principles, however, problems can arise in specific application. In agricultural policy, for example, it sometimes seems that government's efforts to maintain individual free enterprise result in greater government controls. A contemporary farmer does not work for the government, but to "protect" agriculture the federal bureaucracy may tell the farmer how much to plant, decide how the farmer can market products, and greatly influence expenditures on land and equipment through loan programs. A comparable situation exists with many defense-oriented industries. Lockheed Aircraft Corporation and General Dynamics are part of our private free enterprise system, but their survival can depend on government loans and free use of government manufacturing and research facilities. Government's generosity toward many large corporations has led some critics to describe the government's policy as "socialism for the rich and free enterprise for the poor."

Perhaps the most controversial policy relating to the government's commitment to free enterprise is the use of wage and price controls. During World War II and the Korean War, to prevent shortages and sharp price increases, the national government placed numerous controls on the economy. Wages, rents, food, gasoline prices, and most other consumer-goods prices were set by government order. Such action was considered a drastic, emergency measure, and regulations were gradually removed following the wars. In 1970 the Economic Stabilization Act

---

[22] An inflation rate of 4 or 5 percent may not seem like much on a yearly basis, but over a long period it can really add up. In 1977, the Federal Reserve Bank of St. Louis calculated what prices would look like in forty-five years given a 5 percent inflation rate. Your local supermarket would, for example, be selling a gallon of milk for $12.49, a dozen eggs would go for $7.64, and four rolls of toilet paper would set you back $7.10. Nobody would believe you when you told them that when you were young you could still buy a nickel candy bar for 20 cents.

gave the President, for a limited period, the power to impose government controls on the economy during peacetime. In August 1971, only a few days after he publicly denounced economic controls, President Nixon put a 90-day freeze on all salaries, prices, and rents. A few months later Nixon created the Cost of Living Council and other agencies to monitor these controls. Eventually these controls were dismantled and guidelines became voluntary, not government-enforced.

PRESERVATION OF THE MIDDLE CLASS

The United States has sometimes been described as a middle-class nation. The essential characteristics of middle class are not, however, precisely clear. One observer with a touch of humor defined the middle class as "people who own their own homes, live in the suburbs, don't have large families, send their children to nursery school and kindergarten, don't let their teenagers drop out of high school, send their kids to college, have good jobs, retire, take vacations, own washers, dryers, air conditioners, television sets, dishwashers, cars and second cars, have good incomes, play tennis, and get divorced."[23] Using figures on total family income, we see that most citizens are in the "comfortable, not rich, not poor" category. In 1976, for example, the median family income was $14,958 (only about 19 percent earned under $7,000).[24]

The income distribution in the United States is sometimes characterized as diamond-shaped as opposed to pyramid-shaped, with a small number of wealthy people, a slightly larger middle class, and a very large number of poor people. The survival of this diamond-shaped distribution is a pervasive theme in government policy making. The notion that you should "level out" the class structure by sharply increasing taxes on middle-class families has little support in government. Antipoverty programs are essentially designed to raise poor people up to middle-class levels, not redistribute middle-class wealth to poor people. Such middle-class "institutions" as home ownership, public education, automobile travel, suburban growth, and the like, have received extensive government economic aid. Political leaders do not wish to create a situation in which middle-class citizens suddenly find themselves falling back toward a lower-class existence. In many parts of the world such losses of economic standing have caused revolutions.

CONFLICTS AMONG GOALS

These five goals by themselves are generally not controversial. Few citizens oppose moderate growth, low unemployment, low inflation, private enterprise, and a large middle class. Nevertheless, policies designed to achieve these goals frequently generate enormous conflict. Why does such conflict occur if everyone agrees on what the government is supposed to accomplish? One major reason involves the priorities of these goals, that is, which problems should be solved first. Government cannot

[23] Ben J. Wattenberg, *The Real America* (New York: Putman, 1976), p. 68.
[24] *Statistical Abstract of the United States, 1978*, p. 440.

PRICES IN THE SOVIET UNION

In our economy prices are usually established by tens of thousands of individuals acting independently of one another. The person who decides that one pound of Oscar Meyer all-beef hot dogs will cost $1.75 has nothing to do with the cost of hot dog buns. In the economy of the Soviet Union, however, one person and a staff of about 800 control about ten million prices. Nicolai Timofeyevich Glushkov, chairman of the State Prices Committee, will sometimes set as many as 1,000 new prices a day on everything from television sets to machine tools. In 1977, to make sure these prices were enforced, 250,000 prices were checked by central and local inspectors. Western experts do not yet understand just how Glushkov arrives at his prices. A manufacturer may claim that it costs 5,750 rubles to build a tractor. Based on what Glushkov considers the economic value (not manufacturing cost) this tractor might get reduced to only 4,000 rubles. Unlike pricing in the United States, Soviet prices frequently have no relation to supply or demand.

David K. Willis, "The Man Who Sets 10 Million Prices," *The Christian Science Monitor,* June 21, 1978, p. 3.

Trickle-down approach to tax cuts Tax cuts given to the wealthy in the expectation that their increased spending will eventually produce benefits for workers (benefits will "trickle down" to the workers).

do everything at once, and people disagree over which goals should come first.

The classic conflict of this type occurs between business and labor during times of high unemployment. To organized labor the first priority is creating more jobs through public works projects and increased government spending. Many business leaders oppose these programs on the grounds that the result will be more inflation, more encroachment on the private sector, and less real economic growth because of government disruption of the marketplace. Business leaders do not want high levels of unemployment; rather, from their perspective, unemployment is less important than other economic goals.

CONFLICTS OVER HOW GOALS ARE TO BE ACHIEVED

Conflict occurs not only over goal priorities, but also over how the goals are to be achieved. Each goal can be pursued through a number a different mechanisms, and people frequently disagree on specific economic strategies. For example, if the government wants to cut taxes to stimulate economic growth, *whose* taxes should be cut? Many business leaders support what is called the **"trickle-down" approach** — tax cuts for business will generate economic expansion, so benefits such as more jobs and

Bubble-up approach to tax cuts Tax cuts given to workers in the expectation that increased buying power will stimulate the overall economy through increased demand.
Stagflation The situation of high unemployment and a high inflation rate.

higher wages will eventually "trickle down" to ordinary workers. Labor leaders, however, frequently advocate the reverse, or **"bubble-up,"** approach—provide tax rebates directly to workers, whose purchases will spur growth. Both policies may stimulate the economy, but each differs in its immediate benefits.

A related problem concerns the trade-off between a good economic policy and a good humanitarian policy. This type of conflict was illustrated by President Carter's decision that millions of elderly citizens deserve higher social security benefits even though this action would be inflationary. Another conflict occurred over federal regulations of dangerous cotton dust in cotton mills. Economic advisers claimed that stiffer regulations would boost cotton prices, but the President nevertheless supported these changes on the grounds that the well-being of mill employees came first. Proposed government standards for reducing the flammability of upholstered furniture may cost consumers an extra $150 million a year and contribute to inflation.

CONFLICTS DUE TO DIFFERENCES AMONG ECONOMISTS

Adding to the conflict over economic policy making is the fact that many professional economists disagree on how best to achieve these national economic goals. Economics is not a precise science; it is sometimes said that if you put ten economists in a room they will give you eleven different opinions. Especially on basic issues such as preventing depressions, economists will commonly offer different—and sometimes conflicting—advice. Some might emphasize stimulating consumer demand through tax cuts and extensive government spending. Other, equally well-respected economists might claim that these programs would only deepen and prolong the depression. They might instead recommend that the Federal Reserve Board increase the money supply to banks while the government balanced taxes and expenditures. Only half jokingly it is sometimes said that almost any economic policy will be supported by some experts and denounced by others.

The difficulty of translating expert advice into effective public policy is illustrated in the debate over the unemployment-inflation relationship. Until the early 1970s, many prominent economists argued that an inverse relationship existed between inflation and unemployment—if unemployment increased, inflation would decrease, and vice versa. The statistical evidence strongly confirmed this idea, and political leaders acted on the basis of this argument. However, since the early 1970s, the economy has occasionally experienced high unemployment *and* high inflation at the same time (sometimes called **"stagflation"**). Professional economists have made many inaccurate predictions and, thus, few people are willing to accept their pronouncements as the final word.

CONFLICTS OVER IMPLEMENTING ECONOMIC POLICY

Finally, the way in which economic policy is formulated and implemented encourages considerable debate and controversy. The nation's economic program is not made by a single person or small group. Within the government itself Congress, the President, the federal bureaucracy, and semiautonomous agencies such as the Federal Reserve Board and the Interstate Commerce Commission all play substantial roles. Moreover, each of these groups has its own perspectives and goals. Economic policy making also frequently requires the cooperation of nongovernment groups. The government may provide a tax incentive for businesspeople to purchase new equipment, but private businesspeople cannot be forced to buy this equipment. Similar cooperation is also sometimes needed from organized labor. With so many people and interests involved, controversy readily occurs even though basic economic goals are widely accepted.

It should be apparent that despite the clarity of our economic goals, economic policy making is like a complicated juggling act. To appreciate the difficulty of trying to achieve several different goals simultaneously, let us briefly consider how the Carter Administration in 1978 attempted to combat inflation (this was only one of several such programs against inflation). We shall see that fighting high inflation involves making difficult choices among equally laudable goals, deciding which expert advice is worth following, and then selling particular policies to many government and nongovernment decision makers.

Jawboning The use of persuasion and pressure by the President to hold down prices and wages. May involve threats, but emphasis is on voluntary restraint.

CARTER'S ANTI-INFLATION PROGRAM

President Carter's election campaign emphasized economic growth, not inflation, as the number one economic problem. Nevertheless, soon after the election it became apparent to both the Carter Administration and the general public that soaring inflation required immediate government attention. Especially in 1978, the President took several concrete steps to reduce inflation. President Carter's program has consisted of the following elements:

1. Intensive efforts to persuade ("**jawboning**") business to hold down price increases. The President's program, announced on October 24, 1978, called for companies to keep price increases half a percentage point below increases in 1976 and 1977. Much of this exhortation was to be done by the Council on Wage and Price Stability (which was created in 1974 under President Nixon). Alfred E. Kahn was appointed in October 1978 to oversee the anti-inflation program. Jawboning has had some success. For example, when U.S. Steel announced a $10.50 a ton price hike, it and other steel producers were persuaded to settle for about half this increase. However, many economists, including Arthur Okun, chief economic adviser to Lyndon Johnson, and Herbert Stein, chief economic adviser to Richard Nixon, believe that jawboning will have little overall impact.[25]

[25] "Carter's Crisis," *U.S. News and World Report*, April 17, 1978, pp. 21–23. Also see Herbert Stein, "Carter vs. Inflation: Round 3," *The Wall Street Journal*, April 18, 1978.

KEY OFFICIALS IN ECONOMIC POLICY MAKING

Government economic policy is made by several different agencies. Two of the most important are the Department of the Treasury and the Department of Commerce. The head of the Treasury Department is responsible for formulating and recommending domestic and international financial policy, tax policy, and managing the public debt. The Secretary is also the financial agent of the U.S. government and manufactures coins and currency. The Department of Commerce is responsible for promoting national economic development and technological advancement. Among its activities are collecting and analyzing statistical information, promoting research on economic matters, and providing financial assistance for economic development in the United States. Here are brief portraits of the two men who head these cabinet-level agencies.

MALCOLM BALDRIDGE, Secretary of Commerce. Born October 4, 1922, in Omaha, Nebraska. Graduated from Yale University. Father was a Congressman from Nebraska in the 1930s (his sister was social secretary to Jacqueline Kennedy during the Kennedy Administration). After military service in World War II went to work as a mill hand in an iron foundry and eventually became the firm's president, building Scovill Manufacturing Company in Waterbury, Connecticut, into a diversified company with annual sales of a billion dollars. "Mac" Baldridge is also a card-carrying member of the Professional Rodeo Cowboys Association (he still competes in rodeos as part of a two-man steer-roping team). He also wears hand-tooled leather belts with his pin-striped suits. An activist in Connecticut Republican circles, he managed long time-friend George Bush's 1980 Connecticut primary win over Ronald Reagan. Known for his ability to get right to the heart of difficult, complex problems, Baldridge is especially concerned with lagging national productivity, increasing exports, and eliminating excessive government regulation of business.

DONALD T REGAN Secretary of the Treasury. Born December 21, 1918, in Cambridge, Massachusetts. Graduated from Harvard (where he was a classmate of John F. Kennedy) with a degree in English. Joined the Marines and rose to lieutenant colonel. Joined the stock brokerage firm of Merrill Lynch in 1946 and steadily rose in the firm to become chief executive in 1971. As chief executive he greatly expanded the size and range of business activities of the Wall Street firm. Regan has not been active politically, though he has been involved in national and international financial organizations such as the Council on Foreign Relations. Regan has a reputation as being intelligent, imaginative, and tough (one person said that he still thinks like a Marine). His philosophy is one of being pro-free enterprise capitalism but not rigid right wing. Among the programs he most strongly favors are increased deregulation of industry and changing the tax system to provide more incentives to productive economic activities (through such measures as tax cuts). Though Regan occupies a key role in the Reagan Administration, he is not personally close to the President.

2. Jawboning was also to be employed to hold down wages. The October 24th program called for companies not to exceed 7 percent in yearly wage and fringe-benefit increases. However, workers earning less than $4 an hour were excluded from this limit, as were those whose contracts called for higher future increases. Greater increases would be allowed if based on increased productivity.

3. To encourage business compliance with these guidelines the government might use such sanctions as rate reductions in regulated industries (for example, interstate trucking), a relaxation in import quotas, and the modification of wages paid on federal projects. After January 1, 1979, all companies applying for federal contracts of more than $5 million have to show that they are complying with the wage and price guidelines.

4. To encourage worker compliance with these guidelines President Carter on October 24 proposed a "real wage insurance plan." If workers in a company limited their wage increases to 7 percent but inflation exceeded 7 percent, they would receive a tax rebate to make up the difference in real income lost through inflation.

5. Encourage federal regulatory agencies to adopt anti-inflation policies. One response has been a decision by the Civil Aeronautics Board to allow more cut-rate airfares (for example, "Super-Saver" fares). The President also promised that environmental and safety regulations would be issued only when necessary and accomplished at the lowest possible cost.

6. Hold down spending by the federal government. This has entailed such actions as vetoing unnecessary and expensive public works projects, refusing to "bail out" financially troubled companies or industries, and reorganizing the executive branch to make it more cost effective. Carter also proposed a 5.5 percent limit on pay raises for white-collar federal employees and filling only one of every two federal job vacancies to eliminate 20,000 government jobs. This desire to stop inflation by holding down government spending is most clearly demonstrated in the budget Carter proposed for fiscal 1980. That budget had only a $29 billion deficit compared to a $48.8 billion deficit in 1978. Moreover, while the 1978 budget took 22.1 percent of the gross national product, and 1980 proposed budget would take only 21.2 percent.

Though high levels of inflation are opposed by nearly everyone, the President's program has run into serious opposition on several fronts. First, the "real wage insurance" program has met congressional opposition and has been bottled up in the House Ways and Means Committee for several months. Many organized labor leaders oppose it as well as members of Congress who fear that it may cost the government an extra $15 billion a year. Second, Carter's policy of not giving government contracts to firms doing $5 million worth of government business has been challenged in the courts by private industry and denounced in Congress as an illegal usurpation of legislative authority. Efforts to reduce inflation by reducing expensive regulations have also run into trouble. For example, when the Interior Department sought to relax strip-mining regulations to reduce the price of coal, it was sued by three environmental groups.

President Carter's vetoes of inflationary legislation have been bitterly attacked. In early October, for example, his vetoes angered textile manufacturers and cattlemen. The head of the National Cattlemen's Association called the veto a "short-term political expediency" that would contribute to inflation.[26] When the President vetoed $10.2 billion worth of pork-barrel legislation in October 1978, he had to go against House Democratic leaders. Opposition to the President was especially strong among legislators from western states where federally funded dams and irrigation projects are economically important.

Perhaps the strongest opposition to Carter's anti-inflation program has been generated by his 1980 "lean and austere" budget. This budget would eliminate 158,000 public service jobs, cut back government-subsidized housing by 25,000 units, trim $600 million in social security benefits, and otherwise reduce the federal commitment to social welfare programs (however, the military budget was increased 10 percent). Many people had harsh judgments of the proposed anti-inflation budget. Vernon Jordan of the National Urban League (a black civil rights group) said that it would make blacks and poor people "common fodder in the war on inflation."[27] The vice president of the American Council on Education called cutbacks in health personnel programs "a disaster" and added that the budget "raise[d] serious questions about the future of our medical schools." George Meany, president of the AFL-CIO, said it is "a major attack on the living standards of average Americans." Dozens of groups and several prominent political leaders—including Ted Kennedy—have organized to fight these proposals in Congress.[28]

Analyses of Carter's 1978 anti-inflation program illustrate several things about making economic policy. First, despite a widespread demand to reduce inflation, this goal can be pursued only to a limited degree. As Carter moved against inflation, many people worried that government cutbacks would lead to a recession. Especially among less well-off citizens, even a mild recession might result in much higher levels of unemployment. Second, economists are not in agreement on whether Carter's programs will work or what the consequences will be. Some, like Alfred E. Kahn, the President's chief inflation fighter, believe that jawboning can work; other economists disagree. If so many economists disagree over the value of voluntary wage and price limitations, why should workers and businesspeople make sacrifices to follow these guidelines?

Third, almost every anti-inflation policy has had political costs to the President. Reducing quotas on the amount of cheaper beef the United States can import was not a policy designed to make U.S. cattlemen happy (such a policy also upset people concerned about our trade deficit). When the President eliminated 250,000 summer jobs in his proposed 1980 budget, many black leaders were angry. Assuming that President Carter wants to win reelection, enacting policies that hurt specific

[26] Quoted in Brooks Jackson, "3 Inflation Vetoes," *Champaign-Urbana News-Gazette*, November 12, 1978.

[27] Quoted in *Newsweek*, January 29, 1979, p. 20.

[28] These and other reactions are reported in *Congressional Quarterly Weekly Report*, January 27, 1978, pp. 125–126.

Belmont, Massachusetts

BOUGHT 1972	SOLD 1977
$39,500	**$65,000**

Inflation has been particularly severe for the cost of private homes. While most home-owners have made high paper profits due to inflation, many prospective home buyers find themselves priced out of the housing market.

Santa Monica, California

BOUGHT 1974	SOLD 1977
$61,000	**$131,500**

groups a lot (but that help everyone a little) is not an effective strategy. Finally, the fate of many anti-inflation policies shows that even the President can do only so much without the cooperation of Congress, independent regulatory commissions, bureaucrats, and the courts. A two-thirds majority in both houses of Congress could implement a totally different 1980 budget than the one proposed by Carter. Agencies can continue to enforce expensive regulations despite presidential pleas. The limits of presidential power were well illustrated when Carter called for increased timber harvests from federal land, a program that would, it was estimated, reduce new housing prices by 2 percent a year (a saving of $1.5 billion a year). Congress, however, blocked the funds necessary to implement the plans.[29]

[29] "Timber Angle," *Forbes*, July 24, 1978.

In sum, it is one thing to agree on an economic goal and quite another to carry it out. The issue for the President is not how to reduce inflation. The question is, How do we reduce inflation without using extensive coercion, meet other equally important goals, and keep most people happy?

Has the federal government become too involved in the economy?

Despite the controversy surrounding economic policy making, most national political leaders accept the principle of government economic intervention. Controversies generally concern the amount and type of intervention, not intervention itself. It would be a mistake, however, to conclude that extensive government economic intervention goes unchallenged. A long and distinguished intellectual tradition asserts that when government meddles in the economy, the ultimate result is economic ruin and loss of personal freedom. Especially in recent years, as the federal government has shown less ability to achieve its economic objectives, this position has received more attention. Let us briefly consider the arguments made by one of the best-known critics of government economic intervention, Milton Friedman.[30]

FRIEDMAN'S ECONOMIC PHILOSOPHY

The paramount value in Friedman's analysis of politics and economics is individual freedom. For Friedman the ability to do what one wants to do subject to minimal restrictions (for example, laws against killing other citizens) is more important than any other value, including social equality or prosperity. Anarchy—the absence of all formal government—is, however, strongly rejected. Government is essential if a free society is to exist. The major problem, according to Friedman, is how to maintain freedom while having a government strong enough to enforce the laws and provide essential services.

Limiting government
The problem of controlling government is resolved through several mechanisms. One is to limit severely the scope of government action. Government exists only to perform functions that citizens acting independently cannot do themselves. These include maintaining national defense, keeping law and order, enforcing agreements between private individuals, fostering competitive markets, and occasionally undertak-

---

[30] Our analysis of Friedman's philosophy is drawn largely from his *Capitalism and Freedom* (Chicago: University of Chicago Press, 1962). Other arguments against extensive government economic intervention are offered in George J. Stigler, *The Citizen and the State* (Chicago: University of Chicago Press, 1975).

ing projects beyond the capacity of individual citizens (for example, collecting gasoline tax revenue to maintain public roads). The government should not tell a citizen how to live, what to eat, or otherwise impinge on individual freedom.

A second important way to balance government power with individual freedom is to disperse the power of government as widely as possible. Specifically, political power is better concentrated at the local rather than the state level, and, in turn, state political power is preferred to concentration at the national level. Friedman argues that if things get oppressive in the local community you can always leave. The same is true at the state level—if you don't like the policies of New York, you can always move to New Jersey. If you don't like the policies made in Washington, D.C., however, your freedom to choose is much more constrained.

Capitalism and freedom

To this point much of Friedman's analysis is not very different from some of the principles found in the Constitution. What causes controversy is the next step in Friedman's analysis—the linking of individual freedom to a particular economic system, namely, competitive capitalism. Friedman defines competitive capitalism as a system in which exchanges are voluntary for all parties and people are informed in their actions. If you and your father, freely and knowingly, agree that you can use the family car on Saturday in exchange for mowing the grass, you are operating under a system of competitive capitalism. Friedman argues that without competitive capitalism there can be no freedom, though the mere existence of competitive capitalism does not guarantee individual freedom.

Capitalism and freedom are linked in the following two ways. First, the economic freedom provided by capitalism is a crucial freedom in and of itself. You are not free, according to Friedman, if the government can determine such things as your conditions of employment or how you spend your income. Second, capitalism separates political and economic power, so one can offset the other. In a capitalistic system you can hold antigovernment or otherwise unpopular opinions, yet because the government does not control the economy, you can still find employment. A well-known Communist could survive economically in a capitalist system, but an advocate of capitalism could not in a Communist system. Moreover, in a competitive system characteristics such as political opinion, race, religion, sex, and the like, are irrelevant to transactions. In fact, Friedman argues that historically there has been less racial, ethnic, and religious discrimination in economically competitive segments of society. The desire to make a buck drives out irrational prejudices.

Friedman's analysis of the relationship between economic freedom and political freedom leads him to oppose virtually all government intervention in the economy. He would, among other things, abolish all government subsidies, remove all foreign-trade tariffs and import restrictions, eliminate compulsory social security contributions, abolish the peacetime draft, and have toll roads run by private enterprise. Friedman would not, however, give private enterprise an absolutely free hand.

THE FEDERAL RESERVE SYSTEM

Congress and the President must share their economic policy making with the Federal Reserve Board (the Fed, as it is commonly called). The Fed was established in 1913 and is designed to act as a national bank for the United States. The overall operation of the Fed is supervised by a Board of Governors consisting of seven members serving fourteen-year terms. The terms of appointment are staggered so a term expires every two years. The appointments are made by the President and confirmed by the Senate. One member of the Board of Governors is designated its chair (presently Paul A. Volcker, who succeeded G. William Miller in mid-1979). In addition to the Board of Governors, there is also the Federal Open Market Committee, which buys and sells securities—mostly government bonds and other obligations. Most of the business of the Fed is carried out through twelve regional branches.

The Fed performs several important economic tasks. It is legally charged with supervising the activities of banks affiliated with the

Former Chairman of the Board of Governors of the Federal Reserve System G. William Miller meets with the Fed and aides.

Federal Reserve System (about 5,700). This includes fixing maximum interest rates on deposits, regulating bank mergers, determining how much a bank must keep in reserve, and generally setting standards for "good banking practices." One recent Fed action was to allow member banks to transfer money automatically from savings to checking accounts. The Fed also helps maintain the commercial banking system by providing such services as clearing checks, transferring funds, and making loans to banks.

Perhaps the most important function performed by the Fed is regulating the supply of money in the economy (a function usually known as **monetary policy**). As of June 1978 there was approximately $92.8 billion of currency and $257.1 billion in checking accounts for a total of $349.9 billion in circulation. The amount of money in circulation can have a major impact on the economy. With lots of money around businesses can borrow money at low interest rates and easily expand. Rapid expansion of business, however, can also bring inflation. Yet too little money can encourage recession and high unemployment. The money supply must be continually adjusted to encourage economic development but at the same time limit inflation.

The Fed can control the money supply through a variety of techniques. Allowing banks to pay high interest rates on deposits can encourage people to remove their money from circulation temporarily. The Fed also determines how much banks must hold in reserve and how much they can lend. Also, the price banks must pay for loans from the Fed affects the willingness of banks to lend money. The most important money-control mechanism, however, is open-market purchases. Here the Fed can purchase government obligations owned by private individuals and thereby convert, say, a $10,000 government bond into $10,000 in checking account deposits. This is $10,000 more that can be used to purchase goods and services.

The Fed has frequently been in conflict with Congress and the President. In general, the Board of Governors has taken a cautious approach to expanding the money supply while political leaders have been more worried about recession than about inflation. The Fed's independence is reinforced by the fact that it is entirely self-supporting from the profits from its open-market operations. On more than one occasion Presidents have been warned by the Federal Reserve chair that attempts to overstimulate the economy through increased government spending will be countered by Fed policies to slow down the growth of the money supply.

Monetary policy Policies affecting the amount of money and credit in the economy. When money and credit are reduced, money is frequently called "tight." Monetary policy is sometimes contrasted with fiscal policy—the use of government expenditures to shape the economy.

Since monopolies limit free choice, they should be prevented by government action—unless for technical reasons they are economically essential (for example, a unified telephone system). Another limitation derives from what Friedman calls "neighborhood effects"—the effects of transactions on people not a party to the transaction. For example, a polluting steel mill can harm everyone in the area, and these people have no say about the situation. In such instances Friedman recommends case-by-case solutions with a careful weighing of the costs and benefits of government intervention.

Friedman's defense of competitive capitalism is not based solely on its maximization of individual freedom. He also believes that free enterprise is more effective than government intervention in solving social and economic problems. For example, Friedman argues that if we abolished government licensing of doctors (that is, anyone could practice medicine), medical care for the population would be more plentiful, of better quality, and cheaper than under present rules. Similarly, racial and ethnic discrimination would decline faster if the government stopped issuing antidiscrimination rules and instead encouraged greater economic competition. Friedman claims that the economic costs incurred by discriminatory behavior are a more powerful (and much cheaper) solution to discrimination than a multitude of regulations and court orders.

The arguments advanced by Friedman and his associates are not always viewed as unrealistic, "pie-in-the-sky" schemes. Increasingly, the case for getting government out of the economy is being stated and applauded. The deregulation of airlines and natural gas has recently been given serious attention, and proposals have even been made regarding less government intervention in welfare and public aid. The question that now comes up is: How far can we carry Friedman's analysis of capitalism and freedom? If it were politically possible to disengage government and the economy, would this be a goal worth pursuing? In other words, is Friedman correct in claiming that competitive capitalism, freedom, and effectiveness all go hand in hand?

CRITICISMS OF MINIMAL GOVERNMENT AND UNRESTRICTED CAPITALISM

A basic criticism of Friedman's position concerns his conception of freedom. Recall that his definition of freedom entails the right to do what you want except for actions such as murder or not fulfilling legal obligations. Critics point out that such "freedom" is meaningless without a certain amount of economic equality. A poor person and a millionaire do not bargain in the marketplace as equals. Eventually, unrestrained economic competition will result in a large class of impoverished, exploited citizens, totally dependent on the wealthy. Thus, if freedom is to be meaningful, some degree of economic equality must be assured, and this requires government intervention. Government programs such as progressive taxation and social services are required to maintain (not diminish) individual freedom.

A second criticism focuses on Friedman's view of government as a kind of neutral policeman to enforce the rules and maintain physical safety. This view is unrealistic, according to Friedman's critics, because wealthy interests will soon gain control of government and use its coercive capacity for their own selfish purposes. A government controlled by the rich would soon rewrite the laws to weaken the bargaining position of workers in the name of enhancing free enterprise. The proper role of government in a free society is to redress the imbalance between rich and poor. Government in a purely capitalist society would only deepen the discrepancies of power.

Finally, the assertion that capitalism can be an effective provider of goods and the amenities of life has no historical foundation, according to Friedman's critics. Capitalistic societies such as nineteenth-century England or the United States experienced repeated economic crises during which fortunes were wiped out and millions of people suffered severe hardships. Moreover, some critics of capitalism claim that the capitalist system by its very nature encourages war and **imperialism** to solve its economic problems. Without strong government planning and management, the economic system goes from one crisis to the next.[31]

Imperialism The policy of one country dominating another for purposes of economic exploitation. Usually applied to advanced industrial societies controlling underdeveloped countries.

RESOLVING THE CONFLICT BETWEEN CAPITALISM AND STATE INTERVENTION

The debate between advocates of capitalism and state intervention is unlikely ever to be conclusively resolved. One reason is that neither system has ever—or is likely to in the future—existed in its pure form. Most, perhaps all, economies are mixtures of free enterprise and government control. Even the Communist economy of the Soviet Union contains a small class of officially tolerated capitalists who provide essential services in agriculture and industry. Nor has any country ever been run solely on the principles of competitive capitalism. Moreover, both sides disagree sharply on the meaning of key terms. Because of differing interpretations of words like "freedom" and "equality," participants in this debate usually talk past one another. Hence, it is unlikely that either side could convince the other of its arguments.

A conclusion: economics and politics

The U.S. economy is incredibly complex. Almost everything is somehow related to everything else, and many important factors, for example, the weather and the actions of foreign nations, are difficult to predict. This

---

[31] These arguments do not exhaust the debate. Several additional criticisms of the capitalistic economy are offered in Richard C. Edwards, Michael Reich, and Thomas E. Weisskopf, *The Capitalist System*, 2d ed. (Englewood Cliffs, N.J.: Prentice-Hall, 1978). Also see Leonard Silk, *Capitalism: The Moving Target* (New York: Praeger, 1974).

complexity is reinforced by the technical nature of contemporary economics. Though every citizen makes economic decisions regarding production and consumption, the language of professional economists leaves most people baffled. Even elementary economic terms, for example, "marginal utility" and "opportunity cost," are too sophisticated to be part of most public debate. And as students of Economics 101 know, it is easy to be impressed by experts with their econometric models and elaborate statistical analyses.

All of this makes it tempting to leave economic policy making to trained experts. One could treat economic problems like one would treat automobile problems: discover that something is wrong, but leave it to an expert to diagnose and correct the problem. You pay the bill, but you don't tell the mechanic how to do the job.

We have argued in this chapter that political decisions affecting the economy take precedence over purely technical decisions. The U.S. economy is *not* like a car that has to be correctly tuned up by master technicians following a service manual. There are many different ways, not a single "correct" way, of solving economic problems. Through the political process we establish our priorities and the particular solutions we shall employ. A professional economist could show us that production is exceeding demand and suggest a tax cut as a solution. However, the seriousness of this problem and the question of *who* will get the benefit of a tax reduction are political, not technical, questions. Similarly, an economist might claim that federal programs must be curtailed to reduce inflation, but which programs should be reduced? Should we prune the budget for the National Park Service or cut expenditures for medical care?

All solutions to economic problems have costs and benefits. A tolerable cost for one person may be an intolerable disaster for another. A manual worker on a salary can easily accept a 10 percent increase in the capital gains tax; for a real estate developer, however, this might be a calamity. Naturally, the beneficiaries of economic policies will probably justify their good fortune on the basis of "sound economic policy as proven by experts." We are not claiming that expert opinion is irrelevant or serves only as a rationalization for personal gain. Rather, basic questions regarding who is to benefit at whose expense are issues decided in the *political* process. They are not technical matters better left to trained experts.

Major questions raised

1. How does the government affect the economy? The major ways government affects the economy are through promoting economic development, taxes and subsidies, regulations, government consumption, and government-owned enterprises.

2. What are the economic goals of government? The federal government is committed to the goals of moderate growth, full employment, low inflation, private enterprise, and the preservation of the middle class.

While these five goals are widely accepted, the means to accomplish them are controversial. Different solutions favor some interests more than others, and experts disagree on the best economic strategies.

3. Has the government become too involved in the economy? Most political leaders do not seriously question the existing economic role of government. Differences of opinion occur over specific policies. However, this position has been challenged. Critics such as Milton Friedman argue that government economic intervention leads to a loss of individual freedom and greater inefficiency. Friedman, in turn, has been criticized for his conception of personal freedom and his unrealistic expectations of what would happen to a government under competitive capitalism.

QUESTIONS FOR FURTHER DISCUSSION

1. What would you do if you were in Senator Frank Church's shoes? In December 1979, the United States and eighty other nations signed a new International Sugar Agreement. This treaty has to be approved by the Senate, but it first must pass through the Senate Foreign Relations Committee, of which Church is chairperson. Here is Church's situation. Church represents Idaho, a state with many sugarbeet growers and processors. The International Sugar Agreement does not set prices high enough to satisfy Idaho sugar producers. They would like an extra 3½ cents a pound increase, which would cost American consumers up to $1 billion a year (and thus contribute to inflation). Church is up for reelection in 1980. If you were Church, would you risk electoral defeat and support lower sugar prices? Would you oppose the agreement to keep the Idaho producers happy but stop short of using all your influence and power to block it? Would you be out of town giving a speech against the agreement when the Foreign Relations Committee takes its vote?

2. An important component of the middle-class life-style is home ownership. Because mortgage interest and local property taxes are deductible on federal income taxes, home ownership (as opposed to renting) is indirectly subsidized by the federal government. These deductions will cost the government an estimated $15.9 billion in fiscal 1980 (*Congressional Quarterly Weekly Report*, February 24, 1979, p. 342). Would you favor eliminating this incentive and simply reducing taxes by $15.9 billion? Or should the government provide a tax incentive for home ownership?

3. For several years the federal government has been involved in legal action against IBM on the grounds that IBM is a monopoly (IBM controls about three quarters of the U.S. computer business). The government, and many smaller computer companies, contend that by virtue of its size IBM can unfairly compete for business. IBM responds by saying that it has become so large by supplying better products at lower prices. Companies much larger than IBM (RCA and GE, for example) have tried but failed to provide better products at less cost. If IBM is right, would you still break up IBM on the grounds that such monopoly is a potential threat to our economy? That is, would you be willing to tolerate higher prices and less innovation to prevent the excessive accumulation of power? How do you respond to IBM's claim that antimonopoly laws penalize efficient companies?

4. The Energy Act of 1978 allows individuals credits on their tax pay-

ments of up to $300 for investments in storm windows, weather stripping, furnace-ignition systems, and other energy-saving devices installed in their private homes and residences. The purpose of the act is to use tax incentives to reduce energy consumption. Wouldn't it be much easier just to raise the price of fuel? This strategy would eliminate paper work and legal confusions over what is a legitimate energy-saving device as well as provide a more direct incentive to save energy. What are the principle advantages of tax incentives over higher prices? Why would leaders enact rules that require even more paper work?

BIBLIOGRAPHY

Best, Michael H., and William E. Connolly. *The Politicized Economy.* Lexington, Mass.: Heath, 1976.
   A radical interpretation of the U.S. economic system which argues that our present problems cannot be solved by more government welfare programs. Maintains that the present system encourages inequality, job dissatisfaction, and misuse of the environment.

Edwards, Richard C., Michael Reich, and Thomas E. Weisskopf, eds. *The Capitalist System: A Radical Analysis of American Society,* 2d ed. Englewood Cliffs, N.J.: Prentice-Hall, 1978.
   A large collection of articles highly critical of present-day economic conditions and policies. Describes such things as the alienation of workers, the irrationality of present policies, U.S. imperialism, and alternatives to the present system. Contains a bibliography.

Friedman, Milton. *Capitalism and Freedom.* Chicago: University of Chicago Press, 1962.
   A provocative and widely read book defending minimal government intervention in economic affairs. Argues that we would have more freedom, better health care, less poverty, and less racial discrimination if government would not try to run our lives.

Haveman, Robert H. *The Economics of the Public Sector.* New York: Wiley, 1970.
   Basically examines the impact of federal spending and tax programs on U.S. society. Frequently asks who loses and who wins in particular economic decisions. Some elementary knowledge of economics is helpful but not essential.

Melloan, George, and Joan Melloan. *The Carter Economy.* New York: Wiley, 1978.
   Analyzes Carter's economic policies in the first year of his Administration. Useful for describing backgrounds of advisers, contending approaches in the Administration, and the relationship of economic to noneconomic goals.

Musolf, Lloyd D. *Government and the Economy: Promoting the General Welfare.* Chicago: Scott, Foresman, 1965.
   A good, straightforward description of how the government affects the economy. Describes government promotion of various enterprises, federal regulations, things that the government buys, and how government officials run various ventures. Contains a bibliography.

North, Douglas C. *Growth and Welfare in the American Past.* Englewood Cliffs, N.J.: Prentice-Hall, 1966.
   A clearly written review of economic events and policies from colonial times to the mid-1960s. Thought rich in information, no prior knowledge of economics or statistics is required.

North, Douglas, and Roger LeRoy Miller. *The Economics of Public Issues,* 2d ed. New York: Harper & Row, 1973.
   Briefly considers the economic aspects of 33 public issues. Included are such topics as abortion repeal, prostitution, medical care, sports, oil spills, marriage, and distributing free bread.

Pechman, Joseph A. *Federal Tax Policy*, 3d ed. Washington, D.C.: The Brookings Institution, 1977.

An expert analysis of how tax policy is made, the nature of different (including state and local) taxes, and the impact of taxation policy. Contains a considerable amount of statistical data, but does not require knowledge of statistics or economics. Contains a bibliography.

Stern, Philip M. *The Rape of the Taxpayer: Why You Pay More While the Rich Pay Less*. New York: Vintage Books, 1974.

A somewhat sensationalist but carefully documented study of how wealthy citizens manipulate the tax laws to their advantage. Contains numerous fascinating examples.

Stigler, George J. *The Citizen and the State: Essays on Regulation*. Chicago: University of Chicago Press, 1975.

Stigler argues that expansion of government regulation – even if motivated by the best of intentions – diminishes our freedom. Moreover, regulatory efforts are frequently ineffective and wasteful. Case studies on government regulations of electricity, the stock market, and consumer protection are presented. Good coverage of different approaches to regulation.

Taxes, Jobs and Inflation. Washington, D.C.: Congressional Quarterly, 1978.

An excellent overview of government economics in the mid-1970s. Examines topics such as social security policy, tax policy, airline deregulation, and farm policy and presents a chronology of economic policy from 1973 to 1977. Contains a bibliography.

Tufte, Edward R. *Political Control of the Economy*. Princeton, N.J.: Princeton University Press, 1978.

Argues that politics, particularly elections, has a major impact on such economic matters as income levels, economic expansion, unemployment, and size of national budgets. Occasionally gets technical.

PREVIEW

How is U.S. foreign policy made?

Foreign policy consists of actions that involve relations between the United States and foreign governments. The line between foreign and domestic policy is not always clear. Foreign policy decisions involve five major participants: the President, the executive branch advisers and departments, Congress, interest groups, and the general public. The roles these actors play usually depend on whether or not a situation is a crisis demanding an immediate U.S. response. Crisis decision making is characterized by presidential domination, a limited number of other participants, rapid decisions, and a heightened concern for the national interest. In contrast, noncrisis decision making is marked by the participation of many actors, a concern for public opinion, extensive bargaining, and divergent views on overall policy goals. Noncrisis decision making usually resembles domestic policy making.

What are the goals of U.S. foreign policy?

The basic goal is maintaining national security. Before World War II this goal did not require active involvement in world affairs. Since World War II the focus of national security has been the containment of Soviet expansion through military alliances, overseas bases, military intervention, and the maintenance of a large military force. Promoting peace and international stability is a third major goal. Supporting the United Nations, mediating armed conflicts, and, most important, reaching agreements with the Soviet Union have contributed to this goal. Through such policies as foreign aid, technical assistance, and reduced trade restrictions the United States has sought to promote world-wide economic development. Furthering U.S. economic interests is a fourth major foreign policy goal. This policy has been criticized as promoting U.S. imperialistic domination of less developed nations.

Have American foreign policy obligations been achieved?

Overall, the United States has had limited success in implementing its goals. It has contained Soviet expansion, has helped to resolve many world tensions and has had successes in providing economic assistance, and U.S. economic interests have prospered overseas. There have, however, been many failures. Major wars still occur, much of the world remains poor despite billions in U.S. aid, and overseas corporate success has had mixed results for the U.S. domestic economy. Improving the performance of U.S. foreign policy may be difficult. International affairs are filled with uncertainty, and many problems require complex solutions beyond present capacities. Moreover, foreign policy objectives frequently conflict with domestic goals. Finally, major foreign policy goals can sometimes collide.

CHAPTER NINETEEN

GOVERNMENT AND FOREIGN RELATIONS

For most of U.S. history political leaders were far more concerned with domestic than with foreign policy. Until World War II the policy of isolationism—noninvolvement with other nations unless to protect clear national interests—was a reasonably accurate description of American foreign policy. The last forty years, however, have seen a major change. Many of the most basic aspects of our existence, for example, energy, food, clothing, and security, are dependent on international agreements. The American farmer, once a virtual symbol of isolationism, has become keenly interested in the intricacies of foreign trade. Foreign policy issues regarding military commitments, arms agreements, and trade frequently play a significant role in state and national electoral campaigns. Even more important, the advent of nuclear weapons and the missile systems to deliver these weapons has dramatically raised the stakes of foreign policy making. Whereas a domestic policy mistake can waste billions of dollars or cause numerous people to feel outraged, foreign policy mistakes can bring nuclear holocaust. In many ways the politics of national security is *the* high-stake game in politics. The making of U.S. foreign policy is exceptionally complex, but our analysis will consider three basic aspects of this process:

1. How is U.S. foreign policy made?
2. What are the goals of U.S. foreign policy?
3. Have American foreign policy objectives been achieved?

How is U.S. foreign policy made?

Before we address the question of how foreign policy is made, we must first ask: What exactly is foreign policy? In the past the answer to this question was clear—foreign policy consisted of those policies directly involving foreign governments. When the President signed a treaty with Great Britain regulating trade, this was foreign policy. Foreign policy involved such questions as declarations of war, military alliances, diplomatic recognition, and matters relating to foreign trade.

Today, however, the distinction is frequently less clear. Many domestic issues have important implications for U.S. relations with other nations, and agreements with other nations can have immediate domestic consequences. For example, in 1973, the U.S. government decided to sell the Soviet Union a substantial quantity of wheat. This decision affected the strength of the dollar (which affected world trade) and was part of an overall U.S. policy of improving relations with the USSR. On the domestic side, by decreasing the supply of wheat the sale increased the price of food and encouraged wheat farmers to expand production (which, in turn, had financial and political consequences when wheat prices eventually declined). Overall, it is more useful to think of a policy continuum ranging from purely domestic (for example, building a highway) to purely foreign (for example, a military alliance). In between are many policies, for example, energy-conservation programs designed to reduce oil imports, with both domestic and foreign consequences.

Let us begin our analysis of the making of U.S. foreign policy by considering the role of the five participants (or "actors" as they are frequently called). The actors are (1) the President; (2) executive branch advisers and departments; (3) Congress; (4) interest groups; and (5) the general public. These are not, of course, the only participants who have an impact on foreign policy. On occasion the courts have made decisions that limit presidential power over foreign policy (and they administer international law). Private governments such as labor unions or corporations can also have an impact (for example, some dock-workers' unions threatened to refuse to load wheat sold to the Soviet Union in 1973). Nevertheless, these five actors represent the major participants in foreign policy making.

THE PRESIDENT

More than any one person, the President is responsible for making U.S. foreign policy. While the President cannot dictate policy, our overall foreign policy orientation must have presidential approval. Other actors such as Congress or interest groups may occasionally frustrate part of the President's program, but positive action requires presidential support. In fact, it is sometimes argued that the United States has two presidencies—a domestic President who frequently finds it difficult to control policy and a President for foreign affairs who has considerable power to achieve his goals.

The President's preeminence in foreign affairs derives from several sources. The Constitution grants the President several important powers relevant to foreign policy. As commander-in-chief of the armed forces the President can dispatch troops anywhere in the world. It was this constitutional provision that allowed President Truman to involve the United States in Korea in 1950 and President Johnson to make a similar commitment in Vietnam in the mid-1960s. Article II, section 2 also gives the President the power to make treaties (subject to Senate approval) and appoint ambassadors. The importance of these provisions was highlighted by President Carter's negotiation of the Panama Canal Treaty in 1977 and his appointment of the controversial Andrew Young as U.S. Ambassador to the United Nations. Section 3 of Article II further authorizes the President to receive ambassadors. This power has generally been interpreted to mean the power of diplomatic recognition of foreign nations. President Carter, for example, has refused diplomatic recognition to Vietnam, thus hindering trade and travel between the two nations.

The President's constitutional power is not limited to the powers explicitly granted. The Founding Fathers clearly realized that the system of checks and balances and separation of powers designed to prevent domestic tyranny were less appropriate for foreign relations. Thus, the federal government was left relatively free to protect national sovereignty. And by federal government in this instance the Founding Fathers meant the President. In the words of John Marshall, the President is "the Nations' organ for foreign affairs." In practice this has meant that a determined President can almost always push to their limits the meaning of constitutional grants of power relating to foreign policy without legislative or judicial interference. Even explicit limitations, for example, the congressional prerogative to declare war, can sometimes be overcome by a determined President.

The Constitution is but one source of presidential preeminence in foreign policy. The President's claim to speak for the nation is buttressed by several more practical claims. Dealing effectively with foreign powers requires a unified voice, and only the President can provide such unity. Imagine what might happen if congressional leaders or cabinet officials acted independently of the President in negotiating, say, an arms-limitation agreement with the Soviet Union. These leaders may attempt to influence presidential policy, but they would be risking confusion if they acted on their own. Congressional or cabinet leaders, unless speaking on behalf of the President, would also lack the prestige that is so necessary in international negotiations.

Another practical reason for presidential preeminence concerns the speed at which foreign affairs can move. Many international events requiring a U.S. response must receive immediate attention, and it is much easier for one person to act decisively than a committee or two legislative houses. Even advocates of a stronger congressional role in foreign policy acknowledge that the necessity for extensive consultation or debate during a crisis would be detrimental to our national welfare.

The sensitive nature of many foreign policy decisions also helps the

KEY OFFICIALS IN FOREIGN POLICY MAKING

Two of the key officials in the making of U.S. foreign policy are the Secretary of State and the Director of the Central Intelligence Agency (CIA). The Secretary of State is in charge of the State Department, an agency with far-ranging world responsibilities. Besides running diplomatic missions and providing advice to the President, State negotiates treaties and represents the United States in more than fifty major international organizations. The CIA is responsible for collecting and evaluating intelligence relating to national security. Here are brief portraits of the two men who head these agencies.

ALEXANDER M. HAIG, JR., Secretary of State. Born December 2, 1924, in Bala Cynwyd, Pennsylvania. Attended Notre Dame University, but graduated from West Point in 1947. Obtained a master's degree in international relations from Georgetown University in 1961. Has spent almost his entire adult life in the military. Besides a variety of administrative positions Haig saw extensive combat in Korea and Vietnam. His first major political job was military assistant to the Secretary of the Army, Cyrus Vance, in 1964 (he was later Deputy Secretary of Defense under Robert McNamara). After extensive action in Vietnam and duties at West Point, he joined Henry Kissinger's staff and began a rapid rise in the Nixon Administration, eventually becoming Nixon's last White House chief of staff. Haig played a major role in keeping things together during the last months of the Nixon presidency. He then served as commander of NATO forces and later as president of United Telephone Corporation, a $9 billion-a-year firm. Haig has frequently been described as an exceptionally hard-working "new breed" military man who grasps politics and can work well with people. He is also highly regarded by many European leaders.

WILLIAM J. CASEY, Director of the CIA. Born March 13, 1913, in New York City. Graduated from Fordham University and St. John's University Law School. Became involved with the Office of Strategic Services (forerunner of the CIA) in World War II. Rose to chief of intelligence operations for the European theater. Remained very interested in espionage following the war but became a very successful and wealthy lawyer specializing in tax law. Casey has also written several books on tax law. Under President Richard Nixon he served as chairman of the Securities and Exchange Commission, Undersecretary for Economic Affairs, and president of the Export-Import Bank. Managed Ronald Reagan's presidential campaign where he gained a reputation as a gruff, not very diplomatic but decisive manager. At times Casey appears as an inarticulate, bewildered old-timer, but this masks a razor-sharp mind. He is personally close to Reagan, and the President is sufficiently concerned with the CIA to give Casey cabinet rank.

President maintain his key position. Much of the information used in making decisions cannot be stated openly, and the odds of this information remaining secret are much greater if it remains in the White House. Some of this information, for example, evaluations of Soviet missile strength, may be shared with key congressional leaders, but it would be extremely risky to release it to all 535 members of Congress. Nor could the U.S. bargaining position in international negotiations be widely discussed without serious risk. All in all, then, by virtue of both his powers and the nature of world politics, the President is the preeminent figure in formulating foreign policy.

EXECUTIVE BRANCH ADVISERS AND DEPARTMENTS

Though the President dominates the foreign policy-making process, he does not act all by himself. Surrounding the President are numerous advisers, cabinet-level departments, and special agencies that provide everything from detailed technical information to serving as sounding boards for new policies. Advisers and cabinet departments are a key link in determining the policies that will be followed and how they will be implemented. Many a presidential directive came to naught when top aides or middle-level bureaucrats chose to ignore or distort it.

Every President had advisers who are especially important in the creation of foreign policy. The precise titles of these advisers vary from President to President and may change in the course of an administration. President Carter, for example, sought advice from many people, including Zbigniew Brzezinski (national security advisor) and Cyrus Vance (Secretary of State). President Ford relied much more heavily on one person, Secretary of State Henry Kissinger. Important foreign policy advisers may even come from domestic departments. President Nixon during his first term frequently consulted with his Attorney General, John Mitchell. A key adviser may not even have an official position — men like former Ambassador W. Averell Harriman and former Secretary of State Dean Acheson advised Presidents Kennedy and Johnson but never received formal titles describing their positions.

The closest thing to an "official" foreign policy advising group is the National Security Council (NSC). A part of the Executive Office of the President, the NSC was created in 1947 to insure coordination in national security policy making. The original membership consisted of the President, Vice President, Secretaries of Defense and State, the national security adviser, chairman of the Joint Chiefs of Staff, the director of the Central Intelligence Agency, and the director of the Office of Emergency Preparedness. More recently the Secretary of the Treasury and the chairman of the Council of Economic Advisors have been added to the NSC. Despite the design of this Council and the illustrious people who serve on it, the NSC rarely has a major impact on policy. The principal reason for this is that the group of "inner advisers" on whom the President relies rarely corresponds to this legally defined group. In some ways convening the NSC is more a signal to the outside world than an attempt to get the best possible advice.

Beyond the NSC and other White House advisers are several large bureaucracies that deal with much of the routine (though highly important) business of foreign policy. The most relevant to foreign policy is the Department of State, which in 1977 employed almost 30,000 people.[1] It is the State Department that runs the world-wide network of U.S. embassies and consulates and oversees relations with international organizations such as the United Nations and the Organization of American States. The State Department also has numerous world-wide research and intelligence responsibilities. If, for example, the President is contemplating a new policy regarding South America, he might receive legal, political, and economic assessments developed by State Department experts. Perhaps due to its sheer size and unwieldiness, however, in recent years the State Department has rarely played a significant role in major foreign policy decisions. President Kennedy once described it as a "bowl of jelly." Its inability to act quickly is well illustrated by the fact that in the early 1960s twenty-nine separate signatures were required to approve an outgoing telegram concerning milk exports.[2]

Another large bureaucracy with a special foreign policy relevance is the Central Intelligence Agency (CIA). Established in 1947, it is charged with collecting intelligence and advising the President and the NSC on intelligence matters. On occasion the CIA has also engaged in more direct actions, for example, assassinations of foreign leaders or revolutions, but is is unclear just how much of this behavior was explicitly authorized by the President. As with other government departments, the importance of its official functions does not automatically guarantee its great influence with the President. Following the aborted 1961 invasion of Cuba in which the CIA supposedly played a significant part, President Kennedy paid less attention to CIA assessments and advice.

The Department of Defense is also an important element in the making of foreign policy. Over the years top Defense officials have been among the President's closest advisers (for example, President Johnson initially relied heavily on the advice of his Defense Secretary, Robert McNamara). The military services also maintain their own intelligence organizations, and, as mentioned, the chairman of the Joint Chiefs of Staff is a member of the NSC. The military has played an important role in arms-limitations negotiations and in providing assessments of both U.S. and foreign military capabilities. The lengthy and costly involvement of the United States in Vietnam resulted, in part, from overly optimistic evaluations of American intervention provided by the Pentagon.

Other government agencies with foreign policy responsibilities include the Arms Control and Disarmament Agency, the Agency for International Development (AID), which administers economic aid to foreign nations, the United States Information Agency (USIA), the United States International Trade Commission, and the Export-Import Bank of the United States, which facilitates exports and imports. There are even

[1] *Statistical Abstract of the United States 1978*, p. 270.

[2] These incidents plus a more general evaluation of the State Department can be found in Cecil V. Crabb, Jr., *American Foreign Policy in the Nuclear Age*, 3d ed. (New York: Harper & Row, 1972), pp. 65–73.

government-financed, but technically private, advisory agencies outside government. These include the well-known "think tanks"—the Rand Corporation and the Hudson Institute—as well as research organizations at major universities.

CONGRESS

Like the President, Congress derives much of its role in foreign policy making from explicit constitutional grants of power. Article I, section 8 gives Congress the power to regulate foreign commerce, declare war, and define and punish offenses against the Law of Nations. In Article II, which describes presidential power, the Senate is given responsibility for approving treaties (by a two-thirds vote) made by the President and the right to approve "Ambassadors, other public Ministries and Consuls." Equally relevant to the conduct of foreign affairs is the power over appropriations. Since many foreign policies require money, refusing to appropriate funds requested by the President is a powerful weapon.

Many of the congressional powers that have evolved over the years also contribute to the role of Congress in foreign policy. Congressional oversight—legislative monitoring of the executive bureaucracy—has allowed legislators to influence foreign policy through their involvement with the State Department, the CIA, and more specialized agencies such as the Export-Import Bank. During the 1960s, on the issue of foreign military aid the Secretaries of State and Defense had to maintain close relationships with ten separate congressional committees and subcommittees. Moreover, each legislative house has several committees with jurisdictions in aspects of foreign policy (for example, the House Committee on International Relations). Finally, the congressional power to investigate can sometimes be a potent weapon. During much of the war in Vietnam the Senate Foreign Relations Committee's investigation of the war provided a public forum for those opposed to U.S. intervention.[3]

Limits on congressional power over foreign policy

The formal foreign policy powers of Congress are considerable, but it has often been maintained that the gap between formal and actual power is usually large. While Congress can sometimes thwart presidential goals, historically Congress has been the junior partner to the President in making foreign policy. This contention is supported by several different pieces of information. In the area of treaty ratification, for example, one study found that between 1789 and 1963 the Senate approved without change 69 percent of the treaties submitted to it.[4] Many important international agreements have been enacted by executive agreements that do not require Senate approval but have the same level standing as treaties.

---

[3] A more detailed analysis of the role of Congress in making foreign policy is presented in James A. Robinson, *Congress and Foreign Policy-Making*, rev. ed. (Homewood, Ill.: Dorsey Press, 1967).

[4] Cited in Crabb, p. 106.

Regarding Senate confirmation of diplomatic appointments, the Senate almost always goes along with the President. Even if the Senate resisted, the President has available such tactics as "interim" appointments (appointments made after congressional adjournment that do not require Senate approval until forty days after the start of the next legislative session) or can simply appoint a person as his "personal representative" to important diplomatic missions.

Perhaps the most significant area in which congressional foreign policy initiative has eroded is in declaring war. Two of the costliest wars in American history—the Korean and Vietnam wars—were never declared by Congress. In both instances the President relied on his powers as commander-in-chief to dispatch U.S. troops (though President Johnson claimed legislative approval through the Tonkin Gulf Resolution of August 10, 1964, which empowered the President to protect U.S. military security in Southeast Asia). As a result of what it perceived as excessive presidential war power, Congress passed the War Powers Act of 1973 to curb undeclared wars. The heart of this act is a provision requiring a President to obtain congressional authorization of a troop commitment within sixty days; approval for an additional thirty days may be given without a formal declaration of war, but after ninety days Congress can require disengagement of all troops and the action cannot be vetoed by the President. However, doubt remains as to whether Congress would actually resist presidential military initiatives if national security was clearly involved.

Congressional control over appropriations has also proved to be more a limited weapon than a major instrument of control. On several occasions congressional efforts to use appropriations to set foreign policy have been met by presidential vetoes or outright refusal to spend the money. Presidents have also avoided legislative interference through the appropriations process by transferring funds across programs or by subterfuge (for example, declaring military equipment "obsolete" so it can be given away or sold without congressional authorization). Moreover, by its very nature Congress is ill-equipped to offer the President a budget that reflects its own coherent foreign policy goals. The type of financial control Congress is capable of was illustrated by its refusal in January 1976 to allow military aid to pro-Western forces in Angola (a similar action had been to ban military aid to Turkey). Such actions are not insignificant, but they hardly constitute overall control, and a determined President can probably surmount these obstacles.

INTEREST GROUPS

At one time it was customary to dismiss the role of interest groups in foreign policy. Foreign policy involved such momentous decisions as war, peace treaties, and diplomatic alliances, while interest group behavior supposedly concerned more mundane, closer-to-home politics. It is perhaps still true that on "big" foreign policy decisions (for example, whether the Korean War should have been expanded into China) interest groups play a very limited role. Nevertheless, short of these "big" decisions, pressure groups do affect policy outcomes. Moreover, if the trend of

An attempt to pressure the Japanese government to restrict the killing of whales through a boycott of Japanese-made goods in the United States. Such boycotts can allow citizens a method of influencing foreign governments directly.

growing interdependence between foreign and domestic policy (where interest groups are important) continues, the role of pressure groups will increase correspondingly.

The impact of interest groups on foreign policy

Interest group behavior relevant to foreign policy takes several forms. The most obvious is probably in the area of international trade. Especially in recent years, with increased world-wide economic competition, numerous U.S. industries depend on trade agreements for their survival. These industries, through such trade associations as the Corduroy Council of America or the National Frozen Pizza Institute (which is concerned with cheese imports), can exert considerable pressure regarding import duties, export subsidies, import quotas, and other details of trade. Often these battles involve far more than the price of television sets or pizzas. To a nation that depends heavily on exports to the United States — for example, Japan, Great Britain — increased import duties may be interpreted as a very hostile action. Similarly, if the government were to give in to various group demands for lower food prices by curtailing soybean exports to Japan, the repercussions for U.S.-Japanese ties would be far-reaching (soybeans are a major food source in Japan).

Other types of interest groups that have had a voice in making U.S. foreign policy are ethnic or nationality groups. Millions of Americans have special ties to foreign nations, and groups representing these citizens frequently lobby government. For example, when Turkey invaded the Greek-held island of Cyprus in 1974, Greek organizations waged a successful campaign to cut off U.S. military aid to Turkey. Over the years numerous Jewish groups have run a well-orchestrated campaign in support of U.S. aid to Israel. More recently several black civil rights groups have focused their attention on U.S. policy in Africa (especially on the issue of sanctions against the Union of South Africa and Rhodesia).

A third type of interest group that is oriented toward foreign policy can best be described as the political-cause group. These groups concentrate on policies such as nuclear disarmament or an international treaty pro-

639

tecting whales from extinction. These groups have varied in organization and tactics. Some, like the American Friends Service Committee, maintain low-key operations devoted to such noncontroversial issues as world hunger or the plight of refugees. Others, however, view their role as that of marshaling public pressure on Congress or the President. In

THE
MULTINATIONAL
CORPORATION
AND FOREIGN
POLICY

Traditionally, foreign policy involves relations between nations. Citizens, interest groups, and businesses might try to affect this policy, but they would operate through government, not as independent actors. The rise of multinational corporations with large assets in several countries is, however, changing the nature of the foreign policy-making process.

One dramatic illustration of this change was the events involving the International Telephone and Telegraph Company (ITT) in Chile in 1970–1971. ITT had about $200 million in assets in Chile that were threatened by the election of the Marxist-oriented Salvador Allende as president. An established American company facing economic loss from a new government is not, of course, a new situation. Many corporations have had similar problems, and the usual solution has been to seek U.S. government protection or to solve the problem by threats, bribes, or negotiations. The actions of ITT, however, went beyond the usual tactics and show that private corporations can behave almost as if they were sovereign governments.

First, ITT saw the conflict with Allende as much more than a dispute over company property. To top ITT officials the survival of the Allende government posed a national security threat to the United States, the rest of Latin America, and the private enterprise system. Even if no commercial loss were to be suffered, Allende would have to be overthrown. This view of the potential danger from Allende differed substantially from the views of many U.S. government leaders. If the U.S. government would not accept ITT's view of the situation, ITT was prepared to go it alone even if this course meant opposition from the State Department and possible damage to overall U.S. foreign policy in Latin America. ITT did not view itself as governed by U.S. foreign policy; it perceived itself as an entity with its own foreign policy.

Second, ITT's action against the Allende government went far beyond normal commercial practices. Among other tactics, it offered a million dollars to the CIA for its assistance, it vigorously supported the

the early 1960s, for instance, the Fair Play for Cuba Committee tried (unsuccessfully) to create a more favorable climate for Fidel Castro's Cuba. The war in Vietnam gave birth to several groups both for and against U.S. military involvement. In general, the political-cause interest group has had less success than the other groups.

---

leading anti-Allende newspaper, and it otherwise financed an extensive propaganda program (in November 1978 it was convicted in U.S. courts of paying $400,000 in illegal payments to Chilean officials in order to overthrow Allende). It also sought to create anti-Allende alliances among Chilean businesspeople and members of the military. Many of these actions involved the CIA (this link was probably facilitated by the fact that John McCone—ex-head of the CIA but still secretly on the CIA payroll—was a director of ITT). ITT officials also suggested an alliance of other American companies to deny credit to Allende, to delay payments, to stop delivery of spare parts, to withdraw technical assistance, and otherwise to subvert the Chilean government. Such actions were much more aggressive than those of other U.S.-based firms in Chile.

Finally, like a sovereign nation ITT ran its own intelligence service that was concerned with the whole range of events in Chile. At times ITT seemed more interested in struggles within Chilean political parties, newspaper reports, military matters, and economic conditions than in information directly affecting company investments. On occasion ITT intelligence reports concerned the size of the Russian embassy staff and the arrival of Cuban political police. Here again the evidence suggests that ITT's interests in Chile went well beyond protecting its financial investment.

Incidents such as these could become commonplace in the future. Many multinationals, especially the oil giants such as EXXON, Gulf, and Texaco, do not always see their interests as identical to U.S. foreign policy goals, despite the fact that they are U.S. corporations. In a future energy or monetary crisis these corporations may behave like independent nations complete with their own currency, intelligence networks, treaties, ambassadors, and ever-changing alliances. An American President may have to negotiate with the head of EXXON as well as with foreign leaders regarding the price and availability of oil.

Our analysis here is drawn from P. G. Bock, "The Transnational Corporation and Private Foreign Policy," *Society*, Jan./Feb. 1974. Also see Anthony Sampson. *The Sovereign State of ITT* (New York: Stein and Day, 1973), Chap. 11.

FOREIGN MANIPULATION OF AMERICAN TELEVISION

The impact of public opinion on American foreign policy is difficult to measure. Nevertheless, several foreign governments attribute enough importance to public opinion to spend millions of dollars each year to influence it. Much of this money is spent on influencing TV viewers, but rarely do people realize they are watching foreign propaganda.

The most direct method of influence is the packaging of "news" that goes out over the air in the same form as the usual news story. For example, the British Information Service (a government agency) makes available to the networks news films about Northern Ireland that reflect the position of the British government on this issue. Some networks have sent out edited versions of these propaganda films to their local affiliates as part of their regular news service. Programs featuring news-oriented interviews (for example, *Today, Good Morning America, Meet the Press*) are sometimes used to promote the perspective of a foreign government in the guise of a "spontaneous interview with a political personality." (These personalities will sometimes give long, previously memorized speeches defending their nation's actions regardless of the questions asked them.)

Another popular method of attempted influence is the nonpolitical travelogue show that gives a good impression of a nation and leaves out any negative elements. The TV show *Journey to Adventure,* hosted by Gunther Less, which appears in eighty areas of the country is a frequent vehicle for such propaganda. On four shows Less ran programs highly favorable to Iran and Iran's former leader, the Shah, but no mention was made that Less was a paid consultant to the of-

THE GENERAL PUBLIC

The remaining actor in foreign policy making that we shall consider is the American public. Compared to our previous analyses, assessing the role of public opinion is much more difficult. Actions of the President, members of Congress, or interest group leaders can be observed or otherwise ascertained, but not so with public opinion. Despite the power sometimes attributed to public opinion, to show concretely how this influence has been exerted is almost impossible. Measuring the role of public opinion is frequently akin to measuring the impact of an invisible and mysterious force. The task is frequently complicated by the fact that leaders who are pursuing unpopular policies will nevertheless insist that they are acting in accord with public opinion.

ficial Iran airline. *Journey to Adventure* has also run favorable shows on the Union of South Africa (South Africa supplied the film and bought commercial time for the show). Overall, in 1977, the South African government placed twelve government-made films on television and showed them to thirty million American viewers. Viewers of station KOIN-TV in Portland, Oregon, once saw eight shows on lifestyles in Taiwan. These shows came about because the government of Taiwan brought the show's host (Mike Donahue) and the film crew to Taiwan at government expense.

Perhaps the most common means of attempted influence is creating general feelings of good will among television producers and reporters. The news staffs of CBS, NBC, and ABC are forbidden from taking free all-expense paid trips from foreign governments, but reporters from local affiliates have accepted free trips to South Korea, Israel, Taiwan, Egypt, Italy, Ireland, Greece, France, and Japan. Many reporters argue that they are inevitably influenced in a positive direction by such graciousness. Another indirect method of influence is to develop close ties to a reporter (this is also an advantage to the reporter for getting stories). The Palestine Liberation Organization (PLO) has, for example, developed such ties with Peter Jennings of ABC. People like Walter Cronkite, Barbara Walters, and important television executives are also regularly invited to diplomatic receptions and embassy parties. Do these efforts actually work? Many people think so. In the words of one ABC reporter, "I don't go to many embassy functions. I don't want to get over-wooed."

John Wiseman, "Foreign Lobbyists: How They Try To Manipulate U.S. Television," *TV Guide,* November 18, 1978, pp. 7–14; and "Buying Good Will and More," *TV Guide,* November 25, 1978, pp. 30–36.

Public opinion and broad foreign policy objectives

Does public opinion have an impact on U.S. foreign policy? Most experts would probably agree that the greatest impact of the public is in defining broad policy boundaries.[5] That is, the public holds leaders responsible for meeting general foreign policy objectives, and leaders understand that to ignore these objectives is to risk almost certain electoral defeat or disgrace. Among these objectives are maintenance of our national sovereignty, preventing the spread of communism, promoting world peace, protecting traditional allies such as Great Britain, and upholding U.S. world prestige and influence. Of course, many different policies can be

[5] See, for example, Gabriel A. Almond, *The American People and Foreign Policy* (New York: Praeger, 1960), especially Chapter 1.

consistent with these broad goals. Some leaders, for example, might pursue world peace by intervening militarily in the affairs of other nations. Emphasis on the peace-keeping role of the United Nations would also be consistent with the goal of world peace. Though such goals can be vague, they can be important. Imagine the results if a political leader said it was fine with him if the Communists took over Italy.

Public opinion and specific policy goals

When it comes to more specific policies, however, the role of the public is more constrained. An overwhelming majority of citizens may favor a strong U.S. military presence overseas to thwart Communist aggression, but whether this will be accomplished through diplomatic alliances (for example, NATO) or independent action (for example, a strong Sixth Fleet in the Mediterranean Sea) is not a question likely to be decided by public opinion. That public opinion is less relevant in foreign than domestic affairs is quite understandable. For one thing, citizens are frequently less informed about foreign affairs than domestic issues, and leaders are undoubtedly aware of this lack of knowledge.[6] Second, under most circumstances foreign policy choices have less impact on people's lives than domestic policy. Thus, the consequences of leaders ignoring public opinion may be less severe. You may not want the United States to sign an arms-limitation treaty with the Soviet Union, but if the President did sign such a treaty, your anger would not be as great compared to, say, a 25 percent increase in your taxes.

We are not suggesting that leaders therefore have a free hand in specific foreign policy decisions. Especially when foreign and domestic issues are interconnected, public opinion can be crucial. During the war in Vietnam, for example, leaders paid close attention to the results of opinion polls. Similarly, as U.S. farmers have grown increasingly dependent on exports they have become much more vocal on the details of foreign agricultural trade. If President Carter were to cut off U.S. sales of grain to the Soviet Union in retaliation for its actions in Africa, the outcry would be immediate and very loud.

THE RELATIONSHIP AMONG FOREIGN POLICY ACTORS

Thus far we have described the five major participants in the foreign policy process. The important question we now face is: How do these different participants interact? If the President, presidential advisers, Congress, pressure groups, and public opinion are the actors, what are the scripts? Those who have observed the making of U.S. foreign policy have distinguished between two basic policy-making patterns: crisis and noncrisis decision making. Each usually has its own style and cast of players.

[6] Data on this point are presented in Robert Weissberg, *Public Opinion and Popular Government* (Englewood Cliffs, N.J.: Prentice-Hall, 1976), pp. 33–34.

Crisis policy making

A crisis situation is the occurrence of an unexpected event that could substantially affect U.S. interests. Almost always these events involve large-scale violence (or the threat of violence) and require a prompt U.S. response. Such crises are a regular feature of international relations. In 1946, the Soviet blockade of West Berlin sharply increased world tension and resulted in a massive U.S. airlift of supplies to Berlin. The invasion of South Korea by North Korea in 1950 (and the subsequent Communist Chinese intervention) also raised immediate questions that required a rapid response. In 1955 and 1958, the United States again faced the possibility of war with China over the islands of Quemoy and Matsu, which belonged to Nationalist China (Taiwan) but were under attack by the Communists. The Cuban missile crisis of 1962 brought a direct confrontation between the United States and the Soviet Union over whether Soviet offensive missiles would be based in Cuba. Numerous civil wars and border disputes have also precipitated crisis situations. Our involvement in Vietnam generated numerous such crises, the last being the Cambodian seizure of the American merchant ship *Mayagüez* in 1975, which resulted in a U.S. military operation to secure its release. On the average, there seems to be at least one such crisis every couple of years.

Policy making during a crisis tends to have certain characteristics. Without exception it is the President who dominates decision making. Whether the United States will send troops, authorize other military action, dispatch an emergency diplomatic mission, or issue a public warning must be decided by the President. Congress, pressure groups, large government bureaucracies, and public opinion have almost no immediate role during a crisis. Moreover, the President rarely involves more than a few aides and advisers and maybe a few congressional leaders to help him make these decisions. These key participants are usually among the President's inner circle of advisers and rarely correspond exactly to the official foreign policy advising apparatus.[7] Finally, a concern for the national interest is the dominant (though not exclusive) theme of decision making. Goals such as personal advancement, bureaucratic expansion, economic gain, or favorable publicity tend to be subordinate.[8]

Noncrisis decision making

Noncrisis policy making involves a much larger and more diverse set of participants. For example, a decision on whether to sell the Soviet Union the latest computer as part of a "normalization of relations" program would involve the State Department, the Department of Defense, the Department of Commerce (since commerce officials are interested in overall U.S.-Soviet trade), the Export-Import Bank, Congress (since there

[7] For an excellent description of crisis activity written by a participant, see Robert F. Kennedy, *Thirteen Days: A Memoir of the Cuban Missile Crisis* (New York: Norton, 1969).

[8] John Spanier and Eric M. Uslaner, *How American Foreign Policy Is Made*, 2d ed. (New York: Holt, Rinehart and Winston, 1978), pp. 114–115.

are laws covering the sale of militarily relevant goods to foreign nations), numerous businesses and issue-oriented organizations, and the President and his staff. Noncrisis decisions also frequently involve a major concern for public opinion (though not an absolute adherence to it). During our negotiations with Panama over a new canal treaty, for example, there was much talk of "selling" or "educating" the public, and opinion surveys were used to pressure Senators undecided on their votes.

Typically, since participants do not share the same perspective on an issue, policy making is characterized by conflict and bargaining. On an issue such as selling the Russians U.S. computers the Defense Department may find itself opposed by the State and Commerce Departments. A division of opinion is also likely in Congress—"get-tough-with-Russia" legislators may oppose those interested in greater trade and legislators from the state in which computers are manufactured. Extensive bargaining may occur over what computers should be sold, the terms of the sales, and the political concessions to be extracted from the Russians as part of the deal. Unlike decisions reached in crisis situations, the debate can go on for months or even years. Greater disagreement over what best serves the national interest is also likely. Would the sharing of our technology with the Russians help reduce U.S.-Soviet hostility, or would a technologically stronger Russia be more aggressive and belligerent?

As we move from the "big" crisis decisions in foreign policy toward those not involving immediate threats to U.S. security, foreign and domestic decision-making processes converge. The way in which funds for antipoverty programs and foreign aid are decided have many parallels. The President is important, but he does not dominate the process (and may have a limited interest in the outcome). Numerous people are involved, and the final outcome results from many compromises and the skillful advancement of particular interests. Finally, issues like foreign aid, trade agreements, overseas military deployment, and other noncrisis policies are part of an ongoing debate, with no decision likely to have immediate and dramatic consequences. This is in contrast to situations such as the 1968 crisis when North Korea seized the U.S. intelligence-gathering ship *Pueblo* in international waters. Here the President had a day or so to decide whether U.S. military intervention (which could have triggered a war) was necessary (no military action was taken).

What are the goals of U.S. foreign policy?

Every year government officials make hundreds of decisions involving foreign policy that cost billions of dollars. What overall goals motivate these decisions? What is U.S. foreign policy supposed to accomplish? Basically, we can distinguish four broad goals: (1) maintaining national security; (2) promoting peace and international stability; (3) providing economic assistance; and (4) furthering U.S. economic interests. Frequently these goals overlap, for example, U.S. aid to a developing nation can also help U.S. corporations that provide this aid, but this distinction of goals provides a useful way of approaching a variety of government and private political actions.

NATIONAL SECURITY

The protection of the United States from foreign aggression has been the preeminent goal of U.S. foreign policy. Without a secure territory none of the other goals are possible. For most of American history this goal was not the major item on the agenda despite its unquestioned priority. Until World War II our geographical isolation plus the nature of warfare allowed U.S. political leaders the benefit of not having to make difficult (and expensive) decisions regarding alliances or military commitments.

The end of World War II, however, brought a fundamental change in U.S. national security policy. First, the advent of the atomic bomb and long-range bombers (and later intercontinental ballistic missiles) ended the luxury of being able to take a year or two to decide whether we should enter a war and then fighting the war on somebody else's territory. A Pearl Harbor with atomic weapons is a terrifying thought. Second, the emergence of the Soviet Union and other Eastern European Communist countries presented the United States with a formidable adversary explicitly committed to expansion by subversion, military invasion, or even free elections. This threat was given concrete meaning in 1947 when Soviet-backed forces seized power in Czechoslovakia and instituted a civil war in Greece to accomplish the same goal.

The doctrine of containing the Soviet Union

For all practical purposes since World War II the central feature of U.S. national security policy has been the containment of Communist expansion. This goal, first clearly stated by President Truman in a 1947 speech before Congress, was for many years known as the **Truman Doctrine.** As Truman himself put it: "I believe that it must be the policy of the United States to support free peoples who are resisting attempted subjugation by armed minorities or by outside pressures." Though recent Presidents have sought to reduce U.S.-Soviet tensions, blocking Soviet advances in Asia, Africa, or Latin America continues to be the key theme of our national security policy.

The U.S. response to Soviet expansion has taken a variety of forms. Following World War II, when the possibility of Russian military intervention in a devastated Europe seemed very real, the United States launched the Marshall Plan to provide economic assistance to war-ravaged European countries (named after George C. Marshall, who as Secretary of State first proposed such aid). Between 1947 and 1952, about $15 billion was given to Western European nations (the Soviet Union was asked to participate in the plan but it declined). In other aid programs designed to thwart Communist threats in the late 1940s, $400 million was given to Greece and Turkey and over $2 billion to Nationalist China (which proved to be futile because the Communists seized control

Truman doctrine The doctrine first proposed by President Harry Truman which called for free people throughout the world to resist subjugation by force. Directed at Communist subversion and armed intervention.

The U.S. Marines near Beirut, Lebanon, 1958. Troops were sent to prevent a possible collapse of the pro-U.S. government.

in 1949). In more recent times economic and military assistance has been given to Thailand, Pakistan, Korea, and many other nations to help prevent Communist takeovers.

Alliances have been a second major response to the threat of Communist expansion. The 1947 Rio Treaty signed by the United States, Mexico, and virtually all of South America provided for mutual assistance in case of attack originating inside or outside the Western Hemisphere. NATO—the North Atlantic Treaty Organization—was created in 1949 among the United States, Canada, Western European nations, and Iceland, Turkey, Portugal, and Greece. SEATO—the Southeast Asia Treaty Organization—which involved the United States, Great Britain, France, Pakistan, Australia, Thailand, and the Philippines—was formed in 1954. The United States also helped to create but did not actually join CENTO (Central Treaty Organization) in 1959 among Great Britain, Pakistan, Iran, and Turkey. In addition to these large-scale defensive alliances, the United States entered into bilateral treaties with Japan, South Korea, Taiwan, and other nations.

With the exception of NATO, these alliances have proved of little or no national security value. While the United States might come to the aid of treaty members, the likelihood of a SEATO or Rio Treaty member reciprocating is quite small. Moreover, military assistance supplied through treaty obligations has frequently been used for purposes other than containing communism. For example, Pakistan has usually deployed its military not against possible Soviet or Chinese attack but against India. Given the lack of political consensus among many treaty members, plus a decline in the immediacy of Communist aggression in many areas, most of these alliances—except for NATO—have become moribund or officially dissolved.[9]

A third response to the perceived Communist threat was the establishment of numerous overseas military bases. Since World War II American political and military leaders have held that the best deterrent to Soviet aggression was the threat of devastating U.S. thermonuclear retaliation. To make the threat credible in the days before long-range missiles, the United States surrounded the Soviet Union with large air force bases from which a retaliatory attack could be launched. Military installations were established in Libya, Spain, the Azores (owned by Portugal), Turkey, Japan, Iran, and several other nations as part of a "ring" around the Soviet Union. In many instances this policy of foreign bases had far-reaching implications. Having made this expensive investment, the United States frequently felt obligated to protect this investment by granting the host nations trade concessions, foreign aid, or support for local political elite. During the 1950s, for example, despite pressures to the contrary at home and abroad, we supported the Spanish dictator Francisco Franco on the grounds that our NATO air bases in Spain were essential to U.S. national security.

The United States has also engaged in numerous military operations in the name of stopping Communist expansion. The most notable, of course, were the Korean and Vietnam wars. In many other instances, however, U.S. intervention was less overt. For example, military supplies and training were given to anti-Communist insurgents in Iran, Chile, Guatemala, Cuba, and several African nations. In 1958, when it appeared that pro-Communist forces might seize control of Lebanon, President Eisenhower ordered the marines to Lebanon. President Johnson took similar action in 1965 when it appeared that the Dominican Republic might fall to Communist revolutionaries. Such intervention, even in areas far from U.S. borders with little economic relevance to American interests, has occasionally been justified by what is called the "**domino theory.**" Essentially, this perspective holds that one Communist victory will lead to another, and eventually, if unchecked, the whole world will go Communist, much as one tipped domino can trigger the fall of other dominos in a row.

Contemporary containment policy

Present-day national security policy remains based on containing Communist expansion, though the means to this end have changed considerably since the 1950s. Except for our traditional Western European allies (plus West Germany), military alliances are no longer a high priority. The development of long-range missiles that can be launched from within the United States, plus submarine-launched missiles, allows massive retaliation without extensive commitments to foreign bases. In the wake of Vietnam, America's commitment to military intervention to stop communism anywhere in the world has also been reassessed. In 1977, when

Domino theory The argument that if one country in an area is taken over by the Communists, neighboring countries will similarly soon fall. Used to justify intervention in seemingly non-important nations.

[9] A critical analysis of this alliance policy is presented in Henry A. Kissinger, *American Foreign Policy,* expanded edition (New York: Norton, 1974), pp. 66–76.

Cuban-backed pro-Communist forces seemed ready to seize control in Angola, Congress refused to authorize U.S. support to the pro-Western factions (some aid was given, but the end result was defeat for the Western-backed forces). Finally, defining national security solely in terms of containing communism has increasingly been questioned. The recent energy crisis and the Arab-led oil embargo of 1973 showed that communism is not the only world threat to vital U.S. interests. Stopping Communist expansion remains important, but it is no longer a simple question of the United States versus the Red Menace.

PROMOTING PEACE AND INTERNATIONAL STABILITY

A second goal of U.S. foreign policy has been to promote world peace. Preventing war has always been an important goal, but the growing interdependence of nations of the world plus the horrible consequences of nuclear warfare have made the goal even more crucial. Whereas a war between two obscure countries could have once been safely ignored, today there is always the possibility that the conflict could spread and be the spark that touches off World War III.

U.S. support for the United Nations

Following World War II U.S. leaders had great hope that world peace could be maintained through the United Nations. The American government was one of the moving forces in its creation and has since provided the UN with considerable financial and material support. On numerous occasions the goal of reducing armed conflict by UN intervention has been realized. Between 1947 and 1949, for example, the UN helped end the conflict between the Dutch and the Indonesians. Likewise, between 1948 and 1965, the UN played an important role in preventing a war between India and Pakistan over the disputed territory of Kashmir. On innumerable occasions UN troops have supervised armistices or provided a neutral buffer zone between opposing forces, for example, in Korea in 1953, in Cyprus in 1964, and in the Middle East in 1948, 1967, and 1973.

The American goal of creating an international peace-keeping force in the UN has not, however, had great success when world powers have been in direct conflict. Separating Indians and Pakistanis is considerably easier than preventing U.S.-Soviet military confrontations. When the Communist North Koreans invaded South Korea in 1950 the UN was powerless to stop a rapid escalation of military involvement. The UN was equally impotent when the Soviet Union invaded Hungary in 1956 and Czechoslovakia in 1968. Nor did the UN fare much better in mediating U.S. involvement in Southeast Asia. Overall, the UN has fulfilled American expectations in keeping peace when the issues or participants do not directly threaten U.S. or Communist bloc interests.

Direct U.S. intervention in conflicts

Besides working through the UN, the United States has on numerous occasions directly entered conflicts to promote peace. In 1973 and early 1974, for example, the American Secretary of State Henry Kissinger dramatically intervened in the Arab-Israeli war to arrange a ceasefire and an eventual agreement on the Israeli use of the Suez Canal and partial Israeli withdrawal from the Sinai desert. Perhaps the most spectacular recent U.S. peace-keeping effort occurred in September 1978 when President Carter brought Egyptian President Anwar Sadat and Israeli Prime Minister Menachem Begin together at Camp David to resolve several long-standing Arab-Israeli disputes. U.S. influence was also employed to mediate Turkish-Greek conflict over Cyprus, civil war in Nicaragua, and several Pakistani-Indian border disputes.

U.S.-Soviet accords

The most important diplomatic efforts directed at achieving world peace, however, have directly involved the Soviet Union. In the late 1950s, American leaders increasingly came to realize that avoiding World War III required some accommodation with the Soviet Union. Since then U.S. and Soviet leaders have taken several important diplomatic steps (frequently in conjunction with other nations) to reduce the possibility of nuclear holocaust. The first was the Antarctic Treaty signed by the United States in 1959, which took effect in 1961, making Antarctica international territory, prohibiting its military use, and allowing inspections to enforce this prohibition.[10] In 1963, the United States and Russia agreed to establish a telegraphic "hotline" between Washington, D.C., and Moscow for emergency communications (during the 1967 Middle East war it was used by the United States to prevent Soviet misunderstanding of U.S. fleet movements in the Mediterranean).

Since the late 1960s, the issue of arms control, especially the control of nuclear weapons, has occupied center stage as a means of reducing the risk of war. In 1967, the United States and Russia agreed to ban atomic weapons from space as well as to prohibit the military use of outer space. This was quickly followed in 1968 by the Treaty on the Non-Proliferation of Nuclear Weapons signed by the United States, the Soviet Union, and almost all the nations of the world. This treaty was intended to stop the spread of nuclear weapons to more and more nations and to insure that nuclear energy facilities for peaceful uses would not be misused for weapons production. In 1971 Russia and the United States, working through the UN, agreed not to install nuclear or other weapons of mass destruction on the ocean floor. The development, production, and stockpiling of biological weapons was likewise banned by almost all nations in 1972.

Of the various agreements relating to weapons, those with the farthest-reaching consequences are the Strategic Arms Limitation Talks (SALT) that have been going on with the Soviet Union with occasional interruption since late 1969. These talks are solely between the United States and the Soviet Union and concern the truly big weapons in each nation's military arsenal. First, these negotiations are in part motivated

[10] The full text of the Antarctic Treaty and other key arms-limitation treaties described here can be found in U.S. Arms Control and Disarmament Agency, *Arms Control and Disarmament Agreements* (Washington, D.C.: Government Printing Office, 1975).

THE HIDDEN SIDE OF AMERICAN FOREIGN POLICY

Though most Americans abhor ''dirty tricks'' in politics, the U.S.-Soviet conflict has frequently led to tactics of questionable legal and ethical value. Both sides justify these actions on the grounds that they are necessary to combat the other side's even-worse tactics. Many of the operations on the U.S. side are conducted by the Central Intelligence Agency (CIA) and, until recent exposés, were completely hidden from the general public and most high officials. Since the CIA has had some success in censoring these revelations (even prior to publication), our knowledge of its activities remains incomplete. These secret operations on behalf of U.S. interests have taken several forms.

Covert military operations

The CIA has supplied advice, training, weapons, and occasionally personnel to help establish pro-U.S. governments. Following World War II, CIA-trained agents were sent to Albania, Poland, and the Ukraine to organize resistance to Communist-controlled governments. Due to strict security measures in these countries, however, this infiltration was unsuccessful. In 1958, the CIA played a significant role in organizing a rebellion against President Sukarno of Indonesia. This involvement was denied by President Eisenhower, who stated, regarding the Indonesian rebellion, ''Our policy is one of careful neutrality and proper deportment all the way through so as not to be taking sides where it is none of our business.'' When the Tibetans rebelled against the Chinese Communists in 1959, the CIA not only trained and equipped Tibetan troops but CIA-operated planes helped direct and cover sabotage raids into Red China. Tibetan troops were also secretly brought to Colorado for more extensive training. Secret military operations against China (and North Vietnam) were also conducted by the CIA from bases in Laos during the early 1960s.

Covert military operations have been especially common in Latin American nations. In 1954, the CIA was largely responsible for a successful *coup d-état* that overthrew the socialist-leaning government of Guatemala. The most famous (and most disastrous) Latin American operation was the Bay of Pigs invasion of Cuba in 1961, which involved thousands of CIA-armed and trained Cuban refugees. Even after this dramatic failure the CIA continued to support refugee sabotage and espionage raids into Cuba. When guerrillas threatened the government of Peru in the early 1960s, the CIA trained a highly successful antiguerrilla army. In 1967, CIA agents were dispatched to Bolivia to help hunt down the Cuban revolutionary leader Che Guevera. The CIA likewise played a major role in the "destabilization" of the Salvador Allende regime in Chile in 1970.

Africa has also been the scene of several CIA interventions. When insurgents threatened the pro-U.S. government of the Congo in the early 1960s, the CIA created an "instant air force" of World War II-vintage B-26s piloted by Cubans. When troops from Castro's Cuba became involved in the Angolan civil war in 1976, the CIA again supplied arms and training to pro-U.S. forces.

Spying and espionage

The CIA and other government agencies, especially the National Security Agency (NSA), spend considerable effort monitoring the communications of other nations (including many of our allies). In many Latin American nations the CIA regularly intercepts telephone messages between officials and "bugs" their homes and offices. Sophisticated electronic listening posts exist in the United States and around the world to monitor the diplomatic communications of other nations. The FBI, working with the Chesapeake and Potomac Telephone Company, regularly monitors the phones of foreign embassies in Washington.

Since most messages are sent in code, effort must be devoted to breaking foreign codes. Most of this work is done by computers at the NSA, but the CIA has also stolen foreign codebooks, bugged embassy radio rooms, or secretly enlisted the aid of foreign code clerks. The United States also sells encoding and cryptographic devices to other nations, and knowledge of these devices is used by the United States to break the codes of these nations.

The CIA's Technical Services Division has also helped by developing a variety of James Bond-like spying devices. Among other things, it has built a radio transmitter designed as a false tooth, an ordinary-looking pencil that can write invisibly on special paper, and a rear-view automobile mirror that secretly provides a view of back seat passengers. One contraption that never got off the ground was a one-man airplane designed to be packed into two large suitcases (its purpose was to allow an agent to flee after the espionage). The CIA also has a section that works on forgeries, and these have been used on several occasions to cause confusion and undermine governments (U.S. reporters are sometimes inadvertently taken in by these forgeries).   *(Continued on p. 654)*

(Continued from p. 653)

Attacks on foreign leaders

Of all the "dirty tricks" in international relations the most controversial are assassination attempts on foreign leaders. Cuban Prime Minister Fidel Castro was the object of repeated CIA-organized assassination attempts during the Eisenhower, Kennedy, and Johnson Administrations. This was frequently done through CIA contacts with Mafia leaders such as Sam Giancona and John Rosselli. The Technical Service Division tried to lend a hand by developing such devices as exploding seashells and a poisoned fountain pen. In 1963, the CIA prepared a diving suit to be presented to Castro as a gift. The inside was dusted with a fungus to produce a chronic skin disease while the breathing apparatus contained tuberculosis bacteria.

The plot against Castro is not an isolated exception. Evidence points to some CIA involvement in "executive action" (as assassinations were called) against Patrice Lumumba (a leftist leader of the Congo), Rafael Trujillo, dictator of the Dominican Republic, Ngo Dinh Diem of South Vietnam, and General René Schneider of Chile. The CIA has also worked on plans to kill much larger numbers of people. For example, the CIA once flooded the New York subway system with a "harmless stimulant" of a disease-carrying gas to test the vulnerability of subway riders to a sneak attack.

These incidents are drawn from Victor Marchetti and John D. Marks, *The CIA and the Cult of Intelligence* (New York: Dell, 1975); and Morton W. Halperin, Jerry J. Berman, Robert L. Borosage, and Christine M. Marwick, *The Lawless State: The Crimes of the U.S. Intelligence Agencies* (Middlesex, England: Penguin Books, 1976).

by the huge costs of the arms race—the deployment of a new and expensive Soviet offensive weapon calls for an even more expensive U.S. defense, which in turn leads to new Soviet deployments, and on and on. Such weapons systems can cost tens of billions of dollars. Second, both sides have come to realize that increased military capacity does not automatically lead to greater security or reduce the outbreak of war. The United States and the Soviet Union have long since passed the point where each can inflict enormous damage on the other, so that multiplying this capacity provides few (if any) strategic benefits at a staggering cost.

Negotiations have been slow and complicated. The stakes are extremely high for both sides, and technical complexities abound. For example, is a U.S. medium-range bomber stationed in Europe a "strategic offensive weapon" because it can reach the Soviet Union, while a comparable Soviet bomber is not a strategic offensive weapon because from Russia it cannot reach the United States? Despite numerous problems and mutual suspicion (especially over how compliance is to be verified), the first SALT agreement was reached in 1972. This agreement limited each country to two (eventually changed to one) antiballistic missile (ABM) sites (and limited the number of missiles at each site). One site could protect the capitol while the other would protect an offensive missile base. Nor was each side allowed to develop and deploy ABM systems based on new technology. This agreement not only stopped the growth of a weapons system costing tens of billions of dollars but also prevented one side from risking war on the grounds that it was invulnerable to counterattack. In addition, a five-year interim agreement was also signed that essentially froze the number of intercontinental missile launchers possessed by each side.

After the 1972 set of agreements SALT talks were begun again (these sessions were known as SALT II) to resolve the issue of just how many strategic weapons each side should eventually possess and of what design (for example, submarine-launched missiles versus manned bombers). Agreements on these issues have come in piecemeal form. In late 1974, for example, President Ford signed an agreement putting a ceiling of 2,400 offensive strategic delivery vehicles (though the nature of these "vehicles" was left undecided for the moment). In 1978–1979, SALT II negotiators were wrestling with such problems as how to treat the U.S. cruise missile, a newly developed and very accurate air-launched missile. Also being debated was whether the latest Soviet manned bomber is a "strategic delivery vehicle," as well as the perceived problem of enforcing agreements.

In June 1979 President Carter and Soviet President Leonid Brezhnev signed the SALT II agreement in Vienna. This treaty limited both the development and deployment of missiles and bombers of various sizes and contained provisions to insure some degree of treaty enforcement (for example, data from test missile launches cannot be encoded).

Of course, it is difficult to say precisely how much these various agreements have contributed to world peace. Wars still occur, and a nuclear World War III remains a real possibility. Nevertheless, it is probably fair to say that these actions, ranging from the Antarctic Treaty to SALT II, have helped reduce world tension. At a minimum, they have provided an element of control in what could easily be a runaway military situation.

PROVIDING ECONOMIC ASSISTANCE

As the world's richest nation the United States has long had a commitment to helping other nations achieve higher standards of living. Of course, in many instances, for example, post-World War II help to Europe, economic assistance was largely motivated by the goal of blocking Communist expansion. Nevertheless, the United States has not been motivated solely by political expediency. On many occasions the U.S.

Corn meal waiting to be sent abroad as part of the U.S. "Food for Peace" program. Since 1954 the United States has sent about a billion dollars a year worth of food to those in need.

government has provided financial assistance or help in rebuilding after a natural disaster to nations that differed substantially with U.S. foreign policy.

Foreign aid

Much of our support for world-wide economic development has come through foreign aid money appropriated annually by Congress. Between 1949 and 1976, the United States made outright grants of over $76 billion and loans of over $39 billion (many such loans are never repaid).[11] Immediately following World War II aid was largely given to European nations, but since the mid-1950s the emphasis has been on helping underdeveloped nations. Some of the major recipients of foreign aid in recent years have been Egypt, Jordan, Guatemala, Indonesia, and the Philippines.[12] In recent years, however, there has been a trend toward using semiautonomous multinational agencies to channel U.S. economic aid. These include the World Bank, regional bodies such as the African Development Fund, and UN agencies (in 1976 the United States gave over $1 billion to such international organizations).[13]

[11] *Statistical Abstract of the United States, 1978,* p. 861.
[12] *Statistical Abstract of the United States, 1978,* p. 862.
[13] *Statistical Abstract of the United States, 1978,* p. 858.

In addition to regular foreign aid assistance, the United States has enacted special programs to meet particular problems or the needs of specific areas. For example, President Kennedy was greatly concerned with U.S.-Latin American relations and helped create the Alliance for Progress, with an American commitment of $10 billion over a ten-year period to foster industrialization and economic growth in Latin America (subsequent Presidents have extended this commitment). For many years through the U.S. Food for Peace Program surplus farm products have been given to nations in need. On several occasions surplus U.S. wheat prevented famine in India, Egypt, and several African nations. In 1961, President Kennedy by executive order created the Peace Corps. Under this program thousands of Americans have worked overseas to provide technical assistance on a person-to-person basis, frequently in remote areas.

Foreign aid through international trade

One area of enormous relevance for economic assistance is international trade. Many leaders of underdeveloped nations have argued that concessions in trade are far more valuable for economic progress than an occasional foreign aid handout. They maintain that if the United States really wanted to help, say, Ghana, it would import more cocoa beans from that country. This policy is frequently called "trade, not aid," and it is strongly endorsed by the United States. The United States insists, however, that trade concessions be reciprocal; that is, if we cut cocoa bean duties, Ghana should cut its duties on U.S. soybeans. The underdeveloped nations have largely rejected this position on the grounds that it would favor the industrialized nations who would flood poor nations with their goods, thus preventing local economic development. To date, while the United States has occasionally helped an underdeveloped nation by modifying its trade policy, it has not abandoned its policy of reciprocal trade concessions.

FURTHERING U.S. ECONOMIC INTERESTS

As we saw in Chapter Eighteen, the federal government has traditionally been an important promoter of U.S. industry, even to the extent of ensuring that U.S. business can effectively compete in overseas markets. In fact, several critics of U.S. foreign policy have claimed that the promotion of U.S. commercial interests throughout the world is *the* preeminent goal of American foreign policy. These critics characterize American foreign policy as imperialistic, that is, geared to systematically exploiting the rest of the world to turn profits for giant U.S. corporations. Whether government assistance is merely a helping hand or part of a comprehensive imperialist strategy is an important question that we shall consider once we have described how government promotes U.S. business interests abroad.

Megaton The explosive power of a million tons of TNT. Smaller weapons are described in terms of kilotons—thousands of tons of TNT.
Overkill The capacity to kill people which exceeds the number of people who can be killed. An overkill of five means that you could kill five times as many people as there actually are in a given place.
Second strike An attack on the enemy made after the enemy has attacked first.

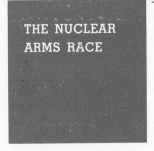

THE NUCLEAR ARMS RACE

One of the most controversial military developments since World War II has been the build-up of U.S. and Soviet strategic nuclear arsenals. Presently the United States maintains 1,054 Minuteman land-based missiles, 656 submarine-based missiles, and 380 plus long-range bombers. These weapons could deliver 9,000 nuclear warheads (with an explosive capacity of 6,500 **megatons**) on 11,000 Soviet targets. The United States also possesses some 22,000 nuclear weapons designed for battlefield use. To appreciate the devastating power of this arsenal, one Department of Defense study estimated that an attack by "only" twenty of our forty-one submarines could kill seventy-four million Russians and destroy three-quarters of Soviet industry.

The building of this arsenal has been criticized as a needless, and very expensive, exercise in **"overkill."** Such power could readily kill every person on earth several times. And despite arms-limitation talks like SALT, the overkill is increasing. Can this system be justified? Defenders of massive overkill point to the goals of all this weaponry and the relationship between weapons and the likelihood of World War III.

It is argued that the ultimate purpose of these weapons is to *deter* aggressive enemy action, not to kill each Soviet citizen five times over. Deterrence requires that even if the enemy launches a powerful first strike on the United States, and even manages to destroy most U.S. military installations, the U.S. retaliation—or **"second strike"**—will be equally devastating. If the enemy knows that even if it knocks out 85 percent of U.S. fire power on the first strike it will still suffer an unacceptable loss, it will think long and hard before striking first. Hence, each side needs enough missiles to absorb the massive initial attack and still launch an effective second strike.

It is also argued that the diversity of weapons—land-based missiles, submarine-based missiles, and manned bombers—is essential to prevent a technological breakthrough from rendering obsolete our entire deterrence capacity. For example, technological advances and spy satellites have recently made land-based missiles more vulnerable to attack. However, U.S. submarines are still beyond such detection. For

U.S. overseas investments

Anyone who has traveled overseas has observed U.S. brand name products—ranging from Coca Cola to Caterpillar bulldozers—in almost every country. The penetration of foreign markets is neither accidental

this reason it is also important to develop new weapons-delivery systems to insure further invulnerability to technological advances (for example, Missile X, a proposed $20 billion system of 200 missiles that would be moved randomly through underground passages to 4,000 silos spread over a large area).

Advocates of maintaining the present nuclear deterrent system also claim that having more and better weapons *decreases* the likelihood of nuclear war. They argue that if each side had only a few missiles, the temptation to launch a first strike would be much greater. First, a small force has little second-strike value, so that if it is to be used, it must be used as a first-strike force. Moreover, as a first strike against an equally small force it might be possible to wipe out the enemy (and even if this failed, the retaliatory strike would be small). However, a Russian leader would have to be insane to believe that a first strike could destroy over a thousand American ground missile sites, forty-one submarines, and numerous bomber bases. Spending vast sums to make these installations invulnerable to attack also decreases the probability of war. Because U.S. missile sites have been "hardened," that is, missiles are buried in concrete silos, they can survive a virtual direct hit. Thus, the chances of a first strike succeeding are made even more remote.

Given this logic, it is easy to see why nuclear systems can expand at an astronomical rate. When the United States deployed its submarine missiles the Russians responded with more missiles of their own to maintain their margin for a second strike in case of an initial U.S. attack. Of course, the Russian missiles now changed our vulnerability to a Russian first strike, so we had to construct yet more missile bases as well as develop techniques of multiple warheads for each missile. This, in turn, generated a similar response by the Russians. Since neither side was gaining any real strategic advantage from this escalation (and the costs were huge), SALT made considerable sense.

For a further analysis of these issues, see Philip Morrison and Paul F. Walker, "A New Strategy for Military Spending," *Scientific American,* October 1978, pp. 48–61; and "Nuclear Hardware Debate Masks SALT II Political Issues," *Congressional Quarterly Weekly Report,* January 6, 1979, pp. 3–10.

or due to the appeal of U.S. goods. The federal government has taken several steps to insure that General Motors or Boeing can sell products in Europe, Asia, South America, or Africa. The U.S. tax code, for example, contains provisions that encourage U.S. overseas expansion. When a

U.S. business located abroad pays taxes to a foreign government, these taxes are credited against the company's U.S. taxes as opposed to being treated as ordinary business expenses.[14] American overseas businesses also enjoy a deferral privilege, which delays U.S. taxes on earned income until the earnings are actually brought back into the United States. This provision grants to companies what amounts to interest-free loans. Both tax credits and deferred income provide major monetary incentives to do business overseas. Moreover, under some conditions portions of various antimonopoly laws are suspended when U.S. businesses cooperate with one another to engage in foreign trade.

The U.S. government has also acted to prevent foreign nations from leveling excessive import duties on American products. The well-known "Open Door" policy toward China advocated in the 1890s called for all commercial interests, whether British, French, or American, to be given equal treatment. The most significant modern manifestation of this policy has been the General Agreement on Tariffs and Trade (GATT), which the U.S. played a major role in creating in 1947. This agreement, which includes most non-Communist nations, regulates tariff policy on thousands of items in world trade. Members of GATT agree not to discriminate against countries in their tariff rates, not to use internal taxes to substitute for tariffs, not to impose import quotas (except in special circumstances), and not to flood foreign markets (that is, dump) with artificially cheap goods. Though GATT contains several important escape clauses, overall it has acted to open up world trade.

In many instances government officials have directly negotiated (or served as intermediaries) on behalf of U.S. business interests. Recently, for example, in response to large trade imbalances between the United States and Japan, American officials have tried to convince Japan to import more U.S. beef and citrus products and in general make it easier for U.S. companies to sell in Japan. Perhaps the most obvious government efforts on behalf of U.S. corporations occurs in the sales of military hardware. For example, when General Dynamics was trying to sell its F-16 fighter plane to several European air forces (in competition with the French F1 M53) it received full government cooperation (the U.S. Army even gave procurement orders for machine guns to a Belgian company to further the deal).

The foreign aid program is yet another means of opening up the world

---

[14] The importance of this provision can be made clear by a simple example. Suppose that an American corporation earns $100 million and its U.S. corporate income tax bill is $50 million. Also suppose that $20 million was earned in Japan where it paid $5 million in Japanese taxes. This $5 million is then credited against the federal government claim of $50 million (reducing the corporation's U.S. taxes to $45 million). If, however, the company has located its operation in, say, New Jersey and paid $5 million in New Jersey state taxes, this $5 million would be deducted from the company's $100 million earnings as a business expense. With a federal tax rate of 50 percent, this $5 million deduction saves the company $2.5 million while a tax credit of $5 million saves $5 million. In this example the company has a $2.5 million incentive to do business in Japan rather than in New Jersey.

"I see. Due to your corrupt mis-management, the people of your country are starving and rebellious, and you urgently require American aid. Right. How many machine guns?"
Reproduced by special permission of PLAYBOY Magazine; © 1967 by Playboy.

for American business interests.[15] This occurs in several different ways. In some instances the free aid and technical assistance sets up a future market — it is easier to sell a nation American tractors, airplanes, or computers, once the nation has become accustomed to using U.S. technology. Foreign aid programs also pay for U.S. corporations to explore overseas investment opportunities. It was under such a program, for example, that Colgate Palmolive, Union Carbide, and other U.S. firms first located in Nigeria. The granting of U.S. aid (or the threat of withdrawal once granted) has also been widely used to guarantee protection for U.S. interests overseas. When Peru decided to withdraw a tax concession given to the international subsidiary of Standard Oil of New Jersey, U.S. financial assistance was stopped. In addition, the overseas investments of many U.S. corporations are frequently protected by the Investment Guaranty Program, which is part of the Agency for International Development (AID).

Perhaps the most controversial use of foreign aid on behalf of U.S. commercial interests occurs when aid is used to support a dictatorial government that is sympathetic to U.S. businesses. For example, in 1964, the socialist-oriented government of Brazil was overthrown by military officers trained by the United States and sympathetic to U.S. interests. Foreign aid subsequently jumped by more than $100 million despite

[15] This discussion of the role of foreign aid in opening up trade relations is drawn largely from Harry Magdoff, *The Age of Imperialism: The Economics of U.S. Foreign Policy* (New York: Modern Reader, 1969), Chap. 4.

claims by some Brazilians that the new government was repressive. Military aid (and CIA assistance) ostensibly given for self-defense or as part of an anti-Communist treaty obligation has allegedly been used to maintain dictators that, in turn, help U.S. companies. Current governments in Taiwan and South Korea, for example, are both strongly pro-U.S. business and have both received substantial military assistance (some of which has been used to intimidate political opponents).

Overseas investments: the imperialism argument

That many U.S. foreign policy decisions are directed toward helping U.S. private economic interests is beyond doubt. Controversy does occur, however, on the scope and intensity of this government commitment to private interests. On the one hand are those who see U.S. government help as essentially no different from the help given by the Japanese, French, or British government to their corporations. Also, because American prosperity depends in part on the success of U.S. businesses, it is reasonable for the government to provide assistance in overseas ventures. Moreover, such assistance contributes to overall world economic development by creating jobs and skills in underdeveloped nations. In short, some people believe that there is nothing abnormal or evil about government promoting the penetration of overseas markets by U.S. corporations.

Opposed to this perspective are several scholars who view current U.S. foreign policy as a continuation, though by different methods, of a long-standing policy of imperialism. In the past imperialism meant the blatant control of other nations, usually by military force, in order to exploit local resources. An African or Asian colony would be forced to buy goods manufactured by the controlling nation, labor would be paid as little as possible, local leaders would be repressed or manipulated, and natural resources would be extracted until exhausted. Nations and private economic interests were virtually inseparable, and nations competed to carve up the underdeveloped portion of the world.

Following World War II the old system of outright control was destroyed as nations in Asia and Africa achieved self-rule. Nevertheless, proponents of the imperialism argument claim that the same goals are still being pursued, though now the chief culprit is the multinational U.S. corporation. That is, it is no longer necessary for the United States to own outright or directly administer an underdeveloped nation. Instead, a few multinational corporations, supported by the ever-present threat of U.S. government intervention, can make huge profits by controlling key industries. In Central America, for example, United Brands has long dominated banana growing and marketing and has thus controlled several nations without actually running them (United Brands markets the Chiquita bananas). Especially in technologically dependent industries, for example, telecommunications and electronics, the American multinational corporation frequently dominates the local economy.[16]

[16] A good description of the world-wide reach of the multinational corporation is presented in Richard J. Barnet and Roland E. Muller, *Global Reach: The Power of the Multinational Corporation* (New York: Simon & Schuster, 1974).

Proponents of the U.S. imperialism argument do not stop, however, with charges of government intervention to aid a foreign business venture. Imperialism can also result in wars such as the ones in Vietnam or Korea. These wars, the argument goes, are fought not only to preserve the specific investments of U.S. companies but to preserve U.S. economic influence over much greater areas. In Vietnam, for example, the immediate goal was holding on to extensive rubber and oil resources, but the long-range goal was control over an area of 200 million people and one and a half million square miles of territory.[17] In Africa imperialism is expressed by supporting conservative or racist regimes that allow U.S. corporations free access to supplies of copper, uranium, diamonds, and oil.

The counterargument

Is the United States guilty of imperialism? On the whole, the more extreme claims by those who believe that it is have not been well documented. It certainly is not true that the U.S. government in conjunction with the giant multinational corporations is seeking to take over the world. Recently the federal government has cracked down on the payment of bribes by American corporations to obtain foreign business despite corporate claims that bribery is essential to doing business in many nations (convicted companies are subject to a million dollar fine). The imperialism argument also fails to explain continued U.S. support for Israel when economic self-interest would dictate stronger support for the oil-producing Arab states. The argument that imperialism leads to war in order to protect U.S. domination is also open to serious questions. Both the Korean and Vietnam wars undoubtedly cost more than these nations were worth economically (the war in Vietnam cost U.S. taxpayers at least $118 billion).[18] In addition, the willingness of U.S. corporations to do business with Communist governments suggests that so-called imperialistic wars may be unnecessary. After all, why go to war with China if you can sell the Chinese Boeing jets and IBM computers at a handsome profit without generating ill feeling?

Have American foreign policy objectives been achieved?

We will consider now how successful the United States has been in achieving the foreign policy goals just outlined. We must realize that U.S. foreign policy has involved thousands of separate decisions and hundreds of programs, so a complete evaluation can obviously not be given here. Our emphasis is on the accomplishment of overall goals, not the successes or failures of specific programs. On the whole, it is proba-

---

[17] Magdoff, pp. 7–8. The imperialism position is also expounded in Gabriel Kolko, *The Roots of American Foreign Policy* (Boston: Beacon Press, 1969), especially Chap. 3.

[18] *Statistical Abstract of the United States, 1978*, p. 361.

bly fair to say that U.S. foreign policy objectives have been moderately well met, though there have been some major failures.

NATIONAL SECURITY

Certainly the preeminent goal of national security appears to be fulfilled. The United States does not find itself facing a militarily superior Soviet Union that can influence U.S. action by threatening a show of force. Western Europe also seems reasonably secure from a military perspective. Moreover, the fear that the United States would face an aggressive, expansionist, and monolithic Communist bloc led by the Soviet Union has generally receded. While Communist governments have come to power in some nations, for example, Cuba and Vietnam, Soviet expansion in underdeveloped nations has had few successes. Major efforts to extend Russian influence in Egypt, Ghana, Indonesia, Somalia, and several other countries failed. Equally important, sharp divisions, most notably the Soviet-Chinese rift, have occurred within the Communist bloc. Of course, many of these disputes are caused by disputes over Communist ideology, but in many instances the United States has taken advantage of the situation. For example, economic assistance was given to Yugoslavia despite its Communist government when it asserted its independence from Moscow. More recently, the United States and the People's Republic of China established diplomatic and commercial relationships (much to the displeasure of the Soviet Union).

PEACE AND INTERNATIONAL STABILITY

The major accomplishment in promoting peace and international stability has been the prevention of World War III. At one time, as the United States and the Soviet Union engaged in an all-out nuclear arms race, such a war seemed almost inevitable. Today, thanks to a policy of **détente,** U.S. and Communist leaders have worked to reduce international tensions and the likelihood of nuclear war. As we have seen, these efforts have involved several treaties and arms-limitations agreements (SALT). Tensions have also been reduced by diplomatic initiatives, for example, President Nixon's historic visit to Communist China in 1972 and various summit meetings between top U.S. and Soviet leaders, as well as numerous scientific and cultural exchanges.

At the same time, however, conventional wars show no signs of becoming archaic. When the United States finally withdrew from Vietnam the new Communist government in that country soon found itself in late 1978 fighting with the Communist government in Cambodia. In early 1979, Vietnam went to war with the People's Republic of China. The Middle East has been the scene of several wars between Israel and the Arab countries as well as of major conflicts among Arab nations and Arabs and Christians in Lebanon. India and Pakistan have likewise had a history of armed conflict, and conditions producing these conflicts remain unresolved. Africa has been an especially fertile environment for wars, and many of these, for instance, the Biafran secession from Nigeria in 1969 and the civil war in Rhodesia, have been long and costly. Though the United Nations and the United States have occasionally successfully mediated these disputes, nobody seems capable of preventing them.

ECONOMIC ASSISTANCE

The U.S. goal of providing world-wide economic assistance has had mixed results. The most striking successes involved the rebuilding of Western Europe and Japan following World War II. So successful were programs like the Marshall Plan that it was once jokingly said that the best way of insuring economic development was to declare war on the United States and lose. American policy has also occasionally been successful in responding to world hunger and widespread disease. On more than one occasion India was saved from extensive starvation by large shipments of grain through the Food for Peace program, and when national disasters struck in Yugoslavia and Guatemala, U.S. economic assistance helped prevent widespread starvation.

Beyond these accomplishments, however, the record is less impressive. The expectation that American technical know-how is exportable no longer seems self-evident. Though U.S. economic assistance has produced many concrete accomplishments—highways, dams, university buildings—it has not succeeded in transforming poor nations into economically well-off ones. In many instances the problems of economic development proved far more difficult to solve than first imagined. For example, how do you convince a farmer that although his past practice of beating a water buffalo might get results, beating a tractor with a stick will not accomplish anything? Moreover, a major hope underlying economic assistance—that economic development will encourage political democracy—has not been realized. Such assistance has even helped stabilize undemocratic regimes.

FURTHERING U.S. ECONOMIC INTERESTS

Finally, as measured by the standards of corporate growth and return on investment, the government has successfully promoted the world-wide vitality of U.S. economic interests. In 1966, the foreign affiliates of major U.S.-owned manufacturing industries reported sales of $47.4 billion. By 1975, this figure had risen to $175.7 billion. Total foreign sales during this period (including agricultural products) rose from $97.8 billion to $458.3 billion.[19] Tariff barriers to U.S. goods, especially exports to Western Europe, have been reduced substantially in the last twenty years. The one-time fear that U.S. industries might be cut off from essential overseas resources by hostile governments has not materialized. As we have seen, a variety of government actions (and threats) has kept American industry supplied with copper, cobalt, oil, nickel, chromium, tungsten, and other essential products.

The successes of the giant U.S.-based multinational corporations have, however, also produced several problems for American policy makers. In some ways government through its own actions has created a powerful

[19] *Statistical Abstract of the United States, 1978*, p. 564.

economic force that it can no longer control. It has been argued, for example, that multinationals have substantially hurt the domestic economy by transferring jobs out of the United States to foreign countries such as Mexico, Haiti, and South Korea where labor is cheap. These job transfers also worsen the U.S. trade deficit (the difference between the values of imports and exports) since what was previously manufactured at home must now be imported. American multinationals have also been accused of exporting U.S. technology for the sake of a quick dollar. By selling or manufacturing abroad such things as computers, jet engines, and the like, they help undermine the traditional U.S. technological advantage in world trade.[20] Much of the recent decline of the dollar has also been blamed on U.S. multinationals. The dumping of U.S. dollars in the international currency exchanges is not solely the result of foreigners wanting to hold marks or yen instead of dollars. American companies with large overseas investments such as R. J. Reynolds and Dow Chemical have also contributed to the decline of the dollar through currency speculations.[21] In short, the assistance given U.S. industry to compete world-wide has resulted in mixed blessings.

CAN U.S. FOREIGN POLICY PERFORMANCE BE IMPROVED?

An inevitable question arises in viewing the results of American foreign policy: Can we do better? Is this record of mixed success and failure the best we can do? In the abstract, of course, there is always room for improvement. In practice, however, American policy makers face some major constraints. The situation is comparable to the problems faced in economic policy making: there is no one "best" solution, just a variety of partial solutions that resolve some problems better than others. Certainly there are no sure-fire "master plans" that will resolve all issues equally well.

Perhaps the major problem facing foreign policy makers is the unpredictability of events. On numerous occasions the most informed calculations of what other nations would do have proved dead wrong. During the Korean War, for example, U.S. political and military leaders strongly believed that the Communist Chinese would not enter the war if the United States advanced into North Korea. Their miscalculation was extremely costly. Throughout the Vietnam war the United States made several miscalculations regarding the determination of North Vietnam and the willingness of the Soviet Union to supply its ally. No doubt even the most sophisticated intelligence system and careful weighing of alternatives cannot be 100 percent accurate in predicting the behavior of other

[20] Extensive data on how American multinational corporations might have harmed the domestic economy are presented in "Multinational Corporations and United States Foreign Policy," Hearings before the Subcommittee on Multinational Corporations of the Committee on Foreign Relations, U.S. Senate, 94th Congress, first sess., part 13 (Washington, D.C.: Government Printing Office, 1976).

[21] This subject is described more fully in "Stateless Money: A New Force in World Economics," *Business Week*, August 21, 1978, pp. 76–85.

THE FOREIGN POLICY PRICE OF CLEAN AIR

The trade-off between domestic policy objectives and foreign policy goals can sometimes be unpredictable. Consider the relationship between lowering environmental pollution and helping the economies of the Soviet Union and South Africa. The Clean Air Act—as amended in 1970—commits U.S. car manufacturers to increasingly strict antipollution standards. This has led to a continuing search for new technology, for example, the stratified-charge engine (developed by Honda). The 1981 pollution standard is particularly stringent, but one promising solution is a new type of catalytic converter that uses the rare metal rhodium. Not only is rhodium expensive—$600 an ounce—but the Soviet Union and South Africa are the major sources of this metal. Meeting the 1981 pollution standards using rhodium would not only worsen the U.S. balance of payments and economically help two countries opposed to overall U.S. foreign policy objectives, but the U.S. would become vulnerable to threatened rhodium price increases or embargos. These costs and risks, however, may be the price of clean air.

More on the consequences of using rhodium to reduce air pollution is presented in Jean A. Briggs, "Detroit and Congress: Eyeball to Eyeball," *Forbes*, February 15, 1977; and Douglas Starr, "A Rare, Rare Metal Cuts Auto Emissions," *The Christian Science Monitor*, November 15, 1978.

nations. Given the hundreds of decisions that must be made each year, mistakes are bound to occur.

Along with the uncertainty of international affairs, many of our foreign policy goals require knowledge that has yet to be discovered. Both the United States and the Soviet Union view the spread of nuclear weapons as a threat to world peace. Yet nuclear technology is spreading rapidly. How can the peaceful use of atomic energy be controlled so that it is not used for military purposes? This is a key, but thus far largely unresolved, problem. Recall the lack of success the United States has had with its economic aid to underdeveloped nations. One major reason for these failures is that despite our knowledge of economics and technology, we still do not know what precisely leads to economic development. Regarding the control of U.S. multinational corporations, experts divide sharply over what measures would correct the problems. Policy makers must, therefore, continue to employ hit or miss tactics in many important areas.

A third factor limiting the effectiveness of foreign policy is that foreign policy goals can conflict with domestic goals. The clearest example is the trade-off between maintaining a strong but expensive military capacity versus spending more money for domestic programs such as education, health care, and urban improvement. During the early 1970s a frequently debated issue was whether the United States should begin full-scale production of the very expensive B-1 long-range bomber. Critics of the program argued (successfully) that the tens of billions would be better spent on human needs than on a slight improvement in national security. A similar type of argument is sometimes made regarding foreign aid — why spend billions in Asia or South America when comparable domestic programs need greater funding. Moreover, overseas economic or military commitments are sometimes made with an eye toward upcoming elections, not the overall foreign policy program.

Finally, the four general foreign policy goals we described can frequently collide. Consider the goals of furthering world peace, blocking the expansion of Communist influence, and promoting U.S. overseas business interests. Selling military equipment to nations like Saudi Arabia might block Communist expansion and help the U.S. economy, but would increased military strength further peace? Some people would argue that it might if it contributed to a balance of military strength in the region. It is equally plausible, however, that such arms sales could encourage the use of military solutions to international disputes. On more than one occasion, for example, in the conflict between Israel and Jordan in 1967 and in that between Turkey and Greece over Cyprus in 1974, both sides fought with U.S.-supplied weapons. Supporters of the U.S. policy of selling arms abroad contend that if we did not provide military hardware the Russians (or the French or British) would, and at least this way we get the sales and can exercise some influence.

Another situation in which overall goals conflict concerns maintaining pro-Western governments in power versus promoting economic development. Recall that economic assistance was frequently used to reward our friends and punish our enemies. This policy may have blocked Communist expansion, but it was not always an effective economic-assistance policy. Especially during the 1950s, when being neutral in the U.S.-USSR conflict was viewed negatively by American leaders, several nations pursuing economic development were denied large-scale assistance because of their neutrality. On the other hand, adamantly anti-Communist nations sometimes received considerable assistance (much of it purchased from U.S. corporations) despite the lack of commitment to economic development. Which goal is more important, helping pro-U.S. leaders or promoting economic growth? A reasonable case can be made for either one.

In summary, the United States has long been committed to four general foreign policy goals: maintaining national security, promoting peace and international stability, providing economic assistance, and furthering U.S. economic interests. Each goal has taken a variety of forms, and the overall record of achievement has been mixed. A certain amount of failure is to be expected, however, given the uncertainty of international events, our lack of knowledge in many important areas, the constraints imposed by domestic policies, and conflicts among the major goals.

A conclusion: American foreign policy

Our analysis of America's foreign policy has reviewed a wide range of goals and problems. Beneath all of these specific issues, however, is a long-standing controversy over how U.S. foreign policy *ought* to be oriented. We have not thus far considered this question, but it is fundamental. Essentially, the issue involves the role of morality in international affairs. We can basically distinguish two opposing perspectives in this debate: the "power-politics" position and what might be called the "democratic-idealism" perspective.

Advocates of the power-politics position see international affairs as competition among nations without rules. Whereas domestic conflict is regulated by explicit laws enforced by police, no such provisions exist among nations except for relatively unimportant matters (for example, postal rates). Ultimately, as in the jungle, power is decisive. In a crisis organizations like the UN are powerless because they cannot marshal force. Under such circumstances the primary national goal is survival. Helping other nations, unless such aid directly helps you, is wasteful or even dangerous. Advocating vague idealistic goals such as world freedom will only lead to disaster. The goal of national survival should be pursued by whatever means possible. Policy making typically involves secrecy, deception, shows of force, "dirty tricks," and whatever else is necessary. Foreign policy is the pursuit of national self-interest.

In contrast, is the position we have called democratic idealism. The ultimate goal here is the creation of an international order based on humanitarian principles where disputes are settled by law, not violence. Merely because previous efforts such as the League of Nations have failed does not preclude future successes. After all, at one time the idea of a United States of America seemed impossible. U.S. relations with other nations should be determined by how well those nations adhere to peaceful, humanitarian goals. Under no conditions should we support repressive, dictatorial regimes. U.S. foreign policy ought to be made openly and be governed by the same principles as domestic policy. Strategies such as assassinations, blackmail, and "dirty tricks" are not used at home and should not be employed abroad. A humanitarian world order cannot be achieved by unscrupulous means.

Both perspectives have enjoyed popularity among American leaders at different times. We are all familiar with Woodrow Wilson's idealistic efforts to bring world peace following World War I. More recently, President Carter's emphasis on the promotion of human rights as a cornerstone of U.S. diplomacy is also in the tradition of democratic idealism. The power-politics position has also had its advocates. Many of America's staunchest allies have been repressive dictatorships, and U.S. military aid has frequently been used by these leaders to crush opponents. Moreover, as events in Cuba and Vietnam showed, American leaders are quite willing to make secret agreements, engage in clandestine military operations, and even encourage the assassinations of foreign leaders. Even President Carter has found it necessary in negotiating

Israeli-Egyptian differences to use secrecy and to wheel and deal to accomplish his goal of peace in the Middle East.

Obviously, it is difficult to decide which approach the United States ought to follow. It seems apparent, however, that American foreign policy will continue to employ both. In fact, it frequently seems that we sometimes combine the two perspectives in a strange blend: we practice power politics but call it democratic idealism. For example, we enter into alliances with dictatorships to protect the "free world." In Vietnam the United States justified its massive and highly destructive intervention on the grounds that the Vietnamese ought to be free to decide their own fate. We sell billions of dollars in arms ($13.4 billion in fiscal 1978) at a considerable profit in the name of world peace.[22] We are not suggesting that U.S. foreign policy is an evil conspiracy justified by high-sounding phrases. Rather, both the power-politics and democratic-idealist perspectives have strong appeals to leaders, and it is sometimes difficult to separate one from the other.

Major questions raised

1. How is U.S. foreign policy made? In crisis situations the President and his immediate advisers make the key decisions. However, in noncrisis situations foreign policy choices can involve Congress, the bureaucracy, interest groups, and the general public.

2. What are the goals of U.S. foreign policy? The preeminent goal has been national security, which since 1947 has meant containing Communist expansion. Other important goals are promoting world peace, encouraging economic development, and helping U.S. economic interests overseas.

3. Have American foreign policy objectives been achieved? The United States has successfully maintained its national security, but for other goals the record has been mixed. Foreign policy makers face several important constraints, including the uncertainty of international events, a lack of knowledge on many questions, domestic political demands, and conflict among foreign policy objectives.

QUESTIONS FOR FURTHER DISCUSSION

1. In the old days "gunboat diplomacy" was common. If the United States wished to punish a nation, the Navy might bombard its capitol for a few hours to teach it a lesson. Today, of course, such action is not tolerated. Nevertheless, it can still be argued that the use of physical force is justified if the vital interests of the United States are threatened. The frequent problem is: What are our "vital" interests? Would force be justified if certain Middle Eastern nations refused to sell us oil essential to our economy? Would force be necessary if a nearby country gave substantial assistance to terrorists who repeatedly attacked U.S. cities? What if some nation decided to explode a hydrogen bomb in the Pacific that would

[22] *The Christian Science Monitor*, October 4, 1978.

eventually shower the United States with dangerous radioactivity? In other words, other than defending ourselves from attack, when can military action be justified?

2. What would you do if you were the President? The United States is presently trying to expand U.S.-Chinese trade. One item China exports to America is wooden clothespins. In the last few years foreign clothespins have sharply increased their share of the U.S. market (from about 25 percent to almost half the market between 1973 and 1977). U.S. wooden clothespins are manufactured in Vermont and Maine where levels of unemployment are high, and few economic alternatives exist for hundreds of clothespin workers. Chinese clothespins could easily end the U.S. industry completely. Should the President act to help American companies and workers? Should duties be put on cheaper imports, even if this might harm future U.S.-China trade? Should the U.S. government provide public jobs for unemployed clothespin makers in a pinch?

3. Great controversy arose when it was publicly acknowledged that the U.S. government had been involved in attempts to assassinate Premier Fidel Castro of Cuba. A few people defended these plans on the basis that the principle of assassinating foreign leaders is not necessarily a bad principle. The real issue is *who* should be assassinated, not whether there should be assassinations. For example, think of all the lives that would have been saved if Adolf Hitler could have been assassinated in 1939. Do you accept this position? Or should the U.S. government never engage in such behavior?

4. It is sometimes argued that the United States does not use its foreign economic assistance effectively. In particular, we frequently allow this aid to be squandered or used to maintain inefficient economic systems. On occasion a nation may not make needed agricultural improvements because it knows that if disaster does strike, the United States will be there to provide the needed help. Should the United States insist that aid be used in the most efficient way to maximize long-term benefits? Or does each country have the right to run its own affairs without outsiders telling it about land reform, educational programs, and other purely internal matters? If the people of a nation want to use U.S.-supplied powdered milk to line their soccer fields, that's their decision.

BIBLIOGRAPHY

Allison, Graham. *Essence of Decision: Explaining the Cuban Missile Crisis.* Boston: Little, Brown, 1971.
> Uses the Cuban missile crisis of 1962 as a case study of how crisis decisions are made. Considers actions from the perspective of national decision making, organizational factors, and bargaining among different interests.

Coplin, William D., and Charles W. Kegley, Jr. eds., *Analyzing International Relations: A Multimethod Introduction.* New York: Praeger, 1975.
> A diverse collection of articles dealing with some of the major issues in foreign relations. Articles cover such issues as how to explain the Cuban missile crisis, the origins of U.S. involvement in Vietnam, the role of international organizations, and the use of nuclear deterrence. Contains a bibliography.

Crabb, Cecil V., Jr. *American Foreign Policy in the Nuclear Age*, 3d ed., New York: Harper & Row, 1972.
> A comprehension, detailed description of almost every aspect of U.S. foreign policy. Can be employed like a reference book to look up key events, laws, treaties, and descriptions of organizations.

Fulbright, J. William. *The Crippled Giant: American Foreign Policy and its Domestic Consequences.* New York: Vintage Books, 1972.

> Fulbright is the former chairman of the Senate Foreign Relations Committee, and he had a ringside seat at foreign policy making. Fulbright opposes our national obsession to defeat communism and our use of military force to accomplish our goals. Emphasizes the moral dimensions of foreign policy.

Keenan, George F. *American Diplomacy: 1900–1950.* New York: New American Library, n.d.

> Keenan is a former U.S. ambassador to the Soviet Union and a renowned scholar. He presents an overview of U.S. diplomacy from the Spanish-American War to the Cold War with the Soviet Union. Concludes with a pessimistic assessment of improving U.S.-Soviet relations. A widely read and influential book.

Kennedy, Robert F. *Thirteen Days: A Memoir of the Cuban Missile Crisis.* New York: Norton, 1969.

> A fascinating, behind-the-scenes account of decision making during an international crisis written by a major participant. Day-by-day, hour-by-hour events are described as they led to a U.S.-Soviet confrontation and possible nuclear war.

Magdoff, Harry. *The Age of Imperialism: The Economics of U.S. Foreign Policy.* New York: Modern Reader, 1969.

> Argues that the basic purpose of U S. foreign policy is to dominate less well-developed nations. Analyses provide extensive documentation of alleged U.S. imperialism. Useful for describing the relationship between the U.S. government and overseas private enterprise even if one does not accept Magdoff's conclusions concerning imperialism.

Marchetti, Victor, and John D. Marks. *The CIA and the Cult of Intelligence.* New York: Dell, 1975.

> A detailed expose of CIA activities. Covers everything from the CIA's "clandestine mentality" to concrete actions and policies. Also considers how the CIA might be controlled. The CIA went to court to prevent publication of much of this information, and 168 items (indicated in text) were removed.

Morgenthau, Hans J. *A New Foreign Policy for the United States.* New York: Praeger, 1969.

> A leading authority on international relations examines recent U.S. foreign policies and their underlying assumptions. Believes that foreign policy should be based on national self-interest. Concludes with several recommendations for improving our foreign policy.

O'Leary, Michael Kent. *The Politics of American Foreign Aid.* New York: Atherton Press, 1967.

> Thorough treatment of U.S. foreign aid policy. Examines foreign aid in terms of the American culture, how Americans now view foreign aid, and foreign aid politics in Congress and the executive branch.

Spanier, John, and Larry Elowitz. *Understanding American Foreign Policy: A Concise History Since World War II.* New York: Praeger, 1975.

> A clearly written historical overview of U.S. foreign policy. Especially useful for providing information of specific events, alliances, and policies.

Spanier, John, and Eric M. Uslaner. *How American Foreign Policy Is Made,* 2d ed. New York: Holt, Rinehart and Winston, 1978.

> A brief but well-documented analysis of foreign policy making. Considers who participates, different explanations of decisions, and the appropriate role of different institutions and organizations in deciding foreign policy.

Waltz, Kenneth N. *Foreign Policy and Democratic Politics: The American and British Experience.* Boston: Little, Brown, 1967.

> A comparison of foreign policy making in the United States and Great Britain. Considers such factors as the differences in forms of government, attitudes of leaders, the roles of political parties, differences between the prime minister and the President, and the differing roles of public opinion.

PREVIEW

How are state and local governments organized?

States follow the national model of separate legislative, executive, and judicial branches. However, the specifics of government organization vary considerably from state to state. Within a state there are numerous types of political jurisdictions—counties, townships, cities, special districts, and even metropolitan governments. Legally, the state government is supreme over these units, but in practice contemporary fiscal federalism has provided these jurisdictions a degree of independence from state authority (and areas once completely under state control have now at least partially come under federal control).

What are the major responsibilities of state and local governments?

In terms of expenditures, education constitutes the most important state activity followed by public welfare, highways, and health and hospitals. Considerable variation exists, however, on how much states spend in these areas. These variations are due to such factors as the nature of the problems faced by states, differences in financial resources, and what citizens want. The other side of expenditures is raising revenue, and here too we find sizable differences among the states. Some states stress regressive sales taxes; others more progressive income taxes.

Is the present system adequate for solving contemporary problems?

Much of the present state and local governmental system has its roots in the eighteenth and nineteenth centuries, and it has been criticized as inadequate. Among the major criticisms are that existing geographical boundaries are no longer relevant, the multiplicity of governments leads to unnecessary complexity, government responsibilities and capacities are frequently mismatched, and state and local governments are overwhelmed by modern problems. The adequacy of the present system can, however, be defended. Many people see the system as adaptable to new demands, no worse than making all key decisions in Washington, and the arrangement that most citizens prefer. It is important to keep in mind that much of the debate over who should be responsible for a certain policy really involves what policy is to be chosen.

CHAPTER TWENTY

THE POLITICS OF STATE AND LOCAL GOVERNMENTS

The national government is the dominant government in the United States; it is more visible and holds the ultimate power. Nevertheless, state and local governments are equally, if not more, important in their daily impact on the lives of citizens. Such issues as the amount of money for education, construction and maintenance of roads, law enforcement, public assistance to the needy, licensing of lawyers and doctors, and zoning and land use are decided by state and local governments. Despite the popular image of an ever more powerful Washington dominating state and local governments, states and municipalities have held their own. In fact, they have expanded much more rapidly than the national government. For example, in 1950 combined state and local government spending was 40 percent of all government spending in the United States (the national government spent $42 billion; state and local governments $28 billion). By 1975, the spending of state and local governments was equal to federal spending (and in 1976, 81 percent of all government employees worked for state and local governments). State and local governments in the United States are far from being insignificant. Our analysis examines three important questions regarding governments below the national level:

1. How are state and local governments organized?
2. What are the major responsibilities of state and local governments?
3. Is the present system adequate for solving contemporary problems?

How are state and local governments organized?

Most citizens believe that state and local governments follow the organizational pattern of the government in Washington, D.C. There is a governor instead of a President; there is the state legislature instead of Congress; and a state court system corresponding to the federal court system. At the local level equivalent government offices would be the mayor, city council, and municipal court. Moreover, many people also believe that the system of national-state-local government is organized like a pyramid: local governments are subordinate to the states in the same way that states are subordinate to the national government.

This image of fifty miniature national governments which in turn govern many smaller, similarly organized local governments is only partially correct. State and local governments may sometimes appear to be this way, but in fact these governments are varied and complex. To understand state and local politics we must begin by examining this diversity and complexity. Our analysis will first consider the various forms government structures take at the state levels. We shall then examine how governments at different levels are related to each other.

THE STRUCTURE OF GOVERNMENT IN THE FIFTY STATES

State governments are generally modeled on the national system of separate executive, legislative, and judicial branches. However, the specifics, such as terms of office, which state officials are elected, and the powers of the branches of government, vary from state to state. Each state seems to have developed its own system, and these differences can frequently explain why politics is not the same in, say, California as it is in Tennessee.

The office of governor

Consider, for example, the office of governor in the fifty states. In four states the governor can serve for only two years. In the remaining states there is a four-year term, but the states differ about whether a governor can run for more than one term. Seventeen states do not limit terms, twenty-one limit a governor to two terms, and eight prohibit only consecutive terms. Salaries of governors vary considerably—in 1975 they ranged from $10,000 in Arkansas to $85,000 in New York (most fall between $35,000 and $49,000). A major departure from the national model occurs in twenty-one states where the lieutenant governor is elected separately from the governor. Since an independently elected lieutenant governor frequently has his or her own political ambitions and can be of a different political party than the governor, this can heighten political conflict.[1]

---

[1] Unless otherwise noted, all information on the characteristics of state governments is drawn from *Book of the States* (Lexington, Ky.: Council of State Governments, various years).

The power of the state's chief executive varies even more. While the President can appoint his or her Cabinet-level administrators, in many states these top administrators are elected independently. For example, in forty-two states the important position of attorney general is elected; in thirty-seven states the state treasurer is elected; and in twenty states the superintendent of education is elected. Some states even make top executive positions civil service positions (for example, in Colorado the important departments of agriculture, labor, and health are headed by civil service appointees). Many states also make it difficult for a governor to remove an appointee; they require that the governor give some concrete reason—not just a disagreement over policy—to the legislature for such removal (a President does not have to provide any explanation for removing top executive branch officials). Also, while the President maintains complete control over preparing the national budget, governors in ten states must share budgeting power with the legislature, a civil service appointee, or an independent agency.

The governor's relationship to the state legislature also differs from the national model. All states except North Carolina give the governor veto power over legislation, but wide variations exist on how large a legislative vote is necessary to override a veto. Most states specify a two-thirds vote; others a simple majority; while Alaska requires a three-quarters majority to override. The President lacks one important power given to thirty-nine governors, the **item veto**—the power to veto a portion of a bill while leaving the rest of the legislation intact (the governor in Wisconsin can even veto a sentence or a word). Most governors can also call a special session of the state legislature (and frequently decide the agenda of the session). Especially where state legislative service is a part-time job, the governor can use a special session as a potent weapon since few legislators want to spend more time than necessary at the state capitol. The President can likewise call a special session of Congress, but this power has become less relevant as congressional sessions now occupy most of the year.

The state legislature

Like Congress, the responsibility of the legislatures of the fifty states is to create legislation. The procedures in state legislatures also generally follow the pattern of Congress—after a bill is introduced, it goes to committee where it is debated, changed, and then passed on for a floor vote. Of course, many states have their own special rules and customs. For example, in Tennessee two-thirds of the membership, not the usual one-half, is needed for a legislative quorum; in 1977 North Carolina had seventy-seven legislative committees. Also like Congress, state legislatures generally have two chambers. The one exception is Nebraska, which has been a **unicameral** (one-house) legislature since 1934. All but twelve state senators have four-year terms, while all but four lower-house legislators have two-year terms. The size of the state legislature differs considerably from state to state. The lower house of the New Hampshire legislature has 400 members, compared to the lower houses of Alaska and Nevada where there are only 40 members (state senates are much smaller—most are in the 40–60 range).

Item veto   The power of a governor to veto only a portion of a bill, leaving the rest intact.

Unicameral   A one-house legislature. A two-house legislature like the U.S. Congress is called a bicameral legislature.

A major difference between Congress and the average state legislature is the demands made on the legislator. Serving in the U.S. Congress is a full-time job; serving as a state legislator is usually a part-time job. In the past it was customary for a state legislature to meet once every two years, and while this has changed in most states, seven states still hold only one session every two years. Even where there is an annual session, this session is likely to run for only a few months (North Dakota in 1976 responded to the press of legislative business by increasing its legislative session from sixty to eighty days). Also, since state legislators are usually within an automobile drive of home, the legislative week may be a short one (and frequent absences are encouraged by the fact that most legislators have other full-time occupations).

Another difference between members of Congress and state legislators is that a state legislator receives less support than a member of Congress. This is most notable in legislative salaries. Many states still pay legislators less than $10,000 per biennial (two-year) session. New Hampshire pays the lowest, $200, followed by Rhode Island at $600 per bien-

NOW LET'S HEAR IT FOR TONTO AND SILVER

Though state legislatures are not concerned with international problems, their interests can range far from home. The Illinois legislature, for example, recently became involved in a controversy about Clayton Moore, the actor who portrayed the Lone Ranger in the television series of the 1950s. The question was whether Clayton Moore could wear his mask when he toured college campuses to describe his acting career. Owners of the rights to the Lone Ranger character stopped Moore from wearing his mask in these tours on the grounds that Moore was too old and harmed the Lone Ranger image. Moore got around this restriction by wearing sunglasses, not a mask. The plight of Moore generated much sympathy. As the following Illinois state senate resolution shows, in his campaign the old ranger was not alone.

Senate Resolution No. 13
Offered by Senator Rhoads and Senator Rock, President of the Senate; and Senators Becker, Berman, Berning, Bloom, Bowers, Bruce, Buzbee, Carroll, Chew, Coffey, Collins, D'Arco, Daley, Davidson, DeAngelis, Demuzio, Donnewald, Egan, Geo-Karis, Gitz, Graham, Grotberg, Hall, Johns, Jeremiah Joyce, Jerome Joyce, Keats, Lemke, Maitland, Maragos, Martin, McLendon, McMillan, Merlo, Mitchler, Moore, Nash, Nedza, Nega, Netsch, Newhouse, Nimrod, Ozinga, Philip, Regner, Rupp, Sangmeister, Savickas, Schaffer, Shapiro, Sommer, Vadalabene, Walsh, Washington, Weaver and Wooten.

nial session. On the high end of the pay scale are Illinois ($46,000), New York ($47,000), and California ($61,599) per two-year session. In most states, however, legislative pay would not be considered a good income for a skilled worker or college graduate. Legislative staffs and other resources are also limited in most states. Support facilities of the type enjoyed by Congress (research services, organizations to make investigations, expert legal advice, and the like) are generally found in the larger, more industrialized states such as New York and California. Given low salaries and meager legislative resources, it is not surprising that the turnover in state legislatures is fairly high. For example, the average turnover in lower houses in 1976 was 29 percent. New Hampshire, with its $200 per biennial pay, had a 44 percent turnover.

One final important distinction between Congress and state legislatures concerns legislative **apportionment** (how many people per district and the shape of legislative districts). While U.S. Senators represent different numbers of people, representation within a state for both houses must closely follow population size. Before 1962 lower state

Apportionment The allocation of legislative seats according to a standard such as population size or area.

Whereas, the distinguished actor, Mr. Clayton Moore, is a native of the City of Chicago and State of Illinois; and

Whereas, Mr. Clayton Moore for many years portrayed the character known as the "Lone Ranger" in a popular television series during the 1950's; and

Whereas, Mr. Clayton Moore's portrayal of that character was instrumental in teaching the values of right conduct and good moral character to a generation of American young people; and

Whereas, Mr. Clayton Moore continues today to win the admiration and affection of millions of Americans in his personal appearances around the country; and

Whereas, Mr. Clayton Moore continues to be known as an inspiration to young people around the country and particularly to his loyal fans in the State of Illinois; therefore, be it

Resolved, by the senate of the eighty-first general assembly of the State of Illinois, that we commend Mr. Clayton Moore for his fine acting career and for his efforts to set an outstanding example for American youth; and that we congratulate Mr. Moore for the qualities of courage and honor which he has exemplified and for the credit he has brought to his native State, the Land of Lincoln; and be it further

Resolved, that a suitable engrossed copy of this resolution be presented to Mr. Clayton Moore.

Adopted by the Senate, September 6, 1979.

_____
President of the Senate

_____
Secretary of the Senate

houses frequently experienced severe **malapportionment**—one state representative would be elected by a few thousand voters, another by 10 or 20 times that number. State senates—like the U.S. Senate—tended to represent geographical units (for example, counties), and they too did not accurately translate population into legislative voting strength. Beginning with the *Baker* v. *Carr* decision in 1962, however, several key Supreme Court decisions forced state legislatures to apportion *both* houses strictly on the basis of population. The analogy between the U.S. Senate and a state senate was declared invalid in the *Reynolds* v. *Sims* (1964) case because political subdivisions of states, unlike the states themselves, were never sovereign entities.

The state judicial system

Like the office of governor and the bicameral state legislature, the state judicial system generally resembles the federal system. At the top of each state's court system is a final court of appeals of three to nine judges (it is given a variety of names—supreme court, court of appeals, or even supreme court of errors). Below this state version of the Supreme Court, twenty-seven states have an intermediate court of appeals. The bulk of state judicial business is conducted in district courts which cover a specific geographical area (a variety of names are used—circuit court, district court, superior court, or chancery court). Most states also maintain several specialized courts to deal with such matters as juvenile crime, the probation of wills, and family relations.

The area in which the practices of state court systems differ the most from federal court customs is in the selection of judges. All federal judges are appointed by the President and confirmed by the Senate. In the states, however, some judges are elected. This election can take a variety of forms. Most states elect almost all state judges in either **partisan** or **nonpartisan elections.** Several states use a combination of appointment and election. For example, the governor of Arizona, upon recommendation of a special commission, appoints judges to the state supreme, appellate, and certain district courts; judges for all other state courts are elected. Some states follow the federal model; the governor, with the consent of the state senate, appoints all judges. In a few states the legislature itself appoints judges. In other cases there is a division of labor—some judges are appointed by the governor, others by the state legislature.

Ten states use an interesting variation for selecting judges, called the **Missouri plan,** or **merit plan.** Under this plan a committee of distinguished judges, lawyers, and citizens gives a list of possible judges to the governor. The governor selects one judge from the list; after one year on the bench, the judge must be approved by the voters (there is no competing candidate, just "approve" or "disapprove"). The purpose of this plan is to balance expert judgment, input from the governor, and popular participation. Almost without exception judges chosen by the Missouri plan gain popular approval and serve long terms through repeated reelection.

Do these variations in selecting state judges make much difference?

Malapportionment A situation in which legislative seats are not allocated according to an appropriate standard. In contemporary politics this usually means that legislative districts have populations that differ substantially in size.

Partisan elections Elections in which candidates are identified by political party label, and parties are allowed to campaign. In a *nonpartisan election* there is no party designation on the ballot.

Missouri plan (or *merit plan*) A method of choosing judges in which a committee prepares a list of nominees, the governor chooses one, and the public, after a time period, is allowed to accept or reject this choice.

A rural justice of the peace. Justice dispensed by these officials frequently reflected local customs rather than state law. Institutions like the one pictured here are disappearing.

Apparently not, according to several studies. One study of alternative selection plans found that they resulted in few differences in education, experience, or social background of judges (with the exception that state legislatures were more likely to appoint their colleagues to the bench). Nor do the judges seem to decide cases differently. Elected judges, for example, are no more likely to decide in favor of defendants in criminal trials, in favor of weaker economic interests, or against corporations than appointed judges. How a judge is selected also has little impact on his or her tenure in office—elected judges are rarely defeated for reelection. Like appointed judges, they have long careers. However, unlike federal judges, most state judges face mandatory retirement ages.[2]

Finally, while states are sometimes willing to have part-time, poorly paid, and insufficiently staffed legislatures, state courts are generally more professional. Though only four states require judges to be lawyers, higher-level state judges are usually lawyers who work at their jobs full time (most nonlawyer judges are in the rural Southeast and West).

___

[2] Information on the consequences of methods of judicial selection can be found in Richard A. Watson and Rondal G. Downing, *The Politics of the Bench and Bar: Judicial Selection under the Missouri Nonpartisan Court Plan* (New York: Wiley, 1969); Burton M. Atkins and Henry R. Glick, "Formal Judicial Recruitment and State Supreme Court Decisions," *American Politics Quarterly*, Vol. 2 (1974), pp. 427–449; and Bradley Cannon, "The Impact of Formal Selection Processes on Characteristics of Judges—Reconsidered," *Law and Society Review*, Vol. 13 (1972), pp. 570–573.

Judges are also fairly well paid, usually earning between $25,000 and $50,000 a year (sometimes more, depending on whether counties supplement state salaries). Only in municipal courts, especially **justice of the peace courts** in rural areas, is justice occasionally dispensed by part-time, poorly trained, nonlawyer judges who depend more on their wits than expert assistance.

THE RELATIONSHIP OF GOVERNMENTS WITHIN THE FIFTY STATES

Though each of the fifty state governments conducts the business of politics in its own way, this variety is modest compared to the variation (and complexity) of governments *within* each of the fifty states. In 1977 the number of governments below the state level was 79,862, and a county or township in one state could be quite different from a county or township in a neighboring state (or even in the same state).[3] Some of the key political units below the state level are described below.

Counties

All states except Connecticut and Rhode Island have a system of county government (in Louisiana counties are called parishes and in Alaska boroughs). This form of government, which goes back to William the Conqueror of England, came to America during the colonial period. In 1977 there were some 3,042 counties; they varied enormously by size. Los Angeles County, for example, has 7 million people; Cook County, which includes Chicago, has 5.1 million citizens. But there are also hundreds of counties in the West and Southwest with 10,000 or fewer citizens. The variation in population is matched by the diversity in administrative organization. Most counties are run by committees with such names as board of supervisors, county commissioners, or just county board (very few counties have a single executive). Counties also have various elected or appointed officials with countywide responsibilities (for example, county attorney, assessor, sheriff, judge, and treasurer). There were some 63,000 elected county officials in 1977. In many states there are also countywide boards with authority over hospitals, public welfare, taxes, and libraries.

County government plays a vital political role, especially in rural areas. The county handles law enforcement and road construction and maintenance, administers elections, records legal information such as deeds and mortgages, and provides help to the poor. County seats in rural areas are frequently impressive places with economic importance since they are magnets for people. Urban county governments more closely resemble city government; they are responsible for such things

[3] Unless otherwise noted, all statistical data on the number of governments in the United States come from U.S. Department of Commerce, Bureau of the Census, 1977 Census of Governments, Popularly Elected Officials, "Introduction."

WHY, ARIZONA? WHY NOT, MISSISSIPPI?

The enormous diversity of U.S. local government is reflected in the names of towns and cities. Though some names are used often (for example, there are nineteen Springfields), others reflect the peculiarities of the area. Here are some of the more interesting place names in the United States:

Ben Hur, Arizona
Why, Arizona
Peanut, California
Coffee Pot Rapids, Idaho
Rural, Indiana
Ordinary, Kentucky
Monkey's Eyebrow, Kentucky

Whynot, Mississippi
Double Trouble, New Jersey
Glen Campbell, Pennsylvania
Scalp Level, Pennsylvania
Looneyville, West Virginia
Dull Center, Wyoming

Source: These and other interesting names are reported in "61 Curious Place Names in the United States," in David Wallechinsky and Irving Wallace, *The People's Almanac #2* (New York: Bantam Books, 1978), p. 1124.

as providing recreation, flood control, sewage-treatment facilities, and countywide fire and police protection.

Township or town government

About one out of every five Americans lives in a town or township. This type of government is found in twenty states, especially New England and the Midwest. Townships are subdivisions of a county and carry out many functions of county government (for example, education, highways, fire protection, and law enforcement). In 1977 there were 16,822 townships. Rural townships can cover many square miles of territory and provide important government service to villages.

The best-known town form of government is the democratic town meeting in New England states. These meetings are open to all eligible voters who collectively make important policy decisions. The voters appoint a board, whose members are usually called selectmen, to administer these decisions. As government has become more complex, these town meetings have given greater power and discretion to the selectmen. Outside New England, however, rural township governments have become less important as school boards have taken over what was once a major responsibility of township government. Nevertheless, there are still parts of the country outside of New England where township government remains important. In some suburban areas they play a key role in delivering government services.

A town meeting in Victory, Vermont. In many New England areas these meetings provide citizens with a direct voice in their government. Though widely admired, they have not been successfully imitated.

Special district government

County and township governments have deep roots in U.S. history. Special districts, however, are more recent innovations. They have arisen from both America's transition from rural to urban life and the desire of existing governments to shift the costs of certain services to the users of these services. Special districts are a popular new arrangement. Between 1952 and 1977 the number of special district governments (other than school districts) doubled to 26,000. The most popular type of special district government is the school district, which might run schools involving several towns and thousands of students. In 1977 there were 15,000 school districts with 87,000 elected officials. Other popular responsibilities of special district governments are fire protection, soil conservation, housing, cemeteries, flood control, hospitals, and libraries.

The powers and responsibilities of these special-purpose governments vary considerably. Perhaps the most important difference among these governments concerns their independent power to raise revenue. Many special districts are limited to user charges, for example, a charge for supplying water or fire protection. But over half can levy property taxes or special assessments on property rather than a direct charge for services or benefits. Others have the additional power to raise revenue by issuing bonds. The rules regulating the creation of these districts and the selection of people to run them are enormously varied. Some districts are created by the state; others are created by the municipal governments. Members of some districts are appointed; others are elected.

Cities

In contemporary society cities are generally the most important political unit below the level of state government. In 1977 there were some 18,862 cities where more than 132 million Americans lived (but over half of these cities had less than 1,000 residents). These cities had 134,017 elected officials. Cities are not only where most of us live, they also contain many of our social and economic problems. Crime, air pollution, drug addiction, inadequate transportation, and other problems are largely, though not exclusively, urban problems.

It is important to realize that a city is not merely a large number of people living near each other. "City" is a legal term. To become a city a group of people must meet the requirements of incorporation specified in state law. Typically this involves the filing of an incorporation petition with the state, verification that petition signers are a majority of the residents, a state review of the adequacy of the proposed city (for example, population density, impact in adjacent areas), and, finally, proclamation that the area is a city. The number of people necessary to become a city is usually fairly low—frequently less than 1,000.

Once the residents have crossed the legal dividing line to become a city, they can now form a local government and take actions. They can make local laws **(ordinances)**, grant licenses and permits in the name of the city, and provide their own police, fire, and social services. However, despite these opportunities to exercise political power, the city is not an independent entity, sovereign within its borders. What cities can and cannot do always depends on state law. Cities can do no more than what their state-granted charters spell out. Cities frequently do have significant discretion in some areas (for example, their form of government), but the states grant such discretion and can take it away by acts of the state legislatures. In some cases cities are allowed significant discretion, and this is frequently called **home rule.** Home rule is found in about two-thirds of all cities with populations greater than 250,000.

Metropolitan governments

Many problems such as mass transportation, air and water pollution, and education have grown beyond the borders and financial resources of individual cities. As a result, a new form of government called metropolitan government has received widespread attention. The basic idea behind metropolitan government is to preserve the identity and local functions of established cities, but to provide efficient, large-scale solutions to problems beyond the capacity of these individual governments. This solution has taken two forms: metropolitan government and metropolitan area coordination. The special district governments described earlier are a third "metro" solution when they include several cities within their service jurisdiction.

Metropolitan government is presently found in only about two dozen areas, mainly in the South. These metropolitan governments have usually been created from county governments. The county government is turned into a metropolitan government with wider responsibilities and greater legal powers. In 1957, for example, voters of Dade County,

Ordinances Laws passed by a city government.

Home rule Autonomy granted by the state to cities in certain policy areas (for example, the right to decide their own form of government).

FORMS OF CITY GOVERNMENT

Government at both the national and state levels is organized into the familiar legislative-executive-judicial pattern. That is, there is a single executive, a sizable legislature, and a judiciary. At the municipal level, however, there are some important variations on this single executive, separate legislature arrangement. Cities have one of three types of governmental structure: mayor-council, council-manager, or a commission form of government.

The mayor-council system has an independently elected mayor and an independently elected city council. This is the most traditional form of government and it typically—but not always—encourages strong executive leadership. This form of government is most popular in large cities and in the East (79.2 percent of all cities of 500,000 or more people in 1977 had this form of government). Graphically, the mayor-council system is as follows:

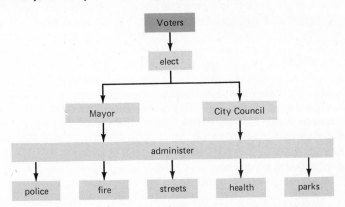

The mayor-council form of government also has two variations: strong-mayor and weak-mayor systems. The distinction is not absolute, but strong-mayor systems allow mayors considerable power in administering, appointing department heads, preparing the budget, and vetoing actions of the city council. A weak mayor, however, must share administrative decision making with the city council.

The council-manager form of government has no elected chief executive. Instead, voters elect a council, and this council chooses a professionally trained city manager who runs the day-to-day business of the city (the manager can be fired by the city council).

This system is intended to separate policy making (the job of the council) from administration (the job of the manager). This system is especially popular in middle-sized cities in the West; a little more than half of the cities of 25,000 or more have this system of government. The council-manager system can be depicted as follows:

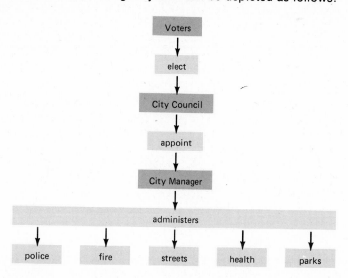

The third, and least common, form of government is the commission form. This system combines executive and legislative authority into a single council of commissioners. One commissioner may be designated as mayor, but he or she has little special power. Typically, each commissioner is responsible for a specific city service. Less than 10 percent of U.S. cities have this form of government. Here is how the commission form of government appears:

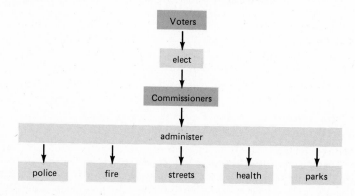

Metropolitan councils of
government Associations
of government officials
from an area who meet to
discuss and coordinate
their actions. These
councils have no inde-
pendent power.

Florida (in which the city of Miami is located), made their government into a metro government with jurisdiction over the area's water supply, sewage, traffic, transportation, central planning, and several other services. Cities within this metro system retain their powers over other services, though the Miami metro government can set minimal standards. This Dade Metro government is run by a commission of five members elected at large, five from districts, and one commissioner elected by each city. A similar metro solution was adopted in Jacksonville, Florida, in 1967.

A second approach to metropolitan government is the creation of **metropolitan councils of government** (or COGs). These COGs are associations of government officials in a geographical area. Their purpose is to discuss, research, and coordinate efforts to solve common problems. Though these councils may have a budget and a professional staff, they are not true governments. They can only make recommendations, but cannot make laws, raise revenue, or otherwise act as governments. In the last fifteen years the national government has encouraged the creation of these councils as a means of coordinating grant proposals made by local governments (some states have also encouraged these COGs). Nevertheless, without any legal powers and given the need for voluntary cooperation from groups with diverse viewpoints, these councils have had only a limited impact.

Power of government units within the states

We have seen that states may have numerous types of governments within their borders. Moreover, the jurisdictions of these governments frequently overlap—a citizen may simultaneously be ruled by city, town, county, special district, and metropolitan officials (and also pay taxes and fees to all these authorities). How can all these forms of political life coexist? Is there a sort of political chain of command in which one unit dominates the one below it, which in turn dominates the one below it?

Understanding the relationship among hundreds or even thousands of governments is both simple and complex. If we take a purely legal view of the distribution of political power in a state, the relationships among different political units are simple. Without exception, state government ultimately controls political subdivisions in the state, whether these subdivisions are huge cities, sewer districts, or hamlets of five residents. The relationship among these subdivisions is also defined by state government. Local jurisdictions over taxes, the delivery of services, form of government, educational curriculum, zoning, pollution control, and taxes exist at the pleasure of the state government. Unlike a state in the federal system, a city or county in a state has no claim of ultimate authority in some policy, though in practice it may exercise wide discretion.

The nature of contemporary federalism has made the relationship among governments within a state highly complex. In particular, the national government's willingness to provide grants-in-aid directly to

COULDN'T THEY MERGE THE AIRPORT AND MOSQUITO COMMISSIONS?

The complexity of government in the United States is illustrated by the situation faced by residents of Fridley, Minnesota. As well as being residents of the United States and the state of Minnesota, the people of Fridley also had to contend with nine other government bodies, all of which were extracting taxes from them. Here's the way the situation might appear to Fridley residents:

The United States of America
State of Minnesota
Metropolitan Mosquito Control District
Minneapolis-St. Paul Metropolitan Airport Commission
Anoka County
Soil Conservation District
North Suburban Hospital District
Minneapolis-St. Paul Sanitary District
North Suburban Sanitary Sewer District
14 Independent School Districts
FRIDLEY

political subdivisions of a state free of state control has in practice enhanced local independence (though legally the state is dominant). In 1976, for example, when local governments needed money to combat unemployment they appealed to Washington for relief, not to the state capitals. By 1976 cities were receiving some $6.5 billion in direct federal money through the grant system.[4] Such recourse to federal funds has fostered a new sense of political independence among city and county officials.

Equally important, it is the national legislature and court system that now make the key decisions on such local issues as school integration, regulation of health and safety, housing regulations, crime control, waste disposal, and other areas once considered largely under complete state control. Hence, a mayor may be legally subservient to the state government, but he or she is also likely to pay great attention to national edicts on how to integrate a school or clean the water. In short, in legal theory local governments are completely subservient to the state government; in practice, however, financial intervention by the national government has freed local governments to a large degree.

[4] *Statistical Abstract of the United States, 1978*, p. 300.

What are the major responsibilities of state and local governments?

We have seen that state and local governments have not disappeared as a result of the enormous growth of the government in Washington. In fact, in several areas (for example, number of employees) state and local governments have kept pace with or even surpassed the national government. The question that we now confront is: What is it that all of these governments do? We shall approach this complex question by focusing on money. Rather than list all the thousands of services and functions performed by state and local governments, we ask instead how money is allocated—how much for welfare, police protection, and so on. This way we can see where governments make their major commitments. Our analysis of state and local government responsibilities begins with spending. Subsequently we shall examine the other side of expenditures—how all this money is raised.

SPENDING IN STATES AND CITIES

What do states and local governments spend their money on? In fiscal 1977 the fifty states and all the governments within them spent some $273 billion. As Figure 20.1 shows, the largest expenditures were on education—$102.8 billion in fiscal 1977, or 37.6 percent of all state and local expenditures. No other state or local cost comes close to the cost of education. Public welfare, the second largest expenditure category, comprised only 12.7 percent of all expenditures. The domination of education is not new, though the slice of the budget going to education has gradually risen in the twentieth century. In 1902, for instance, education comprised 25.2 percent of all expenditures (highways were second with 17.3 percent); in 1950 education was up to 30.1 percent (highways were again second with 16.7 percent).[5] In terms of expenditures per person, in 1977 state and local governments spent some $1,262 per person on average, of which $475 was spent on education.

This general analysis is not true for all states and localities. Considerable variation exists in how state and local governments fulfill their obligations to their citizens. Table 20.1 shows the per capita (per person) expenditures for the five states with the largest levels of spending and the five states with the lowest levels. Note that Alaska spends two and a half the national average for governmental services and 3.7 times as much as Arkansas. New York spends about twice per citizen as does Arkansas. In general, states in the South tend to spend less per person on services such as education, public welfare, health care, and police protection.

[5] Unless otherwise indicated, all data on state and city finances come from *Facts and Figures on Government Finance*, 20th ed. (Washington, D.C.: Tax Foundation, 1979).

FIGURE 20.1

STATE AND LOCAL DIRECT EXPENDITURES, BY FUNCTION, FISCAL 1977

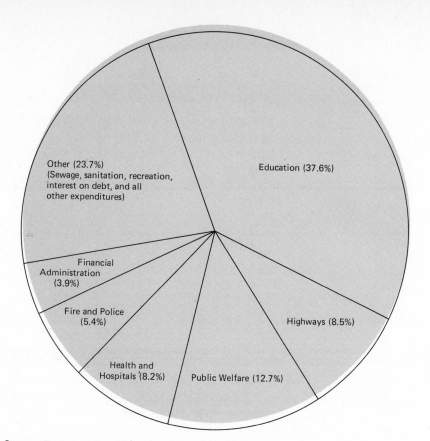

Other (23.7%)
(Sewage, sanitation, recreation, interest on debt, and all other expenditures)

Education (37.6%)

Financial Administration (3.9%)

Fire and Police (5.4%)

Highways (8.5%)

Health and Hospitals (8.2%)

Public Welfare (12.7%)

Source: *Facts and Figures on Government Finance,* 20th ed. (Washington, D.C.: Tax Foundation, 1979), pp. 138–139.

Data on per capita expenditures in major urban areas show a greater range of governmental expenditures for services. In 1977, for the largest forty-six cities, the average per capita expenditure for all city services was $734. However, New York City spends more than twice that amount per resident ($1,629); other cities spending much more than average were Baltimore, Boston, Cincinnati, and San Francisco. At the other end of the scale are cities like El Paso, Texas ($181 per capita); San Antonio, Texas; San Diego; Houston; and Omaha, Nebraska.

These figures indicate a wide discrepancy among states and localities in the spending of money. We must be cautious, however, in interpreting the meaning of this type of information. It is misleading to assert that merely because a state or city spends more (or less) money on, say, education, it therefore better serves its citizens. Several factors must be kept in mind when examining differences in how states and cities spend their money.

One factor is the cost of providing a given level of service. In sparsely populated western states, for example, states must construct hundreds

TABLE 20.1

PER CAPITA STATE AND LOCAL DIRECT GENERAL EXPENDITURE BY FUNCTION, FIVE HIGHEST AND FIVE LOWEST STATE LEVELS, FISCAL 1977

		Category						
Five states with largest per capita expenditure level	**Total**	**Education**	**Highways**	**Public Welfare**	**Health and Hospitals**	**Police and Fire**	**Financial Admin.**	**Other***
Alaska	$3,275	$1,073	$469	$141	$111	$126	$225	$1,130
Hawaii	1,915	534	149	212	119	82	79	740
New York	1,795	538	82	297	156	99	56	567
Wyoming	1,672	637	276	66	141	56	70	426
California	1,486	558	69	237	107	95	70	350
Five states with lowest per capita expenditure level								
Arkansas	$ 876	$ 354	$122	$111	$ 83	$ 35	$ 32	$ 139
Missouri	942	382	106	94	87	55	32	186
Indiana	953	429	93	89	99	46	35	162
South Carolina	979	398	196	102	79	36	58	257
North Carolina	982	438	93	78	95	43	37	200
National average	$1,262	$ 475	$107	$160	$104	$ 68	$ 49	$ 301

*Includes sewage, sanitation, parks and recreation, interest on general debt, and all other expenditures.

Source: Facts and Figures on Government Finance, 20th ed. (Washington, D.C.: Tax Foundation, 1979), p. 143.

of miles of highway among towns with relatively low populations. This is expensive when calculated on a per person basis. Wyoming in fiscal 1977, for example, spent $276 per person on highways; Rhode Island, however, given its small size and great population density, got by with $67 per person. Citizens of both states may have equally decent highways, but decent highways cost more than four times as much in Wyoming as they do in Rhode Island. Another good example of this difference in service costs can occur with police protection. Nevada, due to the presence of gambling and millions of visitors, spent $121 per resident in 1977 in police protection; North Dakota spent $37 per citizen for law enforcement. Factors such as climate, population density, terrain, soil types, and availability of water can all affect state expenditure levels. Such factors help explain why, for example, Alaska and Hawaii must spend so much more than the other forty-eight states.

A second element that helps to account for the range of expenditures is the problems facing a particular government. Consider state support for higher education. Since World War II the states have increasingly provided opportunities for higher education. In many eastern states numerous privately supported colleges and universities have taken much of the burden of support for higher education off state government. In many western states, however, no extensive system of private colleges existed, so after World War II, as the demand for a college education increased, states had to enter the education business. In 1975, for example, 74 percent of all students enrolled in institutions of higher learning in California were enrolled in publicly supported colleges; in Massachusetts, thanks to the existence of numerous private colleges, only 45 percent of college students were in tax-supported schools. A similar pattern occurs at the local level—many cities in Florida and Arizona have low educational expenditures since most residents are elderly people with no school-age children.[6]

A third factor that helps to explain why states and localities can differ so much in their financial policies is that financial resources vary considerably across states and local governments. In 1976, for example, the average per capita income in Connecticut was $7,373. In Mississippi, however, the figure was $4,575, almost $2,800 less than Connecticut. Large differences also exist with respect to value of real estate, value of manufacturing facilities, and locations of business offices (in 1977, for example, there was $4,406 in assessed property value for every citizen of New York state; in Alabama there was only $1,602 of assessed property value per resident). These differences in wealth cause differences in what problems are approached and how they are solved. New York state, thanks to its huge tax base, could afford to spend $2,527 per pupil in 1977–1978, while much poorer Vermont spent about $1,000 per pupil. Wealthy towns may solve the problem of recreation by hiring a recreation staff and building tennis courts. Less affluent towns may post a sign warning motorists of children playing in the streets.

Examining how states and communities spend money in terms of their financial resources can provide an interesting picture. Some governments are more generous than others. Consider the expenditures of Utah. Overall, in terms of population size, Utah in 1977 was slightly below the national norm for total expenditures on various state services ($1,201 per capita versus $1,262 nationally). However, for every $1,000 per personal income in Utah, state and local governments spent $232, while the average for all states was $199. In terms of personal income the state and local governments of Utah spent more than any other state on education ($116 per $1,000 of personal income versus a nationwide average of $75). In other words, compared to their resources, citizens of Utah give a great deal toward educating their children.

A fourth consideration to keep in mind when viewing differences in state and local financial commitments is that state and local expenditures tell only part of the story of how much money is spent. Our analysis has focused on *direct* state and local financial efforts. Recall, however, that the national government, through grants and revenue sharing, contributes significantly to state and local services. In fiscal 1977 the federal government provided some $62.6 billion in aid. The importance of this federal aid is that it can sometimes help reduce some of the sharper differences in expenditure patterns among the states, or at least provide minimal levels of services. While nationally the federal government contributes 21.9 percent of all state and local expenditures, in

[6] *Statistical Abstract of the United States, 1978,* p. 156.

poorer states this figure is much higher (28.5 percent of state and local expenditures in Alabama, for example). In fiscal 1976, for every dollar of federal tax money sent to Washington, the citizens of Mississippi received back $1.79. Wealthier states such as Illinois and New Jersey, however, got back only about seventy cents on the tax dollar sent to Washington.[7] Such federal expenditures do *not* necessarily equalize spending for education, health care, welfare, and the like. Rather, these federal contributions allow states and localities to offer services that are not reflected in their own direct expenditures.

The final point about how state and local governments provide services is that these services do not solely reflect financial or situational factors. In contemporary society all governments must provide certain types and levels of services. Imagine public reaction if a local government decided to not offer police protection or education because such services had become too expensive. However, beyond these minimal levels (which are frequently legally required) and the constraints imposed by limits on resources, much discretion exists. Some states, for example, California, may want an extensive system of higher education, while others (for example, New Jersey) may decide that such a system is not needed. In the field of public welfare, Wisconsin, with its long tradition of government involvement in social problems, spent more than twice as much per capita in 1977 on social welfare as Utah, which has a tradition of greater reliance on the private sector. In New York City garbage removal is a service provided by the government; in San Francisco it is a service provided by private companies.

How much money will be spent and on what projects are frequently decided through the political process. In the 1960s, as governor of New York, Nelson A. Rockefeller committed the state to ambitious new projects in higher education, the construction of public buildings, increased aid for the needy, and other expensive innovative projects. Despite all the increased tax burdens, Rockefeller was elected for four consecutive terms. In other parts of the country, however, candidates try to outdo one another with promises of lower taxes and balanced budgets. Interestingly, this process does not seem to depend greatly on such factors as party affiliation of leaders, political competition in a state, or amount of citizen participation.[8] That is, a Republican-dominated state is not automatically likely to spend more (or less) than a Democratic-dominated state.

TAXING IN STATES AND CITIES

So far our analysis has focused on the expenditure side of state and local government activity. We have seen how much money states and

---

[7] I. M. Labavitz, "Federal Expenditures and Revenues in Regions and States," *Intergovernmental Perspective*, Vol. 4 (1978), pp. 16–23.

[8] For more on the political factors that affect state differences in expenditure level, see Ira Sharkansky, *The Politics of Taxing and Spending* (Indianapolis: Bobbs-Merrill, 1969), especially Chaps. 4 and 5.

localities spend on different functions and why variations occur. Besides being consumers of education, highways, and the like, however, as taxpayers we are also the ultimate supporters of all these services. And since the question of "Who pays?" is certainly as relevant as "What do we get?" we must also examine the revenue side of state and local government. First we will analyze the different ways state and local revenue can be raised. We shall then consider how such revenue is actually generated as well as differences among states in the amount of money raised.

State and local governments can use a variety of methods to finance their services. Many services can be supported by charging a fee for their use. Parents of school children can pay tuition for the schooling, highway users can either pay tolls, license fees, or a special tax on gasoline, people who had fires can be assessed fees for fire department services, and so on. A different method of raising money would be for governments to operate income-producing businesses—liquor stores, hospitals, or even state lotteries (a variation would be to collect fees for things like oil, gas, or coal taken from the state). A third method is taxation; taxes can be levied on everything from income to property to consumer purchases.

All three of these ways of raising money can be found in the United States. Though all three are used, it would be a mistake to believe that a dollar raised one way is the same as a dollar raised another way. Each method of raising money has benefits for some people and disadvantages for others. Some techniques, such as taxes on property, taxes on food and other necessities, or fees for state licenses, are usually regressive (poor people pay a larger proportion of their income to taxes than do wealthy people). User fees (for example, school tuition) can sometimes place a heavy burden on small groups of citizens while those who benefit indirectly pay nothing. From the perspective of poor citizens, government revenue derived wholly from a graduated income tax would be most desirable since they would pay comparatively little—absolutely and in percentage terms—compared to the wealthy.

What types of taxes are used most commonly by state and local governments? In fiscal 1978 sales taxes of one type or another accounted for half of all state revenue (31.1 percent from general sales taxes and 20.3 percent from special taxes such as fuel taxes). State income (both individual and corporate) taxes in general brought in 35.2 percent of state revenue (most states have state corporation income taxes, but they are financially significant in only three states—New York, Pennsylvania, and California). The property tax is the most important source of tax revenue for local governments (more than 60 percent of local tax revenue). The property tax contributed only slightly (2.1 percent) to state government revenue. Revenue from licenses contributed 6.8 percent of state tax-generated revenue.

Predictably, considerable variation exists in states' reliance on different techniques of raising revenue. Oregon, for example, receives 70 percent of its tax revenues from the income tax (other states relying on the income tax for more than half their revenue in fiscal 1978 were

Delaware, Massachusetts, New York, and Wisconsin). On the other hand, Nevada, Texas, and Wyoming have no state income tax. Several states— Connecticut, Florida, and Mississippi, for example—collected 70 percent or more of their state taxes from sales taxes.

States and localities also differ significantly in key details of taxation. While a sales tax is generally regressive, it can be made even more regressive if the rate is high and if it is applied to food (because food expenses typically comprise a large proportion of expenditures for poor people). In 1978 state sales taxes varied from 2 percent (Oklahoma) to 7 percent (Connecticut). However, about half of the states allowed localities to add to the general sales tax so citizens of some areas were paying as much as 9 percent in sales taxes on their purchases. Half the states taxed food, and ten even taxed prescription drugs. Income tax rates and provisions display an even greater variety among the states. Illinois, for example, has a simple system of 2.5 percent regardless of income. Iowa has a sharply graduated system that begins at 0.5 percent for incomes under $1,000, while incomes over $75,000 are taxed at a 13 percent rate. A resident of Delaware must pay 19.8 percent on income above $100,000. Many cities such as New York, Detroit, Philadelphia, and Kansas City add their own city income taxes to the burden.

When considering types of taxes, the question is: How much does it cost the taxpayer? In fiscal 1977 the average per capita state and local tax burden in the United States was $813.01 (up from $308.29 in 1967 and $169.14 in 1957). Citizens of Alaska, California, Massachusetts, and New York have the heaviest tax burdens. Many southern states placed a much lighter burden on their citizens (Arkansas' per capita taxes amounted to only $494.08). However, this does not necessarily mean that citizens of high-tax states are being overwhelmed by their state taxes. States differ considerably in their taxable wealth. Thus a low tax bite in a poor state could be as much of a burden on citizens as a large bite in a wealthy state. For the most part, states with high per capita tax burdens (for example, New York and California) are also states with the greatest wealth. Therefore, the discrepancy between, say, California and Arkansas should not be interpreted to mean that Californians are being impoverished by their taxes, although they are twice as high.

What can we conclude from the numerous figures on state and local expenditures and revenue collection? While all state and local governments provide certain crucial services—education, public welfare, highways, and recreation, for example—there is no one fixed level of these services. Education may be funded lavishly in some states while in others little more than the minimum is provided. Such variations depend on both nonpolitical factors (for example, difficulty of providing the service) and factors expressed through the political system (for example, a desire by elderly citizens to keep taxes to a minimum). A second point is that a given level of services can be financed many different ways. Regressive property and sales taxes or progressive income taxes are all capable of raising sufficient revenue, but each type of tax has its costs and benefits to different citizens. In short, providing services to citizens requires numerous choices.

Is the present system adequate for solving contemporary problems?

Our basic form of state and local government derives from decisions made over a hundred years ago. Such "modern" innovations as the unicameral legislature, special districts, metro government, and the federal grant-in-aid system are minor adjustments in a nineteenth- or even eighteenth-century system. It is not surprising, then, especially as the burdens of government continue to mount, that the present system has been challenged. Such challenges involve far more than a call for a new law or increased financial assistance to a city; they question such matters as state boundaries, the legal division between city and suburbs, and other core aspects of the present system. Let us begin our analysis of the adequacy of the present system by reviewing some major criticisms of it. We shall then consider some possible defenses.

GEOGRAPHICAL DIVISIONS ARE NO LONGER RELEVANT OR USEFUL

The boundaries of the thirteen original states frequently derived from charters granted by English kings, early political disputes, and decisions by surveyors. Rivers, migration patterns, and military victories against foreign nations commonly defined the boundaries of subsequent states. Within states, city and county boundaries often depended on railroad routes, river junctions, and other aspects of the transportation system. Although there have been enormous population shifts in the last fifty years, the basic legal jurisdictions of state and local governments still largely reflect the decisions and circumstances of the eighteenth and nineteenth centuries.

It can be argued that these well-established boundaries are not the most efficient way of dividing political authority in contemporary society. One problem with existing boundaries is that population centers frequently cross state lines. For example, there is a Kansas City, Missouri and Kansas City, Kansas. East St. Louis, an important industrial suburb of St. Louis, is across the river in Illinois. In terms of its work force, transportation facilities, and economic impact, New York City is located in three states—New Jersey, Connecticut, and New York. This situation is reflected in the following humorous conversation between two couples on vacation:

FIRST PERSON: I hear you are from New York.
SECOND PERSON: Yes, I am. Are you?
FIRST PERSON: Oh, yes, we're from Stamford, Connecticut. What part of New York are you from?
SECOND PERSON: Why, we're practically neighbors. We're from Tenafly, New Jersey.[9]

[9] Adapted from Ben J. Wattenberg with Richard M. Scammon, *This U.S.A.* (New York: Doubleday, 1965), p. 72.

The existence of inappropriate legal boundaries has greater significance than producing "New Yorkers" from Connecticut and New Jersey. The historical accidents of boundaries can provide major artificial obstacles to solving contemporary problems, such as in the area of air and water pollution. For example, several small communities in northern New Jersey are almost wall-to-wall chemical factories and oil refineries whose pollution greatly affects residents of New York City. Despite bearing much of the cost of such pollution (health problems, damaged property, and so on), residents of New York City have no say on this matter except, perhaps, by trying to obtain federal legislation. Given that most of these New Jersey cities (and the state, to a lesser extent) enjoy substantial tax revenue from these polluting industries, revenues that help offset their costs, the motivation to help the politically irrelevant New York residents is small.

Another policy area where existing geographical borders can create unnecessary problems is transportation routes. For example, two states may design a perfectly good road system for the needs of each state, yet unless these two systems are coordinated, the overall result can be inefficient. This problem was illustrated several years ago when Connecticut and Rhode Island decided that there should be a road between New London, Connecticut, and Providence, Rhode Island. Acting according to its best economic interests, Connecticut built a northerly oriented route; Rhode Island decided it needed a more southerly oriented route. For a few years neither of these modern highways met, and motorists traveling between New London and Providence could not take advantage of this highway system. Eventually, however, the two highways were connected.[10]

Such problems are not limited to relationships among states. Consider, for instance, how the existence of separate cities and towns can play havoc with the racial integration of schools. It is now public policy to eliminate racial segregation of schools. But what if whites move out of a town leaving the entire school system virtually all black? Because the school systems of most cities (or special districts) are separate from one another, nothing can be done. This is true even if blacks live near the schools that lie outside their city or school district. In other words, the existence of legal—not physical—boundaries blocks a public goal. And since people who flee integrated schools realize this, these legal divisions may in fact help create the problem. We are not claiming that a single statewide school system would bring instant social integration; rather, eliminating artificial district lines could remove one barrier to this goal.

THE MULTIPLICITY OF GOVERNMENTS LEADS TO UNNECESSARY COMPLEXITY

While the first criticism of the existing system focused on the inappropriate boundaries of state and local governments, the sheer number of

[10] This conflict is described more fully in Ira Sharkansky, *The Maligned States* (New York: McGraw-Hill, 1972), pp. 47–48.

governing authorities is itself a problem. That is, when travel was time consuming and population widely dispersed, it may have made sense to have lots of cities and counties. However, as the populations of towns expand toward each other and eventually merge, and modern transportation allows a "nearby" government to be thirty miles away, there is little justification for almost eighty thousand government units. This is especially true in large metropolitan areas where the only divisions between hundreds of communities are legally defined boundaries. In 1975, for example, there were some 1,214 local governments in the Chicago, Illinois, metropolitan area (and 7,815 elected officials for these governments). The New York City metropolitan area was "governed" by some 363 governments and almost three thousand elected officials.

One of the unfortunate consequences of so many governments, most with their own rule-making and taxing power, is a bewildering variety of rules and regulations. Consider, for instance, the present building code situation. A building code is a locally designed and enforced set of standards that details the building practices permitted in a particular area. A building code deals with such things as what types of pipes can be used (plastic or copper), the materials of electrical wiring, septic systems, inspection requirements, and much more. There are presently four widely recognized "model" building codes, but only 15 percent of all governments of five thousand or more citizens use these or similar codes. Thanks to pressures from local builders, modern prefabrication techniques and innovative materials are generally prohibited. The impact of this diversity of building codes and the power of local interests is that it is nearly impossible for manufacturers of housing to market inexpensive mass-produced preassembled parts of buildings. Because of these local requirements, each unit must be custom built, and this adds substantially to housing costs.[11]

The existence of hundreds of independent communities, each with the power to define land use in its jurisdiction (called zoning power) can also discourage rational economic planning. Consider the problems of matching housing, commercial, and transportation needs in most multi-government suburban areas. Community A encourages building office buildings or factories. But the workers in these offices or factories may have to travel thirty miles to work because neighboring communities, by limiting lot size, prohibiting multioccupancy dwellings, and the like, effectively keep these new workers out. Meanwhile, communities between Community A and where the workers in the new facilities live find their roads overcrowded. Getting numerous independent governments to agree on such issues as location of new industry, placement of low-income housing, roads improvement, and so on, is difficult because local officials must face their own voters at election time, not the voters of the larger geographical area.

[11] Arthur F. Schreiber, Paul K. Gatons, and Richard B. Clemmer, *Economics of Urban Problems: An Introduction,* 2d ed. (Boston: Houghton Mifflin, 1976), p. 156.

UNDER THE PRESENT SYSTEM THE RESPONSIBILITIES AND CAPABILITIES OF GOVERNMENT ARE FREQUENTLY NOT MATCHED

During the 1960s many local government officials were fond of saying that the federal government had the money, the state government had the power, and city governments had the problems. Thanks to greatly increased federal aid to state and local governments in the 1970s, this characterization is now less accurate. Nevertheless, if one examines the problems faced by many government units and then considers their legal and financial capacities to handle these problems, it is clear that mismatches persist. Such mismatches are especially evident in the field of education, where money and power are not in the hands of the educators.

NEW JERSEY RESIDENTS GLOW IN FINANCIAL WINDFALL

One of the consequences of our present system of property taxes is that a small town can find itself deluged with money if a major industry locates there. Teterboro, New Jersey, for example, has only a few hundred residents yet it is very well off thanks to the fact that almost the entire town consists of industrial and commercial property. It is a good deal for Teterboro residents — they pay no property taxes — and an even better deal for business — their taxes are low since town needs are virtually nonexistent (Teterboro's few children are sent to neighboring schools).

Another example of such a windfall is Lower Alloways Creek Township, New Jersey. Thanks to a large nuclear plant in its jurisdiction, the township collects $7 million in utility taxes, or $4,375 for each of its 1,600 residents. The township cannot possibly spend all this money on itself so it has been charitable to some neighboring communities. It has given $75,000 for a new county courthouse roof, $1 million to area hospitals, and funds for special education programs in nearby communities. Nevertheless, such generosity does not satisfy the governor of New Jersey, who would like Lower Alloway's $7 million distributed more evenly to communities facing financial difficulties.

In short, the present system encourages industries to locate where financial demands are few, which in turn further weakens the tax base of communities that need the money.

Source: The Lower Alloways story was reported in "Catchall," *EPO: The Magazine for Elected Public Officials*, March/April 1979, p. 8.

Though the federal government has funneled huge amounts of money into state and local communities for public education, state governments retain ultimate legal control. In education states remain the dominant unit of government. In 1977 the federal contributions to primary and secondary schools comprised less than 8 percent of all expenditures.[12] In all fifty states the ultimate control of education firmly rests in state hands, though the responsibility for schooling is given to local authorities. The states control such things as length of school term, minimum teacher salaries, operation of local school boards, qualifications of teachers, and general curriculum content. Some states even regulate what books can be used, acceptable methods of teaching, and approved type of penmanship. Through its overall power to regulate local finances, the state exercises a powerful influence over local school revenue raising. Local educational autonomy exists only when the state allows it to exist.

The difficulty with this state domination is that local communities with the largest educational problems are very limited in their ability to respond to these problems. For example, poor communities with many disadvantaged students must follow state, not community, standards. They also must finance a major educational effort from their limited tax base, since on average almost half of all school revenues come from local property taxes. When local residents want to use unconventional teaching techniques, have a longer school term, or develop new textbooks, they probably will be frustrated by state regulations and the limits imposed by an inadequate property tax base. The mismatch between need and capability can be seen by examining spending differences between a wealthy and poor community in New Jersey. In 1974 Englewood Cliffs had $246,000 in assessed property value for each pupil and was able to spend $2,000 a year for each student. The much poorer city of Camden had only $18,000 of assessed property per student and, despite a tax rate almost twice that of Englewood Cliffs, could spend only $1,000 per student.[13] In short, it is the poor communities that must solve major education problems, yet a city like Camden lacks the political power and the financial capacity.

STATE AND LOCAL GOVERNMENTS ARE OVERWHELMED BY THE DEMANDS OF MODERN SOCIETY

The argument is that states and localities may have been perfectly capable of solving problems of the nineteenth and early twentieth centuries, and they still may be able to handle some contemporary problems, but the tough problems are beyond them. Especially in such areas as public welfare, economic planning, crime control, and enforcement of civil rights, state and local governments cannot be effective in meeting

[12] *Statistical Abstract of the United States, 1978*, p. 129.
[13] Murray S. Stedman, Jr., *State and Local Government* (Cambridge, Mass.: Winthrop, 1976), p. 315.

Two major problems faced by city government are pollution and crime. Cities must somehow cope, but they lack the resources and jurisdiction to solve these problems. They are frequently criticized for dirt and crime, but many of the critics wouldn't give cities the money and power to deal effectively with these problems.

their responsibilities. This argument is supported by several pieces of evidence.

Recall from our previous discussion of state governments that the office of governor is frequently very limited. Governors typically must live with independently elected cabinet officials and autonomous powerful boards. Moreover, many states limit the time a governor can serve. Terry Sanford, governor of North Carolina from 1961 to 1965, put it this way: "Almost no governor in the country has authority that even approaches his responsibility. The state constitutions fairly adequately prevent the governor from committing evil. That was perhaps the intent. They also hinder his attempt to pursue excellence."[14] Nor, for that matter, are many state legislatures equipped to deal effectively with complex modern problems. As we saw, state legislatures tend to be characterized by high turnover, part-time legislators, and limited staff resources.

Another aspect of state government that tends to limit effectiveness is the existence of lengthy, detailed state constitutions. A constitution should describe basic institutions, their interrelationships, and key principles of government. It cannot provide specific rules for each situation without running the risk of creating a rigid legal straitjacket for future action (remember that one of the virtues of the U.S. Constitution is its generality). Unfortunately, many state constitutions are lengthy documents that unnecessarily hinder effective governing. Oklahoma, for example, has a 63,569 word constitution; the Texas constitution runs to 54,000 words. Lengthy constitutions such as these can spell out details of taxation policy, regulate public utilities and insurance companies, put ceilings on taxes and debts, and in the case of South Carolina, define what is to be a hard-surface road in Greenville.[15]

[14] Terry Sanford, *Storm Over the States* (New York: McGraw-Hill, 1967), p. 31.
[15] Cited in Sanford, p. 29.

Finally, some people question the capacity of state and local government to raise sufficient revenue. Three points are usually made. First, the federal government can readily borrow needed money, but states and local governments typically operate under tight debt restrictions (many of these are in the state constitution itself). Second, unlike the national government, a state must worry that increased taxes will put it at a competitive disadvantage vis-à-vis other states. Industry and wealth will "migrate" if state and local taxes become too high. Third, the sources of tax revenue readily available to states and communities — sales and property taxes in particular — are much more limited due to their regressive character. While an income tax can exclude poor people, sales and property taxes will almost always fall on poor people, and if these taxes are too high, poor people will enter the welfare system. The possibility exists of relying more on state income taxes. Many states are moving in this direction, but the already high federal income tax rates probably preclude large state income tax rates. In sum, meeting modern needs requires a capacity to raise large sums of money, and states and cities lack a capacity comparable to that of the national government.

DEFENDING THE ADEQUACY OF THE EXISTING SYSTEM OF STATE AND LOCAL GOVERNMENT

Few people claim that the existing system is perfect. Attempts to make major changes are an enduring tradition — one delegate to the Constitutional Convention of 1787 even suggested that the thirteen original states redraw their boundaries so that each would have equal population. Nevertheless, despite all the obvious flaws, the present system can be defended. Let us briefly consider three general defenses of our system of state and local government.

The system can adapt to changing circumstances

The legal and geographic roots of state and local governments go back hundreds of years, and few would argue that a nineteenth-century system could handle the problems of the 1980s. Yet if we look closely at the present arrangement, we can see that significant changes have occurred to allow an old system to meet new needs. New government authorities were created to solve problems beyond the legal and financial power of existing governments. For example, in response to the difficulties of coordinating the transportation and shipping problems of New York City, New York State and New Jersey created the Port of New York Authority, a powerful agency with its own sources of income. To meet the problem of fragmentation of government public officials have joined together in such organizations as the National League of Cities, the National Governors Conference, and the National Conference of State Legislatures. Also recall that since the 1960s many adjacent local governments have created councils of government to discuss and coordinate their actions.

Perhaps the most important adaptation of the old system to meet modern needs has been the federal government's financial help to state and local governments. This assistance has frequently allowed governments with limited resources to tackle expensive problems such as pollution,

A NEW, IMPROVED UNITED STATES OF AMERICA

The problems with present state boundaries has led G. Etzel Pearcy, a geography professor at California State University Los Angeles, to propose a new 38-state United States. These boundaries are drawn to reflect population densities, location of metropolitan areas, and common orientations. These 38 states would be approximately equal in size, be compact in shape, and provide many financial savings. Here is what this 38-state United States would look like:

Source: G. Etzel Pearcy, *A Thirty-Eight State U.S.A.* (Fullerton, Calif.: Plycon Press, 1973), pp. 22–23.

vocational education, and hospital construction. This federal intervention has been especially important in the field of helping the needy. At one time "helping the poor" was strictly a state or local matter, but as many poor began congregating in large cities and the costs of providing assistance rose, the national government stepped in. In 1976, for example, the federal government contributed over $90 billion for such welfare benefits as Social Security and Medicare (another $18 billion was given for various types of public assistance).[16] To be sure, cities and counties themselves still must fund a large burden of welfare costs, but providing adequate services will now no longer exhaust local resources.

[16] *Statistical Abstract of the United States, 1978,* p. 319.

Shifting power to Washington is not necessarily a cure

A major criticism of our present system is that with so many state and local officials each having "a piece of the action" and each jealously guarding his or her turf, the coordination necessary to solve problems is impossible. Thus, some claim, a necessary first step in resolving many contemporary problems is to centralize power in Washington. However, this line of reasoning may be challenged on the grounds that shifting power to Washington merely substitutes a new set of problems for some old problems.

First, the image of replacing dozens of narrow-minded state and local officials with a central, all-powerful Washington authority is highly misleading. When it comes to dealing with issues such as education, welfare, and transportation, there are numerous officials in Washington, each with his or her own perspective and power. Thus, instead of having to get dozens of local officials to agree to a plan, one now has to get dozens of Washington officials to agree, and this is not always easy. A regional solution to water transport proposed by the Army Corps of Engineers could easily get bogged down in disputes involving the Environmental Protection Agency, the Department of Transportation, and 535 members of Congress. Washington may be as unable to make as rapid, encompassing decisions as state and local officials, despite the image of "centralized power" in the national government.

Second, even if Washington could exercise centralized power, experience has shown that solutions made in Washington are not always better than choices made in Smallville. Consider, for example, the problems with the federal urban renewal program. Created by the Housing Act of 1949, this program poured billions of dollars into cities to rebuild slums and to provide adequate housing for the poor. Despite these intentions and much federal effort, the net impact of urban renewal has been to decrease the well-being of poor central city residents. Typically, slum housing was replaced with high-income housing or commercial property, while the relocation of slum residents helped to create new slums but with higher rents. When low-income housing was built, it frequently helped to increase problems of crime, sanitation, and feelings of alienation. The disaster of this Washington-made policy has, in fact, directed people toward a new emphasis on programs involving more decentralization (for example, giving neighborhood groups a voice in planning).

The present system is what most citizens want

Though feelings of loyalty toward one's state and community are undoubtedly not as great as they were a hundred years ago, few citizens are so imbued with national spirit that they would willingly abolish existing states and localities to create more national entities. How many New Yorkers are willing to merge with, say, New Jersey, for the purpose of saving money and better coordinating state services? Even though some towns may have physically merged into one (for example, Bloomington and Normal, Illinois), legal mergers are rare. Efforts to create "consolidated" government in metropolitan areas by merging county and city governments have also had only limited success (success that has occurred frequently is racially motivated—whites want to keep city government out the hands of blacks).[17]

We must also realize that one person's defects may be another person's virtues. For example, from the perspective of someone wanting complete racial integration of schools, the existence of numerous autonomous school districts is a problem. However, to the individual who believes that racial integration will harm educational quality, the existence of separate educational districts is a great virtue. A similar situation can occur in the area of transportation policy. While everyone wants a "good" network of highways, nobody wants modern highways going through his or her own neighborhood. To the extent that each small town has some control over highway location, citizens can better protect themselves from a possible forced relocation (of course, the net impact of such protection is frequently inaction on new roads).

A system of numerous small governments may also have political benefits for many people. In particular, while dozens of separate governments in an area may discourage overall coordination, the smallness of such governments allows each citizen a greater role in affecting his or her political destiny. A citizen concerned about education, law enforcement, and zoning stands a better chance of being effective politically in a town of 10,000 than in a metropolitan area government of one million. This chance to make one's voice heard may well be worth the costs of some overall inefficiency. Moreover, a local political group with some degree of local influence would probably lose much of its power if local governments were consolidated. In short, to change the current system might require many citizens to lose a degree of political influence.

To return to our original question of whether or not the existing system of state and local government is adequate for solving contemporary problems, obviously, the evidence is mixed. Certainly there are many drawbacks to the present system—geographical boundaries do not always make sense; there has been a proliferation of governments; governments do not always have the power to match their responsibilities; and governments below the national level can be overwhelmed by modern problems. Nevertheless, to acknowledge these problems is not to endorse drastic and large-scale changes. The present system can be defended, if only on the grounds that proposed remedies are worse or at least no better. Ultimately, "adequacy" seems to come down to the balance between weaknesses and strengths. For some people, especially those who seek change, the multiplicity of governments, limitations on state and local governments, and the like, are grave weaknesses that overshadow any virtues. However, for someone largely content with existing policies the present system offers protection against rapid change and is thus a good system worthy of preservation.

[17] For evidence on this point, see Vincent L. Marando and Carl Whitley, "City-County Consolidation: An Overview of Voter Response," *Urban Affairs Quarterly*, Vol. 8 (1972), pp. 181–203.

A conclusion: state and local governments

The debate between those who would shift power toward Washington and those who would strengthen state and local government has been an enduring one. Much of this debate has focused on the capacities of the different governments. Supporters of a larger federal role usually speak of the national government's greater financial capacity, the national talent it can draw on, its ability to provide overall coordination, and other advantages that come with size. Proponents of state and local government typically stress that such governments are "closer to the people," have a better grasp of local problems, and can act faster and with less red tape. To advocates of local government, Washington means clumsy bureaucracy. To those in Washington, state and local politics is colored by small-town provincialism, amateurism, and domination by local economic interests.

This debate is more than a philosophical discussion over the merits of local rule versus a central government. The debate has practical consequences. Whether the decision is made on a federal or a local level greatly affects the outcome. People who want political decisions made in one place typically also want a certain *type* of decision. For example, advocates of tax reduction would generally favor giving greater power over tax policy to state and local officials, since these officials have traditionally resisted increased taxes. Supporters of greater government action, however, would prefer to see tax power in the hands of the national government. However, if we look behind many of the conflicts over education, taxes, welfare, and criminal justice, we find that the policy, not where the decision is made, is the true cause of the conflict.

Major questions raised

1. How are state and local governments organized? In general, states follow the federal plan of governmental organization, but each state has its own variations. Below the state level there are numerous types of political jurisdictions, and the forms and powers of these units differ considerably across states. Legally, all these jurisdictions are subservient to state government, though money from Washington has provided the local jurisdictions with some autonomy.

2. What are the major responsibilities of state and local governments? Education, followed by public welfare, highways, and health care are the major areas of state and local policy. What is important, however, is that states and communities vary considerably in how they meet their responsibilities—their response depends on many factors, including needs, resources, and people's values as they are transmitted through the political process. Wide variations also exist in how the necessary revenue is generated.

3. Is the present system adequate for solving contemporary problems? There are clearly some problems with the present system. A few criticisms are that geographical boundaries do not always make contemporary sense, there are probably too many local governments, and not all local governments can handle their responsibilities. However, the system can be defended on the grounds that it is adaptable; centralization is not necessarily a solution; and it is a system that most of us want.

QUESTIONS FOR FURTHER DISCUSSION

1. An agreement advanced by many officials of large cities is that residents of suburbs enjoy city benefits without paying taxes to support these benefits. That is, city governments must provide police protection, streets, and other essential services to keep a city functioning, yet those who live outside the city but visit it frequently (for work or pleasure) pay little of this upkeep. Should such suburbanites be required to contribute some of their property taxes toward maintaining the central city? Should the federal government insure city vitality on the grounds that they are national resources much like a national park?

2. A major power of local governments is the zoning power—the power to restrict land use. This power has frequently been criticized because it can be used to keep poor people out of a community. This type of restriction, it is argued, dooms many people to live in crowded, substandard conditions. Should a community of wealthy citizens be allowed to set building and lot size standards so high that poor people cannot move to their community? Should a landowner be restricted from selling land if the sale will encourage poor people to move in? Who should have the power to decide who can live where?

3. A current issue in higher education concerns whether a state can discriminate against nonresidents in admission and fees for its state-funded universities. A New Jerseyite visiting Wisconsin does not have to pay extra for using Wisconsin highways, bridges, police protection, and so on. Why should a college student from New Jersey be made to meet higher academic standards and pay a higher tuition? Doesn't such discrimination violate Article IV, section 2 of the Constitution—"The Citizens of each State shall be entitled to all Privileges and Immunities of Citizens in the several States"?

BIBLIOGRAPHY

Banfield, Edward C., *The Unheavenly City Revisited.* Boston: Little, Brown, 1974.
>   A widely read and controversial analysis of urban politics and problems. Deals with the issues of race, poverty, education, and violence. Concludes with an analysis of some possible solutions to urban problems.

Burby, Raymond J. III, and Shirley F. Weiss, *New Communities U.S.A.* Lexington, Mass.: Lexington Books, 1976.
>   A detailed analysis of recently created communities. Covers everything from who lives in these communities to how they are governed to how services are provided to the quality of life in them, and much more.

Caputo, David A., *Urban America: The Policy Alternatives.* San Francisco: Freeman, 1976.

A comprehensive analysis of the problems facing contemporary cities. Also reviews several possible solutions to these problems—revenue sharing, greater citizen participation, and various institutional changes. Well written and carefully documented.

Derthick, Martha, *Between State and Nation.* Washington, D.C.: Brookings Institution, 1974.

Describes and evaluates several multistate regional organizations such as the Tennessee Valley Authority and the Appalachian Regional Commission. Good analysis of the limits and prospects of such organizations for solving contemporary problems.

Dye, Thomas R., *Politics in States and Communities,* 3d ed. Englewood Cliffs, N.J.: Prentice-Hall, 1977.

A leading comprehensive text on state and community politics. Covers the institutions of government, citizen participation, and various policy areas such as crime, education, and welfare.

The Fiscal Outlook for Cities: Implications of a National Urban Policy, ed. Roy Bahl. Syracuse, N.Y.: Syracuse University Press, 1978.

A collection of articles analyzing the financial situation of cities. Lots of statistical information but not overly technical. An appendix provides a statement of Carter's urban assistance program.

Lineberry, Robert L., and Ira Sharkansky, *Urban Politics and Public Policy,* 2d ed. New York: Harper & Row, 1974.

A popular and comprehensive urban government text with a major emphasis on policy. Among the policies considered are education, crime, poverty, the environment, and urban growth.

Pettengill, Robert B., and Joginder S. Uppal, *Can Cities Survive? The Fiscal Plight of American Cities.* New York: St. Martin's Press, 1974.

A data-rich analysis of urban expenditures, urban revenue problems, and the relationship between central cities and suburbs. Contains a good chapter on possible alternatives to present political arrangements.

Politics in the American States, 3d ed., ed. Herbert Jacob and Kenneth Vines. Boston: Little, Brown, 1976.

A collection of essays on important aspects of state government—from parties to institutions to various public policies. Much of the analysis stresses differences and similarities among states. A fair amount of statistical data but analysis is nontechnical.

Schreiber, Arthur F., Paul K. Gatons, and Richard B. Clemmer, *Economics of Urban Problems: An Introduction,* 2d ed. Boston: Houghton Mifflin, 1976.

Analyzes such urban problems as poverty, housing, transportation, and air pollution from an economic perspective. For example, various economic solutions to the urban transportation problem are described and evaluated. Some limited knowledge of economics is helpful but not essential.

Sharkansky, Ira, *The Maligned States: Accomplishments, Problems, and Opportunities,* 2d ed. New York: McGraw-Hill, 1978.

A sympathetic analysis of state politics. Discusses various criticisms of state government, the fiscal capacity of state governments, and the state role in education and urban affairs.

Weinberg, Martha Wagner, *Managing the State.* Cambridge, Mass.: MIT Press, 1977.

An in-depth analysis of how the governor of Massachusetts (Francis Sargent) managed various state agencies. Useful for showing the mix of personality, politics, and the nature of the situation in affecting a governor's actions. Analysis is occasionally complex but not too technical.

Part five

American government: events, issues, and decisions

PREVIEW

Why Carter versus Reagan? Though many citizens were dissatisfied with these alternatives, both the rules for obtaining party nominations and public evaluations encouraged this final choice. As the better-organized, better-known front runners, Carter and Reagan could survive numerous primaries and benefited from laws limiting campaign expenditures. Moreover, both received the widest support among their party's adherents of those running for the presidency.

Why did Reagan win in 1980? Numerous voters who traditionally supported the Democratic candidate defected to the Republican Reagan or did not vote. Reagan did well, however, among traditional Republican supporters and Independents. Much of this behavior was motivated by economic issues—especially inflation and unemployment and international events such as our inability to free the hostages held captive in Iran.

How much difference will the outcome make? Reagan's victory, coupled with major Republican House and Senate victories, will undoubtedly shift many policy areas in a conservative direction. The fact that Reagan will appoint many like-minded people to high positions in the executive branch will also mean a conservative shift in day-to-day policy. However, several key factors—international events, inertia of the bureaucracy, and existing financial commitments, for example—will prevent dramatic across-the-board changes.

CHAPTER TWENTY-ONE

THE 1980 ELECTION

o two national elections are alike, but the 1980 election will probably be remembered as one of the most different in modern history. For the first time in one hundred years, since 1880 and the defeat of Grover Cleveland, an incumbent Democratic President was defeated. Not only was an incumbent defeated by a 69-year-old former movie actor, but the defeat was sizable (51 to 41 percent in popular vote, 483 to 49 in the electoral college), and it encompassed more than the presidency itself (Republicans gained 11 Senate seats, 33 House seats, and 4 governorships). Because Ronald Reagan was a self-proclaimed conservative and because many defeated Democratic congressional candidates were liberals, much was said about the election as heralding a dramatic shift toward more conservative politics. At the same time, however, many Americans were not overly excited about the possibility of a dramatic political change. Only about 53 percent of the voting-age population of 160.5 million bothered to vote—the lowest turnout since 1948. Nor did the campaign emphasize sharp ideological differences among the parties despite Reagan's avowed conservative philosophy—Reagan even quoted Franklin Roosevelt, long the arch enemy of conservatives. Our analysis considers three questions regarding the 1980 election:

1. Why Carter versus Reagan?

2. Why did Reagan win?

3. How much difference will the outcome make?

Why Carter versus Reagan

When 84.5 million citizens voted on November 4, their choice for President was limited. In principle, most voters had at least a half dozen choices, if minor party candidates are included, but, in practice, the choice for most people was between Jimmy Carter and Ronald Reagan. This narrowing of choices was one of the crucial aspects of the contest for the presidency. It was also a choice that disturbed many people. More than one commentator asked how it was possible, of all the potential candidates, to come up with two such as Carter and Reagan. According to a June 1980 CBS poll, only 48 percent of the voting-age population felt satisfied with Reagan and Carter as the major party choices. Many voting decisions were probably justified in terms of "lesser of two evils." One citizen even went so far as to put a "Slim Pickens for President" bumper sticker on his car. (Slim Pickens is a movie actor.)

To understand why the final realistic choice came down to Carter versus Reagan as opposed to, say, Edward Kennedy versus George Bush, Jerry Brown versus Howard Baker, or Henry Jackson versus John Anderson, we must examine three key features of the 1980 presidential race: (1) the basic roles and procedures governing the Democratic and Republican parties' selection of their nominees, (2) federal government regulations of campaign expenditures, and (3) public views on the alternatives to Carter and Reagan.

PARTY NOMINATION RULES

To become President of the United States one must first win the nomination of the Democratic or Republican Party. This is crucial—no independent candidate regardless of popularity or resources has ever come close to winning the presidency. Over the years the major parties have employed a variety of methods to choose nominees. The most commonly used procedure has been for state party organizations to select national nominating convention delegates who then pick the party's nominee. This method pretty much excluded ordinary citizens and gave considerable power to state party leaders who dominated the delegate-selection process. A nominee could be chosen even if he did no campaigning for the party's nomination.

In 1980 both parties relied heavily on the primary as a way of selecting nominating convention delegates. The Democratic Party held primaries in 34 states, the Republican Party in 36 states. Seventy-one percent of all Democratic convention delegates were chosen in primaries. Moreover, even where primaries were not held and delegates were chosen through caucuses, widespread participation by voters frequently was encouraged. In 1968, Hubert H. Humphrey was able to win the Democratic

Party nomination without winning a single primary election. This was impossible in 1980—a party's nominee had to do well in numerous primaries.

A second significant feature of the 1980 party nomination process was that the winner-take-all rule was virtually abolished in Democratic primaries and weakened in GOP primaries. In the past it was possible for a candidate to receive less than a majority but still win the bulk of a state's delegates so long as he won more votes than any other candidate. For example, in the 1976 Texas primary Carter won less than a majority but came away with 126 of 152 convention delegates.

A third important feature of the 1980 nomination process was that most delegates in both conventions were legally bound to support the person to whom they were pledged (at least for the first convention vote). This rule usually held for delegates whether they were selected through primaries or caucuses. In other words, a delegate selected as a Carter delegate in the New Hampshire primary could not suddenly decide to support Kennedy or Brown at the convention without breaking state law.

What were the consequences of these 1980 nomination rules? First, obtaining the presidential nomination required a sustained electoral effort. Running in and even winning only a few primaries meant certain defeat. A candidate had to do reasonably well in numerous primaries to get delegates. This meant that candidates with only regional support, or those with limited organizational support, were severely disadvantaged. The protracted character of this electoral battle was also encouraged by the reduction of the number of winner-take-all primaries. No longer was it possible to finish off a rival by winning a few bare majorities at the beginning of the campaign. Finally, because most delegates were legally bound to support the candidate to whom they were pledged, a dramatic last come-from-behind effort was extremely difficult.

All three of the consequences favored the candidacies of Carter and Reagan. Because each was initially well known and began the quest for the nomination with well-established election organizations (recall that Reagan had almost won the GOP nomination in 1976), each was in a good position to survive a long and demanding campaign. On the Republican side, candidates like George Bush, Howard Baker, Philip Crane, Robert Dole, and John Anderson, with their low name recognition and limited campaign organizations, were unable to survive 36 separate elections against the well-established, well-organized Ronald Reagan. Such a challenge might have been possible under the old rules under which an all-out effort in a few states could have resulted in winning a major share of the available delegates (or at least convinced uncommitted delegates that one was a "winner"). On the Democratic side, Carter as an incumbent President had a decided edge over a late-starting Ted Kennedy in a campaign of numerous separate elections. Had the Democratic nomination depended on winning only a half dozen or so primaries, Kennedy might have overcome the President's greater resources (such as patronage) and organizational strength.

In short, the nominating procedures of both parties gave the advantage to "established" candidates as opposed to "upstarts" or "dark horses." To be successful one had to win lots of elections, and this was difficult if one began the campaign without extensive resources.

RULES REGULATING THE FINANCING OF PRIMARIES

In Chapter 7 we described why rules regulating the financing of elections can never be neutral. A campaign finance rule, even if enforced impartially, will always favor some candidates over others. In the 1980 elections, there was a new set of campaign finance laws and thus a new set of biases. The basic finance rules for the primary period concerned both how candidates for the nominations could *raise money* and how they could *spend money*. The rules for *raising* money were as follows:

1. No candidate for the nomination could accept more than $1000 from an individual or $5000 from a political action committee (PAC). If a candidate accepted public funding of their campaign (see below), they could not contribute more than $50,000 of their own money.

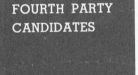

FOURTH PARTY CANDIDATES

Though the realistic choices for President on election day were Carter, Reagan, and perhaps Anderson, the actual number of choices was far greater. There were at least 10 other presidential tickets on the ballots of at least two states. These candidates were interested in conveying a point of view or building for the future rather than winning the election. Here is a sample of what might be called fourth party candidates.

Libertarian Party, Ed Clark and David Koch
Founded in 1971, the Libertarian Party has grown to a point that it was on the ballot in all 50 states in 1980 and fielded some 550 candidates for other offices. The party's philosophy is to reduce government involvement in society to an absolute minimum—no regulation of business, no laws regulating personal behavior, very limited military commitments, and the abolishment of almost all government programs. The Clark-Koch ticket received about 900,000 votes in the 1980 election.

Citizens Party, Barry Commoner and LaDonna Harris
On the ballot in 29 states, the Citizens Party had 22 other candidates running on the party's label. The party advocates public control of energy issues, banning all nuclear power, price controls on all necessities, and drastic cuts in military spending. The party philosophy is populist and anti-big business. The Citizens Party received about 220,000 votes.

2. To qualify for a federal campaign subsidy, at least $5000 in 20 states must be raised from individuals in donations no larger than $250 each. Once this qualification was met, the federal government matched on a dollar-for-dollar basis all contributions of $250 or less. But, if a candidate drew less than 10 percent of the vote in two consecutive primaries, this subsidy was withdrawn.

The rules regarding *spending* of campaign monies were as follows:

1. In the preconvention period, a candidate who accepted a government subsidy could spend up to $14.7 million (plus 20 percent of this figure to raise money and an unlimited amount for accounting and legal expenses).

2. Preconvention spending was also limited in each state. In small states such as New Hampshire, Vermont, and Nevada, the spending ceiling was $294,400. On the other extreme, a candidate in California could spend as much as $3,880,192.

3. However, candidates could not spend the maximum in each state since the state-by-state total is more than twice the overall national campaign expenditure ceiling of $14.7 million.

Four socialist parties also ran candidates. The Socialist Workers Party, the Communist Party, the Socialist Party, and the Workers World Party. Though all parties managed to get on several state ballots, their extreme left wing philosophy drew negligible public support.

On the right were two parties whose roots go back to George Wallace's 1968 bid for the presidency—the American Party and the American Independent Party. Neither of these parties drew significant support in 1980.

The 1980 election also saw several parties concerned with only a single issue. The National Statesman Party is a new version of the Prohibition Party and supports some other conservative measures besides antidrinking laws. The Right to Life Party is against abortion and has had some electoral success in certain states.

Not all candidates in 1980 were serious, however. One declared candidate was "Zippy the Pinhead" whose slogan was "Am I elected yet?". If elected, he pledged that no one will have to do the dishes or take out the garbage. On the subject of nuclear power, Zippy noted: "Nuclear power is·like an empty box of Ding Dongs. It smells funny and we wish it would go away."

For more on these candidates, see "Alternate Party Candidates May Have Substantial Impact on 1980 Presidential Election," *Congressional Quarterly Weekly Report,* October 18, 1980, pp. 3143–3149. The "Zippy the Pinhead" story is reported in detail in *Mother Jones,* September/October 1980, p. 6.

AND NOBODY DOES IT ANY BETTER, TOO

Though many Americans complained about the poor choices on election day, some people took a step further. On election day, across from the White House, led by Hugh Romney (also known as "Wavy Gravy"), there occurred a "Nobody for President" rally. The purpose of the demonstration was to have a "none of the above" alternative on the next presidential ballot. In defense of "Nobody" for President, Mr. Gravy pointed out that Nobody makes better apple pie than Mom and Nobody will love you when you're down and out.

Reported in the *New York Times*, November 5, 1980, p. 23.

In the 1980 primary battle all candidates except Republican John Connally accepted federal government matching funds and were thus bound by both fund-raising rules and spending ceilings. (Connally's campaign was, however, limited by the fund-raising rules.) What were the consequences of these rules in terms of who won the major party nominations? At first glance it might appear that rules limiting donations and providing federal subsidies might help less established candidates such as George Bush, John Anderson, Philip Crane, and Robert Dole on the Republican side or Ted Kennedy and Jerry Brown on the Democratic side. In fact, the very opposite was true. Just as the party nomination rules helped Reagan and Carter, the campaign finance rules helped these two candidates get the nomination.

To understand why Reagan and Carter benefited by these rules, we must realize two things. First, these rules favor candidates who get off to a good early start. A good start means it is easier to raise funds which are then matched by the government. A poor start, however, could mean that federal matching funds are withdrawn, which could seriously weaken a campaign. This is in fact what happened to Democrat Brown and Republicans Crane and Dole after their poor early showings. In other words, matching funds with a performance-based cut-off helped to make the rich richer. Coming from behind in the larger later primaries such as those in California, New Jersey, or Michigan thus was made more difficult—one now had to beat federally subsidized candidates to win.

Second, even if candidates did reasonably well in the early primaries, the per state spending ceilings provided a built-in advantage to well-established candidates. For example, in the February 26 New Hampshire primary, Reagan received 49.7 percent of the vote, Bush 22.9 percent, and Baker 12.9 percent. The next major primary was Florida on March 11. Since Reagan was the frontrunner and also had the greatest name recognition and in-place campaign organization in Florida, to beat Reagan in Florida, both Bush and Baker would have had to make enormous campaign efforts. However, since only about $1.5 million could be spent on a Florida campaign by Bush or Baker (a relatively small amount for a modern, mass media-oriented campaign), playing "catch-up" was difficult. In fact, Baker withdrew from the nomination contest shortly before the Florida primary. On the Democratic side, Ted Kennedy was likewise hindered by the state-by-state campaign limits. He had to battle an incumbent President who had numerous advantages such as the power to generate free publicity for himself, yet Kennedy was limited to spending no more than the President.

In sum, the 1980 campaign finance regulations were intended to make the preconvention process "fairer." While these laws may have helped several candidates financially, their overall impact was one of helping Carter and Reagan secure their parties' nominations. These rules discouraged late-starting dark horse victories and prevented candidates like Kennedy and Bush from overcoming the advantages of the frontrunners by spending far greater amounts of campaign money.

PUBLIC VIEWS ON THE ALTERNATIVES TO CARTER AND REAGAN

We have seen that both the party nominations and campaign finance rules were biased toward the two candidates who were the best known and best organized—President Jimmy Carter and the nearly successful 1976 Republican nominee, Ronald Reagan. These rule biases, however, did not preclude other candidates capturing party nomination. A string of convincing primary victories could have overcome these biases. Given the widespread feelings of dissatisfaction with the prospect of a Carter versus Reagan presidential election, why didn't a different set of candidates take advantage of these dissatisfactions to depose these frontrunners?

The answer to this question seems to be that though neither Carter nor Reagan drew enthusiastic, widespread support, their opponents were even less well regarded. In other words, Carter and Reagan may have fallen short of the ideal, but for most people they were better than any of the alternatives.

Strong evidence for this claim comes from opinion poll data collected during the primary period. Table 21.1 indicates how Republicans viewed various Republican candidates for their party's nomination and how Democrats viewed Carter, Kennedy, and Brown. We examine Republican views of Republican candidates and Democratic views of Democratic candidates since voters in a party's primary are usually people who identify with that party; hence, a Republican must appeal to Republicans to win the GOP nomination.

On the Republican side, note that Ronald Reagan is clearly the most favorably viewed of the seven candidates during the six-month period. In January, for example, 59 percent of the Republicans have a favorable image of Reagan; this compares with 20 percent for Bush, 7 percent for

TABLE 21.1

PUBLIC EVALUATION OF CANDIDATES IN 1980 PRESIDENTIAL PRIMARIES*

Candidate	Date				
	January (%)	February (%)	March (%)	April (%)	June (%)
Republican					
Reagan					
Favorable	52	51	53	61	70
Unfavorable	25	32	24	21	12
Bush					
Favorable	20	41	32	29	34
Unfavorable	14	16	24	27	21
Anderson					
Favorable	7	5	21	23	20
Unfavorable	12	15	24	34	33
Baker					
Favorable	30	31	—	—	—
Unfavorable	15	17	—	—	—
Dole					
Favorable	11	11	—	—	—
Unfavorable	18	12	—	—	—
Crane					
Favorable	4	7	—	—	—
Unfavorable	8	13	—	—	—
Connally					
Favorable	36	23	—	—	—
Unfavorable	34	43	—	—	—
Democratic					
Carter					
Favorable	56	71	63	53	43
Unfavorable	24	21	30	41	49
Kennedy					
Favorable	51	31	36	36	40
Unfavorable	38	48	52	54	46
Brown					
Favorable	20	19	11	—	—
Unfavorable	45	48	40	—	—

* The question asked was: "I'm going to name some possible Presidential candidates and ask what you think of them. If you haven't heard about someone I name, just tell me. Do you have a favorable or unfavorable opinion about . . ., or don't you know enough about him to have an opinion?" Source: CBS News/New York Times National Surveys.

Anderson, 30 percent for Baker, 11 percent for Dole, 4 percent for Crane, and 36 percent for Connally. With the exception of February when favorable ratings of Bush doubled and Reagan's ratings dropped 8 percentage points, Reagan continued to maintain his lead in favorable ratings among Republican citizens. The only Republican who did significantly better than Reagan among Republicans was former President Gerald Ford; he led Reagan 72 percent to 53 percent according to a March CBS/New York Times poll. However, since Ford was not running and thus could not win primary delegates, his greater popularity had no impact.

On the Democratic side the gap between the frontrunner and the nearest challengers is somewhat closer. Among Democrats, President Carter leads Senator Kennedy in terms of favorable opinions throughout the entire primary period, though at the end, when the race is nearly over, the difference is a mere 3 percentage points. Governor Brown of California, a formidable challenge to Carter in 1976, can make no headway in 1980 and, in fact, loses support as the campaign progresses. What is especially interesting on the Democratic side is that by June there are more Democrats with unfavorable opinions about both Carter and Kennedy.

What these and similar poll data add up to is that Reagan and Carter were the preferred choices of citizens identifying with these candidates' parties. To be sure, Ford drew a more favorable response among Republicans, and Carter's image was not positive among a substantial number of Democrats. Nevertheless, it is fair to say that among all the alternatives, Carter and Reagan come out the best. It certainaly was not true that some highly regarded candidates other than Carter and Reagan were deprived of the nomination despite wide public popularity.

To return to our original question of why the election was a choice between Carter and Reagan, the answer lies in the rules governing how parties selected their nominees, in government regulations of campaign finance, and in the greater degree of public support for these candidates compared with other candidates. No single factor guaranteed Carter or Reagan the nominations, but all three pointed in the same direction and thus resulted in the choice of Carter or Reagan.

Why did Reagan win in 1980?

The reasons behind Ronald Reagan's 9 million vote victory over Jimmy Carter are very complex. More than 84 million citizens voted, and each probably voted the way he or she did for different reasons. Equally important, about 75 million Americans did not vote, and these nonvoters also had their own explanation of their behavior. Nevertheless, despite the multitude of reasons behind each vote, it is possible to better understand the outcome if we examine (1) how 1980 presidential voting behavior patterns differed from past patterns and (2) some of the major issues of the campaign and which candidate benefited from these issues.

THE 1980 ELECTION AND THE TRADITIONAL DEMOCRATIC COALITION

Since the 1930s, Democratic and Republican candidates for the presidency have faced different problems in getting elected. With Franklin

D. Roosevelt's overwhelming victories in 1932 and 1936, the Democratic Party became the dominant party in terms of citizen loyalty. This attachment, or partisan identification as it is sometimes called, was especially common in certain groups—manual workers, members of labor unions, blacks, Catholics, Jews, and those with only a high school or less education. Even more than 40 years after the Roosevelt landslides, the Democratic disposition of these groups remains largely intact.

Given the domination of the Democratic Party in terms of psychological attachments, the major problem faced by the Democratic nominee has been to mobilize these Democratically disposed groups. Jimmy Carter in 1976, like Truman in 1948 and John F. Kennedy in 1960, did effectively mobilize these traditionally Democratic groups. For example, in 1976 Carter received 64 percent of the vote cast by Jews, 82 percent of the black vote, 58 percent of the vote from those with incomes below $10,000, 59 percent of the vote from those in union households, and 57 percent of the vote among those in blue-collar jobs. These margins provided Carter a thin victory over the incumbent, Gerald R. Ford, in 1976.

As a member of the minority party in terms of party loyalty, a Republican candidate faces a different situation. To win, a Republican candidate must, at least temporarily, (1) convert large numbers of voters whose normal inclination would be to cast Democratic votes, (2) win a major share of the independent vote, and (3) still hold on to core Republicans. In 1956, for example, the considerable personal popularity of Eisenhower caused many traditionally Democratic voters to vote Republican, and this defection gave Eisenhower a substantial victory over Stevenson. In 1972 many Democrats had serious doubts about some of Senator George McGovern's proposals and voted for President Richard Nixon. In sum, for a Democrat to win, he (or she) must hold substantial numbers of voters from traditionally Democratic groups within the party; a Republican, however, must do reasonably well in these Democratically disposed groups and win big among independents and Republicans.

What happened in 1980? Table 21.2 shows how Carter, Reagan, and Anderson did among various types of voters (and also presents comparisons for the 1976 election). As in the past, the Democratic nominee—President Carter—did well among Democrats; he won 66 percent of the group's vote. The Republican—Reagan—did very well among Republicans, winning 84 percent of their vote. Even though there are many more Democrats than Republicans, Carter's 2 to 1 victory among Democrats was not good enough. Reagan's very strong showing among Independents (54 percent versus 30 percent for Carter) coupled with his strong Republican showing more than offset Carter's Democratic strength. Note that in 1976 when he just defeated Gerald Ford, Carter beat the Republican Ford by a 3½ to 1 margin among Democrats. (This 3½ to 1 margin could offset poor showings among Independents and Republicans.)

The erosion of support for Carter among groups that have traditionally sided with the Democratic nominee is well displayed in Table 21.2. Only

	1980			1976		TABLE 21.2
	Carter	Reagan	Anderson	Carter	Ford	HOW DIFFERENT GROUPS VOTED IN 1976 AND 1980
Party Identification						
Democrats (43%)	66	26	6	77	22	
Independents (23%)	30	54	12	43	54	
Republicans (28%)	11	84	4	9	90	
Race						
Blacks (10%)	82	14	3	82	16	
Hispanics (2%)	54	36	7	75	24	
Whites (88%)	36	55	18	47	52	
Religion						
Catholic (25%)	40	51	7	54	44	
Jewish (5%)	45	39	14	64	34	
Protestant (63%)	36	59	5	44	55	
Family Income						
Less than $10,000 (13%)	50	41	6	58	40	
$10,000 - $14,999 (14%)	47	42	8	55	43	
$15,000 - $24,999 (30%)	38	53	7	48	50	
$25,000 - $50,000 (24%)	32	58	8	38	62	
Over $50,000 (18%)	25	65	8	—	—	
Occupation						
Professional/manager (40%)	33	56	9	41	57	
Clerical, sales, or other white collar (17%)	42	48	8	46	53	
Blue collar worker (17%)	46	47	5	57	41	
Agriculture (3%)	29	66	3	—	—	
Looking for work (3%)	55	35	7	65	34	
Education						
High school or less (39%)	46	48	4	57	43	
Some college (28%)	35	55	8	51	49	
College graduate (27%)	35	51	11	45	55	
Union Membership						
Labor union household (26%)	47	44	7	59	39	
No member of household in union (62%)	35	55	11	45	55	

Source: New York Times/CBS News poll.

among blacks does Carter receive the type of voting support usually given Democratic nominees. Among Jews, a group that went 2 to 1 for Carter in 1976, Carter won in 1980 by a bare 6 percent of the vote. Among Catholics, another pro-Carter group in 1976, Reagan beat Carter by 11 points. Reagan ran just about even with Carter among blue-collar workers and only slightly behind among voters from households in which

Though Ronald Reagan won with only slight black support, it is expected that the President will pay attention to all significant groups regardless of their voting behavior. Here President Reagan and Vice President George Bush meet with various black leaders.

there was a union member. This is significant since blue-collar workers in general, and union households in particular, were long considered part of the very core of the Democratic electoral coalition.

In contrast to President Carter's poor showing among groups that traditionally supported the Democratic Party, Reagan did quite well among groups that traditionally supported the GOP. For example, among those with professional or managerial jobs, Reagan beat Carter by 23 points. Of those with incomes greater than $25,000, Reagan beat Carter by a margin of about 2 to 1. Reagan also did well among college graduates — another traditional Republican group despite some recent talk about liberal or radical college students.

On top of these defections of traditional Democratic voters to Reagan, the Carter candidacy was also unable to generate enthusiasm to vote among many of these likely to support Carter. The decline in turnout between 1976 and 1980 was not uniform across all groups. Among Jews, union members, and blacks — all key groups for a Carter victory — turnout was down from 1976.[1] What made this lower turnout especially important was that many of these nonvoters lived in populous eastern states with large electoral college votes. For a Carter victory, these states were absolutely essential. (In New York, turnout was down by about a half million, and Carter lost it and its 41 electoral votes by 160,000 out of 5.86 million votes cast.)

[1] Cited in *Newsweek*, November 17, 1980, p. 32.

ISSUES IN THE 1980 ELECTION

The previous analysis depicted President Carter's failure to win sufficient support among groups that had traditionally given Democratic
candidates their victories. The task now is one of accounting for these
substantial defections. In other words, what drove millions of people
who were normally predisposed to vote Democratic into the arms of a
conservative Republican? To understand what happened let us examine
two of the major issue clusters of the campaign and how these issues
affected voting.

The debate between Jimmy Carter and Ronald Reagan. One week prior to the election
the candidates met face to face to respond to questions from reporters. Some 105
million Americans watched the 90-minute event. Carter's answers to questions emphasized that he was the President and that he had to make life-or-death decisions in the
White House, while his opponent had ideas that were "dangerous," "disturbing," and
"radical." Besides frequent mention of the war-and-peace issue, Carter also emphasized
that he is a mainstream Democrat and that the Democratic Party has had a traditional
concern for women, blacks, workers, Hispanics, and southerners. Reagan spent much
of the time defending his proposals and his record as governor of California, only
briefly attacking Carter's record on the economy and foreign affairs. The thrust of
Reagan's message seemed to be: I am a reasonable, benign person, not an elderly
irresponsible anxious to use the bomb. Neither Carter nor Reagan decisively won the
debate—the public by a 34 to 26 percent margin (with 31 percent saying "neither")
gave the nod to Reagan, but political experts were closely divided. However, prior to
the debate Carter did seem to be making major gains on Reagan's lead in the opinion
polls. After the debate Reagan's lead grew larger. One possibility was that Reagan
supporters, previously unsure of his character, were reassured by the debate that the
candidate was a warm human being who could be trusted as President. In other words,
the debate helped turn a small but significant number of Reagan supporters into
Reagan voters.

Sharp increases in the cost of energy are a major reason for high rates of inflation. High energy costs are also very visible and motivate people to do things such as install wood-burning stoves.

Economic issues

Perhaps more than any other type of issue, economic issues can have a powerful impact on people's behavior. One may grumble about a decline in public morality, racial violence in the inner city, or the plight of the whales, but these issues do not affect one the same way as the loss of one's job or a reduced standard of living. In 1980 there were two economic issues that concerned a great many people: inflation and unemployment.

When Jimmy Carter defeated Gerald Ford in 1976, Carter had emphasized that he could reduce the then-current inflation rate of 5–6 percent. By 1980 inflation was running between 12 and 13 percent (and even touched 18 percent at one time). In concrete terms, this high inflation meant that food bills were up sharply, gasoline prices had nearly tripled between 1976 and 1980, and home ownership was quickly becoming an unaffordable luxury for middle-income families, to name just a few consequences. Since incomes for most people had not risen at the same rate as inflation, inflation constituted a financial loss for most people.

Though Carter made an effort to convince voters that the major reasons for inflation were beyond his control (for example, increased costs of foreign oil), this tactic was unsuccessful, and many voters, worried about these high inflation rates, voted for Reagan. According to an NBC/Associated Press poll, 41 percent of voters felt that inflation was the decisive issue, and among this group, Reagan beat Carter by a 3 to 1 margin. (This poll also found that most voters believed that a President *could* cope with inflation.[2])

[2] Cited in *Newsweek*, November 17, 1980, p. 30.

The concern for unemployment was perhaps not as widespread as worries over inflation, but this concern was especially common in large electoral-vote-rich industrial states such as Michigan, New Jersey, Illinois, New York, Ohio, and Pennsylvania. Automobile workers in Michigan, steel workers in Ohio, and other once solidly blue-collar Democratic supporters defected to Reagan in substantial numbers as a result of the economic problems experienced by American heavy industry. The high unemployment rate in the steel industry led one Pennsylvania steel worker union president to say on election day: "Carter ignored the steel workers for 3½ years, and now he comes around asking for our votes. Well, he's not getting them."[3]

The importance of economic factors in voting defection is clearly demonstrated by the data in Table 21.3. Those Democrats whose economic position improved in the last year supported Carter over Reagan by an almost 5 to 1 margin. However, among Democrats whose economic situation had declined, Carter ran only 8 points ahead of Reagan. Among independents and Republicans, as well, Carter did comparatively better among those whose financial situation had improved. Note, however, that among Democrats, Independents, and Republicans, people whose financial situation had declined are in the overwhelming majority. Ronald Reagan clearly benefited from the poor economic conditions.

Family financial situation and political party	Voted for		
	Carter	Reagan	Anderson
Democrats *better* off now than a year ago (7% of the sample)	77	16	6
Democrats *worse* off now than a year ago (13%)	47	39	10
Independents *better* off (3%)	45	36	12
Independents *worse* off (9%)	21	65	11
Republicans *better* off (4%)	18	77	5
Republicans *worse* off (11%)	6	89	4

TABLE 21.3

FINANCIAL SITUATION, POLITICAL PARTY, AND VOTE

Source: New York Times/CBS News poll.

[3] Quoted in *Time*, November 17, 1980, p. 24.

THE ANDERSON DIFFERENCE

Though the contest for the presidency is in practice a two-party race, there exists a long tradition of individuals who try to make it a three-party race. These third party candidates, unlike the Socialist or single-issue parties, honestly believe that they might win or at least significantly affect the final election outcome. In 1968, for example, George Wallace, running under the American Independent Party label, received about 13 percent of the popular vote. In 1980, the heir to this third party tradition was John Anderson, the ten-term Republican Congressman from Illinois who had been unsuccessful in the Republican primaries.

The Anderson candidacy was one of many contrasts. He began his Congressional career in 1960 as a solid conservative, a stance that was well suited to the people in his district. In Congress, he voted against Medicare, food stamps, the war on poverty, and all other liberal measures except civil rights. He began to change in the late 1960s with more vigorous support of civil rights and opposition to the war in Vietnam (though he continued to support the war effort in his voting). By the 1970s he was generally among the most liberal Republicans in Congress.

His independent candidacy for the presidency seemed to be motivated by moral conviction. He believed that most Americans were genuinely dissatisfied with the system that gave them a choice between Carter and Reagan. Anderson disdained the politics of backroom deals, horse trading, and saying what people want to hear—in Detroit, the automobile capital of the United States, he spoke out against government assistance to Chrysler and for a 50-cents-a-gallon tax on gasoline. (In the House, he was sometimes called "Saint John the Righteous.")

International relations

In addition to a concern over the economic matters of inflation and unemployment, several aspects of America's international relations also had an impact on voting behavior. One such issue was the feeling among many people that the United States was falling behind the Soviet Union in military strength and was not responding effectively to Soviet intervention in places like Afghanistan. In his campaign Reagan frequently stressed a commitment to increased military spending, scrapping the SALT II agreement because it conceded too much to the Soviet Union, and in general increasing America's prestige and power throughout the world.

Anderson at Yale.

Though Anderson offered the American people a 317-page platform with a wide range of solutions to almost every conceivable problem, Anderson himself with his "high class" (some would say arrogant or "preachy") style seems to be the main element in his appeal. Like the (unsuccessful) Eugene McCarthy candidacy of 1968, Anderson does best among young, highly educated, liberal voters who consider themselves independents. On November 4 Anderson received about 5.5 million votes (about 7 percent of the total), running best in the New England area. Because he did not win a plurality in any state, the 5.5 million votes translated into zero electoral votes.

Reagan's strategy proved to be an effective one. A CBS/New York Times poll shortly after the election found that 77 percent of all registered voters believed that Reagan would see to it that the United States would be respected by other nations, while only 11 percent disagreed. (An October poll found that only 49 percent believed that Carter could create this respect.) Among those who felt that the United States should be more forceful in dealing with the Soviet Union even if this increased the likelihood of war—and 54 percent of voters agreed with this proposition—Reagan beat Carter better than 2 to 1 (64 percent to 28 percent). However, among the 31 percent who rejected this argument, Carter beat Reagan by a 56 to 32 margin.

Though Reagan benefited among some from his image of "getting tough with the Russians," it was also a grave potential danger for him if he was perceived as being too trigger-happy. In fact, one of President Carter's major campaign tactics was to emphasize Reagan's willingness to involve the United States militarily in situations that could lead to nuclear war. Two weeks prior to the election a CBS/New York Times poll reported that 39 percent of all registered voters believed that if elected, Reagan would involve the United States in war (compared with 18 percent who believed this of Carter). However, following the televised debate between Carter and Reagan, and despite Carter's repeated emphasis of this issue, the proportion believing that a Reagan victory would mean war dropped to 31 percent. Overall, this image of "getting tough with the Russians" cut both ways for Reagan. He probably lost votes among those worried about nuclear war, yet he probably gained even more among those who believed that the United States had become weak in international affairs.

The final international issue that significantly affected voting behavior was President Carter's handling of the Americans held captive by the government of Iran. The inability of the Administration to make any sort of progress on the hostage situation for nearly a year had resulted in widespread frustration. By election day, voters by a 3 to 2 margin disapproved of Carter's handling of the Iranian crisis, and, among these dissatisfied voters, 4 of 5 chose Reagan. Moreover, many of those who made up their minds late in the campaign gave the Iran situation as a major reason for their decision, and here, too, Reagan came out ahead.[4]

In sum, though the 1980 election had numerous issues, the issues of inflation, unemployment, America's stature in the world, and the hostages in Iran were particularly important in affecting voting decisions. In all cases, Carter came out the loser to Reagan. Inflation was high, unemployment was high in key industrial states, the United States seemed to be losing out to the Soviets, and the hostage situation remained unresolved. With all these issues pushing in the same direction, it was no wonder that many traditional Democrats decided that it was time for a change.

How much difference will the outcome make?

Many citizens who voted on November 4 believed that it was time for a change—and, indeed, the election did produce many changes in addition to a new President. The key question, however, is, will these changes make a difference? Will we have a continuation of more or less the same policies enacted by a new set of people? Or will changes in people mean changes in policy? To answer this question we shall consider three factors that will have a bearing on possible changes resulting from the

[4] Cited in *Newsweek*, November 17, 1980, p. 32.

1980 election: (1) changes in Congress, (2) changes in top leadership in the executive branch, and (3) the limits of presidential power in contemporary politics.

Changes in Congress

Besides winning the presidency, the Republican Party made substantial inroads in capturing the legislative branch of government. In the House Republicans won 37 seats previously held by Democrats and lost four to Democrats, representing a net gain of 33 seats. This constituted the largest GOP gain since 1966 and reduced the Democratic margin from 276–159 to 243–192. In the Senate Republicans picked up 12 seats, gaining a 53 to 47 majority. The last time the Republican Party held a Senate majority was in 1952 (and the last time the two houses of Congress were split between two parties was under Herbert Hoover in 1931–1933).

These numbers do not tell the whole story, however. When we examine the types of legislators defeated and the resultant changes in Congress, the changes brought by the 1980 election are even more substantial. Consider the Republican victories in the House. Many of the 33 defeated Democrats were liberal or moderate Democrats who lost to more conservative Republicans. Moreover, some of these defeated liberal Democrats (for example, Robert Eckhardt of Texas, Lester L. Wolff of New York) chaired important House committees or subcommittees. Though they will be replaced by other Democrats, an overall movement in a conservative direction is likely among committee chairmen. Also defeated was John Brademas of Ohio, a liberal Democrat who was the Democratic Whip. In general, the substitution of Republicans for Democrats, especially liberal Democrats, will probably mean a more conservative House. Conservative proposals such as antibusing measures or tax cut proposals that once lost by a dozen or so votes will probably now pass.

In the Senate, the conservative shift due to Republican electoral gains will be even clearer. Several of the most liberal Democratic Senators were defeated in 1980—George McGovern of South Dakota, Warren Magnuson of Washington, Frank Church of Idaho, John Culver of Iowa, Birch Bayh of Indiana, and Gaylord Nelson of Wisconsin. Almost all of these legislators were replaced by more conservative men. Moreover, in situations where a Republican replaced another Republican (for example, in New York and Oklahoma), the new Republican was more conservative than the one he replaced.

This new, conservatively oriented Republican majority will make its impact felt in two ways. First, Republicans will now succeed Democrats as heads of all committees and subcomittees, and committee membership will reflect the Republican majority. In some cases, for example, the Armed Services Committee, changes will not be great since not much difference existed between senior Democrats and senior Republicans. However, on several key committees, especially Foreign Relations, Judiciary, and Budget, the shift to GOP domination will have a clear impact. For example, the Senate Judiciary Committee, which deals with civil rights legislation and the appointment of federal judges, will now be headed by the conservative Strom Thurmond of South Carolina (who has opposed all civil rights legislation in the past) instead of the much more liberal Ted Kennedy.

A second consequence of the New Senate Republican majority will be major changes in Senate staffs. A prerogative of the majority party is to fill two-thirds of all staff positions. Recall from Chapter 10 that these staff members play a vital role in the law-making process (for example, supervising legislative investigations and running much committee work). No doubt, the replacement of hundreds of Democrats with Republicans in staff positions will further contribute to the new conservative orientation of the Senate.

Though there is no question that Congress will be more conservatively disposed following the 1980 election, this conservative disposition cannot be equated with dramatic legislative success in enacting conservative policy goals into law. We saw in Chapter 10 that power in Congress is highly fragmented and more negative than positive. This holds whether Congress is highly liberal, moderate, or highly conservative. A powerful member of the House cannot intimidate a Senator; an all-powerful committee chairperson still must persuade his or her colleagues to accept committee decisions. Senator Thurmond as chairman of the Senate Judiciary Committee may block all future civil rights bills, but he cannot by himself repeal those on the books. In short, the 1980 election is likely to produce a more conservative Congress, yet it is unlikely that Congress will be able to undertake systematically a major overhaul of programs and policies enacted by previous, and more liberal, Congresses.

Changes in top executive branch leadership

The replacement of Jimmy Carter by Ronald Reagan by the electorate means far more than replacing a single person. With Reagan there comes a whole new top leadership in the executive branch. Voters not only changed Presidents, they changed presidencies. This change will be most apparent in the President's "inner circle" of advisers. For President Carter, men like Hamilton Jordan, Jody Powell, and Stuart Eizenstat constituted this inner circle. For Reagan, people like James Baker, Ed Meese, and Mike Deaver comprise part of this circle. Such close advisers may not even have official government positions—one of Reagan's long-time trusted advisers is Holmes Tuttle, a California auto dealer.

Beyond this inner circle are important advisers to the President and heads of agencies in the Executive Office of the President such as the Office of Management and Budget. They typically have titles like "Assistant to the President for National Security Affairs," but their power lies less in formal titles and authority than in their access to the President himself. Presidents have considerable discretion in whom they appoint to these positions. It will also be largely up to Ronald Reagan who will occupy some 5000 "policy-making" positions in the federal bureaucracy. These include heads of the thirteen cabinet level departments and executive agencies such as the CIA plus numerous lesser officials not covered by civil service. Virtually all of these appointees will be Republicans generally in accord with Reagan's own philosophy.

The changing of some 5000 officials, from members of the President's inner circle to the most minor assistant, is significant for at least two reasons. First, numerous important political decisions are made entirely by these subordinates. For example, the Justice Department under President Carter vigorously prosecuted many cases involving suspected civil rights violations. Likewise, the Environmental Protection Agency made a major effort to control industrial pollution. President Carter himself did not actually make these decisions though he probably favored them. Rather, he appointed people to key positions who "on their own" would make these decisions. Through such appointments the President is able "to make" thousands of decisions each month.

Second, these 5000 officials constitute a communications network that helps define presidential alternatives. By the time a President confronts a choice, it has typically passed through the hands of numerous lower officials and each one has made his or her own impact on the information alternatives given the President. It is entirely likely that when President Reagan deals with inflation or unemployment his available options, perceptions of costs of different solutions, and judgments of what is possible will be quite different from those perceived by President Carter, even if the problems are virtually identical. In other words, the shift from 5000 Carter appointees to 5000 Reagan appointees also means a change in political reality as seen from the White House. An important problem in the Carter Administration may not be an important problem in the Reagan presidency.

Both of these factors mean that policy-making will have a more conservative orientation. In the past the Attorney General might have committed considerable Justice Department resources to lawsuits involving racial discrimination or water pollution, and the President might have been pressed by his aides to use his prestige to increase funding from Congress for even more such suits. Under President Reagan, the Attorney General is likely to see such suits as less important than other matters (for example, investigating subversive activities), and Reagan will not be sent messages from subordinates about the lack of progress in racial discrimination or water pollution lawsuits.

In sum, the voters in November elected far more than Ronald Reagan and George Bush; they also changed some 5000 other policy-makers ranging from close advisers to heads of dozens of executive branch agencies and their subordinates. These nonelected officials will make thousands of decisions that the President will never see and help shape the political environment.

The limits of presidential power in contemporary politics

We have thus far shown how the election of Ronald Reagan, the changes in Congress, and the changes in the bureaucracy will shift policy-making in a conservative direction. Such conservative policies as reducing spending by the national government, removing many regulations on business, limiting the number of national government employees, lowering taxes, strengthening the U.S. military, vigorously combating Soviet expansion, and making less use of government intervention to achieve sexual and racial equality will certainly be pursued by Reagan, his advisers, and those he appoints to positions of power. Moreover, as we described in Chapter 12, a modern President has enormous powers at his disposal—he is Commander-in-Chief, chief U.S. diplomat, a major force in setting the legislative agenda, and the focal point of public attention. Will Ronald Reagan be able to use all of these formal and informal powers to accomplish his policy objectives? No doubt there will be major changes compared with the Carter years, but several factors will prevent the wholesale changes frequently demanded by some of Reagan's most conservative supporters.

One major limiting factor will be international events. The President has considerable formal power in foreign affairs, and recent Presidents have had much more discretion in foreign than domestic affairs. But no President—whether liberal or conservative—can dominate overseas events. President Reagan's commitment to reducing inflation may come to naught if, for example, Middle Eastern nations double or triple the price of oil. Changes in top Soviet leadership may involve the United States in a huge arms race which would dash completely Reagan's goals of reducing government deficit spending and balancing the budget.

Another limitation Reagan faces will be trying to control the vast federal bureaucracy in order to accomplish specific objectives. Unquestionably, President Reagan and the people he appoints will be able to prevent the federal bureaucracy from pursuing many past policies, for example, pressuring small businesses to develop elaborate plans to hire more minorities. However, Reagan will probably be less successful in achieving positive goals (for example, turning over government-performed jobs to private industry). Here Reagan will face the same types of problems faced by all Presidents, regardless of philosophy—the complex nature of government bureaucracy makes it possible for subordinates to avoid carrying out their assigned tasks or even to take contrary actions.

A third problem that Reagan will encounter will be gaining cooperation from Congress. Our system of government with its separation of powers and checks and balances makes such cooperation both essential and difficult. Even if the President and Congress share the same philosophical goals, differences in specifics are bound to emerge, and these can cause a stalemate. For example, when Reagan proposes reducing "unnecessary" public works programs, many a conservative legislator will probably say: "Great idea, but fortunately all the projects in *my* district are necessary." The necessity of winning cooperation from hundreds of legislators, each with his or her own priorities, will force President Reagan to adjust his policy goals.

A fourth problem faced by the President, especially one committed to reducing federal government expenditures, is that many of the government's financial obligations are precommitted well into the future. Reagan and the new Congress will not start with a clean slate—huge amounts of money are going to be spent unless the government violates thousands of contracts and hundreds of laws. For example, tens of billions must legally be allocated for veterans and Social Security pensions. The government is also legally obligated to pay the huge interest on the national debt. Sharply reducing the number of federal employees would also violate civil service regulations. Many projects begun years ago (building the Trident missile submarine) will require payments well into the future. Only a relatively small portion of the federal budget is thus open to significant reduction.

Finally, the need to keep his own re-election possibilities plus those of his followers in Congress will moderate many of Reagan's more conservative proposals. Few people find tax cuts objectionable, but when we look at other Reagan-backed proposals, we can see that they might prove to be an eventual electoral liability. For instance, reducing "waste" might in fact become reducing service to tourists in national parks, raising the cost of private medical care by reducing government aid, closing post offices, or letting the national highway system deteriorate. These actions might be costly on subsequent election days and are thus to be avoided. Many people who oppose big government in the abstract can be outraged when their government jobs or subsidies are cut back.

In general, the Reagan victory will probably have a moderate effect in many areas. The Reagan Administration will probably have its greatest impact on stopping certain types of national government actions (for example, lawsuits against schools that refuse to hire more minorities). It will also be effective in revising or at least slowing many trends—for example, the proliferation of regulatory bodies in government. The agenda of problems faced by the President will also change—reducing taxes will be more important than guaranteeing everyone adequate health care. Nevertheless, the overall impact will be far short of revolutionary. The President is not a king, and both the constitutional system and the nature of our political process prevent rapid and extensive change, regardless of the philosophy behind the change.

Major questions raised

1. Why Carter versus Reagan? Each of these candidates started as the frontrunner in their quest for their party's nomination, and both party nomination rules and campaign contribution laws helped these better-organized candidates. Moreover, though neither was extremely well regarded by party identifiers, compared with the alternatives in the race each had the best image among citizens.

2. Why did Reagan win? President Carter was unsuccessful in mobilizing strong majorities within many traditionally Democratic groups. Reagan, however, received much of this traditional Democratic support plus strong support among Independents and Republicans. The issues of the economy and foreign affairs played a key role in the defection of voters from the Democratic nominee.

3. How much difference will the outcome make? Reagan's victory, together with major victories by conservatives in Congress, will make a difference. On a day-to-day basis decisions will have a different orientation both in Congress and in the executive branch. However, President Reagan will face severe problems in implementing major overhauls of the existing system. Many conservative policy goals are not feasible or are politically too costly under the present system of government.

The Declaration of Independence
In Congress, July 4, 1776

The unanimous Declaration of the thirteen united States of America,

When in the Course of human events, it becomes necessary for one people to dissolve the political bands which have connected them with another, and to assume the Powers of the earth, the separate and equal station to which the Laws of Nature and of Nature's God entitle them, a decent respect to the opinions of mankind requires that they should declare the causes which impel them to the separation.

We hold these truths to be self-evident, that all men are created equal, that they are endowed by their Creator with certain unalienable Rights, that among these are Life, Liberty and the pursuit of Happiness. That to secure these rights, Governments are instituted among Men, deriving their just powers from the consent of the governed. That whenever any Form of Government becomes destructive of these ends, it is the Right of the People to alter or to abolish it, and to institute new Government, laying its foundation on such principles and organizing its powers in such form, as to them shall seem most likely to effect their Safety and Happiness. Prudence, indeed, will dictate that Governments long established should not be changed for light and transient causes; and accordingly all experience hath shown, that mankind are more disposed to suffer, while evils are sufferable, than to right themselves by abolishing the forms to which they are accustomed. But when a long train of abuses and usurpations, pursuing invariably the same Object evinces a design to reduce them under absolute Despotism, it is their right, it is their duty, to throw off such Government, and to provide new Guards for their future security. — Such has been the patient sufferance of these Colonies; and such is now the necessity which constrains them to alter their former Systems of Government. The history of the present King of Great Britain is a history of repeated injuries and usurpations, all having in direct object the establishment of an absolute Tyranny over these States. To prove this, let Facts be submitted to a candid world.

He has refused his Assent to Laws, the most wholesome and necessary for the public good.

He has forbidden his Governors to pass Laws of immediate and pressing importance, unless suspended in their operation till his Assent should be obtained; and when so suspended, he has utterly neglected to attend to them.

He has refused to pass other Laws for the accommodation of large districts of people, unless those people would relinquish the right of Representation in the Legislature, a right inestimable to them and formidable to tyrants only.

He has called together legislative bodies at places unusual, uncomfortable, and distant from the depository of their Public Records, for the sole purpose of fatiguing them into compliance with his measures.

He has dissolved Representative Houses repeatedly, for opposing with manly firmness his invasions on the rights of the people.

He has refused for a long time, after such dissolutions, to cause others to be elected; whereby the Legislative Powers, incapable of Annihilation, have returned to the People at large for their exercise; the State remaining in the mean time exposed to all the dangers of invasion from without, and convulsions within.

He has endeavoured to prevent the population of these States; for that purpose obstructing the Laws for Naturalization of Foreigners; refusing to pass others to encourage their migrations hither, and raising the conditions of new Appropriations of Lands.

He has obstructed the Administration of Justice, by refusing his Assent to Laws for establishing Judiciary Powers.

He has made Judges dependent on his Will alone, for the tenure of their offices, and the amount and payment of their salaries.

He has erected a multitude of New Offices, and sent hither swarms of Officers to harass our people, and eat out their substance.

He has kept among us, in times of peace, Standing Armies without the Consent of our legislatures.

He has affected to render the Military independent of and superior to the Civil Power.

He has combined with others to subject us to a jurisdiction foreign to our constitution, and unacknowledged by our laws; giving his Assent to their acts of pretended Legislation:

For quartering large bodies of armed troops among us:

For protecting them, by a mock Trial, from Punishment for any Murders which they should commit on the inhabitants of these States:

For cutting off our Trade with all parts of the world:

For imposing taxes on us without our Consent:

For depriving us in many cases, of the benefits of Trial by Jury:

For transporting us beyond Seas to be tried for pretended offences:

For abolishing the free System of English Laws in a neighbouring Province, establishing therein an Arbitrary government, and enlarging its Boundaries so as to render it at once an example and fit instrument for introducing the same absolute rule into these Colonies:

For taking away our Charters, abolishing our most valuable Laws, and altering fundamentally the Forms of our Governments:

For suspending our own Legislatures, and declaring themselves invested with Power to legislate for us in all cases whatsoever.

He has abdicated Government here, by declaring us out of his Protection and waging War against us.

He has plundered our seas, ravaged our Coasts, burnt our towns, and destroyed the lives of our people.

He is at this time transporting large armies of foreign mercenaries to compleat the works of death, desolation and tyranny, already begun with circumstances of Cruelty & perfidy scarcely parallelled in the most barbarous ages, and totally unworthy the Head of a civilized nation.

He has constrained our fellow Citizens taken Captive on the high Seas to bear Arms against their Country, to become the executioners of their friends and Brethren, or to fall themselves by their Hands.

He has excited domestic insurrections amongst us, and has endeavoured to bring on the inhabitants of our frontiers, the merciless Indian Savages, whose known rule of warfare, is an undistinguished destruction of all ages, sexes and conditions.

In every stage of these Oppressions We have Petitioned for Redress in the most humble terms: Our repeated Petitions have been answered only by repeated injury. A Prince, whose character is thus marked by every act which may define a Tyrant, is unfit to be the ruler of a free people.

Nor have We been wanting in attentions to our British brethren. We have warned them from time to time of attempts by their legislature to extend an unwarrantable jurisdiction over us. We have reminded them of the circumstances of our emigration and settlement here. We have appealed to their native justice and magnanimity, and we have conjured them by the ties of our common kindred to disavow these usurpations which, would inevitably interrupt our connections and correspondence. They too have been deaf to the voice of justice and of consanguinity. We must, therefore, acquiesce in the necessity, which denounces our Separation, and hold them, as we hold the rest of mankind, Enemies in War, in Peace Friends.

We, therefore, the Representatives of the united States of America, in General Congress, Assembled, appealing to the Supreme Judge of the world for the rectitude of our intentions, do, in the Name, and by authority of the good People of these Colonies, solemnly publish and declare, That these United Colonies are, and of Right ought to be Free and Independent States; that they are Absolved from all Allegiance to the British Crown, and that all political connection between them and the State of Great Britain, is and ought to be totally dissolved; and that as Free and Independent States, they have full power to levy War, conclude Peace, contract Alliances, establish Commerce, and to do all other Acts and Things which Independent States may of right do. And for the support of this Declaration, with a firm reliance on the Protection of Divine Providence, we mutually pledge to each other our Lives, our Fortunes and our sacred Honor.

The Constitution of the United States of America

[Preamble]

We the People of the United States, in Order to form a more perfect Union, establish Justice, insure domestic Tranquility, provide for the common defence, promote the general Welfare, and secure the Blessings of Liberty to ourselves and our Posterity, do ordain and establish this Constitution for the United States of America.

Article I
Section 1
[Legislative Powers]

All legislative Powers herein granted shall be vested in a Congress of the United States, which shall consist of a Senate and House of Representatives.

Section 2
[House of Representatives, How Constituted, Power of Impeachment]

The House of Representatives shall be composed of Members chosen every second Year by the People of the several States, and the Electors in each State shall have the Qualifications requisite for Electors of the most numerous Branch of the State Legislature.

No Person shall be a Representative who shall not have attained to the Age of twenty-five Years, and been seven Years a Citizen of the United States, and who shall not, when elected, be an inhabitant of that State in which he shall be chosen.

Representatives and *direct Taxes*[1] shall be apportioned among the several states which may be included within this Union, according to their respective Numbers, *which shall be determined by adding to the whole Number of free Persons, including those bound to Service for a Term of Years, and excluding Indians not taxed, three fifths of all other Persons.*[2] The actual Enumeration shall be made within three Years after the first Meeting of the Congress of the United States, and within every subsequent Term of ten Years, in such manner as they shall by Law direct. The Number of Representatives shall not exceed one for every thirty Thousand, but each State shall have at Least one Representative; *and until such enumeration shall be made, the State of New Hampshire shall be entitled to chuse three, Massachusetts eight, Rhode-Island and Providence Plantations one, Connecticut five, New-York six, New Jersey four, Pennsylvania eight, Deleware one, Maryland six, Virginia ten, North Carolina five, South Carolina five, and Georgia three.*[3]

When vacancies happen in the Representation from any State, the Executive Authority thereof shall issue Writs of Election to fill such Vacancies.

The House of Representatives shall chuse their Speaker and other Officers; and shall have the sole Power of Impeachment.

Section 3
[The Senate, How Constituted, Impeachment Trials]

The Senate of the United States shall be composed of two Senators from each State, *chosen by the Legislative thereof,*[4] for six Years; and each Senator shall have one Vote.

Immediately after they shall be assembled in Consequence of the first Election, they shall be divided as equally as may be into three Classes. The Seats of the Senators of the first Class shall be vacated at the Expiration of the second Year, of the second Class at the Expiration of the fourth Year, and of the third Class at the Expiration of the sixth Year, so that one third may be chosen every second Year: *and if vacancies happen by Resignation, or otherwise, during the Recess of the Legislature of any State, the Executive thereof may make temporary Appointments until the next Meeting of the Legislature, which shall then fill such Vacancies.*[5]

[1] Modified by Sixteenth Amendment.
[2] Modified by Fourteenth Amendment.
[3] Temporary provision.
[4] Modified by Seventeenth Amendment.
[5] *Ibid.*

No person shall be a Senator who shall not have attained to the Age of thirty Years, and been nine Years a Citizen of the United States, and who shall not, when elected, be an Inhabitant of that State for which he shall be chosen.

The Vice President of the United States shall be President of the Senate, but shall have no Vote, unless they be equally divided.

The Senate shall chuse their other Officers, and also a President pro tempore in the Absence of the Vice President, or when he shall exercise the Office of President of the United States.

The Senate shall have the sole Power to try all Impeachments. When sitting for that Purpose, they shall be on Oath of Affirmation. When the President of the United States is tried, the Chief Justice shall preside: And no Person shall be convicted without the Concurrence of two thirds of the Members present.

Judgment in Cases of Impeachment shall not extend further than to removal from Office, and disqualification to hold and enjoy any Office of honor, Trust or Profit under the United States: but the Party convicted shall nevertheless be liable and subject to Indictment, Trial, Judgment and Punishment, according to Law.

Section 4
[Election of Senators and Representatives]

The Times, Places and Manner of holding Elections for Senators and Representatives, shall be prescribed in each State by the Legislature thereof; but the Congress may at any time by Law make or alter such Regulations, except as to the Places of chusing Senators.

The Congress shall assemble at least once in every Year, and such Meeting shall be on the first Monday in December, unless they shall by Law appoint a different Day.[6]

Section 5
[Quorum, Journals, Meetings, Adjournments]

Each House shall be the Judge of the Elections, Returns and Qualifications of its own Members, and a Majority of each shall constitute a Quorum to do Business; but a smaller Number may adjourn from day to day, and may be authorized to compel the Attendence of absent Members, in such Manner, and under the Penalties as each House may provide.

Each House may determine the Rules of its Proceedings, punish its Members for disorderly Behavior, and, with the Concurrence of two thirds, expel a Member.

Each House shall keep a Journal of its Proceedings, and from time to time publish the same, excepting such Parts as may in their Judgment require Secrecy; and the Yeas and Nays of the Members of either House on any question shall, at the Desire of one fifth of the present, be entered on the Journal.

Neither House, during the Session Congress, shall, without the Consent of the other, adjourn for more than three days, nor to any other Place than that in which the two Houses shall be sitting.

Section 6
[Compensation, Privileges, Disabilities]

The Senators and Representatives shall receive a Compensation for their Services, to be ascertained by Law, and paid out of the Treasury of the United States. They shall in Cases, except Treason, Felony and Breach of the Peace, be privileged from Arrest during their Attendence at the Session of their respective Houses and in going to and returning from the same; and for any Speech or Debate in either House, they shall not be questioned in any other Place.

No Senator or Representative shall, during the time for which he was elected, be appointed to any civil Office under the authority of the United States, which shall have been created, or the Emoluments whereof shall have been encreased during such time; and no Person holding any Office under the United States shall be a Member of either House during his Continuance in Office.

Section 7
[Procedure in Passing Bills of Resolutions]

All Bills for raising Revenue shall originate in the House of Representatives; but the Senate may propose or concur with Amendments as on other Bills.

[6] Modified by Twentieth Amendment.

Every Bill which shall have passed the House of Representatives and the Senate, shall, before it becomes a Law, be presented to the President of the United States; if he approve he shall sign it, but if not he shall return it, with his Objections to that House in which it shall have originated, who shall enter the Objections at large on their Journal, and proceed to reconsider it. If after such Reconsideration two thirds of that House shall agree to pass the Bill, it shall be sent, together with the Objections, to the other House, by which it shall likewise be reconsidered, and if approved by two thirds of that House, it shall become a Law. But in all such Cases the Votes of both Houses shall be determined by Yeas and Nays, and the Names of the Persons voting for and against the Bill shall be entered on the Journal of each House respectively. If any Bill shall not be returned by the President within ten Days (Sundays excepted) after it shall have been presented to him, the Same shall be a Law, in like Manner as if he had signed it, unless the Congress by their Adjournment prevent its Return, in which Case it shall not be a Law.

Every Order, Resolution, or Vote to which the Concurrence of the Senate and House of Representatives may be necessary (except on a question of Adjournment) shall be presented to the President of the United States; and before the Same shall take Effect, shall be approved by him, or being disapproved by him, shall be repassed by two thirds of the Senate and House of Representatives, according to the Rules and Limitations prescribed in the case of a Bill.

Section 8
[Power of Congress]

The Congress shall have Power

To lay and collect Taxes, Duties, Imposts and Excises, to pay the Debts and provide for the common Defense and general Welfare of the United States; but all Duties, Imposts and excises shall be uniform throughout the United States;

To borrow Money on the Credit of the United States;

To regulate Commerce with foreign Nations, and among the several States, and with the Indian Tribes;

To establish an uniform Rule of Naturalization, and uniform Laws on the subject of Bankruptcies throughout the United States;

To coin Money, regulate the Value thereof, and of foreign Coin, and fix the Standard of Weights and Measures;

To provide for the Punishment of counterfeiting the Securities and current Coin of the United States;

To establish Post Offices and post Roads;

To promote the Progress of Science and useful Arts, by securing for limited Times to Authors and Inventors the exclusive Rights to their respective Writings and Discoveries;

To constitute Tribunals inferior to the supreme Court;

To define and Punish Piracies and Felonies committed on the high Seas, and Offences against the Law of Nations;

To declare War, grant Letters of Marque and Reprisal, and make Rules concerning Captures on Land and Water;

To raise and support Armies, but no Appropriation of Money to that Use shall be for a longer Term than two Years;

To provide and maintain a Navy;

To make Rules for the Government and Regulation of the land and naval forces;

To provide for calling forth the Militia to execute the Laws of the Union, suppress Insurrections and repel Invasions;

To provide for organizing, arming, and disciplining, the Militia, and for governing such Part of them as may be employed in the Service of the United States, reserving to the States respectively, the Appointment of the Officers, and the Authority of training the Militia according to the discipline prescribed by Congress;

To exercise exclusive Legislation in all Cases whatsoever, over such District (not exceeding ten Miles square) as may, by Cession of particular States, and the Acceptance of Congress, become the Seat of the Government of the United States, and to exercise like Authority over all Places purchased by the Consent of the Legislature of the State in which the Same shall be, for the Erection of Forts, Magazines, Arsenals, dock-Yards, and other needful Buildings;- And

To make all Laws which shall be necessary and proper for carrying into Execution the foregoing Powers, and all other Powers vested by this Constitution in the Government of the United States, or in any Department or Officer thereof.

Section 9

The Migration or Importation of such Persons as any of the States now existing shall think proper to admit, shall not be prohibited by the Congress prior to the Year one thousand eight hundred and eight, but a Tax or Duty may be imposed on such Importation, not exceeding ten dollars for each Person.[7]

The privilege of the Writ of Habeas Corpus shall not be suspended, unless when in Cases of Rebellion or Invasion the public Safety may require it.

No Bill of Attainder or ex post facto Law shall be passed.

No Capitation, or other direct, Tax shall be laid, unless in Proportion to the Census or Enumeration herein before directed to be taken.[8]

No Tax or Duty shall be laid on Articles exported from any State.

No Preference shall be given by any Regulation of Commerce or Revenue to the Ports of one State over those of another; nor shall vessels bound to, or from, one State, be obliged to enter, clear, or pay Duties in another.

No Money shall be drawn from the Treasury, but in Consequence of Appropriations made by Law; and a regular Statement and Account of the Receipts and Expenditures of all public Money shall be published from time to time.

No Title of Nobility shall be granted by the United States: And no Person holding any Office or Profit or Trust under them, shall, without the Consent of the Congress, accept of any present, Emolument, Office, or Title, of any kind whatever, from any King, Prince, or foreign State.

Section 10
[Restrictions Upon Powers of States]

No State shall enter into any Treaty, Alliance, or Confederation; grant Letters of Marque and Reprisal; coin Money; emit Bills of Credit; make any Thing but gold and silver Coin a Tender in Payment of Debts; pass any Bill of Attainder, ex post facto Law, or Law impairing the Obligation of Contracts, or grant any Title of Nobility.

No State shall, without the Consent of the Congress, lay any Imposts or Duties on Imports or Exports, except what may be absolutely necessary for executing its inspection Laws: and the net Produce of all Duties and Imposts, laid by any State on Imports or Exports, shall be for the use of the Treasury of the United States; and all such Laws shall be subject to the Revision and Control of the Congress.

No State shall, without the Consent of Congress, lay any Duty of Tonnage, keep Troops, or Ships of War in time of Peace, enter into any Agreement or Compact with another State, or with a foreign Power, or engage in War, unless actually invaded, or in such imminent Danger as will not admit of Delay.

Article II
Section 1
[Executive Power, Election, Qualifications of the President]

The executive Power shall be vested in a President of the United States of America. *He shall hold his Office during the Term of four years and, together with the Vice President, chosen for the same Term, be elected as follows.*[9]

Each State shall appoint, in such Manner as the Legislature thereof may direct, a Number of Electors, equal to the whole Number of Senators and Representatives to which the State may be entitled in the Congress; but no Senator or Representative, or Person holding an Office of Trust or Profit under the United States, shall be appointed an Elector.

The electors shall meet in their respective States, and vote by ballot for two Persons, of whom one at least shall not be an Inhabitant of the same State with themselves. And they shall make a List all of the Persons voted for, and of the Number of Votes for each; which List they shall sign and certify, and transmit sealed to the Seat of the Government of the United States, directed to the President of the Senate. The President of the Senate shall, in the Presence of the Senate and House of Representatives, open all the Certificates, and the Votes shall then be counted. The Person having the greatest Number of Votes shall be the President, if such Number be a Majority of the whole Number of Electors appointed; and if

---

[7] Temporary provision.

[8] Modified by Sixteenth Amendment.

[9] Number of terms limited to two by Twenty-second Amendment.

there be more than one who have such Majority and have an equal Number of Votes, then the House of Representatives shall immediately chuse by Ballot one of them for President; and if no person have a Majority, then from the five highest on the list the said House shall in like Manner chuse the President. But in chusing the President, the Votes shall be taken by States, the Representation for each State having one Vote; A quorum for this Purpose shall consist of a Member or Members from two-thirds of the States, and a Majority of all the States shall be necessary to a Choice. In every Case, after the Choice of the President, the person having the greatest Number of Votes of the Electors shall be the Vice President. But if there should remain two or more who have equal vote, the Senate shall chuse from them by Ballot the Vice President.[10]

The Congress may determine the Time of chusing the Electors, and the Day on which they shall give their Votes; which Day shall be the same throughout the United States.

No Person except a natural born Citizen, or a Citizen of the United States, at the time of the Adoption of this Constitution, shall be eligible to the Office of President, neither shall any Person be eligible to that Office who shall not have attained to the Age of thirty-five Years, and been fourteen Years a Resident within the United States.

In Case of the Removal of the President from Office, or his Death, Resignation, or Inability to discharge the Power and Duties of the said Office, the same shall devolve on the Vice President, and the Congress may by Law provide for the Case of Removal, Death, Resignation, or Inability, both of the President and Vice President, declaring what Officer shall then act as President, and such Officer shall act accordingly, until the Disability be removed, or a President shall be elected.

The President shall, at stated Times, receive for his Services, a Compensation, which shall neither be encreased nor diminished during the Period of which he shall have been elected, and he shall not receive within that Period any other Emolument from the United States, or any of them.

Before he enter on the Execution of his Office, he shall take the following oath or Affirmation:-"I do solemnly swear (or affirm) that I will faithfully execute the Office of President of the United States, and will to the best of my Ability, preserve, protect and defend the Constitution of the United States."

Section 2
[Powers of the President]

The President shall be Commander in Chief of the Army and Navy of the United States, and of the Militia of the several States, when called into the actual Service of the United States; he may require the Opinion, in writing, of the principal Officer in each of the executive Departments, upon any Subject relating to the Duties of their respective Offices, and he shall have Power to grant Reprieves and Pardons for Offences against the United States, except in Cases of Impeachment.

He shall have Power, by and with the Advice and Consent of the Senate to make Treaties, provided two thirds of the Senators present concur; and he shall nominate, and by and with the Advice and Consent of the Senate, shall appoint Ambassadors, other public Ministers and Consuls, Judges of the Supreme Court, and all other Officers of the United States, whose Appointments are not herein otherwise provided for, and which shall be established by Law: but the Congress may by Law vest the Appointment of such inferior Officers, as they think proper, in the President alone, in the Courts of Law, or in the Heads of Departments.

The President shall have Power to fill up all Vacancies that may happen during the Recess of the Senate, by granting Commissions which shall expire at the End of their next Session.

Section 3
[Powers and Duties of the President]

He shall from time to time give to the Congress Information of the State of the Union, and recommend to their Consideration such Measures as he shall judge necessary and expedient; he may, on extraordinary Occasions, convene both Houses, or either of them, and in Case of Disagreement between them, with Respect to the Time of Adjournment, he may adjourn them to such Time as he shall think proper; he shall receive Ambassadors and other public Ministers; he shall take Care that the Laws be faithfully executed, and shall Commission all the Officers of the United States.

[10] Modified by Twelfth and Twentieth Amendments.

Section 4
[Impeachment]

The President, Vice President and all civil Officers of the United States shall be removed from Office on Impeachment for, and Conviction of, Treason, Bribery, or other high Crimes and Misdemeanors.

Article III
Section 1
[Judicial Power, Tenure of Office]

The judicial Power of the United States, shall be vested in one supreme Court, and in such inferior Courts as the Congress may from time to time ordain and establish. The Judges, both of the supreme and inferior Courts, shall hold their Offices during good Behavior, and shall, at stated Times, receive for their Services, a Compensation, which shall not be diminished during their Continuance in Office.

Section 2
[Jurisdiction]

The judicial Power shall extend to all Cases, in Law and Equity, arising under this Constitution, the Laws of the United States, and Treaties made, of which shall be made, under their Authority;—to all Cases affecting Ambassadors, other public Ministers and Consuls;—to all Cases of admiralty and maritime Jurisdiction;—to Controversies to which the United States shall be a party—to Controversies between two or more States;—*between a State and Citizens of another State;*—between Citizens of different States;—between Citizens of the same State claiming Lands under Grants of different States, *and between a State,* or the Citizens thereof, *and foreign States, Citizens or Subjects.*[11]

In all Cases affecting Ambassadors, other public Ministers and Consults, and those in which a State shall be Party, the supreme Court shall have original Jurisdiction. In all the other Cases before mentioned, the supreme Court shall have appelate Jurisdiction, both as to Law and Fact, with such Exceptions, and under such Regulations as Congress shall make.

The Trial of all Crimes, except in Cases of Impeachment, shall be by Jury; and such Trial shall be held in the State where the said Crimes shall have been committed; but when not committed within any State, the Trial shall be at such Place or Places as the Congress may by Law have directed.

Section 3
[Treason, Proof and Punishment]

Treason against the United States, shall consist only in levying War against them, or in adhering to their Enemies, giving them Aid and Comfort. No Person shall be convicted of Treason unless on the Testimoney of two Witnesses to the same overt Act, or on Confession in open Court.

The Congress shall have Power to declare the Punishment of Treason, but no Attainder of Treason shall work Corruption of Blood, or Forfeiture except during the Life of the Person attained.

Article IV
Section 1
[Faith and Credit Among States]

Full Faith and Credit shall be given in each State to the public Acts, Records, and judicial Proceedings of every other State. And the Congress may by general Laws prescribe the Manner in which such Acts, Records and Proceedings shall be proved, and the Effect thereof.

Section 2
[Privileges and Immunities, Fugitives]

The Citizens of each State shall be entitled to all Privileges and Immunities of Citizens in the several States.

A person charged in any State with Treason, Felony or other Crime, who shall flee from Justice, and be found in another State, shall on Demand of the executive Authority of the

---

[11] Modified by Eleventh Amendment.

State from which he fled, be delivered up to be removed to the State having Jurisdiction of the Crime.

No person held to Service or Labour in one State, under the Laws thereof, escaping into another, shall in Consequence of any Law or Regulation therein, be discharged from such Service or Labour, but shall be delivered up on Claim of the Party to whom such Service or Labour may be due.[12]

Section 3
[Admission of New States]

New States may be admitted by the Congress into this Union; but no new State shall be formed or erected within the Jurisdiction of any other State; nor any State be formed by the Junction of two or more States, or Parts of States, without the Consent of the Legislatures of the States concerned as well as of the Congress.

Section 4
[Guarantee of Republican Government]

The United States shall guarantee to every State in this Union a Republican Form of Government, and shall protect each of them against Invasion; and on Application of Legislature, or of the Executive (when the Legislature cannot be convened) against domestic Violence.

Article V
[Amendment of the Constitution]

The Congress, whenever two thirds of both Houses shall deem it necessary, shall propose Amendments to this Constitution, or, on the Application of the Legislatures of two thirds of the several States, shall call a Convention for proposing Amendments, which, in either Case, shall be valid to all Intents and Purposes, as Part of this Constitution, when ratified by the Legislatures of three fourths of the several States, or by Conventions in three fourths thereof, as the one or the other Mode of Ratification may be proposed by the Congress; *Provided that no Amendment which may be made prior to the Year One thousand eight hundred and eight shall in any Manner affect the first and fourth Clauses in the Ninth Section of the first Article,*[13] and that no State, without its Consent, shall be deprived of its equal Suffrage in the Senate.

Article VI
[Debts, Supremacy, Oath]

All Debts contracted and Engagements entered into, before the Adoption of this Constitution, shall be as valid against the United States under this Constitution, as under the Confederation.

This Constitution, and the Laws of the United States which shall be made in Pursuance thereof; and all Treaties made, or which shall be made, under the Authority of the United States, shall be the supreme Law of the Land; and the Judges in every State shall be bound thereby, any thing in the Constitution or Laws of any State to the Contrary notwithstanding.

The Senators and Representatives before mentioned, and the Members of the several State Legislatures, and all executive and judicial Officers, both of the United States and of the several States, shall be bound by Oath or Affirmation, to support this Constitution; but no religious Test shall be required as a Qualification to any Office or public Trust under the United States.

Article VII
[Ratification & Establishment]

The Ratification of the Conventions of nine States, shall be sufficient for the Establishment of this Constitution between the States so ratifying the Same.[14]

done in Convention by the Unanimous Consent of the States present the Seventeenth Day of September in the Year of our Lord one thousand seven hundred and Eighty seven and of the

[12] Repealed by the Thirteenth Amendment.
[13] Temporary provision.
[14] The Constitution was submitted on September 17, 1787, by the Constitutional Conventions, was ratified by the conventions of several states at various dates up to May 29, 1790, and became effective on March 4, 1789.

Independence of the United States of America the Twelfth. *In Witness* whereof We have hereunto subscribed our Names.

G:⁰WASHINGTON— *Presidt, and Deputy from Virginia*

New Hampshire	John Langdon, Nicholas Gilman
Massachusetts	Nathaniel Gorham, Rufus King
Connecticut	Wm Saml Johnson, Roger Sherman
New York	Alexander Hamilton
New Jersey	Wil: Livingston, David Brearley, Wm Paterson, Jona: Dayton, B Franklin, Thomas Mifflin, Robt Morris, Geo. Clymer
Pennsylvania	Thos. FitzSimons, Jared Ingersoll, James Wilson, Gouv Morris
Delaware	Geo Read, Gunning Bedfor Jun, John Dickinson, Richard Bassett, Jaco: Broom
Maryland	James McHenry, Dan of St Thos. Jenifer, Danl Carroll
Virginia	John Blair, James Madison Jr.
North Carolina	Wm Blount, Richd Dobbs Spaight, Hu Williamson
South Carolina	J. Rutledge, Charles Cotesworth Pinckney, Charles Pickney, Pierce Butler
Georgia	William Few, Abr Baldwin

Amendments to the Constitution

The first ten amendments were proposed by Congress on September 25, 1789; ratified and adoption certified on December 15, 1791.

Amendment I
[Freedom of Religion, of Speech, and of the Press]

Congress shall make no law respecting an establishment of religion, or prohibiting the free exercise thereof; or abridging the freedom of speech, or of the press; or the right of the people peaceably to assemble, and to petition the Government for a redress of grievances.

Amendment II
[Right to Keep and Bear Arms]

A well regulated Militia, being necessary to the security of a free State, the right of the people to keep and bear Arms, shall not be infringed.

Amendment III
[Quartering of Soldiers]

No Soldier shall, in time of peace be quartered in any house, without the consent of the Owner, nor in time of war, but in a manner to be prescribed by law.

Amendment IV
[Security from Unwarrantable Search and Seizure]

The right of the people to be secure in their persons, houses, papers, and effects, against unreasonable searches and seizures, shall not be violated, and no Warrants shall issue, but upon probable cause, supported by Oath or affirmation, and particularly describing the place to be searched, and the persons or things to be seized.

Amendment V
[Rights of Accused Persons in Criminal Proceedings]

No person shall be held to answer for a capital, or otherwise infamous crime, unless on a presentment or indictment of a Grand Jury, except in cases arising in the land or naval forces, or in the Militia, when in actual service in time of War or in public danger; nor shall any person be subject for the same offence to be twice put in jeopardy of life or limb; nor shall be compelled in any criminal case to be a witness against himself, nor be deprived of life, liberty, or property, without due process of law; nor shall private property be taken for public use, without just compensation.

Amendment VI
[Right to Speedy Trial, Witnesses, Etc.]

In all criminal prosecutions, the accused shall enjoy the right to a speedy and public trial, by an impartial jury of the State and district wherein the crime shall have been committed, which district shall have been previously ascertained by law, and to be informed of the nature and cause of accusation; to be confronted with the witnesses against him; to have compulsory process for obtaining Witnesses in his favor, and to have the Assistance of Counsel for his defence.

Amendment VII
[Trial by Jury in Civil Cases]

In suits at common law, where the value in controversy shall exceed twenty dollars, the right of trial by jury shall be preserved, and no fact tried by a jury shall be otherwise re-examined in any Court of the United States, than according to the rules of the common law.

Amendment VIII
[Bails, Fines, Punishments]

Excessive bail shall not be required, nor excessive fines imposed, nor cruel and unusual punishments inflicted.

Amendment IX
[Reservation of Rights of People]

The enumeration in the Constitution, of certain rights, shall not be construed to deny or disparage others retained by the people.

Amendment X
[Powers Reserved to States or People]

The powers not delegated to the United States by the Constitution, nor prohibited by it to the States, are reserved to the States respectively, or to the people.

Amendment XI

[Proposed by Congress on March 4, 1794; declared ratified on January 8, 1798.]

[Restriction of Judicial Power]

The Judicial power of the United States shall not be construed to extend to any suit in law or equity, commenced or prosecuted against one of the United States by Citizens of another State, or by Citizens or Subjects of any Foreign State.

Amendment XII

[Proposed by Congress on December 8, 1803; declared ratified on September 24, 1804.]

[Election of President and Vice President]

The Electors shall meet in their respective state, and vote by ballot for President and Vice-President, one of whom, at least, shall not be an inhabitant of the same state with themselves; they shall name in their ballots the person voted for as President, and in distinct ballots the person voted for as Vice-President, and they shall make distinct lists of all persons voted for as

President, and all persons voted for as Vice-President, and of the number of votes for each, which lists they shall sign and certify, and transmit sealed to the seat of the government of the United States, directed to the President of the Senate; — The President of the Senate shall, in presence of the Senate and House of Representatives, open all the certificates and the votes shall then be counted; — The person having the greatest number of votes for President, shall be the President, if such number be a majority of the whole number of Electors appointed; and if no person have such majority, then from the persons having the highest numbers not exceeding three on the list of those voted for as President, the House of Representatives shall choose immediately, by ballot, the President. But in choosing the President, the votes shall be taken by states, the representation from each state having one vote; a quorum for this purpose shall consist of a member or members from two-thirds of the states, and a majority of all states shall be necessary to a choice. And if the House of Representatives shall not choose a President whenever the right of choice shall devolve upon them, before the fourth day of March next following, then the Vice-President, shall act as President, as in the case of the death or other constitutional disability of the President. The person having the greatest number of votes as Vice-President, shall be the Vice-President, if such a number be a majority of the whole numbers of Electors appointed, and if no person have a majority, then from the two highest numbers on the list, the Senate shall choose the Vice-President; a quorum for the purpose shall consist of two-thirds of the whole number of Senators, and a majority of the whole number shall be necessary to a choice. But no person constitutionally ineligible to the office of President shall be eligible to that of Vice-President of the United States.

Amendment XIII

[Proposed by Congress on January 31, 1865; declared ratified on December 18, 1865.]

Section 1
[Abolition of Slavery]

Neither slavery nor involuntary servitude, except as a punishment for crime whereof the party shall have been duly convicted, shall exist within the United States, or any place subject to their jurisdiction.

Section 2
[Power to Enforce this Article]

Congress shall have power to enforce this article by appropriate legislation.

Amendment XIV

[Proposed by Congress on June 13, 1866; declared ratified on July 28, 1868.]

Section 1
[Citizenship Rights not to be Abridged by States]

All persons born or naturalized in the United States, and subject to the jurisdiction thereof, are citizens of the United States and of the State wherein they reside. No state shall make or enforce any law which shall abridge the privileges or immunities of citizens of the United States; nor shall any State deprive any person of life, liberty, or property, without due process of law; nor deny to any person within its jurisdiction the equal protection of the laws.

Section 2
[Apportionment of Representatives in Congress]

Representatives shall be apportioned among the several States according to their respective numbers, counting the whole number of persons in each State, excluding Indians not taxed. But when the right to vote at any election for the choice of electors for President and Vice President of the United States, Representatives in Congress, the Executive and Judicial officers of a State, or the members of the Legislature thereof, is denied to any of the male inhabitants of such State, being twenty-one years of age, and citizens of the United States, or in any way abridged, except for participation in rebellion, or other crime, the basis of representation therein shall be reduced in the proportion which the number of such male citizens shall bear to the whole number of male citizens twenty-one years of age in such State.

Section 3
[Persons Disqualified from Holding Office]

No person shall be a Senator or Representative in Congress, or elector of President and Vice-President, or hold any office, civil or military, under the United States, or under any State, who, having previously taken an oath, as a member of Congress, or as an officer of the United States, or as a member of any State legislature, or as an executive or judical officer of any State, to support the Constitution of the United States, shall have engaged in insurrection or rebellion against the same, or given aid or comfort to the enemies thereof. But Congress may by a vote of two-thirds of each House, remove such disability.

Section 4
[What Public Debts are Valid]

The validity of the public debt of the United States, authorized by law, including debts incurred for payment of pensions and bounties for services in suppressing insurrection or rebellion, shall not be questioned. But neither the United States nor any State shall assume or pay any debt or obligation incurred in aid of insurrection or rebellion against the United States, or any claim for the loss of emancipation of any slave; but all such debts, obligations and claims shall be held illegal and void.

Section 5
[Power to Enforce this Article]

The Congress shall have power to enforce, by appropriate legislation, the provisions of this article.

Amendment XV

[Proposed by Congress on February 26, 1869; declared ratified on March 30, 1870.]

Section 1
[Negro Suffrage]

The right of citizens of the United States to vote shall not be denied or abridged by the United States or by any State on account of race, color, or previous condition of servitude.

Section 2
[Power to Enforce this Article]

The Congress shall have power to enforce this article by appropriate legislation.

Amendment XVI

[Proposed by Congress on July 12, 1909; declared ratified on February 25, 1913.]

Authorizing Income Taxes]

The Congress shall have power to lay and collect taxes on incomes, from whatever source derived, without apportionment among the several States, and without regard to any census or enumeration.

Amendment XVII

[Proposed by Congress on May 13, 1912; declared ratified on May 31, 1913.]

[Popular Election of Senators]

The Senate of the United States shall be composed of two Senators from each State, elected by the people thereof, for six years, and each Senator shall have one vote. The electors in each State shall have the qualifications requisite for electors of the most numerous branch of the State Legislature.

When vacancies happen in the representation of any State in the Senate, the executive authority of such State shall issue writs of election to fill such vacancies: Provided, That the Legislature of any State may empower the executive thereof to make temporary appointment until the people fill the vacancies by election as the Legislature may direct.

This amendment shall not be so construed as to affect the election or term of any Senator chosen before it becomes valid as part of the Constitution.

Amendment XVIII

[Proposed by Congress December 18, 1917; declared ratified on January 29, 1919.]

Section 1
[National Liquor Prohibition]

After one year from ratificiation of this article the manufacture, sale, or transportation of intoxicating liquors within, the importation thereof into, or the exportation thereof from the United States and all territory subject to the jurisdiction thereof for beverage purposes is hereby prohibited.

Section 2
[Power to Enforce this Article]

The Congress and the several states shall have concurrent power to enforce this article by appropriate legislation.

Section 3
[Ratification within Seven Years]

This article shall be inoperative unless it shall have been ratified as an amendment to the Constitution by the legislatures of the several states, as provided in the Constitution, within seven years from the date of the submission hereof to the states by the Congress.

Amendment XIX

[Proposed by Congress on June 4, 1919; declared ratified on August 26, 1920.]

[Women Suffrage]

The right of the citizens of the United States to vote shall not be denied or abridged by the United States or by any state on account of sex.

Congress shall have power, by appropriate legislation, to enforce the provision of this article.

Amendment XX

[Proposed by Congress on March 2, 1932; declared ratified on February 6, 1933.]

Section 1
[Terms of Office]

The terms of the President and Vice-President shall end at noon on the 20th day of January, and the terms of the Senators and Representatives at noon on the 3rd day of January, of the years in which such terms would have ended if this article had not been ratified; and the terms of their successors shall then begin.

Section 2
[Time of Convening Congress]

The Congress shall assemble at least once in every year, and such meeting shall begin at noon on the 3rd day of January, unless they shall by law appoint a different day.

Section 3
[Death of President-Elect]

If, at the time fixed for the beginning of the term of the President, the President elect shall have died, the Vice-President elect shall become President. If a President shall not have been chosen before the time fixed for the beginning of his term, or if the President elect shall have failed to qualify, then the Vice-President elect shall act as President until a President shall have qualified; and the Congress may by law provide for the case wherein neither a President elect nor a Vice-President elect shall have qualified, declaring who shall then act as President, or the manner in which one who is to act shall be selected, and such person shall act accordingly until a President or Vice-President shall have qualified.

Section 4
[Election of the President]

The Congress may by law provide for the case of the death of any of the persons from whom the House of Representatives may choose a President whenever the right of choice shall have devolved upon them, and for the case of the death of any of the persons from whom the Senate may choose a Vice-President whenever the right of choice shall have devolved upon them.

Section 5

Sections 1 and 2 shall effect on the 15th day of October following ratification of this article.

Section 6

This article shall be inoperative unless it shall have been ratified as an amendment to the Constitution by the legislatures of three-fourths of the several States within seven years from the date of its submission.

Amendment XXI

[*Proposed by Congress on February 20, 1933; declared ratified on December 5, 1933.*]

Section 1
[National Liquor Prohibition Repealed]

The eighteenth article of amendment to the Constitution of the United States is hereby repealed.

Section 2
[Transporation of Liquor into "Dry" States]

The transportation or importation into any State, Territory, or Possession of the United States for delivery or use therein of intoxicating liquors, in violation of the laws thereof, is hereby prohibited.

Section 3

This article shall be inoperative unless it shall have been ratified as an amendment to the Constitution by conventions in the several States, as provided in the Constitution, within seven years from the date of the submission hereof to the States by the Congress.

Amendment XXII

[*Proposed by Congress on March 21, 1947; declared ratified on February 26, 1951.*]

Section 1
[Tenure of President Limited]

No person shall be elected to the office of President more than twice, and no person who has held the office of President, or acted as President, for more than two years of a term to which some other person was elected President shall be elected to the Office of the President more than once. But this Article shall not apply to any person holding the Office of President when this Article was proposed by the Congress, and shall not prevent any person who may be holding the office of President, during the term within which this Article becomes operative from holding the office of President or acting as President during the remainder of such term.

Section 2

This Article shall be inoperative unless it shall have been ratified as an amendment to the

Constitution by the legislatures of three-fourths of the several states within seven years from the date of its submission to the States by the Congress.

Amendment XXIII

[Proposed by Congress on June 21, 1960; declared ratified on March 29, 1961.]

Section 1
[Electoral College Votes for the District of Columbia]

The District constituting the seat of Government of the United States shall appoint in such manner as the Congress may direct:

A number of electors of President and Vice President equal to the whole number of Senators and Representatives in Congress to which the District would be entitled if it were a State, but in no event more than the least populous State; they shall be in addition to those appointed by the States, but they shall be considered, for the purposes of the election of President and Vice President, to be electors appointed by a State; and they shall meet in the District and perform such duties as provided by the twelfth article of amendment.

Section 2

The Congress shall have power to enforce this article by appropriate legislation.

Amendment XXIV

[Proposed by Congress on August 27, 1963; declared ratified on January 23, 1964.]

Section 1
[Anti-Poll Tax]

The right of citizens of the United States to vote in any primary or other election for President or Vice President, for electors for President or Vice President, or for Senators or Representative of Congress, shall not be denied or abridged by the United States or any State by reasons of failure to pay any poll tax or other tax.

Section 2

The Congress shall have power to enforce this article by appropriate legislation.

Amendment XXV

[Proposed by Congress on July 7, 1965; declared ratified on February 10, 1967.]

Section 1
[Vice President to Become President]

In case of the removal of the President from office or his death or resignation, the Vice President shall become President.

Section 2
[Choice of a New Vice President]

Whenever there is a vacancy in the office of the Vice President, the President shall nominate a Vice President who shall take the office upon confirmation by a majority vote of both houses of Congress.

Section 3
[President may Declare own Disability]

Whenever the President transmits to the President pro tempore of the Senate and the Speaker of the House of Representatives has written declaration that he is unable to discharge the powers and duties of his office, and until he transmits to them a written declaration to the contrary, such powers and duties shall be discharged by the Vice President as Acting President.

Section 4
[Alternative Procedures to Declare and to End Presidental Disability]

Whenever the Vice President and a majority of either the principal officers of the executive departments, or of such other body as Congress may by law provide, transmit to the President pro tempore of the Senate and the Speaker of the House of Representatives their written declaration that the President is unable to discharge the powers and duties of his office, the Vice President shall immediately assume the powers and duties of the office as Acting President.

Thereafter, when the President transmits to the President pro tempore of the Senate and the Speaker of the House of Representatives his written declaration that no inability exists, he shall resume the powers and duties of his office unless the Vice President and majority of either the principal officers of the executive department, or of such other body as Congress may by law provide, transmit within four days to the President pro tempore of the Senate and the Speaker of the House of Representatives their written declaration that the President is unable to discharge the powers and duties of his office. Thereupon Congress shall decide the issue, assembling within 48 hours for that purpose if not in session. If the Congress, within 21 days after receipt of the latter written declaration, or, if Congress is not in session, within 21 days after Congress is required to assemble, determines by two-thirds vote of both houses that the President is unable to discharge the powers and duties of his office, the Vice President shall continue to discharge the same as Acting President; otherwise, the President shall resume the powers and duties of his office.

Amendment XXVI

[Proposed by Congress on March 23, 1971; declared ratified on June 30, 1971.]

Section 1

The right of citizens of the United States, who are eighteen years of age or older, to vote shall not be denied or abridged by the United States or by any State on account of age.

Section 2

The Congress shall have the power to enforce this article by appropriate legislation.

Proposed Amendment XXVII

[Proposed by Congress on March 22, 1972.]

Section 1

Equality of rights under the law shall not be denied or abridged by the United States or by any State on account of sex.

Section 2

The Congress shall have power to enforce, by appropriate legislation, the provisions of this article.

Section 3

This amendment shall take effect two years after date of ratification. *[To become effective this amendment must be ratified by 38 state legislatures prior to September 1982.]*

Name index[1]

---

[1] n following page number indicates entry appears in a footnote; italic page numbers indicate entries appearing in illustration captions.

Subject index[2]

[2] Terms in boldface type are defined in the running glossaries on the text pages on which the terms first appear.

Political Divisions of the Senate and House, 1855-1981

Congress	Years	Senate					House of Representatives				
		Number of Senators	Democrats	Republicans	Other parties	Vacant	Number of Representatives	Democrats	Republicans	Other parties	Vacant
34th	1855-57	62	42	15	5		234	83	108	43	
35th	1857-59	64	39	20	5		237	131	92	14	
36th	1859-61	66	38	26	2		237	101	113	23	
37th	1861-63	50	11	31	7	1	178	42	106	28	2
38th	1863-65	51	12	39			183	80	103		
39th	1865-67	52	10	42			191	46	145		
40th	1867-69	53	11	42			193	49	143		1
41st	1869-71	74	11	61		2	243	73	170		
42d	1871-73	74	17	57			243	104	139		
43d	1873-75	74	19	54		1	293	88	203		2
44th	1875-77	76	29	46		1	293	181	107	3	2
45th	1877-79	76	36	39	1		293	156	137		
46th	1879-81	76	43	33			293	150	128	14	1
47th	1881-83	76	37	37	2		293	130	152	11	
48th	1883-85	76	36	40			325	200	119	6	
49th	1885-87	76	34	41		1	325	182	140	2	1
50th	1887-89	76	37	39			325	170	151	4	
51st	1889-91	84	37	47			330	156	173	1	
52d	1891-93	88	39	47	2		333	231	88	14	
53d	1893-95	88	44	38	3	3	356	220	126	10	
54th	1895-97	88	39	44	5		357	104	246	7	
55th	1897-99	90	34	46	10		357	134	206	16	1
56th	1899-1901	90	26	53	11		357	163	185	9	
57th	1901-03	90	29	56	3	2	357	153	198	5	1
58th	1903-05	90	32	58			386	178	207		1
59th	1905-07	90	32	58			386	136	250		
60th	1907-09	92	29	61		2	386	164	222		
61st	1909-11	92	32	59		1	391	172	219		
62d	1911-13	92	42	49		1	391	228	162	1	
63d	1913-15	96	51	44	1		435	290	127	18	
64th	1915-17	96	56	39	1		435	231	193	8	3
65th	1917-19	96	53	42	1		435	210	216	9	
66th	1919-21	96	47	48	1		435	191	237	7	
67th	1921-23	96	37	59			435	132	300	1	2
68th	1923-25	96	43	51	2		435	207	225	3	
69th	1925-27	96	40	54	1	1	435	183	247	5	
70th	1927-29	96	47	48	1		435	195	237	3	
71st	1929-31	96	39	56	1		435	163	267	1	4
72d	1931-33	96	47	48	1		435	216	218	1	
73d	1933-35	96	59	36	1		435	313	117	5	
74th	1935-37	96	69	25	2		435	322	103	10	
75th	1937-39	96	75	17	4		435	333	89	13	
76th	1939-41	96	69	23	4		435	262	169	4	
77th	1941-43	96	66	28	2		435	267	162	6	
78th	1943-45	96	57	38	1		435	222	209	4	
79th	1945-47	96	57	38	1		435	243	190	2	
80th	1947-49	96	45	51			435	188	246	1	
81st	1949-51	96	54	42			435	263	171	1	
82d	1951-53	96	48	47	1		435	234	199	2	
83d	1953-55	96	46	48	2		435	213	221	1	
84th	1955-57	96	48	47	1		435	232	203		
85th	1957-59	96	49	47			435	234	201		
86th	1959-61	98	64	34			436	283	153		
87th	1961-63	100	64	36			437	262	175		
88th	1963-65	100	67	33			435	258	176		1
89th	1965-67	100	68	32			435	295	140		
90th	1967-69	100	64	36			435	248	187		
91st	1969-71	100	58	42			435	243	192		
92d	1971-73	100	54	44	2		435	255	180		
93d	1973-75	100	56	42	2		435	242	192	1	
94th	1975-77	100	61	37	2		435	291	144		
95th	1977-79	100	61	38	1		435	292	143		
96th	1979-81	100	58	41	1		435	275	158	(2 undecided)	
97th	1981-83	100	47	53			435	243	192		

(1) Democrats organized House with help of other parties. (2) Democrats organized House due to Republican deaths. (3) Proclamation declaring Alaska a State issued Jan. 3, 1959. (4) Proclamation declaring Hawaii a State issued Aug. 21, 1959.